THE BROADVIEW ANTHOLOGY OF EXPOSITORY
PROSE

Second Edition

Library and Archives Canada Cataloguing in Publication

The Broadview anthology of expository prose / editors Laura Buzzard ... [et al].

Includes bibliographical references and index.
ISBN 978-1-55481-037-6

1. Essays. 2. Exposition (Rhetoric). 3. College readers.
I. Buzzard, Laura

PN6142.B76 2011   808.84   C2011-902620-1

Broadview Press is an independent, international publishing house, incorporated in 1985.

We welcome comments and suggestions regarding any aspect of our publications—please feel free to contact us at the addresses below or at broadview@broadviewpress.com.

North America   PO Box 1243, Peterborough, Ontario, Canada K9J 7H5
2215 Kenmore Ave., Buffalo, New York, USA 14207
Tel: (705) 743-8990; Fax: (705) 743-8353
email: customerservice@broadviewpress.com

UK, Europe, Central Asia,   Eurospan Group, 3 Henrietta St., London WC2E 8LU, UK
Middle East, Africa, India,   Tel: 44 (0) 1767 604972; Fax: 44 (0) 1767 601640
and Southeast Asia   email: eurospan@turpin-distribution.com

Australia and New Zealand   NewSouth Books, c/o TL Distribution
15-23 Helles Ave., Moorebank, NSW, Australia 2170
Tel: (02) 8778 9999; Fax: (02) 8778 9944
email: orders@tldistribution.com.au

www.broadviewpress.com

Broadview Press acknowledges the financial support of the Government of Canada through the Canada Book Fund for our publishing activities.

This book is printed on paper containing 50% post-consumer fibre.

PRINTED IN CANADA

PREFACE

This anthology has its origin in the space between books. For many years the Broadview Press list has included three outstanding readers designed for first-year composition and literature courses at post-secondary institutions: *The Broadview Reader* (edited by Herbert Rosengarten and Jane Flick) and *Clear Writing* (edited by Marjorie Mather and Brett McLenithan), each comprising an excellent selection of every sort of non-fiction prose except scholarly writing; and *Academic Reading* (edited by Janet Giltrow), comprising an excellent selection of purely scholarly writing. Another attractive option, it seemed to us, would be an anthology combining a wide range of literary and other non-scholarly essays with a good selection of academic writing.

Central to the idea of this anthology, then, is the inclusion of a substantial selection of academic writing. Very frequently, anthologies which make a stab at including academic writing end up selecting journalistic writing by academics rather than "real" academic writing. Granted, it is not easy to find examples of purely academic discourse that are at all accessible to a first- or second-year student who is unlikely to be familiar with the conventions of the given discipline. But it is not impossible. One guideline we have followed in searching out such essays has been to look for academic pieces which have ended up exerting considerable influence on a public much broader than that within the discipline. Essays such as those by Milgram on obedience and conformity; Luis and Walter Alvarez on the extinction of the dinosaurs (their hypothesis of an asteroid impact was at first met with incredulity); Putnam on social capital in modern American society; and Judith Rich Harris on the importance of peer influence to the formation of personality have all presented ideas that have ended by being widely discussed and widely influential outside academia. Also included here are many pieces which, while they may not have reached the general public in any form, have been widely influential within their discipline.

A second central principle of the book is variety. At the heart of the anthology are a wide range of essays that attempt in one way or another to persuade the reader of something. But a variety of other modes of prose writing are also included. The reader will find personal essays, occasional pieces, letters, and humorous sketches. Selections range from less than a page in length to more than twenty pages. In some essays the writing is almost transparent in its simplicity; in others the reader may be challenged by complex syntax as well as by difficulty of material. In many cases the intended audience is clearly the general reader, but some selections aim at a much narrower readership. And the anthology includes a wide range of subject matter, with a number of essays on scientific subjects in addition to many on subjects in the humanities and social sciences. Most of the selections are of course written in English, but we have also included a handful of pieces first written in other languages either because (as in the case of Montaigne) they have been extraordinarily influential in shaping the history of the essay, or because of the central position of their authors in shaping intellectual discourse in Western society (as in the case of Barthes).

In choosing new selections for the second edition, we have tried to maintain the balance of style, length, and difficulty that proved to work well in the first edition, while updating our contemporary content to reflect the scientific developments and political events of the past ten years. Other changes have been made in response to extremely helpful advice we received from a number of academics who have been using the book in their classes. One of these suggestions was that we include work from a greater range of academic disciplines; our new selections include influential articles from geology, neuroscience, and engineering. We are also pleased to include paired articles, intended to help students examine how a single topic can be approached in more than one way. In most cases, this involves similar material treated for different anticipated audiences; the pairings for the most part include one scholarly paper and one article written for lay readers.

One category of expository writing that is not represented in this anthology is the student essay. For instructors who would like to include discussion of student work in their courses, however, we have posted on an associated website a selection of excellent student essays; simply go to <http://www.broadviewpress.com> and follow the links to the websites that accompany this book. Also appearing online are several essays included in the first edition of this book that we have not been able to find room for in the second, and a few essays that appear in neither edition of the bound book anthology.

Most essay anthologies designed for university use are arranged either by broad subject category ("Nature," "Science," and so on) or by rhetorical category ("Descriptive essays," "Persuasive essays," etc.). On the good advice of the majority of academics we consulted on this matter, we have instead adopted a loosely chronological arrangement, in the interests both of simplicity and of flexibility. In an anthology where the grouping is by subject or by rhetorical category each essay must of necessity appear as part of only one grouping—whereas in reality, of course, many of the finest and most interesting essays will have two or more subjects, many of the best persuasive essays also employ description or narration, and so on. The chronological approach, by contrast, allows the instructor to group the essays in whatever combinations seem most interesting or appropriate, and to change those groupings as desired each time a course is taught. (Tables of contents by subject category and by rhetorical category—in both of which each essay is likely to appear two or three times—appear following this preface.) A chronological organization is flexible in another respect too; it lends itself to use in courses on the history of the essay or on non-fiction prose as a genre as well as in courses on composition and rhetoric.

One issue in assembling almost any anthology is whether or not to excerpt. If the book is to be essentially an anthology of essays, does the integrity of the form demand that all essays selected for inclusion be included in their entirety? Should selections taken from full-length books be excluded on the grounds of their provenance? To both these questions we have answered in the negative. If an anthology such as this is to do the best possible job of presenting the widest possible range within a manageable compass, practical and pedagogical concerns seem to us to justify the occasional decision to excerpt a very long essay, or to select a discrete section from a full-length book. We have, however, included a considerable number of longer essays in their entirety.

We should say something, finally, about the book's title. There may be no satisfactory solution to naming a book of this sort. "Anthology of Prose" is obviously inappropriate, since prose fiction is excluded. "Anthology of Essays" becomes unsuitable once the decision has been made to include selections from longer works as well. "Anthology of Non-Fiction Prose" is clunky, and would argue for the inclusion of a much wider variety of forms of non-fiction prose than are presented here (among them interview transcripts, car maintenance manuals, and truthful advertising copy); conversely, it would argue for the exclusion of pieces such as the "essays" in this collection by David Sedaris and Daniel Heath Justice, both of which hover on the border between fiction and non-fiction.

In the end we have settled on "Anthology of Expository Prose." That too is a title that if taken narrowly would argue for the exclusion of certain of the selections in the anthology. Defined according to traditional rhetorical categories, expository writing is an umbrella category of writing that involves explanation. It has been taken to include writing engaged in comparison or contrast, definition, analysis, and persuasion or argument—but not to include purely descriptive or narrative forms of non-fiction prose. More broadly, though, "expository prose" is often used nowadays as a short form for "non-fiction prose that aims to set something forth for a public readership." There are good grounds on which to base this more inclusive meaning; "exposition" may refer simply to "setting forth," and that is certainly what descriptive and even some narrative prose may fairly be said to do, quite as much as prose that attempts to argue or persuade sets something forth. (Though much argument attempts to explain, often the line between explanation and assertion is exceedingly thin—a good deal thinner in many cases than that separating, say, description from explanation.) In any case, writing that falls within the traditional criteria of expository prose constitutes the overwhelming majority of the prose that appears in these pages; we beg the indulgence of the purist who would have it approach more nearly to one hundred per cent.

* * *

Tammy Roberts was the central coordinating force for the first edition of the anthology, and to her goes pride of place in the list of the editors for that edition. This time around, the greatest single contributor has been Laura Buzzard, who has been instrumental not only in coordinating editorial and market research for the new edition and in making the selections but also in drafting head notes, questions, and other material.

We would also like to acknowledge the work of a number of others who helped very substantially in the preparation of the first edition: Lynne Churchill-Frail, Chris Enright, Jennifer Ford, Trevor Rueger, Christine Schill, Janet Sisson, Shari Wattling, and Nicole Zylstra. Kathryn Brownsey and Eileen Eckert are both to be thanked for excellent work in editing, designing, and setting the book. Finally, we would particularly like to thank the following for the helpful advice they provided along the way: Gisele Baxter, University of British Columbia; Candace Fertile, Camosun College;

Richard Harrison, Mount Royal University; Suzanne James, University of British Columbia; Heather Marcovitch, Red Deer College; David McNeil, Dalhousie University; Natalie Meisner, Mount Royal University; Kenneth Phillips, Okanagan University College; Lisa Salem-Wiseman, Humber College; Beth Staley, West Virginia University; Randall Tessier, University of Michigan; Susan Willens, George Washington University; Michael John Martin, San Francisco State University; Alison Wariner, California State University, East Bay; and four academics at Vancouver Island University: Terri Doughty, Gwyneth Evans, Craig Tapping, and Deborah Torkko.

* * *

We welcome the comments and suggestions of all readers—instructors or students—about any and all aspects of this book, from the selections themselves to the book's organization, questions, and ancillary material; please feel free to email us at broadview@broadviewpress.com. We hope you will enjoy the book as it stands—but we also want to think of possible improvements for a third edition.

Don LePan
March 25, 2011

CONTENTS

CONTENTS BY SUBJECT

Children and Students / Culture(s) and Race(s) / Death and Life / The Earth, Humans, and Other Animals / History, and Other Ways of Looking at the Past / The Human Psyche / Issues of Ethics and Conscience / Language and Communication / Literature and the Arts / Personal Experience / Philosophical Perspectives / Religion / Science, Technology, and Change / Social Patterns, Social Issues / Sport / Women in Society / Work and Business

Note: Many selections deal with two or more of these subjects.

Children and Students

Culture(s) and Race(s)

History, and Other Ways of Looking at the Past

The Human Psyche

Issues of Ethics and Conscience

Language and Communication

Literature and the Arts

Personal Experience

Philosophical Perspectives

Religion

Science, Technology, and Change

Social Patterns, Social Issues

Sport

Women in Society

Work and Business

CONTENTS BY RHETORICAL CATEGORY

Essays that employ: Analysis / Cause and Effect /
Comparison and Contrast / Classification / Definition / Description /
Humor and Satire / Narration / Persuasion and Argument

Note: Many selections employ two or more of these modes.

Analysis

Cause and Effect

Comparison and Contrast

Classification

Definition

Description

Humor and Satire

Narration

Persuasion and Argument

MICHEL DE MONTAIGNE

OF DEMOCRITUS AND HERACLITUS

*Montaigne, a sixteenth-century French aristocrat,
is commonly regarded as the originator of the
essay form. The following selections are from
Charles Cotton's 1685-86 translation.*

❧

The judgment is an utensil proper for all subjects, and will have an oar in everything: which is the reason, that in these essays I take hold of all occasions where, though it happen to be a subject I do not very well understand, I try however, sounding it at a distance, and finding it too deep for my stature, I keep me on the shore; and this knowledge that a man can proceed no further, is one effect of its virtue, yea, one of those of which it is most proud. One while in an idle and frivolous subject, I try to find out matter whereof to compose a body, and then to prop and support it; another while, I employ it in a noble subject, one that has been tossed and tumbled by a thousand hands, wherein a man can scarce possibly introduce anything of his own, the way being so beaten on every side that he must of necessity walk in the steps of another: in such a case, 'tis the work of the judgment to take the way that seems best, and of a thousand paths, to determine that this or that is the best. I leave the choice of my arguments to fortune, and take that she first presents to me; they are all alike to me, I never design to go through any of them; for I never see all of anything: neither do they who so largely promise to show it to others. Of a hundred members and faces that everything has, I take one, one while to look it over only, another while to ripple up the skin, and sometimes to pinch it to the bones: I give a stab, not so wide but as deep as I can, and am for the most part tempted to take it in hand by some new light I discover in it. Did I know myself less, I might perhaps venture to handle something or other to the bottom, and to be deceived in my own inability; but sprinkling here one word and there another, patterns cut from several pieces and scattered without design and without engaging myself too far, I am not responsible for them, or obliged to keep close to my subject, without varying at my own liberty and pleasure, and giving up myself to doubt and uncertainty, and to my own gover[n]ing method, ignorance.

All motion discovers us: the very same soul of Caesar, that made itself so conspicuous in marshaling and commanding the battle of Pharsalia, was also seen as solicitous and busy in the softer affairs of love and leisure. A man makes a judgment of a horse, not only by seeing him when he is showing off his paces, but by his very walk, nay, and by seeing him stand in the stable.

Among the functions of the soul, there are some of a lower and meaner form; he who does not see her in those inferior offices as well as in those of nobler note, never fully discovers her; and, peradventure, she is best shown where she moves her simpler pace. The winds of passions take most hold of her in her highest flights; and the rather by reason that she wholly applies herself to, and exercises her whole virtue upon, every particular subject, and never handles more than one thing at a time, and that not according to it, but according to herself. Things in respect to themselves have, peradventure, their weight, measures and conditions; but when we once take them into us, the soul forms them as she pleases. Death is terrible to Cicero, coveted by Cato, indifferent to Socrates. Health, conscience, authority, knowledge, riches, beauty, and their contraries, all strip themselves at their entering into us, and receive a new robe, and of another fashion, from the soul; and of what color, brown, bright, green, dark, and of what quality, sharp, sweet, deep, or superficial, as best pleases each of them, for they are not agreed upon any common standard of forms, rules, or proceedings; every one is a queen in her own dominions. Let us, therefore, no more excuse ourselves upon the external qualities of things; it belongs to us to give ourselves an account of them. Our good or ill has no other dependence but on ourselves. 'Tis there that our offerings and our vows are due, and not to fortune: she has no power over our manners; on the contrary, they draw and make her follow in their train, and cast her in their own mold. Why should not I judge of Alexander at table, ranting and drinking at the prodigious rate he sometimes used to do? Or, if he played at chess? what string of his soul was not touched by this idle and childish game? I hate and avoid it, because it is not play enough, that it is too grave and serious a diversion, and I am ashamed to lay out as much thought and study upon it as would serve to much better uses. He did not more pump his brains about his glorious expedition into the Indies, nor than another in unraveling a passage upon which depends the safety of mankind. To what a degree does this ridiculous diversion molest the soul, when all her faculties are summoned together upon this trivial account! and how fair an opportunity she herein gives everyone to know and to make a right judgment of himself? I do not more thoroughly sift myself in any other posture than this: what passion are we exempted from in it? Anger, spite, malice, impatience, and a vehement desire of getting the better in a concern wherein it were more excusable to be ambitious of being overcome; for to be eminent, to excel above the common rate in frivolous things, nowise befits a man of honor. What I say in this example may be said in all others. Every particle, every employment of man manifests him equally with any other.

Democritus and Heraclitus were two philosophers, of whom the first, finding human condition ridiculous and vain, never appeared abroad but with a jeering and laughing countenance; whereas Heraclitus commiserating that same condition of ours, appeared always with a sorrowful look, and tears in his eyes:

> *Alter Ridebat, quoties a limine moverat unum*
> *Protuleratque pedem; flebat contrarius alter.*[1]

I am clearly for the first humor: not because it is more pleasant to laugh than to weep, but because it expresses more contempt and condemnation than the other, and I think we can never be despised according to our full desert. Compassion and bewailing seem to imply some esteem of and value for the thing bemoaned; whereas the things we laugh at are by that expressed to be of no moment. I do not think that we are so unhappy as we are vain, or have in us so much malice as folly; we are not so full of mischief as inanity; nor so miserable as we are vile and mean. And therefore Diogenes, who passed away his time in rolling himself in his tub, and made nothing of the great Alexander esteeming us no better than flies, or bladders puffed up with wind, was a sharper and more penetrating, and, consequently in my opinion, a juster judge than Timon, surnamed the Man-hater; for what a man hates he lays to heart. This last was an enemy to all mankind, who passionately desired our ruin, and avoided our conversation as dangerous, proceeding from wicked and depraved natures: the other valued us so little that we could neither trouble nor infect him by our example; and left us to herd one with another, not out of fear, but from contempt of our society: concluding us incapable of doing good as ill.

5

---

1   *Alter Ridebat ... contrarius alter*   Latin: "The one was always laughing whenever he put a foot outside the door, the other, his opposite, was always weeping" (Juvenal *Satires* X. 28ff).

Of the same strain was Statilius' answer, when Brutus courted him into the conspiracy against Caesar; he was satisfied that the enterprise was just, but he did not think mankind worthy of a wise man's concern; according to the doctrine of Hegesias, who said, that a wise man ought to do nothing but for himself, forasmuch as he only was worthy of it: and to the saying of Theodorus, that it was not reasonable a wise man should hazard himself for his country, and endanger wisdom for a company of fools. Our condition is as ridiculous as risible.[2]

(1580)

from OF EXPERIENCE

There is no desire more natural than that of knowledge. We try all ways that can lead us to it; where reason is wanting, we therein employ experience.

> *Per varios usus artem experientia fecit,*
> *Exemplo monstrante viam,*[3]

which is a means much more weak and cheap; but truth is no great thing, that we ought not to disdain any mediation that will guide us to it. Reason has so many forms, that we know not to which to take; experience has no fewer; the consequence we would draw from the comparison of events is unsure, by reason they are always unlike. There is no quality so universal in this image of things, as diversity and variety. Both the Greeks and the Latins, and we, for the most express example of similitude, employ that of eggs: and yet there have been men, particularly one at Delphos, who could distinguish marks of difference among eggs so well, that he never mistook one for another; and, having many hens, could tell which had laid it. Dissimilitude intrudes itself of itself in our works; no art can arrive at perfect

---

2 *Of the same ... as risible* The story of Statilius comes from Plutarch's *Lives*, life of Brutus 12. 3. The doctrines of Hegesias and Theodorus can be found in Diogenes Laertius' life of Aristippus, *Lives of the Eminent Philosophers* II. 8; the views of Hegesias are stated at §95, and those of Theodorus at §98.

3 *Per varios ... monstrante viam* Latin: "Through various exercises, experience produces art, with example showing the way" (Minilius *Astronomica* I. 61-2).

similitude: neither Perrozet, nor any other cardmarker, can so carefully polish and blanch the backs of his cards, that some gamesters will not distinguish them by seeing them only shuffled by another. Resemblance does not so much make one, as difference makes another. Nature has obliged herself to make nothing other, that was not unlike.

And yet I am not much pleased with his opinion, who thought by the multitude of laws to curb the authority of judges, in cutting out for them their several parcels; he was not aware that there is as much liberty and latitude in the interpretation of laws, as in their form; and they but fool themselves, who think to lessen and stop our disputes by recalling us to the express words of the Bible: forasmuch as our mind does not find the field less spacious wherein to controvert the sense of another, than to deliver his own; and as if there were less animosity and tartness in commentary than in invention. We see how much he was mistaken; for we have more laws in France than all the rest of the world put together, and more than would be necessary for the government of all the worlds of Epicurus: *Ut olim flagitiis, sic nunc legibus laboramus:*[4] and yet we have left so much to the opinions and decisions of our judges, that there never was so full a liberty or so full a license. What have our legislators gained by culling out a hundred thousand particular cases, and by applying to these a hundred thousand laws? This number holds no manner of proportion with the infinite diversity of human actions; the multiplication of our inventions will never arrive at the variety of examples; add to these a hundred times as many more, it will still not happen, that of events to come, there shall one be found that, in this vast number of millions of events so chosen and recorded, shall so tally with any other one, and be so exactly coupled and matched with it, that there will not remain some circumstance and diversity which will require a diverse judgment. There is little relation between our actions, which are in perpetual mutation, and fixed and immutable laws; the most to be desired, are those that are the most rare, the most simple and general: and I am even of opinion, that we had better have none at all, than to have them in so prodigious a number as we have.

Nature always gives them better and happier than those we make ourselves. Witness the picture of the Golden Age of the poets, and the state wherein we see nations live, who have no other: some there are, who for their only judge, take the first passer-by that travels along their mountains,

---

4   *Ut olim ... laboramus*   Latin: "Previously we suffered from crimes, now we suffer from laws" (Tacitus *Annals* III. 25).

to determine their cause: and others who, on their market day, choose out some one among them upon the spot to decide their controversies. What danger would there be, that the wisest among us should so determine ours, according to occurrences, and at sight, without obligation of example and consequence? For every foot, its own shoe. King Ferdinand, sending colonies[5] to the Indies, wisely provided that they should not carry along with them any students of the long-robe,[6] for fear lest suits should get footing in that new world, as being a science in its own nature, the mother of altercation and division: judging with Plato, "that lawyers and physicians are the pests of a country."

Whence does it come to pass that our common language, so easy for all other uses, becomes obscure, and unintelligible in wills and contracts? and that he who so clearly expresses himself, in whatever else he speaks or writes, cannot find in these, any way of declaring himself that does not fall into doubt and contradiction? if it be not that the princes of that art, applying themselves with a peculiar attention to cull out portentous words and to contrive artificial sentences, have so weighed every syllable, and so thoroughly sifted every sort of quirking connection, that they are now confounded and entangled in the infinity of figures and minute divisions, and can no more fall within any rule or prescription, nor any certain intelligence: *Confusum est, quidquid usque in pulverem sectum est.*[7] As you see children trying to bring a mass of quicksilver to a certain number of parts; the more they press and work it, and endeavor to reduce it to their own will, the more they irritate the liberty of this generous metal; it evades their endeavor, and sprinkles itself into so many separate bodies as frustrate all reckoning; so is it here; for in subdividing these subtleties, we teach men to increase their doubts; they put us into a way of extending and diversifying difficulties, and lengthen and disperse them. In sowing and retailing questions, they make the world fructify and increase in uncertainties and disputes, as the earth is made fertile by being crumbled and dug deep: *Difficultatim facit doctrina.*[8] We doubted of Ulpian,[9] and are now still more perplexed with

---

5   *colonies*   Colonists.

6   *students of the long-robe*   Those knowledgeable in the law.

7   *Confusum est ... sectum est*   Latin: "Whatever is ground to dust becomes confused" (Seneca *Letters* 89. 3).

8   *Difficultatim facit doctrina*   Latin: "Learning creates a problem" (Quintilian *Institutiones Oratoriae* (or else *Declamationes*) X. iii. 16).

9   *Ulpian*   Roman jurist.

Bartolus and Baldus.[10] We should efface the trace of this innumerable diversity of opinions; not adorn ourselves with it, and fill posterity with crotchets. I know not what to say to it; but experience makes it manifest, that so many interpretations dissipate truth, and break it. Aristotle wrote to be understood; if he could not do this, much less will another that is not so good at it; and a third than he who expressed his own thoughts. We open the matter, and spill it in pouring out: of one subject we make a thousand, and in multiplying and subdividing them, fall again into the infinity of atoms of Epicurus. Never did two men make the same judgment of the same thing; and 'tis impossible to find two opinions exactly alike, not only in several men, but in the same man, at diverse hours. I often find matter of doubt in things of which the commentary has disdained to take notice; I am most apt to stumble in an even country, like some horses that I have known, that make most trips in the smoothest way.

Who will not say that glosses augment doubts and ignorance, since there's no one book to be found, either human or divine, which the world busies itself about, whereof the difficulties are cleared by interpretation. The hundredth commentator passes it on to the next, still more knotty and perplexed than he found it. When were we ever agreed among ourselves: "this book has enough; there is now no more to be said about it?" This is most apparent in the law; we give the authority of law to infinite doctors, infinite decrees, and as many interpretations: yet do we find any end of the need of interpreting? is there, for all that, any progress or advancement toward peace, or do we stand in need of any fewer advocates and judges, than when this great mass of law was yet in its first infancy? On the contrary, we darken and bury intelligence; we can no longer discover it, but at the mercy of so many fences and barriers. Men do not know the natural disease of the mind; it does nothing but ferret and inquire, and is eternally wheeling, juggling, and perplexing itself like silkworms, and then suffocates itself in its work; *Mus in pice*.[11] It thinks it discovers at a great distance, I know not what glimpse of light and imaginary truth; but while running to it, so many difficulties, hindrances and new inquisitions cross it, that it loses its way, and is made drunk with the motion: not much unlike Aesop's dogs, that seeing something like a dead body floating in the sea, and not being able to approach it, set to work to drink the water and lay the passage dry, and so choked themselves. To which, what one Crates said of the writings of

5

---

10   *Bartolus and Baldus*   Medieval scholars of the law.

11   *Mus in pice*   Latin: A mouse [stuck] in pitch.

Heraclitus, falls pat enough, "that they required a reader who could swim well," so that the depth and weight of his doctrine might not overwhelm and stifle him. 'Tis nothing but particular weakness that makes us content with what others or ourselves have found out in this chase after knowledge: one of better understanding will not rest so content; there is always room for one to follow, nay, even for ourselves; and another road: there is no end of our inquisitions; our end is in the other world. 'Tis a sign either that the mind has grown short-sighted when it is satisfied, or that it has got weary. No generous mind can stop in itself; it will still tend further, and beyond its power; it has sallied beyond its effects; if it do not advance and press forward, and retire, and rush and wheel about, 'tis but half alive: its pursuits are without bound or method; its aliment is admiration, the chase, ambiguity, which Apollo sufficiently declared in always speaking to us in a double, obscure, and oblique sense; not feeding, but amusing and puzzling us. 'Tis an irregular and perpetual motion, without model and without aim; its inventions heat, pursue, and interproduce one another.

(1588)

Questions

1. "Of Democritus and Heraclitus" is the essay in which Montaigne first referred to "essais"—literally, "attempts." Express in your own words what Montaigne thinks of himself as attempting in these "essais."

2. Is the topic of "Of Democritus and Heraclitus" really Democritus and Heraclitus? What other title(s) might be given to this piece?

3. To what extent are the various ideas that Montaigne throws out in "Of Democritus and Heraclitus" connected?

4. Whereas "Of Democritus and Heraclitus" is reprinted here in its entirety, the passage from "Of Experience" is a selection from a much longer essay. To what extent does this passage provide a fuller sense of Montaigne's notions of intellectual endeavor?

5. As you sift through Montaigne's wide variety of observations and assertions, which strike you as being particularly astute? Which (if any) strike you as being no longer relevant, and which (if any) strike you as being unhelpful or simply wrong?

Francis Bacon

Of Studies

Bacon was one of the first to try in English the form that had been pioneered by Montaigne. "Of Studies" remains one of the most widely quoted essays in English.

☙

Studies serve for delight, for ornament, and for ability. Their chief use for delight is in privateness and retiring; for ornament, is in discourse; and for ability, is in the judgment and disposition of business. For expert men can execute, and perhaps judge of particulars, one by one; but the general counsels, and the plots and marshalling of affairs, come best from those that are learned. To spend too much time in studies is sloth; to use them too much for ornament is affectation; to make judgment wholly by their rules is the humor of a scholar. They perfect nature, and are perfected by experience, for natural abilities are like natural plants, that need pruning by study; and studies themselves do give forth directions too much at large, except they be bounded in by experience. Crafty men contemn studies, simple men admire them, and wise men use them, for they teach not their own use; but that is a wisdom without them and above them, won by observation. Read not to contradict and confute, nor to believe and take for granted, nor to find talk and discourse, but to weigh and consider. Some books are to be tasted, others to be swallowed, and some few to be chewed and digested; that is, some books are to be read only in parts, others to be read, but not curiously,[1] and some few to be read wholly, and with diligence and attention. Some books also may be read by deputy, and extracts made of them by others; but that would be only in the less important arguments and the meaner sort of books; else distilled books are, like common distilled waters, flashy things. Reading maketh a full man, conference[2] a

---

1   *curiously*   With curiosity and care.

2   *conference*   Discussion.

ready man, and writing an exact man. And therefore if a man write little, he had need have a great memory; if he confer little, he had need have a present wit; and if he read little, he had need have much cunning, to seem to know that he doth not. Histories make men wise; poets, witty; the mathematics, subtle; natural philosophy, deep; moral, grave; logic and rhetoric, able to contend.[3] *Abeunt studia in mores.*[4] Nay, there is no stond[5] or impediment in the wit but may be wrought out by fit studies, like as diseases of the body may have appropriate exercises. Bowling is good for the stone and reins,[6] shooting for the lungs and breast, gentle walking for the stomach, riding for the head, and the like. So if a man's wit be wandering, let him study the mathematics, for in demonstrations, if his wit be called away never so little, he must begin again. If his wit be not apt to distinguish or find differences, let him study the Schoolmen,[7] for they are *cymini sectores.*[8] If he be not apt to beat over matters,[9] and to call up one thing to prove and illustrate another, let him study the lawyers' cases. So every defect of the mind may have a special receipt.

(1613)

---

3   *contend*   Argue effectively.

4   *Abeunt studia in mores*   Latin: Study affects one's habits (and character).

5   *stond*   Obstacle.

6   *reins*   Kidneys.

7   *the Schoolmen*   Theologians of the late medieval period (e.g., St. Thomas Aquinas) known for making fine distinctions.

8   *cymini sectores*   Latin: Splitters of seeds; hair-splitters.

9   *not apt to beat over matters*   Not skilled at discussion.

Questions

1. Comment on the organization (or lack thereof) in this essay. What are some of the ways in which the essay has evolved as a form since Bacon's time?

2. This essay is filled with confident generalizations. Which of these in particular seem to you to be well founded? Are there any that you would strongly disagree with? How much value do you see in generalizing to the extent that Bacon does?

3. Comment on the use by Bacon of parallelism and balance in structuring his sentences. To what extent does the effectiveness of this essay stem from stylistic matters such as this (as opposed to the ideas themselves)?

JOHN DONNE

from FOR WHOM THIS BELL TOLLS (MEDITATION XVII)

*In this famous meditation, the dean of St. Paul's in London
reflects on the significance of the tolling of church bells.*

☙

NUNC LENTO SONITU DICUNT, MORIERIS[1]

Perchance he for whom this bell tolls may be so ill, as that he knows not it tolls for him; and perchance I may think myself so much better than I am, as that they who are about me, and see my state, may have caused it to toll for me, and I know not that. The church is Catholic, universal, so are all her actions; all that she does belongs to all. When she baptizes a child, that action concerns me; for that child is thereby connected to that body which is my head too, and engrafted into that body whereof I am a member. And when she buries a man, that action concerns me: all mankind is of one author, and is one volume; when one man dies, one chapter is not torn out of the book, but translated into a better language; and every chapter must be so translated; God employs several translators; some pieces are translated by age, some by sickness, some by war, some by justice; but God's hand is in every translation, and his hand shall bind up all our scattered leaves again for that library where every book shall lie open to one another. As therefore the bell that rings to a sermon calls not upon the preacher only, but upon the congregation to come, so this bell calls us all; but how much more me, who am brought so near the door by this sickness. There was a contention as far as a suit (in which both piety and dignity, religion and estimation, were mingled), which of the religious orders should ring to prayers first in the

---

1   *Nunc lento ... morieris*   Latin: Now this bell tolling softly for another, says to me: thou must die.

morning; and it was determined, that they should ring first that rose earliest. If we understand aright the dignity of this bell that tolls for our evening prayer, we would be glad to make it ours by rising early, in that application, that it might be ours as well as his, whose indeed it is. The bell doth toll for him that thinks it doth; and though it intermit again, yet from that minute that that occasion wrought upon him, he is united to God. Who casts not up his eye to the sun when it rises? but who takes off his eye from a comet when that breaks out? Who bends not his ear to any bell which upon any occasion rings but who can remove it from that bell which is passing a piece of himself out of this world? No man is an island, entire of himself; every man is a piece of the continent, a part of the main. If a clod be washed away by the sea, Europe is the less, as well as if a promontory were, as well as if a manor of thy friend's or of thine own were: any man's death diminishes me, because I am involved in mankind, and therefore never send to know for whom the bell tolls; it tolls for thee.

(1626)

Questions

1. In Donne's world, the Christian church was indeed "catholic" in the sense of being near universally present in society. Can you think of any in Donne's time who were outside this frame of reference? To what extent is it possible to translate Donne's observations made in this context into the pluralistic world of modern Western society?

2. Comment on Donne's use of metaphor here.

3. Comment on the rhythm and structure of Donne's sentences.

MARGARET CAVENDISH

ON SOCIAL CLASS AND HAPPINESS

In her preface to Sociable Letters *Margaret Cavendish writes*
that she has "endeavored under the cover of letters to express
the humors of mankind ... by the correspondence of two ladies,
living at some short distance from each other, which make it not
only their chief delight and pastime, but their tie in friendship,
to discourse by letters, as they would do if they were
personally together." The following is one of those letters.

☙

MADAM,

You were pleased in your last letter to tell me, that you had been in the country, and that you did almost envy the peasants for living so merrily; it is a sign, Madam, they live happily, for mirth seldom dwells with troubles and discontents, neither doth riches nor grandeur live so easily, as that unconcerned freedom that is in low and mean[1] fortunes and persons, for the ceremony of grandeur is constrained and bound with forms and rules, and a great estate and high fortune is not so easily managed as a less, a little is easily ordered,[2] where much doth require time, care, wisdom and study as considerations; but poor, mean peasants that live by their labor, are for the most part happier and pleasanter than great rich persons, that live in luxury and idleness, for idle time is tedious, and luxury is unwholesome, whereas labor is healthful and recreative, and surely country housewives take more pleasure in milking their cows, making their butter and cheese, and feeding their poultry, than great ladies do in painting, curling, and adorning themselves, also they have more quiet and peaceable minds and thoughts, for they never, or seldom, look in a glass to view their faces, they regard not their complexions,

---

1   *mean*   Poor.

2   *ordered*   Put into order.

nor observe their decays, they defy time's ruins of their beauties, they are not peevish and froward if they look not as well one day as another, a pimple or spot in their skin tortures not their minds, they fear not the sun's heat, but out-face the sun's power, they break not their sleeps to think of fashions, but work hard to sleep soundly, they lie not in sweats to clear their complexions, but rise to sweat to get them food, their appetites are not queasy with surfeits, but sharpened with fasting, they relish with more savor their ordinary coarse fare, than those who are pampered do their delicious rarities; and for their mirth and pastimes, they take more delight and true pleasure, and are more inwardly pleased and outwardly merry at their wakes, than the great ladies at their balls, and though they dance not with such art and measure, yet they dance with more pleasure and delight, they cast not envious, spiteful eyes at each other, but meet friendly and lovingly. But great ladies at public meetings take not such true pleasures, for their envy at each other's beauty and bravery disturbs their pastimes; and obstructs their mirth, they rather grow peevish and froward through envy, than loving and kind through society, so that whereas the country peasants meet with such kind hearts and unconcerned freedom as they unite in friendly jollity, and depart with neighborly love, the greater sort of persons meet with constrained ceremony, converse with formality, and for the most part depart with enmity; and this is not only amongst women, but amongst men, for there is amongst the better sort a greater strife[3] for bravery than for courtesy, for place[4] than friendship, and in their societies there is more vainglory than pleasure, more pride than mirth, and more vanity than true content; yet in one thing the better sort of men, as the nobles and gentry, are to be commended, which is, that though they are oftener drunken and more debauched than peasants, having more means to maintain their debaucheries, yet at such times as at great assemblies, they keep themselves more sober and temperate than peasants do, which are for the most part drunk at their departing; but to judge between the peasantry and nobles for happiness, I believe where there's one noble that is truly happy, there are a hundred peasants; not that there be more peasants than nobles, but that they are more happy, number for number, as having not the envy, ambition, pride, vainglory, to cross, trouble, [and] vex them, as nobles have; when I say nobles, I mean those that have been ennobled by time as well as title, as the gentry. But, Madam, I am not a fit judge

---

3   *strife*   Striving.

4   *place*   Social position.

for the several sorts or degrees, or courses of lives, or actions of mankind, as to judge which is happiest, for happiness lives not in outward show or concourse, but inwardly in the mind, and the minds of men are too obscure to be known, and too various and inconstant to fix a belief in them, and since we cannot know ourselves, how should we know others? Besides, pleasure and true delight lives in everyone's own delectation; but let me tell you, my delectation is, to prove myself,

    Madam,

Your Faithful Fr. and S.

I, M.N.

(1664)

Questions

1. Looked at from one angle, this letter might be seen as an essay on wealth and privilege being no guarantee of happiness—but from another angle it is possible to see Cavendish's arguments as providing a rationalization for the continuance of injustice. Form an argument supporting one or the other of these two approaches to Cavendish's letter.

2. It was common when Cavendish wrote to use expressions such as "the greater sort of persons" and "the better sort" to refer to the nobility, contrasted with the "lower orders." Comment on this hierarchy as expressed in language, and on the implications of the terms we use nowadays with which to discuss social class (middle class, working class, etc.).

3. Comment on the way in which Cavendish structures her sentences.

4. Write a short essay about the way in which you perceive the relationship between wealth and happiness.

JONATHAN SWIFT

A MODEST PROPOSAL

FOR PREVENTING THE CHILDREN OF POOR PEOPLE IN IRELAND, FROM BEING A BURDEN TO THEIR PARENTS OF COUNTRY; AND FOR MAKING THEM BENEFICIAL TO THE PUBLIC

This piece setting forth arguments in favor of a particular course of public policy in Ireland in the early eighteenth century remains the most widely reprinted English language essay.

❧

It is a melancholy object to those who walk through this great town[1] or travel in the country, when they see the streets, the roads and cabin doors crowded with beggars of the female sex, followed by three, four, or six children, all in rags and importuning every passenger for an alms. These mothers, instead of being able to work for their honest livelihood, are forced to employ all their time in strolling to beg sustenance for their helpless infants; who as they grow up either turn thieves for want of work, or leave their dear native country to fight for the Pretender[2] in Spain, or sell themselves to the Barbadoes.[3]

---

1   *town*   Dublin.

2   *the Pretender*   James Francis Edward Stuart, was known as "the old pretender"; his father, James II, had been overthrown in 1688 in the English Revolution. Many Irish-Catholics supported him.

3   *the Barbadoes*   It was common at the time for poverty-stricken Irish citizens to go into debt in order to pay for passage to the West Indies, where they would then pay off the debt through labor.

I think it is agreed by all parties that this prodigious number of children in the arms, or on the backs, or at the heels of their mothers, and frequently of their fathers, is in the present deplorable state of the kingdom a very great additional grievance; and, therefore, whoever could find out a fair, cheap, and easy method of making these children sound and useful members of the Commonwealth, would deserve so well of the public as to have his statue set up for a preserver of the nation.

But my intention is very far from being confined to provide only for the children of professed beggars; it is of a much greater extent, and shall take in the whole number of infants at a certain age who are born of parents in effect as little able to support them as those who demand our charity in the streets.

As to my own part, having turned my thoughts for many years upon this important subject, and maturely weighed the several schemes of other projectors,[4] I have always found them grossly mistaken in their computation. It is true a child, just dropped from its dam, may be supported by her milk for a solar year, with little other nourishment; at most not above the value of two shillings, which the mother may certainly get, or the value in scraps, by her lawful occupation of begging; and it is exactly at one year old that I propose to provide for them in such a manner as instead of being a charge upon their parents or the parish, or wanting food and raiment for the rest of their lives, they shall on the contrary contribute to the feeding, and partly to the clothing, of many thousands.

5   There is likewise another great advantage in my scheme, that it will prevent those voluntary abortions, and that horrid practice of women murdering their bastard children, alas! too frequent among us, sacrificing the poor innocent babes, I doubt,[5] more to avoid the expense than the shame, which would move tears and pity in the most savage and in-human breast.

The number of souls in Ireland being usually reckoned one million and a half, of these I calculate there may be about two hundred thousand couples whose wives are breeders; from which number I subtract thirty thousand couples who are able to maintain their own children (although I apprehend there cannot be so many, under the present distresses of the kingdom); but this being granted, there will remain an hundred and seventy thousand breeders. I again subtract fifty thousand for those women who miscarry, or whose children die by accident or disease within the

---

4   *projectors* People who put forward schemes or projects.

5   *doubt* Suspect.

year. There only remain an hundred and twenty thousand children of poor parents annually born. The question therefore is, how this number shall be reared and provided for? which, as I have already said, under the present situation of affairs, is utterly impossible by all the methods hitherto proposed. For we can neither employ them in handicraft or agriculture; we neither build houses (I mean in the country) nor cultivate land; they can very seldom pick up a livelihood by stealing, till they arrive at six years old, except where they are of towardly parts; although I confess they learn the rudiments much earlier; during which time they can, however, be properly looked upon only as probationers; as I have been informed by a principal gentleman in the county of Cavan, who protested to me that he never knew above one or two instances under the age of six, even in a part of the kingdom so renowned for the quickest proficiency in that art.

I am assured by our merchants, that a boy or a girl before twelve years old is no saleable commodity; and even when they come to this age they will not yield above three pounds or three pounds and half a crown at most on the Exchange; which cannot turn to account either to the parents or the kingdom, the charge of nutriment and rags having been at least four times that value.

I shall now therefore humbly propose my own thoughts, which I hope will not be liable to the least objection.

I have been assured by a very knowing American of my acquaintance in London, that a young healthy child well nursed is, at year old, a most delicious, nourishing, and wholesome food, whether stewed, roasted, baked, or boiled; and I make no doubt that it will equally serve in a fricassee or a ragout.

I do therefore humbly offer it to public consideration that of the hundred and twenty thousand children already computed, twenty thousand may be reserved for breed, whereof only one-fourth part to be males; which is more than we allow to sheep, black cattle, or swine; and my reason is, that these children are seldom the fruits of marriage, a circumstance not much regarded by our savages; therefore one male will be sufficient to serve four females. That the remaining hundred thousand may, at a year old, be offered in sale to the persons of quality and fortune through the kingdom; always advising the mother to let them suck plentifully in the last month, so as to render them plump and fat for a good table. A child will make two dishes at an entertainment for friends; and when the family dines alone, the fore or hind quarter will make a reasonable dish, and seasoned with a little pepper or salt will be very good boiled on the fourth day, especially in winter.

10

I have reckoned upon a medium that a child just born will weigh twelve pounds, and in a solar year, if tolerably nursed, will increase to twenty-eight pounds.

I grant this food will be somewhat dear, and therefore very proper for landlords, who, as they have already devoured most of the parents, seem to have the best title to the children.

Infant's flesh will be in season throughout the year, but more plentiful in March, and a little before and after: for we are told by a grave author,[6] an eminent French physician, that fish being a prolific diet, there are more children born in Roman Catholic countries about nine months after Lent than at any other season; therefore reckoning a year after Lent, the markets will be more glutted than usual, because the number of popish infants is at least three to one in this kingdom: and therefore it will have one other collateral advantage, by lessening the number of Papists among us.

I have already computed the charge of nursing a beggar's child (in which list I reckon all cottagers, laborers, and four-fifths of the farmers) to be about two shillings per annum, rags included; and I believe no gentleman would repine to give ten shillings for the carcass of a good fat child, which, as I have said, will make four dishes of excellent nutritive meat, when he has only some particular friend or his own family to dine with him. Thus the squire will learn to be a good landlord, and grow popular among his tenants; the mother will have eight shillings net profit, and be fit for work till she produces another child.

15 Those who are more thrifty (as I must confess the times require) may flay the carcass; the skin of which artificially[7] dressed will make admirable gloves for ladies, and summer boots for fine gentlemen.

As to our city of Dublin, shambles may be appointed for this purpose in the most convenient parts of it, and butchers we may be assured will not be wanting: although I rather recommend buying the children alive, and dressing them hot from the knife as we do roasting pigs.

A very worthy person, a true lover of his country, and whose virtues I highly esteem, was lately pleased in discoursing on this matter to offer a refinement upon my scheme. He said that many gentlemen of this kingdom, having of late destroyed their deer, he conceived that the want of venison might be well supplied by the bodies of young lads and maidens, not exceeding fourteen years of age nor under twelve; so great a number

---

6   *grave author*   François Rabelais.

7   *artificially*   With artifice or skill.

of both sexes in every county being now ready to starve for want of work and service; and these to be disposed of by their parents, if alive, or otherwise by their nearest relations. But with due deference to so excellent a friend and so deserving a patriot, I cannot be altogether in his sentiments. For as to the males, my American acquaintance assured me from frequent experience that their flesh was generally tough and lean, like that of our schoolboys by continual exercise, and their taste disagreeable; and to fatten them would not answer the charge. Then as to the females, it would, I think, with humble submission be a loss to the public, because they soon would become breeders themselves: and besides, it is not improbable that some scrupulous people might be apt to censure such a practice (although indeed very unjustly) as a little bordering upon cruelty; which, I confess, has always been with me the strongest objection against any project, how well soever intended.

But in order to justify my friend, he confessed that this expedient was put into his head by the famous Salmanaazor,[8] a native of the island Formosa, who came from thence to London above twenty years ago: and in conversation told my friend, that in his country when any young person happened to be put to death, the executioner sold the carcass to persons of quality as a prime dainty; and that in his time the body of a plump girl of fifteen, who was crucified for an attempt to poison the emperor, was sold to his imperial majesty's prime minister of state, and other great mandarins of the court, in joints from the gibbet, at four hundred crowns. Neither indeed can I deny, that if the same use were made of several plump young girls in this town, who without one single groat to their fortunes cannot stir abroad without a chair,[9] and appear at the playhouse and assemblies in foreign fineries which they never will pay for, the kingdom would not be the worse.

Some persons of a desponding spirit are in great concern about that vast number of poor people, who are aged, diseased, or maimed, and I have been desired to employ my thoughts what cause may be taken to ease the nation of so grievous an encumbrance. But I am not in the least pain upon that matter, because it is very well known that they are every day dying and rotting by cold and famine, and filth and vermin, as fast as can be reasonably expected. And as to the young laborers, they are now in as hopeful a

---

8   *Salmanaazor*   Under the false name "George Psalmanazar" a French citizen in 1704 published a popular book about Formosa where he claims to have been born; he was later exposed as an impostor.

9   *chair*   Sedan chair.

condition: they cannot get work, and consequently pine away for want of nourishment, to a degree that if at any time they are accidentally hired to common labor, they have not strength to perform it; and thus the country and themselves are in a fair way of being soon delivered from the evils to come.

20   I have too long digressed, and therefore shall return to my subject. I think the advantages by the proposal which I have made are obvious and many, as well as of the highest importance.

For first, as I have already observed, it would greatly lessen the number of Papists, with whom we are yearly overrun, being the principal breeders of the nation as well as our most dangerous enemies; and who stay at home on purpose with a design to deliver the kingdom to the Pretender, hoping to take their advantage by the absence of so many good Protestants, who have chosen rather to leave their country than stay at home and pay tithes against their conscience to an idolatrous Episcopal curate.

Secondly, the poor tenants will have something valuable of their own, which by law may be made liable to distress and help to pay their landlord's rent, their corn and cattle being already seized, and money a thing unknown.

Thirdly, whereas the maintenance of an hundred thousand children from two years old and upwards, cannot be computed at less than ten shillings apiece per annum, the nation's stock will be thereby increased fifty thousand pounds per annum, beside the profit of a new dish introduced to the tables of all gentlemen of fortune in the kingdom who have any refinement in taste. And the money will circulate among ourselves, the goods being entirely of our own growth and manufacture.

Fourthly, the constant breeders besides the gain of eight shillings sterling per annum by the sale of their children, will be rid of the charge of maintaining them after the first year.

25   Fifthly, this food would likewise bring great custom to taverns, where the vintners will certainly be so prudent as to procure the best receipts[10] for dressing it to perfection, and consequently have their houses frequented by all the fine gentlemen, who justly value themselves upon their knowledge in good eating; and a skilful cook who understands how to oblige his guests, will contrive to make it as expensive as they please.

Sixthly, this would be a great inducement to marriage, which all wise nations have either encouraged by rewards or enforced by laws and penalties. It would increase the care and tenderness of mothers towards their

---

10   *receipts*   Recipes.

children, when they were sure of a settlement for life to the poor babes, provided in some sort by the public, to their annual profit instead of expense. We should soon see an honest emulation among the married women, which of them could bring the fattest child to the market. Men would become as fond of their wives during the time of their pregnancy as they are now of their mares in foal, their cows in calf, their sows when they are ready to farrow; nor offer to beat or kick them (as is too frequent a practice) for fear of a miscarriage.

Many other advantages might be enumerated. For instance, the addition of some thousand carcasses in our exportation of barreled beef, the propagation of swine's flesh, and improvement in the art of making good bacon, so much wanted among us by the great destruction of pigs, too frequent at our tables, and which are no way comparable in taste or magnificence to a well-grown, fat, yearling child, which roasted whole will make a considerable figure at a Lord Mayor's feast or any other public entertainment. But this and many others I omit, being studious of brevity.

Supposing that one thousand families in this city would be constant customers for infant's flesh, besides others who might have it at merry meetings, particularly weddings and christenings, I compute that Dublin would take off annually about twenty thousand carcasses; and the rest of the kingdom (where probably they will be sold somewhat cheaper) the remaining eighty thousand.

I can think of no one objection that will possibly be raised against this proposal, unless it should be urged that the number of people will be thereby much lessened in the kingdom. This I freely own, and it was indeed one principal design in offering it to the world. I desire the reader will observe, that I calculate my remedy for this one individual kingdom of Ireland and for no other that ever was, is, or I think ever can be upon earth. Therefore let no man talk to me of other expedients: of taxing our absentees at five shillings a pound: of using neither clothes nor household furniture except what is of our own growth and manufacture: of utterly rejecting the materials and instruments that promote foreign luxury: of curing the expensiveness of pride, vanity, idleness, and gaming in our women: of introducing a vein of parsimony, prudence, and temperance: of learning to love our country, wherein we differ even from Laplanders and the inhabitants of Topinamboo:[11] of quitting our animosities and factions,

---

11 *Topinamboo* Name given in the eighteenth century to what is now coastal and central Brazil.

nor act any longer like the Jews,[12] who were murdering one another at the very moment their city was taken: of being a little cautious not to sell our country and conscience for nothing: of teaching landlords to have at least one degree of mercy towards their tenants. Lastly, of putting a spirit of honesty, industry, and skill into our shopkeepers; who, if a resolution could now be taken to buy only our native goods, would immediately unite to cheat and exact upon us in the price, the measure, and the goodness, nor could ever yet be brought to make one fair proposal of just dealing, though often and earnestly invited to it.

30   Therefore, I repeat, let no man talk to me of these and the like expedients, till he has at least a glimpse of hope that there will ever be some hearty and sincere attempt to put them in practice.

But as to myself, having been wearied out for many years with offering vain, idle, visionary thoughts, and at length utterly despairing of success, I fortunately fell upon this proposal; which, as it is wholly new, so it has something solid and real, of no expense and little trouble, full in our own power, and whereby we can incur no danger in disobliging England. For this kind of commodity will not bear exportation, the flesh being of too tender a consistence to admit a long continuance in salt, although perhaps I could name a country which would be glad to eat up our whole nation without it.

After all, I am not so violently bent upon my own opinion as to reject any offer proposed by wise men, which shall be found equally innocent, cheap, easy, and effectual. But before something of that kind shall be advanced in contradiction to my scheme, and offering a better, I desire the author or authors will be pleased maturely to consider two points. First, as things now stand, how they will be able to find food and raiment for a hundred thousand useless mouths and backs? And secondly, there being a round million of creatures in human figure throughout this kingdom, whose whole subsistence put into a common stock would leave them in debt two millions of pounds sterling, adding those who are beggars by profession to the bulk of farmers, cottagers, and laborers, with the wives and children who are beggars in effect; I desire those politicians who dislike my overture, and may perhaps be so bold to attempt an answer, that they will first ask the parents of these mortals, whether they would not at this day think it a great happiness to have been sold for food at a year old in the manner I prescribe,

---

12 *like the Jews* The biblical reference is unclear (possible references include II Kings 24, II Chronicles 37); the anti-Semitic sentiment is all too clear.

and thereby have avoided such a perpetual scene of misfortunes as they have since gone through by the oppression of landlords, the impossibility of paying rent without money or trade, the want of common sustenance, with neither house nor clothes to cover them from the inclemencies of weather, and the most inevitable prospect of entailing the like or greater miseries upon their breed forever.

I profess, in the sincerity of my heart, that I have not the least personal interest in endeavoring to promote this necessary work, having no other motive than the public good of my country, by advancing our trade, providing for infants, relieving the poor, and giving some pleasure to the rich. I have no children by which I can propose to get a single penny; the youngest being nine years old, and my wife past child-bearing.

(1729)

Questions

1. At what point does the reader realize that this is a satire? What effect does this delay have?
2. What is it possible to infer about the character of the speaker?
3. What is the purpose of the long list of other "expedients" provided in paragraph 29?
4. Comment on Swift's diction, and in particular on the use of such terms as "dam," "breeders," and "yearling child." Can you think of parallels in the way in which humans refer to the animals they eat?

SAMUEL JOHNSON

TO REIGN ONCE MORE IN OUR NATIVE COUNTRY

Discussions of the Seven Years' War in North America have
focused most often on the main protagonists—the English
and the French. In this essay Johnson attempts to imagine
the point of view of Native North Americans.

ℰ

A s the English army was passing towards Quebec along a soft savanna
between a mountain and a lake, one of the petty chiefs of the inland regions stood upon a rock surrounded by his clan, and from behind the shelter
of the bushes contemplated the art and regularity of European war. It was
evening, the tents were pitched, he observed the security with which the
troops rested in the night, and the order with which the march was renewed
in the morning. He continued to pursue them with his eye till they could be
seen no longer, and then stood for some time silent and pensive.

Then turning to his followers, "My children," said he, "I have often
heard from men hoary with long life, that there was a time when our
ancestors were absolute lords of the woods, the meadows, and the lakes,
wherever the eye can reach or the foot can pass. They fished and hunted,
feasted and danced, and when they were weary lay down under the first
thicket, without danger and without fear. They changed their habitations as
the seasons required, convenience prompted, or curiosity allured them, and
sometimes gathered the fruits of the mountain, and sometimes sported in
canoes along the coast.

"Many years and ages are supposed to have been thus passed in plenty
and security; when at last, a new race of men entered our country from the
great ocean. They enclosed themselves in habitations of stone, which our
ancestors could neither enter by violence, nor destroy by fire. They issued
from those fastnesses, sometimes covered like the armadillo with shells,

26

from which the lance rebounded on the striker, and sometimes carried by mighty beasts which had never been seen in our vales or forests, of such strength and swiftness, that flight and opposition were vain alike. Those invaders ranged over the continent, slaughtering in their rage those that resisted, and those that submitted, in their mirth. Of those that remained, some were buried in caverns, and condemned to dig metals for their masters; some were employed in tilling the ground, of which foreign tyrants devour the produce; and when the sword and the mines have destroyed the natives, they supply their place by human beings of another color, brought from some distant country to perish here under toil and torture.

"Some there are who boast their humanity, and content themselves to seize our chases and fisheries, who drive us from every tract of ground where fertility and pleasantness invite them to settle, and make no war upon us except when we intrude upon our own lands.

"Others pretend to have purchased a right of residence and tyranny; but surely the insolence of such bargains is more offensive than the avowed and open dominion of force. What reward can induce the possessor of a country to admit a stranger more powerful than himself? Fraud or terror must operate in such contracts; either they promised protection which they never have afforded, or instruction which they never imparted. We hoped to be secured by their favor from some other evil, or to learn the arts of Europe, by which we might be able to secure ourselves. Their power they have never exerted in our defense, and their arts they have studiously concealed from us. Their treaties are only to deceive, and their traffic only to defraud us. They have a written law among them, of which they boast as derived from him who made the earth and sea, and by which they profess to believe that man will be made happy when life shall forsake him. Why is not this law communicated to us? It is concealed because it is violated. For how can they preach it to an Indian nation, when I am told that one of its first precepts forbids them to do to others what they would not that others should do to them?

"But the time perhaps is now approaching when the pride of usurpation shall be crushed, and the cruelties of invasion shall be revenged. The sons of rapacity have now drawn their swords upon each other, and referred their claims to the decision of war; let us look unconcerned upon the slaughter, and remember that the death of every European delivers the country from a tyrant and a robber; for what is the claim of either nation, but the claim of the vulture to the leveret, of the tiger to the fawn? Let them then continue to dispute their title to regions which they cannot people, to purchase by

5

danger and blood the empty dignity of dominion over mountains which they will never climb, and rivers which they will never pass. Let us endeavor, in the mean time, to learn their discipline, and to forge their weapons; and when they shall be weakened with mutual slaughter, let us rush down upon them, force their remains to take shelter in their ships, and reign once more in our native country."

(1759)

Questions

1. Like many eighteenth-century writers, Johnson tends towards long "periodic" sentences, such as the second sentence in the last paragraph of this essay. What means does Johnson employ to help the reader follow his train of thought in such a long sentence?

2. Summarize in a single paragraph the case against the Europeans that Johnson puts forward in this essay.

3. Typically we consider it morally praiseworthy to "put oneself in the other person's shoes." Typically as well, however, it is considered presumptuous to try to speak on behalf of people of another culture—and particularly of a culture that has been oppressed by one's own people. How deserving of either praise or blame is it that Johnson has "appropriated the voice" of a Native North American in this essay? Would it have been better (either ethically or aesthetically) for him to have tried to make the same points but without assuming a Native voice?

MARY WOLLSTONECRAFT

TO M. TALLEYRAND-PÉRIGORD, LATE BISHOP OF AUTUN

In the Dedication to her great work, A Vindication of
the Rights of Woman, *Wollstonecraft summarizes
many of the book's main arguments.*

❧

SIR,

Having read with great pleasure a pamphlet which you have lately
published, I dedicate this volume to you; to induce you to reconsider
the subject, and maturely weigh what I have advanced respecting the
rights of woman and national education: and I call with the firm tone of
humanity; for my arguments, Sir, are dictated by a disinterested spirit—I
plead for my sex—not for myself. Independence I have long considered
as the grand blessing of life, the basis of every virtue—and independence
I will ever secure by contracting my wants, though I were to live on a
barren heath.

It is then an affection for the whole human race that makes my pen dart
rapidly along to support what I believe to be the cause of virtue: and the
same motive leads me earnestly to wish to see woman placed in a station in
which she would advance, instead of retarding, the progress of those glorious
principles that give a substance to morality. My opinion, indeed, respecting
the rights and duties of woman, seems to flow so naturally from these simple
principles, that I think it scarcely possible, but that some of the enlarged
minds who formed your admirable constitution, will coincide with me.

In France there is undoubtedly a more general diffusion of knowledge
than in any part of the European world, and I attribute it, in a great measure,
to the social intercourse which has long subsisted between the sexes. It is
true, I utter my sentiments with freedom, that in France the very essence
of sensuality has been extracted to regale the voluptuary, and a kind of

sentimental lust has prevailed, which, together with the system of duplicity that the whole tenor of their political and civil government taught, have given a sinister sort of sagacity to the French character, properly termed finesse; from which naturally flow a polish of manners that injures the substance, by hunting sincerity out of society.—And, modesty, the fairest garb of virtue! has been more grossly insulted in France than even in England, till their women have treated as *prudish* that attention to decency, which brutes instinctively observe.

Manners and morals are so nearly allied that they have often been confounded; but, though the former should only be the natural reflection of the latter, yet, when various causes have produced factitious and corrupt manners, which are very early caught, morality becomes an empty name. The personal reserve, and sacred respect for cleanliness and delicacy in domestic life, which French women almost despise, are the graceful pillars of modesty; but, far from despising them, if the pure flame of patriotism have reached their bosoms, they should labor to improve the morals of their fellow-citizens, by teaching men, not only to respect modesty in women, but to acquire it themselves, as the only way to merit their esteem.

5   Contending for the rights of woman, my main argument is built on this simple principle, that if she be not prepared by education to become the companion of man, she will stop the progress of knowledge and virtue; for truth must be common to all, or it will be inefficacious with respect to its influence on general practice. And how can woman be expected to co-operate unless she know why she ought to be virtuous? unless freedom strengthen her reason till she comprehend her duty, and see in what manner it is connected with her real good? If children are to be educated to understand the true principle of patriotism, their mother must be a patriot; and the love of mankind, from which an orderly train of virtues spring, can only be produced by considering the moral and civil interest of mankind; but the education and situation of woman, at present, shuts her out from such investigations.

In this work I have produced many arguments, which to me were conclusive, to prove that the prevailing notion respecting a sexual character[1] was subversive of morality, and I have contended, that to render the human body and mind more perfect, chastity must more universally prevail, and that chastity will never be respected in the male world till the person of a woman is not, as it were, idolized, when little virtue or sense embellish

---

1   *prevailing notion respecting a sexual character*   I.e., prevailing notion regarding what is natural and appropriate for the two sexes.

it with the grand traces of mental beauty, or the interesting simplicity of affection.

Consider, Sir, dispassionately, these observations—for a glimpse of this truth seemed to open before you when you observed, "that to see one half of the human race excluded by the other from all participation of government, was a political phenomenon that, according to abstract principles, it was impossible to explain." If so, on what does your constitution rest? If the abstract rights of man will bear discussion and explanation, those of woman, by a parity of reasoning, will not shrink from the same test: though a different opinion prevails in this country, built on the very arguments which you use to justify the oppression of woman—prescription.

Consider, I address you as a legislator, whether, when men contend for their freedom, and to be allowed to judge for themselves respecting their own happiness, it be not inconsistent and unjust to subjugate women, even though you firmly believe that you are acting in the manner best calculated to promote their happiness? Who made man the exclusive judge, if woman partake with him the gift of reason?

In this style, argue tyrants of every denomination, from the weak king to the weak father of a family; they are all eager to crush reason; yet always assert that they usurp its throne only to be useful. Do you not act a similar part, when you *force* all women, by denying them civil and political rights, to remain immured in their families groping in the dark? for surely, Sir, you will not assert, that a duty can be binding which is not founded on reason? If indeed this be their destination, arguments may be drawn from reason: and thus augustly supported, the more understanding women acquire, the more they will be attached to their duty—comprehending it—for unless they comprehend it, unless their morals be fixed on the same immutable principle as those of man, no authority can make them discharge it in a virtuous manner. They may be convenient slaves, but slavery will have its constant effect, degrading the master and the abject dependent.

But, if women are to be excluded, without having a voice, from a participation of the natural rights of mankind, prove first, to ward off the charge of injustice and inconsistency, that they want[2] reason—else this flaw in your NEW CONSTITUTION will ever show that man must, in some shape, act like a tyrant, and tyranny, in whatever part of society it rears its brazen front, will ever undermine morality.

I have repeatedly asserted, and produced what appeared to me

10

---

2   *want* Lack.

irrefragable arguments drawn from matters of fact, to prove my assertion, that women cannot, by force, be confined to domestic concerns; for they will, however ignorant, intermeddle with more weighty affairs, neglecting private duties only to disturb, by cunning tricks, the orderly plans of reason which rise above their comprehension.

Besides, whilst they are only made to acquire personal accomplishments, men will seek for pleasure in variety, and faithless husbands will make faithless wives; such ignorant beings, indeed, will be very excusable when, not taught to respect public good, nor allowed any civil rights, they attempt to do themselves justice by retaliation.

The box of mischief thus opened in society, what is to preserve private virtue, the only security of public freedom and universal happiness?

Let there be then no coercion *established* in society, and the common law of gravity prevailing, the sexes will fall into their proper places. And, now that more equitable laws are forming your citizens, marriage may become more sacred: your young men may choose wives from motives of affection, and your maidens allow love to root out vanity.

15   The father of a family will not then weaken his constitution and debase his sentiments, by visiting the harlot, nor forget, in obeying the call of appetite, the purpose for which it was implanted. And, the mother will not neglect her children to practice the arts of coquetry, when sense and modesty secure her the friendship of her husband.

But, till men become attentive to the duty of a father, it is vain to expect women to spend that time in their nursery which they, "wise in their generation," choose to spend at their glass;[3] for this exertion of cunning is only an instinct of nature to enable them to obtain indirectly a little of that power of which they are unjustly denied a share: for, if women are not permitted to enjoy legitimate rights, they will render both men and themselves vicious, to obtain illicit privileges.

I wish, Sir, to set some investigations of this kind afloat in France; and should they lead to a confirmation of my principles, when your constitution is revised the Rights of Woman may be respected, if it be fully proved that reason calls for this respect, and loudly demands JUSTICE for one half of the human race.

I am, SIR,

    Your's respectfully,

                                                M.W.
                                              (1792)

---

3   *glass* Mirror.

Questions

1. In no more than three paragraphs summarize the main points of Wollstonecraft's argument here.

2. What in Wollstonecraft's style of writing do you think might have helped make her work influential?

3. Can you think of additional arguments in support of Wollstonecraft's position?

CHARLES LYELL

from THE PRINCIPLES OF GEOLOGY

*Lyell is often described as the founder of modern geology. In
this selection, the introduction to his magnum opus, Lyell sets
out to define the science and connect it to other disciplines.*

❧

CHAPTER I

*Geology defined—Compared to History—Its relation to other
Physical Sciences—Its distinctness from all—Not to
be confounded with Cosmogony.*

Geology is the science which investigates the successive changes that
have taken place in the organic and inorganic kingdoms of nature; it
enquires into the causes of these changes, and the influence which they
have exerted in modifying the surface and external structure of our planet.

By these researches into the state of the earth and its inhabitants at
former periods, we acquire a more perfect knowledge of its *present* condition, and more comprehensive views concerning the laws *now* governing
its animate and inanimate productions. When we study history, we obtain
a more profound insight into human nature, by instituting a comparison
between the present and former states of society. We trace the long series
of events which have gradually led to the actual posture of affairs; and by
connecting effects with their causes, we are enabled to classify and retain
in the memory a multitude of complicated relations—the various peculiarities of national character—the different degrees of moral and intellectual
refinement, and numerous other circumstances, which, without historical
associations, would be uninteresting or imperfectly understood. As the
present condition of nations is the result of many antecedent changes,
some extremely remote and others recent, some gradual, others sudden and
violent, so the state of the natural world is the result of a long succession of

events, and if we would enlarge our experience of the present economy of nature, we must investigate the effects of her operations in former epochs.

We often discover with surprise, on looking back into the chronicles of nations, how the fortune of some battle has influenced the fate of millions of our contemporaries, when it has long been forgotten by the mass of the population. With this remote event we may find inseparably connected the geographical boundaries of a great state, the language now spoken by the inhabitants, their peculiar manners, laws, and religious opinions. But far more astonishing and unexpected are the connections brought to light, when we carry back our researches into the history of nature. The form of a coast, the configuration of the interior of a country, the existence and extent of lakes, valleys, and mountains, can often be traced to the former prevalence of earthquakes and volcanoes, in regions which have long been undisturbed. To these remote convulsions the present fertility of some districts, the sterile character of others, the elevation of land above the sea, the climate, and various peculiarities, may be distinctly referred. On the other hand, many distinguishing features of the surface may often be ascribed to the operation at a remote era of slow and tranquil causes—to the gradual deposition of sediment in a lake or in the ocean, or to the prolific growth in the same of corals and testacea. To select another example, we find in certain localities subterranean deposits of coal, consisting of vegetable matter, formerly drifted into seas and lakes. These seas and lakes have since been filled up, the lands whereon the forests grew have disappeared or changed their form, the rivers and currents which floated the vegetable masses can no longer be traced, and the plants belonged to species which for ages have passed away from the surface of our planet. Yet the commercial prosperity, and numerical strength of a nation, may now be mainly dependent on the local distribution of fuel determined by that ancient state of things.

Geology is intimately related to almost all the physical sciences, as is history to the moral.[1] An historian should, if possible, be at once profoundly acquainted with ethics, politics, jurisprudence, the military art, theology; in a word, with all branches of knowledge, whereby any insight into human affairs, or into the moral and intellectual nature of man, can be obtained. It would be no less desirable that a geologist should be well versed in chemistry, natural philosophy, mineralogy, zoology, comparative anatomy, botany; in short, in every science relating to organic and inorganic nature. With these accomplishments the historian and geologist would rarely fail

---

1   *to the moral*   I.e., to the moral sciences (ethics, politics, jurisprudence, etc.).

to draw correct and philosophical conclusions from the various monuments transmitted to them of former occurrences. They would know to what combination of causes analogous effects were referable, and they would often be enabled to supply by inference, information concerning many events unrecorded in the defective archives of former ages. But the brief duration of human life, and our limited powers, are so far from permitting us to aspire to such extensive acquisitions, that excellence even in one department is within the reach of few, and those individuals most effectually promote the general progress, who concentrate their thoughts on a limited portion of the field of inquiry. As it is necessary that the historian and the cultivators of moral or political science should reciprocally aid each other, so the geologist and those who study natural history or physics stand in equal need of mutual assistance. A comparative anatomist may derive some accession of knowledge from the bare inspection of the remains of an extinct quadruped, but the relic throws much greater light upon his own science, when he is informed to what relative era it belonged, what plants and animals were its contemporaries, in what degree of latitude it once existed, and other historical details. A fossil shell may interest a conchologist, though he be ignorant of the locality from which it came; but it will be of more value when he learns with what other species it was associated, whether they were marine or fresh-water, whether the strata containing them were at a certain elevation above the sea, and what relative position they held in regard to other groups of strata, with many other particulars determinable by an experienced geologist alone. On the other hand, the skill of the comparative anatomist and conchologist are often indispensable to those engaged in geological research, although it will rarely happen that the geologist will himself combine these different qualifications in his own person.

5   Some remains of former organic beings, like the ancient temple, statue, or picture, may have both their intrinsic and their historical value, while there are others which can never be expected to attract attention for their own sake. A painter, sculptor, or architect, would often neglect many curious relics of antiquity, as devoid of beauty and uninstructive with relation to their own art, however illustrative of the progress of refinement in some ancient nation. It has therefore been found desirable that the antiquary should unite his labors to those of the historian, and similar co-operation has become necessary in geology. The field of inquiry in living nature being inexhaustible, the zoologist and botanist can rarely be induced to sacrifice time in exploring the imperfect remains of lost species of animals and plants, while those still existing afford constant matter of novelty. They

must entertain a desire of promoting *geology* by such investigations, and some knowledge of its objects must guide and direct their studies. According to the different opportunities, tastes, and talents of individuals, they may employ themselves in collecting particular kinds of minerals, rocks, or organic remains, and these, when well examined and explained, afford data to the geologist, as do coins, medals, and inscriptions to the historian.

It was long ere the distinct nature and legitimate objects of geology were fully recognized, and it was at first confounded with many other branches of inquiry, just as the limits of history, poetry, and mythology were ill-defined in the infancy of civilization. Werner appears to have regarded geology as little other than a subordinate department of mineralogy, and Desmarest included it under the head of Physical Geography. But the identification of its objects with those of Cosmogony has been the most common and serious source of confusion. The first who endeavored to draw a clear line of demarcation between these distinct departments, was Hutton, who declared that geology was in no ways concerned "with questions as to the origin of things." But his doctrine on this head was vehemently opposed at first, and although it has gradually gained ground, and will ultimately prevail, it is yet far from being established. We shall attempt in the sequel of this work to demonstrate that geology differs as widely from cosmogony, as speculations concerning the creation of man differ from history. But before we enter more at large on this controverted question, we shall endeavor to trace the progress of opinion on this topic, from the earliest ages, to the commencement of the present century.

(1830)

Questions

1. Discuss Lyell's style of structuring sentences, with particular reference to the sentences that form the third paragraph.

2. Explain in your own words the interaction between geology and other academic disciplines.

3. It has often been said that Lyell is one scientific writer who appeals to the imagination of his readers. Is there any evidence to suggest this here?

HENRY DAVID THOREAU

CIVIL DISOBEDIENCE

*Thoreau's "Civil Disobedience," written in the wake of his brief
imprisonment for refusing to pay a federal poll tax, has become
perhaps the most famous and influential of all American essays.*

❧

I heartily accept the motto,—"That government is best which governs
least"; and I should like to see it acted up to more rapidly and systematically. Carried out, it finally amounts to this, which also I believe,—"That
government is best which governs not at all"; and when men are prepared
for it, that will be the kind of government which they will have. Government is at best but an expedient; but most governments are usually, and
all governments are sometimes, inexpedient. The objections which have
been brought against a standing army, and they are many and weighty, and
deserve to prevail, may also at last be brought against a standing government. The standing army is only an arm of the standing government. The
government itself, which is only the mode which the people have chosen
to execute their will, is equally liable to be abused and perverted before
the people can act through it. Witness the present Mexican war,[1] the work
of comparatively a few individuals using the standing government as
their tool; for, in the outset, the people would not have consented to this
measure.

---

1   *the present Mexican war*   The Mexican-American War of 1846-48 was fought
over a border dispute. Mexico claimed territory north to the Nueces River, while the
Texans claimed that their territory extended south to the Rio Grande. The Americans
were the aggressors in beginning the war when General Zachary Taylor advanced with
his troops into the area under dispute. When the war ended, Mexico gave up not only
its claim to Texas above the Rio Grande, but also New Mexico and California. (The
United States did pay Mexico 15 million dollars for the latter territories as part of the
final agreement under the terms of the Gadsden Purchase.)

This American government,—what is it but a tradition, though a recent one, endeavoring to transmit itself unimpaired to posterity, but each instant losing some of its integrity? It has not the vitality and force of a single living man; for a single man can bend it to his will. It is a sort of wooden gun to the people themselves. But is it not the less necessary for this; for the people must have some complicated machinery or other, and hear its din, to satisfy that idea of government which they have. Governments show thus how successfully men can be imposed on, even impose on themselves, for their own advantage. It is excellent, we must all allow. Yet this government never of itself furthered any enterprise, but by the alacrity with which it got out of its way. *It* does not keep the country free. *It* does not settle the West. *It* does not educate. The character inherent in the American people has done all that has been accomplished; and it would have done somewhat more, if the government had not sometimes got in its way. For government is an expedient by which men would fain succeed in letting one another alone; and, as has been said, when it is most expedient, the governed are most let alone by it. Trade and commerce, if they were not made of India-rubber, would never manage to bounce over the obstacles which legislators are continually putting in their way; and, if one were to judge these men wholly by the effects of their actions and not partly by their intentions, they would deserve to be classed and punished with those mischievous persons who put obstructions on the railroads.

But, to speak practically and as a citizen, unlike those who call themselves no-government men, I ask for, not at once no government, but *at once* a better government. Let every man make known what kind of government would command his respect, and that will be one step toward obtaining it.

After all, the practical reason why, when the power is once in the hands of the people, a majority are permitted, and for a long period continue, to rule is not because they are most likely to be in the right, nor because this seems fairest to the minority, but because they are physically the strongest. But a government in which the majority rule in all cases cannot be based on justice, even as far as men understand it. Can there not be a government in which majorities do not virtually decide right and wrong, but conscience?—in which majorities decide only those questions to which the rule of expediency is applicable? Must the citizen ever for a moment, or in the least degree, resign his conscience to the legislator? Why has every man a conscience, then? I think that we should be men first, and subjects afterward. It is not desirable to cultivate a respect for the law, so much as for the right. The only obligation which I have a right to assume is to do at any time what I think right. It is truly enough said, that a corporation[2] has no conscience; but a corporation of conscientious men is a corporation *with* a conscience. Law never made men a whit more just; and, by means of their respect for it, even the well-disposed are daily made the agents of injustice. A common and natural result of an undue respect for law is, that you may see a file of soldiers, colonel, captain, corporal, privates, powder-monkeys, and all, marching in admirable order over hill and dale to the wars, against their wills, ay, against their common sense and consciences, which makes it very steep marching indeed, and produces a palpitation of the heart. They have no doubt that it is a damnable business in which they are concerned; they are all peaceably inclined. Now, what are they? Men at all? or small movable forts and magazines, at the service of some unscrupulous man in power? Visit the Navy-Yard, and behold a marine, such a man as an American government can make, or such as it can make a man with its black arts,—a mere shadow and reminiscence of humanity, a man laid out alive and standing, and already, as one may say, buried under arms with funeral accompaniments, though it may be,—

> Not a drum was heard, not a funeral note,
>   As his corse to the rampart we hurried;
> Not a soldier discharged his farewell shot
>   O'er the grave where our hero we buried.

5   The mass of men serve the state thus, not as men mainly, but as machines, with their bodies. They are the standing army, and the militia, jailers, constables, posse comitatus, etc. In most cases there is no free exercise whatever of the judgment or of the moral sense; but they put themselves on a level with wood and earth and stones; and wooden men can perhaps be manufactured that will serve the purpose as well. Such command no more respect than men of straw or a lump of dirt. They have the same sort of worth only as horses and dogs. Yet such as these even are commonly esteemed good citizens. Others—as most legislators, politicians, lawyers, ministers, and office-holders—serve the state chiefly with their heads; and, as they rarely make any moral distinctions, they are as likely to serve the Devil, without *intending* it, as God. A very few, as heroes, patriots, martyrs, reformers in the great sense, and *men*, serve the state with their consciences

---

2   *corporation* I.e., in the sense of any "body of associated persons" (not formed specifically for business ends).

also, and so necessarily resist it for the most part; and they are commonly treated as enemies by it. A wise man will only be useful as a man, and will not submit to be "clay," and "stop a hole to keep the wind away," but leave that office to his dust at least:—

> I am too high-born to be propertied,
> To be a secondary at control,
> Or useful serving-man and instrument
> To any sovereign state throughout the world.

He who gives himself entirely to his fellow-men appears to them useless and selfish; but he who gives himself partially to them is pronounced a benefactor and philanthropist.

How does it become a man to behave toward this American government to-day? I answer, that he cannot without disgrace be associated with it. I cannot for an instant recognize that political organization as *my* government which is the *slave's* government also.

All men recognize the right of revolution; that is, the right to refuse allegiance to, and to resist, the government, when its tyranny or its inefficiency are great and unendurable. But almost all say that such is not the case now. But such was the case, they think, in the Revolution of '75. If one were to tell me that this was a bad government because it taxed certain foreign commodities brought to its ports, it is most probable that I should not make an ado about it, for I can do without them. All machines have their friction; and possibly this does enough good to counterbalance the evil. At any rate, it is a great evil to make a stir about it. But when the friction comes to have its machine, and oppression and robbery are organized, I say, let us not have such a machine any longer. In other words, when a sixth of the population of a nation which has undertaken to be the refuge of liberty are slaves, and a whole country is unjustly overrun and conquered by a foreign army, and subjected to military law, I think that it is not too soon for honest men to rebel and revolutionize. What makes this duty the more urgent is the fact that the country so overrun is not our own, but ours is the invading army.

Paley, a common authority with many on moral questions, in his chapter on the "Duty of Submission to Civil Government," resolves all civil obligation into expediency; and he proceeds to say, "that so long as the interest of the whole society requires it, that is, so long as the established government cannot be resisted or changed without public inconveniency, it is the will of God that the established government be obeyed, and no longer.... This principle being admitted, the justice of every particular case of resistance is reduced to a computation of the quantity of the danger and grievance on the one side, and of the probability and expense of redressing it on the other." Of this, he says, every man shall judge for himself. But Paley appears never to have contemplated those cases to which the rule of expediency does not apply, in which a people, as well as an individual, must do justice, cost what it may. If I have unjustly wrested a plank from a drowning man, I must restore it to him though I drown myself. This, according to Paley, would be inconvenient. But he that would save his life, in such a case, shall lose it. This people must cease to hold slaves, and to make war on Mexico, though it cost them their existence as a people.

10   In their practice, nations agree with Paley; but does anyone think that Massachusetts[3] does exactly what is right at the present crisis?

> A drab of state, a cloth-o'-silver slut,
> To have her train borne up, and her soul trail in the dirt.

Practically speaking, the opponents to a reform in Massachusetts are not a hundred thousand politicians at the South, but a hundred thousand merchants and farmers here, who are more interested in commerce and agriculture than they are in humanity, and are not prepared to do justice to the slave and to Mexico, *cost what it may*. I quarrel not with far-off foes, but with those who, near at home, co-operate with, and do the bidding of, those far away, and without whom the latter would be harmless. We are accustomed to say, that the mass of men are unprepared; but improvement is slow, because the few are not materially wiser or better than the many. It is not so important that many should be as good as you, as that there be some absolute goodness somewhere; for that will leaven the whole lump. There are thousands who are *in opinion* opposed to slavery and to the war, who yet in effect do nothing to put an end to them; who, esteeming themselves children of Washington and Franklin, sit down with their hands in their pockets, and say that they know not what to do, and do nothing; who even postpone the question of freedom to the question of free-trade, and quietly read the prices-current along with the latest advices from

---

3   *Massachusetts*   Thoreau was born and raised in Concord, Massachusetts, attended Harvard University in Cambridge, Massachusetts, and then returned to Concord for much of his adult life.

Mexico, after dinner, and, it may be, fall asleep over them both. What is the price-current of an honest man and patriot to-day? They hesitate, and they regret, and sometimes they petition; but they do nothing in earnest and with effect. They will wait, well disposed, for others to remedy the evil, that they may no longer have it to regret. At most, they give only a cheap vote, and a feeble countenance and Godspeed, to the right, as it goes by them. There are nine hundred and ninety-nine patrons of virtue to one virtuous man. But it is easier to deal with the real possessor of a thing than with the temporary guardian of it.

All voting is a sort of gaming, like checkers or backgammon, with a slight moral tinge to it, a playing with right and wrong, with moral questions; and betting naturally accompanies it. The character of the voters is not staked. I cast my vote, perchance, as I think right; but I am not vitally concerned that that right should prevail. I am willing to leave it to the majority. Its obligation, therefore, never exceeds that of expediency. Even voting *for the right* is *doing* nothing for it. It is only expressing to men feebly your desire that it should prevail. A wise man will not leave the right to the mercy of chance, nor wish it to prevail through the power of the majority. There is but little virtue in the action of masses of men. When the majority shall at length vote for the abolition of slavery, it will be because they are indifferent to slavery, or because there is but little slavery left to be abolished by their vote. *They* will then be the only slaves. Only *his* vote can hasten the abolition of slavery who asserts his own freedom by his vote.

I hear of a convention to be held in Baltimore, or elsewhere, for the selection of a candidate for the Presidency, made up chiefly of editors, and men who are politicians by profession; but I think, what is it to any independent, intelligent, and respectable man what decision they may come to? Shall we not have the advantage of his wisdom and honesty, nevertheless? Can we not count upon some independent votes? Are there not many individuals in the country who do not attend conventions? But no: I find that the respectable man, so called, has immediately drifted from his position, and despairs of his country, when his country has more reason to despair of him. He forthwith adopts one of the candidates thus selected as the only *available* one, thus proving that he is himself *available* for any purposes of the demagogue. His vote is of no more worth than that of any unprincipled foreigner or hireling native, who may have been bought. O for a man who is a *man*, and, as my neighbor says, has a bone in his back which you cannot pass your hand through! Our statistics are at fault: the population has been returned too large. How many *men* are there to a square thousand miles in this country? Hardly one. Does not America offer any inducement for men to settle here? The American has dwindled into an Odd Fellow,—one who may be known by the development of his organ of gregariousness, and a manifest lack of intellect and cheerful self-reliance; whose first and chief concern, on coming into the world, is to see that the Almshouses are in good repair; and, before yet he has lawfully donned the virile garb, to collect a fund for the support of the widows and orphans that may be; who, in short, ventures to live only by the aid of the Mutual Insurance company, which has promised to bury him decently.

It is not a man's duty, as a matter of course, to devote himself to the eradication of any, even the most enormous wrong; he may still properly have other concerns to engage him; but it is his duty, at least, to wash his hands of it, and, if he gives it no thought longer, not to give it practically his support. If I devote myself to other pursuits and contemplations, I must first see, at least, that I do not pursue them sitting upon another man's shoulders. I must get off him first, that he may pursue his contemplations too. See what gross inconsistency is tolerated. I have heard some of my townsmen say, "I should like to have them order me out to help put down an insurrection of the slaves, or to march to Mexico;—see if I would go"; and yet these very men have each, directly by their allegiance, and so indirectly, at least, by their money, furnished a substitute. The soldier is applauded who refuses to serve in an unjust war by those who do not refuse to sustain the unjust government which makes the war; is applauded by those whose own act and authority he disregards and sets at naught; as if the state were penitent to that degree that it hired one to scourge it while it sinned, but not to that degree that it left off sinning for a moment. Thus, under the name of Order and Civil Government, we are all made at last to pay homage to and support our own meanness. After the first blush of sin comes its indifference; and from immoral it becomes, as it were, *un*moral, and not quite unnecessary to that life which we have made.

The broadest and most prevalent error requires the most disinterested virtue to sustain it. The slight reproach to which the virtue of patriotism is commonly liable, the noble are most likely to incur. Those who, while they disapprove of the character and measures of a government, yield to it their allegiance and support are undoubtedly its most conscientious supporters, and so frequently the most serious obstacles to reform. Some are petitioning the state to dissolve the Union, to disregard the requisitions of the President. Why do they not dissolve it themselves,—the union between themselves and the state,—and refuse to pay their quota into its treasury? Do not they stand in the same relation to the state that the state does to the Union? And have not the same reasons prevented the state from resisting the Union which have prevented them from resisting the state?

How can a man be satisfied to entertain an opinion merely, and enjoy *it*? Is there any enjoyment in it, if his opinion is that he is aggrieved? If you are cheated out of a single dollar by your neighbor, you do not rest satisfied with knowing that you are cheated, or with saying that you are cheated, or even with petitioning him to pay you your due; but you take effectual steps at once to obtain the full amount, and see that you are never cheated again. Action from principle, the perception and the performance of right, changes things and relations; it is essentially revolutionary, and does not consist wholly with anything which was. It not only divides states and churches, it divides families; ay, it divides the *individual*, separating the diabolical in him from the divine.

Unjust laws exist: shall we be content to obey them, or shall we endeavor to amend them, and obey them until we have succeeded, or shall we transgress them at once? Men generally, under such a government as this, think that they ought to wait until they have persuaded the majority to alter them. They think that, if they should resist, the remedy would be worse than the evil. But it is the fault of the government itself that the remedy *is* worse than the evil. *It* makes it worse. Why is it not more apt to anticipate and provide for reform? Why does it not cherish its wise minority? Why does it cry and resist before it is hurt? Why does it not encourage its citizens to be on the alert to point out its faults, and *do* better than it would have them? Why does it always crucify Christ, and excommunicate Copernicus and Luther, and pronounce Washington and Franklin rebels?

One would think, that a deliberate and practical denial of its authority was the only offense never contemplated by government; else, why has it not assigned its definite, its suitable and proportionate penalty? If a man who has no property refuses but once to earn nine shillings for the state, he is put in prison for a period unlimited by any law that I know, and determined only by the discretion of those who placed him there; but if he should steal ninety times nine shillings from the state, he is soon permitted to go at large again.

If the injustice is part of the necessary friction of the machine of government, let it go: perchance it will wear smooth,—certainly the machine will wear out. If the injustice has a spring, or a pulley, or a rope, or a crank, exclusively for itself, then perhaps you may consider whether the remedy will not be worse than the evil; but if it is of such a nature that it requires you to be the agent of injustice to another, then, I say, break the law. Let your life be a counter friction to stop the machine. What I have to do is to see, at any rate, that I do not lend myself to the wrong which I condemn.

As for adopting the ways which the state has provided for remedying the evil, I know not of such ways. They take too much time, and a man's life will be gone. I have other affairs to attend to. I came into this world, not chiefly to make this a good place to live in, but to live in it, be it good or bad. A man has not everything to do, but something; and because he cannot do *everything*, it is not necessary that he should do *something* wrong. It is not my business to be petitioning the Governor or the Legislature any more than it is theirs to petition me; and if they should not hear my petition, what should I do then? But in this case the state has provided no way: its very Constitution is the evil. This may seem to be harsh and stubborn and unconciliatory; but it is to treat with the utmost kindness and consideration the only spirit that can appreciate or deserves it. So is all change for the better, like birth and death, which convulse the body.

20 I do not hesitate to say, that those who call themselves Abolitionists should at once effectually withdraw their support, both in person and property, from the government of Massachusetts, and not wait till they constitute a majority of one, before they suffer the right to prevail through them. I think that it is enough if they have God on their side, without waiting for that other one. Moreover, any man more right than his neighbors constitutes a majority of one already.

I meet this American government, or its representative, the state government, directly, and face to face, once a year—no more—in the person of its tax-gatherer; this is the only mode in which a man situated as I am necessarily meets it; and it then says distinctly, Recognize me; and the simplest, the most effectual, and, in the present posture of affairs, the indispensablest mode of treating with it on this head, of expressing your little satisfaction with and love for it, is to deny it then. My civil neighbor, the tax-gatherer, is the very man I have to deal with,—for it is, after all, with men and not with parchment that I quarrel,—and he has voluntarily chosen to be an agent of the government. How shall he ever know well what he is and does as an officer of the government, or as a man, until he is obliged to consider whether he shall treat me, his neighbor, for whom he has respect, as a neighbor and well-disposed man, or as a maniac and disturber of the peace, and see if he can get over this obstruction to his neighborliness without a ruder and more impetuous thought or speech corresponding with his action. I know this well, that if one thousand, if one hundred, if ten men whom I could name,—if ten *honest* men only,—ay, if *one* HONEST man, in this State of Massachusetts, *ceasing to hold slaves*, were actually to withdraw from this copartnership, and be locked up in the county jail therefore, it would be the abolition of slavery in America. For it matters not how small the beginning may seem to be: what is once well done is done forever. But we love better to talk about it: that we say is our mission. Reform keeps many scores of newspapers in its service, but not one man. If my esteemed neighbor, the State's ambassador, who will devote his days to the settlement of the question of human rights in the Council Chamber, instead of being threatened with the prisons of Carolina, were to sit down the prisoner of Massachusetts, that State which is so anxious to foist the sin of slavery upon her sister,—though at present she can discover only an act of inhospitality to be the ground of a quarrel with her,—the Legislature would not wholly waive the subject the following winter.

Under a government which imprisons any unjustly, the true place for a just man is also a prison. The proper place to-day, the only place which Massachusetts has provided for her freer and less desponding spirits, is in her prisons, to be put out and locked out of the State by her own act, as they have already put themselves out by their principles. It is there that the fugitive slave, and the Mexican prisoner on parole, and Indian come to plead the wrongs of his race should find them; on that separate, but more free and honorable ground, where the State places those who are not *with* her, but *against* her,—the only house in a slave State in which a free man can abide with honor. If any think that their influence would be lost there, and their voices no longer afflict the ear of the State, that they would not be as an enemy within its walls, they do not know by how much truth is stronger than error, nor how much more eloquently and effectively he can combat injustice who has experienced a little in his own person. Cast your whole vote, not a strip of paper merely, but your whole influence. A minority is powerless while it conforms to the majority; it is not even a minority then; but it is irresistible when it clogs by its whole weight. If the alternative is to keep all just men in prison, or give up war and slavery, the State will not hesitate which to choose. If a thousand men were not to pay their tax-bills this year, that would not be a violent and bloody measure, as it would be to pay them, and enable the State to commit violence and shed innocent blood. This is in fact, the definition of a peaceable revolution, if any such is possible. If the tax-gatherer, or any other public officer, asks me, as one has done, "But what shall I do?" my answer is, "If you really wish to do anything, resign your office." When the subject has refused allegiance, and the officer has resigned his office, then the revolution is accomplished. But even suppose blood should flow. Is there not a sort of blood shed when the conscience is wounded? Through this wound a man's real manhood and immortality flow out, and he bleeds to an everlasting death. I see this blood flowing now.

I have contemplated the imprisonment of the offender, rather than the seizure of his goods,—though both will serve the same purpose,—because they who assert the purest right, and consequently are most dangerous to a corrupt State, commonly have not spent much time in accumulating property. To such the State renders comparatively small service, and a slight tax is wont to appear exorbitant, particularly if they are obliged to earn it by special labor with their hands. If there were one who lived wholly without the use of money, the State itself would hesitate to demand it of him. But the rich man—not to make any invidious comparison—is always sold to the institution which makes him rich. Absolutely speaking, the more money, the less virtue; for money comes between a man and his objects, and obtains them for him; and it was certainly no great virtue to obtain it. It puts to rest many questions which he would otherwise be taxed to answer; while the only new question which it puts is the hard but superfluous one, how to spend it. Thus his moral ground is taken from under his feet. The opportunities of living are diminished in proportion as what are called the "means" are increased. The best thing a man can do for his culture when he is rich is to endeavor to carry out those schemes which he entertained when he was poor. Christ answered the Herodians according to their condition. "Show me the tribute-money," said he;—and one took a penny out of his pocket;—if you use money which has the image of Caesar on it, which he has made current and valuable, that is, *if you are men of the State*, and gladly enjoy the advantages of Caesar's government, then pay him back some of his own when he demands it. "Render therefore to Caesar that which is Caesar's, and to God those things which are God's,"—leaving them no wiser than before as to which was which; for they did not wish to know.

When I converse with the freest of my neighbors, I perceive that, whatever they may say about the magnitude and seriousness of the question, and their regard for the public tranquility, the long and the short of the matter is, that they cannot spare the protection of the existing government, and they dread the consequences to their property and families of disobedience to it. For my own part, I should not like to think that I ever rely on the protection of the State. But, if I deny the authority of the State when it presents its tax-bill, it will soon take and waste all my property, and so harass me and my children without end. This is hard. This makes it impossible for a man to live honestly, and at the same time comfortably, in outward respects. It will not be worth the while to accumulate property; that would be sure to go again. You must hire or squat somewhere, and raise but a small crop, and eat that soon. You must live within yourself, and depend upon yourself always tucked up and ready for a start, and not have many affairs. A man may grow rich in Turkey even, if he will be in all respects a good subject of the Turkish government. Confucius said: "If a state is governed by the principles of reason, poverty and misery are subjects of shame; if a state is not governed by the principles of reason, riches and honors are the subjects of shame." No: until I want the protection of Massachusetts to be extended to me in some distant Southern port, where my liberty is endangered, or until I am bent solely on building up an estate at home by peaceful enterprise, I can afford to refuse allegiance to Massachusetts, and her right to my property and life. It costs me less in every sense to incur the penalty of disobedience to the State than it would to obey. I should feel as if I were worth less in that case.

Some years ago, the State met me in behalf of the Church, and commanded me to pay a certain sum toward the support of a clergyman whose preaching my father attended, but never I myself. "Pay," it said, "or be locked up in the jail." I declined to pay. But unfortunately, another man saw fit to pay it. I did not see why the schoolmaster should be taxed to support the priest, and not the priest the schoolmaster; for I was not the State's schoolmaster, but I supported myself by voluntary subscription. I did not see why the lyceum should not present its tax-bill, and have the State to back its demand, as well as the Church. However, at the request of the selectmen, I condescended to make some such statement as this in writing:—"Know all men by these presents, that I, Henry Thoreau, do not wish to be regarded as a member of any incorporated society which I have not joined." This I gave to the town clerk; and he has it. The State, having thus learned that I did not wish to be regarded as a member of that church, has never made a like demand on me since; though it said that it must adhere to its original presumption that time. If I had known how to name them, I should then have signed off in detail from all the societies which I never signed on to; but I did not know where to find a complete list.

25

I have paid no poll-tax for six years. I was put into a jail on this account, for one night; and, as I stood considering the walls of solid stone, two or three feet thick, the door of wood and iron, a foot thick, and the iron grating which strained the light, I could not help being struck with the foolishness of that institution which treated me as if I were mere flesh and blood and bones, to be locked up. I wondered that it should have concluded at length that this was the best use it could put me to, and had never thought to avail itself of my services in some way. I saw that, if there was a wall of stone between me and my townsmen, there was a still more difficult one to climb or break through before they could get to be as free as I was. I did not for a moment feel confined, and walls seemed a great waste of stone and mortar. I felt as if I alone of all my townsmen had paid my tax. They plainly did not know how to treat me, but behaved like persons who are underbred. In every threat and in every compliment there was a blunder; for they thought that my chief desire was to stand the other side of that stone wall. I could not but smile to see how industriously they locked the door on my meditations, which followed them out again without let or hindrance, and *they* were really all that was dangerous. As they could not reach me, they had resolved to punish my body; just as boys, if they cannot come at some person against whom they have a spite, will abuse his dog. I saw that the State was halfwitted, that it was timid as a lone woman with her silver spoons, and that it did not know its friends from its foes, and I lost all my remaining respect for it, and pitied it.

Thus the State never intentionally confronts a man's sense, intellectual or moral, but only his body, his senses. It is not armed with superior wit or honesty, but with superior physical strength. I was not born to be forced. I will breathe after my own fashion. Let us see who is the strongest. What force has a multitude? They only can force me who obey a higher law than I. They force me to become like themselves. I do not hear of *men* being *forced* to live this way or that by masses of men. What sort of life were that to live? When I meet a government which says to me, "Your money or your life," why should I be in haste to give it my money? It may be in a great strait, and not know what to do: I cannot help that. It must help itself; do as I do. It is not worth the while to snivel about it. I am not responsible for the successful working of the machinery of society. I am not the son of the engineer. I perceive that, when an acorn and a chestnut fall side by side, the one does not remain inert to make way for the other, but both obey their own laws, and spring and grow and flourish as best they can, till one, perchance, overshadows and destroys the other. If a plant cannot live according to its nature, it dies; and so a man.

The night in prison was novel and interesting enough. The prisoners in their shirt-sleeves were enjoying a chat and the evening air in the doorway, when I entered. But the jailer said, "Come, boys, it is time to lock up"; and so they dispersed, and I heard the sound of their steps returning into the hollow apartments. My room-mate was introduced to me by the jailer as "a first-rate fellow and a clever man." When the door was locked, he showed me where to hang my hat, and how he managed matters there. The rooms were whitewashed once a month, and this one, at least, was the whitest, most simply furnished, and probably the neatest apartment in the town. He naturally wanted to know where I came from, and what brought me there; and, when I had told him, I asked in my turn how he came there, presuming him to be an honest man, of course; and, as the world goes, I believe he was. "Why," said he, "they accuse me of burning a barn; but I never did it." As near as I could discover, he had probably gone to bed in a barn when drunk, and smoked his pipe there; and so a barn was burnt. He had the reputation of being a clever man, and been there some three months waiting for his trial to come on, and would have to wait as much longer; but he was quite domesticated and contented, since he got his board for nothing, and thought that he was well treated.

He occupied one window, and I the other; and I saw that if one stayed there long, his principal business would be to look out the window. I had soon read all the tracts that were left there, and examined where former prisoners had broken out, and where a grate had been sawed off, and heard the history of the various occupants of that room; for I found that even here there was a history and a gossip which never circulated beyond the walls of the jail. Probably this is the only house in the town where verses are composed, which are afterward printed in a circular form, but not published. I was shown quite a long list of verses which were composed by some young men who had been detected in an attempt to escape, who avenged themselves by singing them.

I pumped my fellow-prisoner as dry as I could, for fear I should never see him again; but at length he showed me which was my bed, and left me to blow out the lamp.

It was like traveling into a far country, such as I had never expected to behold, to lie there for one night. It seemed to me that I never had heard the town-clock strike before, nor the evening sounds of the village; for we slept with the windows open, which were inside the grating. It was to see my native village in the light of the Middle Ages, and our Concord was turned into a Rhine stream, and visions of knights and castles passed before me. They were the voices of old burghers that I heard in the streets. I was an involuntary spectator and auditor of whatever was done and said in the kitchen of the adjacent village-inn,—a wholly new and rare experience to me. It was a closer view of my native town. I was fairly inside of it. I never had seen its institutions before. This is one of its peculiar institutions; for it is a shire town. I began to comprehend what its inhabitants were about.

In the morning, our breakfasts were put through the hole in the door, in small oblong-square tin pans, made to fit, and holding a pint of chocolate, with brown bread, and an iron spoon. When they called for the vessels again, I was green enough to return what bread I had left; but my comrade seized it, and said that I should lay that up for lunch or dinner. Soon after he was let out to work at haying in a neighboring field, whither he went every day, and would not be back till noon; so he bade me good-day, saying that he doubted if he should see me again.

When I came out of prison,—for someone interfered, and paid that tax,—I did not perceive that great changes had taken place on the common, such as he observed who went in a youth and emerged a tottering and gray-haired man; and yet a change had to my eyes come over the scene,— the town, and State, and country,—greater than any that mere time could effect. I saw yet more distinctly the State in which I lived. I saw to what extent the people among whom I lived could be trusted as good neighbors and friends; that their friendship was for summer weather only; that they did not greatly propose to do right; that they were a distinct race from me by their prejudices and superstitions, as the Chinamen and Malays are; that in their sacrifices to humanity they ran no risks, not even to their property; that after all they were not so noble but they treated the thief as he had treated them, and hoped, by a certain outward observance and a few prayers, and by walking in a particular straight though useless path from time to time, to save their souls. This may be to judge my neighbors harshly; for I believe that many of them are not aware that they have such an institution as the jail in their village.

It was formerly the custom in our village, when a poor debtor came out of jail, for his acquaintances to salute him, looking through their fingers, which were crossed to represent the grating of a jail window, "How do ye do?" My neighbors did not thus salute me, but first looked at me, and then at one another, as if I had returned from a long journey. I was put into jail as I was going to the shoemaker's to get a shoe which was mended. When I was let out the next morning, I proceeded to finish my errand, and, having put on my mended shoe, joined a huckleberry party, who were impatient to put themselves under my conduct; and in half an hour,—for the horse was soon tackled,—was in the midst of a huckleberry field, on one of our highest hills, two miles off, and then the State was nowhere to be seen.

This is the whole history of "My Prisons."

35

I have never declined paying the highway tax, because I am as desirous of being a good neighbor as I am of being a bad subject; and as for supporting schools, I am doing my part to educate my fellow-countrymen now. It is for no particular item in the tax-bill that I refuse to pay it. I simply wish to refuse allegiance to the State, to withdraw and stand aloof from it effectually. I do not care to trace the course of my dollar, if I could, till it buys a man or a musket to shoot one with,—the dollar is innocent,—but I am concerned to trace the effects of my allegiance. In fact, I quietly declare war with the State, after my fashion, though I will still make what use and get what advantage of her I can, as is usual in such cases.

If others pay the tax which is demanded of me, from a sympathy with the State, they do but what they have already done in their own case, or rather they abet injustice to a greater extent than the State requires. If they pay the tax from a mistaken interest in the individual taxed, to save his property, or prevent his going to jail, it is because they have not considered wisely how far they let their private feelings interfere with the public good.

This, then, is my position at present. But one cannot be too much on his guard in such a case, lest his action be biased by obstinacy or an undue regard for the opinions of men. Let him see that he does only what belong to himself and to the hour.

I think sometimes, Why, this people mean well, they are only ignorant; they would do better if they knew how: why give your neighbors this pain to treat you as they are not inclined to? But I think again, This is no reason why I should do as they do, or permit others to suffer much greater pain of a different kind. Again I sometimes say to myself, When many millions of men, without heat,[4] without ill will, without personal feeling of any kind, demand of you a few shillings only, without the possibility, such is their constitution, of retracting or altering their present demand, and without the possibility, on your side, of appeal to any other millions, why expose yourself to this overwhelming brute force? You do not resist cold and hunger,

---

4   *heat*   Anger.

the winds and the waves, thus obstinately; you quietly submit to a thousand similar necessities. You do not put your head into the fire. But just in proportion as I regard this as not wholly a brute force, but partly a human force, and consider that I have relations to those millions as to so many millions of men, and not of mere brute or inanimate things, I see that appeal is possible, first and instantaneously, from them to the Maker of them, and, secondly, from them to themselves. But if I put my head deliberately into the fire, there is no appeal to fire or to the Maker of fire, and I have only myself to blame. If I could convince myself that I have any right to be satisfied with men as they are, and to treat them accordingly, and not according, in some respects, to my requisitions and expectations of what they and I ought to be, then, like a good Mussulman and fatalist, I should endeavor to be satisfied with things as they are, and say it is the will of God. And, above all, there is this difference between resisting this and a purely brute or natural force, that I can resist this with some effect; but I cannot expect, like Orpheus, to change the nature of the rocks and trees and beasts.

40   I do not wish to quarrel with any man or nation. I do not wish to split hairs, to make fine distinctions, or set myself up as better than my neighbors. I seek rather, I may say, even an excuse for conforming to the laws of the land. I am but too ready to conform to them. Indeed, I have reason to suspect myself on this head; and each year, as the tax-gatherer comes round, I find myself disposed to review the acts and position of the general and State governments, and the spirit of the people, to discover a pretext for conformity.

> We must affect our country as our parents,
> And if at any time we alienate
> Our love or industry from doing it honor,
> We must respect effects and teach the soul
> Matter of conscience and religion,
> And not desire of rule or benefit.

I believe that the State will soon be able to take all my work of this sort out of my hands, and then I shall be no better a patriot than my fellow-countrymen. Seen from a lower point of view, the Constitution, with all its faults, is very good; and the law and the courts are very respectable; even this State and this American government are, in many respects, very admirable, and rare things, to be thankful for, such as a great many have described them; but seen from a point of view a little higher, they are what I have described them; seen from a higher still, and the highest, who shall say what they are, or that they are worth looking at or thinking of at all?

However, the government does not concern me much, and I shall bestow the fewest possible thoughts on it. It is not many moments that I live under a government, even in this world. If a man is thought-free, fancy-free, imagination-free, that which *is not* never for a long time appearing *to be* to him, unwise rulers or reformers cannot fatally interrupt him.

I know that most men think differently from myself; but those whose lives are by profession devoted to the study of these or kindred subjects content me as little as any. Statesmen and legislators, standing so completely within the institution, never distinctly and nakedly behold it. They speak of moving society, but have no resting-place without it. They may be men of a certain experience and discrimination, and have no doubt invented ingenious and even useful systems, for which we sincerely thank them; but all their wit and usefulness lie within certain not very wide limits. They are wont to forget that the world is not governed by policy and expediency. Webster[5] never goes behind government, and so cannot speak with authority about it. His words are wisdom to those legislators who contemplate no essential reform in the existing government; but for thinkers, and those who legislate for all time, he never once glances at the subject. I know of those whose serene and wise speculations on this theme would soon reveal the limits of his mind's range and hospitality. Yet compared with the cheap professions of most reformers, and the still cheaper wisdom and eloquence of politicians in general, his are almost the only sensible and valuable words, and we thank Heaven for him. Comparatively, he is always strong, original, and, above all, practical. Still, his quality is not wisdom, but prudence. The lawyer's truth is not Truth, but consistency or a consistent expediency. Truth is always in harmony with herself, and is not concerned chiefly to reveal the justice that may consist with wrong-doing. He well deserves to be called, as he has been called, the Defender of the Constitution. There are really no blows to be given by him but defensive ones. He is not a leader, but a follower. His leaders are the men of '87. "I have never made an effort," he says, "and never propose to make an effort; I have never countenanced an effort, and never mean to countenance an effort, to disturb the arrangement as originally

---

5   *Webster*   Daniel Webster (1782-1852), one of the great politicians of the mid-nineteenth century.

made, by which the various States came into the union." Still thinking of the sanction which the Constitution gives to slavery, he says, "Because it was a part of the original compact,—let it stand." Notwithstanding his special acuteness and ability, he is unable to take a fact out of its merely political relations, and behold it as it lies absolutely to be disposed of by the intellect,—what, for instance, it behooves a man to do here in America to-day with regard to slavery,—but ventures, or is driven, to make some such desperate answer as the following, while professing to speak absolutely, and as a private man,—from which what new and singular code of social duties might be inferred? "The manner," says he, "in which the governments of those States where slavery exists are to regulate it is for their own consideration, under their responsibility to their constituents, to the general laws of propriety, humanity, and justice, and to God. Associations formed elsewhere, springing from a feeling of humanity, or any other cause, have nothing whatever to do with it. They have never received any encouragement from me, and they never will."

They who know of no purer sources of truth, who have traced up its stream no higher, stand, and wisely stand, by the Bible and the Constitution, and drink at it there with reverence and humility; but they who behold where it comes trickling into this lake or that pool, gird up their loins once more, and continue their pilgrimage toward its fountain-head.

No man with a genius for legislation has appeared in America. They are rare in the history of the world. There are orators, politicians, and eloquent men, by the thousand; but the speaker has not yet opened his mouth to speak who is capable of settling the much-vexed questions of the day. We love eloquence for its own sake, and not for any truth which it may utter, or any heroism it may inspire. Our legislators have not yet learned the comparative value of free-trade and of freedom, of union, and of rectitude, to a nation. They have no genius or talent for comparatively humble questions of taxation and finance, commerce and manufactures and agriculture. If we were left solely to the wordy wit of legislators in Congress for our guidance, uncorrected by the seasonable experience and the effectual complaints of the people, America would not long retain her rank among the nations. For eighteen hundred years, though perchance I have no right to say it, the New Testament has been written; yet where is the legislator who has wisdom and practical talent enough to avail himself of the light which it sheds on the science of legislation?

45   The authority of government, even such as I am willing to submit to,— for I will cheerfully obey those who know and can do better than I, and in

many things even those who neither know nor can do so well,—is still an impure one: to be strictly just, it must have the sanctions and consent of the governed. It can have no pure right over my person and property but what I concede to it. The progress from an absolute to a limited monarchy, from a limited monarchy to a democracy, is a progress toward a true respect for the individual. Even the Chinese philosopher was wise enough to regard the individual as the basis of the empire. Is a democracy, such as we know it, the last improvement possible in government? Is it not possible to take a step further towards recognizing and organizing the rights of man? There will never be a really free and enlightened State until the State comes to recognize the individual as a higher and independent power, from which all its own power and authority are derived, and treats him accordingly. I please myself with imagining a State at last which can afford to be just to all men, and to treat the individual with respect as a neighbor; which even would not think it inconsistent with its own repose if a few were to live aloof from it, not meddling with it, nor embraced by it, who fulfilled all the duties of neighbors and fellow-men. A State which bore this kind of fruit, and suffered it to drop off as fast as it ripened, would prepare the way for a still more perfect and glorious State, which also I have imagined, but not yet anywhere seen.

(1849)

Questions

1. Explain in your own words Thoreau's concept of a "patron of virtue" (paragraph 10).

2. Thoreau's anti-government message has often appealed both to Americans who are to the right of center politically and to those who are to the left of center. Do you see any contradiction or paradox in this?

3. Compare "Civil Disobedience" with Martin Luther King's "Letter from Birmingham Jail" in terms of the ideas expressed, the style, and the tone of writing.

4. Discuss the extended metaphor in paragraph 18. How effective do you find the extended metaphor as a literary device? Write a paragraph yourself employing an extended metaphor.

5. Discuss the way in which Thoreau's argument in this essay is gendered. Like other transcendentalists, Thoreau clearly saw courage from a male perspective, and he frequently refers to what a "real man" can or should do. To what extent is this a harmful way of conceptualizing his ideas?

6. To a large degree, modern Western society conceives of difficult ethical issues in passive terms; citizens may have a responsibility to decide where they stand on these difficult issues, but they are not generally believed to have a moral responsibility to become a social activist on behalf of whichever causes they believe to be right. (Among contemporary philosophers, Peter Singer is unique in taking an activist role—see elsewhere in this volume.) To what degree do you think we should have responsibilities to act on behalf of what we believe to be right? When (if ever) are we justified in breaking the law in support of what we perceive to be a just cause?

7. In paragraph 22, Thoreau appears to equate real and metaphorical violence and bloodshed. Comment on this argumentative strategy.

8. Thoreau asserts that when a person becomes rich, the moral ground is "taken from under his feet." To what extent do you believe this to be true? A similar Christian idea is the notion that it is easier for a camel to pass through the eye of a needle than for a rich person to enter into heaven. Discuss the uneasy relationship between organized Christianity and wealth.

CHARLES DARWIN

from ON THE ORIGIN OF SPECIES BY MEANS OF NATURAL SELECTION

OR THE PRESERVATION OF FAVORED RACES IN THE STRUGGLE FOR LIFE

In the concluding section of his great work of natural history,
Darwin cast his gaze on the future of science and of humanity.

℘,

When the views entertained in this volume on the origin of species, or when analogous views are generally admitted, we can dimly foresee that there will be a considerable revolution in natural history. Systematists will be able to pursue their labors as at present; but they will not be incessantly haunted by the shadowy doubt whether this or that form be in essence a species. This I feel sure, and I speak after experience, will be no slight relief. The endless disputes whether or not some fifty species of British brambles are true species will cease. Systematists will have only to decide (not that this will be easy) whether any form be sufficiently constant and distinct from other forms, to be capable of definition; and if definable, whether the differences be sufficiently important to deserve a specific name. This latter point will become a far more essential consideration than it is at present; for differences, however slight, between any two forms, if not blended by intermediate gradations, are looked at by most naturalists as sufficient to raise both forms to the rank of species. Hereafter we shall be compelled to acknowledge that the only distinction between species and well-marked varieties is, that the latter are known, or believed, to be connected at the present day by intermediate gradations, whereas species were formerly thus connected. Hence, without quite rejecting the consideration of the present existence of intermediate gradations between any two forms, we shall be led to weigh more carefully and to value higher the actual amount of difference between them. It is quite possible that forms now generally acknowledged to be merely varieties may hereafter be thought worthy of specific names, as with the primrose and cowslip; and in this case scientific and common language will come into accordance. In short, we shall have to treat species in the same manner as those naturalists treat genera, who admit that genera are merely artificial combinations made for convenience. This may not be a cheering prospect; but we shall at least be freed from the vain search for the undiscovered and undiscoverable essence of the term species.

The other and more general departments of natural history will rise greatly in interest. The terms used by naturalists of affinity, relationship, community of type, paternity, morphology, adaptive characters, rudimentary and aborted organs, etc., will cease to be metaphorical, and will have a plain signification. When we no longer look at an organic being as a savage looks at a ship, as at something wholly beyond his comprehension; when we regard every production of nature as one which has had a history; when we contemplate every complex structure and instinct as the summing up of many contrivances, each useful to the possessor, nearly in the same way as when we look at any great mechanical invention as the summing up of the labor, the experience, the reason, and even the blunders of numerous workmen; when we thus view each organic being, how far more interesting, I speak from experience, will the study of natural history become!

A grand and almost untrodden field of inquiry will be opened, on the causes and laws of variation, on correlation of growth, on the effects of use and disuse, on the direct action of external conditions, and so forth. The study of domestic productions will rise immensely in value. A new variety raised by man will be a far more important and interesting subject for study than one more species added to the infinitude of already recorded species. Our classifications will come to be, as far as they can be so made, genealogies; and will then truly give what may be called the plan of creation. The rules for classifying will no doubt become simpler when we have a definite object in view. We possess no pedigrees or armorial bearings; and we have to discover and trace the many diverging lines of descent in our natural genealogies, by characters of any kind which have long been inherited. Rudimentary organs will speak infallibly with respect to the nature of long-lost structures. Species and groups of species, which are called aberrant, and which may fancifully be called living fossils, will aid us in forming a picture of the ancient forms of life. Embryology will reveal to us the structure, in some degree obscured, of the prototypes of each great class.

When we can feel assured that all the individuals of the same species, and all the closely allied species of most genera, have within a not very remote period descended from one parent, and have migrated from some one birthplace; and when we better know the many means of migration, then, by the light which geology now throws, and will continue to throw, on former changes of climate and of the level of the land, we shall surely be enabled to trace in an admirable manner the former migrations of the inhabitants of the whole world. Even at present, by comparing the differences of the inhabitants of the sea on the opposite sides of a continent, and the nature of the various inhabitants of that continent in relation to their apparent means of immigration, some light can be thrown on ancient geography.

The noble science of Geology loses glory from the extreme imperfection of the record. The crust of the earth with its embedded remains must not be looked at as a well-filled museum, but as a poor collection made at hazard and at rare intervals. The accumulation of each great fossiliferous formation will be recognized as having depended on an unusual concurrence of circumstances, and the blank intervals between the successive stages as having been of vast duration. But we shall be able to gauge with some security the duration of these intervals by a comparison of the preceding and succeeding organic forms. We must be cautious in attempting to correlate as strictly contemporaneous two formations, which include few identical species, by the general succession of their forms of life. As species are produced and exterminated by slowly acting and still existing causes, and not by miraculous acts of creation and by catastrophes; and as the most important of all causes of organic change is one which is almost independent of altered and perhaps suddenly altered physical conditions, namely, the mutual relation of organism to organism,—the improvement of one being entailing the improvement or the extermination of others; it follows, that the amount of organic change in the fossils of consecutive formations probably serves as a fair measure of the lapse of actual time. A number of species, however, keeping in a body might remain for a long period unchanged, whilst within this same period, several of these species, by migrating into new countries and coming into competition with foreign associates, might become modified; so that we must not overrate the accuracy of organic change as a measure of time. During early periods of the earth's history, when the forms of life were probably fewer and simpler, the rate of change was probably slower; and at the first dawn of life, when very few forms of the simplest structure existed, the rate of change may have been slow in an extreme degree. The whole history of the world, as

5

at present known, although of a length quite incomprehensible by us, will hereafter be recognized as a mere fragment of time, compared with the ages which have elapsed since the first creature, the progenitor of innumerable extinct and living descendants, was created.

In the distant future I see open fields for far more important researches. Psychology will be based on a new foundation, that of the necessary acquirement of each mental power and capacity by gradation. Light will be thrown on the origin of man and his history.

Authors of the highest eminence seem to be fully satisfied with the view that each species has been independently created. To my mind it accords better with what we know of the laws impressed on matter by the Creator, that the production and extinction of the past and present inhabitants of the world should have been due to secondary causes, like those determining the birth and death of the individual. When I view all beings not as special creations, but as the lineal descendants of some few beings which lived long before the first bed of the Silurian system was deposited, they seem to me to become ennobled. Judging from the past, we may safely infer that not one living species will transmit its unaltered likeness to a distant futurity. And of the species now living very few will transmit progeny of any kind to a far distant futurity; for the manner in which all organic beings are grouped, shows that the greater number of species of each genus, and all the species of many genera, have left no descendants, but have become utterly extinct. We can so far take a prophetic glance into futurity as to foretell that it will be the common and widely-spread species, belonging to the larger and dominant groups, which will ultimately prevail and procreate new and dominant species. As all the living forms of life are the lineal descendants of those which lived long before the Silurian epoch, we may feel certain that the ordinary succession by generation has never once been broken and that no cataclysm has desolated the whole world. Hence we may look with some confidence to a secure future of equally inappreciable length. And as natural selection works solely by and for the good of each being, all corporeal and mental endowments will tend to progress towards perfection.

It is interesting to contemplate an entangled bank, clothed with many plants of many kinds, with birds singing on the bushes, with various insects flitting about, and with worms crawling through the damp earth, and to reflect that these elaborately constructed forms, so different from each other, and dependent on each other in so complex a manner, have all been produced by laws acting around us. These laws, taken in the largest sense, being Growth with Reproduction; Inheritance which is almost implied by reproduction; Variability from the indirect and direct action of the external conditions of life, and from use and disuse; a Ratio of Increase so high as to lead to a Struggle for Life, and as a consequence to Natural Selection, entailing Divergence of Character and the Extinction of less-improved forms. Thus, from the war of nature, from famine and death, the most exalted object which we are capable of conceiving, namely, the production of the higher animals, directly follows. There is grandeur in this view of life, with its several powers, having been originally breathed into a few forms or into one; and that, whilst this planet has gone cycling on according to the fixed law of gravity, from so simple a beginning endless forms most beautiful and most wonderful have been, and are being, evolved.

(1859)

Questions

1. Although this forms the conclusion to a work on natural history, it is very largely oriented towards the future. Compare the attitudes towards the future—and towards progress—expressed here with those expressed in the piece by Stephen Jay Gould elsewhere in this volume.

2. Darwin tends to write quite long paragraphs. Try in one sentence to summarize the main idea of each of the eight paragraphs in this piece.

3. Explain how the science of biology becomes closely intertwined with that of geology when it comes to deal with evolution. Discuss the connections between the ideas expressed here and the ideas expressed in two other selections in this volume—those by Charles Lyell and by Luis Alvarez et al.

4. Darwin has been proved correct in the prediction he made at the end of the first paragraph that categories such as "species" would come to be regarded as human constructs (albeit as human constructs that do have genuine reference in the "real world"). Think of examples of other sorts in which categories have been thought to embody essential differences but have later been shown to be merely human constructs—sometimes useful or convenient constructs, sometimes misleading or indeed harmful.

MARK TWAIN

A RIVER PILOT LOOKS AT
THE MISSISSIPPI

*In this passage, Twain reflects on how the experience
of working as a Mississippi pilot changed his
attitudes toward the river itself.*

❧

The face of the water, in time, became a wonderful book—a book that
was a dead language to the uneducated passenger, but which told its
mind to me without reserve, delivering its most cherished secrets as clearly
as if it uttered them with a voice. And it was not a book to be read once and
thrown aside, for it had a new story to tell every day. Throughout the long
twelve hundred miles there was never a page that was void of interest, never
one that you could leave unread without loss, never one that you would
want to skip, thinking you could find higher enjoyment in some other thing.
There never was so wonderful a book written by man; never one whose
interest was so absorbing, so unflagging, so sparklingly renewed with every
re-perusal. The passenger who could not read it was charmed with a peculiar sort of faint dimple on its surface (on the rare occasions when he did
not overlook it altogether); but to the pilot that was an *italicized* passage;
indeed, it was more than that, it was a legend of the largest capitals, with
a string of shouting exclamation-points at the end of it, for it meant that a
wreck or a rock was buried there that could tear the life out of the strongest
vessel that ever floated. It is the faintest and simplest expression the water
ever makes, and the most hideous to a pilot's eye. In truth, the passenger
who could not read this book saw nothing but all manner of pretty pictures
in it, painted by the sun and shaded by the clouds, whereas to the trained
eye these were not pictures at all, but the grimmest and most dead-earnest
of reading-matter.

Now when I had mastered the language of this water, and had come to know every trifling feature that bordered the great river as familiarly as I knew the letters of the alphabet, I had made a valuable acquisition. But I had lost something, too. I had lost something which could never be restored to me while I lived. All the grace, the beauty, the poetry, had gone out of the majestic river! I still keep in mind a certain wonderful sunset which I witnessed when steamboating was new to me. A broad expanse of the river was turned to blood; in the middle distance the red hue brightened into gold, through which a solitary log came floating, black and conspicuous; in one place a long, slanting mark lay sparkling upon the water; in another the surface was broken by boiling, tumbling rings, that were as many-tinted as an opal; where the ruddy flush was faintest, was a smooth spot that was covered with graceful circles and radiating lines, ever so delicately traced; the shore on our left was densely wooded, and the somber shadow that fell from this forest was broken in one place by a long, ruffled trail that shone like silver; and high above the forest wall a clean-stemmed dead tree waved a single leafy bough that glowed like a flame in the unobstructed splendor that was flowing from the sun. There were graceful curves, reflected images, woody heights, soft distances; and over the whole scene, far and near, the dissolving lights drifted steadily, enriching it every passing moment with new marvels of coloring.

I stood like one bewitched. I drank it in, in a speechless rapture. The world was new to me, and I had never seen anything like this at home. But as I have said, a day came when I began to cease from noting the glories and the charms which the moon and the sun and the twilight wrought upon the river's face; another day came when I ceased altogether to note them. Then, if that sunset scene had been repeated, I should have looked upon it without rapture, and should have commented upon it, inwardly, after this fashion: "This sun means that we are going to have wind tomorrow; that floating log means that the river is rising, small thanks to it; that slanting mark on the water refers to a bluff reef which is going to kill somebody's steamboat one of these nights, if it keeps on stretching out like that; those tumbling 'boils' show a dissolving bar and a changing channel there; the lines and circles in the slick water over yonder are a warning that that troublesome place is shoaling up dangerously; that silver streak in the shadow of the forest is the 'break' from a new snag, and he has located himself in the very best place he could have found to fish for steamboats; that tall dead tree, with a single living branch, is not going to last long, and then how is a body ever going to get through this blind place at night without the friendly old landmark?"

No, the romance and beauty were all gone from the river. All the value any feature of it had for me now was the amount of usefulness it could furnish toward compassing the safe piloting of a steamboat. Since those days, I have pitied doctors from my heart. What does the lovely flush in a beauty's cheek mean to a doctor but a "break" that ripples above some deadly disease? Are not all her visible charms sown thick with what are to him the signs and symbols of hidden decay? Does he ever see her beauty at all, or doesn't he simply view her professionally, and comment upon her unwholesome condition all to himself? And doesn't he sometimes wonder whether he has gained most or lost most by learning his trade?

(1875)

Questions

1. Through the first paragraph and into the second Twain employs an extended metaphor. Summarize in your own words the ways in which the river is said to resemble a book.

2. What is the essential contrast being discussed in this passage? To what is the change in Twain's reactions to the river to be attributed?

3. Recount a case in which you had been similarly deadened to the effects of the beauty around you, either by being pressed to focus on your surroundings in a different fashion for practical purposes, or simply through familiarity.

Eliza M.

Account of Cape Town, 1863

*The following account is one of the most remarkable literary
descriptions we have of the world of nineteenth-century British
colonialism from the point of view of one of the colonized.
King William's Town was a small town some 500 miles east
of Cape Town, and Eliza M., as she was identified in the* King
William's Town Gazette, *had attended school at St. Matthew's
Mission in the area, where she likely wrote this piece as a
school exercise. The piece was originally in Xhosa, and was
translated for the* Gazette *by an unknown translator.*

℮

We left East London on the Sunday, while it was raining; the sea was
fighting very much, and there were soldiers going to England and
their wives. On the Tuesday we arrived at Algoa Bay, and boats came to
fetch the people who were going there, and other people came in. The
ship went off the same day. A great wind blew, and I thought myself that
if it had been another ship, it would not have been able to go on, but in its
going, it kept twisting about, it did not go straight, but it went well on the
day of our arrival, for the wind was good. We arrived on the Friday. While
I was in the ship, I forgot I was on the water, it was like a house inside, but
outside it was not like a house. There is everything that is kept at home;
there were fowls and sheep and pigs, and slaughtering every day. I kept
looking at the thing which makes the ship go. There are two horses inside,
made of iron, which make it go; and when I looked inside, it was very
frightful. There are many bed-rooms inside. The ship we were in is named
the *Norman*, it is a steamer. It was unpleasant when nothing appeared, but
when we left the Bay, we saw the mountains till we got to the Cape. One
mountain is called the Lion's Head, and another is called Green Point,
and I myself saw those mountains. That which is called the Lion's Head,
is like a lion asleep. And another mountain above the town is that called

Table Mountain; nevertheless it is not like a table, still that name is proper for it.

Before I came into the town, my heart said, "this place is not large," but when I entered it, I wondered, and was afraid. Oh, we slept that day. I have forgotten to relate something I saw the day I arrived. I saw black people, and I thought they were our kind, but they are not; they are Slams, called in English, Malays. Also, I was astonished at their large hats, pointed at the top, and large below. I saw some making baskets of reeds, and I wished I knew how to do it. On the Saturday evening, we went to a shop to buy butter and bread. At night lights were hung up throughout the whole town. I had thought we were going to walk in the darkness. I have not yet seen houses built with grass, like those we live in, they are high beautiful houses. The roads where people walk, are very fine. I have not yet seen a dirty, muddy place in the whole town. On the Sunday, bells sounded; there is one big one, and other small ones; we went to service in the great church.

Early on the Monday, wagons came about to sell things. Really people here get these things for nothing from their owners. A person can get men's trousers for three shilling each, yet in other places a person can never get them for that money. You can get three pairs of stockings for a shilling, a child's cap for a penny; you can get a width of a dress for threepence, if it is five widths, it is a shilling and threepence. There are little wagons, the man who drives the horses sits behind, the proprietor does nothing, he sits so.

Another thing. The shoes of the Malays astonished me. There is a heel, and yonder on before a piece of wood sticks out, and they put it between their toes, and so make a clattering like the Germans. As things are to be got for such little money, how cheap must they be in England!

5   On Friday I saw a man riding in a wagon, there was a barrel inside and a cross-bar, and the water came out there. I don't know how it came out. It watered the new road, which is being made. And on Tuesday I saw people working at slates, taking off their ends—it was a great heap; the people who were at work were four. On the day of our arrival, a house was burnt, the people escaped, but I don't know whether the goods escaped. There are carts which go every day, carrying earth to throw on the road which is being mended, drawn by one horse.

There is a house where there are all kinds of beasts, and there are figures of black people, as if they were alive; their blackness is very ugly; also the bones of a man when he is dead, and birds and elephants, and lions, and tigers and sea-shells. I was afraid of those people, and the skeleton. There is also an ape holding Indian Corn, and there are monkeys.

In the evening we went out again, we went to the houses of the Malays; we went to see their decorations, for they were rejoicing because their days of fasting were ended. They were very beautiful; they had made flowers of paper, you would never think they were made of paper. We went for the sole purpose of seeing these works. They made a great noise, singing as they walked; you would laugh to see the children dancing outside and clapping their hands.

There are also wagons there for the sale of fish. The proprietors sound a thing like a horn to announce that he who wishes to buy let him buy. There are others for collecting dust-heaps, they ring a bell. There are vehicles to convey two people, he who drives the horses, and he who sits inside. In some there are windows and lights lit at night: those windows are two.

There are not many trees in the town; in some places there are not many at all, but in one place it is like the bush; it is pleasant underneath the trees; there are stools to sit on when a person is tired. That path is very long; I saw two Newfoundland dogs. I did not know that I should ever come to see them when I heard them spoken of. They are dogs with large heads and great long ears; the hair is like sheep's wool, and they have great claws; they are suited to assist people. It seemed as if they could swallow me without chewing; I was very much afraid, but one was not very big, it was about the size of the dogs of black people, when it barks, it says so with a great voice. Also, I saw sheep rather unlike others, in the tail here it was very large, the head was small, and the body was large and fat.

I have forgotten to mention something which I ought to have said before; when I came out of the ship and walked on land the earth seemed to move, and when I entered a house, it seemed to imitate the sailing of a ship, and when I lay down it seemed to move. 10

I saw an ox-wagon here, but I had not imagined that I should see a wagon.

We go to a very large beautiful Church; I don't forget the people who sing, the English; the prayers are said with thin voices as if it were singing; but the chief thing done is singing frequently, all the while there is continually singing, and then sitting. There is a Kafir school here; I went one day, they were reading; they can read well; there are also carpenters &c.

There is another place besides that which I said is like the bush, and in that place there are trees and flowers, and two fountains; a thing is stuck in, and the water comes out above. I saw the date-tree when it is young; it is one leaf, yet when it is grown, it is a very large tree. In that place there are wild birds, doves are there, and those birds which the English call canaries, and a very beautiful bird, its tail is long, its bill is red.

Yesterday the soldiers had sports, the music-band played, and when they finished playing they fired. They were many, and they fired together. And as we were walking, they fired; I was very much startled and afraid. And to-day they are playing the music. It seems to-day it exceeds in sweetness, I mean its sound.

15   There came a person here who is a Kafir. I rejoiced very much when I heard that he too was one. He asked me what I had come to do here; I said "I am only traveling." He asked whether I was a prisoner, and I said "No." He said he was very glad, he had thought I was a prisoner. I told him that I was going away again, and he said "May you go in peace, the Lord preserve you well till you arrive whence you came." I never saw a person like him of such kindness; he said he had come here to learn, he came from where I did; but I should not have known him to be a Kafir, and he did not know that I was one.

There are creatures which are eaten; they come from the sea, their name is called crawfish, they are frightful in appearance, yet their flesh is very fine and white.

The person of this house is a dyer of clothes, the white he makes red, and the red green, and the brown he makes black. I saw the wood with which they dye. Soap is cut in pieces, and put in water, and heated and boiled well, and continually stirred. This thing—dyeing clothes, is a great work. Water is even in the house; I don't know where it comes from, a person turns a thing, and fresh water comes out as if it were of a river.

There are also carts for selling meat, and for selling bread. I saw the fire-wagon, I did nothing but wonder. I did not know that it was such a big thing. It is long, with many wheels, they are not so large as those of an ox-wagon; people sit in places inside. The wheels run on metal; I say I could do nothing but wonder very much. I had not thought that it was such a great thing. And when it is about to proceed it says "Sh!" I don't know whether it is the boiling of the water; it hastens exceedingly, a person would be unable to notice it well, yet now some people say that this is a small one which I have seen. If it treads on anything, it must smash it, it is a very great thing. I shall never forget it. Where I saw it, the place was fenced on both sides, and I beheld it from the outside. I entered it another week after I had seen it; we went to Somerset West and slept one night. In the morning we returned by it: when I was inside, the earth seemed to move; it is pleasant to ride inside. I end now although this is not all the news about it. When I was in it, I saw a sugar plant; it is not a large plant, it is short with red flowers. I saw other trees at Somerset West which I had never seen before.

One day I saw people going to a burial, the carriages were black, but that people should wear black clothes is done also among the natives where a person has died; there were stuck up black feathers, and on the graves were placed stones with writing; the name of the person was written, and the years of his age, and the year in which he died.

I have seen to-day another thing which I did not know of, that thing   20
which is said to be always done by white people in this month of May. They make themselves black people, they smear themselves with something black, with red patches on the cheeks; a thing is made with evergreens, and a man is put inside, and two people carry it, and another man carries a pan, and goes begging for money.

Another thing which I saw during the past month, was people going to the Governor's house—little chiefs, and chiefs of the soldiers, some had hats with red and white feathers, and silver coats, and gold swords, and the bishop went too. I heard it said that they were going to hear the things which were about to be spoken by people who had come from Graham's Town, King William's Town, Beaufort, and other places; it was said that these people were going to speak of the state of those towns and the doings of the people who live there. I do not say that those coats were really of gold, I say there was gold on some parts of them, on the arms and the back.

Also I have seen the fruit of the tree which the English call the chestnut; I did not see what the tree is like, the fruit is nice, the outside of it is hard; when you eat it, it is sweet and edible like the potato, you can roast it or boil it. There is another fruit called Banana in English, it also is a nice fruit; it is not boiled or roasted, it is eaten like other fruits. There is a great white sweet potato, it is called Sweet Potato; those potatoes are very large, I had never seen them before, they are nearly all long: I do not know whether they are the potatoes named "Medicine" by the Fingoes.

I am puzzled to know how to begin to relate what was done yesterday, but I will try. Yesterday was said to be the wedding-day of the Great Son of Victoria, but it was not really the day of his marriage, for he has been married some time. The thing first done was arranging the children of the schools and I was there too. All walked in threes, going from one street to another. When we left the school-house we took up our station on an open piece of ground, other people climbed on the houses, and others looked on from below. On one house where we were standing there was the figure of a man like a king, a red cloth was put as if it were held by him, it is called in English a flag. Amongst all of us there were flags of different beautiful kinds; we stood there a great while, till we saw a multitude of soldiers and their officers and little chiefs and different sorts of people: one set wore clothes all alike, another had different clothes and ancient hats which were worn by the people of that time. All these now went in front, a very long line, then followed the ranks of another school, and we came after them. When we had finished going through many streets, we went to stand in another open spot of ground. All the time we were walking we were singing the song of Victoria. And there we saw the Governor and his wife; we all saluted. Although it seems that I have written a great deal I have not yet wondered at the things done at night, but let me finish those of the day. We were given food. We saw boats going along with people inside and boys wearing red clothes; there followed one with an old man, his hairs were long and white. There was a woman at his side wearing short clothes. Other boats followed with people in them, all the time they were appearing the drum and trumpets were sounded. I don't know how I shall make myself understood. I never saw such a beautiful thing; some of the men wore short dresses and short coats, and others wore short trousers like those of the French. All these things were red. When we had finished walking we went to stand in an open piece of ground, then we all went home. I do not know if any other things were done.

We went out again in the evening to see the fireworks. First we went into the gardens, where there were what I shall call candles; but nevertheless they are not called so in English. They were lights put inside little red and green glasses—When I was at a distance I thought they were little round things, all these were hung up and fastened in the trees,—there were some large ones and there were others not put in glasses.

25   We walked and went to a great crowd of people, we could not tell what we should do to see that which we came to see. There we saw a tall man with a high hat, I did not understand how it was made, and another man wearing women's clothes continually playing with that tall man. All these things have their names in English, some were called *Punch & Judy*, *Spectre*, *Father of the Doomed Arm-chair*, or *The Maid, the Murderer and the Midnight Avenger*,[1] and many other plays besides these. We passed on from that woman and man and went to see white people smeared with soot, they went into a house made of a tent where there were stools, and two came out and spoke to the people saying, "Ladies and gentlemen, come in and see what we have got here inside." Some went in and others did not, afterwards

---

1   *Punch & Judy ... Midnight Avenger*   Popular plays of the period.

they opened that the people might see; there were black people sitting on chairs and singing. So we left; at the entrance of the garden there was written in letters of fire, "GOD bless Albert and Alexandra." In another place there were other things of fire, that place is called in English the Parade, where there was a thing like a light-house, on all sides there were candles. Some people sent up fire from Table Mountain, others from Green Point, others sent up fire in the midst of the town, it went up and came down again.

Besides these things there was another thing done, an ox was baked whole, the legs were not removed, only the inside and the hoofs. Many tables were set underneath the trees; that ox was intended for the poor people.

I am going to end now; I am very glad that I was brought here to see things which I never thought I should see.

There is another thing which has lately taken place, the birthday of Queen Victoria. Two balloons were made, no one went in them, there were only lights. That sort is called fire-balloons. The first was sent up; it rose very high till it was like a star: I did not see it again where it went. The other reappeared, it did not rise high like the first, it burnt, and fire came down like two stars.

I saw where newspapers are printed; four people were at work. I do not know what I shall say to tell about it. There is a thing which folds the papers and another thing which continually receives them. It made us sleepy.

E.M.

(1863)

Questions

1. Eliza M. describes a "fire-wagon" without naming it. What is the "fire-wagon"? Does the fact that she doesn't give the conventional name make you read the description differently? If so, how?

2. Daymond et al. of the *Women Writing Africa Project* speculate that this piece originally would have been published in the *Gazette* "partly because its naiveté was amusing to the whites." Give an example from the article that shows how Eliza M.'s outsider perspective affects her observations. What is she unable to see, and in what ways does she see with exceptional clarity?

3. Daymond et al. also suggest that Eliza M.'s 1863 English readers would have appreciated this piece as "proof of the success of the civilizing policies" of the British missionaries. Based on her writing, how much do you think that Eliza M. has been shaped by her missionary education? To what extent are these effects positive?

4. Choose a practice or a technology from your own culture and give a brief description of it as someone with no previous experience of your way of life might see it.

Lady Agnes Macdonald

By Car and Cowcatcher

*The wife of Canada's first Prime Minister displays her
taste for adventure on an official trip along
the Canadian Pacific Railway.*

℮

The evening is warm and moonlit, the wide Ottawa's dark water glides
swiftly between high wooded banks; the pale foam of a rapid gleams
in mid-distance; the Chaudière Falls break the silence with their muffled
roar, and above them, in dim outline, on a cedar-covered cliff, stand the tall
towers of the stately building where Parliament assembles in the Dominion
of Canada.

It is the 10th of July—long anticipated as the day of our departure for
the Pacific coast, and now everything is ready and the hour is at hand. All
sorts of luggage, necessary for convenience and comfort, during a journey
extending over many thousand miles, is already on its way to the Ottawa
station of the Canadian Pacific Railway, and our party, six in number, is
only waiting for coffee and the evening papers before bringing up the
rear. All day long each intending traveler has been diligently employed in
making special packing arrangements suited to his or her particular taste,
and while the writer, in capacity of general manager, has given particular
care to hampers and grocery lists, others of the party have selected new
books, illustrated papers, maps, games, and embroidery, mindful that for
at least three weeks during our absence we shall have no home but the
railway car.

Off at last! a town clock is striking eleven, and the moon, unsteady with
moving clouds, lights us to the station. There a long row of gleaming lamps
marks out the whereabouts of our "Special," which, five minutes after we
have stepped on board, has glided out among the soft shadows of a summer
night, and is bearing us swiftly westward.

How pleasant it is to recall the sense of novelty and freedom which delighted at least one of our party as we walked through the length of the train and inspected our accommodation. The "Special" (consisting of a large private car named the "Jamaica," a Pullman and a baggage car, with engine and tender complete) looked very cozy. In the baggage car our larger trunks were neatly set in rows; and in the brightly lighted Pullman, curtained bed-places alternated with velvet-cushioned seats, while traveling bags, writing cases, small portmanteaus, and alas! tobacco-boxes too, were symmetrically arranged on small fixed tables. In the rear end a separate enclosure looked very like a smoking-room, and a tell-tale embroidered cap already graced a peg.

5   The "Jamaica"—her large fixed lamps brightening each little sitting-room—had a very homelike effect. Baskets of flowers stood on either side of the entrance-doors. In a tiny kitchen the white-aproned cook stood superintending the stowage of sundry useful packages into a neat little cupboard fitted behind two cozy bedrooms placed *dos à dos* in the center of the car, with a door opening into each parlor. These small apartments contained excellent beds, good washing apparatus, with taps for hot and cold water connecting with the kitchen-stove and a tank overhead—all somewhat resembling the cabin of a fine ship, everything being as richly colored and effective as black walnut and gilding could make it.

Eighty feet over all, and wide in proportion, smoothly painted and varnished outside of a deep golden brown color, the "Jamaica," though more spacious and certainly safer in its accommodations than the "Cowcatcher" of days to come, was, as will be seen in the sequel, not half so much fun! But that glorious ride through the wild passes of the mighty mountains, round curving bends of magnificent rivers, under towering snow-tipped peaks, and amid the rich green gloom of endless valleys—surrounded on all sides by scenery of striking grandeur and beauty—was a thing of the future, for twenty-three hundred miles of woodland, river, rock, lake, and prairie lay between us and the eastern base of the Rocky Mountains, where the soft ineffable beauty of those blue and white summits shall first gladden our longing eyes....

We are [at last] among the "Foot hills," or lowest range of the Rockies—great, mound-like, smooth, softly-tinted hills that swelled into many a lovely curved shape, holding in their wide folds winding blue rivers and great stretches of fine grazing land, over which, as the sweet morning air stirred through the grass, little billows of pale green seemed to pass. These are some of the cattle ranches of which we have "heard tell" so often lately.

As we travel slowly onward—slowly, so as to enjoy all to the fullest extent—these plains widen and stretch away into flat quiet distances, soft and misty, lying below farther hills outlined against the sky. Sharper risings and rougher edges appear. By and by the wide valleys change into broken ravines and lo! through an opening in mist made rosy with early sunlight, we see far away up in the sky, its delicate pearly tip clear against the blue, a single snow-peak of the Rocky Mountains! There is a general rush to see it;—perhaps general disappointment. Surely that fragile, almost quivering point rising so high over the pink drapery that sweeps to the valley below, can have nothing to do with the rugged heights and mountains we have come to see!

Our coarse natures cannot at first appreciate the exquisite aerial grace of that solitary peak that seems on its way to heaven; but as we look, its fading, gauzy mist passes over, and has vanished.

On again we go, now through long stretches of park-like country, now near great mountain shoulders, half-misty, half-defined, with occasional gleams of snowy peaks far away before us like kisses on the morning sky.

The Kananaskis River flows directly across the pass that leads into the mountains which here begin to close in around us. We stopped at the Kananaskis Station, and walking across a meadow, behold the wide river a mass of foam leaping over ledges of rocks into the plains below.

We reach Canmore,—sixty-eight miles from Calgary. Here the pass we are traveling through has narrowed suddenly to four miles, and as mists float upwards and away, we see great masses of scarred rock rising on each side—ranges towering one above another. Very striking and magnificent grows the prospect as we penetrate into the mountains at last, each curve of the line bringing fresh vistas of endless peaks, rolling away before and around us, all tinted rose, and blush pink, and silver, as the sun lights their snowy tips. Every turn becomes a fresh mystery, for some huge mountain seems to stand right across our way, barring it for miles, with a stern face frowning down upon us; and yet a few minutes later we find the giant has been encircled and conquered, and soon lies far away in another direction.

Mount Cascade is perhaps one of the most remarkable of these peaks. Approaching its perpendicular massive precipice-front, streaked with a thousand colors which glow in the sunshine, we half shrink from what seems an inevitable crash! From this precipice falls a narrow cascade making a

10

leap of about 1800 feet. Surely it will presently burst over us!—but no; a few minutes later Mount Cascade has mysteriously moved away to the right, and its silver waterfall soon gleams in the distance.

Many of the mountains were skirted with low dark forests. Some had a vegetation of small evergreens marking out wide ledges; but beyond a certain height, fissured rock, in which tiny glaciers and snow-beds found a resting place, rose alone into the sky. Sometimes this bristling beard of rugged trees was sharply defined against great walls of white and grey above, with crags and peaks and ledges, in all sorts of fantastic forms, breaking the outline. Below, all was in deep shade, but above, sunlight fell in a sharp, bright line across those mighty walls, and glistened, with beauty inconceivable, upon fairy-like points in the sky.

15   At Banff, six miles from Canmore, sulphur springs of great medicinal value had been only lately discovered; but already, from our car window, we can see the timbers for an hotel awaiting transportation up the winding road to the springs. One of our party informs us that the Government has reserved 20,000 acres for a public park in this beautiful place, and that arrangements are already being made to render it available for this purpose. It is an enchanting spot, encircled by mountains—said to contain many more valuable springs—the air fragrant with sweet odors from low spruce-trees clothing their sides.

Here the Bow River, which we have skirted since leaving Calgary, winds through the wide green plateau, its waters of a dull China blue. About five miles farther on Castle Mountain is before us, standing a sheer precipice 5000 feet high—a giant's "keep," with turrets, bastions, and battlements complete, reared against the sky.

As we rise toward the summit, near Stephen, about thirty-five miles farther on, the railway's grade gets steeper, tall forests gather round us, and a curious effect is produced by glimpses of snowy spurs and crests peeping through the trees, and of which, though apparently near us, we see no base. This conveyed to me an idea of our elevation, and it was delightful to think of oneself as hidden away among those solitary mountains, even for a few short hours, with all the troubles and worries of life left in noisy bustling cities far away!

At the Laggan Station, more than thirty miles from the summit, a huge engine,—in curious black contrast to a small white house nearby,—stood on a siding with all steam up, waiting for our train. I then learned that this monster is necessary for the steep grades, both ascending and descending, over which we have to go.

The General Superintendent ... in an unlucky moment suggested I should walk forward, examine this big "mountain" engine, and see its heavy proportions and fine machinery. I say "unlucky," because from the instant my eyes rested on the broad shining surface of its buffer-beam and cowcatcher, over which a bright little flag waved from a glossy brass pole, I decided to travel there and nowhere else for the remaining 600 miles of my journey!

From Calgary to Laggan I had traveled in the car of the engine, accompanied by a victimized official. Perched on a little feather bench, well in front, and close to the small windows, I had enjoyed an excellent opportunity of seeing everything. Besides this, I had gained a great deal of useful information about engines, boilers, signals, &c., which may come in "handy" some day. During our stoppages the engineer and firemen had not failed to explain these things, and I had even ventured to whistle "caution" at a "crossing." The signal went very well for an amateur, but the Chief's quick ear had detected a falter, and at the next halt he sent a peremptory message, desiring me "not to play tricks," which, addressed to a discreet matron, was really quite insulting. I had even questioned the engineer as to the probable effect of a bad collision while I occupied this post. He promptly suggested, "most likely killed"; and added, reflectively, as he carefully oiled an already dripping valve, "which would be a bad job"!

When I announced my desire to travel on the cowcatcher, Mr. E seemed to think that a very bad job indeed. To a sensible, level-headed man as he is, such an innovation on all general rules of traveling decorum was no doubt very startling. He used many ineffectual persuasions to induce me to abandon the idea, and almost said I should not run so great a risk; but at last, being a man of few words, and seeing time was nearly up, he so far relented as to ask what I proposed using as a seat. Glancing round the station platform I beheld a small empty candle-box lying near, and at once declared that was "just the thing." Before Mr. E could expostulate further, I had asked a brakesman to place the candle-box on the buffer-beam, and was on my way to the "Jamaica" to ask the Chief's permission. The Chief, seated on a low chair on the rear platform of the car, with a rug over his knees and a magazine in his hand, looked very comfortable and content. Hearing my request, he pronounced the idea "rather ridiculous," then remembered it was dangerous as well, and finally asked if I was sure I could hold on. Before the words were well out

20

of his lips, and taking permission for granted by the question, I was again standing by the cowcatcher, admiring the position of the candle-box, and anxiously asking to be helped on.

Before I take my seat, let me try, briefly, to describe the "Cowcatcher." Of course everyone knows that the buffer-beam is that narrow, heavy iron platform, with the sides scooped out, as it were, on the very forefront of the engine over which the headlight glares, and in the corner of which a little flag is generally placed. In English engines, I believe, the buffers proper project from the front of this beam. In Canadian engines another sort of attachment is arranged, immediately below the beam, by which the engine can draw trains backwards as well as forwards. The beam is about eight feet across, at the widest part, and about three feet deep. The description of a cowcatcher is less easy. To begin with, it is misnamed, for it catches no cows at all. Sometimes, I understand, it throws up on the buffer-beam whatever maimed or mangled animal it has struck, but in most cases it clears the line by shoving forward, or tossing aside, any removable obstruction. It is best described as a sort of barred iron beak, about six feet long, projecting close over the track in a V shape, and attached to the buffer-beam by very strong bolts. It is sometimes sheathed with thin iron plates in winter, and acts then as a small snow-plough.

Behold me now, enthroned on the candle-box, with a soft felt hat well over my eyes, and a linen carriage-cover tucked round me from waist to foot. Mr. E had seated himself on the other side of the headlight. He had succumbed to the inevitable, ceased further expostulation, disclaimed all responsibility, and, like the jewel of a Superintendent he was, had decided on sharing my peril! I turn to him, peeping round the headlight, with my best smile. "This is *lovely*," I triumphantly announce, seeing that a word of comfort is necessary, "*quite lovely*: I shall travel on this cowcatcher from summit to sea!"

Mr. Superintendent, in his turn, peeps round the headlight and surveys me with solemn and resigned surprise. "I—suppose—you—will," he says slowly, and I see that he is hoping, at any rate, that I shall live to do it!

25   With a mighty snort, a terribly big throb, and shrieking whistle, No. 374 moves slowly forward. The very small population of Laggan have all come out to see. They stand in the hot sunshine, and shade their eyes as the stately engine moves on. "It is an awful thing to do!" I hear a voice say, as the little group lean forward; and for a moment I feel a thrill that is very like fear; but it is gone at once, and I can think of nothing but the novelty, the excitement, and the fun of this mad ride in glorious sunshine and intoxicating air, with

magnificent mountains before and around me, their lofty peaks smiling down on us, and never a frown on their grand faces!

The pace quickens gradually, surely, swiftly, and then we are rushing up to the summit. We soon stand on the "Great Divide"—5300 feet above sea-level—between two great oceans. As we pass, Mr. E by a gesture, points out a small river (called Bath Creek, I think) which, issuing from a lake on the narrow summit-level, winds near the track. I look, and lo! the water, flowing *eastward* towards the Atlantic side, turns in a moment as the Divide is passed, and pours *westward* down the Pacific slope!

Another moment and a strange silence has fallen round us. With steam shut off and brakes down, the 60-ton engine, by its own weight and impetus alone, glides into the pass of the Kicking Horse River, and begins a descent of 2800 feet in twelve miles. We rush onward through the vast valley stretching before us, bristling with lofty forests, dark and deep, that, clinging to the mountain side, are reared up into the sky. The river, widening, grows white with dashing foam, and rushes downwards with tremendous force. Sunlight flashes on glaciers, into gorges, and athwart huge, towering masses of rock crowned with magnificent tree crests that rise all round us of every size and shape. Breathless—almost awe-stricken—but with a wild triumph in my heart, I look from farthest mountain peak, lifted high before me, to the shining pebbles at my feet! Warm wind rushes past; a thousand sunshine colors dance in the air. With a firm right hand grasping the iron stanchion, and my feet planted on the buffer beam, there was not a yard of descent in which I faltered for a moment. If I had, then assuredly in the wild valley of the Kicking Horse River, on the western slope of the Rocky Mountains, a life had gone out that day! I did not think of danger, or remember what a giddy post I had. I could only gaze at the glaciers that the mountains held so closely, 5000 feet above us, at the trace of snow avalanches which had left a space a hundred feet wide massed with torn and prostrate trees; on the shadows that played over the distant peaks; and on a hundred rainbows made by the foaming, dashing river, which swirls with tremendous rapidity down the gorge on its way to the Columbia in the valley below.

We have left the North-West Territories, and are now in the Province of British Columbia. Field—Ottertail—Leanchoile flit past us. Steam has been up for ten miles now; we have left the Kicking Horse pass behind us and are gliding into the wide Columbia Valley, full of rich, new beauty, of green tall waving grass and blue water. A lower range of Rockies, streaked and capped with snow, stretches away on either side. The roadway is very level, and the rails gleam before us, narrowing in a distant point to a silver thread. I hear the engineer piling in fuel, and whistle with shrillest note. Then, with trebly quickened pace, we dart along in the sunshine. For a second only I feel a quickening of the heart-pulse, and a hot color mounts to my face, but it is gone in a moment, and I am none the worse for that "spurt" at the rate of fifty miles an hour.

Halted at Palliser. The Chief and his friends walked up to the cow-catcher to make a morning call. I felt a little "superior" and was rather condescending. Somewhat flushed with excitement, but still anxious to be polite, I asked "would the Chief step up and take a drive?" To the horror of the bystanders he carelessly consented, and in another moment had taken the place of Mr. E, the latter seating himself at our feet on the buffer-beam. There was a general consternation among our little group of friends and the few inhabitants of Palliser—the Chief rushing through the flats of the Columbia on a cowcatcher! and, worse still, possibly even among the wild Selkirk Mountains—those mountains of which scarcely three years before, in his charming book, "From Old Westminster to New," my friend Mr. Sandford Fleming[1] had said, "no one had been through the western slope of the Selkirks"! Everyone is horrified. It is a comfort to the other occupant of the buffer to find someone else willful, and as we steamed away towards Donald, at the eastern base of the Selkirks, I felt not so bad after all!

30 Following the valley of the Eagle River, we wind gaily through the cedar forests of the Gold Range, gemmed with lakes blue and shining, its tall darkly clothed summits often lit by small cascades gleaming through the trees. Crossing and recrossing the Eagle River seven or eight times, we reach the Sicamous Narrows, into which its dark hurrying waters are emptied. We presently sweep into an immense valley, through which, for many miles, the line skirts beautiful stretching lakes—grand sheets of blue water, glacier fed, lying in the folds of the Gold Range. These lakes close, as it were, into the south branch of the Thompson River. Many tunnels lie in our way as we rush by them, and during a halt I am told one of the tunnels is "wet." This being interpreted, means that the arching rock is full of springs, which pour on the train as it passes. An umbrella and waterproof are therefore necessary for me—now the sole occupant of the cowcatcher;

---

1   *Sandford Fleming*   Sir Sandford Fleming (1827-1915) was a civil engineer and surveyor involved in the planning of the Canadian Pacific Railway.

and with praiseworthy economy I take off my hat, tuck it safely under my wraps, and prepare to encounter the "wet" tunnel thus equipped! We plunge into a few moments' darkness—water splashing and dripping on every side; and as we emerge into sunlight again, and stop just beyond the tunnel, I see a party of young English sportsmen standing near the roadside. They have evidently just climbed the bank, guns in hand, leaving a large canoe with two Indian paddlers on the lake below. Fine, tall young Saxons they are, in sporting attire somewhat the worse for long travel, but very conventional in style notwithstanding. Just imagine the feelings with which these well-regulated young men beheld a lady, bareheaded, and with an umbrella, seated in front of an engine, at the mouth of a tunnel in the Gold Range of British Columbia! I am sorely afraid I laughed outright at the blank amazement on their rosy faces, and longed to tell them what fun it was; but not being "introduced, you know," I contented myself with acknowledging their presence by a solemn little bow—which was quite irresistible under the circumstances!

On we go, speeding forward to the coast, meeting the sweet breath of ocean mingled with rich scent of pine boughs, their delicate tips waving welcome as we pass—on, on, steadily, swiftly down to the sea! Now nearly 3000 miles from our starting-point, Ottawa, we are nearing Port Moody on Burrard Inlet, where, alas! I must bid good-bye to candle-box and cow-catcher, and content myself with an easy-chair on the deck of a steamer bound for Victoria.

(1887)

Questions

1. Find examples in "By Car and Cowcatcher" of the following poetic devices: personification, metaphor, alliteration, juxtaposition. Explain the effect of the poetic device in each example.

2. Describe Macdonald's personality as she portrays it in the essay. How do you get this impression of her character?

3. Many authorities on writing advise essay writers to avoid an enthusiastic tone—and to avoid the exclamation mark, in particular. Argue for or against, with reference to this selection.

4. Comment on how expectations of gender and class contribute to the humor in this essay.

5. a) Compare and contrast Macdonald's approach to descriptive writing with that of Mark Twain in "A River Pilot Looks at the Mississippi" (included elsewhere in this volume).

   b) How does each piece portray the relationship between beauty and novelty?

OSCAR WILDE

THE NEW AESTHETIC

In the final speech of his 1889 work "The Decay
of Lying," Wilde puts forward a manifesto
for a new set of aesthetic principles.

℮

Briefly, then, [the doctrines of the new aesthetics] are these. Art never expresses anything but itself. It has an independent life, just as Thought has, and develops purely on its own lines. It is not necessarily realistic in an age of realism, nor spiritual in an age of faith. So far from being the creation of its time, it is usually in direct opposition to it, and the only history that it preserves for us is the history of its own progress. Sometimes it returns upon its footsteps, and revives some antique form, as happened in the archaistic movement of late Greek Art, and in the pre-Raphaelite movement of our own day. At other times it entirely anticipates its age, and produces in one century work that it takes another century to understand, to appreciate, and to enjoy. In no case does it reproduce its age. To pass from the art of a time to the time itself is the great mistake that all historians commit.

The second doctrine is this. All bad art comes from returning to Life and Nature, and elevating them into ideals. Life and Nature may sometimes be used as part of Art's rough material, but before they are of any real service to Art they must be translated into artistic conventions. The moment Art surrenders its imaginative medium it surrenders everything. As a method Realism is a complete failure, and the two things that every artist should avoid are modernity of form and modernity of subject-matter.[1] To us, who live in the nineteenth century, any century is a suitable subject for art except

---

1   *Realism ... subject-matter*   In the late nineteenth century realism was the dominant aesthetic principle; leading writers and visual artists attempted to portray "real life" as convincingly as possible. (In the early twentieth century, the movement that became known as "modernism" turned radically away from realism.)

our own. The only beautiful things are the things that do not concern us. It is, to have the pleasure of quoting myself, exactly because Hecuba[2] is nothing to us that her sorrows are so suitable a motive for a tragedy. Besides, it is only the modern that ever becomes old-fashioned. M. Zola sits down to give us a picture of the Second Empire.[3] Who cares for the Second Empire now? It is out of date. Life goes faster than Realism, but Romanticism is always in front of Life.

The third doctrine is that Life imitates Art far more than Art imitates Life. This results not merely from Life's imitative instinct, but from the fact that the self-conscious aim of Life is to find expression, and that Art offers it certain beautiful forms through which it may realize that energy. It is a theory that has never been put forward before, but it is extremely fruitful, and throws an entirely new light upon the history of Art.

It follows, as a corollary from this, that external Nature also imitates Art. The only effects that she can show us are effects that we have already seen through poetry, or in paintings. This is the secret of Nature's charm, as well as the explanation of Nature's weakness.

5 The final revelation is that Lying, the telling of beautiful untrue things, is the proper aim of Art.

(1889)

---

2 *Hecuba* In Shakespeare's *Hamlet*, Hamlet makes the following speech while observing the players dramatize the death of Hecuba (in Greek mythology, the wife of Priam, King of Troy, who was taken prisoner when the Greeks captured Troy):

> O, what a rogue and peasant slave am I:
> Is it not monstrous that this player here,
> But in a fiction, in a dream of passion,
> Could force his soul so as to his own conceit
> That from her working all his visage wann'd
> Tears in his eyes, distraction in's aspect,
> A broken voice, and his whole function suiting
> With forms to his conceit? And all for nothing!
> For Hecuba!
> What's Hecuba to him or he to Hecuba
> That he should weep for her?

(I. iv. 584-92)

3 *the Second Empire* Louis Napoleon, nephew of Napoleon 1st, and heir to the Napoleonic title, was elected president of France in 1848, and in 1852 dismissed Parliament and declared himself emperor. The Second Empire ended when he was forced from power after France's defeat at the hands of Prussia in 1871. Emile Zola was the leading novelist of the period in France.

Questions

1. Wilde's approach stands on its head the notion of Plato that poets had no proper place in society because they were liars. From the late medieval period through the twentieth century the prevailing view has been that the "lying" engaged in by literary writers is of an entirely different order from lies with which people attempt to deceive each other in everyday life. Are there any grounds for regarding the two forms of lying as in any way similar?

2. Should artists (writers as well as visual and other sorts of artists) strive in some sense to tell the truth? Why?

JANE ADDAMS

ON HALSTED STREET

Hull-House, established by Addams in 1889 and located on Halsted Street in a depressed area of Chicago, represented a successful and influential effort to improve the lot of the urban poor in nineteenth-century America—in intellectual, social, and spiritual terms as well as economic ones. The following forms the conclusion of Addams's book Twenty Years at Hull-House.

❧

In those early days we were often asked why we had to come to live on Halsted Street when we could afford to live somewhere else. I remember one man who used to shake his head and say it was "the strangest thing he had met in his experience," but who was finally convinced that it was "not strange but natural." In time it came to seem natural to all of us that the Settlement should be there. If it is natural to feed the hungry and care for the sick, it is certainly natural to give pleasure to the young, comfort to the aged, and to minister to the deep-seated craving for social intercourse that all men feel. Whoever does it is rewarded by something which, if not gratitude, is at least spontaneous and vital and lacks that irksome sense of obligation with which a substantial benefit is too often acknowledged.

In addition to the neighbors who responded to the receptions and classes, we found those who were too battered and oppressed to care for them. To these, however, was left that susceptibility to the bare offices of humanity which raises such offices into a bond of fellowship.

From the first it seemed understood that we were ready to perform the humblest neighborhood services. We were asked to wash the new-born babies, and to prepare the dead for burial, to nurse the sick, and to "mind the children."

Occasionally these neighborly offices unexpectedly uncovered ugly human traits. For six weeks after an operation we kept in one of our three bedrooms a forlorn little baby who, because he was born with a cleft palate, was most unwelcome even to his mother, and we were horrified when he died of neglect a week after he was returned to his home; a little Italian bride of fifteen sought shelter with us one November evening, to escape her husband who had beaten her every night for a week when he returned home from work, because she had lost her wedding ring; two of us officiated quite alone at the birth of an illegitimate child because the doctor was late in arriving, and none of the honest Irish matrons would "touch the likes of her"; we ministered at the deathbed of a young man, who during a long illness of tuberculosis had received so many bottles of whiskey through the mistaken kindness of his friends, that the cumulative effect produced wild periods of exultation, in one of which he died.

We were also early impressed with the curious isolation of many of the immigrants; an Italian woman once expressed her pleasure in the red roses that she saw at one of our receptions in surprise that they had been "brought so fresh all the way from Italy." She would not believe for an instant that they had been grown in America. She said that she had lived in Chicago for six years and had never seen any roses, whereas in Italy she had seen them every summer in great profusion. During all that time, of course, the woman had lived within ten blocks of a florist's window; she had not been more than a five-cent car ride away from the public parks; but she had never dreamed of faring forth for herself, and no one had taken her. Her conception of America had been the untidy street in which she lived and had made her long struggle to adapt herself to American ways.

But in spite of some untoward experiences, we were constantly impressed with the uniform kindness and courtesy we received. Perhaps these first days laid the simple human foundations which are certainly essential for continuous living among the poor: first, genuine preference for residence in an industrial quarter to any other part of the city, because it is interesting and makes the human appeal; and second, the conviction, in the words of Canon Barnett,[1] that the things which make men alike are finer and better than the things that keep them apart, and that these basic likenesses, if they are properly accentuated, easily transcend the less essential differences of race, language, creed and tradition.

Perhaps even in those first days we made a beginning toward that object which was afterwards stated in our charter: "To provide a center for a higher

5

---

1   *Canon Barnett*   Samuel A. Barnett, an English cleric and reformer, and the founder of Toynbee Hall, on which Addams modeled Hull-House.

civic and social life; to institute and maintain educational and philanthropic enterprises, and to investigate and improve the conditions in the industrial districts of Chicago."

(1910)

Questions

1. Comment on the way in which Addams alternates between the general and the particular in her observations in this passage.

2. The contrary argument to that made by Addams in the second last paragraph of this passage is often put forward: that in order to appeal to all different sorts of human beings, it is often necessary to appeal to the "lowest common denominator." Argue in a more extended way for one or the other of these positions.

3. To what extent do you see differences such as race and language as forming essential dividing lines between human groups?

4. Beyond what Addams states explicitly, what are we able to infer from this passage about the Chicago of the late nineteenth century?

W.E.B. Du Bois

A Mild Suggestion

This short piece is among the most biting essays by
the famous American civil rights activist.

❧

They were sitting on the leeward deck of the vessel and the colored man was there with his usual look of unconcern. Before the seasickness his presence aboard had caused some upheaval. The Woman, for instance, glancing at the Southerner, had refused point blank to sit beside him at meals, so she had changed places with the Little Old Lady. The Westerner, who sat opposite, said he did not care a ——, then he looked at the Little Old Lady, and added in a lower voice to the New Yorker that there was no accounting for tastes. The Southerner from the other table broadened his back and tried to express with his shoulders both ancestors and hauteur. All this, however was half forgotten during the seasickness, and the Woman sat beside the colored man for a full half hour before she noticed it, and then was glad to realize that the Southerner was too sick to see. Now again with sunshine and smiling weather, they all quite naturally reverted (did the Southerner suggest it?) to the Negro problem. The usual solutions had been suggested: education, work, emigration, etc.

They had not noticed the back of the colored man, until the thoughtless Westerner turned toward him and said breezily: "Well, now, what do you say? I guess you are rather interested." The colored man was leaning over the rail and about to light his cigarette—he had several such bad habits, as the Little Old Lady noticed. The Southerner simply stared. Over the face of the colored man went the shadow of several expressions; some the New Yorker could interpret, others he could not.

"I have," said the colored man, with deliberation, "a perfect solution." The Southerner selected a look of disdain from his repertoire, and assumed it. The Woman moved nearer, but partly turned her back. The Westerner and

91

the Little Old Lady sat down. "Yes," repeated the colored man, "I have a perfect solution. The trouble with most of the solutions which are generally suggested is that they aggravate the disease." The Southerner could not help looking interested. "For instance," proceeded the colored man, airily waving his hand, "take education; education means ambition, dissatisfaction and revolt. You cannot both educate people and hold them down."

"Then stop educating them," growled the Southerner aside.

5   "Or," continued the colored man, "if the black man works, he must come into competition with whites ——"

"He sure will, and it ought to be stopped," returned the Westerner. "It brings down wages."

"Precisely," said the speaker, "and if by underselling the labor market he develops a few millionaires, how now would you protect your residential districts or your select social circles or—your daughters?"

The Southerner started angrily, but the colored man was continuing placidly with a far-off look in his eyes. "Now, migration is both costly and inhuman; the transportation would be the smallest matter. You must buy up perhaps a thousand millions' worth of Negro property; you must furnish some capital for the masses of poor; you must get some place for them to go; you must protect them there, and here you must pay not only higher wages to white men, but still higher on account of the labor scarcity. Meantime, the Negroes suddenly removed from one climate and social system to another climate and utterly new conditions would die in droves—it would be simply prolonged murder at enormous cost."

"Very well," continued the colored man, seating himself and throwing away his cigarette, "listen to my plan," looking almost quizzically at the Little Old Lady; "you must not be alarmed at its severity—it may seem radical, but really it is—it is—well, it is quite the only practical thing and it has surely one advantage: it settles the problem once, suddenly, and forever. My plan is this: You now outnumber us nearly ten to one. I propose that on a certain date, shall we say next Christmas, or possibly Easter, 1912? No, come to think of it, the first of January, 1913, would, for historical reasons, probably be best. Well, then, on the first of January, 1913, let each person who has a colored friend invite him to dinner. This would take care of a few; among such friends might be included the black mammies and faithful old servants of the South; in this way we could get together quite a number. Then those who have not the pleasure of black friends might arrange for meetings, especially in 'white' churches and Young Men's and Young Women's Christian Associations, where Negroes are not expected. At such meetings, contrary to custom, the black people should not be seated by themselves, but distributed very carefully among the whites. The remaining Negroes who could not be flattered or attracted by these invitations should be induced to assemble among themselves at their own churches or at little parties and house warmings.

"The few stragglers, vagrants and wanderers could be put under careful 10 watch and ward. Now, then, we have the thing in shape. First, the hosts of those invited to dine should provide themselves with a sufficient quantity of cyanide of potassium, placing it carefully in the proper cups, and being careful not to mix the cups. Those at church and prayer meeting could choose between long sharp stilettoes and pistols—I should recommend the former as less noisy. Those who guard the colored assemblies and the stragglers without should carefully surround the groups and use Winchesters. Then, at a given signal, let the colored folk of the United States be quietly dispatched; the signal might be a church bell or the singing of the national hymn; probably the bell would be best, for the diners would be eating."

By this time the auditors of the colored man were staring; the Southerner had forgotten to pose; the Woman had forgotten to watch the Southerner; the Westerner was staring with admiration; there were tears in the eyes of the Little Old Lady, while the New Yorker was smiling; but the colored man held up a deprecating hand: "Now don't prejudge my plan," he urged. "The next morning there would be ten million funerals, and therefore no Negro problem. Think how quietly the thing would be settled; no more bother, no more argument; the whole country united and happy. Even the Negroes would be a great deal happier than they are at present. Instead of being made heirs to hope by education, or ambitious by wealth, or exiled invalids on the fever coast, they would all be happily ensconced in Heaven. Of course, I admit that at first the plan may seem a little abrupt and cruel, and yet is it more cruel than present conditions, and would it not be well to be a little more abrupt in our social solutions? At any rate think it over," and the colored man dropped lazily into his steamer chair and felt for another cigarette.

The crowd slowly dispersed; the Southerner chose the Woman, but was heard to say something about fools. The Westerner turned to the New Yorker and said: "Now, what in hell do you suppose that darky meant?" But the Little Old Lady went silently to her cabin.

(1912)

Questions

1. This essay is similar in several respects to "A Modest Proposal" by Jonathan Swift. What are some of these similarities? Are there also significant differences between the two essays in tone and approach?

2. "A Mild Suggestion" was published almost 50 years after "emancipation"; in what ways were African-Americans evidently still not fully free in 1912? What reflections, if any, does this prompt about the nature of freedom?

3. Comment on the tone and diction of Du Bois's prose in this piece. What can you say about the choice of verbs when the crucial part of the proposal is set out ("provide themselves with," "choose between," "carefully surround the groups," "be quietly dispatched")?

WINSTON CHURCHILL

from BLOOD, TOIL, TEARS AND SWEAT

*Given three days after the beginning of the German offensive
in Western Europe, this was the first speech Churchill
gave to the House of Commons as Prime Minister.*

❧

To form an Administration of this scale and complexity is a serious undertaking in itself, but it must be remembered that we are in the preliminary stage of one of the greatest battles in history, that we are in action at many other points in Norway and in Holland, that we have to be prepared in the Mediterranean, that the air battle is continuous and that many preparations, such as have been indicated by my honorable Friend below the Gangway, have to be made here at home. In this crisis I hope I may be pardoned if I do not address the House at any length today. I hope that any of my friends and colleagues, or former colleagues, who are affected by the political reconstruction, will make allowance, all allowance, for any lack of ceremony with which it has been necessary to act. I would say to the House, as I said to those who have joined this government: "I have nothing to offer but blood, toil, tears and sweat."

We have before us an ordeal of the most grievous kind. We have before us many, many long months of struggle and of suffering. You ask, what is our policy? I can say: It is to wage war, by sea, land and air, with all our might and with all the strength that God can give us; to wage war against a monstrous tyranny, never surpassed in the dark, lamentable catalogue of human crime. That is our policy. You ask, what is our aim? I can answer in one word: It is victory, victory at all costs, victory in spite of all terror, victory, however long and hard the road may be; for without victory, there is no survival. Let that be realized; no survival for the British Empire, no survival for all that the British Empire has stood for, no survival for the urge and impulse of the ages, that mankind will move forward towards its goal.

But I take up my task with buoyancy and hope. I feel sure that our cause will not be suffered to fail among men. At this time I feel entitled to claim the aid of all, and I say, "come then, let us go forward together with our united strength."

(13 May 1940)

from WE SHALL FIGHT ON THE BEACHES

Churchill gave this speech after a large-scale evacuation of Allied troops from France. At this point, it appeared likely that the French would withdraw from the war and possible that the Germans would then attempt an invasion of England.

❧

. . . We have found it necessary to take measures of increasing stringency, not only against enemy aliens and suspicious characters of other nationalities, but also against British subjects who may become a danger or a nuisance should the war be transported to the United Kingdom. I know there are a great many people affected by the orders which we have made who are the passionate enemies of Nazi Germany. I am very sorry for them, but we cannot, at the present time and under the present stress, draw all the distinctions which we should like to do. If parachute landings were attempted and fierce fighting attendant upon them followed, these unfortunate people would be far better out of the way, for their own sakes as well as for ours. There is, however, another class, for which I feel not the slightest sympathy. Parliament has given us the powers to put down Fifth Column activities with a strong hand, and we shall use those powers subject to the supervision and correction of the House, without the slightest hesitation until we are satisfied, and more than satisfied, that this malignancy in our midst has been effectively stamped out.

Turning once again, and this time more generally, to the question of invasion, I would observe that there has never been a period in all these long centuries of which we boast when an absolute guarantee against invasion, still less against serious raids, could have been given to our people. In the days of Napoleon the same wind which would have carried his transports across the Channel might have driven away the blockading fleet. There was always the chance, and it is that chance which has excited and befooled the imaginations of many Continental tyrants. Many are the tales that are told. We are assured that novel methods will be adopted, and when we see the originality of malice, the ingenuity of aggression, which our enemy displays, we may certainly prepare ourselves for every kind of novel stratagem and every kind of brutal and treacherous maneuver. I think that no idea is so outlandish that it should not be considered and viewed with a searching, but at the same time, I hope, with a steady eye. We must never forget the solid assurances of sea power and those which belong to air power if it can be locally exercised.

I have, myself, full confidence that if all do their duty, if nothing is neglected, and if the best arrangements are made, as they are being made, we shall prove ourselves once again able to defend our Island home, to ride out the storm of war, and to outlive the menace of tyranny, if necessary for years, if necessary alone. At any rate, that is what we are going to try to do. That is the resolve of His Majesty's Government—every man of them. That is the will of Parliament and the nation. The British Empire and the French Republic, linked together in their cause and in their need, will defend to the death their native soil, aiding each other like good comrades to the utmost of their strength. Even though large tracts of Europe and many old and famous States have fallen or may fall into the grip of the Gestapo and all the odious apparatus of Nazi rule, we shall not flag or fail. We shall go on to the end, we shall fight in France, we shall fight on the seas and oceans, we shall fight with growing confidence and growing strength in the air, we shall defend our Island, whatever the cost may be, we shall fight on the beaches, we shall fight on the landing grounds, we shall fight in the fields and in the streets, we shall fight in the hills; we shall never surrender, and even if, which I do not for a moment believe, this Island or a large part of it were subjugated and starving, then our Empire beyond the seas, armed and guarded by the British Fleet, would carry on the struggle, until, in God's good time, the New World, with all its power and might, steps forth to the rescue and the liberation of the old.

(4 June 1940)

from THIS WAS THEIR FINEST HOUR

This speech was delivered to the House of Commons
the day after France declared its intention to
seek an armistice with Germany.

❧

... **D**uring the first four years of the last war the Allies experienced nothing but disaster and disappointment. That was our constant fear: one blow after another, terrible losses, frightful dangers. Everything miscarried. And yet at the end of those four years the morale of the Allies was higher than that of the Germans, who had moved from one aggressive triumph to another, and who stood everywhere triumphant invaders of the lands into which they had broken. During that war we repeatedly asked ourselves the question: How are we going to win? and no one was able ever to answer it with much precision, until at the end, quite suddenly, quite unexpectedly, our terrible foe collapsed before us, and we were so glutted with victory that in our folly we threw it away.

We do not yet know what will happen in France or whether the French resistance will be prolonged, both in France and in the French Empire overseas. The French Government will be throwing away great opportunities and casting adrift their future if they do not continue the war in accordance with their Treaty obligations, from which we have not felt able to release them. The House will have read the historic declaration in which, at the desire of many Frenchmen—and of our own hearts—we have proclaimed our willingness at the darkest hour in French history to conclude a union of common citizenship in this struggle. However matters may go in France or with the French Government, or other French Governments, we in this Island and in the British Empire will never lose our sense of comradeship with the French people. If we are now called upon to endure what they have been suffering, we shall emulate their courage, and if final victory rewards our toils they shall share the gains, aye, and freedom shall be restored to all. We abate nothing of our just demands; not one jot or tittle do we recede. Czechs, Poles, Norwegians, Dutch, Belgians have joined their causes to our own. All these shall be restored.

What General Weygand called the Battle of France is over. I expect that the Battle of Britain is about to begin. Upon this battle depends the survival of Christian civilization. Upon it depends our own British life, and the long continuity of our institutions and our Empire. The whole fury and might of the enemy must very soon be turned on us. Hitler knows that he will have to break us in this Island or lose the war. If we can stand up to him, all Europe may be free and the life of the world may move forward into broad, sunlit uplands. But if we fail, then the whole world, including the United States, including all that we have known and cared for, will sink into the abyss of a new Dark Age made more sinister, and perhaps more protracted, by the lights of perverted science. Let us therefore brace ourselves to our duties, and so bear ourselves that, if the British Empire and its Commonwealth last for a thousand years, men will still say, "This was their finest hour."

(18 June 1940)

Questions

1. Define the following rhetorical devices and find an example from Churchill's speeches: anadiplosis, anaphora, euphemism, assonance, and metaphor. Explain the effect of the rhetorical device in each example.

2. Churchill equates a German victory with the end "of Christian civilization" in which "the whole world ... will sink into the abyss of a new Dark Age made more sinister, and perhaps more protracted, by the lights of perverted science." What does he mean by this? Given the context in which he was speaking, should he have made these claims?

3. Churchill delivered these speeches at a very difficult time in British history. How does he balance the need to explain the seriousness of Britain's position in the war with the need to avoid inciting panic?

4. Write a speech in the style of Churchill that defines your nation's role in a current political situation.

5. Compare these speeches with Barack Obama's speech "A More Perfect Union," included later in this volume, with a focus on tone, style, and rhetorical technique.

Virginia Woolf

Professions for Women

*This lecture to a society of professional women
touches on themes developed at greater length
in Woolf's* A Room of One's Own.

ତ

When your secretary invited me to come here, she told me that your Society is concerned with the employment of women and she suggested that I might tell you something about my own professional experiences. It is true that I am a woman; it is true I am employed; but what professional experiences have I had? It is difficult to say. My profession is literature; and in that profession there are fewer experiences for women than in any other, with the exception of the stage—fewer, I mean, that are peculiar to women. For the road was cut many years ago—by Fanny Burney, by Aphra Behn, by Harriet Martineau, by Jane Austen, by George Eliot—many famous women, and many more unknown and forgotten, have been before me, making the path smooth, and regulating my steps. Thus, when I came to write, there were very few material obstacles in my way. Writing was a reputable and harmless occupation. The family peace was not broken by the scratching of a pen. No demand was made upon the family purse. For ten and sixpence one can buy paper enough to write all the plays of Shakespeare—if one has a mind that way. Pianos and models, Paris, Vienna, and Berlin,[1] masters and mistresses, are not needed by a writer. The cheapness of writing paper is, of course, the reason why women have succeeded as writers before they have succeeded in the other professions.

But to tell you my story—it is a simple one. You have only got to figure to yourselves a girl in a bedroom with a pen in her hand. She had only to move that pen from left to right—from ten o'clock to one. Then it occurred

---

1   *Paris, Vienna, and Berlin*   All three are cities that Britons frequently traveled to for training in art and music.

to her to do what is simple and cheap enough after all—to slip a few of those pages into an envelope, fix a penny stamp in the corner, and drop the envelope into the red box at the corner. It was thus that I became a journalist; and my effort was rewarded on the first day of the following month—a very glorious day it was for me—by a letter from an editor containing a check for one pound ten shillings and sixpence. But to show you how little I deserve to be called a professional woman, how little I know of the struggles and difficulties of such lives, I have to admit that instead of spending that sum upon bread and butter, rent, shoes and stockings, or butcher's bills, I went out and bought a cat—a beautiful cat, a Persian cat, which very soon involved me in bitter disputes with my neighbors.

What could be easier than to write articles and to buy Persian cats with the profits? But wait a moment. Articles have to be about something. Mine, I seem to remember, was about a novel by a famous man. And while I was writing this review, I discovered that if I were going to review books I should need to do battle with a certain phantom. And the phantom was a woman, and when I came to know her better I called her after the heroine of a famous poem, The Angel in the House. It was she who used to come between me and my paper when I was writing reviews. It was she who bothered me and wasted my time and so tormented me that at last I killed her. You who come of a younger and happier generation may not have heard of her—you may not know what I mean by the Angel in the House. I will describe her as shortly as I can. She was intensely sympathetic. She was immensely charming. She was utterly unselfish. She excelled in the difficult arts of family life. She sacrificed herself daily. If there was chicken, she took the leg; if there was a draft she sat in it—in short she was so constituted that she never had a mind or a wish of her own, but preferred to sympathize always with the minds and wishes of others. Above all—I need not say it—she was pure. Her purity was supposed to be her chief beauty—her blushes, her great grace. In those days—the last of Queen Victoria—every house had its Angel. And when I came to write I encountered her with the very first words. The shadow of her wings fell on my page; I heard the rustling of her skirts in the room. Directly, that is to say, I took my pen in my hand to review that novel by a famous man, she slipped behind me and whispered: "My dear, you are a young woman. You are writing about a book that has been written by a man. Be sympathetic; be tender; flatter; deceive; use all the arts and wiles of our sex. Never let anybody guess that you have a mind of your own. Above all, be pure." And she made as if to guide my pen. I now record the one act for which I take some credit to myself, though the credit rightly belongs to some excellent ancestors of mine who left me a certain sum of money—shall we say five hundred pounds a year?—so that it was not necessary for me to depend solely on charm for my living. I turned upon her and caught her by the throat. I did my best to kill her. My excuse if I were to be had up at a court of law, would be that I acted in self-defense. Had I not killed her she would have killed me. She would have plucked the heart out of my writing. For as I found directly I put pen to paper, you cannot review even a novel without having a mind of your own, without expressing what you think to be the truth about human relations, morality, sex. And all these questions, according to the Angel of the House cannot be dealt with freely and openly by women; they must charm, they must conciliate, they must—to put it bluntly—tell lies if they are to succeed. Thus, whenever I felt the shadow of her wing or the radiance of her halo upon my page, I took up the inkpot and flung it at her. She died hard. Her fictitious nature was of great assistance to her. It is far harder to kill a phantom than a reality. She was always creeping back when I thought I had dispatched her. Though I flatter myself that I killed her in the end, the struggle was severe; it took much time that had better have been spent upon learning Greek grammar; or in roaming the world in search of adventures. But it was a real experience; it was an experience that was bound to befall all writers at that time. Killing the Angel in the House was part of the occupation of a woman writer.

But to continue my story. The Angel was dead; what then remained? You may say that what remained was a simple and common object—a young woman in a bedroom with an inkpot. In other words, now that she had rid herself of falsehood, that young woman had only to be herself. Ah, but what is "herself"? I mean, what is a woman? I assure you, I do not know. I do not believe that you know. I do not believe that anybody can know until she has expressed herself in all the arts and professions open to human skill. That indeed is one of the reasons why I have come here—out of respect for you, who are in process of showing us by your experiments what a woman is, who are in process of providing us, by your failures and successes, with that extremely important piece of information.

5   But to continue the story of my professional experiences. I made one pound ten and six by my first review; and I bought a Persian cat with the proceeds. Then I grew ambitious. A Persian cat is all very well, I said; but a Persian cat is not enough. I must have a motor-car. And it was thus that I became a novelist—for it is a very strange thing that people will give you a motor-car if you will tell them a story. It is a still stranger thing that there is

nothing so delightful in the world as telling stories. It is far pleasanter than writing reviews of famous novels. And yet, if I am to obey your secretary and tell you my professional experiences as a novelist, I must tell you about a very strange experience that befell me as a novelist. And to understand it you must try first to imagine a novelist's state of mind. I hope I am not giving away professional secrets if I say that a novelist's chief desire is to be as unconscious as possible. He has to induce in himself a state of perpetual lethargy. He wants life to proceed with the utmost quiet and regularity. He wants to see the same faces, to read the same books, to do the same things day after day, month after month, while he is writing, so that nothing may break the illusion in which he is living—so that nothing may disturb or disquiet the mysterious nosings about, feelings round, darts, dashes, and sudden discoveries of that very shy and illusive spirit, the imagination. I suspect that this state is the same both for men and women. Be that as it may, I want you to imagine me writing a novel in a state of trance. I want you to figure to yourselves a girl sitting with a pen in her hand, which for minutes, and indeed for hours, she never dips into the inkpot. The image that comes to my mind when I think of this girl is the image of a fisherman lying sunk in dreams on the verge of a deep lake with a rod held out over the water. She was letting her imagination sweep unchecked round every rock and cranny of the world that lies submerged in the depths of our unconscious being. Now came the experience that I believe to be far commoner with women writers than with men. The line raced through the girl's fingers. Her imagination had rushed away. It had sought the pools, the depths, the dark places where the largest fish slumber. And then there was a smash. There was an explosion. There was foam and confusion. The imagination had dashed itself against something hard. The girl was roused from her dream. She was indeed in a state of the most acute and difficult distress. To speak without figure, she had thought of something, something about the body, about the passion, which it was unfitting for her as a woman to say. Men, her reason told her, would be shocked. The consciousness of what men will say of a woman who speaks the truth about her passions had roused her from her artist's state of consciousness. She could write no more. The trance was over. Her imagination could work no longer. This I believe to be a very common experience with women writers—they are impeded by the extreme conventionality of the other sex. For though men sensibly allow themselves great freedom in these respects, I doubt that they realize or can control the extreme severity with which they condemn such freedom in women.

These then were two very genuine experiences of my own. These were two of the adventures of my professional life. The first—killing the Angel in the House—I think I solved. She died. But the second, telling the truth about my own experiences as a body, I do not think I solved. I doubt that any woman has solved it yet. The obstacles against her are still immensely powerful—and yet they are very difficult to define. Outwardly, what is simpler than to write books? Outwardly, what obstacles are there for a woman rather than for a man? Inwardly, I think the case is very different; she has still many ghosts to fight, many prejudices to overcome. Indeed it will be a long time still, I think, before a woman can sit down to write a book without finding a phantom to be slain, a rock to be dashed against. And if this is so in literature, the freest of all professions for women, how is it in the new professions which you are now for the first time entering?

Those are the questions that I should like, had I time, to ask you. And indeed, if I have laid stress upon these professional experiences of mine, it is because I believe that they are, though in different forms, yours also. Even when the path is nominally open—when there is nothing to prevent a woman from being a doctor, a lawyer, a civil servant—there are many phantoms and obstacles, as I believe, looming in her way. To discuss and define them is I think of great value and importance; for thus only can the labor be shared, the difficulties be solved. But besides this, it is necessary also to discuss the ends and the aims for which we are fighting, for which we are doing battle with these formidable obstacles. Those aims cannot be taken for granted; they must be perpetually questioned and examined. The whole position, as I see it—here in this hall surrounded by women practicing for the first time in history I know not how many different professions—is one of extraordinary interest and importance. You have won rooms of your own in the house hitherto exclusively owned by men. You are able, though not without great labor and effort, to pay the rent. You are earning your five hundred pounds a year. But this freedom is only a beginning; the room is your own, but it is still bare. It has to be furnished; it has to be decorated; it has to be shared. How are you going to furnish it, how are you going to decorate it? With whom are you going to share it, and upon what terms? These, I think are questions of the utmost importance and interest. For the first time in history you are able to ask them; for the first time you are able to decide for yourselves what the answers should be. Willingly would I stay and discuss those questions and answers—but not tonight. My time is up; and I must cease.

(1930)

THE DEATH OF THE MOTH

*A famous novelist's observations of the final living
moments of a moth lead her to reflect upon the
nature of life and the inevitability of death.*

❧

Moths that fly by day are not properly to be called moths; they do not excite that pleasant sense of dark autumn nights and ivy-blossom which the commonest yellow-underwing asleep in the shadow of the curtain never fails to rouse in us. They are hybrid creatures, neither gay like butter-flies nor somber like their own species. Nevertheless the present specimen, with his narrow hay-colored wings, fringed with a tassel of the same color, seemed to be content with life. It was a pleasant morning, mid-September, mild, benignant, yet with a keener breath than that of the summer months. The plough was already scoring the field opposite the window, and where the share had been, the earth was pressed flat and gleamed with moisture. Such vigor came rolling in from the fields and down beyond that it was difficult to keep the eyes strictly turned upon the book. The rooks too were keeping one of their annual festivities; soaring round the tree tops until it looked as if a vast net with thousands of black knots in it had been cast up into the air; which, after a few moments sank slowly down upon the trees until every twig seemed to have a knot at the end of it. Then, suddenly, the net would be thrown into the air again in a wider circle this time, with the utmost clamor and vociferation, as though to be thrown into the air and settle slowly down upon the tree tops were a tremendously exciting experience.

The same energy which inspired the rooks, the ploughmen, the horses, and even, it seemed, the lean bare-backed downs, sent the moth fluttering from side to side of his square of the window pane. One could not help watching him. One was, indeed, conscious of a queer feeling of pity for him. The possibilities of pleasure seemed that morning so enormous and so various that to have only a moth's part in life, and a day moth's at that, appeared a hard fate, and his zest in enjoying his meager opportunities to the full, pathetic. He flew vigorously to one corner of his compartment, and, after waiting there for a second, flew across to the other. What remained for him but to fly to a third corner and then to a fourth? That was all he could do, in spite of the size of the downs, the width of the sky, the far-off smoke of houses, and the romantic voice, now and then, of a steamer out at sea. What he could do he did. Watching him, it seemed as if a fiber, very thin but pure, of the enormous energy of the world had been thrust into his frail and diminutive body. As often as he crossed the pane, I could fancy that a thread of vital light became visible. He was little or nothing but life.

Yet, because he was so small, and so simple a form of the energy that was rolling in at the open window and driving its way through so many narrow and intricate corridors in my own brain and in those of other human beings, there was something marvelous as well as pathetic about him. It was as if someone had taken a tiny bead of pure life and decking it as lightly as possible with down and feathers, had set it dancing and zig-zagging to show us the true nature of life. Thus displayed one could not get over the strangeness of it. One is apt to forget all about life, seeing it humped and bossed and garnished and cumbered so that it has to move with the greatest circumspection and dignity. Again, the thought of all that life might have been had he been born in any other shape caused one to view his simple activities with a kind of pity.

After a time, tired by his dancing apparently, he settled on the window ledge in the sun, and, the queer spectacle being at an end, I forgot about him. Then, looking up, my eye was caught by him. He was trying to resume his dancing, but seemed either so stiff or so awkward that he could only flutter to the bottom of the window-pane; and when he tried to fly across it he failed. Being intent on other matters I watched these futile attempts for a time without thinking, unconsciously waiting for him to resume his flight, as one waits for a machine, that has stopped momentarily, to start again without considering the reason of its failure. After perhaps a seventh attempt he slipped from the wooden ledge and fell, fluttering his wings, on to his back on the window sill. The helplessness of his attitude roused me. It flashed upon me that he was in difficulties; he could no longer raise himself; his legs struggled vainly. But, as I stretched out a pencil, meaning to help him to right himself, it came over me that the failure and awkward- ness were the approach of death. I laid the pencil down again.

5   The legs agitated themselves once more. I looked as if for the enemy against which he struggled. I looked out of doors. What had happened there? Presumably it was midday, and work in the fields had stopped. Stillness and quiet had replaced the previous animation. The birds had taken themselves off to feed in the brooks. The horses stood still. Yet the power was there all the same, massed outside indifferent, impersonal, not attending to anything in particular. Somehow it was opposed to the little hay-colored moth. It

was useless to try to do anything. One could only watch the extraordinary efforts made by those tiny legs against an oncoming doom which could, had it chosen, have submerged an entire city, not merely a city, but masses of human beings; nothing, I knew, had any chance against death. Nevertheless after a pause of exhaustion the legs fluttered again. It was superb this last protest, and so frantic that he succeeded at last in righting himself. One's sympathies, of course, were all on the side of life. Also, when there was nobody to care or to know, this gigantic effort on the part of an insignificant little moth, against a power of such magnitude, to retain what no one else valued or desired to keep, moved one strangely. Again, somehow, one saw life, a pure bead. I lifted the pencil again, useless though I knew it to be. But even as I did so, the unmistakable tokens of death showed themselves. The body relaxed, and instantly grew stiff. The struggle was over. The insignificant little creature now knew death. As I looked at the dead moth, this minute wayside triumph of so great a force over so mean an antagonist filled me with wonder. Just as life had been strange a few minutes before, so death was now as strange. The moth having righted himself now lay most decently and uncomplainingly composed. O yes, he seemed to say, death is stronger than I am.

(1942)

Questions

1. The title of the first of these essays suggests a focus on the economic and the practical. How relevant do Woolf's reflections seem to you to be to the stated topic? To what extent do you feel it appropriate to surprise one's audience in a public address by approaching the stated topic from unexpected angles?

2. Comment on the tone with which Woolf describes her own situation in paragraphs 2 and 3 in "Professions for Women." What is the effect of this tone on the reader? Would the effect be heightened in a public speech?

3. What do you think Woolf means when she refers in "Professions for Women" to "telling the truth about my own experiences as a body" (paragraph 6)? Write an essay concerning a "phantom" that you feel you (and people like you) must struggle with.

4. To what extent is "the Angel in the House" still alive for women today?

5. In paragraph 6 of "Professions for Women" Woolf employs a variety of sentence structures. Comment on the structures of individual sentences—and on structural connections between the various sentences in the paragraph.

6. Explain the phrase, "He was little or nothing but life," in paragraph 2 of "The Death of the Moth."

7. What is Woolf's attitude toward the moth? How does she inform the reader of this attitude?

8. What are the stages of the moth's life, according to this essay?

9. Describe Woolf's use of irony in the second of these essays.

10. Explain the use of juxtaposition in "The Death of the Moth." What effect does this have on the reader?

11. Have you ever had an experience similar to Woolf's in watching an insect die? What were your feelings and observations?

George Orwell

Shooting an Elephant

*In the most famous of his anti-imperialist essays,
Orwell uses a personal story to describe the
effects of imperialism on its perpetrators.*

❧

In Moulmein, in lower Burma, I was hated by large numbers of people—
the only time in my life that I have been important enough for this to
happen to me. I was sub-divisional police officer of the town, and in an
aimless, petty kind of way anti-European feeling was very bitter. No one
had the guts to raise a riot, but if a European woman went through the
bazaars alone somebody would probably spit betel juice over her dress. As
a police officer I was an obvious target and was baited whenever it seemed
safe to do so. When a nimble Burman tripped me up on the football field
and the referee (another Burman) looked the other way, the crowd yelled
with hideous laughter. This happened more than once. In the end the sneer-
ing yellow faces of young men that met me everywhere, the insults hooted
after me when I was at a safe distance, got badly on my nerves. The young
Buddhist priests were the worst of all. There were several thousands of
them in the town and none of them seemed to have anything to do except
stand on street corners and jeer at Europeans.

All this was perplexing and upsetting. For at that time I had already
made up my mind that imperialism was an evil thing and the sooner I
chucked up my job and got out of it the better. Theoretically—and secretly,
of course—I was all for the Burmese and all against their oppressors, the
British. As for the job I was doing, I hated it more bitterly than I can perhaps make clear. In a job like that you see the dirty work of Empire at close
quarters. The wretched prisoners huddling in the stinking cages of the lock-
ups, the grey, cowed faces of the long-term convicts, the scarred buttocks
of the men who had been flogged with bamboos—all these oppressed me

with an intolerable sense of guilt. But I could get nothing into perspective. I was young and ill-educated and I had had to think out my problems in the utter silence that is imposed on every Englishman in the East. I did not even know that the British Empire is dying, still less did I know that it is a great deal better than the younger empires that are going to supplant it. All I knew was that I was stuck between my hatred of the empire I served and my rage against the evil-spirited little beasts who tried to make my job impossible. With one part of my mind I thought of the British Raj as an unbreakable tyranny, as something clamped down, *in saecula saeculorum*,[1] upon the will of prostrate peoples; with another part I thought that the greatest joy in the world would be to drive a bayonet into a Buddhist priest's guts. Feelings like these are the normal by-products of imperialism; ask any Anglo-Indian official, if you can catch him off duty.

One day something happened which in a roundabout way was enlightening. It was a tiny incident in itself, but it gave me a better glimpse than I had had before of the real nature of imperialism—the real motives for which despotic governments act. Early one morning the sub-inspector at a police station the other end of the town rang me up on the phone and said that an elephant was ravaging the bazaar. Would I please come and do something about it? I did not know what I could do, but I wanted to see what was happening and I got on to a pony and started out. I took my rifle, an old .44 Winchester and much too small to kill an elephant, but I thought the noise might be useful *in terrorem*.[2] Various Burmans stopped me on the way and told me about the elephant's doings. It was not, of course, a wild elephant, but a tame one which had gone "must." It had been chained up, as tame elephants always are when their attack of "must" is due, but on the previous night it had broken its chain and escaped. Its mahout, the only person who could manage it when it was in that state, had set out in pursuit, but had taken the wrong direction and was now twelve hours' journey away, and in the morning the elephant had suddenly reappeared in the town. The Burmese population had no weapons and were quite helpless against it. It had already destroyed somebody's bamboo hut, killed a cow, and raided some fruit-stalls and devoured the stock; also it had met the municipal rubbish van and, when the driver jumped out and took to his heels, had turned the van over and inflicted violences upon it.

---

1   *in saecula saeculorum*   Latin: forever and ever.
2   *in terrorem*   Latin: in order to frighten.

The Burmese sub-inspector and some Indian constables were waiting for me in the quarter where the elephant had been seen. It was a very poor quarter, a labyrinth of squalid bamboo huts, thatched with palmleaf, winding all over a steep hillside. I remember that it was a cloudy, stuffy morning at the beginning of the rains. We began questioning the people as to where the elephant had gone and, as usual, failed to get any definite information. That is invariably the case in the East; a story always sounds clear enough at a distance, but the nearer you get to the scene of events the vaguer it becomes. Some of the people said that the elephant had gone in one direction, some said that he had gone in another, some professed not even to have heard of any elephant. I had almost made up my mind that the whole story was a pack of lies, when we heard yells a little distance away. There was a loud, scandalized cry of "Go away, child! Go away this instant!" and an old woman with a switch in her hand came round the corner of a hut, violently shooing away a crowd of naked children. Some more women followed, clicking their tongues and exclaiming; evidently there was something that the children ought not to have seen. I rounded the hut and saw a man's dead body sprawling in the mud. He was an Indian, a black Dravidian coolie,[3] almost naked, and he could not have been dead many minutes. The people said that the elephant had come suddenly upon him round the corner of the hut, caught him with its trunk, put its foot on his back and ground him into the earth. This was the rainy season and the ground was soft, and his face had scored a trench a foot deep and a couple of yards long. He was lying on his belly with arms crucified and head sharply twisted to one side. His face was coated with mud, the eyes wide open, the teeth bared and grinning with an expression of unendurable agony. (Never tell me, by the way, that the dead look peaceful. Most of the corpses I have seen looked devilish.) The friction of the great beast's foot had stripped the skin from his back as neatly as one skins a rabbit. As soon as I saw the dead man I sent an orderly to a friend's house nearby to borrow an elephant rifle. I had already sent back the pony, not wanting it to go mad with fright and throw me if it smelt the elephant.

The orderly came back in a few minutes with a rifle and five cartridges, and meanwhile some Burmans had arrived and told us that the elephant was in the paddy fields below, only a few hundred yards away. As I started forward practically the whole population of the quarter flocked out of the houses and followed me. They had seen the rifle and were all shouting

5

---

3   *coolie*   I.e., manual laborer.

excitedly that I was going to shoot the elephant. They had not shown much interest in the elephant when he was merely ravaging their homes, but it was different now that he was going to be shot. It was a bit of fun to them, as it would be to an English crowd; besides they wanted the meat. It made me vaguely uneasy. I had no intention of shooting the elephant—I had merely sent for the rifle to defend myself if necessary—and it is always unnerving to have a crowd following you. I marched down the hill, looking and feeling a fool, with the rifle over my shoulder and an ever-growing army of people jostling at my heels. At the bottom, when you got away from the huts, there was a metalled road and beyond that a miry waste of paddy fields a thousand yards across, not yet ploughed but soggy from the first rains and dotted with coarse grass. The elephant was standing eight yards from the road, his left side towards us. He took not the slightest notice of the crowd's approach. He was tearing up bunches of grass, beating them against his knees to clean them and stuffing them into his mouth.

I had halted on the road. As soon as I saw the elephant I knew with perfect certainty that I ought not to shoot him. It is a serious matter to shoot a working elephant—it is comparable to destroying a huge and costly piece of machinery—and obviously one ought not to do it if it can possibly be avoided. And at that distance, peacefully eating, the elephant looked no more dangerous than a cow. I thought then and I think now that his attack of "must" was already passing off; in which case he would merely wander harmlessly about until the mahout came back and caught him. Moreover, I did not in the least want to shoot him. I decided that I would watch him for a little while to make sure that he did not turn savage again, and then go home.

But at that moment I glanced round at the crowd that had followed me. It was an immense crowd, two thousand at the least and growing every minute. It blocked the road for a long distance on either side. I looked at the sea of yellow faces above the garish clothes—faces all happy and excited over this bit of fun, all certain that the elephant was going to be shot. They were watching me as they would watch a conjurer about to perform a trick. They did not like me, but with the magical rifle in my hands I was momentarily worth watching. And suddenly I realized that I should have to shoot the elephant after all. The people expected it of me and I had got to do it; I could feel their two thousand wills pressing me forward, irresistibly. And it was at this moment, as I stood there with the rifle in my hands, that I first grasped the hollowness, the futility of the white man's dominion in the East. Here was I, the white man with his gun, standing in front of the unarmed native crowd—seemingly the leading actor of the piece; but in reality I was only an absurd puppet pushed to and fro by the will of those yellow faces behind. I perceived in this moment that when the white man turns tyrant it is his own freedom that he destroys. He becomes a sort of hollow, posing dummy, the conventionalized figure of a sahib. For it is the condition of his rule that he shall spend his life in trying to impress the "natives," and so in every crisis he has got to do what the "natives" expect of him. He wears a mask, and his face grows to fit it. I had got to shoot the elephant. I had committed myself to doing it when I sent for the rifle. A sahib has got to act like a sahib; he has got to appear resolute, to know his own mind and do definite things. To come all that way, rifle in hand, with two thousand people marching at my heels, and then to trail feebly away, having done nothing—no, that was impossible. The crowd would laugh at me. And my whole life, every white man's life in the East, was one long struggle not to be laughed at.

But I did not want to shoot the elephant. I watched him beating his bunch of grass against his knees, with that preoccupied grandmotherly air that elephants have. It seemed to me that it would be murder to shoot him. At that age I was not squeamish about killing animals, but I had never shot an elephant and never wanted to. (Somehow it always seems worse to kill a large animal.) Besides, there was the beast's owner to be considered. Alive, the elephant was worth at least a hundred pounds; dead, he would only be worth the value of his tusks, five pounds, possibly. But I had got to act quickly. I turned to some experienced-looking Burmans who had been there when we arrived, and asked them how the elephant had been behaving. They all said the same thing: he took no notice of you if you left him alone, but he might charge if you went too close to him.

It was perfectly clear to me what I ought to do. I ought to walk up to within, say, twenty-five yards of the elephant and test his behavior. If he charged, I could shoot; if he took no notice of me, it would be safe to leave him until the mahout came back. But also I knew that I was going to do no such thing. I was a poor shot with a rifle and the ground was soft mud into which one would sink at every step. If the elephant charged and I missed him, I should have about as much chance as a toad under a steam-roller. But even then I was not thinking particularly of my own skin, only of the watchful yellow faces behind. For at that moment, with the crowd watching me, I was not afraid in the ordinary sense, as I would have been if I had been alone. A white man mustn't be frightened in front of "natives"; and so, in general, he isn't frightened. The sole thought in my mind was that if anything went wrong those two thousand Burmans would see me pursued, caught, trampled on and reduced to a grinning corpse like that Indian up the hill. And if that happened it was quite probable that some of them would laugh. That would never do.

10   There was only one alternative. I shoved the cartridges into the magazine and lay down on the road to get a better aim. The crowd grew very still, and a deep, low, happy sigh, as of people who see the theater curtain go up at last, breathed from innumerable throats. They were going to have their bit of fun after all. The rifle was a beautiful German thing with cross-hair sights. I did not then know that in shooting an elephant one would shoot to cut an imaginary bar running from ear-hole to ear-hole. I ought, therefore, as the elephant was sideways on, to have aimed straight at his ear-hole, actually I aimed several inches in front of this, thinking the brain would be further forward.

When I pulled the trigger I did not hear the bang or feel the kick—one never does when a shot goes home—but I heard the devilish roar of glee that went up from the crowd. In that instant, in too short a time, one would have thought, even for the bullet to get there, a mysterious, terrible change had come over the elephant. He neither stirred nor fell, but every line of his body had altered. He looked suddenly stricken, shrunken, immensely old, as though the frightful impact of the bullet had paralyzed him without knocking him down. At last, after what seemed a long time—it might have been five seconds, I dare say—he sagged flabbily to his knees. His mouth slobbered. An enormous senility seemed to have settled upon him. One could have imagined him thousands of years old. I fired again into the same spot. At the second shot he did not collapse but climbed with desperate slowness to his feet and stood weakly upright, with legs sagging and head drooping. I fired a third time. That was the shot that did for him. You could see the agony of it jolt his whole body and knock the last remnant of strength from his legs. But in falling he seemed for a moment to rise, for as his hind legs collapsed beneath him he seemed to tower upward like a huge rock toppling, his trunk reaching skyward like a tree. He trumpeted, for the first and only time. And then down he came, his belly towards me, with a crash that seemed to shake the ground even where I lay.

I got up. The Burmans were already racing past me across the mud. It was obvious that the elephant would never rise again, but he was not dead. He was breathing very rhythmically with long rattling gasps, his great mound of a side painfully rising and falling. His mouth was wide open—I could see far down into caverns of pale pink throat. I waited a long time for him to die, but his breathing did not weaken. Finally I fired my two remaining shots into the spot where I thought his heart must be. The thick blood welled out of him like red velvet, but still he did not die. His body did not even jerk when the shots hit him, the tortured breathing continued without a pause. He was dying, very slowly and in great agony, but in some world remote from me where not even a bullet could damage him further. I felt that I had got to put an end to that dreadful noise. It seemed dreadful to see the great beast lying there, powerless to move and yet powerless to die, and not even to be able to finish him. I sent back for my small rifle and poured shot after shot into his heart and down his throat. They seemed to make no impression. The tortured gasps continued as steadily as the ticking of a clock.

In the end I could not stand it any longer and went away. I heard later that it took him half an hour to die. Burmans were bringing dash and baskets even before I left, and I was told they had stripped his body almost to the bones by the afternoon.

Afterwards, of course, there were endless discussions about the shooting of the elephant. The owner was furious, but he was only an Indian and could do nothing. Besides, legally I had done the right thing, for a mad elephant has to be killed, like a mad dog, if its owner fails to control it. Among the Europeans opinion was divided. The older men said I was right, the younger men said it was a damn shame to shoot an elephant for killing a coolie, because an elephant was worth more than any damn Coringhee coolie. And afterwards I was very glad that the coolie had been killed; it put me legally in the right and it gave me a sufficient pretext for shooting the elephant. I often wondered whether any of the others grasped that I had done it solely to avoid looking a fool.

(1936)

Questions

1. What is Orwell arguing about the nature of imperialism?
2. Orwell uses an autobiographical story in order to make a political claim. How does he accomplish this? Find places in the text where he signals the connection between his personal experience and his political argument.
3. What might the elephant symbolize?

4. Orwell describes the dead Indian man and the death of the elephant in vivid detail. How do these graphic descriptions of violence change the impact of the essay?

5. What does Orwell mean when he says, "All I knew was that I was stuck between my hatred of the empire I served and my rage against the evil-spirited little beasts who tried to make my job impossible"?

6. Find examples of racist language in the essay. Do you think such language was used intentionally or unconsciously? What effect does it have on the essay?

7. Read Jamaica Kincaid's essay "On Seeing England for the First Time," elsewhere in this anthology. How does Orwell's experience of colonialism compare with Kincaid's?

POLITICS AND THE ENGLISH LANGUAGE

*Orwell's essay deploring the state of English usage
in the 1940s became one of the most widely read
and influential essays of the twentieth century.*

☙

Most people who bother with the matter at all would admit that the English language is in a bad way, but it is generally assumed that we cannot by conscious action do anything about it. Our civilization is decadent and our language—so the argument runs—must inevitably share in the general collapse. It follows that any struggle against the abuse of language is a sentimental archaism, like preferring candles to electric light or hansom cabs to airplanes. Underneath this lies the half-conscious belief that language is a natural growth and not an instrument which we shape for our own purposes.

Now, it is clear that the decline of a language must ultimately have political and economic causes: it is not due simply to the bad influence of this or that individual writer. But an effect can become a cause, reinforcing the original cause and producing the same effect in an intensified form, and so on indefinitely. A man may take to drink because he feels himself to be a failure, and then fail all the more completely because he drinks. It is rather the same thing that is happening to the English language. It becomes ugly and inaccurate because our thoughts are foolish, but the slovenliness of our language makes it easier for us to have foolish thoughts. The point is that the process is reversible. Modern English, especially written English, is full of bad habits which spread by imitation and which can be avoided if one is willing to take the necessary trouble. If one gets rid of these habits one can think more clearly, and to think clearly is a necessary first step towards political regeneration: so that the fight against bad English is not frivolous and is not the exclusive concern of professional writers. I will come back to this presently, and I hope that by that time the meaning of what I have said here will have become clearer. Meanwhile, here are five specimens of the English language as it is now habitually written.

These five passages have not been picked out because they are especially bad—I could have quoted far worse if I had chosen—but because they illustrate various of the mental vices from which we now suffer. They are a little below the average, but are fairly representative samples. I number them so that I can refer back to them when necessary:

(1) I am not, indeed, sure whether it is not true to say that the Milton who once seemed not unlike a seventeenth-century Shelley had not become, out of an experience ever more bitter in each year, more alien [*sic*] to the founder of that Jesuit sect which nothing could induce him to tolerate.

Professor Harold Laski (Essay in *Freedom of Expression*).

(2) Above all, we cannot play ducks and drakes with a native battery of idioms which prescribes such egregious collocations of vocables as the Basic *put up with* for *tolerate* or *put at a loss* for *bewilder*.

Professor Lancelot Hogben (*Interglossa*).

(3) On the one side we have the free personality: by definition it is not neurotic, for it has neither conflict nor dream. Its desires, such as they are, are transparent, for they are just what institutional approval keeps in the forefront of consciousness; another institutional pattern would alter their number and intensity; there is little in them that is natural, irreducible, or culturally dangerous. But *on the other side*, the social bond itself is nothing but the mutual reflection of these self-secure integrities. Recall the definition of love. Is not this

the very picture of a small academic? Where is there a place in this hall of mirrors for either personality or fraternity?

> Essay on psychology in *Politics* (New York).

(4) All the "best people" from the gentlemen's clubs, and all the frantic fascist captains, united in common hatred of Socialism and bestial horror of the rising tide of the mass revolutionary movement, have turned to acts of provocation, to foul incendiarism, to medieval legends of poisoned wells, to legalize their own destruction of proletarian organizations, and rouse the agitated petty-bourgeoisie to chauvinistic fervor on behalf of the fight against the revolutionary way out of the crisis.

> Communist pamphlet.

(5) If a new spirit *is* to be infused into this old country, there is one thorny and contentious reform which must be tackled, and that is the humanization and galvanization of the B.B.C. Timidity here will bespeak canker and atrophy of the soul. The heart of Britain may be sound and of strong beat, for instance, but the British lion's roar at present is like that of Bottom in Shakespeare's *Midsummer Night's Dream*—as gentle as any sucking dove. A virile new Britain cannot continue indefinitely to be traduced in the eyes or rather ears, of the world by the effete languors of Langham Place, brazenly masquerading as 'standard English.' When the Voice of Britain is heard at nine o'clock, better far and infinitely less ludicrous to hear aitches honestly dropped than the present priggish, inflated, inhibited, school-ma'amish arch braying of blameless bashful mewing maidens!

> Letter in *Tribune*.

Each of these passages has faults of its own, but, quite apart from avoidable ugliness, two qualities are common to all of them. The first is staleness of imagery: the other is lack of precision. The writer either has a meaning and cannot express it, or he inadvertently says something else, or he is almost indifferent as to whether his words mean anything or not. This mixture of vagueness and sheer incompetence is the most marked characteristic of modern English prose, and especially of any kind of political writing. As soon as certain topics are raised, the concrete melts into the abstract and no one seems able to think of turns of speech that are not hackneyed: prose consists less and less of *words* chosen for the sake of their meaning, and more and more of *phrases* tacked together like the sections of a prefabricated hen-house. I list below, with notes and examples, various of the tricks by means of which the work of prose-construction is habitually dodged:

Dying Metaphors. A newly invented metaphor assists thought by evoking a visual image, while on the other hand a metaphor which is technically "dead" (e.g., *iron resolution*) has in effect reverted to being an ordinary word and can generally be used without loss of vividness. But in between these two classes there is a huge dump of worn-out metaphors which have lost all evocative power and are merely used because they save people the trouble of inventing phrases for themselves. Examples are: *Ring the changes on, take up the cudgels for, toe the line, ride roughshod over, stand shoulder to shoulder with, play into the hands of, no axe to grind, grist to the mill, fishing in troubled waters, on the order of the day, Achilles' heel, swan song, hotbed.* Many of these are used without knowledge of their meaning (what is a "rift," for instance?), and incompatible metaphors are frequently mixed, a sure sign that the writer is not interested in what he is saying. Some metaphors now current have been twisted out of their original meaning without those who use them even being aware of the fact. For example, *toe the line* is sometimes written *tow the line.* Another example is *the hammer and the anvil,* now always used with the implication that the anvil gets the worst of it. In real life it is always the anvil that breaks the hammer, never the other way about: a writer who stopped to think what he was saying would be aware of this, and would avoid perverting the original phrase.

Operators or *verbal false limbs.* These save the trouble of picking out appropriate verbs and nouns, and at the same time pad each sentence with extra syllables which give it an appearance of symmetry. Characteristic phrases are: *render inoperative, militate against, make contact with, be subjected to, give rise to, give grounds for, have the effect of, play a leading part (role) in, make itself felt, take effect, exhibit a tendency to, serve the purpose of, etc., etc.* The keynote is the elimination of simple verbs. Instead of being a single word, such as *break, stop, spoil, mend, kill,* a verb becomes a *phrase,* made up of a noun or adjective tacked on to some general-purpose verb such as *prove, serve, form, play, render.* In addition, the passive voice is wherever possible used in preference to the active, and noun constructions are used instead of gerunds (*by examination of* instead of *by examining*). The range of verbs is further cut down by means of the

5

-*ize* and *de-* formations, and the banal statements are given an appearance of profundity by means of the *not un-* formation. Simple conjunctions and prepositions are replaced by such phrases as *with respect to, having regard to, the fact that, by dint of, in view of, in the interests of, on the hypothesis that*; and the ends of sentences are saved from anti-climax by such resounding commonplaces as *greatly to be desired, cannot be left out of account, a development to be expected in the near future, deserving of serious consideration, brought to a satisfactory conclusion*, and so on and so forth.

Pretentious diction. Words like *phenomenon, element, individual* (as noun), *objective, categorical, effective, virtual, basic, primary, promote, constitute, exhibit, exploit, utilize, eliminate, liquidate*, are used to dress up simple statements and give an air of scientific impartiality to biased judgments. Adjectives like *epoch-making, epic, historic, unforgettable, triumphant, age-old, inevitable, inexorable, veritable*, are used to dignify the sordid processes of international politics, while writing that aims at glorifying war usually takes on an archaic color, its characteristic words being: *realm, throne, chariot, mailed fist, trident, sword, shield, buckler, banner, jackboot, clarion*. Foreign words and expressions such as *cul de sac, ancien régime, deus ex machina, mutatis mutandis, status quo, Gleichschaltung, Weltanschauung*, are used to give an air of culture and elegance. Except for the useful abbreviations *i.e., e.g.*, and *etc.*, there is no real need for any of the hundreds of foreign phrases now current in English. Bad writers, and especially scientific, political and sociological writers, are nearly always haunted by the notion that Latin or Greek words are grander than Saxon ones, and unnecessary words like *expedite, ameliorate, predict, extraneous, deracinated, clandestine, subaqueous* and hundreds of others constantly gain ground from their Anglo-Saxon opposite numbers.[4] The jargon peculiar to Marxist writing (*hyena, hangman, cannibal, petty bourgeois, these gentry, lacquey, flunkey, mad dog, White Guard*, etc.) consists largely of words and phrases translated from Russian, German or French; but the normal way of coining a new word is to use a Latin or Greek root with the appropriate affix and, where necessary, the *-ize* formation. It is often easier to make up words of this kind (*deregionalize, impermissible,*

---

4   An interesting illustration of this is the way in which the English flower names which were in use till very recently are being ousted by Greek ones, *snapdragon* becoming *antirrhinum, forget-me-not* becoming *myosotis*, etc. It is hard to see any practical reason for this change of fashion; it is probably due to an instinctive turning-away from the more homely word and a vague feeling that the Greek word is scientific. [author's note]

extramarital, non-fragmentatory and so forth) than to think up the English words that will cover one's meaning. The result, in general, is an increase in slovenliness and vagueness.

Meaningless words. In certain kinds of writing, particularly in art criticism and literary criticism, it is normal to come across long passages which are almost completely lacking in meaning.[5] Words like *romantic, plastic, values, human, dead, sentimental, natural, vitality,* as used in art criticism, are strictly meaningless, in the sense that they not only do not point to any discoverable object, but are hardly ever expected to do so by the reader. When one critic writes, "The outstanding feature of Mr. X's work is its living quality," while another writes, "The immediately striking thing about Mr. X's work is its peculiar deadness," the reader accepts this as a simple difference of opinion. If words like *black* and *white* were involved, instead of the jargon words *dead* and *living,* he would see at once that language was being used in an improper way. Many political words are similarly abused. The word *Fascism* has now no meaning except in so far as it signifies "something not desirable." The words *democracy, socialism, freedom, patriotic, realistic, justice,* have each of them several different meanings which cannot be reconciled with one another. In the case of a word like *democracy,* not only is there no agreed definition, but the attempt to make one is resisted from all sides. It is almost universally felt that when we call a country democratic we are praising it: consequently the defenders of every kind of régime claim that it is a democracy, and fear that they might have to stop using the word if it were tied down to any one meaning. Words of this kind are often used in a consciously dishonest way. That is, the person who uses them has his own private definition, but allows his hearer to think he means something quite different. Statements like *Marshal Pétain was a true patriot, The Soviet Press is the freest in the world, The Catholic Church is opposed to persecution,* are almost always made with intent to deceive. Other words used in variable meanings, in most cases more or less dishonestly, are: *class, totalitarian, science, progressive, reactionary, bourgeois, equality.*

---

5   Example: "Comfort's catholicity of perception and image, strangely Whitmanesque in range, almost the exact opposite in aesthetic compulsion, continues to evoke that trembling atmospheric hinting at a cruel, an inexorably serene timelessness.... Wrey Gardiner scores by aiming at simple bully's-eyes with precision. Only they are not so simple, and through this contented sadness runs more than the surface bitter-sweet of resignation" (*Poetry Quarterly*). [author's note]

Now that I have made this catalogue of swindles and perversions, let me give another example of the kind of writing that they lead to. This time it must of its nature be an imaginary one. I am going to translate a passage of good English into modern English of the worst sort. Here is a well-known verse from *Ecclesiastes*:

I returned and saw under the sun, that the race is not to the swift, nor the battle to the strong, neither yet bread to the wise, nor yet riches to men of understanding, nor yet favor to men of skill; but time and chance happeneth to them all.

10   Here it is in modern English:

Objective consideration of contemporary phenomena compels the conclusion that success or failure in competitive activities exhibits no tendency to be commensurate with innate capacity, but that a considerable element of the unpredictable must invariably be taken into account.

This is a parody, but not a very gross one. Exhibit (3), above, for instance, contains several patches of the same kind of English. It will be seen that I have not made a full translation. The beginning and ending of the sentence follow the original meaning fairly closely, but in the middle the concrete illustrations—race, battle, bread—dissolve into the vague phrase "success or failure in competitive activities." This had to be so, because no modern writer of the kind I am discussing—no one capable of using phrases like "objective consideration of contemporary phenomena"—would ever tabulate his thoughts in that precise and detailed way. The whole tendency of modern prose is away from concreteness. Now analyze these two sentences a little more closely. The first contains forty-nine words but only sixty syllables, and all its words are those of everyday life. The second contains thirty-eight words of ninety syllables: eighteen of its words are from Latin roots, and one from Greek. The first sentence contains six vivid images, and only one phrase ("time and chance") that could be called vague. The second contains not a single fresh, arresting phrase, and in spite of its ninety syllables it gives only a shortened version of the meaning contained in the first. Yet without a doubt it is the second kind of sentence that is gaining ground in modern English. I do not want to exaggerate. This kind of writing is not yet universal, and outcrops of simplicity will occur here and there in the worst-written page. Still, if you or I were told to write a few lines on the uncertainty of human fortunes, we should probably come much nearer to my imaginary sentence than to the one from *Ecclesiastes*.

As I have tried to show, modern writing at its worst does not consist in picking out words for the sake of their meaning and inventing images in order to make the meaning clearer. It consists in gumming together long strips of words which have already been set in order by someone else, and making the results presentable by sheer humbug. The attraction of this way of writing is that it is easy. It is easier—even quicker, once you have the habit—to say *In my opinion it is a not unjustifiable assumption that* than to say *I think*. If you use ready-made phrases, you not only don't have to hunt about for words; you also don't have to bother with the rhythms of your sentences, since these phrases are generally so arranged as to be more or less euphonious. When you are composing in a hurry—when you are dictating to a stenographer, for instance, or making a public speech—it is natural to fall into a pretentious, Latinized style. Tags like *a consideration which we should do well to bear in mind* or *a conclusion to which all of us would readily assent* will save many a sentence from coming down with a bump. By using stale metaphors, similes and idioms, you save much mental effort, at the cost of leaving your meaning vague, not only for your reader but for yourself. This is the significance of mixed metaphors. The sole aim of a metaphor is to call up a visual image. When these images clash—as in *The Fascist octopus has sung its swan song, the jackboot is thrown into the melting pot*—it can be taken as certain that the writer is not seeing a mental image of the objects he is naming; in other words he is not really thinking. Look again at the examples I gave at the beginning of this essay. Professor Laski (1) uses five negatives in fifty-three words. One of these is superfluous, making nonsense of the whole passage, and in addition there is the slip *alien* for akin, making further nonsense, and several avoidable pieces of clumsiness which increase the general vagueness. Professor Hogben (2) plays ducks and drakes with a battery which is able to write prescriptions, and, while disapproving of the everyday phrase *put up with*, is unwilling to look *egregious* up in the dictionary and see what it means. (3), if one takes an uncharitable attitude towards it, is simply meaningless: probably one could work out its intended meaning by reading the whole of the article in which it occurs. In (4), the writer knows more or less what he wants to say, but an accumulation of stale phrases chokes him like tea leaves blocking a sink. In (5), words and meaning have almost parted company. People who write in this manner usually have a general emotional meaning—they dislike one thing and want to express solidarity with another—but they are not interested in the detail of what they are saying. A scrupulous writer, in every sentence that he writes, will ask himself at least four questions, thus: What am I trying to say? What words will express it? What image or idiom will make it clearer? Is this image fresh enough to have an effect? And he will probably ask himself two more: Could I put it more shortly? Have I said anything that is avoidably ugly? But you are not obliged to go to all this trouble. You can shirk it by simply throwing your mind open and letting the ready-made phrases come crowding in. They will construct your sentences for you—even think your thoughts for you, to a certain extent—and at need they will perform the important service of partially concealing your meaning even from yourself. It is at this point that the special connection between politics and the debasement of language becomes clear.

In our time it is broadly true that political writing is bad writing. Where it is not true, it will generally be found that the writer is some kind of rebel, expressing his private opinions and not a "party line." Orthodoxy, of whatever color, seems to demand a lifeless, imitative style. The political dialects to be found in pamphlets, leading articles, manifestos, White Papers and the speeches of under-secretaries do, of course, vary from party to party, but they are all alike in that one almost never finds in them a fresh, vivid, home-made turn of speech. When one watches some tired hack on the platform mechanically repeating the familiar phrases—*bestial atrocities, iron heel, bloodstained tyranny, free peoples of the world, stand shoulder to shoulder*—one often has a curious feeling that one is not watching a live human being but some kind of dummy: a feeling which suddenly becomes stronger at moments when the light catches the speaker's spectacles and turns them into blank discs which seem to have no eyes behind them. And this is not altogether fanciful. A speaker who uses that kind of phraseology has gone some distance towards turning himself into a machine. The appropriate noises are coming out of his larynx, but his brain is not involved as it would be if he were choosing his words for himself. If the speech he is making is one that he is accustomed to make over and over again, he may be almost unconscious of what he is saying, as one is when one utters the responses in church. And this reduced state of consciousness, if not indispensable, is at any rate favorable to political conformity.

In our time, political speech and writing are largely the defense of the indefensible. Things like the continuance of British rule in India, the Russian purges and deportations, the dropping of the atom bombs on Japan, can indeed be defended, but only by arguments which are too brutal for most people to face, and which do not square with the professed aims of political parties. Thus political language has to consist largely of euphemism, question-begging and sheer cloudy vagueness. Defenseless villages are bombarded from the air, the inhabitants driven out into the countryside, the cattle machine-gunned, the huts set on fire with incendiary bullets: this is called *pacification*. Millions of peasants are robbed of their farms and sent trudging along the roads with no more than they can carry: this is called *transfer of population* or *rectification of frontiers*. People are imprisoned for years without trial, or shot in the back of the neck or sent to die of scurvy in Arctic lumber camps: this is called *elimination of unreliable elements*. Such phraseology is needed if one wants to name things without calling up mental pictures of them. Consider for instance some comfortable English professor defending Russian totalitarianism. He cannot say outright, "I believe in killing off your opponents when you can get good results by doing so." Probably, therefore, he will say something like this:

> "While freely conceding that the Soviet regime exhibits certain features which the humanitarian may be inclined to deplore, we must, I think, agree that a certain curtailment of the right to political opposition is an unavoidable concomitant of transitional periods, and that the rigors which the Russian people have been called upon to undergo have been amply justified in the sphere of concrete achievement."

The inflated style is itself a kind of euphemism. A mass of Latin words falls upon the facts like soft snow, blurring the outlines and covering up all the details. The great enemy of clear language is insincerity. When there is a gap between one's real and one's declared aims, one turns as it were instinctively to long words and exhausted idioms, like a cuttlefish squirting out ink. In our age there is no such thing as "keeping out of politics." All issues are political issues, and politics itself is a mass of lies, evasions, folly, hatred and schizophrenia. When the general atmosphere is bad, language must suffer. I should expect to find—this is a guess which I have not sufficient knowledge to verify—that the German, Russian and Italian languages have all deteriorated in the last ten or fifteen years, as a result of dictatorship.

But if thought corrupts language, language can also corrupt thought. A bad usage can spread by tradition and imitation, even among people who should and do know better. The debased language that I have been discussing is in some ways very convenient. Phrases like *a not unjustifiable assumption, leave much to be desired, would serve no good purpose, a consideration which we should do well to bear in mind*, are a continuous temptation, a packet of aspirins always at one's elbow. Look back through this essay, and for certain you will find that I have again and again committed the very faults I am protesting against. By this morning's post I have received a pamphlet dealing with conditions in Germany. The author tells me that he "felt impelled" to write it. I open it at random, and here is almost the first sentence that I see: "(The Allies) have an opportunity not only of achieving a radical transformation of Germany's social and political structure in such a way as to avoid a nationalistic reaction in Germany itself, but at the same time of laying the foundations of a co-operative and unified Europe." You see, he "feels impelled" to write—feels, presumably, that he has something new to say—and yet his words, like cavalry horses answering the bugle, group themselves automatically into the familiar dreary pattern. This invasion of one's mind by ready-made phrases (*lay the foundations, achieve a radical transformation*) can only be prevented if one is constantly on guard against them, and every such phrase anaesthetizes a portion of one's brain.

I said earlier that the decadence of our language is probably curable. Those who deny this would argue, if they produced an argument at all, that language merely reflects existing social conditions, and that we cannot influence its development by any direct tinkering with words and constructions. So far as the general tone or spirit of a language goes, this may be true, but it is not true in detail. Silly words and expressions have often disappeared, not through any evolutionary process but owing to the conscious action of a minority. Two recent examples were *explore every avenue* and *leave no stone unturned*, which were killed by the jeers of a few journalists. There is a long list of flyblown metaphors which could similarly be got rid of if enough people would interest themselves in the job; and it should also be possible to laugh the *not un-* formation out of existence,[6] to reduce the amount of Latin and Greek in the average sentence, to drive out foreign phrases and strayed scientific words, and, in general, to make pretentiousness unfashionable. But all these are minor points. The defense of the English language implies more than this, and perhaps it is best to start by saying what it does *not* imply.

---

6   One can cure oneself of the *not un-* formation by memorizing this sentence: *A not unblack dog was chasing a not unsmall rabbit across a not ungreen field*. [author's note]

To begin with it has nothing to do with archaism, with the salvaging of obsolete words and turns of speech, or with the setting up of a "standard English" which must never be departed from. On the contrary, it is especially concerned with the scrapping of every word or idiom which has outworn its usefulness. It has nothing to do with correct grammar and syntax, which are of no importance so long as one makes one's meaning clear, or with the avoidance of Americanisms, or with having what is called a "good prose style." On the other hand it is not concerned with fake simplicity and the attempt to make written English colloquial. Nor does it even imply in every case preferring the Saxon word to the Latin one, though it does imply using the fewest and shortest words that will cover one's meaning. What is above all needed is to let the meaning choose the word, and not the other way about. In prose, the worst thing one can do with words is to surrender to them. When you think of a concrete object, you think wordlessly, and then, if you want to describe the thing you have been visualizing you probably hunt about till you find the exact words that seem to fit it. When you think of something abstract you are more inclined to use words from the start, and unless you make a conscious effort to prevent it, the existing dialect will come rushing in and do the job for you, at the expense of blurring or even changing your meaning. Probably it is better to put off using words as long as possible and get one's meaning as clear as one can through pictures or sensations. Afterwards one can choose—not simply *accept*—the phrases that will best cover the meaning, and then switch round and decide what impression one's words are likely to make on another person. This last effort of the mind cuts out all stale or mixed images, all prefabricated phrases, needless repetitions, and humbug and vagueness generally. But one can often be in doubt about the effect of a word or a phrase, and one needs rules that one can rely on when instinct fails. I think the following rules will cover most cases:

(i) Never use a metaphor, simile or other figure of speech which you are used to seeing in print.

(ii) Never use a long word where a short one will do.

(iii) If it is possible to cut a word out, always cut it out.

(iv) Never use the passive where you can use the active.

(v) Never use a foreign phrase, a scientific word or a jargon word if you can think of an everyday English equivalent.

(vi) Break any of these rules sooner than say anything outright barbarous.

These rules sound elementary, and so they are, but they demand a deep change of attitude in anyone who has grown used to writing in the style now fashionable. One could keep all of them and still write bad English, but one could not write the kind of stuff that I quoted in those five specimens at the beginning of this article.

20   I have not here been considering the literary use of language, but merely language as an instrument for expressing and not for concealing or preventing thought. Stuart Chase and others have come near to claiming that all abstract words are meaningless, and have used this as a pretext for advocating a kind of political quietism. Since you don't know what Fascism is, how can you struggle against Fascism? One need not swallow such absurdities as this, but one ought to recognize that the present political chaos is connected with the decay of language, and that one can probably bring about some improvement by starting at the verbal end. If you simplify your English, you are freed from the worst follies of orthodoxy. You cannot speak any of the necessary dialects, and when you make a stupid remark its stupidity will be obvious, even to yourself. Political language—and with variations this is true of all political parties, from Conservatives to Anarchists—is designed to make lies sound truthful and murder respectable, and to give an appearance of solidity to pure wind. One cannot change this all in a moment, but one can at least change one's own habits, and from time to time one can even, if one jeers loudly enough, send some worn-out and useless phrase—some *jackboot, Achilles' heel, hotbed, melting pot, acid test, veritable inferno* or other lump of verbal refuse—into the dustbin where it belongs.

(1946)

Questions

1. As Orwell sees it, why does it matter how political material is presented verbally?

2. What examples can you give of euphemisms being used to disguise unpleasant aspects of political actions?

3. Aside from implications for political discourse, what arguments does Orwell put forward for "the defense of the English language"?

4. What are the principles underlying the six rules that Orwell presents in paragraph 18?

5. Orwell and many others have argued for simplicity of expression, shorter words over longer ones, and so on. The contrary argument, however, has also been often made: that the extraordinarily large vocabulary of the English language, including many long and complex words of Latin origin, allows for greater precision in expressing one's meaning than do languages with much smaller vocabularies. Write one paragraph arguing each side of this argument, in each case referring to passages from other essays in this anthology.

6. At several points Orwell distinguishes between words of Anglo-Saxon origin and words of Latin origin. What are some of the characteristics of the two? Why does Orwell prefer one to the other?

7. Aside from the examples Orwell gives, think of some "ready-made phrases" (paragraph 12) that "construct your sentences for you" aside from the examples Orwell gives.

8. Describe the tone of Orwell's writing in this essay.

9. Orwell advises using concrete words or phrases whenever possible. Write two or three sentences expressing abstract principles, and then re-write so as to express them in more concrete language, or using concrete examples.

10. Express in your own words the difference between live metaphors and those that are stale, dead, or dying. Think of three dead metaphors not mentioned by Orwell, and think up three fresh metaphors in sentences of your own. (See for reference paragraphs 5 and 12.)

11. Explain how the confusion between "toe the line" and "tow the line" would have arisen.

STANLEY MILGRAM

from BEHAVIORAL STUDY OF OBEDIENCE

*In this famous essay, a social psychologist reports
the surprising results of an experiment on obedience
conducted at Yale University.*

❧

Obedience is as basic an element in the structure of social life as one can point to. Some system of authority is a requirement of all communal living, and it is only the man dwelling in isolation who is not forced to respond, through defiance or submission, to the commands of others. Obedience, as a determinant of behavior, is of particular relevance to our time. It has been reliably established that from 1933-45 millions of innocent persons were systematically slaughtered on command. Gas chambers were built, death camps were guarded, daily quotas of corpses were produced with the same efficiency as the manufacture of appliances. These inhumane policies may have originated in the mind of a single person, but they could only be carried out on a massive scale if a very large number of persons obeyed orders....

General Procedure

A procedure was devised which seems useful as a tool for studying obedience (Milgram, 1961). It consists of ordering a naive subject to administer electric shock to a victim. A simulated shock generator is used, with 30 clearly marked voltage levels that range from 15 to 450 volts. The instrument bears verbal designations that range from Slight Shock to Danger: Severe Shock. The responses of the victim, who is a trained confederate of the experimenter, are standardized. The orders to administer shocks are given to the naive subject in the context of a "learning experiment" ostensibly set up to study the effects of punishment on memory. As the experiment proceeds the naive subject is commanded to administer increasingly more intense shocks to the victim, even to a point of reaching the level marked Danger: Severe Shock. Internal resistances become stronger, and at a certain point the subject refuses to go on with the experiment. Behavior prior to this rupture is considered "obedience," in that the subject complies with the commands of the experimenter. The point of rupture is the act of disobedience. A quantitative value is assigned to the subject's performance based on the maximum intensity shock he is willing to administer before he refuses to participate further. Thus for any particular subject and for any particular experimental condition the degree of obedience may be specified with a numerical value. The crux of the study is to systematically vary the factors believed to alter the degree of obedience to the experimental commands....

METHOD

Subjects

The subjects were 40 males between the ages of 20 and 50, drawn from New Haven and surrounding communities. Subjects were obtained by a newspaper advertisement and direct mail solicitations. Those who responded to the appeal believed they were to participate in a study of memory and learning at Yale University. A wide range of occupations is represented in the sample. Typical subjects were postal clerks, high school teachers, salesmen, engineers, and laborers. Subjects ranged in educational level from one who had not finished elementary school, to those who had doctorate and other professional degrees. They were paid $4.50 for their participation in the experiment. However, subjects were told that payment was simply for coming to the laboratory, and that the money was theirs no matter what happened after they arrived....

Personnel and Locale

The experiment was conducted on the grounds of Yale University in the elegant interaction laboratory. (This detail is relevant to the perceived legitimacy of the experiment. In further variations, the experiment was dissociated from the university, with consequences for performance.) The role of experimenter was played by a 31-year-old high school teacher of biology. His manner was impassive, and his appearance somewhat stern throughout the experiment. He was dressed in a gray technician's coat. The victim was played by a 47-year-old accountant, trained for the role; he was of Irish-American stock, whom most observers found mild-mannered and likeable.

Procedure

5   One naive subject and one victim (an accomplice) performed in each experiment. A pretext had to be devised that would justify the administration of electric shock by the naive subject. This was effectively accomplished by the cover story. After a general introduction on the presumed relation between punishment and learning, subjects were told:

> But actually, we know *very little* about the effect of punishment on learning, because almost no truly scientific studies have been made of it in human beings.
>
> For instance, we don't know how *much* punishment is best for learning—and we don't know how much difference it makes as to who is giving the punishment, whether an adult learns best from a younger or an older person than himself—or many things of that sort.
>
> So in this study we are bringing together a number of adults of different occupations and ages. And we're asking some of them to be teachers and some of them to be learners.
>
> We want to find out just what effect different people have on each other as teachers and learners, and also what effect *punishment* will have on learning in this situation.
>
> Therefore, I'm going to ask one of you to be the teacher here tonight and the other one to be the learner.
>
> Does either of you have a preference?

Subjects then drew slips of paper from a hat to determine who would be the teacher and who would be the learner in the experiment. The drawing was rigged so that the naive subject was always the teacher and the accomplice always the learner. (Both slips contained the word "Teacher.") Immediately after the drawing, the teacher and learner were taken to an adjacent room and the learner was strapped into an "electric chair" apparatus.

The experimenter explained that the straps were to prevent excessive movement while the learner was being shocked. The effect was to make it impossible for him to escape from the situation. An electrode was attached to the learner's wrist, and electrode paste was applied "to avoid blisters and burns." Subjects were told that the electrode was attached to the shock generator in the adjoining room.

In order to improve credibility the experimenter declared, in response to a question by the learner: "Although shocks can be extremely painful, they cause no permanent tissue damage."

Learning task. The lesson administered by the subject was a paired-associate learning task. The subject read a series of word pairs to the learner, and then read the first word of the pair along with four terms. The learner was to indicate which of the four terms had originally been paired with the first word. He communicated his answer by pressing one of four switches in front of him, which in turn lit up one of four numbered quadrants in a answer-box located atop the shock generator.

Shock generator. The instrument panel consists of 30 lever switches set in a horizontal line. Each switch is clearly labeled with a voltage designation that ranges from 15 to 450 volts. There is a 15-volt increment from one switch to the next going from left to right. In addition, the following verbal designations are clearly indicated for groups of four switches going from left to right: Slight Shock, Moderate Shock, Strong Shock, Intense Shock, Extremely Intense Shock, Danger: Severe Shock. (Two switches after this last designation are simply marked XXX.)

Upon depressing a switch: a pilot light corresponding to each switch is illuminated in bright red; an electric buzzing is heard; an electric blue light, labeled "voltage energizer," flashes; the dial on the voltage meter swings to the right; various relay clicks are sounded.

The upper left-hand corner of the generator is labeled Shock generator, Type ZLB, Dyson Instrument Company, Waltham, Mass. Output 15 volts-450 volts.

Details of the instrument were carefully handled to insure an appearance of authenticity. The panel was engraved by precision industrial engravers, and all components were of high quality. No subject in the experiment suspected that the instrument was merely a simulated shock generator.

Sample shock. Each naive subject is given a sample shock on the shock generator, prior to beginning his run as teacher. This shock is always 45 volts, and is applied by pressing the third switch of the generator. The shock is applied to the wrist of the naive subject, and has its source in a 45-volt battery wired to the generator. This further convinces the subject of the authenticity of the generator.

15   *Shock instructions.* The subject is told to administer a shock to the learner each time he gives a wrong response. Moreover—and this is the key command—the subject is instructed to "move one level higher on the shock generator each time the learner flashes a wrong answer." He is also instructed to announce the voltage level before administering a shock. This serves to continually remind subjects of the increasing intensity of shocks administered to the learner.

    Preliminary and regular run. Pretests revealed that the procedure of reading words and administering shocks requires some practice before it can be handled smoothly. Therefore, immediately preceding the regular run, the teacher is given a preliminary series of 10 words to read to the learner. There are 3 neutral words in the practice series (i.e., words that the learner answers correctly), so that the shocks are administered for 7 of the words, with the maximum shock of 105 volts (moderate shock). Almost all subjects master the procedure by the time the preliminary run is over.

    Subjects are then presented with a second list, and are told that the procedure is the same as for the first list; the experimenter adds however:

> When you get to the bottom of the list, repeat it over again, and continue giving shocks, until the learner has learned all the pairs correctly.

The experimenter instructs the subject to,

> start from 15 volts and increase the shock level one step each time the learner gives a wrong answer.

    Feedback from the victim. In all conditions the learner gives a predetermined set of responses to the word pair test, based on a schedule of approximately three wrong answers to one correct answer. In the present experimental condition no vocal response or other sign of protest is heard from the learner until Shock Level 300 is reached. When the 300-volt shock is administered, the learner pounds on the wall of the room in which he is bound to the electric chair. The pounding can be heard by the subject. From this point on, the learner's answers no longer appear on the four-way panel.

At this juncture, subjects ordinarily turn to the experimenter for guidance. The experimenter instructs the subject to treat absence of a response as a wrong answer, and to shock the subject according to the usual schedule. He advises the subject to allow 5-10 seconds before considering no response as a wrong answer, and to increase the shock level one step each time the learner fails to respond correctly. The learner's pounding is repeated after the 315-volt shock is administered; afterwards he is not heard from, nor do his answers reappear on the four-way signal box.

Experimenter feedback. At various points in the experiment the subject   20
may turn to the experimenter for advice on whether he should continue to administer shocks. Or he may indicate that he does not wish to go on. It was important to standardize the experimenter's responses to these inquiries and reactions.

If the subject indicated his unwillingness to go on, the experimenter responded with a sequence of "prods," using as many as necessary to bring the subject into line.

Prod 1: Please continue. *or* Please go on.

Prod 2: The experiment requires that you continue.

Prod 3: It is absolutely essential that you continue.

Prod 4: You have no other choice, you *must* go on.

The prods were always made in sequence: Only if Prod 1 had been unsuccessful, could Prod 2 be used. If the subject still refused to obey the experimenter after Prod 4, the experiment was terminated. The experimenter's tone of voice was at all times firm, but not impolite. The sequence was begun anew on each occasion that the subject balked or showed reluctance to follow orders.

Special prods. If the subject asked if the learner was liable to suffer permanent physical injury, the experimenter said:

Although the shocks may be painful, there is no permanent tissue damage, so please go on. [Followed by Prods 2, 3, and 4 if necessary.]

If the subject said that the learner did not want to go on, the experimenter replied:

Whether the learner likes it or not, you must go on until he has learned all the word pairs correctly. So please go on. [Followed by Prods 2, 3, and 4 if necessary.]

Dependent Measures

25   The primary dependent measure for any subject is the maximum shock he administers before he refuses to go any further. In principle this may vary from 0 (for a subject who refuses to administer even the first shock) to 30 (for a subject who administers the highest shock on the generator). A subject who breaks off the experiment at any point prior to administering the thirtieth shock level is termed a *defiant subject*. One who complies with experimental command fully, and proceeds to administer all shock levels commanded, is termed an *obedient* subject....

Interview and dehoax. Following the experiment, subjects were interviewed; open-ended questions, projective measures, and attitude scales were employed. After the interview, procedures were undertaken to assure that the subject would leave the laboratory in a state of well being. A friendly reconciliation was arranged between the subject and the victim, and an effort was made to reduce any tensions that arose as a result of the experiment.

RESULTS

Preliminary Notions

Before giving an account of the experimental results, it is instructive to consider how persons predict others will perform when commanded to administer powerful shocks to another person. Fourteen Yale seniors, all psychology majors, were provided with a detailed description of the experimental situation. They were asked to reflect carefully on it, and to predict the behavior of 100 hypothetical subjects. More specifically, they were instructed to plot the distribution of obedience of "100 Americans of diverse occupations, and ranging in age from 20 to 50 years," who were placed in the experimental situation.

There was considerable agreement among the respondents on the expected behavior or hypothetical subjects. All respondents predicted that only an insignificant minority would go through to the end of the shock series. (The estimates ranged from 0 to 3%; i.e., the most "pessimistic" member of the class predicted that of 100 persons, 3 would continue through to the most potent shock available on the shock generator—450 volts.) The class mean was 1.2%. The question was also posed informally to colleagues of the author, and the most general feeling was that few if any subjects would go beyond the designation Very Strong Shock.

Result of Experiment 1

Subjects accept situation. With few exceptions subjects were convinced of the reality of the experimental situation, that they were administering shocks to another person, and the most potent shocks were extremely painful. In the post-experimental interview subjects were asked: "How painful to the learner were the last few shocks that you administered to him?" Subjects were instructed to indicate their answers on a printed 14-point scale ranging from "Not at all painful" to "Extremely painful." The modal response was 14 (Extremely painful) with the mean at 13.42.

Signs of extreme tension. Many subjects showed signs of nervousness in the experimental situation, and especially upon administering the more powerful shocks. In a large number of cases the degree of tension reached extremes that are rarely seen in sociopsychological laboratory studies. Subjects were observed to sweat, tremble, stutter, bite their lips, groan, and dig their fingernails into their flesh. These were characteristic rather than exceptional responses to the experiment.

One sign of tension was the regular occurrence of nervous laughing fits. Fourteen of the 40 subjects showed definite signs of nervous laughter and smiling. The laughter seemed entirely out of place, even bizarre. Full-blown, uncontrollable seizures were observed for 3 subjects. On one occasion we observed a seizure so violently convulsive that it was necessary to call a halt to the experiment. The subject, a 46-year-old encyclopedia salesman, was seriously embarrassed by his untoward and uncontrollable behavior. In the post-experimental interviews subjects took such pains to point out that they were not sadistic types, and that the laughter did not mean they enjoyed shocking the victim.

30

TABLE 1
Distribution of Breakoff Points

Verbal designation and voltage indication	Number of subjects for whom this was maximum shock
Slight Shock	
15	0
30	0
45	0
60	0
Moderate Shock	
75	0
90	0
105	0
120	0
Strong Shock	
135	0
150	0
165	0
180	0
Very Strong Shock	
195	0
210	0
225	0
240	0
Intense Shock	
255	0
270	0
285	0
300	5
Extreme Intensity Shock	
315	4
330	2
345	1
360	1
Danger: Severe Shock	
375	1
390	0
405	0
420	0
XXX	
435	0
450	26

5

Distribution of scores. It had been conjectured that persons would not, in general, agree to administer shocks beyond the level designated Very Strong Shock. The distribution of maximum shocks for this experiment is shown in Table 1. The obtained distribution of scores deviates radically from the prediction.

Upon command of the experimenter, each of the 40 subjects went beyond the expected breakoff point. No subject stopped prior to administering Shock Level 20. (At this level—300 volts—the victim kicks on the wall and no longer provides answers to the teacher's multiple-choice questions.)

Of the 40 subjects, 5 refused to obey the experimental commands beyond the 330-volt level. Four more subjects administered one further shock, and then refused to go on. Two broke off at the 330-volt level, and 1 each at 345, 360, and 375 volts. Thus a total of 14 subjects defied the experimenter. It is instructive to reprint their remarks at the point of defiance, as transcribed from the tape recordings:

[0124] I think he's trying to communicate, he's knocking.... Well it's not fair to shock the guy ... these are terrific volts. I don't think this is very humane.... Oh, I can't go on with this; no this isn't right. It's a hell of an experiment. The guy is suffering in there. No, I don't want to go on. This is crazy. [Subject refused to administer more shocks.]

[0123] He's banging in there. I'm gonna chicken out. I'd like to continue, but I can't do that to a man.... I'm sorry I can't do that to a man. I'll hurt his heart. You take your check.... No really, I couldn't do it.

These subjects were frequently in a highly agitated and even angered state. Sometimes, verbal protest was at a minimum, and the subject simply got up from his chair in front of the shock generator, and indicated that he wished to leave the laboratory.

Of the 40 subjects, 26 obeyed the orders of the experimenter to the end, proceeding to punish the victim until they reached the most potent shock available on the shock generator. At that point, the experimenter called a halt to the sessions. (The maximum shock is labeled 450 volts, and is two steps beyond the designation: Danger: Severe Shock.) Although obedient subjects continued to administer shocks, they often did so under extreme stress. Some expressed reluctance to administer shocks beyond the 300-volt level, and displayed fears similar to those who defied the experimenter; yet they obeyed.

After the maximum shocks had been delivered, and the experimenter called a halt to the proceedings, many obedient subjects heaved sighs of relief, mopped their brows, rubbed their fingers over their eyes, or nervously fumbled cigarettes. Some shook their heads, apparently in regret. Some subjects had remained calm throughout the experiment, and displayed only minimal signs of tension from beginning to end.

DISCUSSION

The experiment yielded two findings that were surprising. The first finding concerns the sheer strength of obedient tendencies manifested in this situation. Subjects have learned from childhood that it is a fundamental breach of moral conduct to hurt another person against his will. Yet, 26 subjects abandon this tenet in following the instructions of an authority who has no special powers to enforce his commands. To disobey would bring no material loss to the subject; no punishment would ensue. It is clear from the remarks and outward behavior of many participants that in punishing the victim they are often acting against their own values. Subjects often expressed deep disapproval of shocking a man in the face of his objections, and others denounced it as stupid and senseless. Yet the majority complied with the experimental commands. This outcome was surprising from two perspectives: first, from the standpoint of predictions made in the questionnaire described earlier. (Here, however, it is possible that the remoteness of the respondents from the actual situation, and the difficulty of conveying to them the concrete details of the experiment, could account for the serious underestimation of obedience.)

But the results were also unexpected to persons who observed the experiment in progress, through one-way mirrors. Observers often uttered expressions of disbelief upon seeing a subject administrate more powerful shocks to the victim. These persons had a full acquaintance with the details of the situation, and yet systematically underestimated the amount of obedience that subjects would display.

The second unanticipated effect was the extraordinary tension generated by the procedures. One might suppose that a subject would simply break off or continue as his conscience dictated. Yet, this is very far from what happened. There were striking reactions of tension and emotional strain.

(1961)

Questions

1. What was the purpose of the experiment conducted at Yale?

2. What elements were included to make the experiment seem authentic? How did the experimenters signify authority to the naive subjects?

3. What is the effect of the very scientific style in which this paper is written?

4. What does the term "naive subject" refer to, literally? What does it seem to imply figuratively?

5. What effect does the contrast between the subjects' nervous laughter and the seriousness of their situation have? What is Milgram implying about human behavior under stress?

6. How did the experiment's actual outcome compare to your own expectations? Were you as surprised as the Yale academics? What do you think might account for the discrepancy between the expected outcome and the actual one? How do you feel you would have performed? Can you honestly predict whether you would have been as obedient or less so?

RAYMOND WILLIAMS

CORRECTNESS AND THE ENGLISH LANGUAGE

This short piece is taken from Williams's book The Long
Revolution, *in which he argues that the cultural revolution
which extended literacy and advanced communication through
the Western world was as important as either the growth of
democracy or the industrial revolution.*

❧

The late seventeenth and eighteenth centuries saw a strenuous effort to
rationalize English, by a number of differently motivated groups. The
Royal Society's Committee "for improving the English tongue" (1664)
represents the effort of a new scientific philosophy to clarify the language
for the purposes of its own kind of discourse. A different group, running
from Addison and Swift to Pope and Johnson, were concerned with the
absence of a "polite standard" in the new society. Yet behind these intellectual groups there was the practical pressure of a newly powerful and
self-conscious middle class which, like most groups which find themselves
suddenly possessed of social standing but deficient in social tradition,
thought "correctness" a systematic thing which had simply to be acquired.
Eighteenth-century London abounded in spelling-masters and pronuncia-
tion-coaches: many of them, as it happened, ignorant men. Yet if they had
all been scholars, within the concepts of their period, the result might not
have been greatly different. The scholarly teaching of grammar was locked
in the illusion that Latin grammatical rules were the best possible guide
to correctness in English. And Johnson himself emphatically expounded
a doctrine equally false: that the spelling of a word is the best guide to
its pronunciation, "the most elegant speakers ... [those] who deviate least
from the written words." The new "standard," therefore, was not, as the
earlier common language had been, the result mainly of growth through

contact and actual relationships, but to a considerable extent an artificial creation based on false premises. The habits of a language are too strong to be wholly altered by determined yet relatively ignorant teachers, but the mark of their effort is still on us, and the tension they created is still high.

Common pronunciation (as distinct from regional variations) changed considerably during this period: partly through ordinary change, partly through the teaching of "correctness." English spelling, as is now well known, is in fact extremely unreliable as a guide to pronunciation, for not only, at best, does it frequently record sounds that have become obsolete, but in fact many of these were obsolete when the spellings were fixed, and moreover certain plain blunders have become embedded by time. *Iland, sissors, sithe, coud,* and *ancor* were altered, by men ignorant of their origins, confident of false origins, to *island, scissors, scythe, could,* and *anchor,* but in these cases, fortunately, pronunciation has not been affected. Similar false alterations, however, such as *fault, vault, assault* (which need no l's), or *advantage* and *advance* (which need no d's) have perpetuated their errors not only into spelling but into sound. The principle of following the spelling changed the sound *offen* into *often, forrid* into *forehead, summat* into *somewhat, lanskip* into *landscape, yumer* into *humor, at ome* into *at home, weskit* into *waistcoat,* and so on, in a list that could be tediously prolonged. Words like these are among the pressure points of distinction between "educated" and "uneducated" speech, yet the case is simply that the uneducated, less exposed to the doctrines of "correctness," have preserved the traditional pronunciation.

(1961)

Questions

1. List examples of words that have been added to the English language, or whose spelling or meaning have changed, in your lifetime. How do you think these changes occur?

2. In your opinion, what is the difference between "educated" and "uneducated" speech? Do you feel there is a value in this distinction?

3. How would you describe Williams's writing style? Who do you think is his intended audience?

4. Express in your own words some of the irony inherent in the history of "correct" pronunciation, according to Williams.

Martin Luther King, Jr.

Letter from Birmingham Jail[1]

This long letter is perhaps the best known exposition of the principles of the American Civil Rights Movement.

❧

My Dear Fellow Clergymen:

While confined here in the Birmingham city jail, I came across your recent statement calling my present activities "unwise and untimely." Seldom do I pause to answer criticism of my work and ideas. If I sought to answer all the criticisms that cross my desk, my secretaries would have little time for anything other than such correspondence in the course of the day, and I would have no time for constructive work. But since I feel that you are men of genuine good will and that your criticisms are sincerely set forth, I want to try to answer your statement in what I hope will be patient and reasonable terms.

I think I should indicate why I am here in Birmingham, since you have been influenced by the view which argues against "outsiders coming in." I have the honor of serving as president of the Southern Christian Leadership Conference, an organization operating in every southern state, with headquarters in Atlanta, Georgia. We have some eighty-five affiliated organizations across the South, and one of them is the Alabama Christian

---

1   This response to a published statement by eight fellow clergymen from Alabama (Bishop C.C.J. Carpenter, Bishop Joseph A. Durick, Rabbi Milton L. Grafman, Bishop Paul Hardin, Bishop Holan B. Harmon, the Reverend George M. Murray, the Reverend Edward Ramage and the Reverend Earl Stallings) was composed under somewhat constricting circumstances. Begun on the margins of the newspaper in which the statement appeared while I was in jail, the letter was continued on scraps of writing paper supplied by a friendly Negro trusty, and concluded on a pad my attorneys were eventually permitted to leave me. Although the text remains in substance unaltered, I have indulged in the author's prerogative of polishing it for publication. [author's note]

Movement for Human Rights. Frequently we share staff, educational, and financial resources with our affiliates. Several months ago the affiliate here in Birmingham asked us to be on call to engage in a nonviolent direct-action program if such were deemed necessary. We readily consented, and when the hour came we lived up to our promise. So I, along with several members of my staff, am here because I was invited here. I am here because I have organizational ties here.

But more basically, I am in Birmingham because injustice is here. Just as the prophets of the eighth century BC left their villages and carried their "thus saith the Lord" far beyond the boundaries of their home towns, and just as the Apostle Paul left his village of Tarsus and carried the gospel of Jesus Christ to the far corners of the Greco-Roman world, so am I compelled to carry the gospel of freedom beyond my own home town. Like Paul, I must constantly respond to the Macedonian call for aid.

Moreover, I am cognizant of the interrelatedness of all communities and states. I cannot sit idly by in Atlanta and not be concerned about what happens in Birmingham. Injustice anywhere is a threat to justice everywhere. We are caught in an inescapable network of mutuality, tied in a single garment of destiny. Whatever affects one directly, affects all indirectly. Never again can we afford to live with the narrow, provincial "outside agitator" idea. Anyone who lives inside the United States can never be considered an outsider anywhere within its bounds.

You deplore the demonstrations taking place in Birmingham. But your statement, I am sorry to say, fails to express a similar concern for the conditions that brought about the demonstrations. I am sure that none of you would want to rest content with the superficial kind of social analysis that deals merely with effects and does not grapple with underlying causes. It is unfortunate that demonstrations are taking place in Birmingham, but it is even more unfortunate that the city's white power structure left the Negro community with no alternative.

In any nonviolent campaign there are four basic steps: collection of the facts to determine whether injustices exist; negotiation; self-purification; and direct action. We have gone through all these steps in Birmingham. There can be no gainsaying the fact that racial injustice engulfs this community. Birmingham is probably the most thoroughly segregated city in the United States. Its ugly record of brutality is widely known. Negroes have experienced grossly unjust treatment in the courts. There have been more unsolved bombings of Negro homes and churches in Birmingham than in any other city in the nation. These are the hard, brutal facts of the case.

5

On the basis of these conditions, Negro leaders sought to negotiate with the city fathers. But the latter consistently refused to engage in good-faith negotiation.

Then, last September, came the opportunity to talk with leaders of Birmingham's economic community. In the course of the negotiations, certain promises were made by the merchants—for example, to remove the stores' humiliating racial signs. On the basis of these promises, the Reverend Fred Shuttlesworth and the leaders of the Alabama Christian Movement for Human Rights agreed to a moratorium on all demonstrations. As the weeks and months went by, we realized that we were the victims of a broken promise. A few signs, briefly removed, returned; the others remained.

As in so many past experiences, our hopes had been blasted, and the shadow of deep disappointment settled upon us. We had no alternative except to prepare for direct action, whereby we could present our very bodies as a means of laying our case before the conscience of the local and the national community. Mindful of the difficulties involved, we decided to undertake a process of self-purification. We began a series of workshops on nonviolence, and we repeatedly asked ourselves: "Are you able to accept blows without retaliating?" "Are you able to endure the ordeal of jail?" We decided to schedule our direct-action program for the Easter season, realizing that except for Christmas, this is the main shopping period of the year. Knowing that a strong economic-withdrawal program would be the by-product of direct action, we felt that this would be the best time to bring pressure to bear on the merchants for the needed change.

Then it occurred to us that Birmingham's mayoral election was coming up in March, and we speedily decided to postpone action until after election day. When we discovered that the Commissioner of Public Safety, Eugene "Bull" Connor, had piled up enough votes to be in the run-off, we decided again to postpone action until the day after the run-off so that the demonstrations could not be used to cloud the issues. Like many others, we wanted to see Mr. Connor defeated, and to this end we endured postponement after postponement. Having aided in this community need, we felt that our direct-action program could be delayed no longer.

10   You may well ask, "Why direct action? Why sit-ins, marches, and so forth? Isn't negotiation a better path?" You are quite right in calling for negotiation. Indeed, this is the very purpose of direct action. Nonviolent direct action seeks so to create such a crisis and foster such tension that a community which has constantly refused to negotiate is forced to

confront the issue. It seeks to dramatize the issue that it can no longer be ignored. My citing the creation of tension as part of the work of the nonviolent-resister may sound rather shocking. But I must confess that I am not afraid of the word "tension." I have earnestly opposed violent tension, but there is a type of constructive, nonviolent tension which is necessary for growth. Just as Socrates felt that it was necessary to create a tension in the mind so that individuals could rise from the bondage of myths and half-truths to the unfettered realm of creative analysis and objective appraisal, so must we see the need for nonviolent gadflies to create the kind of tension in society that will help men rise from the dark depths of prejudice and racism to the majestic heights of understanding and brotherhood.

The purpose of our direct-action program is to create a situation so crisis-packed that it will inevitably open the door to negotiation. I therefore concur with you in your call for negotiation. Too long has our beloved Southland been bogged down in a tragic effort to live in monologue rather than dialogue.

One of the basic points in your statement is that the action that I and my associates have taken in Birmingham is untimely. Some have asked: "Why didn't you give the new city administration time to act?" The only answer that I can give to this query is that the new Birmingham administration must be prodded about as much as the outgoing one, before it will act. We are sadly mistaken if we feel that the election of Albert Boutwell as mayor will bring the millennium to Birmingham. While Mr. Boutwell is a much more gentle person than Mr. Connor, they are both segregationists, dedicated to maintenance of the status quo. I have hoped that Mr. Boutwell will be reasonable enough to see the futility of massive resistance to desegregation. But he will not see this without pressure from devotees of civil rights. My friends, I must say to you that we have not made a single gain in civil rights without determined legal and nonviolent pressure. Lamentably, it is an historical fact that privileged groups seldom give up their privileges voluntarily. Individuals may see the moral light and voluntarily give up their unjust posture; but, as Reinhold Niebuhr has reminded us, groups tend to be more immoral than individuals.

We know through painful experience that freedom is never voluntarily given by the oppressor; it must be demanded by the oppressed. Frankly, I have yet to engage in a direct-action campaign that was "well timed" in the view of those who have not suffered unduly from the disease of segregation. For years now I have heard the word "Wait!" It rings in the ear of every Negro with piercing familiarity. This "Wait" has almost always meant "Never." We must come to see, with one of our distinguished jurists, that "justice too long delayed is justice denied."

We have waited for more than 340 years for our constitutional and God-given rights. The nations of Asia and Africa are moving with jet-like speed toward gaining political independence, but we still creep at horse-and-buggy pace toward gaining a cup of coffee at a lunch counter. Perhaps it is easy for those who have never felt the stinging darts of segregation to say, "Wait." But when you have seen vicious mobs lynch your mothers and fathers at will and drown your sisters and brothers at whim; when you have seen hate-filled policemen curse, kick, and even kill your black brothers and sisters; when you see the vast majority of your twenty million Negro brothers smothering in an airtight cage of poverty in the midst of an affluent society; when you suddenly find your tongue twisted and your speech stammering as you seek to explain to your six-year-old daughter why she can't go to the public amusement park that has just been advertised on television, and see tears welling up in her eyes when she is told that Funtown is closed to colored children, and see ominous clouds of inferiority beginning to form in her little mental sky, and see her beginning to distort her personality by developing an unconscious bitterness toward white people; when you have to concoct an answer for a five-year-old son who is asking, "Daddy, why do white people treat colored people so mean?"; when you take a cross-country drive and find it necessary to sleep night after night in the uncomfortable corners of your automobile because no motel will accept you; when you are humiliated day in and day out by nagging signs reading "white" and "colored"; when your first name becomes "nigger," your middle name becomes "boy" (however old you are) and your last name becomes "John," and your wife and mother are never given the respected title "Mrs."; when you are harried by day and haunted by night by the fact that you are a Negro, living constantly at tiptoe stance, never quite knowing what to expect next, and are plagued with inner fears and outer resentments; when you are forever fighting a degenerating sense of "nobodiness"—then you will understand why we find it difficult to wait. There comes a time when the cup of endurance runs over, and men are no longer willing to be plunged into the abyss of despair. I hope, sirs, you can understand our legitimate and unavoidable impatience.

15   You express a great deal of anxiety over our willingness to break laws. This is certainly a legitimate concern. Since we so diligently urge people to

obey the Supreme Court's decision of 1954[2] outlawing segregation in the public schools, at first glance it may seem rather paradoxical for us consciously to break laws. One may well ask: "How can you advocate breaking some laws and obeying others?" The answer lies in the fact that there are two types of laws: just and unjust. I would be the first to advocate obeying just laws. One has not only a legal but a moral responsibility to obey just laws. Conversely, one has a moral responsibility to disobey unjust laws. I would agree with St. Augustine that "an unjust law is no law at all."

Now, what is the difference between the two? How does one determine whether a law is just or unjust? A just law is a man-made code that squares with the moral law or the law of God. An unjust law is a code that is out of harmony with the moral law. To put it in the terms of St. Thomas Aquinas: An unjust law is a human law that is not rooted in eternal law and natural law. Any law that uplifts human personality is just. Any law that degrades human personality is unjust. All segregation statutes are unjust because segregation distorts the soul and damages the personality. It gives the segregator a false sense of superiority and the segregated a false sense of inferiority. Segregation, to use the terminology of the Jewish philosopher Martin Buber, substitutes an "I-it" relationship for an "I-thou" relationship and ends up relegating persons to the status of things. Hence segregation is not only politically, economically, and sociologically unsound, it is morally wrong and sinful. Paul Tillich has said that sin is separation. Is not segregation an existential expression of man's tragic separation, his awful estrangement, his terrible sinfulness? Thus it is that I can urge men to obey the 1954 decision of the Supreme Court, for it is morally right; and I can urge them to disobey segregation ordinances, for they are morally wrong.

Let us consider a more concrete example of just and unjust laws. An unjust law is a code that a numerical or power majority group compels a minority group to obey but does not make binding on itself. This is *difference* made legal. By the same token, a just law is a code that a majority compels a minority to follow and that it is willing to follow itself. This is *sameness* made legal.

Let me give another explanation. A law is unjust if it is inflicted on a minority that, as a result of being denied the right to vote, had no part in

---

2   *Supreme Court's decision of 1954*   Brown v. Board of Education. Prior to 1954 the courts had allowed states to follow policies according to which Black and White were supposedly "separate but equal."

enacting or devising the law. Who can say that the legislature of Alabama which set up that state's segregation laws was democratically elected? Throughout Alabama all sorts of devious methods are used to prevent Negroes from becoming registered voters, and there are some counties in which, even though Negroes constitute a majority of the population, not a single Negro is registered. Can any law enacted under such circumstances be considered democratically structured?

Sometimes a law is just on its face and unjust in its application. For instance, I have been arrested on a charge of parading without a permit. Now, there is nothing wrong in having an ordinance which requires a permit for a parade. But such an ordinance becomes unjust when it is used to maintain segregation and to deny citizens the First-Amendment privilege of peaceful assembly and protest.

20   I hope you are able to see the distinction I am trying to point out. In no sense do I advocate evading or defying the law, as would the rabid segregationist. That would lead to anarchy. One who breaks an unjust law must do so openly, lovingly, and with a willingness to accept the penalty. I submit that an individual who breaks a law that conscience tells him is unjust, and who willingly accepts the penalty of imprisonment in order to arouse the conscience of the community over its injustice, is in reality expressing the highest respect for law.

Of course, there is nothing new about this kind of civil disobedience. It was evidenced sublimely in the refusal of Shadrach, Meshach, and Abednego to obey the laws of Nebuchadnezzar, on the ground that a higher moral law was at stake. It was practiced superbly by the early Christians, who were willing to face hungry lions and the excruciating pain of chopping blocks rather than submit to certain unjust laws of the Roman Empire. To a degree, academic freedom is a reality today because Socrates practiced civil disobedience. In our own nation, the Boston Tea Party represented a massive act of civil disobedience.

We should never forget that everything Adolf Hitler did in Germany was "legal" and everything the Hungarian freedom fighters[3] did in Hungary was "illegal." It was "illegal" to aid and comfort a Jew in Hitler's Germany. Even so, I am sure that, had I lived in Germany at the time, I would have aided and comforted my Jewish brothers. If today I lived in a Communist country where certain principles dear to the Christian faith

---

3   *Hungarian freedom fighters*   The Hungarian Rebellion in 1956 against an oppressive government was brutally suppressed with the help of the Soviet army.

are suppressed, I would openly advocate disobeying that country's anti-religious laws.

I must make two honest confessions to you, my Christian and Jewish brothers. First, I must confess that over the past few years I have been gravely disappointed with the white moderate. I have almost reached the regrettable conclusion that the Negro's great stumbling block in his stride toward freedom is not the White Citizen's Counciler or the Ku Klux Klanner, but the white moderate, who is more devoted to "order" than to justice; who prefers a negative peace which is the absence of tension to a positive peace which is the presence of justice; who constantly says, "I agree with you in the goal you seek, but I cannot agree with your methods of direct action"; who paternalistically believes he can set the timetable for another man's freedom; who lives by a mythical concept of time and who constantly advises the Negro to wait for a "more convenient season." Shallow understanding from people of good will is more frustrating than absolute misunderstanding from people of ill will. Lukewarm acceptance is much more bewildering than outright rejection.

I had hoped that the white moderate would understand that law and order exist for the purpose of establishing justice and that when they fail in this purpose they become the dangerously structured dams that block the flow of social progress. I had hoped that the white moderate would understand that the present tension in the South is a necessary phase of the transition from an obnoxious negative peace, in which the Negro passively accepted his unjust plight, to a substantive and positive peace, in which all men will respect the dignity and worth of human personality. Actually, we who engage in nonviolent direct action are not the creators of tension. We merely bring to the surface the hidden tension that is already alive. We bring it out in the open, where it can be seen and dealt with. Like a boil that can never be cured so long as it is covered up but must be opened with all its ugliness to the natural medicines of air and light, injustice must be exposed, with all the tension its exposure creates, to the light of human conscience and the air of national opinion, before it can be cured.

In your statement you assert that our actions, even though peaceful, must be condemned because they precipitate violence. But is this a logical assertion? Isn't this like condemning a robbed man because his possession of money precipitated the evil act of robbery? Isn't this like condemning Socrates because his unswerving commitment to truth and his philosophical inquiries precipitated the act by the misguided populace in which they

25

made him drink hemlock? Isn't this like condemning Jesus because his unique God-consciousness and never-ceasing devotion to God's will precipitated the evil act of crucifixion? We must come to see that, as the federal courts have consistently affirmed, it is wrong to urge an individual to cease his efforts to gain his basic constitutional rights because the quest may precipitate violence. Society must protect the robbed and punish the robber.

I had also hoped that the white moderate would reject the myth concerning time in relation to the struggle for freedom. I have just received a letter from a white brother in Texas. He writes: "All Christians know that the colored people will receive equal rights eventually, but it is possible that you are in too great a religious hurry. It has taken Christianity almost two thousand years to accomplish what it has. The teachings of Christ take time to come to earth." Such an attitude stems from a tragic misconception of time, from the strangely irrational notion that there is something in the very flow of time that will inevitably cure all ills. Actually, time itself is neutral; it can be used either destructively or constructively. More and more I feel that the people of ill will have used time much more effectively than have the people of good will. We will have to repent in this generation not merely for the hateful words and actions of the bad people, but for the appalling silence of the good people. Human progress never rolls in on wheels of inevitability; it comes through the tireless efforts of men willing to be co-workers with God, and without this hard work, time itself becomes an ally of the forces of social stagnation. We must use time creatively, in the knowledge that the time is always ripe to do right. Now is the time to make real the promise of democracy and transform our pending national elegy into a creative psalm of brotherhood. Now is the time to lift our national policy from the quicksand of racial injustice to the solid rock of human dignity.

You speak of our activity in Birmingham as extreme. At first I was rather disappointed that fellow clergymen would see my nonviolent efforts as those of an extremist. I began thinking about the fact that I stand in the middle of two opposing forces in the Negro community. One is a force of complacency, made up in part of Negroes who, as a result of long years of oppression, are so drained of self-respect and a sense of "somebodiness" that they have adjusted to segregation; and in part of a few middle-class Negroes who, because of a degree of academic and economic security and because in some ways they profit by segregation, have become insensitive to the problems of the masses. The other force is one of bitterness and hatred, and it comes perilously close to advocating violence. It is expressed in the various black nationalist groups that are springing up across the nation, the largest and best-known being Elijah Muhammad's Muslim movement. Nourished by the Negro's frustration over the continued existence of racial discrimination, this movement is made up of people who have lost faith in America, who have absolutely repudiated Christianity, and who have concluded that the white man is an incorrigible "devil."

I have tried to stand between these two forces, saying that we need emulate neither the "do-nothingism" of the complacent nor the hatred and despair of the black nationalist. For there is the more excellent way of love and nonviolent protest. I am grateful to God that, through the influence of the Negro church, the way of nonviolence became an integral part of our struggle.

If this philosophy had not emerged, by now many streets of the South would, I am convinced, be flowing with blood. And I am further convinced that if our white brothers dismiss as "rabblerousers" and "outside agitators" those of us who employ nonviolent direct action, and if they refuse to support our nonviolent efforts, millions of Negroes will, out of frustration and despair, seek solace and security in black-nationalist ideologies—a development that would inevitably lead to a frightening racial nightmare.

Oppressed people cannot remain oppressed forever. The yearning for freedom eventually manifests itself, and that is what has happened to the American Negro. Something within has reminded him of his birthright of freedom, and something without has reminded him that it can be gained. Consciously or unconsciously, he has been caught up by the *Zeitgeist*, and with his black brothers of Africa and his brown and yellow brothers of Asia, South America, and the Caribbean, the United States Negro is moving with a sense of great urgency toward the promised land of racial justice. If one recognizes this vital urge that has engulfed the Negro community, one should readily understand why public demonstrations are taking place. The Negro has many pent-up resentments and latent frustrations, and he must release them. So let him march; let him make prayer pilgrimages to the city hall; let him go on freedom rides—and try to understand why he must do so. If his repressed emotions are not released in nonviolent ways, they will seek expression through violence; this is not a threat but a fact of history. So I have not said to my people, "Get rid of your discontent." Rather, I have tried to say that this normal and healthy discontent can be channeled into the creative outlet of nonviolent direct action. And now this approach is being termed extremist.

But though I was initially disappointed at being categorized as an extremist, as I continued to think about the matter I gradually gained a measure of satisfaction from the label. Was not Jesus an extremist for love: "Love your enemies, bless them that curse you, do good to them that hate you, and pray for them which despitefully use you, and persecute you." Was not Amos an extremist for justice: "Let justice roll down like waters and righteousness like an ever-flowing stream." Was not Paul an extremist for the Christian gospel: "I bear in my body the marks of the Lord Jesus." Was not Martin Luther an extremist: "Here I stand; I cannot do otherwise, so help me God." And John Bunyan: "I will stay in jail to the end of my days before I make a butchery of my conscience." And Abraham Lincoln: "This nation cannot survive half slave and half free." And Thomas Jefferson: "We hold these truths to be self-evident, that all men are created equal...." So the question is not whether we will be extremists, but what kind of extremists we will be. Will we be extremists for hate or for love? Will we be extremists for the preservation of injustice or for the extension of justice? In that dramatic scene on Calvary's hill three men were crucified. We must never forget that all three were crucified for the same crime—the crime of extremism. Two were extremists for immorality, and thus fell below their environment. The other, Jesus Christ, was an extremist for love, truth, and goodness, and thereby rose above his environment. Perhaps the South, the nation, and the world are in dire need of creative extremists.

I had hoped that the white moderate would see this need. Perhaps I was too optimistic; perhaps I expected too much. I suppose I should have realized that few members of the oppressor race can understand the deep groans and passionate yearnings of the oppressed race, and still fewer have the vision to see that injustice must be rooted out by strong, persistent, and determined action. I am thankful, however, that some of our white brothers in the South have grasped the meaning of this social revolution and committed themselves to it. They are still all too few in quantity, but they are big in quality. Some—such as Ralph McGill, Lillian Smith, Harry Golden, James McBridge Dabbs, Ann Braden, and Sarah Patton Boyle—have written about our struggle in eloquent and prophetic terms. Others have marched with us down nameless streets of the South. They have languished in filthy, roach-infested jails, suffering the abuse and brutality of policemen who view them as "dirty nigger-lovers." Unlike so many of their moderate brothers and sisters, they have recognized the urgency of the moment and sensed the need for powerful "action" antidotes to combat the disease of segregation.

Let me take note of my other major disappointment. I have been so greatly disappointed with the white church and its leadership. Of course, there are some notable exceptions. I am not unmindful of the fact that each of you has taken some significant stands on this issue. I commend you, Reverend Stallings, for your Christian stand on this past Sunday, in welcoming Negroes to your worship service on a nonsegregated basis. I commend the Catholic leaders of this state for integrating Spring Hill College several years ago.

But despite these notable exceptions, I must honestly reiterate that I have been disappointed with the church. I do not say this as one of those negative critics who can always find something wrong with the church. I say this as a minister of the gospel, who loves the church; who was nurtured in its bosom; who has been sustained by its spiritual blessings and who will remain true to it as long as the cord of life shall lengthen.

When I was suddenly catapulted into the leadership of the bus protest in Montgomery, Alabama,[4] a few years ago, I felt we would be supported by the white church. I felt that the white ministers, priests, and rabbis of the South would be among our strongest allies. Instead, some have been outright opponents, refusing to understand the freedom movement and misrepresenting its leaders; all too many others have been more cautious than courageous and have remained silent behind the anesthetizing security of stained glass windows.

In spite of my shattered dreams, I came to Birmingham with the hope that the white religious leadership of this community would see the justice of our cause and, with deep moral concern, would serve as the channel through which our just grievances could reach the power structure. I had hoped that each of you would understand. But again I have been disappointed.

I have heard numerous southern religious leaders admonish their worshippers to comply with a desegregation decision because it is the law, but I have longed to hear white ministers declare: "Follow this decree because integration is morally right and because the Negro is your brother." In the midst of blatant injustices inflicted upon the Negro, I have watched white churchmen stand on the sideline and mouth pious irrelevancies and sanctimonious trivialities. In the midst of a mighty struggle to rid our nation of racial and economic injustice, I have heard many ministers say: "Those

35

---

4   *bus protest in Montgomery, Alabama*   In December 1955, Rosa Lee Parks, a 42-year-old Civil Rights activist, refused to give her seat on a local bus to a white man, sparking a year-long boycott by African-Americans of the Montgomery buses.

are social issues, with which the gospel has no real concern." And I have watched many churches commit themselves to a completely otherworldly religion which makes a strange un-Biblical distinction between the body and soul, between the sacred and the secular.

I have traveled the length and breadth of Alabama, Mississippi, and all the other southern states. On sweltering summer days and crisp autumn mornings I have looked at the South's beautiful churches with their lofty spires pointing heavenward. I have beheld the impressive outlines of her massive religious-education buildings. Over and over I have found myself asking: "What kind of people worship here? Who is their God? Where were their voices when the lips of Governor Barnett dripped with words of interposition and nullification? Where were they when Governor Wallace gave a clarion call for defiance and hatred? Where were their voices of support when bruised and weary Negro men and women decided to rise from the dark dungeons of complacency to the bright hills of creative protest?"

Yes, these questions are still in my mind. In deep disappointment I have wept over the laxity of the church. But be assured that my tears have been tears of love. There can be no deep disappointment where there is not deep love. Yes, I love the church. How could I do otherwise? I am in the rather unique position of being the son, the grandson, and the great-grandson of preachers. Yes, I see the church as the body of Christ. But, oh! How we have blemished and scarred that body through social neglect and through fear of being nonconformists.

40   There was a time when the church was very powerful—in the time when the early Christians rejoiced at being deemed worthy to suffer for what they believed. In those days the church was not merely a thermometer that recorded the ideas and principles of popular opinion; it was a thermostat that transformed the mores of society. Whenever the early Christians entered a town, the people in power became disturbed and immediately sought to convict the Christians of being "disturbers of the peace" and "outside agitators." But the Christians pressed on, in the conviction that they were "a colony of heaven," called to obey God rather than man. Small in number, they were big in commitment. They were too God-intoxicated to be "astronomically intimidated." By their effort and example they brought an end to such ancient evils as infanticide and gladiatorial contests.

Things are different now. So often the contemporary church is a weak, ineffectual voice with an uncertain sound. So often it is an arch-defender of the status quo. Far from being disturbed by the presence of the church, the power structure of the average community is consoled by the church's silent—and often even vocal—sanction of things as they are.

But the judgment of God is upon the church as never before. If today's church does not recapture the sacrificial spirit of the early church, it will lose its authenticity, forfeit the loyalty of millions, and be dismissed as an irrelevant social club with no meaning for the twentieth century. Every day I meet young people whose disappointment with the church has turned into outright disgust.

Perhaps I have once again been too optimistic. Is organized religion too inextricably bound to the status quo to save our nation and the world? Perhaps I must turn my faith to the inner spiritual church, the church within the church, as the true *ekklesia*[5] and the hope of the world. But again I am thankful to God that some noble souls from the ranks of organized religion have broken loose from the paralyzing chains of conformity and joined us as active partners in the struggle for freedom. They have left their secure congregations and walked the streets of Albany, Georgia, with us. They have gone down the highways of the South on tortuous rides for freedom. Yes, they have gone to jail with us. Some have been dismissed from their churches, have lost the support of their bishops and fellow ministers. But they have acted in the faith that right defeated is stronger than evil triumphant. Their witness has been the spiritual salt that has preserved the true meaning of the gospel in these troubled times. They have carved a tunnel of hope through the dark mountain of disappointment.

I hope the church as a whole will meet the challenge of this decisive hour. But even if the church does not come to the aid of justice, I have no despair about the future. I have no fear about the outcome of our struggle in Birmingham, even if our motives are at present misunderstood. We will reach the goal of freedom in Birmingham and all over the nation, because the goal of America is freedom. Abused and scorned though we may be, our destiny is tied up with America's destiny. Before the pilgrims landed at Plymouth, we were here. Before the pen of Jefferson etched the majestic words of the Declaration of Independence across the pages of history, we were here. For more than two centuries our forebears labored in this country without wages; they made cotton king; they built the homes of their masters while suffering gross injustice and shameful humiliation—and yet out of a bottomless vitality they continued to thrive and develop. If the inexpressible cruelties of slavery could not stop us, the opposition we now

---

5   *ekklesia*   Christian church in its original form.

face will surely fail. We will win our freedom because the sacred heritage of our nation and the eternal will of God are embodied in our echoing demands.

45   Before closing I feel impelled to mention one other point in your statement that has troubled me profoundly. You warmly commended the Birmingham police for keeping "order" and "preventing violence." I doubt that you would have so warmly commended the police force if you had seen its dogs sinking their teeth into unarmed, nonviolent Negroes. I doubt that you would so quickly commend the policemen if you were to observe their ugly and inhumane treatment of Negroes here in the city jail; if you were to watch them push and curse old Negro women and young Negro girls; if you were to see them slap and kick old Negro men and young boys; if you were to observe them, as they did on two occasions, refuse to give us food because we wanted to sing our grace together. I cannot join you in your praise of the Birmingham police department.

It is true that the police have exercised a degree of discipline in handling the demonstrators. In this sense they have conducted themselves rather "nonviolently" in public. But for what purpose? To preserve the evil system of segregation. Over the past few years I have consistently preached that nonviolence demands that the means we use must be as pure as the ends we seek. I have tried to make clear that it is wrong to use immoral means to attain moral ends. But now I must affirm that it is just as wrong, or perhaps even more so, to use moral means to preserve immoral ends. Perhaps Mr. Connor and his policemen have been rather nonviolent in public, as was Chief Pritchett in Albany, Georgia, but they have used moral means of nonviolence to maintain the immoral end of racial injustice. As T.S. Eliot has said, "The last temptation is the greatest treason: To do the right deed for the wrong reason."[6]

I wish you had commended the Negro sit-inners and demonstrators of Birmingham for their sublime courage, their willingness to suffer, and their amazing discipline in the midst of great provocation. One day the South will recognize its real heroes. They will be the James Merediths,[7] with the noble sense of purpose that enables them to face jeering and hostile mobs, and with the agonizing loneliness that characterizes the life of the

---

6   *The last ... wrong reason*   These lines are part of the response of St. Thomas à Becket to the fourth tempter in T.S. Eliot's play *Murder in the Cathedral*.

7   *James Merediths*   In 1962 James H. Meredith became the first African-American student at the University of Mississippi.

pioneer. They will be old, oppressed, battered Negro women, symbolized in a seventy-two-year-old woman in Montgomery, Alabama, who rose up with a sense of dignity and with her people decided not to ride segregated buses, and who responded with ungrammatical profundity to one who inquired about her weariness: "My feets is tired, but my soul is at rest." They will be the young high school and college students, the young ministers of the gospel and a host of their elders, courageously and nonviolently sitting in at lunch counters and willingly going to jail for conscience' sake. One day the South will know that when these disinherited children of God sat down at lunch counters, they were in reality standing up for what is best in the American dream and for the most sacred values in our Judaeo-Christian heritage, thereby bringing our nation back to those great wells of democracy which were dug deep by the founding fathers in their formulation of the Constitution and the Declaration of Independence.

Never before have I written such a long letter. I'm afraid it is much too long to take your precious time. I can assure you that it would have been much shorter if I had been writing from a comfortable desk, but what else can one do when he is alone in a narrow jail cell, other than write long letters, think long thoughts, and pray long prayers?

If I have said anything in this letter that overstates the truth and indicates an unreasonable impatience, I beg you to forgive me. If I have said anything that understates the truth and indicates my having a patience that allows me to settle for anything less than brotherhood, I beg God to forgive me.

I hope this letter finds you strong in the faith. I also hope that circumstances will soon make it possible for me to meet each of you, not as an integrationist or a civil-rights leader but as a fellow clergyman and a Christian brother. Let us all hope that the dark clouds of racial prejudice will soon pass away and the deep fog of misunderstanding will be lifted from our fear-drenched communities, and in some not too distant tomorrow the radiant stars of love and brotherhood will shine over our great nation with all their scintillating beauty.

50

Yours for the cause of Peace and Brotherhood,
MARTIN LUTHER KING, JR.
(Written 16 April 1963; published 1964)

Questions

1. Summarize the various reasons King gives, first of all for the Birming-ham protest, and second for the means through which the protest is pursued.

2. To what extent is it ever desirable or indeed possible to separate ethi-cal from political questions?

3. Find at least three examples of parallel structure in King's writing, involving words, phrases, or clauses.

DINNER WITH
MY CELEBRATED PEN PAL
T.S. ELIOT

In this letter to his brother Gummo,
Groucho Marx recounts meeting his pen pal T.S. Eliot.

e

DEAR GUMMO:

Last night Eden and I had dinner with my celebrated pen pal T.S. Eliot. It was a memorable evening.

The poet met us at the door with Mrs. Eliot, a good-looking, middle-aged blonde whose eyes seemed to fill up with adoration every time she looked at her husband. He, by the way, is tall, lean and rather stooped over; but whether this is from age, illness or both, I don't know.

At any rate, your correspondent arrived at the Eliots' fully prepared for a literary evening. During the week I had read "Murder in the Cathedral" twice; "The Waste Land" three times; and just in case of a conversational bottleneck, I brushed up on "King Lear."

Well, sir, as cocktails were served, there was a momentary lull—the kind that is more or less inevitable when strangers meet for the first time. So, apropos of practically nothing (and "not with a bang but a whimper")[1] I tossed in a quotation from "The Waste Land." That, I thought, will show him I've read a thing or two besides my press notices from vaudeville.

---

1   *not with ... a whimper*   A famous poem by Eliot dealing with the "emptiness" of twentieth-century life, "The Hollow Men," ends with the lines, "This is the way the world ends / Not with a bang but a whimper."

5   Eliot smiled faintly—as though to say he was thoroughly familiar with his poems and didn't need me to recite them. So I took a whack at "King Lear." I said the king was an incredibly foolish old man, which God knows he *was*; and that if he'd been *my* father I would have run away from home at the age of eight—instead of waiting until I was ten.

That, too, failed to bowl over the poet. He seemed more interested in discussing "Animal Crackers" and "A Night at the Opera." He quoted a joke—one of mine—that I had long since forgotten. Now it was my turn to smile faintly. I was not going to let anyone—not even the British poet from St. Louis—spoil my Literary Evening. I pointed out that King Lear's opening speech was the height of idiocy. Imagine (I said) a father asking his three children: Which of you kids loves me the most? And then disowning the youngest—the sweet, honest Cordelia—because, unlike her wicked sister, she couldn't bring herself to gush out insincere flattery. And Cordelia, mind you, had been her father's favorite!

The Eliots listened politely. Mrs. Eliot then defended Shakespeare; and Eden, too, I regret to say, was on King Lear's side, even though I am the one who supports her. (In all fairness to my wife, I must say that, having played the Princess in a high school production of "The Swan," she has retained a rather warm feeling for all royalty.)

As for Eliot, he asked if I remembered the courtroom scene in "Duck Soup." Fortunately I'd forgotten every word. It was obviously the end of the Literary Evening, but very pleasant none the less. I discovered that Eliot and I had three things in common: (1) an affection for good cigars and (2) cats; and (3) a weakness for making puns—a weakness that for many years I have tried to overcome. T.S., on the other hand, is an unashamed—even proud—punster. For example, there's his Gus, the Theater Cat, whose "real name was Asparagus."

Speaking of asparagus, the dinner included good, solid English beef, very well prepared. And, although they had a semi-butler serving, Eliot insisted on pouring the wine himself. It was an excellent wine and no maitre d' could have served it more graciously. He is a dear man and a charming host.

10   When I told him that my daughter Melinda was studying his poetry at Beverly High, he said he regretted that, because he had no wish to become compulsory reading.

We didn't stay late, for we both felt that he wasn't up to a long evening of conversation—especially mine.

Did I tell you we called him Tom?—possibly because that's his name. I, of course, asked him to call me Tom too, but only because I loathe the name Julius.

Yours,
TOM MARX
(1964)

Questions

1. What were Marx's assumptions about T.S. Eliot prior to his meeting?

2. Why do you suppose T.S. Eliot had no wish to become compulsory reading?

3. Marx says of his dinner: "It was a memorable evening." Why was it memorable? Is this statement positive or negative?

4. Unlike a formal essay written for a public audience, this letter is written for the private audience of the author's brother. How does this affect the style of the writing?

5. What expectation does Marx set up at the beginning of his letter?

6. What would be your assumptions about Marx's relationship with his brother Gummo, based on this letter?

Margaret Laurence

Where the World Began

*In this descriptive essay a famous novelist evokes a sense of
life in a small prairie town, and explores the effect that her
experience has had on her as a person and as an author.*

❧

A strange place it was, that place where the world began. A place of incredible happenings, splendors and revelations, despairs like multitu-
dinous pits of isolated hells. A place of shadow-spookiness, inhabited by
the unknowable dead. A place of jubilation and of mourning, horrible and
beautiful.

It was, in fact, a small prairie town.

Because that settlement and that land were my first and for many years
my only real knowledge of this planet, in some profound way they remain
my world, my way of viewing. My eyes were formed there. Towns like
ours, set in a sea of land, have been described thousands of times as dull,
bleak, flat, uninteresting. I have had it said to me that the railway trip across
Canada is spectacular, except for the prairies, when it would be desirable
to go to sleep for several days, until the ordeal is over. I am always unable
to argue this point effectively. All I can say is—well, you really have to
live there to know that country. The town of my childhood could be called
bizarre, agonizingly repressive or cruel at times, and the land in which it
grew could be called harsh in the violence of its seasonal changes. But
never merely flat or uninteresting. Never dull.

In winter, we used to hitch rides on the back of the milk sleigh, our
moccasins squeaking and slithering on the hard rutted snow of the roads,
our hands in ice-bubbled mitts hanging onto the box edge of the sleigh for
dear life, while Bert grinned at us through his great frosted mustache and
shouted the horse into speed, daring us to stay put. Those mornings, rising,
there would be the perpetual fascination of the frost feathers on windows,

164

the ferns and flowers and eerie faces traced there during the night by unseen artists of the wind. Evenings, coming back from skating, the sky would be black but not dark, for you could see a cold glitter of stars from one side of the earth's rim to the other. And then the sometime astonishment when you saw the Northern Lights flaring across the sky, like the scrawled signature of God. After a blizzard, when the snowplow hadn't yet got through, school would be closed for the day, the assumption being that the town's young could not possibly flounder through five feet of snow in the pursuit of education. We would then gaily don snowshoes and flounder for miles out into the white dazzling deserts, in pursuit of a different kind of knowing. If you came back too close to night, through the woods at the foot of the town hill, the thin black branches of poplar and chokecherry now meringued with frost, sometimes you heard coyotes. Or maybe the banshee wolf-voices were really only inside your head.

Summers were scorching, and when no rain came and the wheat became 5 bleached and dried before it headed, the faces of farmers and townsfolk would not smile much, and you took for granted, because it never seemed to have been any different, the frequent knocking at the back door and the young men standing there, mumbling or thrusting defiantly their requests for a drink of water and a sandwich if you could spare it. They were riding the freights, and you never knew where they had come from, or where they might end up, if anywhere. The Drought and Depression were like evil deities which had been there always. You understood and did not understand.

Yet the outside world had its continuing marvels. The poplar bluffs and the small river were filled and surrounded with a zillion different grasses, stones, and weed flowers. The meadowlarks sang undaunted from the twanging telephone wires along the gravel highway. Once we found an old flat-bottomed scow, and launched her, poling along the shallow brown waters, mending her with wodges of hastily chewed Spearmint, grounding her among the tangles of yellow marsh marigolds that grew succulently along the banks of the shrunken river, while the sun made our skins smell dusty-warm.

My best friend lived in an apartment above some stores on Main Street (its real name was Mountain Avenue, goodness knows why), an elegant apartment with royal-blue velvet curtains. The back roof, scarcely sloping at all, was corrugated tin, of a furnace-like warmth on a July afternoon, and we would sit there drinking lemonade and looking across the back lane at the Fire Hall. Sometimes our vigil would be rewarded. Oh joy! Somebody's house burning down! We had an almost-perfect callousness in some ways.

Then the wooden tower's bronze bell would clonk and toll like a thousand speeded funerals in a time of plague, and in a few minutes the team of giant black horses would cannon forth, pulling the fire wagon like some scarlet chariot of the Goths, while the firemen clung with one hand, adjusting their helmets as they went.

The oddities of the place were endless. An elderly lady used to serve, as her afternoon tea offering to other ladies, soda biscuits spread with peanut butter and topped with a whole marshmallow. Some considered this slightly eccentric, when compared with chopped egg sandwiches, and admittedly talked about her behind her back, but no one ever refused these delicacies or indicated to her that they thought she had slipped a cog. Another lady dyed her hair a bright and cheery orange, by strangers often mistaken at twenty paces for a feather hat. My own beloved stepmother wore a silver fox neckpiece, a whole pelt, *with the embalmed head still on*. My Ontario Irish grandfather said, "sparrow grass," a more interesting term than asparagus. The town dump was known as "the nuisance grounds," a phrase fraught with weird connotations, as though the effluvia of our lives was beneath contempt but at the same time was subtly threatening to the determined and sometimes hysterical propriety of our ways.

Some oddities were, as idiom had it, "funny ha ha"; others were "funny peculiar." Some were not so very funny at all. An old man lived, deranged, in a shack in the valley. Perhaps he wasn't even all that old, but to us he seemed a wild Methuselah figure, shambling among the underbrush and the tall couchgrass, muttering indecipherable curses or blessings, a prophet who had forgotten his prophecies. Everyone in town knew him, but no one knew him. He lived among us as though only occasionally and momentarily visible. The kids called him Andy Gump, and feared him. Some sought to prove their bravery by tormenting him. They were the medieval bear baiters, and he the lumbering bewildered bear, half blind, only rarely turning to snarl. Everything is to be found in a town like mine. Belsen, writ small but with the same ink.

10   All of us cast stones in one shape or another. In grade school, among the vulnerable and violent girls we were, the feared and despised were those few older girls from what was charmingly termed "the wrong side of the tracks." Tough in talk and tougher in muscle, they were said to be whores already. And may have been, that being about the only profession readily available to them.

The dead lived in that place, too. Not only the grandparents who had in local parlance, "passed on" and who gloomed, bearded or bonneted, from the sepia photographs in old albums, but also the uncles, forever eighteen or nineteen, whose names were carved on the granite family stones in the cemetery, but whose bones lay in France. My own young mother lay in that graveyard, beside other dead of our kin, and when I was ten, my father, too, only forty, left the living town for the dead dwelling on the hill.

When I was eighteen, I couldn't wait to get out of that town, away from the prairies. I did not know then that I would carry the land and town all my life within my skull, that they would form the mainspring and source of the writing I was to do, wherever and however far away I might live.

This was my territory in the time of my youth, and in a sense my life since then has been an attempt to look at it, to come to terms with it. Stultifying to the mind it certainly could be, and sometimes was, but not to the imagination. It was many things, but it was never dull.

The same, I now see, could be said for Canada in general. Why on earth did generations of Canadians pretend to believe this country dull? We knew perfectly well it wasn't. Yet for so long we did not proclaim what we knew. If our upsurge of so-called nationalism seems odd or irrelevant to outsiders, and even to some of our own people (*what's all the fuss about?*), they might try to understand that for many years we valued ourselves insufficiently, living as we did under the huge shadows of those two dominating figures, Uncle Sam and Britannia. We have only just begun to value ourselves, our land, our abilities. We have only just begun to recognize our legends and to give shape to our myths.

There are, God knows, enough aspects to deplore about this country. When I see the killing of our lakes and rivers with industrial wastes, I feel rage and despair. When I see our industries and natural resources increasingly taken over by America, I feel an overwhelming discouragement, especially as I cannot simply say "damn Yankees." It should never be forgotten that it is ourselves who have sold such a large amount of our birthright for a mess of plastic Progress. When I saw the War Measures Act being invoked in 1970, I lost forever the vestigial remains of the naïve wish-belief that repression could not happen here, or would not. And yet, of course, I had known all along in the deepest and often hidden caves of the heart that anything can happen anywhere, for the seeds of both man's freedom and his captivity are found everywhere, even in the microcosm of a prairie town. But in raging against our injustices, our stupidities, I do so *as family*, as I did, and still do in writing, about those aspects of my town which I hated and which are always in some ways aspects of myself.

15

The land still draws me more than other lands. I have lived in Africa and in England, but splendid as both can be, they do not have the power to move me in the same way as, for example, that part of southern Ontario where I spent four months last summer in a cedar cabin beside a river. "Scratch a Canadian, and you find a phony pioneer," I used to say to myself in warning. But all the same it is true, I think, that we are not yet totally alienated from physical earth, and let us only pray we do not become so. I once thought that my lifelong fear and mistrust of cities made me a kind of old-fashioned freak; now I see it differently.

The cabin has a long window across its front western wall, and sitting at the oak table there in the mornings, I used to look out at the river and at the tall trees beyond, green-gold in the early light. The river was bronze; the sun caught it strangely, reflecting upon its surface the near-shore sand ripples underneath. Suddenly, the crescenting of a fish, gone before the eye could clearly give image to it. The old man next door said these leaping fish were carp. Himself, he preferred muskie, for he was a real fisherman and the muskie gave him a fight. The wind most often blew from the south, and the river flowed toward the south, so when the water was wind-riffled, and the current was strong, the river seemed to be flowing both ways. I liked this, and interpreted it as an omen, a natural symbol.

A few years ago, when I was back in Winnipeg, I gave a talk at my old college. It was open to the public, and afterward a very old man came up to me and asked me if my maiden name had been Wemyss. I said yes, thinking he might have known my father or my grandfather. But no. "When I was a young lad," he said, "I once worked for your great-grandfather, Robert Wemyss, when he had the sheep ranch at Raeburn." I think that was a moment when I realized all over again something of great importance to me. My long-ago families came from Scotland and Ireland, but in a sense that no longer mattered so much. My true roots were here.

I am not very patriotic, in the usual meaning of that word. I cannot say "My country right or wrong" in any political, social or literary context. But one thing is inalterable, for better or worse, for life.

20   This is where my world began. A world which includes the ancestors—both my own and other people's ancestors who become mine. A world which formed me, and continues to do so, even while I fought it in some of its aspects, and continue to do so. A world which gave me my own lifework to do, because it was here that I learned the sight of my own particular eyes.

(1972)

Questions

1. What does Laurence mean by the phrase, "My eyes were formed there"?

2. What comparison does Laurence make between a small prairie town and the nation of Canada in general?

3. What argument does Laurence put forth in this essay against prairie life being dull?

4. How does Laurence achieve a transition between discussion of small-town prairie life and discussion of Canada on a national scale?

5. Find examples of simile and metaphor in the essay. How does Laurence utilize figurative language to develop her argument that prairie life was never dull?

ROLAND BARTHES

THE WORLD OF WRESTLING

*In this essay, Roland Barthes examines the spectacle of
professional wrestling and the carefully constructed
meanings contained within its gestures.*

❧

> The grandiloquent truth of gestures
> on life's great occasions.
> BAUDELAIRE

The virtue of all-in wrestling is that it is the spectacle of excess. Here we find a grandiloquence which must have been that of the ancient theaters. And in fact wrestling is an open-air spectacle, for what makes the circus or the arena what they are is not the sky (a romantic value suited rather to fashionable occasions), it is the drenching and vertical quality of the flood of light. Even hidden in the most squalid Parisian halls, wrestling partakes of the nature of the great solar spectacles, Greek drama and bull-fights: in both, a light without shadow generates an emotion without reserve.

There are people who think that wrestling is an ignoble sport. Wrestling is not a sport, it is a spectacle, and it is no more ignoble to attend a wrestled performance of Suffering than a performance of the sorrows of Arnolphe or Andromaque. Of course, there exists a false wrestling, in which the participants unnecessarily go to great lengths to make a show of a fair fight; this is of no interest. True wrestling, wrongly called amateur wrestling, is performed in second-rate halls, where the public spontaneously attunes itself to the spectacular nature of the contest, like the audience at a suburban cinema. Then these same people wax indignant because wrestling is a stage-managed sport (which ought, by the way, to mitigate its ignominy). The public is completely uninterested in knowing whether the contest is rigged or not, and rightly so; it abandons itself to the primary virtue of the spectacle, which is to abolish all motives and all consequences: what matters is not what it thinks but what it sees.

This public knows very well the distinction between wrestling and boxing; it knows that boxing is a Jansenist sport, based on a demonstration of excellence. One can bet on the outcome of a boxing-match: with wrestling, it would make no sense. A boxing-match is a story which is constructed before the eyes of the spectator; in wrestling, on the contrary, it is each moment which is intelligible, not the passage of time. The spectator is not interested in the rise and fall of fortunes; he expects the transient image of certain passions. Wrestling therefore demands an immediate reading of the juxtaposed meanings, so that there is no need to connect them. The logical conclusion of the contest does not interest the wrestling-fan, while on the contrary a boxing-match always implies a science of the future. In other words, wrestling is a sum of spectacles, of which no single one is a function: each moment imposes the total knowledge of a passion which rises erect and alone, without ever extending to the crowning moment of a result.

Thus the function of the wrestler is not to win; it is to go exactly through the motions which are expected of him. It is said that judo contains a hidden symbolic aspect; even in the midst of efficiency, its gestures are measured, precise but restricted, drawn accurately but by a stroke without volume. Wrestling, on the contrary, offers excessive gestures, exploited to the limit of their meaning. In judo, a man who is down is hardly down at all, he rolls over, he draws back, he eludes defeat, or, if the latter is obvious, he immediately disappears; in wrestling, a man who is down is exaggeratedly so, and completely fills the eyes of the spectators with the intolerable spectacle of his powerlessness.

This function of grandiloquence is indeed the same as that of ancient theater, whose principle, language and props (masks and buskins) concurred in the exaggeratedly visible explanation of a Necessity. The gesture of the vanquished wrestler signifying to the world a defeat which, far from disguising, he emphasizes and holds like a pause in music, corresponds to the mask of antiquity meant to signify the tragic mode of the spectacle. In wrestling, as on the stage in antiquity, one is not ashamed of one's suffering, one knows how to cry, one has a liking for tears.

Each sign in wrestling is therefore endowed with an absolute clarity, since one must always understand everything on the spot. As soon as the adversaries are in the ring, the public is overwhelmed with the obviousness of the roles. As in the theater, each physical type expresses to excess the part which has been assigned to the contestant. Thauvin, a fifty-year-old

5

with an obese and sagging body, whose type of asexual hideousness always inspires feminine nicknames, displays in his flesh the characters of baseness, for his part is to represent what, in the classical concept of the *salaud*, the "bastard" (the key-concept of any wrestling match), appears as organically repugnant. The nausea voluntarily provoked by Thauvin shows therefore a very extended use of signs: not only is ugliness used here in order to signify baseness, but in addition ugliness is wholly gathered into a particularly repulsive quality of matter: the pallid collapse of dead flesh (the public calls Thauvin *la barbaque*, "stinking meat"), so that the passionate condemnation of the crowd no longer stems from its judgment, but instead from the very depth of its humors. It will thereafter let itself be frenetically embroiled in an idea of Thauvin which will conform entirely with this physical origin: his actions will perfectly correspond to the essential viscosity of his personage.

It is therefore in the body of the wrestler that we find the first key to the contest. I know from the start that all of Thauvin's actions, his treacheries, cruelties and acts of cowardice, will not fail to measure up to the first image of ignobility he gave me; I can trust him to carry out intelligently and to the last detail all the gestures of a kind of amorphous baseness, and thus fill to the brim the image of the most repugnant bastard there is: the bastard-octopus. Wrestlers therefore have a physique as peremptory as those of the characters of the *Commedia dell'Arte*, who display in advance, in their costumes and attitudes, the future contents of their parts: just as Pantaloon can never be anything but a ridiculous cuckold, Harlequin an astute servant and the Doctor a stupid pedant, in the same way Thauvin will never be anything but an ignoble traitor, Reinières (a tall blond fellow with a limp body and unkempt hair) the moving image of passivity, Mazaud (short and arrogant like a cock) that of grotesque conceit, and Orsano (an effeminate teddy-boy first seen in a blue-and-pink dressing-gown) that, doubly humorous, of a vindictive *salope*, or bitch (for I do not think that the public of the Elysée-Montmartre, like Littré, believes the word *salope* to be a masculine).

The physique of the wrestlers therefore constitutes a basic sign, which like a seed contains the whole fight. But this seed proliferates, for it is at every turn during the fight, in each new situation, that the body of the wrestler casts to the public the magical entertainment of a temperament which finds its natural expression in a gesture. The different strata of meaning throw light on each other, and form the most intelligible of spectacles. Wrestling is like a diacritic writing: above the fundamental meaning of his body, the wrestler arranges comments which are episodic but always opportune, and constantly help the reading of the fight by means of gestures, attitudes and mimicry which make the intention utterly obvious. Sometimes the wrestler triumphs with a repulsive sneer while kneeling on the good sportsman; sometimes he gives the crowd a conceited smile which forebodes an early revenge; sometimes, pinned to the ground, he hits the floor ostentatiously to make evident to all the intolerable nature of his situation; and sometimes he erects a complicated set of signs meant to make the public understand that he legitimately personifies the ever-entertaining image of the grumbler, endlessly confabulating about his displeasure.

We are therefore dealing with a real Human Comedy, where the most socially-inspired nuances of passion (conceit, rightfulness, refined cruelty, a sense of "paying one's debts") always felicitously find the clearest sign which can receive them, express them and triumphantly carry them to the confines of the hall. It is obvious that at such a pitch, it no longer matters whether the passion is genuine or not. What the public wants is the image of passion, not passion itself. There is no more a problem of truth in wrestling than in the theater. In both, what is expected is the intelligible representation of moral situations which are usually private. This emptying out of interiority to the benefit of its exterior signs, this exhaustion of the content by the form, is the very principle of triumphant classical art. Wrestling is an immediate pantomime, infinitely more efficient than the dramatic pantomime, for the wrestler's gesture needs no anecdote, no decor, in short no transference in order to appear true.

Each moment in wrestling is therefore like an algebra which instanta- 10 neously unveils the relationship between a cause and its represented effect. Wrestling fans certainly experience a kind of intellectual pleasure in *seeing* the moral mechanism function so perfectly. Some wrestlers, who are great comedians, entertain as much as a Molière character, because they succeed in imposing an immediate reading of their inner nature: Armand Mazaud, a wrestler of an arrogant and ridiculous character (as one says that Harpagon is a character), always delights the audience by the mathematical rigor of his transcriptions, carrying the form of his gestures to the furthest reaches of their meaning, and giving to his manner of fighting a kind of vehemence and precision found in a great scholastic disputation, in which what is at stake is at once the triumph of pride and the formal concern with truth.

What is thus displayed for the public is the great spectacle of Suffering, Defeat, and Justice. Wrestling presents man's suffering with all the amplification of tragic masks. The wrestler who suffers in a hold which is reputedly cruel (an arm-lock, a twisted leg) offers an excessive portrayal of Suffering; like a primitive Pietà, he exhibits for all to see his face, exaggeratedly contorted by an intolerable affliction. It is obvious, of course, that in wrestling reserve would be out of place, since it is opposed to the voluntary ostentation of the spectacle, to this Exhibition of Suffering which is the very aim of the fight. This is why all the actions which produce suffering are particularly spectacular, like the gesture of a conjuror who holds out his cards clearly to the public. Suffering which appeared without intelligible cause would not be understood; a concealed action that was actually cruel would transgress the underwritten rules of wrestling and would have no more sociological efficacy than a mad or parasitic gesture. On the contrary suffering appears as inflicted with emphasis and conviction, for everyone must not only see that the man suffers, but also and above all understand why he suffers. What wrestlers call a hold, that is, any figure which allows one to immobilize the adversary indefinitely and to have him at one's mercy, has precisely the function of preparing in a conventional, therefore intelligible, fashion the spectacle of suffering, of methodically establishing the conditions of suffering. The inertia of the vanquished allows the (temporary) victor to settle in his cruelty and to convey to the public this terrifying slowness of the torturer who is certain about the outcome of his actions; to grind the face of one's powerless adversary or to scrape his spine with one's fist with a deep and regular movement, or at least to produce the superficial appearance of such gestures: wrestling is the only sport which gives such an externalized image of torture. But here again, only the image is involved in the game, and the spectator does not wish for the actual suffering of the contestant; he only enjoys the perfection of an iconography. It is not true that wrestling is a sadistic spectacle: it is only an intelligible spectacle.

There is another figure, more spectacular still than a hold; it is the forearm smash, this loud slap of the forearm, this embryonic punch with which one clouts the chest of one's adversary, and which is accompanied by a dull noise and the exaggerated sagging of a vanquished body. In the forearm smash, catastrophe is brought to the point of maximum obviousness, so much so that ultimately the gesture appears as no more than a symbol; this is going too far, this is transgressing the moral rules of wrestling, where all signs must be excessively clear, but must not let the intention of clarity be seen. The public then shouts "He's laying it on!," not because it regrets the absence of real suffering, but because it condemns artifice: as in the theater, one fails to put the part across as much by an excess of sincerity as by an excess of formalism.

We have already seen to what extent wrestlers exploit the resources of a given physical style, developed and put to use in order to unfold before the eyes of the public a total image of Defeat. The flaccidity of tall white bodies which collapse with one blow or crash into the ropes with arms flailing, the inertia of massive wrestlers rebounding pitiably off all the elastic surfaces of the ring, nothing can signify more clearly and more passionately the exemplary abasement of the vanquished. Deprived of all resilience, the wrestler's flesh is no longer anything but an unspeakable heap spread out on the floor, where it solicits relentless reviling and jubilation. There is here a paroxysm of meaning in the style of antiquity, which can only recall the heavily underlined intentions in Roman triumphs. At other times, there is another ancient posture which appears in the coupling of the wrestlers, that of the suppliant who, at the mercy of his opponent, on bended knees, his arms raised above his head, is slowly brought down by the vertical pressure of the victor. In wrestling, unlike judo, Defeat is not a conventional sign, abandoned as soon as it is understood; it is not an outcome, but quite the contrary, it is a duration, a display, it takes up the ancient myths of public Suffering and Humiliation: the cross and the pillory. It is as if the wrestler is crucified in broad daylight and in the sight of all. I have heard it said of a wrestler stretched on the ground: "He is dead, little Jesus, there, on the cross," and these ironic words revealed the hidden roots of a spectacle which enacts the exact gestures of the most ancient purifications.

But what wrestling is above all meant to portray is a purely moral concept: that of justice. The idea of "paying" is essential to wrestling, and the crowd's "Give it to him" means above all else "Make him pay." This is therefore, needless to say, an immanent justice. The baser the action of the "bastard," the more delighted the public is by the blow which he justly receives in return. If the villain—who is of course a coward—takes refuge behind the ropes, claiming unfairly to have a right to do so by a brazen mimicry, he is inexorably pursued there and caught, and the crowd is jubilant at seeing the rules broken for the sake of a deserved punishment. Wrestlers know very well how to play up to the capacity for indignation of the public by presenting the very limit of the concept of Justice, this outermost zone of confrontation where it is enough to infringe the rules a little more to open the gates of a world without restraints. For a wrestling-fan, nothing is finer than the revengeful fury of a betrayed fighter who throws himself vehemently not on a successful opponent but on the smarting image of foul play. Naturally, it is the pattern of Justice which matters here, much more than its content: wrestling is above all a quantitative sequence of compensations (an eye for an eye, a tooth for a tooth). This explains why sudden changes of circumstances have in the eyes of wrestling habitués a sort of moral beauty: they enjoy them as they would enjoy an inspired episode in a novel, and the greater the contrast between the success of a move and the reversal of fortune, the nearer the good luck of a contestant to his downfall, the more satisfying the dramatic mime is felt to be. Justice is therefore the embodiment of a possible transgression; it is from the fact that there is a Law that the spectacle of the passions which infringe it derives its value.

15   It is therefore easy to understand why out of five wrestling-matches, only about one is fair. One must realize, let it be repeated, that "fairness" here is a role or a genre, as in the theater: the rules do not at all constitute a real constraint; they are the conventional appearance of fairness. So that in actual fact a fair fight is nothing but an exaggeratedly polite one: the contestants confront each other with zeal, not rage; they can remain in control of their passions, they do not punish their beaten opponent relentlessly, they stop fighting as soon as they are ordered to do so, and congratulate each other at the end of a particularly arduous episode, during which, however, they have not ceased to be fair. One must of course understand here that all these polite actions are brought to the notice of the public by the most conventional gestures of fairness: shaking hands, raising the arms, ostensibly avoiding a fruitless hold which would detract from the perfection of the contest.

Conversely, foul play exists only in its excessive signs: administering a big kick to one's beaten opponent, taking refuge behind the ropes while ostensibly invoking a purely formal right, refusing to shake hands with one's opponent before or after the fight, taking advantage of the end of the round to rush treacherously at the adversary from behind, fouling him while the referee is not looking (a move which obviously only has any value or function because in fact half the audience can see it and get indignant about it). Since Evil is the natural climate of wrestling, a fair fight has chiefly the value of being an exception. It surprises the aficionado, who greets it when he sees it as an anachronism and a rather sentimental throwback to the sporting tradition ("Aren't they playing fair, those two"); he feels suddenly moved at the sight of the general kindness of the world, but would probably die of boredom and indifference if wrestlers did not quickly return to the orgy of evil which alone makes good wrestling.

Extrapolated, fair wrestling could lead only to boxing or judo, whereas true wrestling derives its originality from all the excesses which make it a spectacle and not a sport. The ending of a boxing-match or a judo-contest is abrupt, like the full-stop which closes a demonstration. The rhythm of wrestling is quite different, for its natural meaning is that of rhetorical amplification: the emotional magniloquence, the repeated paroxysms, the exasperation of the retorts can only find their natural outcome in the most baroque confusion. Some fights, among the most successful kind, are crowned by a final charivari, a sort of unrestrained fantasia where the rules, the laws of the genre, the referee's censuring and the limits of the ring are abolished, swept away by a triumphant disorder which overflows into the hall and carries off pell-mell wrestlers, seconds, referee and spectators.

It has already been noted that in America wrestling represents a sort of mythological fight between Good and Evil (of a quasi-political nature, the "bad" wrestler always being supposed to be a Red). The process of creating heroes in French wrestling is very different, being based on ethics and not on politics. What the public is looking for here is the gradual construction of a highly moral image: that of the perfect "bastard." One comes to wrestling in order to attend the continuing adventures of a single major leading character, permanent and multiform like Punch or Scapino, inventive in unexpected figures and yet always faithful to his role. The "bastard" is here revealed as a Molière character or a "portrait" by La Bruyère, that is to say as a classical entity, an essence, whose acts are only significant epiphenomena arranged in time. This stylized character does not belong to any particular nation or party, and whether the wrestler is called Kuzchenko (nicknamed Moustache after Stalin), Yerpazian, Gaspardi, Jo Vignola or Nollières, the aficionado does not attribute to him any country except "fairness"—observing the rules.

What then is a "bastard" for this audience composed in part, we are told, of people who are themselves outside the rules of society? Essentially someone unstable, who accepts the rules only when they are useful to him and transgresses the formal continuity of attitudes. He is unpredictable, therefore asocial. He takes refuge behind the law when he considers that it is in his favor, and breaks it when he finds it useful to do so. Sometimes he rejects the formal boundaries of the ring and goes on hitting an adversary legally protected by the ropes, sometimes he reestablishes these boundaries and claims the protection of what he did not respect a few minutes earlier. This inconsistency, far more than treachery or cruelty, sends the audience beside itself with rage: offended not in its morality but in its logic, it considers the contradiction of arguments as the basest of crimes. The forbidden move becomes dirty only when it destroys a quantitative equilibrium and disturbs the rigorous reckoning of compensations; what is condemned by the audience is not at all the transgression of insipid official rules, it is the lack of revenge, the absence of a punishment. So that there is nothing more exciting for a crowd than the grandiloquent kick given to a vanquished "bastard"; the joy of punishing is at its climax when it is supported by a mathematical justification; contempt is then unrestrained. One is no longer dealing with a *salaud* but with a *salope*—the verbal gesture of the ultimate degradation.

20   Such a precise finality demands that wrestling should be exactly what the public expects of it. Wrestlers, who are very experienced, know perfectly how to direct the spontaneous episodes of the fight so as to make them conform to the image which the public has of the great legendary themes of its mythology. A wrestler can irritate or disgust, he never disappoints, for he always accomplishes completely, by a progressive solidification of signs, what the public expects of him. In wrestling, nothing exists except in the absolute, there is no symbol, no allusion, everything is presented exhaustively. Leaving nothing in the shade, each action discards all parasitic meanings and ceremonially offers to the public a pure and full signification, rounded like Nature. This grandiloquence is nothing but the popular and age-old image of the perfect intelligibility of reality. What is portrayed by wrestling is therefore an ideal understanding of things; it is the euphoria of men raised for a while above the constitutive ambiguity of everyday situations and placed before the panoramic view of a univocal Nature, in which signs at last correspond to causes, without obstacle, without evasion, without contradiction.

When the hero or the villain of the drama, the man who was seen a few minutes earlier possessed by moral rage, magnified into a sort of metaphysical sign, leaves the wrestling hall, impassive, anonymous, carrying a small suitcase and arm-in-arm with his wife, no one can doubt that wrestling holds that power of transmutation which is common to the Spectacle and to Religious Worship. In the ring, and even in the depths of their voluntary ignominy, wrestlers remain gods because they are, for a few moments, the key which opens Nature, the pure gesture which separates Good from Evil, and unveils the form of a Justice which is at last intelligible.

(1972)

Questions

1. Barthes draws frequent comparisons between wrestling, judo, and boxing. In what way(s) do the sports differ?

2. What use does Barthes make of analogy in this essay? Give examples.

3. From this essay, would you say that Barthes is a wrestling fan? How do you reach your conclusion? In what ways does Barthes indicate his position?

4. Comment on the closing paragraph of the essay. Does it effectively sum up the main points of Barthes's argument?

5. Do you agree with Barthes's assessment that wrestling is not a sport but a spectacle? Why?

PABLO PICASSO

Flanner's many years of writing for The New Yorker *were distinguished not least of all by her brief biographical portraits, frequently written upon the death of the subject.*

☙

APRIL 21, 1973 Pablo Picasso was born and died a phenomenon. "What is a painter?" he once asked, in front of others, while talking to himself. Having asked his question, he then answered it: "He is someone who founds his art collection by painting it himself." Picasso was that kind of painter. Another time, he overheard someone say, "I don't like Picasso," obviously referring to his paintings, and intruded to ask, "Which Picasso?"

During his career, Picasso, according to André Malraux, produced well over six thousand paintings. Of the multiple art styles that were then employed in France, he made use of all, especially those most filled with his own deformations. When he was approaching his eightieth birthday, he decided that, having gone through so many years, he should have the privilege of choosing for the rest of his life the age he preferred. "I have decided," he said, settling the problem, "that from now on I shall be aged thirty." His energies were so great that even in his bogus-thirties period his habitual creation continued pouring out, though it was mostly audible in his wit and visible in his psychological showmanship and legerdemain, all of which were trivialities compared to what he had produced in his previous era. Many of the wittiest things he said occurred in conversations in which he had the opportunity to cap what someone else had said. During the nineteen-thirties, when the fabrication of counterfeit Picassos was at its height—his works being the most often counterfeited because they rated the highest prices—an old journalist friend took a small Picasso painting belonging to some poor devil of an artist to Picasso himself for authentication, so the impoverished artist could sell it. "It's false," Picasso said. The friend took him another little Picasso, from a different source, and then a third. "It's false," Picasso said each time. "Now, listen, Pablo," the friend said. "I watched you paint this last picture with my own eyes." "I can paint false Picassos just as well as anybody," Picasso replied. He then bought the first Picasso at four times the price the poor artist might have hoped it would fetch. When another person took Picasso a counterfeit etching to sign, he signed it so many times that the man was able to sell it only as a curiosity to an autograph dealer.

When Stalin died, Picasso, who had by then joined the Communist Party, drew an imaginary portrait of a young Stalin with a neck like a column of steel and a brooding Georgian look on his face, and it was published in the Communist *Lettres Françaises*. It drew a chorus of complaints from the weekly's loyal readers, who sensed that this sketch was unofficial and therefore disloyal. On being asked by a friend who was a French Party member what he would do if France became Communized and he found himself forbidden to continue working as an artist except on Party cultural lines, Picasso answered, "If they stopped my painting, I would draw on paper. If they put me in prison without paper or pencil, I would draw with spit on the cell walls."

A remarkable description of the young Picasso came from the pen of Fernande Olivier, who was a member of the Montmartre Bateau-Lavoir group of artists and writers, to which Picasso belonged. She wrote, "Small, dark, thickset, unquiet, disquieting, with somber eyes, deep-set, piercing, strange, almost fixed. Awkward gestures, a woman's hands; ill-dressed, careless. A thick lock of hair, black and glossy, cut across his intelligent, obstinate forehead. Half bohemian, half workman in his clothes; his hair, which was too long, brushing the collar of his worn-out coat." With time, his large, impressive head became a bronzed, hairless dome. An artist friend described Picasso's way of beginning a new picture: "His eyes widen, his nostrils flare, he frowns, he attacks the canvas like a picador sticking a bull."

Picasso painted his world, and often his people, to suit his own style, which, of course, rarely looked natural to the eyes of others. He said, "We all know that art is not truth. Art is a lie that makes us realize truth—at least, the truth that is given us to understand. People speak of naturalism's being in opposition to modern painting. I would like to know if anyone has ever seen a natural work of art. Nature and art, being two different things, cannot be the same thing. Through art we express our conception of what nature is not. There is no abstract art. You must always start with

5

something. Afterward, you can remove all the traces of reality; the danger is past in any case, because the idea of the object has left its ineffaceable mark. Academic training in beauty is a sham. When we love a woman, we don't start measuring her legs."

Picasso was a great conversationalist, and especially a noted solo talker. His recollections of his poverty in his early Montmartre days still make warming, valiant tales. Once, he and Fernande Olivier, who lived with him, had had no food for a day or so when some early Picasso admirer rapped on the studio door. Opening it, they found leaning against it a long loaf of bread, a bottle of wine, and a tin of sardines. In a few years, Picasso's pictures began selling at magically high prices. Thus, he was able to fulfill one of his earlier stated desires: "I should like to live like a poor man, with a great deal of money."

Picasso will rank as the most prodigious artist of our time. He was a man fortunately composed in terms of excess. Even as a genius, he had more gifts than he needed.

(1973)

MME. MARIE CURIE
(1866-1934)

The death of Mme. Curie here was an international death. A native of Poland, a worker in France, with radium donated by America, she was a terrifying example of strict scientific fidelity to each of those lands, to all civilized lands. During the early years of her marriage, "I did the housework," she said, "for we had to pay for our scientific research out of our own pockets. We worked in an abandoned shed. It was only a wooden shack with a skylight roof which didn't always keep the rain out." In winter, the poor Curies worked in their overcoats to keep warm; they were then, as always, very much in love with each other and with chemistry.

Today, in America, radium is characteristically supposed to have been found by Mme. Curie, and in France, naturally, the discovery is accredited to Monsieur. Probably both discovered it together, since they were never apart until he was killed in 1906 on a Paris street by a truck. Certainly the husband's first work was with crystals. And no Curie at all, but a friend of theirs, Henri Becquerel, discovered uranium rays. Still, it was Mme. Curie, intrigued and alone, who devised a method of measuring this radioactivity, as she named it; her proving that it contained essential atomic properties instituted a new method of chemical research, altered the conceptions of the nineteenth century, and for the twentieth gave the base for all modern theories concerning matter and energy. Eventually her husband deserted crystals to work with her on the discovery of polonium (which they named after her native land; Madame, *née* Sklodowska, was always a patriotic Pole); then she or he or they discovered radium. Madame thereupon determined the atomic weight of radium and obtained radium in metallic form. For this she was crowned with the Nobel Chemistry Prize. She was the only woman ever permitted to hold the post of university professor in France.

She called fame a burden, was busy, sensible, shy, had no time for polite palaver, was a good mother to her two girls. The younger, Ève, is beautiful and a professional pianist. The older daughter, Irène, carried on her mother's tradition by also marrying a scientist, Fred Joliot; they are the most promising laboratory couple here today, and have already made extremely important discoveries concerning the neutron.

When the Curies were first wed, Madame put her wedding money into a tandem bicycle; later they got around, financially, to two bicycles. Early snapshots show her young, fetching, in short skirt, mutton-leg sleeves, and an incredible hat, flat as a laboratory saucepan. Later in life, her husband said, "No matter what it does to one, even if it makes of one a body without a soul, one must go on with one's work."

Mme. Curie had long since been in that zealous condition before she finally died.

5

(1934)

Questions

1. What does the word "naturally" (paragraph 2, "Mme. Marie Curie") imply about the attitudes Flanner believed to be common in France when she was writing?

2. Much of the effectiveness of brief biographical profiles rests on the degree to which the author is able to select telling details. What can you say about the way in which the details given here about Curie and about Picasso serve to suggest a fully-rounded person?

3. Compare the piece on Curie with the piece on Picasso. Which leaves a stronger impression with the reader? To what extent is this the result of content and to what extent the result of Flanner's writing being stronger or weaker?

4. Write a brief description of someone who has died—either someone you knew yourself or a public figure who you have not known personally.

5. What effect does the lack of adjectives in Flanner's style (especially pronounced in her piece on Curie) have on the reader? Would the impression created of Curie be stronger or weaker if Flanner employed more adjectives to describe her for us?

6. Flanner is essentially uncritical of her subjects here. In the case of Picasso in particular, do you think the material Flanner draws on could be recast so as to create a rather different impression of the subject?

MARVIN HARRIS

PIG LOVERS AND PIG HATERS

In this essay a leading anthropologist puts forth possible
explanations for widely varying attitudes in different cultures
towards pig eating.

❧

Everyone knows examples of apparently irrational food habits. Chinese like dog meat but despise cow milk; we like cow milk but we won't eat dogs; some tribes in Brazil relish ants but despise venison. And so it goes around the world.

The riddle of the pig strikes me as a good follow-up to mother cow.[1] It presents the challenge of having to explain why certain people should hate, while others love, the very same animal.

The half of the riddle that pertains to pig haters is well known to Jews, Moslems, and Christians. The god of the ancient Hebrews went out of His way (once in the Book of Genesis and again in Leviticus) to denounce the pig as unclean, a beast that pollutes if it is tasted or touched. About 1,500 years later, Allah told His prophet Mohammed that the status of swine was to be the same for the followers of Islam. Among millions of Jews and hundreds of millions of Moslems, the pig remains an abomination, despite the fact that it can convert grains and tubers into high-grade fats and protein more efficiently than any other animal.

Less commonly known are the traditions of the fanatic pig lovers. The pig-loving center of the world is located in New Guinea and the South Pacific Melanesian islands. To the village-dwelling horticultural tribes of this region, swine are holy animals that must be sacrificed to the ancestors and eaten on all important occasions, such as marriages and funerals. In many tribes, pigs must be sacrificed to declare war and to make peace. The

---

1   *follow-up to mother cow*   This essay occurs as the second in a volume which begins with a piece on why cows are regarded as sacred in some cultures.

tribesmen believe that their departed ancestors crave pork. So overwhelming is the hunger for pig flesh among both the living and the dead that from time to time huge feasts are organized and almost all of a tribe's pigs are eaten at once. For several days in a row, the villagers and their guests gorge on great quantities of pork, vomiting what they cannot digest in order to make room for more. When it is all over, the pig herd is so reduced in size that years of painstaking husbandry are needed to rebuild it. No sooner is this accomplished than preparations are made for another gluttonous orgy. And so the bizarre cycle of apparent mismanagement goes on.

5   I shall begin with the problem of the Jewish and Islamic pig haters. Why should gods so exalted as Jahweh and Allah have bothered to condemn a harmless and even laughable beast whose flesh is relished by the greater part of mankind? Scholars who accept the biblical and Koranic condemnation of swine have offered a number of explanations. Before the Renaissance, the most popular was that the pig is literally a dirty animal—dirtier than others because it wallows in its own urine and eats excrement. But linking physical uncleanliness to religious abhorrence leads to inconsistencies. Cows that are kept in a confined space also splash about in their own urine and feces. And hungry cows will eat human excrement with gusto. Dogs and chickens do the same thing without getting anyone very upset, and the ancients must have known that pigs raised in clean pens make fastidious house pets. Finally, if we invoke purely aesthetic standards of "cleanliness," there is the formidable inconsistency that the Bible classifies locusts and grasshoppers as "clean." The argument that insects are aesthetically more wholesome than pigs will not advance the cause of the faithful.

These inconsistencies were recognized by the Jewish rabbinate at the beginning of the Renaissance. To Moses Maimonides, court physician to Saladin during the twelfth century in Cairo, Egypt, we owe the first naturalistic explanation of the Jewish and Moslem rejection of pork. Maimonides said that God had intended the ban on pork as a public health measure. Swine's flesh "has a bad and damaging effect upon the body," wrote the rabbi. Maimonides was none too specific about the medical reasons for this opinion, but he was the emperor's physician, and his judgment was widely respected.

In the middle of the nineteenth century, the discovery that trichinosis was caused by eating undercooked pork was interpreted as a precise verification of the wisdom of Maimonides. Reform-minded Jews rejoiced in the rational substratum of the biblical codes and promptly renounced the taboo on pork. If properly cooked, pork is not a menace to public health, and so its consumption cannot be offensive to God. This provoked rabbis of more fundamentalist persuasion to launch a counter-attack against the entire naturalistic tradition. If Jahweh had merely wanted to protect the health of His people, He would have instructed them to eat only well-cooked pork rather than no pork at all. Clearly, it is argued, Jahweh had something else in mind—something more important than mere physical well-being.

In addition to this theological inconsistency, Maimonides' explanation suffers from medical and epidemiological contradictions. The pig is a vector for human disease, but so are other domestic animals freely consumed by Moslems and Jews. For example, under-cooked beef is a source of parasites, notably tapeworms, which can grow to a length of sixteen to twenty feet within a man's intestines, induce severe anemia, and lower resistance to other infectious diseases. Cattle, goats, and sheep are also vectors for brucellosis, a common bacterial infection in underdeveloped countries that is accompanied by fever, chills, sweats, weakness, pain, and aches. The most dangerous form is *Brucellosis melitensis*, transmitted by goats and sheep. Its symptoms are lethargy, fatigue, nervousness, and mental depression often mistaken for psychoneurosis. Finally, there is anthrax, a disease transmitted by cattle, sheep, goats, horses, and mules, but not by pigs. Unlike trichinosis, which seldom has fatal consequences and which does not even produce symptoms in the majority of infected individuals, anthrax often runs a rapid course that begins with body boils and terminates in death through blood poisoning. The great epidemics of anthrax that formerly swept across Europe and Asia were not brought under control until the development of the anthrax vaccine by Louis Pasteur in 1881.

Jahweh's failure to interdict contact with the domesticated vectors of anthrax is especially damaging to Maimonides' explanation, since the relationship between this disease in animals and man was known during biblical times. As described in the Book of Exodus, one of the plagues sent against the Egyptians clearly relates the symptomology of animal anthrax to a human disease:

> ... and it became a boil breaking forth with blains upon man and beast. And the magicians could not stand before Moses because of the boils, for the boils were upon the magicians, and upon all the Egyptians.

Faced with these contradictions, most Jewish and Moslem theologians have abandoned the search for a naturalistic basis of pig hatred. A frankly

10

mystical stance has recently gained favor, in which the grace afforded by conformity to dietary taboos is said to depend upon not knowing exactly what Jahweh had in mind and in not trying to find out.

Modern anthropological scholarship has reached a similar impasse. For example, with all his faults, Moses Maimonides was closer to an explanation than Sir James Frazer, renowned author of *The Golden Bough*. Frazer declared that pigs, like "all so-called unclean animals, were originally sacred; the reason for not eating them was that many were originally divine." This is of no help whatsoever, since sheep, goats, and cows were also once worshiped in the Middle East, and yet their meat is much enjoyed by all ethnic and religious groups in the region. In particular, the cow, whose golden calf was worshiped at the foot of Mt. Sinai, would seem by Frazer's logic to make a more logical unclean animal for the Hebrews than the pig.

Other scholars have suggested that pigs along with the rest of the animals tabooed in the Bible and the Koran, were once the totemic symbols of different tribal clans. This may very well have been the case at some remote point in history, but if we grant that possibility, we must also grant that "clean" animals such as cattle, sheep, and goats might also have served as totems. Contrary to much writing on the subject of totemism, totems are usually not animals valued as a food resource. The most popular totems among primitive clans in Australia and Africa are relatively useless birds like ravens and finches, or insects like gnats, ants, and mosquitoes, or even inanimate objects like clouds and boulders. Moreover, even when a valuable animal is a totem, there is no invariant rule that requires its human associates to refrain from eating it. With so many options available, saying that the pig was a totem doesn't explain anything. One might as well declare: "The pig was tabooed because it was tabooed."

I prefer Maimonides' approach. At least the rabbi tried to understand the taboo by placing it in a natural context of health and disease where definite mundane and practical forces were at work. The only trouble was that his view of the relevant conditions of pig hate was constrained by a physician's typical narrow concern with bodily pathology.

The solution to the riddle of the pig requires us to adopt a much broader definition of public health, one that includes the essential processes by which animals, plants, and people manage to coexist in viable natural and cultural communities. I think that the Bible and the Koran condemned the pig because pig farming was a threat to the integrity of the basic cultural and natural ecosystems of the Middle East.

To begin with, we must take into account the fact that the protohistoric   15
Hebrews—the children of Abraham, at the turn of the second millennium
BC—were culturally adapted to life in the rugged, sparsely inhabited arid
areas between the river valleys of Mesopotamia and Egypt. Until their
conquest of the Jordan Valley in Palestine, beginning in the thirteenth
century BC, the Hebrews were nomadic pastoralists, living almost entirely
from herds of sheep, goats, and cattle. Like all pastoral peoples they maintained close relationships with the sedentary farmers who held the oases
and the great rivers. From time to time these relationships matured into a
more sedentary, agriculturally oriented lifestyle. This appears to have been
the case with Abraham's descendants in Mesopotamia, Joseph's followers
in Egypt, and Isaac's followers in the western Negev. But even during the
climax of urban and village life under King David and King Solomon, the
herding of sheep, goats, and cattle continued to be a very important economic activity.

Within the overall pattern of this mixed farming and pastoral complex,
the divine prohibition against pork constituted a sound ecological strategy.
The nomadic Israelites could not raise pigs in their arid habitats, while for
the semi-sedentary and village farming populations, pigs were more of a
threat than an asset.

The basic reason for this is that the world zones of pastoral nomadism
correspond to unforested plains and hills that are too arid for rainfall agriculture and that cannot easily be irrigated. The domestic animals best adapted
to these zones are the ruminants—cattle, sheep, and goats. Ruminants have
sacks anterior to their stomachs which enable them to digest grass, leaves,
and other foods consisting mainly of cellulose more efficiently than any
other mammals.

The pig, however, is primarily a creature of forests and shaded river-
banks. Although it is omnivorous, its best weight gain is from food low
in cellulose—nuts, fruits, tubers, and especially grains, making it a direct
competitor of man. It cannot subsist on grass alone, and nowhere in the
world do fully nomadic pastoralists raise significant numbers of pigs. The
pig has the further disadvantage of not being a practical source of milk and
of being notoriously difficult to herd over long distances.

Above all, the pig is thermodynamically ill-adapted to the hot, dry
climate of the Negev, the Jordan Valley, and the other lands of the Bible and
the Koran. Compared to cattle, goats and sheep, the pig has an inefficient
system for regulating body temperature. Despite the expression "To sweat
like a pig," it has recently been proved that pigs can't sweat at all. Human

beings, the sweatiest of all mammals, cool themselves by evaporating as much as 1,000 grams of body liquid per hour from each square meter of body surface. The best the pig can manage is 30 grams per square meter. Even sheep evaporate twice as much body liquid through their skins as pigs. Sheep also have the advantage of thick white wool that both reflects the sun's rays and provides insulation when the temperature of the air rises above that of the body. According to L.E. Mount of the Agricultural Research Council Institute of Animal Physiology in Cambridge, England, adult pigs will die if exposed to direct sunlight and air temperatures over 98°F. In the Jordan Valley, air temperatures of 110°F occur almost every summer, and there is intense sunshine throughout the year.

20   To compensate for its lack of protective hair and its inability to sweat, the pig must dampen its skin with external moisture. It prefers to do this by wallowing in fresh clean mud, but it will cover its skin with its own urine and feces if nothing else is available. Below 84°F, pigs kept in pens deposit their excreta away from their sleeping and feeding areas, while above 84°F they begin to excrete indiscriminately throughout the pen. The higher the temperature, the "dirtier" they become. So there is some truth to the theory that the religious uncleanliness of the pig rests upon actual physical dirtiness. Only it is not in the nature of the pig to be dirty every- where; rather it is in the nature of the hot, arid habitat of the Middle East to make the pig maximally dependent upon the cooling effect of its own excrement.

Sheep and goats were the first animals to be domesticated in the Middle East, possibly as early as 9,000 BC. Pigs were domesticated in the same general region about 2,000 years later. Bone counts conducted by archeolo- gists at early prehistoric village farming sites show that the domesticated pig was almost always a relatively minor part of the village fauna, constituting only about 5 per cent of the food animal remains. This is what one would expect of a creature which had to be provided with shade and mudholes, couldn't be milked, and ate the same food as man.

As I pointed out in the case of the Hindu prohibition on beef, under preindustrial conditions, any animal that is raised primarily for its meat is a luxury. This generalization applies as well to preindustrial pastoralists, who seldom exploit their herds primarily for meat.

Among the ancient mixed farming and pastoralist communities of the Middle East, domestic animals were valued primarily as sources of milk, cheese, hides, dung, fiber, and traction for plowing. Goats, sheep, and cattle provided ample amounts of these items plus an occasional supplement of lean meat. From the beginning, therefore, pork must have been a luxury food, esteemed for its succulent, tender, and fatty qualities.

Between 7,000 and 2,000 BC pork became still more of a luxury. During this period there was a sixtyfold increase in the human population of the Middle East. Extensive deforestation accompanied the rise in population, especially as a result of permanent damage caused by the large herds of sheep and goats. Shade and water, the natural conditions appropriate for pig raising, became progressively more scarce, and pork became even more of an ecological and economical luxury.

As in the case of the beef-eating taboo, the greater the temptation, the greater the need for divine interdiction. This relationship is generally accepted as suitable for explaining why the gods are always so interested in combating sexual temptations such as incest and adultery. Here I merely apply it to a tempting food. The Middle East is the wrong place to raise pigs, but pork remains a succulent treat. People always find it difficult to resist such temptations on their own. Hence Jahweh was heard to say that swine were unclean, not only as food, but to the touch as well. Allah was heard to repeat the same message for the same reason: It was ecologically maladaptive to try to raise pigs in substantial numbers. Small-scale production would only increase the temptation. Better then, to interdict the consumption of pork entirely, and to concentrate on raising goats, sheep, and cattle. Pigs tasted good but it was too expensive to feed them and keep them cool.

Many questions remain, especially why each of the other creatures interdicted by the Bible—vultures, hawks, snakes, snails, shellfish, fish without scales, and so forth—came under the same divine taboo. And why Jews and Moslems, no longer living in the Middle East, continue—with varying degrees of exactitude and zeal—to observe the ancient dietary laws. In general, it appears to me that most of the interdicted birds and animals fall squarely into one of two categories. Some, like ospreys, vultures, and hawks, are not even potentially significant sources of food. Others, like shellfish, are obviously unavailable to mixed pastoral-farming populations. Neither of these categories of tabooed creatures raises the kind of question I have set out to answer—namely, how to account for an apparently bizarre and wasteful taboo. There is obviously nothing irrational about not spending one's time chasing vultures for dinner, or not hiking fifty miles across the desert for a plate of clams on the half shell.

This is an appropriate moment to deny the claim that all religiously sanctioned food practices have ecological explanations. Taboos also have

25

social functions, such as helping people to think of themselves as a distinctive community. This function is well served by the modern observance of dietary rules among Moslems and Jews outside of their Middle Eastern homelands. The question to be put to these practices is whether they diminish in some significant degree the practical and mundane welfare of Jews and Moslems by depriving them of nutritional factors for which there are no readily available substitutes. I think the answer is almost certainly negative. But now permit me to resist another kind of temptation—the temptation to explain everything. I think more will be learned about pig haters if we turn to the other half of the riddle, to the pig lovers.

Pig love is the soulful opposite of the divine opprobrium that Moslems and Jews heap on swine. This condition is not reached through mere gustatory enthusiasm pork cookery. Many culinary traditions, including the Euro-American and Chinese, esteem the flesh and fat of pigs. Pig love is something else. It is a state of total community between man and pig. While the presence of pigs threatens the human status of Moslems and Jews, in the ambience of pig love one cannot truly be human except in the company of pigs.

Pig love includes raising pigs to be a member of the family, sleeping next to them, talking to them, stroking and fondling them, calling them by name, leading them on a leash to the fields, weeping when they fall sick or are injured, and feeding them with choice morsels from the family table. But unlike Hindu love of cow, pig love also includes obligatory sacrificing and eating of pigs on special occasions. Because of ritual slaughter and sacred feasting, pig love provides a broader prospect for communion between man and beast than is true of the Hindu farmer and his cow. The climax of pig love is the incorporation of the pig as flesh into the flesh of the human host and of the pig as spirit into the spirit of the ancestors.

30   Pig love is honoring your dead father by clubbing a beloved sow to death on his grave site and roasting it in an earth oven dug on the spot. Pig love is stuffing fistfuls of cold, salted belly fat into your brother-in-law's mouth to make him loyal and happy. Above all, pig love is the great pig feast, held once or twice a generation, when to satisfy the ancestors' craving for pork, assuring communal health, and secure victory in future wars, most of the adult pigs are killed off and gluttonously devoured.

Professor Roy Rappaport of the University of Michigan has made a detailed study of the relationship between pigs and pig-loving Maring, a remote group of tribesmen living in the Bismarck Mountains of New Guinea. In his book *Pigs for the Ancestors: Ritual in the Ecology of a New Guinea*

People, Rappaport describes how pig love contributes to the solution of basic human problems. Under the given circumstances of Maring life, there are few viable alternatives.

Each local Maring subgroup or clan holds a pig festival on the average about once every twelve years. The entire festival—including various preparations, small-scale sacrifices, and the final massive slaughter—lasts about a year and is known in the Maring language as a *kaiko*. In the first two or three months immediately following the completion of its *kaiko*, the clan engages in armed combat with enemy clans, leading to many casualties and eventual loss or gain of territory. Additional pigs are sacrificed during the fighting, and both the victors and the vanquished soon find themselves entirely bereft of adult pigs with which to curry favor from their respective ancestors. Fighting ceases abruptly, and the belligerents repair to sacred spots to plant small trees known as *rumbim*. Every adult male clansman participates in this ritual by laying hands on the *rumbim* sapling as it is put into the ground.

The war magician addresses the ancestors, explaining that they have run out of pigs and are thankful to be alive. He assures the ancestors that the fighting is now over and that there will be no resumption of hostilities as long as the *rumbim* remains in the ground. From now on, the thoughts and efforts of the living will be directed toward raising pigs; only when a new herd of pigs has been raised, enough for a mighty *kaiko* with which to thank the ancestors properly, will the warriors think of uprooting the *rumbim* and returning to the battlefield.

By a detailed study of one clan called the Tsembaga, Rappaport has been able to show that the entire cycle—which consists of *kaiko*, followed by warfare, the planting of *rumbim*, truce, the raising of a new pig herd, the uprooting of *rumbim*, and new *kaiko*—is no mere psychodrama of pig farmers gone berserk. Every part of this cycle is integrated within a complex, self-regulating ecosystem, that effectively adjusts the size and distribution of the Tsembaga's human and animal population to conform to available resources and production opportunities.

The one question that is central to the understanding of pig love among the Maring is: How do the people decide when they have enough pigs to thank the ancestors properly? The Maring themselves were unable to state how many years should elapse or how many pigs are needed to stage a proper *kaiko*. Possibility of agreement on the basis of a fixed number of animals or years is virtually eliminated because the Maring have no calendar and their language lacks words for numbers larger than three.

35

The *kaiko* of 1963 observed by Rappaport began when there were 169 pigs and about 200 members of the Tsembaga clan. It is the meaning of these numbers in terms of daily work routines and settlement patterns that provides the key to the length of the cycle.

The task of raising pigs, as well as that of cultivating yams, taro, and sweet potatoes, depends primarily upon the labor of the Maring women. Baby pigs are carried along with human infants to the gardens. After they are weaned, their mistresses train them to trot along behind like dogs. At the age of four or five months, the pigs are turned loose in the forests to scrounge for themselves until their mistresses call them home at night to be fed a daily ration of leftover or substandard sweet potatoes and yams. As each woman's pigs mature and as their numbers increase, she must work harder to provide them with their evening meal.

While the *rumbim* remained in the ground, Rappaport found that the Tsembaga women were under considerable pressure to increase the size of their gardens, to plant more sweet potatoes and yams, and to raise more pigs as quickly as possible in order to have "enough" pigs to hold the next *kaiko* before the enemy did. Mature pigs, weighing about 135 pounds, are heavier than the average adult Maring, and even with their daily scrounging, they cost each woman about as much effort to feed as an adult human. At the time of the uprooting of the *rumbim* in 1963, the more ambitious Tsembaga women were taking care of the equivalent of six 135-pounders in addition to gardening for themselves and their families, cooking, nursing, carrying infants about, and manufacturing household items such as net bags, string aprons, and loincloths. Rappaport calculates that taking care of six pigs alone uses up over 50 per cent of the total daily energy which a healthy, well-fed Maring woman is capable of expending.

The increase in the pig population is normally also accompanied by an increase in the human population, especially among groups that have been victorious in the previous war. Pigs and people must be fed from the gardens which are hacked and burned out of the tropical forest that covers the slopes of the Bismarck Mountains. Like similar horticultural systems in other tropical areas, the fertility of the Maring gardens depends upon the nitrogen that is put into the soil by the ashes left from burning off the trees. These gardens cannot be planted for more than two or three years consecutively, since once the trees are gone, the heavy rains quickly wash away the nitrogen and other soil nutrients. The only remedy is to choose another site and burn off another segment of the forest. After a decade or so, the old gardens get covered over with enough secondary growth so that they can be burned again and replanted. These old garden sites are preferred because they are easier to clear than virgin forest. But as the pig and human populations spurt upward during the *rumbim* truce, the maturation of the old garden sites lags behind and new gardens must be established in the virgin tracts. While there is plenty of virgin forest available, the new garden sites place an extra strain on everybody and lower the typical rate of return for every unit of labor the Maring invest in feeding themselves and their pigs.

The men whose task it is to clear and burn the new gardens must work harder because of the greater thickness and height of the virgin trees. But it is the women who suffer most, since the new gardens are necessarily located at a greater distance from the center of the village. Not only must the women plant larger gardens to feed their families and pigs, but they must consume more and more of their time just walking to work and more and more of their energy hauling piglets and babies up to and down from the garden and the heavy loads of harvested yams and sweet potatoes back to their houses.

A further source of tension arises from the increased effort involved in protecting the gardens from being eaten up by the mature pigs that are let loose to scrounge for themselves. Every garden must be surrounded by a stout fence to keep the pigs out. A hungry 150-pound sow, however, is a formidable adversary. Fences are breached and gardens invaded more frequently as the pig herd multiplies. If caught by an irate gardener, the offending pig may be killed. These disagreeable incidents set neighbor against neighbor and heighten the general sense of dissatisfaction. As Rappaport points out, incidents involving pigs necessarily increase more rapidly than the pigs themselves.

In order to avoid such incidents and to get closer to their gardens, the Maring begin to move their houses farther apart over a wider area. This dispersion lowers the security of the group in case of renewed hostilities. So everyone becomes more jittery. The women begin to complain about being overworked. They bicker with their husbands and snap at their children. Soon the men begin to wonder if perhaps there are "enough pigs." They go down to inspect the *rumbim* to see how tall it has grown. The women complain more loudly, and finally the men, with considerable unanimity and without counting the pigs, agree that the moment has come to begin the *kaiko*.

During the *kaiko* year of 1963, the Tsembaga killed off three-fourths of their pigs by number and seven-eighths by weight. Much of this meat was distributed to in-laws and military allies who were invited to participate in the yearlong festivities. At the climactic rituals held on November 7 and 8, 1963, 96 pigs were killed and their meat and fat were distributed directly or indirectly to an estimated two or three thousand people. The Tsembaga kept about 2,500 pounds of pork and fat for themselves, or 12 pounds for each man, woman, and child, a quantity which they consumed in five consecutive days of unrestrained gluttony.

The Maring consciously use the *kaiko* as an occasion to reward their allies for previous assistance and to seek their loyalty in future hostilities. The allies in turn accept the invitation to the *kaiko* because it gives them an opportunity to decide if their hosts are prosperous and powerful enough to warrant continued support; of course, the allies are also hungry for pig meat.

45   Guests dress up in their finest manner. They wear bead-and-shell necklaces, cowrie-shell garters around their calves, orchid-fiber waistbands, purple-striped loincloths bordered with marsupial fur, and masses of accordion-shaped leaves topped by a bustle on their buttocks. Crowns of eagle and parrot feathers encircle their heads, festooned with orchid stems, green beetles and cowries, and topped with an entire stuffed bird of paradise. Every man has spent hours painting his face in some original design, and wears his best bird-of-paradise plume through his nose along with a favorite disk or a gold-lip crescent shell. Visitors and hosts spend much time showing off to each other by dancing at the specially constructed dance ground, preparing the way for amorous alliances with the female onlookers as well as military alliances with male warriors.

Over a thousand people crowded into the Tsembaga dance ground to participate in the rituals that followed the great pig slaughter witnessed by Rappaport in 1963. Special reward packages of salted pig fat were heaped high behind the window of a three-sided ceremonial building that adjoined the dance grounds. In Rappaport's words:

Several men climbed to the top of the structure and from there proclaimed one by one to the multitude the names and clans of the men being honored. As his name was called, each honored man charged toward the ... window swinging his ax and shouting. His supporters, yelling battle cries, beating drums, brandishing weapons, followed close behind him. At the window the mouth of the honored man was stuffed with cold salted belly-fat by the Tsembaga whom he had come to help in the last fight and who now also passed out to him through the window a package containing additional salted belly for his followers. With the belly fat hanging from his mouth the hero now retired, his supporters close behind him, shouting, singing, beating their drums, dancing. Honored name quickly followed honored name, and groups charging toward the window sometimes became entangled with those retiring.

Within limits set by the basic technological and environmental conditions of the Maring, all of this has a practical explanation. First of all, the craving for pig meat is a perfectly rational feature of Maring life in view of the general scarcity of meat in their diet. While they can supplement their staple vegetables with occasional frogs, rats, and a few hunted marsupials, domesticated pork is their best potential source of high-quality animal fat and protein. This does not mean that the Maring suffer from an acute form of protein deficiency. On the contrary, their diet of yams, sweet potatoes, taro, and other plant foods provides them with a broad variety of vegetable proteins that satisfies but does not far exceed minimum nutritional standards. Getting proteins from pigs is something else, however. Animal protein in general is more concentrated and metabolically more effective than vegetable protein, so for human populations that are mainly restricted to vegetable foods (no cheese, milk, eggs, or fish), meat is always an irresistible temptation.

Moreover, up to a point, it makes good ecological sense for the Maring to raise pigs. The temperature and humidity are ideal. Pigs thrive in the damp, shady environment of the mountain slopes and obtain a substantial portion of their food by roaming freely over the forest floor. The complete interdiction of pork—the Middle Eastern solution—would be a most irrational and uneconomic practice under these conditions.

On the other hand, unlimited growth of the pig population can only lead to competition between man and pig. If permitted to go too far, pig farming overburdens the women and endangers the gardens upon which the Maring depend for survival. As the pig population increases, the Maring women must work harder and harder. Eventually they find themselves working to feed pigs rather than to feed people. As virgin lands are brought into use, the efficiency of the entire agricultural system plummets. It is at this point that the *kaiko* takes place, the role of the ancestors being to encourage a maximum effort at pig raising but at the same time to see to it that the pigs do not destroy the women and the gardens. Their task is admittedly more difficult than Jahweh's or Allah's, since a total taboo is always easier to administer than a partial one. Nonetheless, the belief that a *kaiko* must be held as soon as possible, in order to keep the ancestors happy, effectively rids the Maring of animals that have grown parasitic and helps keep the pig population from becoming "too much of a good thing."

50   If ancestors are so clever, why don't they simply set a limit on the number of pigs that each Maring woman can raise? Would it not be better to keep a constant number of pigs than to permit the pig population to cycle through extremes of scarcity and abundance?

This alternative would be preferable only if each Maring clan had zero growth, no enemies, a wholly different form of agriculture, powerful rulers, and written laws—in short, if they weren't the Maring. No one, not even the ancestors can predict how many pigs are "too much of a good thing." The point at which the pigs become burdensome does not depend upon any set of constants, but rather on a set of variables which changes from year to year. It depends on how many people there are in the whole region and in each clan, on their state of physical and psychological vigor, on the size of their territory, on the amount of secondary forest they have, and on the condition and intentions of the enemy groups in neighboring territories. The Tsembaga's ancestors cannot simply say "thou shalt keep four pigs, and no more," because there is no way of guaranteeing that the ancestors of the Kundugai, Dimbagai, Yimgagai, Tuguma, Aundagai, Kauwasi, Monambant, and all the rest will agree to this number. All of these groups are engaged in a struggle to validate their respective claims to share in the earth's resources. Warfare and the threat of warfare probe and test these claims. The ancestors' insatiable craving for pigs is a consequence of this armed probing and testing by the Maring clans.

To satisfy the ancestors, a maximum effort must be made not only to produce as much food as possible, but to accumulate it in the form of the pig herd. This effort, even though it results in cyclical surpluses of pork, enhances the ability of the group to survive and to defend its territory.

It does this in several ways. First, the extra effort called forth by the pig lust of the ancestors raises the levels of protein intake for the entire group during the *rumbim* truce, resulting in a taller, healthier, and more vigorous population. Furthermore, by linking the *kaiko* to the end of the truce, the ancestors guarantee that massive doses of high-quality fats and proteins are consumed at the period of greatest social stress—in the months immediately prior to the outbreak of intergroup fighting. Finally, by banking large amounts of extra food in the form of nutritionally valuable pig meat, the Maring clans are able to attract and reward allies when they are most needed, again just before the outbreak of war.

The Tsembaga and their neighbors are conscious of the relationship between success in raising pigs and military power. The number of pigs slaughtered at the *kaiko* provides the guests with an accurate basis for judging the health, energy, and determination of the feast givers. A group that cannot manage to accumulate pigs is not likely to put up a good defense of its territory, and will not attract strong allies. No mere irrational premonition of defeat hangs over the battlefield when one's ancestors aren't given enough pork at the *kaiko*. Rappaport insists—correctly, I believe—that in a fundamental ecological sense, the size of a group's pig surplus does indicate its productive and military strength and does validate or invalidate its territorial claims. In other words, the entire system results in an efficient distribution of plants, animals, and people in the region, from a human ecological point of view.

I am sure that many readers will now want to insist that the pig love is maladaptive and terribly inefficient because it is geared to periodic outbreaks of warfare. If warfare is irrational, then so is the *kaiko*. Again, permit me to resist the temptation to explain everything at once. In the next chapter I will discuss the mundane causes of Maring warfare. But for the moment, let me point out that warfare is not caused by pig love. Millions of people who have never even seen a pig wage war; nor does pig hatred (ancient and modern) discernibly enhance the peacefulness of the intergroup relations in the Middle East. Given the prevalence of warfare in human history and prehistory, we can only marvel at the ingenious system devised by New Guinea "savages" for maintaining extensive periods of truce. After all, as long as their neighbor's *rumbim* remains in the ground, the Tsembaga don't have to worry about being attacked. One can perhaps say as much, but not more, about nations that plant missiles instead of *rumbim*.

(1974)

Questions

1. Harris is unusual among academics in aiming his writing both at other academics and at students and general readers with no prior specialized knowledge. Comment on the ways in which the diction, syntax, and organization of ideas in this essay are appropriate to an

audience with no prior familiarity with the topic or with the discipline of anthropology.

2. Express in your own words the logical problem with the argument that pig-eating became taboo in the cultures Harris is discussing because pigs had been regarded as sacred (paragraph 11) or because pigs were regarded as totemic symbols representing tribal clans (paragraph 12).

3. What are the key facts about the physiology of the pig so far as Harris's argument is concerned?

4. In two paragraphs, summarize the practices of the miring of pigs and Harris's explanation as to why these seemingly bizarre practices make sense.

5. Does it "make sense," either from the sort of angle of approach that Harris uses or from other angles, for North American society to consume as much beef and pork as it does?

6. Does the sort of discussion that Harris engages in undermine the foundations of the religions he is discussing in any way?

FRAN LEBOWITZ

CHILDREN: PRO OR CON?

*Like many of Lebowitz's urbane and irreverent pieces on
modern life, this essay purports to have a practical purpose.*

❧

Moving, as I do, in what would kindly be called artistic circles, children are an infrequent occurrence. But even the most artistic of circles includes within its periphery a limited edition of the tenaciously domestic.

As I am generally quite fond of children I accept this condition with far less displeasure than do my more rarefied acquaintances. That is not to imply that I am a total fool for a little grin but simply that I consider myself to be in a position of unquestionable objectivity and therefore eminently qualified to deal with the subject in an authoritative manner.

From the number of children in evidence it appears that people have them at the drop of a hat—for surely were they to give this matter its due attention they would act with greater decorum. Of course, until now prospective parents have not had the opportunity to see the facts spelled out in black and white and therefore cannot reasonably be held accountable for their actions. To this end I have carefully set down all pertinent information in the fervent hope that it will result in a future populated by a more attractive array of children than I have thus far encountered.

Pro

I must take issue with the term "a mere child," for it has been my invariable experience that the company of a mere child is infinitely preferable to that of a mere adult.

* * *

Children are usually small in stature, which makes them quite useful for getting at those hard-to-reach places.

5

* * *

Children do not sit next to one in restaurants and discuss their prepos-terous hopes for the future in loud tones of voice.

* * *

Children ask better questions than do adults. "May I have a cookie?" "Why is the sky blue?" and "What does a cow say?" are far more likely to elicit a cheerful response than "Where's your manuscript?" "Why haven't you called?" and "Who's your lawyer?"

* * *

Children give life to the concept of immaturity.

* * *

Children make the most desirable opponents in Scrabble as they are both easy to beat and fun to cheat.

* * *

10   It is still quite possible to stand in a throng of children without once de-tecting even the faintest whiff of an exciting, rugged after-shave or cologne.

* * *

Not a single member of the under-age set has yet to propose the word *chairchild*.

* * *

Children sleep either alone or with small toy animals. The wisdom of such behavior is unquestionable, as it frees them from the immeasurable tedium of being privy to the whispered confessions of others. I have yet to run across a teddy bear who was harboring the secret desire to wear a maid's uniform.

Con

Even when freshly washed and relieved of all obvious confections, children tend to be sticky. One can only assume that this has something to do with not smoking enough.

* * *

Children have decidedly little fashion sense and if left to their own devices will more often than not be drawn to garments of unfortunate cut. In this respect they do not differ greatly from the majority of their elders, but somehow one blames them more.

* * *

15   Children respond inadequately to sardonic humor and veiled threats.

* * *

Notoriously insensitive to subtle shifts in mood, children will persist in discussing the color of a recently sighted cement-mixer long after one's own interest in the topic has waned.

* * *

Children are rarely in the position to lend one a truly interesting sum of money. There are, however, exceptions, and such children are an excellent addition to any party.

* * *

Children arise at an unseemly hour and are ofttimes in the habit of putting food on an empty stomach.

* * *

Children do not look well in evening clothes.

* * *

All too often children are accompanied by adults.   20

* * *

(1974)

Questions

1. Rephrase a passage of three or four sentences from this essay so as to use shorter sentences and fewer, simpler words. What can you say about the way in which Lebowitz's diction (particularly her choice of adjectives and adverbs) and syntax play a part in lending a humorous tone to her writing?

2. It is often suggested that a key element in humor is the element of the unexpected—and in particular the unexpected flouting of convention. To what extent do you see that generalization as being well-founded?

3. Birth rates in the developed world have been below replacement levels for many years, and birth rates in the developing world are now quickly dropping as well. In all seriousness, discuss the arguments that could be made for and against having children—or, for society as a whole, for or against measures that encourage people to have children.

PETER SINGER

SPECIESISM AND THE
EQUALITY OF ANIMALS

*With his writing about animals, the Australian philosopher
Peter Singer has probably changed the day-to-day behavior of
more people than any other writer of the past generation.*

❧

S*peciesism*—the word is not an attractive one, but I can think of no
better term—is a prejudice or attitude of bias toward the interests of
members of one's own species and against those of members of other species. It should be obvious that the fundamental objections to racism and
sexism made by Thomas Jefferson and Sojourner Truth apply equally to
speciesism. If possessing a higher degree of intelligence does not entitle
one human to use another for his own ends, how can it entitle humans to
exploit nonhumans for the same purpose?

Many philosophers and other writers have proposed the principle of
equal consideration of interests, in some form or other, as a basic moral
principle; but not many of them have recognized that this principle applies
to members of other species as well as to our own. Jeremy Bentham was
one of the few who did realize this. In a forward-looking passage written
at a time when black slaves had been freed by the French but in the British
dominions were still being treated in the way we now treat animals, Bentham wrote:

> The day *may* come when the rest of the animal creation may ac-
> quire those rights which never could have been withholden from
> them but by the hand of tyranny. The French have already discov-
> ered that the blackness of the skin is no reason why a human being
> should be abandoned without redress to the caprice of a tormentor.

It may one day come to be recognized that the number of the legs, the villosity of the skin, or the termination of the *os sacrum* are reasons equally insufficient for abandoning a sensitive being to the same fate. What else is it that should trace the insuperable line? Is it the faculty of reason, or perhaps the faculty of discourse? But a full-grown horse or dog is beyond comparison a more rational, as well as a more conversable animal, than an infant of a day or a week or even a month, old. But suppose they were otherwise, what would it avail? The question is not, Can they *reason*? nor Can they *talk*? but, *Can they suffer*?

In this passage Bentham points to the capacity for suffering as the vital characteristic that gives a being the right to equal consideration. The capacity for suffering—or more strictly, for suffering and/or enjoyment or happiness—is not just another characteristic like the capacity for language or higher mathematics. Bentham is not saying that those who try to mark "the insuperable line" that determines whether the interests of a being should be considered happen to have chosen the wrong characteristic. By saying that we must consider the interests of all beings with the capacity for suffering or enjoyment Bentham does not arbitrarily exclude from consideration any interests at all—as those who draw the line with reference to the possession of reason or language do. The capacity for suffering and enjoyment is a *prerequisite for having interests at all*, a condition that must be satisfied before we can speak of interests in a meaningful way. It would be nonsense to say that it was not in the interests of a stone to be kicked along the road by a schoolboy. A stone does not have interests because it cannot suffer. Nothing that we can do to it could possibly make any difference to its welfare. A mouse, on the other hand, does have an interest in not being kicked along the road, because it will suffer if it is.

If a being suffers there can be no moral justification for refusing to take that suffering into consideration. No matter what the nature of the being, the principle of equality requires that its suffering be counted equally with the like suffering—in so far as rough comparisons can be made—of any other being. If a being is not capable of suffering, or of experiencing enjoyment or happiness, there is nothing to be taken into account. So the limit of sentience (using the term as a convenient if not strictly accurate shorthand for the capacity to suffer and/or experience enjoyment) is the only defensible boundary of concern for the interests of others. To mark this boundary by some other characteristic like intelligence or rationality would be to mark it in an arbitrary manner. Why not choose some other characteristic, like skin color?

The racist violates the principle of equality by giving greater weight to the interests of members of his own race when there is a clash between their interests and the interests of those of another race. The sexist violates the principle of equality by favoring the interests of his own sex. Similarly the speciesist allows the interests of his own species to override the greater interests of members of other species. The pattern is identical in each case.

5   Most human beings are speciesists. Ordinary human beings—not a few exceptionally cruel or heartless humans, but the overwhelming majority of humans—take an active part in, acquiesce in, and allow their taxes to pay for practices that require the sacrifice of the most important interests of members of other species in order to promote the most trivial interests of our own species....

SPECIESISM IN PRACTICE

For the great majority of human beings, especially in urban, industrialized societies, the most direct form of contact with members of other species is at mealtimes: We eat them. In doing so we treat them purely as means to our ends. We regard their life and well-being as subordinate to our taste for a particular kind of dish. I say "taste" deliberately—this is purely a matter of pleasing our palate. There can be no defense of eating flesh in terms of satisfying nutritional needs, since it has been established beyond doubt that we could satisfy our need for protein and other essential nutrients far more efficiently with a diet that replaced animal flesh by soy beans, or products derived from soy beans, and other high protein vegetable products.

It is not merely the act of killing that indicates what we are ready to do to other species in order to gratify our tastes. The suffering we inflict on the animals while they are alive is perhaps an even clearer indication of our speciesism than the fact that we are prepared to kill them. In order to have meat on the table at a price that people can afford, our society tolerates methods of meat production that confine sentient animals in cramped, unsuitable conditions for the entire duration of their lives. Animals are treated like machines that convert fodder into flesh, and any innovation that results in a higher "conversion ratio" is liable to be adopted. As one authority on the subject has said, "cruelty is acknowledged only when profitability ceases." So hens are crowded four or five to a cage with a floor area of twenty inches by eighteen inches, or around the size of a single page of the *New York Times*. The cages have wire floors, since this reduces cleaning costs, though wire is unsuitable for the hens' feet; the floors slope, since this makes the eggs roll down for easy collection, although this makes it difficult for the hens to rest comfortably. In these conditions all the birds' natural instincts are thwarted: They cannot stretch their wings fully, walk freely, dust-bathe, scratch the ground, or build a nest. Although they have never known other conditions, observers have noticed that the birds vainly try to perform these actions. Frustrated at their inability to do so, they often develop what farmers call "vices," and peck each other to death. To prevent this, the beaks of young birds are often cut off.

This kind of treatment is not limited to poultry. Pigs are now also being reared in cages inside sheds. These animals are comparable to dogs in intelligence, and need a varied, stimulating environment if they are not to suffer from stress and boredom. Anyone who kept a dog in the way in which pigs are frequently kept would be liable to prosecution, in England at least, but because our interest in exploiting pigs is greater than our interest in exploiting dogs, we object to cruelty to dogs while consuming the produce of cruelty to pigs. Of the other animals, the condition of veal calves is perhaps worst of all, since these animals are so closely confined that they cannot even turn around or get up and lie down freely. In this way they do not develop unpalatable muscle. They are also made anemic and kept short of roughage, to keep their flesh pale, since white veal fetches a higher price; as a result they develop a craving for iron and roughage, and have been observed to gnaw wood off the sides of their stalls, and lick greedily at any rusty hinge that is within reach.

Since, as I have said, none of these practices cater to anything more than our pleasures of taste, our practice of rearing and killing other animals in order to eat them is a clear instance of the sacrifice of the most important interests of other beings in order to satisfy trivial interests of our own. To avoid speciesism we must stop this practice, and each of us has a moral obligation to cease supporting the practice. Our custom is all the support that the meat industry needs. The decision to cease giving it that support may be difficult, but it is no more difficult than it would have been for a white Southerner to go against the traditions of his society and free his slaves; if we do not change our dietary habits, how can we censure those slaveholders who would not change their own way of living?

The same form of discrimination may be observed in the widespread practice of experimenting on other species in order to see if certain 10 substances are safe for human beings, or to test some psychological theory about the effect of severe punishment on learning, or to try out various new compounds just in case something turns up. People sometimes think that all this experimentation is for vital medical purposes, and so will reduce suffering overall. This comfortable belief is very wide of the mark. Drug companies test new shampoos and cosmetics that they are intending to put on the market by dropping them into the eyes of rabbits, held open by metal clips, in order to observe what damage results. Food additives, like artificial colorings and preservatives, are tested by what is known as the "LD50"—a test designed to find the level of consumption at which 50 per cent of a group of animals will die. In the process, nearly all of the animals are made very sick before some finally die, and others pull through. If the substance is relatively harmless, as it often is, huge doses have to be forcefed to the animals, until in some cases sheer volume or concentration of the substance causes death.

Much of this pointless cruelty goes on in the universities. In many areas of science, nonhuman animals are regarded as an item of laboratory equipment, to be used and expended as desired. In psychology laboratories experimenters devise endless variations and repetitions of experiments that were of little value in the first place. To quote just one example, from the experimenter's own account in a psychology journal: At the University of Pennsylvania, Perrin S. Cohen hung six dogs in hammocks with electrodes taped to their hind feet. Electric shock of varying intensity was then administered through the electrodes. If the dog learned to press its head against a panel on the left, the shock was turned off, but otherwise it remained on indefinitely. Three of the dogs, however, were required to wait periods varying from 2 to 7 seconds while being shocked before making the response that turned off the current. If they failed to wait, they received further shocks. Each dog was given from 26 to 46 "sessions" in the hammock, each session consisting of 80 "trials" or shocks, administered at intervals of one minute. The experimenter reported that the dogs, who were unable to move in the hammock, barked or bobbed their heads when the current was applied. The reported findings of the experiment were that there was a delay in the dogs' responses that increased proportionately to the time the dogs were required to endure the shock, but a gradual increase in the intensity of the shock had no systematic effect in the timing of the response. The experiment was funded by the National Institutes of Health, and the United States Public Health Service.

In this example, and countless cases like it, the possible benefits to mankind are either nonexistent or fantastically remote, while the certain losses to members of other species are very real.

(1977)

Questions

1. Summarize the argument Singer makes in the first six paragraphs here. What are the strengths of the argument? Does it have any weaknesses?

2. What can you say about Singer's recitation of facts concerning the ways in which animals are treated under factory-farming conditions, and the effect these facts have on the reader? If the presentation were different, how might that effect alter?

3. The description of electric shocks being given to dogs near the end of this piece is reminiscent of the research by Stanley Milgram described elsewhere in this volume. Are there any connections between the two in terms of the conclusions one might draw about human nature?

4. Why do you think Singer devotes considerably more space to the issue of animal suffering than to the issue of whether or not humans should eat non-human animals at all?

Adrienne Rich

Taking Women Students Seriously

*In addresses made to a group of women teachers in 1978 and
to a conference at Scripps College in 1984, a famous poet
discusses the place of women in university, and the place of
lesbians both in university and in society as a whole.*

❧

I see my function here today as one of trying to create a context, delineate
a background, against which we might talk about women as students and
students as women. I would like to speak for a while about this background,
and then I hope that we can have, not so much a question period, as a raising of concerns, a sharing of questions for which we as yet may have no
answers, an opening of conversations which will go on and on.

When I went to teach at Douglass, a women's college, it was with
a particular background which I would like briefly to describe to you. I
had graduated from an all-girls' school in the 1940s, where the head and
the majority of the faculty were independent, unmarried women. One or
two held doctorates, but had been forced by the Depression (and by the
fact that they were women) to take secondary school teaching jobs. These
women cared a great deal about the life of the mind, and they gave a great
deal of time and energy—beyond any limit of teaching hours—to those
of us who showed special intellectual interest or ability. We were taken
to libraries, art museums, lectures at neighboring colleges, set to work
on extra research projects, given extra French or Latin reading. Although
we sometimes felt "pushed" by them, we held those women in a kind of
respect which even then we dimly perceived was not generally accorded
to women in the world at large. They were vital individuals, defined not by
their relationships but by their personalities; and although under the pressure of the culture we were all certain we wanted to get married, their lives
did not appear empty or dreary to us. In a kind of cognitive dissonance,

we knew they were "old maids" and therefore supposed to be bitter and lonely; yet we saw them vigorously involved with life. But despite their existence as alternate models of women, the *content* of the education they gave us in no way prepared us to survive as women in a world organized by and for men.

From that school, I went on to Radcliffe, congratulating myself that now I would have great men as my teachers. From 1947 to 1951, when I graduated, I never saw a single woman on a lecture platform, or in front of a class, except when a woman graduate student gave a paper on a special topic. The "great men" talked of other "great men," of the nature of Man, the history of Mankind, the future of Man; and never again was I to experience, from a teacher, the kind of prodding, the insistence that my best could be even better, that I had known in high school. Women students were simply not taken very seriously. Harvard's message to women was an elite mystification: we were, of course, part of Mankind; we were special, achieving women, or we would not have been there; but of course our real goal was to marry—if possible, a Harvard graduate.

In the late sixties, I began teaching at the City College of New York—a crowded, public, urban, multiracial institution as far removed from Harvard as possible. I went there to teach writing in the SEEK Program, which predated Open Admissions and which was then a kind of model for programs designed to open up higher education to poor, black and Third World students. Although during the next few years we were to see the original concept of SEEK diluted, then violently attacked and betrayed, it was for a short time an extraordinary and intense teaching and learning environment. The characteristics of this environment were a deep commitment on the part of teachers to the minds of their students; a constant, active effort to create or discover the conditions for learning, and to educate ourselves to meet the needs of the new college population; a philosophical attitude based on open discussion of racism, oppression, and the politics of literature and language; and a belief that learning in the classroom could not be isolated from the student's experience as a member of an urban minority group in white America. Here are some of the kinds of questions we, as teachers of writing, found ourselves asking:

(1) What has been the student's experience of education in the inadequate, often abusively racist public school system, which rewards passivity and treats a questioning attitude or independent mind as a behavior problem? What has been her

or his experience in a society that consistently undermines the selfhood of the poor and the nonwhite? How can such a student gain that sense of self which is necessary for active participation in education? What does all this mean for us as teachers?

(2) How do we go about teaching a canon of literature which has consistently excluded or depreciated nonwhite experience?

(3) How can we connect the process of learning to write well with the student's own reality, and not simply teach her/him how to write acceptable lies in standard English?

5   When I went to teach at Douglass College in 1976, and in teaching women's writing workshops elsewhere, I came to perceive stunning parallels to the questions I had first encountered in teaching the so-called disadvantaged students at City. But in this instance, and against the specific background of the women's movement, the questions framed themselves like this:

(1) What has been the student's experience of education in schools which reward female passivity, indoctrinate girls and boys in stereotypic sex roles, and do not take the female mind seriously? How does a woman gain a sense of her *self* in a system—in this case, patriarchal capitalism—which devalues work done by women, denies the importance and unique-ness of female experience, and is physically violent toward women? What does this mean for a woman teacher?

(2) How do we, as women, teach women students a canon of lit-erature which has consistently excluded or depreciated female experience, and which often expresses hostility to women and validates violence against us?

(3) How can we teach women to move beyond the desire for male approval and getting "good grades" and seek and write their own truths that the culture has distorted or made taboo? (For women, of course, language itself is exclusive: I want to say more about this further on.)

In teaching women, we have two choices: to lend our weight to the forces that indoctrinate women to passivity, self-depreciation, and a sense of powerlessness, in which case the issue of "taking women students seriously" is a moot one; or to consider what we have to work against, as well as with, in ourselves, in our students, in the content of the curriculum, in the structure of the institution, in the society at large. And this means, first of all, taking ourselves seriously: Recognizing that central responsibility of a woman to herself, without which we remain always the Other, the defined, the object, the victim; believing that there is a unique quality of validation, affirmation, challenge, support, that one woman can offer another. Believing in the value and significance of women's experience, traditions, perceptions. Thinking of ourselves seriously, not as one of the boys, not as neuters, or androgynes, but *as women*.

Suppose we were to ask ourselves, simply: What does a woman need to know? Does she not, as a self-conscious, self-defining human being, need a knowledge of her own history, her much-politicized biology, an awareness of the creative work of women of the past, the skills and crafts and techniques and powers exercised by women in different times and cultures, a knowledge of women's rebellions and organized movements against our oppression and how they have been routed or diminished? Without such knowledge women live and have lived without context, vulnerable to the projections of male fantasy, male prescriptions for us, estranged from our own experience because our education has not reflected or echoed it. I would suggest that not biology, but ignorance of our selves, has been the key to our powerlessness.

But the university curriculum, the high-school curriculum, do not provide this kind of knowledge for women, the knowledge of Womankind, whose experience has been so profoundly different from that of Mankind. Only in the precariously budgeted, much-condescended-to area of women's studies is such knowledge available to women students. Only there can they learn about the lives and work of women other than the few select women who are included in the "mainstream" texts, usually misrepresented even when they do appear. Some students, at some institutions, manage to take a majority of courses in women's studies, but the message from on high is that this is self-indulgence, soft-core education: the "real" learning is the study of Mankind.

If there is any misleading concept, it is that of "coeducation": that because women and men are sitting in the same classrooms, hearing the same lectures, reading the same books, performing the same laboratory experiments, they are receiving an equal education. They are not, first because the content of education itself validates men even as it invalidates women. Its very message is that men have been the shapers and thinkers of the world, and that this is only natural. The bias of higher education, including the so-called sciences, is white and male, racist and sexist; and this bias is expressed in both subtle and blatant ways. I have mentioned already the exclusiveness of grammar itself: "The student should test himself on the above questions"; "The poet is representative. He stands among partial men for the complete man." Despite a few half-hearted departures from custom, what the linguist Wendy Martyna has named "He-Man" grammar prevails throughout the culture. The efforts of feminists to reveal the profound ontological implications of sexist grammar are routinely ridiculed by academicians and journalists, including the professedly liberal *Times* columnist, Tom Wicker, and the professed humanist, Jacques Barzun. Sexist grammar burns into the brains of little girls and young women a message that the male is the norm, the standard, the central figure beside which we are the deviants, the marginal, the dependent variables. It lays the foundation for androcentric thinking, and leaves men safe in their solipsistic tunnel-vision.

10   Women and men do not receive an equal education because outside the classroom women are perceived not as sovereign beings but as prey. The growing incidence of rape on and off the campus may or may not be fed by the proliferations of pornographic magazines and X-rated films available to young males in fraternities and student unions; but it is certainly occurring in a context of widespread images of sexual violence against women, on billboards and in so-called high art. More subtle, more daily than rape is the verbal abuse experienced by the woman student on many campuses—Rutgers for example—where, traversing a street lined with fraternity houses, she must run a gauntlet of male commentary and verbal assault. The undermining of self, of a woman's sense of her right to occupy space and walk freely in the world, is deeply relevant to education. The capacity to think independently, to take intellectual risks, to assert ourselves mentally, is inseparable from our physical way of being in the world, our feelings of personal integrity. If it is dangerous for me to walk home late of an evening from the library, *because I am a woman and can be raped*, how self-possessed, how exuberant can I feel as I sit working in that library? how much of my working energy is drained by the subliminal knowledge that, as a woman, I test my physical right to exist each time I go out alone? Of this knowledge, Susan Griffin has written:

... more than rape itself, the fear of rape permeates our lives. And what does one do from day to day, with *this* experience, which says, without words and directly to the heart, *your existence, your experience, may end at any moment.* Your experience may end, and the best defense against this is not to be, to deny being in the body, as a self, to ... avert your gaze, make yourself, as a presence in the world, less felt.

Finally, rape of the mind. Women students are more and more often now reporting sexual overtures by male professors—one part of our overall growing consciousness of sexual harassment in the workplace. At Yale a legal suit has been brought against the university by a group of women demanding an explicit policy against sexual advances toward female students by male professors. Most young women experience a profound mixture of humiliation and intellectual self-doubt over seductive gestures by men who have the power to award grades, open doors to grants and graduate school, or extend special knowledge and training. Even if turned aside, such gestures constitute mental rape, destructive to a woman's ego. They are acts of domination, as despicable as the molestation of the daughter by the father.

But long before entering college the woman student has experienced her alien identity in a world which misnames her, turns her to its own uses, denying her the resources she needs to become self-affirming, self-defined. The nuclear family teaches her that relationships are more important than selfhood or work; that "whether the phone rings for you, and how often," having the right clothes, doing the dishes, take precedence over study or solitude; that too much intelligence or intensity may make her unmarriageable; that marriage and children—service to others—are, finally, the points on which her life will be judged a success or a failure. In high school, the polarization between feminine attractiveness and independent intelligence comes to an absolute. Meanwhile, the culture resounds with messages. During Solar Energy Week in New York I saw young women wearing "ecology" T-shirts with the legend: CLEAN, CHEAP AND AVAILABLE; a reminder of the 1960s antiwar button which read: CHICKS SAY YES TO MEN WHO SAY NO. Department store windows feature female mannequins in chains, pinned to the wall with legs spread, smiling in positions of torture. Feminists are depicted in the media as "shrill," "strident," "puritanical," or "humorless," and the lesbian choice—the choice of the woman-identified woman—as pathological or sinister. The young woman sitting in the philosophy classroom, the political science lecture, is already gripped by tensions between her nascent sense of self-worth, and the battering force of messages like these.

Look at a classroom: look at the many kinds of women's faces, postures, expressions. Listen to the women's voices. Listen to the silences, the unasked questions, the blanks. Listen to the small, soft voices, often courageously trying to speak up, voices of women taught early that tones of confidence, challenge, anger, or assertiveness, are strident and unfeminine. Listen to the voices of women and the voices of men; observe the space men allow themselves, physically and verbally, the male assumption that people will listen, even when the majority of the group is female. Look at the faces of the silent, and of those who speak. Listen to a woman groping for language in which to express what is on her mind, sensing that the terms of academic discourse are not her language, trying to cut down her thought to the dimensions of a discourse not intended for her (*for it is not fitting that a woman speak in public*); or reading her paper aloud at breakneck speed, throwing her words away, deprecating her own work by a reflex prejudgment: *I do not deserve to take up time and space.*

As women teachers, we can either deny the importance of this context in which women students think, write, read, study, project their own futures; or try to work with it. We can either teach passively, accepting these conditions, or actively, helping our students identify and resist them.

15   One important thing we can do is *discuss* the context. And this need not happen only in a women's studies course; it can happen anywhere. We can refuse to accept passive, obedient learning and insist upon critical thinking. We can become harder on our women students, giving them the kinds of "cultural prodding" that men receive, but on different terms and in a different style. Most young women need to have their intellectual lives, their work, legitimized against the claims of family, relationships, the old message that a woman is always available for service to others. We need to keep our standards very high, not to accept a woman's preconceived sense of her limitations; we need to be hard to please, while supportive of risk-taking, because self-respect often comes only when exacting standards have been met. At a time when adult literacy is generally low, we need to demand more, not less, of women, both for the sake of their futures as thinking beings, and because historically women have always had to be better than men to do half as well. A romantic sloppiness, an inspired lack of rigor, a self-indulgent incoherence, are symptoms of female self-depreciation. We should help our women students to look very critically at such symptoms, and to understand where they are rooted.

Nor does this mean we should be training women students to "think like men." Men in general think badly: in disjuncture from their personal lives, claiming objectivity where the most irrational passions seethe, losing, as Virginia Woolf observed, their senses in the pursuit of professionalism. It is not easy to think like a woman in a man's world, in the world of the professions; yet the capacity to do that is a strength which we can try to help our students develop. To think like a woman in a man's world means thinking critically, refusing to accept the givens, making connections between facts and ideas which men have left unconnected. It means remembering that every mind resides in a body; remaining accountable to the female bodies in which we live; constantly retesting given hypotheses against lived experience. It means a constant critique of language, for as Wittgenstein (no feminist) observed, "The limits of my language are the limits of my world." And it means that most difficult thing of all: listening and watching in art and literature, in the social sciences, in all the descriptions we are given of the world, for the silences, the absences, the nameless, the unspoken, the encoded—for there we will find the true knowledge of women. And in breaking those silences, naming our selves, uncovering the hidden, making ourselves present, we begin to define a reality which resonates to *us*, which affirms *our* being, which allows the woman teacher and the woman student alike to take ourselves, and each other, seriously: meaning, to begin taking charge of our lives.

(1978)

INVISIBILITY IN ACADEME

The history of North American lesbians under white domination begins with the death penalty prescribed for lesbians in 1656 in New Haven, Connecticut. Three hundred years later, in the 1950s, lesbians were being beaten in the city streets, committed to mental institutions, forced to undergo psychosurgery, often at their parents' instigation. Thirty years after that, in the mid-1980s, despite the struggles and visions of both the Women's Liberation movement and the gay liberation movement, lesbians are still being assaulted in the streets—during the past year in the streets of Northampton, Massachusetts, the site of a women's college near which I live. Lesbians are still being forced to endure behavior modification and medical punishment, are still banished from families, are rejected by our ethnic, racial, and religious communities, must pretend to be heterosexual in order to hold jobs, have custody of their children, rent apartments, publicly represent a larger community.

Beside all this, invisibility may seem a small price to pay (as in "All we ask is that you keep your private life private" or "Just don't use the word"). But invisibility is a dangerous and painful condition, and lesbians are not the only people to know it. When those who have power to name and to socially construct reality choose not to see you or hear you, whether you are dark-skinned, old, disabled, female, or speak with a different accent or dialect than theirs, when someone with the authority of a teacher, say, describes the world and you are not in it, there is a moment of psychic disequilibrium, as if you looked into a mirror and saw nothing. Yet you know you exist and others like you, that this is a game with mirrors. It takes some strength of soul—and not just individual strength, but collective understanding—to resist this void, this nonbeing, into which you are thrust, and to stand up, demanding to be seen and heard. And to make yourself visible, to claim that your experience is just as real and normative as any other, as "moral and ordinary" in the words of historian Blanche Cook, can mean making yourself vulnerable. But at least you are not doing the oppressor's work, building your own closet. It is important to me to remember that in the nineteenth century, women—all women—were forbidden by law to speak in public meetings. Society depended on their muteness. But some, and then more and more, refused to be mute and spoke up. Without them, we would not even be here today.

I have been for ten years a very public and visible lesbian. I have been identified as a lesbian in print both by myself and others; I have worked in the lesbian-feminist movement. Here in Claremont, where I have been received with much warmth and hospitality, I have often felt invisible as a lesbian. I have felt my identity as a feminist threatening to some, welcome to others; but my identity as a lesbian is something that many people would prefer not to know about. And this experience has reminded me of what I should never have let myself forget: that invisibility is not just a matter of being told to keep your private life private; it's the attempt to fragment you, to prevent you from integrating love and work and feelings and ideas, with the empowerment that that can bring.

I'm not talking only about this community. There are many places, including Women's Studies programs, where this fragmentation goes on. The basis for dialogue and discussion remains heterosexual, while perhaps a section of a reading list or a single class period is supposed to "include" lesbian experience and thought. In an almost identical way, the experience and thought of women of color is relegated to a special section, added as an afterthought, while the central discourse remains unrelentingly white, usually middle-class in its assumptions and priorities. The name of the second set of blinders is racism; of the first, heterosexism. The Black political scientist Gloria I. Joseph, in a talk on "Third World Women and Feminism," has suggested that *homophobia* is an inaccurate term, implying a form of uncontrollable mental panic, and that *heterosexism* better describes what is really a deeply ingrained prejudice, comparable to racism, sexism, and classism—a political indoctrination which must be recognized as such and which can be re-educated.

I want to suggest that it is impossible for any woman growing up in   5
a gendered society dominated by men to know what heterosexuality really means, both historically and in her individual life, so long as she is kept ignorant of the presence, the existence, the actuality of women who, diverse in so many ways, have centered their emotional and erotic lives on women. A young woman entering her twenties in a blur of stereotypes and taboos, with a vague sense of anxiety centering around the word *lesbian*, is ill equipped to think about herself, her feelings, her options, her relations with men *or* women. This ignorance and anxiety, which affects lesbians and heterosexually identified women alike, this silence, this absence of a whole population, this invisibility, is disempowering for all women. It is not only lesbian students who should be calling for a recognition of their history and presence in the world; it is *all* women who want a more accurate map of the way social relations have been and are, as they try to imagine what might be.

I think that those of us who are lesbians here sense that there are people who want to meet us in our wholeness instead of fragments, and others who do not want to know, who run away, who want us to be quiet, who will use all kinds of indirect and genteel means to keep us that way, including the charge that we never talk about anything else. I believe there is a critical mass in this community—not only lesbians—who recognize the intellectual and moral sterility of heterosexism. I hope that we can find ways of speaking with each other that will strengthen a collective understanding that will keep discussion continuing long after this conference is over.

(1984)

Questions

1. What elements of "Taking Women Students Seriously" reflect the care with which Rich has paid attention to her audience? What sorts of changes in diction, syntax, or tone might be appropriate were an address on the same topic to be made to high school students?

2. In paragraphs 8 and 9 of "Taking Women Students Seriously," Rich flushes out a point about exclusivity in language that she has touched on in paragraph 5. In a paragraph, summarize in your own words Rich's argument about language.

3. How does the ordering of the ideas Rich expresses in the first sentence of paragraph 10 of "Taking Women Students Seriously" intensify their provocative quality? To what extent (if at all) is it an exaggeration to describe women outside the classroom in universities as being perceived as "prey"?

4. Do you believe that men and women think differently? Discuss with reference to paragraph 16 in "Taking Women Students Seriously."

5. To what extent do you think the situation described by Rich in "Taking Women Students Seriously" has altered since 1978?

6. Explain in your own words what Rich means by "invisibility" for lesbians. In a short essay describe the attitude towards gays and lesbians in your own university; is the most common attitude the sort of expectation of invisibility that Rich describes?

MIKE ROYKO

ANOTHER ACCOLADE FOR CHARTER ARMS CORP.

*The occasion for this 1980 newspaper article by a
leading American columnist was the shooting of
John Lennon outside his residence in New York City.*

❧

I was pleased to see that the stories reporting the death of John Lennon were specific and accurate about the kind of gun that was used to murder the world-renowned musician.

It was a .38 caliber pistol made by Charter Arms Corp. of Bridgeport, Conn.

You might ask: What difference does it make what kind of gun was used?

It makes a great deal of difference. Especially to Charter Arms Corp.

There are guns and then there are guns. Cheap guns, ordinary guns, and finely crafted guns.

And when people become emotional about guns, as many do when somebody famous is killed, they tend to lump all guns together. They don't show proper respect for an excellent gun, such as the Charter .38.

It happens this is not the first time a famous person has been shot by this make of weapon. When former Alabama Gov. George C. Wallace was shot and paralyzed for life by another deranged person in 1974, the bullet that tore into his spine came from a Charter .38.

If I'm not mistaken, that makes the Charter .38 the first gun in modern times to have two famous people to its credit. The weapons used to blast President Kennedy, the Rev. Dr. Martin Luther King, Jr., and Sen. Robert F. Kennedy were all of different manufacture.

When Wallace was shot, a CBS reporter made it obvious that he didn't know a fine gun from a cheap gun.

10   The reporter went on network TV and said that Wallace had been wounded by a "cheap handgun." He obviously had in mind the kind of Saturday Night Special that is so popular among the criminal riffraff who have no respect for quality and workmanship.

When the proud executives of Charter Arms Corp. heard the reporter, they became indignant.

They contacted the CBS and demanded an apology. The incident was described in an editorial in the company magazine of the Charter Corp.

The editorial, which was headlined "An Apology from CBS," said:

> "We are too dedicated to high quality in American-made handguns and have poured too much of ourselves into our products to have one of them even casually referred to as a 'cheap handgun.'
>
>   "That was exactly the phrase used in a broadcast description of the handgun used by Arthur Bremer in his assassination attempt on Gov. Wallace, which happened to be one of our Undercover .38 Specials.
>
>   "The broadcast emanated from CBS ... and our public relations people were immediately instructed to bring the error to their attention."

The editorial went on to say that an apology was indeed received from CBS network vice-president, who contritely told Charter Arms Corp., "I am sending a copy of your letter to all our TV producers. In the event that we make reference to the Undercover .38 Special used by Arthur Bremer, we will certainly avoid characterizing it as a 'Saturday Night Special' or any other term which labels it as a 'cheap weapon.'"

15   Presumably that soothed the wounded pride of the gunmakers at Charter Arms Corp., since no further public protests were heard.

And you can't blame them for having felt hurt at such a slur on their product. When Wallace was shot, a Charter .38 cost $105. Today, with rising prices, the gun costs about $180 or $190, depending on where you do your gun shopping.

That is not a cheap gun, especially when compared to the trashy weapons that some gunmen, to whom quality is unimportant, arm themselves with.

Now I don't know if it was mere coincidence that both Bremer, who shot Wallace, and Mark David Chapman, who apparently shot Lennon, used the same weapon. Or if it was that they both recognized quality when they saw it, and were willing to spend money to get the best.

But the fact is, both opted for quality and they got what they paid for. There was no misfiring, no jamming, no bullet flying off line, and no gun exploding in their hands—all of which can happen when one uses a cheap gun.

True, Wallace wasn't killed. That was the fault of Bremer, not the Charter gun. Bremer shot Wallace in the stomach, which isn't the best place to shoot a person if you want to kill him.

But even in that case, the gun did its job—blowing a terrible hole in Wallace's gut and putting him into a wheelchair for good.

In the case of Lennon, you couldn't ask for a better performance from a gun. Lennon was shot several times, but according to the doctor who pronounced him dead, the first bullet hit him in the chest and killed him on the spot. The other shots weren't even necessary.

You can never be sure of getting those kinds of results from a Saturday Night Special.

Now the Charter Arms Corp. has the unique distinction of having two famous people shot by one of their products, I wonder if they have considered using it in their advertising. Something simple and tasteful like: "The .38 that got George Wallace AND John Lennon. See it at your gun dealer now."

If so, they shouldn't wait. With so many handguns—both cheap and of high quality—easily available to Americans, it could be just a matter of time until another manufacturer moves into the lead in the famous-person derby. All it would take would be a few pop-pop-pops from say, a Colt—maybe a politician or two and another rock star or two—and they would have the lead.

On the other hand, maybe Charter Arms Corp. doesn't want recognition—just the kind of pride one feels in a job of fine craftsmanship.

If so, they have a right to feel proud.

Once again, your product really did the job, gents.

(1980)

Questions

1. Compare the paragraphing in this essay with that in other essays in this anthology. To what do you attribute the difference?

2. It is a repeated pattern that popular support for gun control measures rises dramatically after high profile violent incidents such as the

assassinations of Martin Luther King, Jr. and Robert Kennedy in 1968, the killing of Lennon in 1980, the Montreal Massacre in 1989, and the Columbine High School shootings in 1998. With reference to any of these and/or to other incidents you are aware of, write an essay arguing for or against one or more aspects of gun control.

Luis W. Alvarez, Walter Alvarez,
Frank Asaro, and Helen V. Michel

Extraterrestrial Cause for the Cretaceous-Tertiary Extinction

*This scientific article led to a breakthrough concerning the
cause of the great extinction that eliminated the dinosaurs sixty-
five million years ago. The authors posit the hypothesis, now
well-known but extremely controversial at the time,
that an asteroid impact led to the extinction.*

ℯ

Summary

Platinum metals are depleted in the earth's crust relative to their cosmic abundance; concentrations of these elements in deep-sea sediments may thus indicate influxes of extraterrestrial material. Deep-sea limestones exposed in Italy, Denmark, and New Zealand show iridium increases of about 30, 160, and 20 times, respectively, above the background level at precisely the time of the Cretaceous-Tertiary extinctions, 65 million years ago. Reasons are given to indicate that this iridium is of extraterrestrial origin, but did not come from a nearby supernova. A hypothesis is suggested which accounts for the extinctions and the iridium observations. Impact of a large earth-crossing asteroid would inject about 60 times the object's mass into the atmosphere as pulverized rock; a fraction of this dust would stay in the stratosphere for several years and be distributed worldwide. The resulting darkness would suppress photosynthesis, and the expected biological consequences match quite closely the extinctions observed in the paleontological record. One prediction of this hypothesis has been verified: the chemical composition of the boundary clay, which is thought to come from the stratospheric dust, is markedly different from that of clay mixed with the Cretaceous and Tertiary limestones, which are chemically similar to each other. Four different independent estimates of the diameter of the asteroid give values that lie in the range 10 ± 4 kilometers.

In the 570-million-year period for which abundant fossil remains are available, there have been five great biological crises, during which many groups of organisms died out. The most recent of the great extinctions is used to define the boundary between the Cretaceous and Tertiary periods, about 65 million years ago. At this time, the marine reptiles, the flying reptiles, and both orders of dinosaurs died out (*1*), and extinctions occurred at various taxonomic levels among the marine invertebrates. Dramatic extinctions occurred among the microscopic floating animals and plants; both the calcareous planktonic foraminifera and the calcareous nannoplankton[1] were nearly exterminated, with only a few species surviving the crisis. On the other hand, some groups were little affected, including the land plants, crocodiles, snakes, mammals, and many kinds of invertebrates. Russell (*2*) concludes that about half of the genera living at that time perished during the extinction event.

Many hypotheses have been proposed to explain the Cretaceous-Tertiary (C-T) extinctions (*3, 4*) and two recent meetings on the topic (*5, 6*) produced no sign of a consensus. Suggested causes include gradual or rapid changes in oceanographic, atmospheric, or climatic conditions (*7*) due to a random (*8*) or a cyclical (*9*) coincidence of causative factors; a magnetic reversal (*10*); a nearby supernova (*11*); and the flooding of the ocean surface by fresh water from a postulated arctic lake (*12*).

A major obstacle to determining the cause of the extinction is that virtually all the available information on events at the time of the crisis deals with biological changes seen in the paleontological record and is therefore inherently indirect. Little physical evidence is available, and it also is indirect. This includes variations in stable oxygen and carbon isotopic ratios[2] across the boundary in pelagic sediments,[3] which may reflect changes in temperature, salinity, oxygenation, and organic productivity of the ocean

---

1   *calcareous planktonic ... nannoplankton*   Drifting water organisms with shells or other body structures made of calcium carbonate.

2   *isotopic ratios*   Ratios between different atom types of the same chemical element; e.g., an oxygen isotopic ratio is the ratio of oxygen with eight neutrons to that with ten neutrons.

3   *pelagic sediments*   Accumulations of clay and organic matter on the ocean floor.

water, and which are not easy to interpret (*13, 14*). These isotopic changes are not particularly striking and, taken by themselves, would not suggest a dramatic crisis. Small changes in minor and trace element levels at the C-T boundary have been noted from limestone sections in Denmark and Italy (*15*), but these data also present interpretational difficulties. It is noteworthy that in pelagic marine sequences, where nearly continuous deposition is to be expected, the C-T boundary is commonly marked by a hiatus (*3, 16*).

In this article we present direct physical evidence for an unusual event at exactly the time of the extinctions in the planktonic realm. None of the current hypotheses adequately accounts for this evidence, but we have developed a hypothesis that appears to offer a satisfactory explanation for nearly all the available paleontological and physical evidence.

IDENTIFICATION OF EXTRATERRESTRIAL PLATINUM METALS IN DEEP-SEA SEDIMENTS

This study began with the realization that the platinum group elements (platinum, iridium, osmium, and rhodium) are much less abundant in the earth's crust and upper mantle than they are in chondritic meteorites[4] and average solar system material. Depletion of the platinum-group elements in the earth's crust and upper mantle is probably the result of concentration of these elements in the earth's core.

Pettersson and Rotschi (*17*) and Goldschmidt (*18*) suggested that the low concentrations of platinum group elements in sedimentary rocks might come largely from meteoritic dust formed by ablation[5] when meteorites passed through the atmosphere. Barker and Anders (*19*) showed that there was a correlation between sedimentation rate and iridium concentration, confirming the earlier suggestions. Subsequently, the method was used by Ganapathy, Brownlee, and Hodge (*20*) to demonstrate an extraterrestrial origin for silicate spherules in deep-sea sediments. Sarna-Wojeicki *et al.* (*21*) suggested that meteoric dust accumulation in soil layers might enhance the abundance of iridium sufficiently to permit its use as a dating tool. Recently, Crocket and Kuo (*22*) reported iridium abundances in deep-sea sediments and summarized other previous work.

---

4   *chondritic meteorites* Meteorites composed of chondrules, millimeter-sized objects that were originally free-floating in space.

5   *ablation* I.e., the vaporization of outer layers caused by high temperatures.

Considerations of this type (23) prompted us to measure the iridium concentration in the 1-centimeter-thick clay layer that marks the C-T boundary in some sections in the Umbrian Apennines,[6] in the hope of determining the length of time represented by that layer. Iridium can easily be determined at low levels by neutron activation analysis[7] (NAA) (24).... The other platinum group elements are more difficult to determine by NAA.

ITALIAN STRATIGRAPHIC SECTIONS

Many aspects of earth history are best recorded in pelagic sedimentary rocks, which gradually accumulate in the relatively quiet waters of the deep sea as individual grains settle to the bottom. In the Umbrian Apennines of northern peninsular Italy there are exposures of pelagic sedimentary rocks representing the time from Early Jurassic to Oligocene, around 185 to 30 million years ago (25)....

10   In well-exposed, complete sections[8] there is a bed of clay about 1 cm thick between the highest Cretaceous and the lowest Tertiary limestone beds (28). This bed is free of primary $CaCO_3$,[9] so there is no record of the biological changes during the time interval represented by the clay. The boundary is further marked by a zone in the uppermost Cretaceous in which the normally pink limestone is white in color. This zone is 0.3 to 1.0 meter thick, varying from section to section. Its lower boundary is a gradational color change; its upper boundary is abrupt and coincides with the faunal and floral extinctions. In one section (Contessa) we can see that the lower 5 mm of the boundary clay is gray and the upper 5 mm is red, thus placing the upper boundary of the zone in the middle of the clay layer....

RESULTS FROM THE ITALIAN SECTIONS

Our first experiments involved NAA of nine samples from the Bottaccione section (two limestone samples from immediately above and below the boundary plus seven limestone samples spaced over 325 m of the

---

6   *Umbrian Apennines*   A mountain range in the Italian Peninsula.

7   *neutron activation analysis*   A process for determining the composition of elements in a material by bombarding samples with neutrons and measuring the resulting radioactive emissions.

8   *sections*   I.e., stratigraphic sections, sequences of layered rocks and sediment.

9   *$CaCO_3$*   Calcium carbonate, the main component of limestone.

Cretaceous). This was supplemented by three samples from the nearby Contessa section (two from the boundary clay and one from the basal[10] Tertiary bed)....

Figure 5 shows the results of 29 Ir[11] analyses completed on Italian samples. Note that the section is enlarged and that the scale is linear in the vicinity of the C-T boundary, where details are important, but changes to logarithmic to show results from 350 m below to 50 m above the boundary. It is also important to note that analyses from five stratigraphic sections are plotted on the same diagram on the basis of their stratigraphic position above or below the boundary. Because slight differences in sedimentation rate probably exist from one section to the next, the chronologic sequence of samples from different sections may not be exactly correct. Nevertheless, Fig. 5 gives a clear picture of the general trend of iridium concentrations as a function of stratigraphic level.

The pattern, based especially on the samples from the Bottaccione Gorge and Gorgo a Cerbara, shows a steady background level of ~ 0.3 ppb[12] throughout the Upper Cretaceous, continuing into the uppermost bed of the Cretaceous. The background level in the acid-insoluble residues[13] is roughly comparable to the iridium abundance measured by other workers (*19, 22, 32*) in deep-sea clay sediments. This level increases abruptly by a factor of more than 30, to 9.1 ppb, the Ir abundance in the red clay from the Contessa section. Iridium levels are high in clay residues from the first few beds of Tertiary limestone, but fall off to background levels by 1 m above the boundary. For comparison, the upper dashed line in Fig. 5 shows an exponential decay from the boundary clay Ir level with a half-height of 4.6 cm.

To test the possibility that iridium might somehow be concentrated in clay layers, we subsequently analyzed two red clay samples from a short distance below the C-T boundary in the Bottaccione section. One is from a distinctive clay layer 5 to 6 mm thick, 1.73 m below the boundary; the other is from a 1- to 2-mm bedding-plane[14] clay seam 0.85 m below the

---

10 *basal* Lowest.

11 *Ir* Iridium.

12 *ppb* Parts per billion.

13 *acid-insoluble residues* Products of a chemical process used to determine the proportions of mineral components in a rock, such as the quantity of iridium.

14 *bedding-plane* Division between two rock layers.

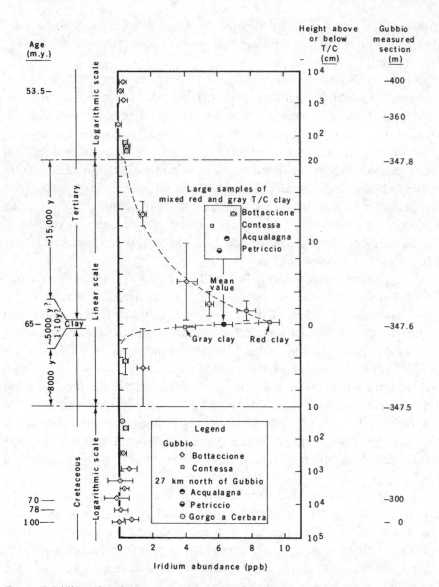

Figure 5. Iridium abundances per unit weight of $2N\ HNO_3$ acid-insoluble residues from Italian limestones near the Tertiary-Cretaceous boundary. Error bars on abundances are the standard deviations in counting radioactivity. Error bars on stratigraphic position indicate the stratigraphic thickness of the sample. The dashed line above the boundary is an "eyeball fit" exponential with a half-height of 4.6 cm. The dashed line below the boundary is a best fit exponential (two points) with a half-height of 0.43 cm. The filled circle and error bar are the mean and standard deviation of Ir abundances in four large samples of boundary clay from different locations.

boundary. The whole-rock analyses[15] of these clays showed no detectable Ir with limits of 0.5 and 0.24 ppb, respectively. Thus neither clay layers from below the C-T boundary nor clay components in the limestone show evidence of Ir above the background level.

THE DANISH SECTION

To test whether the iridium anomaly is a local Italian feature, it was desirable to analyze segments of similar age from another region. The sea cliff of Stevns Klint, about 50 km south of Copenhagen, is a classical area for the C-T boundary and for the Danian or basal stage of the Tertiary. A collection of up-to-date papers on this and nearby areas has recently been published, which includes a full bibliography of earlier works (*6*, vol. 1)....

A SUDDEN INFLUX OF EXTRATERRESTRIAL MATERIAL

To test whether the anomalous iridium at the C-T boundary in the Gubbio sections is of extraterrestrial origin, we considered the increases in 27 of the 28 elements measured by NAA that would be expected if iridium in excess of the background level came from a source with the average composition of the earth's crust. The crustal Ir abundance, less than 0.1 ppb (*19, 22*), is too small to be a worldwide source for material with an Ir abundance of 6.3 ppb, as found near Gubbio. Extraterrestrial sources with Ir levels of hundreds of parts per billion or higher are more likely to have produced the Ir anomaly. Figure 10 shows that if the source had an average earth's crust composition (*46*), increases significantly above those observed would be expected in all 27 elements. However, for a source with average carbonaceous chondrite[16] composition (*46*), only nickel should show an elemental increase greater than that observed. As shown in Fig. 11, such an increase in nickel was not observed, but the predicted effect is small and, given appropriate conditions, nickel oxide would dissolve in seawater (*47*). We conclude that the pattern of elemental abundances in the Gubbio sections

---

15 *whole-rock analyses* Results of a chemical process that, like acid-insoluble residue analysis, can be used to determine the proportion of elements, such as iridium, in a rock.

16 *carbonaceous chondrite* Chondritic meteorite containing high proportions of water and organic compounds.

is compatible with an extraterrestrial source for the anomalous iridium and incompatible with a crustal source....

We next consider whether the Ir anomaly is due to an abnormal influx of extraterrestrial material at the time of the extinctions, or whether it was formed by the normal, slow accumulation of meteoric material (*19*), followed by concentration in the boundary rocks by some identifiable mechanism.

There is prima facie evidence for an abnormal influx in the observations that the excess iridium occurs exactly at the time of one of the extinctions; that the extinctions were clearly worldwide; and that the iridium anomaly is now known from two different areas in western Europe and in New Zealand. Furthermore, we will show in a later section that impact of a 10-km earth-crossing asteroid, an event that probably occurs with about the same frequency as major extinctions, may have produced the observed physical

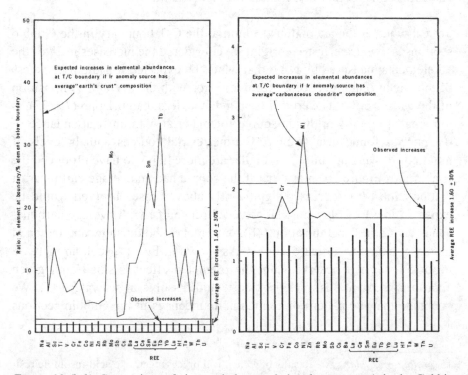

Figure 10 (left). Comparison of observed elemental abundance patterns in the Gubbio section samples with average patterns expected for crustal material (*46*). *Figure 11 (right)*. Comparison of observed elemental abundance patterns in the Gubbio section samples with patterns expected for carbonaceous chondrites (*46*).

and biological effects. Nevertheless, one can invent two other scenarios that might lead to concentration of normal background iridium at the boundary. These appear to be much less likely than the sudden-influx model, but we cannot definitely rule out either one at present.

The first scenario requires a physical or chemical change in the ocean waters at the time of the extinctions, leading to extraction of iridium resident in the seawater. This would require iridium concentrations in seawater that are higher than those presently observed. In addition, it suggests that the positive iridium anomaly should be accompanied by a compensating negative anomaly immediately above, but this is not seen.

The second scenario postulates a reduction in the deposition rate of all components of the pelagic sediment except for the meteoritic dust that carries the concentrated iridium. This scenario requires removal of clay but not of iridium-bearing particles, perhaps by currents of exactly the right velocity. These currents must have affected both the Italian and Danish areas at exactly the time of the C-T extinctions, but at none of the other times represented by our samples. We feel that this scenario is too contrived, a conclusion that is justified in more detail elsewhere (23).

20

In summary, we conclude that the anomalous iridium concentration at the C-T boundary is best interpreted as indicating an abnormal influx of extraterrestrial material....

The Asteroid Impact Hypothesis

After obtaining negative results in our tests of the supernova hypothesis,[17] we were left with the question of what extraterrestrial source within the solar system could supply the observed iridium and also cause the extinctions. We considered and rejected a number of hypotheses (23); finally, we found that an extension of the meteorite impact hypothesis (55, 56) provided a scenario that explains most or all of the biological and physical evidence. In brief, our hypothesis suggests that an asteroid struck the earth, formed an impact crater, and some of the dust-sized material ejected from the crater reached the stratosphere and was spread around the globe. This dust effectively prevented sunlight from reaching the surface for a period of several years, until the dust settled to earth. Loss of sunlight suppressed photosynthesis, and as a result most food chains collapsed and extinctions

---

17 *supernova hypothesis* In the previous section, not included here, Alvarez et al. consider and reject the possibility that a supernova was the source of the iridium.

resulted. Several lines of evidence support this hypothesis, as discussed in the next few sections. The size of the impacting object can be calculated from four independent sets of observations, with good agreement among the four different diameter estimates.

Earth-Crossing Asteroids and Earth Craters

Two quite different data bases show that for the last billion years the earth has been bombarded by a nearly constant flux of asteroids that cross the earth's orbit. One data base comes from astronomical observations of such asteroids and a tabulation of their orbital parameters and their distribution of diameters (57). Öpik (58) computed that the mean time to collision with the earth for a given earth-crossing asteroid is about 200 million years.... Shoemaker (61) estimates that a mean collision time of 100 million years is consistent with a diameter of 10 km, which is the value we will adopt. A discussion of cratering data, which leads to similar estimates, is given in Grieve and Robertson's review article (62) on the size and age distribution of large impact craters on the earth. Rather than present our lengthy justi-fication (23) for the estimates based on the cratering data, we will simply report the evaluation of Grieve (63), who wrote: "I can find nothing in our data that is at odds with your premise." Grieve also estimates that the diam-eter of the crater formed by the impact of a 10-km asteroid would be about 200 km (63). This section of our article has thus been greatly condensed now that we have heard from experienced students of the two data bases involved.

Krakatoa

The largest well-studied terrestrial explosion in historical times was that of the island volcano, Krakatoa, in the Sunda Strait, between Java and Sumatra (64). Since this event provides the best available data on injection of dust into the stratosphere, we give here a brief summary of relevant information.

On 26 and 27 August 1883, Krakatoa underwent volcanic eruptions that shot an estimated 18 km^3 of material into the atmosphere, of which about 4 km^3 ended up in the stratosphere, where it stayed for 2 to 2.5 years. Dust from the explosion circled the globe, quickly giving rise to brilliant sunsets seen worldwide. Recent measurements of the $^{14}C^{18}$ injected into

25

---

18 ^{14}C Carbon-14, a radioactive isotope of carbon.

the atmosphere by nuclear bomb tests confirm the rapid mixing (about 1 year) between hemispheres (65). If we take the estimated dust mass in the stratosphere (4 km^3 times the assumed low density of 2 g/cm^3) and spread it uniformly over the globe, it amounts to 1.6 x 10^{-3} g/cm^2. This layer did not absorb much of the incident radiation[19] on a "straight-through" basis. However, if it were increased by a factor of about 10^3 (a rough prediction of our theory), it is most probable that the sunlight would be attenuated to a high degree.

Since the time for the colored sunsets to disappear after Krakatoa is frequently given as 2 to 2.5 years, we have assumed that the asteroid impact material in the stratosphere settled in a few years. Thus, 65 million years ago, day could have been turned into night for a period of several years, after which time the atmosphere would return relatively quickly to its normal transparent state.

What happened during the Krakatoa explosions can be expected to happen to a much greater extent during the impact of a large asteroid. An interesting difference is that extreme atmospheric turbulence would follow the impact. The asteroid would enter the atmosphere at roughly 25 km/sec and would "punch a hole" in the atmosphere about 10 km across. The kinetic energy of the asteroid is approximately equivalent to that of 10^8 megatons of TNT.

SIZE OF THE IMPACTING OBJECT

If we are correct in our hypothesis that the C-T extinctions were due to the impact of an earth-crossing asteroid, there are four independent ways to calculate the size of the object. The four ways and the results obtained are outlined below.

1) The postulated size of the incoming asteroid was first computed from the iridium measurements in the Italian sections, the tabulated Ir abundances (66) in type I carbonaceous chondrites (CI), which are considered to be typical solar system material, and the fraction of erupted material estimated to end up in the stratosphere....

2) The second estimate comes from data on earth-crossing asteroids and the craters they have made on the earth's surface. In a sense, the second estimate comes from two quite different data bases—one from geology and the other from astronomy. Calculations of the asteroid diameter can be

30

---

19   *incident radiation*   I.e., sunlight.

made from both data bases, but they will not really be independent since the two data bases are known to be consistent with each other. As shown in an earlier section, the most believable calculation of the mean time between collisions of the earth and asteroids equal to or larger than 10 km in diameter is about 100 million years. The smaller the diameter the more frequent are the collisions, so our desire to fit not only the C-T extinction, but earlier ones as well, sets the mean time between extinctions at about 100 million years and the diameter at about 10 km....

3) The third method of estimating the size of the asteroid comes from the possibility that the 1-cm boundary layer at Gubbio and Copenhagen is composed of material that fell out of the stratosphere, and is not related to the clay that is mixed in with the limestone above and below it. This is quite a surprising prediction of the hypothesis, since the most obvious explanation for the origin of the clay is that it had the same source as the clay impurity in the rest of the Cretaceous and Tertiary limestone, and that it is nearly free of primary $CaCo_3$ because the extinction temporarily destroyed the calcite-producing plankton for about 5000 years. But as discussed earlier, the material in the boundary layer is of a different character from the clay above and below it, whereas the latter two clays are very similar....

The first and third methods are independent, even though they both depend on measurements made on the boundary material. This can best be appreciated by noting that if the Ir abundance were about the same in the earth's crust as it is in meteorites, the iridium anomaly seen in Fig. 5 would not exist. Therefore, method 1 would not exist either. The fact that method three could still be used is the indicator of the relative independence of the two methods.

4) The fourth method is not yet able to set close limits on the mass of the incoming asteroid, but it leads to consistent results. This method derives from the need to make the sky much more opaque than it was in the years following the Krakatoa explosion. If it is assumed that the Krakatoa dust cloud attenuated the vertically incident sunlight by about 3 percent, then an explosion involving 33 times as much material would reduce the light intensity to $1/e$. The stratospheric mass due to an explosion of the magnitude calculated in the three earlier methods—about 1000 times that of Krakatoa—would then be expected to reduce the sunlight to $\exp(-30)$ = 10^{-13}. This is, of course, much more light attenuation than is needed to stop photosynthesis. But the model used in this simplistic calculation assumes that the dust is a perfect absorber of the incident light. A reasonable

albedo[20] coupled with a slight reduction in the mass of dust can raise the light intensity under the assumed "optical depth" to 10^{-7} or normal sunlight, corresponding to 10 percent of full moonlight.

Although it is impossible to make an accurate estimate of the asteroid's size from the Krakatoa extrapolation, it would have been necessary to abandon the hypothesis had a serious discrepancy been apparent. In the absence of good measurements of the solar constant in the 1880s, it can only be said that the fourth method leads to asteroid sizes that are consistent with the other three.... We conclude that the data are consistent with an impacting asteroid with a diameter of about 10 ± 4 km.

BIOLOGICAL EFFECTS

A temporary absence of sunlight would effectively shut off photosynthesis and thus attack food chains at their origins. In a general way the effects to be expected from such an event are what one sees in the paleontological record of the extinction. 35

The food chain in the open ocean is based on microscopic floating plants, such as the coccolith-producing[21] algae, which show a nearly complete extinction. The animals at successively higher levels of the food chain were also very strongly affected, with nearly total extinction of the foraminifera and complete disappearance of the belemnites, ammonites,[22] and marine reptiles.

A second food chain is based on land plants. Among these plants, existing individuals would die, or at least stop producing new growth, during an interval of darkness, but after light returned they would regenerate from seeds, spores, and existing root systems. However, the large herbivorous and carnivorous animals that were directly or indirectly dependent on this vegetation would become extinct. Russell (2) states that "no terrestrial vertebrate heavier than about 25 kg is known to have survived the extinctions." Many smaller terrestrial vertebrates did survive, including the ancestral mammals, and they may have been able to do this by feeding on insects and decaying vegetation.

---

20 *albedo* I.e., ratio of light striking the earth to light reflected from the earth.

21 *coccolith* Calcium carbonate plate.

22 *belemnites* Cephalopods similar to cuttlefish; *ammonites* Cephalopods with coiled shells.

The situation among shallow marine bottom-dwelling invertebrates is less clear; some groups became extinct and others survived. A possible base for a temporary food chain in this environment is nutrients originating from the decaying land plants and animals and brought by rivers to the shallow marine waters.

We will not go further into this matter but we will refer the reader to the proceedings of the 1976 Ottawa meeting on the C-T extinction....

IMPLICATIONS

40   Among the many implications of the asteroid impact hypothesis, if it is correct, two stand out prominently. First, if the C-T extinctions were caused by an impact event, the same could be true of the earlier major extinctions as well. There have been five such extinctions since the end of the Precambrian, 570 million years ago, which matches well the probable interval of about 100 million years between collisions with 10-km diameter objects. Discussions of these extinction events generally list the organisms affected according to taxonomic groupings; it would be more useful to have this information given in terms of interpreted ecological or food-chain groupings. It will also be important to carry out iridium analyses in complete stratigraphic sections across these other boundaries. However, E. Shoemaker (private communication) predicts that if some of the extinctions were caused by the collision of a "fresh" comet (mostly ice), the Ir anomaly would not be seen even though the extinction mechanism was via the same dust cloud of crustal material, so the absence of a higher Ir concentration at, for example, the Permian-Triassic boundary would not invalidate our hypothesis. According to Shoemaker, cometary collisions in this size range could be twice as frequent as asteroidal collisions.

Second, we would like to find the crater produced by the impacting object. Only three craters 100 km or more in diameter are known (62). Two of these (Sudbury and Vredefort) are of Precambrian age. For the other, Popigay crater in Siberia, a stratigraphic age of Late Cretaceous to Quaternary and a potassium-aragon date of 28.8 million years (no further details given) have been reported (72, 73). Thus, Popigay crater is probably too young, and at 100-km-diameter probably also too small, to be the C-T impact site. There is about a 2/3 probability that the object fell in the ocean. Since the probable diameter of the object, 10 km, is twice the typical oceanic depth, a crater would be produced on the ocean bottom and pulverized rock would be ejected. However, in this event we are unlikely to find the crater, since bathymetric information[23] is not sufficiently detailed and since a substantial portion of the pre-Tertiary ocean has been subducted.

REFERENCES AND NOTES[24]

1. D.A. Russell, *Geol. Assoc. Can. Spec. Rep. 13* (1975), p. 119.
2. _____, in (*5*), p. 11.
3. M.B. Cita and I. Premoli Silva, *Riv. Ital. Paleontol. Stratigr. Mem. 14* (1974), p. 193.
4. D.A. Russell, *Annu. Rev. Earth Planet. Sci.* 7, 163 (1979).
5. K-TEC group (P. Béland *et al.*), *Cretaceous-Tertiary Extinctions and Possible Terrestrial and Extraterrestrial Causes* (Proceedings of Workshop, National Museum of Natural Sciences, Ottawa, 16 and 17 Nov. 1976).
6. T. Birkelund and R.G. Bromley, Eds., *Cretaceous-Tertiary Boundary Events*, vol. 1, *The Maastrichtian and Danian of Denmark* (Symposium, University of Copenhagen, Copenhagen, 1979); W K Christiansen and T. Birkelund, eds., *ibid.*, vol. 2, *Proceedings*.
7. H. Tappan, *Palaeogeogr. Paleoclimatol. Palaeoecol.* 4, 187 (1968); T.R. Worsley, *Nature (London)* 230, 403 (1977); D.M. McLean, *Science* 200, 1060 (1978); *ibid.* 201, 401 (1978); S. Gartner and J. Keany, *Geology* 6, 708 (1978).
8. E.G. Kauffman, in (*6*), vol. 2, p. 29.
9. A.G. Fischer, in (*6*), vol. 2, p. 11; and M.A. Arthur, *Soc. Econ. Paleontol. Mineral. Spec. Publ. 25* (1977), p. 19.
10. J.F. Simpson, *Geol. Soc. Am. Bull.* 77, 197 (1966); J.D. Hays, *ibid.* 82, 2433 (1971); C.G.A. Harrison and J.M. Prospero, *Nature (London)* 250, 563 (1974).
11. O.H. Schindewolf, *Neues Jahrb. Geol. Paleontol. Monatsh.* 1954, 451 (1954); *ibid.* 1958, 270 (1958); A.R. Leoblich, Jr., and H. Tappan, *Geol. Soc. Am. Bull.* 75, 367 (1964); V.I. Krasovski and I.S. Shivlovsky, *Dokl. Akad. Nauk SSSR* 116, 197 (1957); K.D. Terry and W.H. Tucker, *Science* 159, 421 (1968); H. Laster, *ibid.* 160, 1138 (1968); W.H. Tucker and K.D. Terry, *ibid.*, p. 1138; D. Russell and W.H.

---

23 *bathymetric information*   Measurements of the contours of ocean beds.

24 References have been excerpted to show only those cited in the included material.

Tucker, *Nature (London)* 229, 553 (1971); M.A. Ruderman, *Science* 184, 1079 (1974); R.C. Whitten, J. Cuzzi, W.J. Borucki, J.H. Wolfe, *Nature (London)* 263, 398 (1976).

12. S. Gartner and J.P. McGuirk, *Science* 206, 1272 (1979).

13. A. Boersma and N. Shackleton, in (*6*), vol. 2, p. 50; B. Buchardt and N.O. Jorgensen, in (*6*), vol. 2, p. 54.

14. L. Christensen, S. Fregerslev, A. Simonsen, J. Thiede, *Bull. Geog. Soc. Den* 22, 193 (1973).

15. N.O. Jorgensen, in (*6*), vol. 1, p. 33, vol. 2, p. 62; M. Renard, in (*6*), vol. 2, p. 70.

16. H.P. Luterbacher and I. Premoli Silva, *Riv. Ital. Paleontol. Stratigr.* 70, 67 (1964).

17. H. Pettersson and H. Rotschi, *Geochim. Cosmochim. Acta* 2, 81 (1952).

18. V.M. Goldschmidt, *Geochemistry* (Oxford Univ. Press, New York, 1954).

19. J.L. Barker, Jr., and E. Anders, *Geochim. Cosmochim. Acta* 32, 627 (1968).

20. R. Ganapathy, D.E. Brownlee, P.W. Hodge, *Science* 201, 1119 (1978).

21. A.M. Sarna-Wojcicki, H.R. Bowman, D. Marchand, E. Helley, private communication.

22. J.H. Crocket and H.Y. Kuo, *Geochim. Cosmochim. Acta* 43, 831 (1979).

23. These are briefly discussed in L.W. Alvarez, W. Alvarez, F. Asaro, H.V. Michel, *Univ. Calif. Lawrence Berkeley Lab. Rep. LBL-9666* (1979).

24. A description of the NAA techniques is given in Alvarez *et al.* (*23*), appendix II; I. Perlman and F. Asaro, in *Science and Archaeology*, R.H. Brill, Ed. (MIT Press, Cambridge, Mass., 1971), p. 182.

25. These limestones belong to the Umbrian sequence, of Jurassic to Miocene age, which has been described in V. Bortolotti, P. Passerini, M. Sagri, G. Sestini, *Sediment. Geol.* 4, 341 (1970); A. Jacobacci, E. Centamore, M. Chiocchini, N. Malferrari, G. Martelli, A. Micarelli, *Note Esplicative Carta Geologica d'Italia (1:50,000), Foglio 190: "Cagli"* (Rome, 1974).

32. J.H. Crocket, J.D. McDougall, R.C. Harriss, *Geochim. Cosmochim. Acta* 37, 2547 (1973).

46. *Encyclopaedia Britannica* (Benton, Chicago, ed. 15, 1974), vol. 6, p. 702.

47. K.K. Turekian, *Oceans* (Prentice-Hall, Englewood Cliffs, N.J., 1976), p. 122.

55. H.C. Urey, *ibid.* 242, 32 (1973).

56. E.J. Öpik, *Ir. Astron. J.* 5 (No. 1), 34 (1958).

57. E.M. Shoemaker, J.G. Williams, E.F. Helin, R.F. Wolfe, in *Asteroids*, T. Gehrels, Ed. (Univ. of Arizona Press, Tucson, 1979), pp. 253-282.

58. E.J. Öpik, *Adv. Astron. Astrophys.* 2, 220 (1963); *ibid.* 4, 302 (1964); *ibid.* 8, 108 (1971). These review articles give references to Öpik's extensive bibliography on meteorites, Apollo objects, and asteroids.

61. E.M. Shoemaker, personal communication.

62. R.A.F. Grieve and P.B. Robertson, *Icarus* 38, 212 (1979).

63. R.A.F. Grieve, personal communication.

64. G.J. Symons, Ed., *The Eruption of Krakatoa and Subsequent Phenomena* (Report of the Krakatoa Committee of the Royal Society, Harrison, London, 1888).

65. I.U. Olson and I. Karlen, *Am. J. Sci. Radio-carbon Suppl.* 7 (1965), p. 331; T.A. Rafter and B.J. O'Brien, *Proc. 8th Int. Conf. Radiocarbon Dating* 1, 241 (1972).

66. U. Krähenbühl, *Geochim. Cosmochim. Acta* 37, 1353 (1973).

72. V.L. Masaytis, M.V. Mikhaylov, T.V. Selivanovskaya, *Sov. Geol. No. 6* (1971), pp. 143-147; translated in *Geol. Rev.* 14, 327 (1972).

73. V.L. Masaytis, *Sov. Geol. No. 11* (1975), pp. 52-64; translated in *Int. Geol. Rev.* 18, 1249 (1976).

74. It will be obvious to anyone reading this article that we have benefited enormously from conversations and correspondence with many friends and colleagues throughout the scientific community. We would particularly like to acknowledge the help we have received from E. Anders, J.R. Arnold, M.A. Arthur, A. Buffington, I.S.E. Carmichael, G. Curtis, P. Eberhard, S. Gartner, R.L. Garwin, R.A.F. Grieve, E.K. Hyde, W. Lowrie, C. McKee, M.C. Michel (who was responsible for the mass spectrometric measurements), J. Neil, B.M. Oliver, C. Orth, B. Pardoe, I. Perlman, D.A. Russell, A.M. Sessler, and E. Shoemaker. One of us (W.A.) thanks the National Science foundation for support, the other three authors thank the Department of Energy for support, and one of us (L.W.A.) thanks the National Aeronautics and Space Administration for support. The x-ray fluorescence measurements of trace elements Fe and Ti by R.D. Giaque and of major elements by S. Flexser and M. Sturz were most appreciated. We appreciate the assistance of D. Jackson and C. Nguyen in the sample preparation

procedures. We are grateful to T. Lim and the staff of the Berkeley Research Reactor for many neutron irradiations used in this work. We also appreciate the efforts of G. Pefley and the staff of the Livermore Pool Type Reactor for the irradiations used for the Ir isotopic ratio measurements.

(1980)

Questions

1. In your own words, summarize the asteroid impact hypothesis. What biological and geological events does it explain, and how?

2. Why did Alvarez et al. choose to measure concentrations of iridium, as opposed to another substance?

3. What kinds of organisms died during the mass extinction, and what kinds survived? Why?

4. Compare the style of this article with that of the selection elsewhere in this volume by Charles Lyell on the principles of geology. Comment on diction, sentence structure, and tone. What can you say about the audiences that Lyell and Alvarez et al. were writing for?

5. Alvarez et al. refer to the "many implications of the asteroid impact hypothesis," and they discuss two of these implications. What other implications do you see?

6. Read the selection from *The Principles of Geology* by Charles Lyell, elsewhere in this volume. To what extent does Lyell's description reflect geology as it is practiced by the authors of this article?

Questions on connections between this article and the following essay, "The Sixth Extinction?," can be found at the end of that essay.

ELIZABETH KOLBERT

THE SIXTH EXTINCTION?

In this article for The New Yorker, *an environmentalist
journalist investigates the current worldwide reduction
in natural diversity—and its disturbing resemblance
to the mass extinctions of our planet's past.*

❧

The town of El Valle de Antón, in central Panama, sits in the middle of a volcanic crater formed about a million years ago. The crater is almost four miles across, but when the weather is clear you can see the jagged hills that surround the town, like the walls of a ruined tower. El Valle has one main street, a police station, and an open-air market that offers, in addition to the usual hats and embroidery, what must be the world's largest selection of golden-frog figurines. There are golden frogs sitting on leaves and—more difficult to understand—golden frogs holding cell phones. There are golden frogs wearing frilly skirts, and golden frogs striking dance poses, and ashtrays featuring golden frogs smoking cigarettes through a holder, after the fashion of F.D.R. The golden frog, which is bright yellow with dark brown splotches, is endemic to the area around El Valle. It is considered a lucky symbol in Panama—its image is often printed on lottery tickets—though it could just as easily serve as an emblem of disaster.

In the early nineteen-nineties, an American graduate student named Karen Lips established a research site about two hundred miles west of El Valle, in the Talamanca Mountains, just over the border in Costa Rica. Lips was planning to study the local frogs, some of which, she later discovered, had never been identified. In order to get to the site, she had to drive two hours from the nearest town—the last part of the trip required tire chains—and then hike for an hour in the rain forest.

Lips spent two years living in the mountains. "It was a wonderland," she recalled recently. Once she had collected enough data, she left to work on her dissertation. She returned a few months later, and though nothing seemed to have changed, she could hardly find any frogs. Lips couldn't figure out what was happening. She collected all the dead frogs that she came across—there were only a half dozen or so—and sent their bodies to a veterinary pathologist in the United States. The pathologist was also baffled: the specimens, she told Lips, showed no signs of any known disease.

A few years went by. Lips finished her dissertation and got a teaching job. Since the frogs at her old site had pretty much disappeared, she decided that she needed to find a new location to do research. She picked another isolated spot in the rain forest, this time in western Panama. Initially, the frogs there seemed healthy. But, before long, Lips began to find corpses lying in the streams and moribund animals sitting on the banks. Sometimes she would pick up a frog and it would die in her hands. She sent some specimens to a second pathologist in the US, and, once again, the pathologist had no idea what was wrong.

5   Whatever was killing Lips's frogs continued to move, like a wave, east across Panama. By 2002, most frogs in the streams around Santa Fé, a town in the province of Veraguas, had been wiped out. By 2004, the frogs in the national park of El Copé, in the province of Coclé, had all but disappeared. At that point, golden frogs were still relatively common around El Valle; a creek not far from the town was nicknamed Thousand Frog Stream. Then, in 2006, the wave hit.

Of the many species that have existed on earth—estimates run as high as fifty billion—more than ninety-nine per cent have disappeared. In the light of this, it is sometimes joked that all of life today amounts to little more than a rounding error.

Records of the missing can be found everywhere in the world, often in forms that are difficult to overlook. And yet extinction has been a much contested concept. Throughout the eighteenth century, even as extraordinary fossils were being unearthed and put on exhibit, the prevailing view was that species were fixed, created by God for all eternity. If the bones of a strange creature were found, it must mean that the creature was out there somewhere.

"Such is the economy of nature," Thomas Jefferson wrote, "that no instance can be produced, of her having permitted any one race of her animals to become extinct; of her having formed any link in her great work so weak as to be broken." When, as President, he dispatched Meriwether Lewis and

William Clark to the Northwest, Jefferson hoped that they would come upon live mastodons roaming the region.

The French naturalist Georges Cuvier was more skeptical. In 1812, he published an essay on the "Revolutions of the Surface of the Globe," in which he asked, "How can we believe that the immense mastodons, the gigantic megatheriums, whose bones have been found in the earth in the two Americas, still live on this continent?" Cuvier had conducted studies of the fossils found in gypsum mines in Paris, and was convinced that many organisms once common to the area no longer existed. These he referred to as *espèces perdues*, or lost species. Cuvier had no way of knowing how much time had elapsed in forming the fossil record. But, as the record indicated that Paris had, at various points, been under water, he concluded that the *espèces perdues* had been swept away by sudden cataclysms.

"Life on this earth has often been disturbed by dreadful events," he wrote. "Innumerable living creatures have been victims of these catastrophes." Cuvier's essay was translated into English in 1813 and published with an introduction by the Scottish naturalist Robert Jameson, who interpreted it as proof of Noah's flood. It went through five editions in English and six in French before Cuvier's death, in 1832.

10

Charles Darwin was well acquainted with Cuvier's ideas and the theological spin they had been given. (He had studied natural history with Jameson at the University of Edinburgh.) In his theory of natural selection, Darwin embraced extinction; it was, he realized, essential that some species should die out as new ones were created. But he believed that this happened only slowly. Indeed, he claimed that it took place even more gradually than speciation: "The complete extinction of the species of a group is generally a slower process than their production." In "On the Origin of Species," published in the fall of 1859, Darwin heaped scorn on the catastrophist approach:

> So profound is our ignorance, and so high our presumption, that we marvel when we hear of the extinction of an organic being; and as we do not see the cause, we invoke cataclysms to desolate the world.

By the start of the twentieth century, this view had become dominant, and to be a scientist meant to see extinction as Darwin did. But Darwin, it turns out, was wrong.

Over the past half-billion years, there have been at least twenty mass extinctions, when the diversity of life on earth has suddenly and dramatically contracted. Five of these—the so-called Big Five—were so devastating that they are usually put in their own category. The first took place during the late Ordovician period, nearly four hundred and fifty million years ago, when life was still confined mainly to water. Geological records indicate that more than eighty per cent of marine species died out. The fifth occurred at the end of the Cretaceous period, sixty-five million years ago. The end-Cretaceous event exterminated not just the dinosaurs but seventy-five per cent of all species on earth.

The significance of mass extinctions goes beyond the sheer number of organisms involved. In contrast to ordinary, or so-called background, extinctions, which claim species that, for one reason or another, have become unfit, mass extinctions strike down the fit and the unfit at once. For example, brachiopods, which look like clams but have an entirely different anatomy, dominated the ocean floor for hundreds of millions of years. In the third of the Big Five extinctions—the end-Permian—the hugely successful brachiopods were nearly wiped out, along with trilobites, blastoids, and eurypterids. (In the end-Permian event, more than ninety per cent of marine species and seventy per cent of terrestrial species vanished; the event is sometimes referred to as "the mother of mass extinctions" or "the great dying.")

15   Once a mass extinction occurs, it takes millions of years for life to recover, and when it does it generally has a new cast of characters; following the end-Cretaceous event, mammals rose up (or crept out) to replace the departed dinosaurs. In this way, mass extinctions, though missing from the original theory of evolution, have played a determining role in evolution's course; as Richard Leakey has put it, such events "restructure the biosphere" and so "create the pattern of life." It is now generally agreed among biologists that another mass extinction is under way. Though it's difficult to put a precise figure on the losses, it is estimated that, if current trends continue, by the end of this century as many as half of earth's species will be gone.

The El Valle Amphibian Conservation Center, known by the acronym EVACC (pronounced "e-vac"), is a short walk from the market where the golden-frog figurines are sold. It consists of a single building about the size of an average suburban house. The place is filled, floor to ceiling, with tanks. There are tall tanks for species that, like the Rabb's fringe-limbed tree frog, live in the forest canopy, and short tanks for species that, like the big-headed robber frog, live on the forest floor. Tanks of horned marsupial frogs, which carry their eggs in a pouch, sit next to tanks of casque-headed frogs, which carry their eggs on their backs.

The director of EVACC is a herpetologist named Edgardo Griffith. Griffith is tall and broad-shouldered, with a round face and a wide smile. He wears a silver ring in each ear and has a large tattoo of a toad's skeleton on his left shin. Griffith grew up in Panama City, and fell in love with amphibians one day in college when a friend invited him to go frog hunting. He collected most of the frogs at EVACC—there are nearly six hundred—in a rush, just as corpses were beginning to show up around El Valle. At that point, the center was little more than a hole in the ground, and so the frogs had to spend several months in temporary tanks at a local hotel. "We got a very good rate," Griffith assured me. While the amphibians were living in rented rooms, Griffith and his wife, a former Peace Corps volunteer, would go out into a nearby field to catch crickets for their dinner. Now EVACC raises bugs for the frogs in what looks like an oversized rabbit hutch.

EVACC is financed largely by the Houston Zoo, which initially pledged twenty thousand dollars to the project and has ended up spending ten times that amount. The tiny center, though, is not an outpost of the zoo. It might be thought of as a preserve, except that, instead of protecting the amphibians in their natural habitat, the center's aim is to isolate them from it. In this way, EVACC represents an ark built for a modern-day deluge. Its goal is to maintain twenty-five males and twenty-five females of each species—just enough for a breeding population.

The first time I visited, Griffith pointed out various tanks containing frogs that have essentially disappeared from the wild. These include the Panamanian golden frog, which, in addition to its extraordinary coloring, is known for its unusual method of communication; the frogs signal to one another using a kind of semaphore. Griffith said that he expected between a third and a half of all Panama's amphibians to be gone within the next five years. Some species, he said, will probably vanish without anyone's realizing it: "Unfortunately, we are losing all these amphibians before we even know that they exist."

Griffith still goes out collecting for EVACC. Since there are hardly any frogs to be found around El Valle, he has to travel farther afield, across the Panama Canal, to the eastern half of the country.

20

One day this winter, I set out with him on one of his expeditions, along with two American zookeepers who were also visiting EVACC. The four of us spent a night in a town called Cerro Azul and, at dawn the next morning, drove in a truck to the ranger station at the entrance to Chagres National Park. Griffith was hoping to find females of two species that EVACC is short of. He pulled out his collecting permit and presented it to the sleepy officials manning the station. Some underfed dogs came out to sniff around.

Beyond the ranger station, the road turned into a series of craters connected by ruts. Griffith put Jimi Hendrix on the truck's CD player, and we bounced along to the throbbing beat. (When the driving got particularly gruesome, he would turn down the volume.) Frog collecting requires a lot of supplies, so Griffith had hired two men to help with the carrying. At the very last cluster of houses, in the village of Los Ángeles, they materialized out of the mist. We bounced on until the truck couldn't go any farther; then we all got out and started walking.

The trail wound its way through the rain forest in a slather of red mud. Every few hundred yards, the main path was crossed by a narrower one; these paths had been made by leaf-cutter ants, making millions—perhaps billions—of trips to bring bits of greenery back to their colonies. (The colonies, which look like mounds of sawdust, can cover an area the size of a suburban back yard.) One of the Americans, Chris Bednarski, from the Houston Zoo, warned me to avoid the soldier ants, which will leave their jaws in your shin even after they're dead. "Those'll really mess you up," he observed. The other American, John Chastain, from the Toledo Zoo, was carrying a long hook, for use against venomous snakes. "Fortunately, the ones that can really mess you up are pretty rare," Bednarski said. Howler monkeys screamed in the distance. Someone pointed out jaguar prints in the soft ground.

After about five hours, we emerged into a small clearing. While we were setting up camp, a blue morpho butterfly flitted by, its wings the color of the sky.

25   That evening, after the sun set, we strapped on headlamps and clambered down to a nearby stream. Many amphibians are nocturnal, and the only way to see them is to go looking in the dark, an exercise that's as tricky as it sounds. I kept slipping, and violating Rule No. 1 of rain-forest safety: never grab on to something if you don't know what it is. After one of my falls, Bednarski showed me a tarantula the size of my fist that he had found on a nearby tree.

One technique for finding amphibians at night is to shine a light into the forest and look for the reflecting glow of their eyes. The first amphibian sighted this way was a San José Cochran frog, perched on top of a leaf. San José Cochran frogs are part of a larger family known as "glass frogs," so named because their translucent skin reveals the outline of their internal organs. This particular glass frog was green, with tiny yellow dots. Griffith pulled a pair of surgical gloves out of his pack. He stood entirely still and then, with a heronlike gesture, darted to scoop up the frog. With his free hand, he took what looked like the end of a Q-tip and swabbed the frog's belly. Finally, he put the Q-tip in a little plastic vial, placed the frog back on the leaf, and pulled out his camera. The frog stared into the lens impassively.

We continued to grope through the blackness. Someone spotted a La Loma robber frog, which is an orangey-red, like the forest floor; someone else spotted a Warzewitsch frog, which is bright green and shaped like a leaf. With every frog, Griffith went through the same routine—snatching it up, swabbing its belly, photographing it. Finally, we came upon a pair of Panamanian robber frogs locked in amplexus the amphibian version of sex. Griffith left those two alone.

One of the frogs that Griffith was hoping to catch, the horned marsupial frog, has a distinctive call that's been likened to the sound of a champagne bottle being uncorked. As we sloshed along, the call seemed to be emanating from several directions at once. Sometimes it sounded as if we were right nearby, but then, as we approached, it would fall silent. Griffith began imitating the call, making a cork-popping sound with his lips. Eventually, he decided that the rest of us were scaring the frogs with our splashing. He waded ahead, while we stood in the middle of the stream, trying not to move. When Griffith gestured us over, we found him standing in front of a large yellow frog with long toes and an owlish face. It was sitting on a tree limb, just above eye level. Griffith grabbed the frog and turned it over. Where a female marsupial frog would have a pouch, this one had none. Griffith swabbed it, photographed it, and put it back in the tree.

"You are a beautiful boy," he told the frog.

Amphibians are among the planet's greatest survivors. The ancestors of today's frogs and toads crawled out of the water some four hundred million years ago, and by two hundred and fifty million years ago the earliest representatives of what became the modern amphibian clades—one includes frogs and toads, a second newts and salamanders—had evolved. This

30

means that amphibians have been around not just longer than mammals, say, or birds; they have been around since before there were dinosaurs. Most amphibians—the word comes from the Greek meaning "double life"—are still closely tied to the aquatic realm from which they emerged. (The ancient Egyptians thought that frogs were produced by the coupling of land and water during the annual flooding of the Nile.) Their eggs, which have no shells, must be kept moist in order to develop. There are frogs that lay their eggs in streams, frogs that lay them in temporary pools, frogs that lay them underground, and frogs that lay them in nests that they construct out of foam. In addition to frogs that carry their eggs on their backs and in pouches, there are frogs that carry them in their vocal sacs, and, until recently at least, there were frogs that carried their eggs in their stomachs and gave birth through their mouths. Amphibians emerged at a time when all the land on earth was part of one large mass; they have since adapted to conditions on every continent except Antarctica. Worldwide, more than six thousand species have been identified, and while the greatest number are found in the tropical rain forests, there are amphibians that, like the sandhill frog of Australia, can live in the desert, and also amphibians that, like the wood frog, can live above the Arctic Circle. Several common North American frogs, including spring peepers, are able to survive the winter frozen solid.

When, about two decades ago, researchers first noticed that something odd was happening to amphibians, the evidence didn't seem to make sense. David Wake is a biologist at the University of California at Berkeley. In the early nineteen-eighties, his students began returning from frog-collecting trips in the Sierra Nevadas empty-handed. Wake remembered from his own student days that frogs in the Sierras had been difficult to avoid. "You'd be walking through meadows, and you'd inadvertently step on them," he told me. "They were just everywhere." Wake assumed that his students were just going to the wrong spots, or that they just didn't know how to look. Then a postdoc with several years of experience told him that he couldn't find any, either. "I said, 'OK, I'll go up with you and we'll go out to some proven places,'" Wake recalled. "And I took him out to this proven place and we found, like, two toads."

Around the same time, other researchers, in other parts of the world, reported similar difficulties. In the late nineteen-eighties, a herpetologist named Marty Crump went to Costa Rica to study golden toads; she was forced to change her project because, from one year to the next, the toad essentially vanished. (The golden toad, now regarded as extinct, was actually orange; it is not to be confused with the Panamanian golden frog, which is technically also a toad.) Probably simultaneously, in central Costa Rica the populations of twenty species of frogs and toads suddenly crashed. In Ecuador, the jambato toad, a familiar visitor to back-yard gardens, disappeared in a matter of years. And in northeastern Australia biologists noticed that more than a dozen amphibian species, including the southern day frog, one of the more common in the region, were experiencing drastic declines.

But, as the number of examples increased, the evidence only seemed to grow more confounding. Though amphibians in some remote and—relatively speaking—pristine spots seemed to be collapsing, those in other, more obviously disturbed habitats seemed to be doing fine. Meanwhile, in many parts of the world there weren't good data on amphibian populations to begin with, so it was hard to determine what represented terminal descent and what might be just a temporary dip.

"It was very controversial to say that amphibians were disappearing," Andrew Blaustein, a zoology professor at Oregon State University, recalls. Blaustein, who was studying the mating behavior of frogs and toads in the Cascade Mountains, had observed that some long standing populations simply weren't there anymore. "The debate was whether or not there really was an amphibian population problem, because some people were saying it was just natural variation." At the point that Karen Lips went to look for her first research site, she purposefully tried to steer clear of the controversy.

"I didn't want to work on amphibian decline," she told me. "There were endless debates about whether this was a function of randomness or a true pattern. And the last thing you want to do is get involved when you don't know what's going on."

But the debate was not to be avoided. Even amphibians that had never seen a pond or a forest started dying. Blue poison-dart frogs, which are native to Suriname, had been raised at the National Zoo, in Washington, DC, for several generations. Then, suddenly, the zoo's tank-bred frogs were wiped out.

It is difficult to say when, exactly, the current extinction event—sometimes called the sixth extinction—began. What might be thought of as its opening phase appears to have started about fifty thousand years ago. At that time, Australia was home to a fantastic assortment of enormous animals; these included a wombatlike creature the size of a hippo, a land tortoise nearly as big as a VW Beetle, and the giant short-faced kangaroo, which grew to be ten feet tall. Then all of the continent's largest animals disappeared. Every

35

species of marsupial weighing more than two hundred pounds—there were nineteen of them—vanished, as did three species of giant reptiles and a flightless bird with stumpy legs known as *Genyornis newtoni*.

This die-off roughly coincided with the arrival of the first people on the continent, probably from Southeast Asia. Australia is a big place, and there couldn't have been very many early settlers. For a long time, the coincidence was discounted. Yet, thanks to recent work by geologists and paleontologists, a clear global pattern has emerged. About eleven thousand years ago, three-quarters of North America's largest animals—among them mastodons, mammoths, giant beavers, short-faced bears, and sabre-toothed tigers—began to go extinct. This is right around the time the first humans are believed to have wandered across the Bering land bridge. In relatively short order, the first humans settled South America as well. Subsequently, more than thirty species of South American "megamammals," including elephant-size ground sloths and rhino-like creatures known as toxodons, died out.

And what goes for Australia and the Americas also goes for many other parts of the world. Humans settled Madagascar around two thousand years ago; the island subsequently lost all mammals weighing more than twenty pounds, including pygmy hippos and giant lemurs. "Substantial losses have occurred throughout near time," Ross MacPhee, a curator at the American Museum of Natural History, in New York, and an expert on extinctions of the recent geological past, has written. "In the majority of cases, these losses occurred when, and only when, people began to expand across areas that had never before experienced their presence." The Maori arrived in New Zealand around eight hundred years ago. They encountered eleven species of moas—huge ostrichlike creatures without wings. Within a few centuries—and possibly within a single century—all eleven moa species were gone. While these "first contact" extinctions were most pronounced among large animals, they were not confined to them. Humans discovered the Hawaiian Islands around fifteen hundred years ago; soon afterward, ninety per cent of Hawaii's native bird species disappeared.

40   "We expect extinction when people arrive on an island," David Steadman, the curator of ornithology at the Florida Museum of Natural History, has written. "Survival is the exception."

Why was the first contact with humans so catastrophic? Some of the animals may have been hunted to death; thousands of moa bones have been found at Maori archaeological sites, and man-made artifacts have been uncovered near mammoth and mastodon remains at more than a dozen sites in North America. Hunting, however, seems insufficient to account for so many losses across so many different taxa in so many parts of the globe. A few years ago, researchers analyzed hundreds of bits of emu and *Genyornis newtoni* eggshell, some dating from long before the first people arrived in Australia and some from after. They found that around forty-five thousand years ago, rather abruptly, emus went from eating all sorts of plants to relying mainly on shrubs. The researchers hypothesized that Australia's early settlers periodically set the countryside on fire—perhaps to flush out prey—a practice that would have reduced the variety of plant life. Those animals which, like emus, could cope with a changed landscape survived, while those which, like *Genyornis*, could not died out.

When Australia was first settled, there were maybe half a million people on earth. There are now more than six and a half billion, and it is expected that within the next three years the number will reach seven billion.

Human impacts on the planet have increased proportionately. Farming, logging, and building have transformed between a third and a half of the world's land surface, and even these figures probably understate the effect, since land not being actively exploited may still be fragmented. Most of the world's major waterways have been diverted or dammed or otherwise manipulated—in the United States, only two per cent of rivers run unimpeded—and people now use half the world's readily accessible freshwater runoff. Chemical plants fix more atmospheric nitrogen than all natural terrestrial processes combined, and fisheries remove more than a third of the primary production of the temperate coastal waters of the oceans. Through global trade and international travel, humans have transported countless species into ecosystems that are not prepared for them. We have pumped enough carbon dioxide into the air to alter the climate and to change the chemistry of the oceans.

Amphibians are affected by many—perhaps most—of these disruptions. Habitat destruction is a major factor in their decline, and agricultural chemicals seem to be causing a rash of frog deformities. But the main culprit in the wavelike series of crashes, it's now believed, is a fungus. Ironically, this fungus, which belongs to a group known as chytrids (pronounced "kitrids"), appears to have been spread by doctors.

Chytrid fungi are older even than amphibians—the first species evolved more than six million years ago—and even more widespread. In a manner of speaking, they can be found—they are microscopic—just about everywhere, from the tops of trees to deep underground. Generally, chytrid

45

fungi feed off dead plants; there are also species that live on algae, species that live on roots, and species that live in the guts of cows, where they help break down cellulose. Until two pathologists, Don Nichols and Allan Pessier, identified a weird microorganism growing on dead frogs from the National Zoo, chytrids had never been known to attack vertebrates. Indeed, the new chytrid was so unusual that an entire genus had to be created to accommodate it. It was named *Batrachochytrium dendrobatidis—batrachos* is Greek for "frog"—or Bd for short.

Nichols and Pessier sent samples from the infected frogs to a mycologist at the University of Maine, Joyce Longcore, who managed to culture the Bd fungus. Then they exposed healthy blue poison-dart frogs to it. Within three weeks, the animals had sickened and died.

The discovery of Bd explained many of the data that had previously seemed so puzzling. Chytrid fungi generate microscopic spores that disperse in water; these could have been carried along by streams, or in the runoff after a rainstorm, producing what in Central America showed up as an eastward-moving scourge. In the case of zoos, the spores could have been brought in on other frogs or on tracked-in soil. Bd seemed to be able to live on just about any frog or toad, but not all amphibians are as susceptible to it, which would account for why some populations succumbed while others appeared to be unaffected.

Rick Speare is an Australian pathologist who identified Bd right around the same time that the National Zoo team did. From the pattern of decline, Speare suspected that Bd had been spread by an amphibian that had been moved around the globe. One of the few species that met this condition was *Xenopus laevis*, commonly known as the African clawed frog. In the early nineteen-thirties, a British zoologist named Lancelot Hogben discovered that female *Xenopus laevis*, when injected with certain types of human hormones, laid eggs. His discovery became the basis for a new kind of pregnancy test and, starting in the late nineteen-thirties, thousands of African clawed frogs were exported out of Cape Town. In the nineteen-forties and fifties, it was not uncommon for obstetricians to keep tanks full of the frogs in their offices.

To test his hypothesis, Speare began collecting samples from live African clawed frogs and also from specimens preserved in museums. He found that specimens dating back to the nineteen-thirties were indeed already carrying the fungus. He also found that live African clawed frogs were widely infected with Bd, but seemed to suffer no ill effects from it. In 2004, he co-authored an influential paper that argued that the transmission route for the fungus began in southern Africa and ran through clinics and hospitals around the world.

"Let's say people were raising African clawed frogs in aquariums, and they just popped the water out," Speare told me. "In most cases when they did that, no frogs got infected, but then on that hundredth time, one local frog might have been infected. Or people might have said, 'I'm sick of this frog. I'm going to let it go.' And certainly there are populations of African clawed frogs established in a number of countries around the world, to illustrate that that actually did occur."

At this point, Bd appears to be, for all intents and purposes, unstoppable. It can be killed by bleach—Clorox is among the donors to EVACC—but it is impossible to disinfect an entire rain forest. Sometime in the last year or so, the fungus jumped the Panama Canal. (When Edgardo Griffith swabbed the frogs on our trip, he was collecting samples that would eventually be analyzed for it.) It also seems to be heading into Panama from the opposite direction, out of Colombia. It has spread through the highlands of South America, down the eastern coast of Australia, and into New Zealand, and has been detected in Italy, Spain, and France. In the US, it appears to have radiated from several points, not so much in a wavelike pattern as in a series of ripples.

In the fossil record, mass extinctions stand out, so sharply that the very language scientists use to describe the earth's history derives from them. In 1840, the British geologist John Phillips divided life into three chapters: the Paleozoic (from the Greek for "ancient life"), the Mesozoic ("middle life"), and the Cenozoic ("new life"). Phillips fixed as the dividing point between the first and second eras what would now be called the end-Permian extinction, and between the second and the third the end-Cretaceous event. The fossils from these eras were so different that Phillips thought they represented three distinct episodes of creation.

Darwin's resistance to catastrophism meant that he couldn't accept what the fossils seemed to be saying. Drawing on the work of the eminent geologist Charles Lyell, a good friend of his, Darwin maintained that the apparent discontinuities in the history of life were really just gaps in the archive. In "On the Origin of Species," he argued:

> With respect to the apparently sudden extermination of whole
> families or orders, as of Trilobites at the close of the palaeozoic

period and of Ammonites at the close of the secondary period, we must remember what has been already said on the probable wide intervals of time between our consecutive formations; and in these intervals there may have been much slow extermination.

All the way into the nineteen-sixties, paleontologists continued to give talks with titles like "The Incompleteness of the Fossil Record." And this view might have persisted even longer had it not been for a remarkable, largely inadvertent discovery made in the following decade.

55   In the mid-nineteen-seventies, Walter Alvarez, a geologist at the Lamont Doherty Earth Observatory, in New York, was studying the earth's polarity. It had recently been learned that the orientation of the planet's magnetic field reverses, so that every so often, in effect, south becomes north and then vice versa. Alvarez and some colleagues had found that a certain formation of pinkish limestone in Italy, known as the *scaglia rossa*, recorded these occasional reversals. The limestone also contained the fossilized remains of millions of tiny sea creatures called foraminifera. In the course of several trips to Italy, Alvarez became interested in a thin layer of clay in the limestone that seemed to have been laid down around the end of the Cretaceous. Below the layer, certain species of foraminifera—or forams, for short—were preserved. In the clay layer there were no forams. Above the layer, the earlier species disappeared and new forams appeared. Having been taught the uniformitarian view, Alvarez wasn't sure what to make of what he was seeing, because the change, he later recalled, certainly "looked very abrupt."

Alvarez decided to try to find out how long it had taken for the clay layer to be deposited. In 1977, he took a post at the University of California at Berkeley, where his father, the Nobel prize-winning physicist Luis Alvarez, was also teaching. The older Alvarez suggested using the element iridium to answer the question.

Iridium is extremely rare on the surface of the earth, but more plentiful in meteorites, which, in the form of microscopic grains of cosmic dust, are constantly raining down on the planet. The Alvarezes reasoned that, if the clay layer had taken a significant amount of time to deposit, it would contain detectable levels of iridium, and if it had been deposited in a short time it wouldn't. They enlisted two other scientists, Frank Asaro and Helen Michel, to run the tests, and gave them samples of the clay, Nine months later, they got a phone call. There was something seriously wrong. Much too much iridium was showing up in the samples. Walter Alvarez flew to

Denmark to take samples of another layer of exposed clay from the end of the Cretaceous. When they were tested, these samples, too, were way out of line.

The Alvarez hypothesis, as it became known, was that everything—the clay layer from the *scaglia rossa*, the clay from Denmark, the spike in iridium, the shift in the fossils—could be explained by a single event. In 1980, the Alvarezes and their colleagues proposed that a six-mile-wide asteroid had slammed into the earth, killing off not only the forams but the dinosaurs and all the other organisms that went extinct at the end of the Cretaceous. "I can remember working very hard to make that 1980 paper just as solid as it could possibly be," Walter Alvarez recalled recently. Nevertheless, the idea was greeted with incredulity.

"The arrogance of these people is simply unbelievable," one paleontologist told the *Times*.

"Unseen bodies dropping into an unseen sea are not for me," another declared.

60

Over the next decade, evidence in favor of an enormous impact kept accumulating. Geologists looking at rocks from the end of the Cretaceous in Montana found tiny mineral grains that seemed to have suffered a violent shock. (Such "shocked quartz" is typically found in the immediate vicinity of meteorite craters.) Other geologists, looking in other parts of the world, found small, glasslike spheres of the sort believed to form when molten-rock droplets splash up into the atmosphere. In 1990, a crater large enough to have been formed by the enormous asteroid that the Alvarezes were proposing was found, buried underneath the Yucatán. In 1991, that crater was dated, and discovered to have been formed at precisely the time the dinosaurs died off.

"Those eleven years seemed long at the time, but looking back they seem very brief," Walter Alvarez told me. "Just think about it for a moment. Here you have a challenge to a uniformitarian viewpoint that basically every geologist and paleontologist had been trained in, as had their professors and their professors' professors, all the way back to Lyell. And what you saw was people looking at the evidence. And they gradually did come to change their minds."

Today, it's generally accepted that the asteroid that plowed into the Yucatán led, in very short order, to a mass extinction, but scientists are still uncertain exactly how the process unfolded. One theory holds that the impact raised a cloud of dust that blocked the sun, preventing photosynthesis and causing widespread starvation. According to another theory, the impact kicked up a plume of vaporized rock traveling with so much force that it broke through the atmosphere. The particles in the plume then recondensed, generating, as they fell back to earth, enough thermal energy to, in effect, broil the surface of the planet.

Whatever the mechanism, the Alvarezes' discovery wreaked havoc with the uniformitarian idea of extinction. The fossil record, it turned out, was marked by discontinuities because the history of life was marked by discontinuities.

65 In the nineteenth century, and then again during the Second World War, the Adirondacks were a major source of iron ore. As a result, the mountains are now riddled with abandoned mines. On a gray day this winter, I went to visit one of the mines (I was asked not to say which) with a wildlife biologist named Al Hicks. Hicks, who is fifty-four, is tall and outgoing, with a barrel chest and ruddy cheeks. He works at the headquarters of the New York State Department of Environmental Conservation, in Albany, and we met in a parking lot not far from his office. From there, we drove almost due north.

Along the way, Hicks explained how, in early 2007, he started to get a lot of strange calls about bats. Sometimes the call would be about a dead bat that had been brought inside by somebody's dog. Sometimes it was about a live—or half-alive—bat flapping around on the driveway. This was in the middle of winter, when any bat in the Northeast should have been hanging by its feet in a state of torpor. Hicks found the calls bizarre, but, beyond that, he didn't know what to make of them. Then, in March 2007, some colleagues went to do a routine census of hibernating bats in a cave west of Albany. After the survey, they, too, phoned in.

"They said, 'Holy shit, there's dead bats everywhere,'" Hicks recalled. He instructed them to bring some carcasses back to the office, which they did. They also shot photographs of live bats hanging from the cave's ceiling. When Hicks examined the photographs, he saw that the animals looked as if they had been dunked, nose first, in talcum powder. This was something he had never run across before, and he began sending the bat photographs to all the bat specialists he could think of. None of them could explain it, either.

"We were thinking, Oh boy, we hope this just goes away," he told me. "It was like the Bush Administration. And, like the Bush Administration, it just wouldn't go away." In the winter of 2008, bats with the white powdery substance were found in thirty-three hibernating spots. Meanwhile, bats kept dying. In some hibernacula, populations plunged by as much as ninety-seven per cent.

That winter, officials at the National Wildlife Health Center, in Madison, Wisconsin, began to look into the situation. They were able to culture the white substance, which was found to be a never before identified fungus that grows only at cold temperatures. The condition became known as white-nose syndrome, or W.N.S. White nose seemed to be spreading fast; by March, 2008, it had been found on bats in three more states—Vermont, Massachusetts, and Connecticut—and the mortality rate was running above seventy-five per cent. This past winter, white nose was found to have spread to bats in five more states: New Jersey, New Hampshire, Virginia, West Virginia, and Pennsylvania.

In a paper published recently in *Science*, Hicks and several co-authors observed that "parallels can be drawn between the threat posed by W.N.S. and that from chytridiomycosis, a lethal fungal skin infection that has recently caused precipitous global amphibian population declines."

70

When we arrived at the base of a mountain not far from Lake Champlain, more than a dozen people were standing around in the cold, waiting for us. Most, like Hicks, were from the D.E.C., and had come to help conduct a bat census. In addition, there was a pair of biologists from the US Fish and Wildlife Service and a local novelist who was thinking of incorporating a subplot about white nose into his next book. Everyone put on snowshoes, except for the novelist, who hadn't brought any, and began tromping up the slope toward the mine entrance.

The snow was icy and the going slow, so it took almost half an hour to reach an outlook over the Champlain Valley. While we were waiting for the novelist to catch up—apparently, he was having trouble hiking through the three-foot-deep drifts—the conversation turned to the potential dangers of entering an abandoned mine. These, I was told, included getting crushed by falling rocks, being poisoned by a gas leak, and plunging over a sheer drop of a hundred feet or more.

After another fifteen minutes or so, we reached the mine entrance—essentially, a large hole cut into the hillside. The stones in front of the entrance were white with bird droppings, and the snow was covered with paw prints. Evidently, ravens and coyotes had discovered that the spot was an easy place to pick up dinner.

"Well, shit," Hicks said. Bats were fluttering in and out of the mine, and in some cases crawling on the ground. Hicks went to catch one; it was so lethargic that he grabbed it on the first try. He held it between his thumb and his forefinger, snapped its neck, and placed it in a ziplock bag.

75   "Short survey today," he announced.

At this point, it's not known exactly how the syndrome kills bats. What is known is that bats with the syndrome often wake up from their torpor and fly around, which leads them to die either of starvation or of the cold or to get picked off by predators.

We unstrapped our snowshoes and put on helmets. Hicks handed out headlamps—we were supposed to carry at least one extra—and packages of batteries; then we filed into the mine, down a long, sloping tunnel. Shattered beams littered the ground, and bats flew up at us through the gloom. Hicks cautioned everyone to stay alert. "There's places that if you take a step you won't be stepping back," he warned. The tunnel twisted along, sometimes opening up into concert-hall-size chambers with side tunnels leading out of them. Over the years, the various sections of the mine had acquired names; when we reached something called the Don Thomas section, we split up into groups to start the survey. The process consisted of photographing as many bats as possible. (Later on, back in Albany, someone would have to count all the bats in the pictures.) I went with Hicks, who was carrying an enormous camera, and one of the biologists from the Fish and Wildlife Service, who had a laser pointer. The biologist would aim the pointer at a cluster of bats hanging from the ceiling. Hicks would then snap a photograph. Most of the bats were little brown bats; these are the most common bats in the US, and the ones you are most likely to see flying around on a summer night. There were also Indiana bats, which are on the federal endangered-species list, and small-footed bats, which, at the rate things are going, are likely to end up there. As we moved along, we kept disturbing the bats, which squeaked and started to rustle around, like half-asleep children.

Since white nose grows only in the cold, it's odd to find it living on mammals, which, except when they're hibernating (or dead), maintain a high body temperature. It has been hypothesized that the fungus normally subsists by breaking down organic matter in a chilly place, and that it was transported to bat hibernacula, where it began to break down bats. When news of white nose began to get around, a spelunker sent Hicks photographs that he had shot in Howe's Cave, in central New York. The photographs, which had been taken in 2006, showed bats with clear signs of white nose and are the earliest known record of the syndrome. Howe's Cave is connected to Howe's Caverns, a popular tourist destination.

"It's kind of interesting that the first record we have of this fungus is photographs from a commercial cave in New York that gets about two hundred thousand visits a year," Hicks told me.

Despite the name, white nose is not confined to bats' noses; as we worked our way along, people kept finding bats with freckles of fungus on their wings and ears. Several of these were dispatched, for study purposes, with a thumb and forefinger. Each dead bat was sexed—males can be identified by their tiny penises—and placed in a ziplock bag. 80

At about 7 pm, we came to a huge, rusty winch, which, when the mine was operational, had been used to haul ore to the surface. By this point, we were almost down at the bottom of the mountain, except that we were on the inside of it. Below, the path disappeared into a pool of water, like the River Styx. It was impossible to go any further, and we began working our way back up.

Bats, like virtually all other creatures alive today, are masters of adaptation descended from lucky survivors. The earliest bat fossil that has been found dates from fifty-three million years ago, which is to say twelve million years after the impact that ended the Cretaceous. It belongs to an animal that had wings and could fly but had not yet developed the specialized inner ear that, in modern bats, allows for echolocation. Worldwide, there are now more than a thousand bat species, which together make up nearly a fifth of all species of mammals. Most feed on insects; there are also bats that live off fruit, bats that eat fish—they use echolocation to detect minute ripples in the water—and a small but highly celebrated group that consumes blood. Bats are great colonizers—Darwin noted that even New Zealand, which has no other native mammals, has its own bats—and they can be found as far north as Alaska and as far south as Tierra del Fuego.

In the time that bats have evolved and spread, the world has changed a great deal. Fifty-three million years ago, at the start of the Eocene, the planet was very warm, and tropical palms grew at the latitude of London. The climate cooled, the Antarctic ice sheet began to form, and, eventually, about two million years ago, a period of recurring glaciations began. As recently as fifteen thousand years ago, the Adirondacks were buried under ice.

One of the puzzles of mass extinction is why, at certain junctures, the resourcefulness of life seems to falter. Powerful as the Alvarez hypothesis proved to be, it explains only a single mass extinction.

"I think that, after the evidence became pretty strong for the impact at the end of the Cretaceous, those of us who were working on this naïvely 85 expected that we would go out and find evidence of impacts coinciding with the other events," Walter Alvarez told me. "And, of course, it's turned out to be much more complicated. We're seeing right now that a mass extinction can be caused by human beings. So it's clear that we do not have a general theory of mass extinction."

Andrew Knoll, a paleontologist at Harvard, has spent most of his career studying the evolution of early life. (Among the many samples he keeps in his office are fossils of microorganisms that lived 2.8 billion years ago.) He has also written about more recent events, like the end-Permian extinction, which took place two hundred and fifty million years ago, and the current extinction event.

Knoll noted that the world can change a lot without producing huge losses; ice ages, for instance, come and go. "What the geological record tells us is that it's time to worry when the rate of change is fast," he told me. In the case of the end-Permian extinction, Knoll and many other researchers believe that the trigger was a sudden burst of volcanic activity; a plume of hot mantle rock from deep in the earth sent nearly a million cubic miles' worth of flood basalts streaming over what is now Siberia. The eruption released enormous quantities of carbon dioxide, which presumably led—then as now—to global warming, and to significant changes in ocean chemistry.

"CO_2 is a paleontologist's dream," Knoll told me. "It can kill things directly, by physiological effects, of which ocean acidification is the best known, and it can kill things by changing the climate. If it gets warmer faster than you can migrate, then you're in trouble."

In the end, the most deadly aspect of human activity may simply be the pace of it. Just in the past century, CO_2 levels in the atmosphere have changed by as much—a hundred parts per million—as they normally do in a hundred-thousand year glacial cycle. Meanwhile, the drop in ocean pH levels that has occurred over the past fifty years may well exceed anything that happened in the seas during the previous fifty million. In a single afternoon, a pathogen like Bd can move, via United or American Airlines, halfway around the world. Before man entered the picture, such a migration would have required hundreds, if not thousands, of years—if, indeed, it could have been completed at all.

90   Currently, a third of all amphibian species, nearly a third of reef-building corals, a quarter of all mammals, and an eighth of all birds are classified as "threatened with extinction." These estimates do not include the species that humans have already wiped out or the species for which there are insufficient data. Nor do the figures take into account the projected

effects of global warming or ocean acidification. Nor, of course, can they anticipate the kinds of sudden, terrible collapses that are becoming almost routine.

I asked Knoll to compare the current situation with past extinction events. He told me that he didn't want to exaggerate recent losses, or to suggest that an extinction on the order of the end-Cretaceous or end-Permian was imminent. At the same time, he noted, when the asteroid hit the Yucatán, "it was one terrible afternoon." He went on, "But it was a short-term event, and then things started getting better. Today, it's not like you have a stress and the stress is relieved and recovery starts. It gets bad and then it keeps being bad, because the stress doesn't go away. Because the stress is us."

Aeolus Cave, in Dorset, Vermont, is believed to be the largest bat hibernaculum in New England; it is estimated that, before white nose hit, more than two hundred thousand bats—some from as far away as Ontario and Rhode Island—came to spend the winter here. In late February, I went with Hicks to visit Aeolus. In the parking lot of the local general store, we met up with officials from the Vermont Fish and Wildlife Department, who had organized the trip. The entrance to Aeolus is about a mile and a half from the nearest road, up a steep, wooded hillside. This time, we approached by snowmobile. The temperature outside was about twenty-five degrees—far too low for bats to be active—but when we got near the entrance we could, once again, see bats fluttering around. The most senior of the Vermont officials, Scott Darling, announced that we'd have to put on latex gloves and Tyvek suits before proceeding. At first, this seemed to me to be paranoid; soon, however, I came to see the sense of it.

Aeolus is a marble cave that was created by water flow over the course of thousands of years. The entrance is a large, horizontal tunnel at the bottom of a small hollow. To keep people out, the Nature Conservancy, which owns the cave, has blocked off the opening with huge iron slats, so that it looks like the gate of a medieval fortress. With a key, one of the slats can be removed; this creates a narrow gap that can be crawled (or slithered) through. Despite the cold, there was an awful smell emanating from the cave—half game farm, half garbage dump. When it was my turn, I squeezed through the gap and immediately slid on the ice, into a pile of dead bats. The scene, in the dimness, was horrific. There were giant icicles hanging from the ceiling, and from the floor large knobs of ice rose up, like polyps. The ground was covered with dead bats; some of the ice knobs, I noticed, had bats frozen into them. There were torpid bats roosting on the ceiling, and also wide-awake ones, which would take off and fly by or, sometimes, right into us.

Why bat corpses pile up in some places, while in others they get eaten or in some other way disappear, is unclear. Hicks speculated that the weather conditions at Aeolus were so harsh that the bats didn't even make it out of the cave before dropping dead. He and Darling had planned to do a count of the bats in the first chamber of the cave, known as Guano Hall, but this plan was soon abandoned, and it was decided just to collect specimens. Darling explained that the specimens would be going to the American Museum of Natural History, so that there would at least be a record of the bats that had once lived in Aeolus. "This may be one of the last opportunities," he said. In contrast to a mine, which has been around at most for centuries, Aeolus, he pointed out, has existed for millennia. It's likely that bats have been hibernating there, generation after generation, since the end of the last ice age.

95   "That's what makes this so dramatic—it's breaking the evolutionary chain," Darling said.

He and Hicks began picking dead bats off the ground. Those which were too badly decomposed were tossed back; those which were more or less intact were sexed and placed in two-quart plastic bags. I helped out by holding open the bag for females. Soon, it was full and another one was started. It struck me, as I stood there holding a bag filled with several dozen stiff, almost weightless bats, that I was watching mass extinction in action.

Several more bags were collected. When the specimen count hit somewhere around five hundred, Darling decided that it was time to go. Hicks hung back, saying that he wanted to take some pictures. In the hours we had been slipping around the cave, the carnage had grown even more grotesque; many of the dead bats had been crushed and now there was blood oozing out of them. As I made my way up toward the entrance, Hicks called after me: "Don't step on any dead bats." It took me a moment to realize that he was joking.

(2009)

Questions

1.   What is "the sixth extinction"? Is this an appropriate name?

2. Comment on how Kolbert uses imagery to provoke an emotional response to the deaths of animals.

3. Rather than structure her article as one continuous, flowing piece, Kolbert has divided it into sections. Outline the structure of the article in terms of these divisions. How effective is this structure?

4. Kolbert quotes Hicks, who says of white nose syndrome, "'It's kind of interesting that the first record we have of this fungus is photographs from a commercial cave in New York that gets about two hundred thousand visits a year.'" What is he implying? To what extent does the information in the article support this implication?

5. Kolbert focuses on frogs and bats as illustrative examples of the current extinctions. Find and research another example, and write about it in the style of Kolbert.

6. Does reading this article make you in any way reconsider the impact you have on the environment? Why or why not?

Questions on "Extraterrestrial Causes for the Cretaceous-Tertiary Extinction" and "The Sixth Extinction?"

1. Describe the intended audience for each piece. How can you tell? What differences in style and content reflect the differences in audience?

2. Choose a section from the Alvarez et al. article and summarize it in the style of Kolbert.

3. How does Kolbert's description of Alvarez et al.'s research process differ from their own description of it in their article? Why do you think the descriptions are different?

4. What does Walter Alvarez mean when he says in the Kolbert article that the asteroid impact hypothesis does not provide "'a general theory of mass extinction'"?

5. Both articles make use of numerical data in their arguments. Compare and contrast how they do this. What kind of information is used? How is it presented? Is one presentation more accessible than the other? More persuasive? More objective?

ALICE MUNRO

WHAT IS REAL?

In this essay, Munro attempts to answer the questions
of why and how she uses elements from her
"real" experience in her works of fiction.

❧

Whenever people get an opportunity to ask me questions about my writing, I can be sure that some of the questions asked will be these: "Do you write about real people?"

"Did those things really happen?"

"When you write about a small town are you really writing about Wingham?" (Wingham is the small town in Ontario where I was born and grew up, and it has often been assumed, by people who should know better, that I have simply "fictionalized" this place in my work. Indeed, the local newspaper has taken me to task for making it the "butt of a soured and cruel introspection.")

5   The usual thing, for writers, is to regard these either as very naive questions, asked by people who really don't understand the difference between autobiography and fiction, who can't recognize the device of the first-person narrator, or else as catch-you-out questions posed by journalists who hope to stir up exactly the sort of dreary (and to outsiders, slightly comic) indignation voiced by my home-town paper. Writers answer such questions patiently or crossly according to temperament and the mood they're in. They say, no, you must understand, my characters are composites; no, those things didn't happen the way I wrote about them; no, of course not, that isn't Wingham (or whatever other place it may be that has had the queer unsought-after distinction of hatching a writer). Or the writer may, riskily, ask the questioners what is real, anyway? None of this seems to be very satisfactory. People go on asking these same questions because the subject really does interest and bewilder them. It would seem to be quite true that they don't know what fiction is.

And how could they know, when what it is, is changing all the time, and we differ among ourselves, and we don't really try to explain because it is too difficult?

What I would like to do here is what I can't do in two or three sentences at the end of a reading. I won't try to explain what fiction is, and what short stories are (assuming, which we can't, that there is any fixed thing that it is and they are), but what short stories are to me, and how I write them, and how I use things that are "real." I will start by explaining how I read stories written by other people. For one thing, I can start reading them anywhere; from beginning to end, from end to beginning, from any point in between in either direction. So obviously I don't take up a story and follow it as if it were a road, taking me somewhere, with views and neat diversions along the way. I go into it, and move back and forth and settle here and there, and stay in it for a while. It's more like a house. Everybody knows what a house does, how it encloses space and makes connections between one enclosed space and another and presents what is outside in a new way. This is the nearest I can come to explaining what a story does for me, and what I want my stories to do for other people.

So when I write a story I want to make a certain kind of structure, and I know the feeling I want to get from being inside that structure. This is the hard part of the explanation, where I have to use a word like "feeling," which is not very precise, because if I attempt to be more intellectually respectable I will have to be dishonest. "Feeling" will have to do.

There is no blueprint for the structure. It's not a question of, "I'll make this kind of house because if I do it right it will have this effect." I've got to make, I've got to build up, a house, a story, to fit around the indescribable "feeling" that is like the soul of the story, and which I must insist upon in a dogged, embarrassed way, as being no more definable than that. And I don't know where it comes from. It seems to be already there, and some unlikely clue, such as a shop window or a bit of conversation, makes me aware of it. Then I start accumulating the material and putting it together. Some of the material I may have lying around already, in memories and observations, and some I invent, and some I have to go diligently looking for (factual details), while some is dumped in my lap (anecdotes, bits of speech). I see how this material might go together to make the shape I need, and I try it. I keep trying and seeing where I went wrong and trying again.

I suppose this is the place where I should talk about technical problems and how I solve them. The main reason I can't is that I'm never sure I do solve anything. Even when I say that I see where I went wrong, I'm being

10

misleading. I never figure out how I'm going to change things, I never say to myself, "That page is heavy going, that paragraph's clumsy, I need some dialogue and shorter sentences." I feel a part that's wrong, like a soggy weight; then I pay attention to the story, as if it were really happening somewhere, not just in my head, and in its own way, not mine. As a result, the sentences may indeed get shorter, there may be more dialogue, and so on. But though I've tried to pay attention to the story, I may not have got it right; those shorter sentences may be an evasion, a mistake. Every final draft, every published story, is still only an attempt, an approach, to the story.

I did promise to talk about using reality. "Why, if Jubilee isn't Wingham, has it got Shuter Street in it?" people want to know. Why have I described somebody's real ceramic elephant sitting on the mantel-piece? I could say I get momentum from doing things like this. The fictional room, town, world, needs a bit of starter dough from the real world. It's a device to help the writer—at least it helps me—but it arouses a certain baulked fury in the people who really do live on Shuter Street and the lady who owns the ceramic elephant. "Why do you put in something true and then go on and tell lies?" they say, and anybody who has been on the receiving end of this kind of thing knows how they feel.

"I do it for the sake of my art and to make this structure which encloses the soul of my story, that I've been telling you about," says the writer. "That is more important than anything."

Not to everybody, it isn't.

So I can see there might be a case, once you've written the story and got the momentum, for going back and changing the elephant to a camel (though there's always a chance the lady might complain that you made a nasty camel out of a beautiful elephant), and changing Shuter Street to Blank Street. But what about the big chunks of reality, without which your story can't exist? In the story *Royal Beatings*, I use a big chunk of reality: the story of the butcher, and of the young men who may have been egged on to "get" him. This is a story out of an old newspaper; it really did happen in a town I know. There is no legal difficulty in using it because it has been printed in a newspaper, and besides, the people who figure in it are all long dead. But there is a difficulty about offending people in that town who would feel that use of this story is a deliberate exposure, taunt and insult. Other people who have no connection with the real happening would say, "Why write about anything so hideous?" And lest you think that such an objection could only be raised by simple folk who read nothing but Harlequin Romances, let me tell you that one of the questions most frequently asked at universities is, "Why do you write about things that are so depressing?" People can accept almost any amount of ugliness if it is contained in a familiar formula, as it is on television, but when they come closer to their own place, their own lives, they are much offended by a lack of editing.

There are ways I can defend myself against such objections. I can say, "I do it in the interests of historical reality. That is what the old days were really like." Or, "I do it to show the dark side of human nature, the beast let loose, the evil we can run up against in communities and families." In certain countries I could say, "I do it to show how bad things were under the old system when there were prosperous butchers and young fellows hanging around livery stables and nobody thought about building a new society." But the fact is, the minute I say *to show* I am telling a lie. I don't do it to show anything. I put this story at the heart of my story because I need it there and it belongs there. It is the black room at the center of the house with all other rooms leading to and away from it. That is all. A strange defense. Who told me to write this story? Who feels any need of it before it is written? I do. I do, so that I might grab off this piece of horrid reality and install it where I see fit, even if Hat Nettleton and his friends were still around to make me sorry.

The answer seems to be as confusing as ever. Lots of true answers are. Yes and no. Yes, I use bits of what is real, in the sense of being really there and really happening, in the world, as most people see it, and I transform it into something that is really there and really happening, in my story. No, I am not concerned with using what is real to make any sort of record or prove any sort of point, and I am not concerned with any methods of selection but my own, which I can't fully explain. This is quite presumptuous, and if writers are not allowed to be so—and quite often, in many places, they are not—I see no point in the writing of fiction.

(1982)

Questions

1. Munro's title for this essay is a question rather than a statement. Does she answer her own question in the essay? If so, what is "real" according to Munro?

2. What does Munro mean when she writes, "Every final draft, every published story, is still only an attempt, an approach, to the story"?

3. What is the tone of Munro's essay? How is the tone established?

4. Discuss the use of questions in the essay. What effect do the questions contained in the essay have on the reader?

5. There are several instances where Munro admits an inability to precisely define her process as a writer. Does this weaken or strengthen her argument?

6. We frequently see "fictionalized" versions of actual events in print, on television, and in the movies. Can you envision a situation where fictional stories based on real events can be harmful? How and why?

Robert Darnton

Workers Revolt: The Great Cat Massacre of the Rue Saint-Séverin

*Why would a group of printing apprentices in the 1730s
have launched a murderous attack on their masters' cats?
Endeavoring to answer that question, historian Robert Darnton
explores many aspects of eighteenth-century life.*

❦

The funniest thing that ever happened in the printing shop of Jacques Vincent, according to a worker who witnessed it, was a riotous massacre of cats. The worker, Nicolas Contat, told the story in an account of his apprenticeship in the shop, rue Saint-Séverin, Paris, during the late 1730s.[1] Life as an apprentice was hard, he explained. There were two of them: Jerome, the somewhat fictionalized version of Contat himself, and Léveillé. They slept in a filthy, freezing room, rose before dawn, ran errands all day while dodging insults from the journeymen and abuse from the master, and received nothing but slops to eat. They found the food especially galling. Instead of dining at the master's table, they had to eat scraps from his plate in the kitchen. Worse still, the cook secretly sold the leftovers and gave the boys cat food—old, rotten bits of meat that they could not stomach and so passed on to the cats, who refused it.

---

1   Nicolas Contat, *Anecdotes typographiques où l'on voit la description des coutumes, moeurs et usages singuliers des compagnons imprimeurs*, ed. Giles Barber (Oxford, 1980). The original manuscript is dated 1762. Barber provides a thorough description of its background and of Contat's career in his introduction. The account of the cat massacre occurs on pp. 48-56. [Unless otherwise noted, all notes to this essay are from the author.]

This last injustice brought Contat to the theme of cats. They occupied a special place in his narrative and in the household of the rue Saint-Séverin. The master's wife adored them, especially *la grise* (the gray), her favorite. A passion for cats seemed to have swept through the printing trade, at least at the level of the masters, or *bourgeois* as the workers called them. One bourgeois kept twenty-five cats. He had their portraits painted and fed them on roast fowl. Meanwhile, the apprentices were trying to cope with a profusion of alley cats who also thrived in the printing district and made the boys' lives miserable. The cats howled all night on the roof over the apprentices' dingy bedroom, making it impossible to get a full night's sleep. As Jerome and Léveillé had to stagger out of bed at four or five in the morning to open the gate for the earliest arrivals among the journeymen, they began the day in a state of exhaustion while the bourgeois slept late. The master did not even work with the men, just as he did not eat with them. He let the foreman run the shop and rarely appeared in it, except to vent his violent temper, usually at the expense of the apprentices.

One night the boys resolved to right this inequitable state of affairs. Léveillé, who had an extraordinary talent for mimicry, crawled along the roof until he reached a section near the master's bedroom, and then he took to howling and meowing so horribly that the bourgeois and his wife did not sleep a wink. After several nights of this treatment, they decided they were being bewitched. But instead of calling the curé—the master was exceptionally devout and the mistress exceptionally attached to her confessor—they commanded the apprentices to get rid of the cats. The mistress gave the order, enjoining the boys above all to avoid frightening her *grise*.

Gleefully Jerome and Léveillé set to work, aided by the journeymen. Armed with broom handles, bars of the press, and other tools of their trade, they went after every cat they could find, beginning with *la grise*. Léveillé smashed its spine with an iron bar and Jerome finished it off. Then they stashed it in a gutter while the journeymen drove the other cats across the rooftops, bludgeoning every one within reach and trapping those who tried to escape in strategically placed sacks. They dumped sackloads of half-dead cats in the courtyard. Then the entire workshop gathered round and staged a mock trial, complete with guards, a confessor, and a public executioner. After pronouncing the animals guilty and administering last rites, they strung them up on an improvised gallows. Roused by gales of laughter, the mistress arrived. She let out a shriek as soon as she saw a bloody cat dangling from a noose. Then she realized it might be *la grise*.

Certainly not, the men assured her: they had too much respect for the house to do such a thing. At this point the master appeared. He flew into a rage at the general stoppage of work, though his wife tried to explain that they were threatened by a more serious kind of insubordination. Then master and mistress withdrew, leaving the men delirious with "joy," "disorder," and "laughter."[2]

The laughter did not end there. Léveillé reenacted the entire scene in mime at least twenty times during subsequent days when the printers wanted to knock off for some hilarity. Burlesque reenactments of incidents in the life of the shop, known as *copies* in printers' slang, provided a major form of entertainment for the men. The idea was to humiliate someone in the shop by satirizing his peculiarities. A successful *copie* would make the butt of the joke fume with rage—*prendre la chèvre* (take the goat) in the shop slang—while his mates razzed him with "rough music." They would run their composing sticks across the tops of the type cases, beat their mallets against the chases, pound on cupboards, and bleat like goats. The bleating (*bais* in the slang) stood for the humiliation heaped on the victims, as in English when someone "gets your goat." Contat emphasized that Léveillé produced the funniest *copies* anyone had ever known and elicited the greatest choruses of rough music. The whole episode, cat massacre compounded by *copies*, stood out as the most hilarious experience in Jerome's entire career.

Yet it strikes the modern reader as unfunny, if not downright repulsive. Where is the humor in a group of grown men bleating like goats and banging with their tools while an adolescent reenacts the ritual slaughter of a defenseless animal? Our own inability to get the joke is an indication of the distance that separates us from the workers of preindustrial Europe. The perception of that distance may serve as the starting point of an investigation, for anthropologists have found that the best points of entry in an attempt to penetrate an alien culture can be those where it seems to be most opaque. When you realize that you are not getting something—a joke, a proverb, a ceremony—that is particularly meaningful to the natives, you can see where to grasp a foreign system of meaning in order to unravel it. By getting the joke of the great cat massacre, it may be possible to "get" a basic ingredient of artisanal culture under the Old Regime.

5

---

2   Contat, *Anecdotes typographiques*, p. 53.

It should be explained at the outset that we cannot observe the killing of the cats at firsthand. We can study it only through Contat's narrative, written about twenty years after the event. There can be no doubt about the authenticity of Contat's quasi-fictional autobiography, as Giles Barber has demonstrated in his masterful edition of the text. It belongs to the line of autobiographical writing by printers that stretches from Thomas Platter to Thomas Gent, Benjamin Franklin, Nicolas Restif de la Bretonne, and Charles Manby Smith. Because printers, or at least compositors, had to be reasonably literate in order to do their work, they were among the few artisans who could give their own accounts of life in the working classes two, three, and four centuries ago. With all its misspellings and grammatical flaws, Contat's is perhaps the richest of these accounts. But it cannot be regarded as a mirror-image of what actually happened. It should be read as Contat's version of a happening, as his attempt to tell a story. Like all story telling, it sets the action in a frame of reference; it assumes a certain repertory of associations and responses on the part of its audience; and it provides meaningful shape to the raw stuff of experience. But since we are attempting to get at its meaning in the first place, we should not be put off by its fabricated character. On the contrary, by treating the narrative as fiction or meaningful fabrication we can use it to develop an ethnological *explication de texte*.

The first explanation that probably would occur to most readers of Contat's story is that the cat massacre served as an oblique attack on the master and his wife. Contat set the event in the context of remarks about the disparity between the lot of workers and the bourgeois—a matter of the basic elements in life: work, food, and sleep. The injustice seemed especially flagrant in the case of the apprentices, who were treated like animals while the animals were promoted over their heads to the position the boys should have occupied, the place at the master's table. Although the apprentices seem most abused, the text makes it clear that the killing of the cats expressed a hatred for the bourgeois that had spread among all the workers: "The masters love cats; consequently [the workers] hate them." After masterminding the massacre, Léveillé became the hero of the shop, because "all the workers are in league against the masters. It is enough to speak badly of them [the masters] to be esteemed by the whole assembly of typographers."[3]

---

3   Ibid., pp. 52 and 53.

Historians have tended to treat the era of artisanal manufacturing as an idyllic period before the onset of industrialization. Some even portray the workshop as a kind of extended family in which master and journeymen labored at the same tasks, ate at the same table, and sometimes slept under the same roof.[4] Had anything happened to poison the atmosphere of the printing shops in Paris by 1740?

During the second half of the seventeenth century, the large printing houses, backed by the government, eliminated most of the smaller shops, and an oligarchy of masters seized control of the industry.[5] At the same time, the situation of the journeymen deteriorated. Although estimates vary and statistics cannot be trusted, it seems that their number remained stable: approximately 335 in 1666, 339 in 1701, and 340 in 1721. Meanwhile the number of masters declined by more than half, from eighty-three to thirty-six, the limit fixed by an edict of 1686. That meant fewer shops with larger work forces, as one can see from statistics on the density of presses: in 1644 Paris had seventy-five printing shops with a total of 180 presses; in 1701 it had fifty-one shops with 195 presses. This trend made it virtually impossible for journeymen to rise into the ranks of the masters. About the only way for a worker to get ahead in the craft was to marry a master's widow, for masterships had become hereditary privileges, passed on from husband to wife and from father to son.

The journeymen also felt threatened from below because the masters tended increasingly to hire *alloués*, or underqualified printers, who had not undergone the apprenticeship that made a journeyman eligible, in principle, to advance to a mastership. The *alloués* were merely a source of cheap labor, excluded from the upper ranks of the trade and fixed, in their inferior status, by an edict of 1723. Their degradation stood out in their name: they were *à louer* (for hire), not *compagnons* (journeymen) of the master. They personified the tendency of labor to become a commodity instead of a partnership. Thus Contat served his apprenticeship and wrote his memoirs when times were hard for journeymen printers, when the men in the shop

10

---

4   See, for example, Albert Soboul, *La France à la veille de la Révolution* (Paris, 1966), p. 140; and Edward Shorter, "The History of Work in the West: An Overview" in *Work and Community in the West*, ed. Edward Shorter (New York, 1973).

5   The following discussion is derived from Henri-Jean Martin, *Livre, pouvoirs et société à Paris au XVIIe siècle (1598-1701)* (Geneva, 1969); and Paul Chauvet, *Les Ouviers du livre en France, des origins à la Révolution de 1789* (Paris, 1959). The statistics come from investigations by the authorities of the Old Regime as reported by Martin (II, 699-700) and Chauvet (pp. 126 and 154).

in the rue Saint-Séverin stood in danger of being cut off from the top of the trade and swamped from the bottom.

How this general tendency became manifest in an actual workshop may be seen from the papers of the Société typographique de Neuchâtel (STN). To be sure, the STN was Swiss, and it did not begin business until seven years after Contat wrote his memoirs (1762). But printing practices were essentially the same everywhere in the eighteenth century. The STN's archives conform in dozens of details to Contat's account of his experience. (They even mention the same shop foreman, Colas, who supervised Jerome for a while at the Imprimerie Royale and took charge of the STN's shop for a brief stint in 1779.) And they provide the only surviving record of the way masters hired, managed, and fired printers in the early modern era.

The STN's wage book shows that workers usually stayed in the shop for only a few months.[6] They left because they quarreled with the master, they got in fights, they wanted to pursue their fortune in shops further down the road, or they ran out of work. Compositors were hired by the job, *labeur* or *ouvrage* in printer's slang. When they finished a job, they frequently were fired, and a few pressmen had to be fired as well in order to maintain the balance between the two halves of the shop, the *casse* or composing sector and the *presse* or pressroom (two compositors usually set enough type to occupy a team of two pressmen). When the foreman took on new jobs, he hired new hands. The hiring and firing went on at such a fierce pace that the work force was rarely the same from one week to the next. Jerome's fellow workers in the rue Saint-Séverin seem to have been equally volatile. They, too, were hired for specific *labeurs*, and they sometimes walked off the job after quarrels with the bourgeois—a practice common enough to have its own entry in the glossary of their slang which Contat appended to his narrative: *emporter son Saint Jean* (to carry off your set of tools or quit). A man was known as an *ancien* if he remained in the shop for only a year. Other slang terms suggest the atmosphere in which the work took place: *une chèvre capitale* (a fit of rage), *se donner la grate* (to get in a fight), *prendre la barbe* (to get drunk), *faire la déroute* (to go pub crawling), *promener sa chape* (to knock off work), *faire des loups* (to pile up debts).[7]

---

6   For a more detailed discussion of this material, see Robert Darnton, "Work and Culture in an Eighteenth-Century Printing Shop," an Englehard lecture at the Library of Congress to be published by the Library of Congress.

7   Contat, *Anecdotes typographiques*, pp. 68-73.

The violence, drunkenness, and absenteeism show up in the statistics of income and output one can compile from the STN's wage book. Printers worked in erratic spurts—twice as much in one week as in another, the weeks varying from four to six days and the days beginning anywhere from four in the morning until nearly noon. In order to keep the irregularity within bounds, the masters sought men with two supreme traits: assiduousness and sobriety. If they also happened to be skilled, so much the better. A recruiting agent in Geneva recommended a compositor who was willing to set out for Neuchâtel in typical terms: "He is a good worker, capable of doing any job he gets, not at all a drunkard and assiduous at his labor."[8]

The STN relied on recruiters because it did not have an adequate labor pool in Neuchâtel and the streams of printers on the typographical *tours de France* sometimes ran dry. The recruiters and employers exchanged letters that reveal a common set of assumptions about eighteenth-century artisans: they were lazy, flighty, dissolute, and unreliable. They could not be trusted, so the recruiter should not loan them money for travel expenses and the employer could keep their belongings as a kind of security deposit in case they skipped off after collecting their pay. It followed that they could be discarded without compunction, whether or not they had worked diligently, had families to support, or fell sick. The STN ordered them in "assortments" just as it ordered paper and type. It complained that a recruiter in Lyon "sent us a couple in such a bad state that we were obliged to ship them off"[9] and lectured him about failing to inspect the goods. "Two of those whom you have sent to us have arrived all right, but so sick that they could infect all the rest; so we haven't been able to hire them. No one in town wanted to give them lodging. They have therefore left again and took the route for Besançon, in order to turn themselves in at the *hôpital*."[10] A bookseller in Lyon advised them to fire most of their men during a slack period in their printing in order to flood the labor supply in eastern France and "give us more power over a wild and undisciplinable race, which we cannot control."[11] Journeymen and masters may have lived together as members of a happy family at some time somewhere in

15

8   Christ to STN, Jan. 8, 1773, papers of the Société typographique de Neuchâtel, Bibliothèque de la Ville de Neuchâtel, Switzerland, hereafter cited as STN.

9   STN to Joseph Duplain, July 2, 1777.

10   STN to Louis Vernange, June 26, 1777.

11   Joseph Duplain to STN, Dec. 10, 1778.

Europe, but not in the printing houses of eighteenth-century France and Switzerland.

Contat himself believed that such a state had once existed. He began his description of Jerome's apprenticeship by invoking a golden age when printing was first invented and printers lived as free and equal members of a "republic," governed by its own laws and traditions in a spirit of fraternal "union and friendship."[12] He claimed that the republic still survived in the form of the *chapelle* or workers' association in each shop. But the government had broken up general associations; the ranks had been thinned by *alloués*; the journeymen had been excluded from masterships; and the masters had withdrawn into a separate world of *haute cuisine* and *grasses matinées*. The master in the rue Saint-Séverin ate different food, kept different hours, and talked a different language. His wife and daughters dallied with worldly abbés. They kept pets. Clearly, the bourgeois belonged to a different subculture—one which meant above all that he did not work. In introducing his account of the cat massacre, Contat made explicit the contrast between the worlds of worker and master that ran throughout the narrative: "Workers, apprentices, everyone works. Only the masters and mistresses enjoy the sweetness of sleep. That makes Jerome and Léveillé resentful. They resolve not to be the only wretched ones. They want their master and mistress as associates (associés)."[13] That is, the boys wanted to restore a mythical past when masters and men worked in friendly association. They also may have had in mind the more recent extinction of the smaller printing shops. So they killed the cats.

But why cats? And why was the killing so funny? Those questions take us beyond the consideration of early modern labor relations and into the obscure subject of popular ceremonies and symbolism.

Folklorists have made historians familiar with the ceremonial cycles that marked off the calendar year for early modern man.[14] The most important

---

12 Contat, *Anecdotes typographiques*, pp. 30-31.

13 Ibid., p. 52.

14 For a recent overview of the vast literature on folklore and French history and bibliographic references, see Nicole Belmont, *Mythes et croyances dans l'ancienne France* (Paris, 1973). The following discussion is based primarily on the material collected in Eugène Rolland, *Faune populaire de la France* (Paris, 1881), IV; Paul Sébillot, *Le Folk-lore de France* (Paris, 1904-7), 4 vols., especially III, 72-155 and IV, 90-98; and to a lesser extent Arnold Van Gennep, *Manuel de folklore français contemporain* (Paris, 1937-58), 9 vols.

of these was the cycle of carnival and Lent, a period of revelry followed by a period of abstinence. During carnival the common people suspended the normal rules of behavior and ceremoniously reversed the social order or turned it upside down in riotous procession. Carnival was a time for cutting up by youth groups, particularly apprentices, who organized themselves in "abbeys" ruled by a mock abbot or king and who staged charivaris or burlesque processions with rough music in order to humiliate cuckolds, husbands who had been beaten by their wives, brides who had married below their age group, or someone else who personified the infringement of traditional norms. Carnival was high season for hilarity, sexuality, and youth run riot—a time when young people tested social boundaries by limited outbursts of deviance, before being reassimilated in the world of order, submission, and Lentine seriousness. It came to an end of Shrove Tuesday or Mardi Gras, when a straw mannequin, King Carnival or Caramantran, was given a ritual trial and execution. Cats played an important part in some charivaris. In Burgundy, the crowd incorporated cat torture into its rough music. While mocking a cuckold or some other victim, the youths passed around a cat, tearing its fur to make it howl. *Faire le chat*, they called it. The Germans called charivaris *Katzenmusik*, a term that may have been derived from the howls of tortured cats.[15]

Cats also figured in the cycle of Saint John the Baptist, which took place on June 24, at the time of the summer solstice. Crowds made bonfires, jumped over them, danced around them, and threw into them objects with magical power, hoping to avoid disaster and obtain good fortune during the rest of the year. A favorite object was cats—cats tied up in bags, cats suspended from ropes, or cats burned at the stake. Parisians liked to incinerate cats by the sackful, while the Courimauds (*cour à miaud* or cat chasers) of Saint Chamond preferred to chase a flaming cat through the streets. In parts of Burgundy and Lorraine they danced around a kind of burning May pole with a cat tied to it. In the Metz region they burned a dozen cats at a time in a basket on top of a bonfire. The ceremony took place with great pomp in Metz itself, until it was abolished in 1765. The town dignitaries arrived in procession at the Place du Grand-Saulcy, lit the pyre, and a ring

---

15 In Germany and Switzerland, *Katzenmusik* sometimes included mock trials and executions. The etymology of the term is not clear. See E. Hoffman-Krayer and Hans Bächtold-Stäubli, *Handwörterbuch des deutschen Aberglaubens* (Berlin and Leipzig, 1931-32), IV, 1125-32 and Paul Grebe et al., *Duden Etymologie: Herkunftwörterbuch der deutschen Sprache* (Mannheim, 1963), p. 317.

of riflemen from the garrison fired off volleys while the cats disappeared screaming in the flames. Although the practice varied from place to place, the ingredients were everywhere the same: a *feu de joie* (bonfire), cats, and an aura of hilarious witch-hunting.[16]

20   In addition to these general ceremonies, which involved entire communities, artisans celebrated ceremonies peculiar to their craft. Printers processed and feasted in honor of their patron, Saint John the Evangelist, both on his saint's day, December 27, and on the anniversary of his martyrdom, May 6, the festival of Saint Jean Porte Latine. By the eighteenth century, the masters had excluded the journeymen from the confraternity devoted to the saint, but the journeymen continued to hold ceremonies in their chapels.[17] On Saint Martin's day, November 11, they held a mock trial followed by a feast. Contat explained that the chapel was a tiny "republic," which governed itself according to its own code of conduct. When a worker violated the code, the foreman, who was the head of the chapel and not part of the management, entered a fine in a register: leaving a candle lit, five sous; brawling, three livres; insulting the good name of the chapel, three livres; and so on. On Saint Martin's, the foreman read out the fines and collected them. The workers sometimes appealed their cases before a burlesque tribunal composed of the chapel's "ancients," but in the end they had to pay up amidst more bleating, banging of tools, and riotous laughter. The fines went for food and drink in the chapel's favorite tavern, where the hell-raising continued until late in the night.[18]

Taxation and commensality characterized all the other ceremonies of the chapel. Special dues and feasts marked a man's entry into the shop (*bienvenue*), his exit (*conduite*), and even his marriage (*droit de chevet*). Above all, they punctuated a youth's progress from apprentice to journeyman. Contat described four of these rites, the most important being the first, called the taking of the apron, and the last, Jerome's initiation as a full-fledged *compagnon*.

---

16   Information on the cat burning in Saint Chamond comes from a letter kindly sent to me by Elinor Accampo of Colorado College. The Metz ceremony is described in A. Benoist, "Traditions et anciennes coutumes du pays messin," *Revue des traditions populaires, XV* (1900), 14.

17   Contat, *Anecdotes typographiques*, pp. 30 and 66-67; and Chauvet, *Les Ouviers du livre*, pp. 7-12.

18   Contat, *Anecdotes typographiques*, pp. 65-67.

The taking of the apron (*la prise de tablier*) occurred soon after Jerome joined the shop. He had to pay six livres (about three days' wages for an ordinary journeyman) into a kitty, which the journeymen supplemented by small payments of their own (*faire la reconnaissance*). Then the chapel repaired to its favorite tavern, Le Panier Fleury in the rue de la Huchette. Emissaries were dispatched to procure provisions and returned loaded down with bread and meat, having lectured the shopkeepers of the neighborhood on which cuts were worthy of typographers and which could be left for cobblers. Silent and glass in hand, the journeymen gathered around Jerome in a special room on the second floor of the tavern. The subforeman approached, carrying the apron and followed by two "ancients," one from each of the "estates" of the shop, the *casse* and the *presse*. He handed the apron, newly made from close-woven linen, to the foreman, who took Jerome by the hand and led him to the center of the room, the subforeman and "ancients" falling behind. The foreman made a short speech, placed the apron over Jerome's head and tied the strings behind him, as everyone drank to the health of the initiate. Jerome was then given a seat with the chapel dignitaries at the head of the table. The rest rushed for the best places they could find and fell on the food. They gobbled and guzzled and called out for more. After several Gargantuan rounds, they settled down to shop talk—and Contat lets us listen in:

> "Isn't it true," says one of them, "that printers know how to shovel it in? I am sure that if someone presented us with a roast mutton, as big as you like, we would leave nothing but the bones behind...."
> They don't talk about theology nor philosophy and still less of politics. Each speaks of his job: one will talk to you about the *casse*, another the *presse*, this one of the tympan, another of the ink ball leathers. They all speak at the same time, whether they can be heard or not.

At last, early in the morning after hours of swilling and shouting, the workers separated—sotted but ceremonial to the end: "Bonsoir, Monsieur notre prote [foreman]"; "Bonsoir, Messieurs les compositeurs"; "Bonsoir, Messieurs les imprimeurs"; "Bonsoir Jerome." The text explains that Jerome will be called by his first name until he is received as a journeyman.[19]

---

19   Ibid., pp. 37-41, quotation from pp. 39-40.

That moment came four years later, after two intermediary ceremonies (the *admission à l'ouvrage* and the *admission à la banque*) and a vast amount of hazing. Not only did the men torment Jerome, mocking his ignorance, sending him on wild goose chases, making him the butt of practical jokes, and overwhelming him with nasty chores; they also refused to teach him anything. They did not want another journeyman in their over-flooded labor pool, so Jerome had to pick up the tricks of the trade by himself. The work, the food, the lodging, the lack of sleep, it was enough to drive a boy mad, or at least out of the shop. In fact, however, it was standard treatment and should not be taken too seriously. Contat recounted the catalogue of Jerome's troubles in a light-hearted manner, which suggested a stock comic genre, the *misère des apprentis*.[20] The *misères* provided farcical accounts, in doggerel verse or broadsides, of a stage in life that was familiar and funny to everyone in the artisanate. It was a transitional stage, which marked the passage from childhood to adulthood. A young man had to sweat his way through it so that he would have paid his dues—the printers demanded actual payments, called *bienvenues* or *quatre heures*, in addition to razzing the apprentices—when he reached full membership in a vocational group. Until he arrived at that point, he lived in a fluid or liminal state, trying out adult conventions by subjecting them to some hell-raising of his own. His elders tolerated his pranks, called *copies* and *joberies* in the printing trade, because they saw them as wild oats, which needed to be sown before he could settle down. Once settled, he would have internalized the conventions of his craft and acquired a new identity, which was often symbolized by a change in his name.[21]

---

20   A good example of the genre, *La Misère des apprentis imprimeurs* (1710) is printed as an appendix to Contat, *Anecdotes typographiques*, pp. 101-10. For other examples, see A.C. Cailleau, *Les Misères de ce monde, ou complaints facétieuses sur les apprentissages des différents arts et métiers de la ville et faubourgs de Paris* (Paris, 1783).

21   The classic study of this process is Arnold Van Gennep, *Les Rites de passage* (Paris, 1908). It has been extended by subsequent ethnographic research, notably that of Victor Turner: *The Forest of Symbols: Aspects of Ndembu Ritual* (Ithaca, NY, 1967) and *The Ritual Process* (Chicago, 1969). Jerome's experience fits the Van Gennep-Turner model very well, except in a few respects. He was not considered sacred and dangerous, although the chapel could fine journeymen for drinking with him. He did not live outside adult society, although he left his home for a makeshift room at the edge of the master's household. And he was not exposed to secret *sacra*, although he had to acquire an esoteric lingo and to assimilate a craft ethos after a great deal of tribulation climaxed by a communal meal. Joseph Moxon, Thomas Gent, and Benjamin Franklin mention

Jerome became a journeyman by passing through the final rite, *compa-* 25
gnonnage. It took the same form as the other ceremonies, a celebration over
food and drink after the candidate paid an initiation fee and the journeymen
chipped in with *reconnaissance*. But this time Contat gave a summary of
the foreman's speech:[22]

> The newcomer is indoctrinated. He is told never to betray his col-
> leagues and to maintain the wage rate. If a worker doesn't accept a
> price [for a job] and leaves the shop, no one in the house should do
> the job for a smaller price. Those are the laws among the workers.
> Faithfulness and probity are recommended to him. Any worker
> who betrays the others, when something forbidden, called *marron*
> [chestnut], is being printed, must be expelled ignominiously from
> the shop. The workers blacklist him by circular letters sent around
> all the shops of Paris and the provinces.... Aside from that, anything
> is permitted: excessive drinking is considered a good quality, gal-
> lantry and debauchery as youthful feats, indebtedness as a sign of
> wit, irreligion as sincerity. It's a free and republican territory in
> which everything is permitted. Live as you like but be an *honnête*
> *homme*, no hypocrisy.

Hypocrisy turned out in the rest of the narrative to be the main characteristic of the bourgeois, a superstitious religious bigot. He occupied a
separate world of pharasaical bourgeois morality. The workers defined

---

similar practices in England. In Germany the initiation rite was much more elaborate
and had structural similarities to the rites of tribes in Africa, New Guinea, and North
America. The apprentice wore a filthy headdress adorned with goat's horns and a fox's
tail, indicating that he had reverted to an animal state. As a *Cornut* or *Mittelding*, part
man, part beast, he underwent ritual tortures, including the filing of his fingertips. At the
final ceremony, the head of the shop knocked off the hat and slapped him in the face. He
then emerged newborn—sometimes newly named and even baptized—as a full-fledged
journeyman. Such at least was the practice described in German typographical manuals,
notably Christian Gottlob Täubel, *Praktisches Handbuch der Buchdruckerkunst für An-*
fänger (Leipzig, 1791); Wilhelm Gottlieb Kircher, *Anweisung in der Buchdruckerkunst*
so viel davon das Drucken betrifft (Brunswick, 1793); and Johann Christoph Hildeb-
rand, *Handbuch für Buchdrucker-Lehrlinge* (Eisenach, 1835). The rite was related to an
ancient popular play, the *Depositio Cornuti typographici*, which was printed by Jacob
Redinger in his *Neu aufgesetztes Format Büchlein* (Frankfurt-am-Main, 1679).

22 Contat, *Anecdotes typographiques*, pp. 65-66.

their "republic" against that world and against other journeyman's groups as well—the cobblers, who ate inferior cuts of meat, and the masons or carpenters who were always good for a brawl when the printers, divided into "estates" (the *casse* and the *presse*) toured country taverns on Sundays. In entering an "estate," Jerome assimilated an ethos. He identified himself with a craft; and as a full-fledged journeyman compositor, he received a new name. Having gone through a rite of passage in the full, anthropological sense of the term, he became a *Monsieur*.[23]

So much for ceremonies. What about cats? It should be said at the outset that there is an indefinable *je ne sais quoi* about cats, a mysterious something that has fascinated mankind since the time of the ancient Egyptians. One can sense a quasi-human intelligence behind a cat's eyes. One can mistake a cat's howl at night for a human scream, torn from some deep, visceral part of man's animal nature. Cats appealed to poets like Baudelaire and painters like Manet, who wanted to express the humanity in animals along with the animality of men—and especially of women.[24]

This ambiguous ontological position, a straddling of conceptual categories, gives certain animals—pigs, dogs, and cassowaries as well as cats—in certain cultures an occult power associated with the taboo. That is why Jews do not eat pigs, according to Mary Douglas, and why Englishmen can insult one another by saying "son-of-a-bitch" rather than "son-of-a-cow," according to Edmund Leach.[25] Certain animals are good for swearing, just as they are "good for thinking" in Lévi-Strauss's famous formula. I would add that others—cats in particular—are good for staging ceremonies. They

---

23 The text does not give Jerome's last name, but it stresses the name change and the acquisition of the "Monsieur": "It is only after the end of the apprenticeship that one is called Monsieur; this quality belongs only to journeymen and not to apprentices" (p. 41). In the wage book of the STN, the journeymen always appear with their "Monsieur," even when they were called by nicknames, such as "Monsieur Bonnemain."

24 The black cat in Manet's *Olympia* represents a common motif, the animal "familiar" of a nude. On Baudelaire's cats, see Roman Jakobson and Claude Lévi-Strauss, "*Les Chats* de Charles Baudelaire," *L'Homme*, II (1962), 5-21; and Michel Riffaterre, "Describing Poetic Structures: Two Approaches to Baudelaire's *Les Chats*," in *Structuralism*, ed. Jacques Ehrmann (New Haven, 1966).

25 Mary Douglas, *Purity and Danger: An Analysis of Concepts of Pollution and Taboo* (London, 1966); and E.R. Leach, "Anthropological Aspects of Language: Animal Categories and Verbal Abuse," in *New Directions in the Study of Language*, ed. E.H. Lenneberg (Cambridge, Mass., 1964).

have ritual value. You cannot make a charivari with a cow. You do it with cats: you decide to *faire le chat*, to make *Katzenmusik*.

The torture of animals, especially cats, was a popular amusement throughout early modern Europe. You have only to look at Hogarth's *Stages of Cruelty* to see its importance, and once you start looking you see people torturing animals everywhere. Cat killings provided a common theme in literature, from *Don Quixote* in early seventeenth-century Spain to *Germinal* in late nineteenth-century France.[26] Far from being a sadistic fantasy on the part of a few half-crazed authors, the literary versions of cruelty to animals expressed a deep current of popular culture, as Mikhail Bakhtin has shown in his study of Rabelais.[27] All sorts of ethnographic reports confirm that view. On the *dimanche des brandons* in Semur, for example, children used to attach cats to poles and roast them over bonfires. In the *jeu du chat* at the Fete-Dieu in Aix-en-Provence, they threw cats high in the air and smashed them on the ground. They used expressions like "patient as a cat whose claws are being pulled out" or "patient as a cat whose paws are being grilled." The English were just as cruel. During the Reformation in London, a Protestant crowd shaved a cat to look like a priest, dressed it in mock vestments, and hanged it on the gallows at Cheapside.[28] It would be possible to string out many other examples, but

---

26 Cervantes and Zola adapted traditional cat lore to the themes of their novels. In *Don Quixote* (part II, chap. 46), a sack full of howling cats interrupts the hero's serenade to Altisidora. Taking them for devils, he tries to mow them down with his sword, only to be bested by one of them in single combat. In *Germinal* (part V, chap. 6), the symbolism works in the opposite way. A mob of workers pursues Maigrat, their class enemy, as if he were a cat trying to escape across the rooftops. Screaming "Get the cat! Get the cat!" they castrate his body "like a tomcat" after he falls from the roof. For an example of cat killing as a satire on French legalism, see Friar John's plan to massacre the Furry Lawcats in Rabelais' *Gargantua and Pantagruel*, book V, chap. 15.

27 Mikhail Bakhtin, *Rabelais and His World*, trans. Helene Iswolsky (Cambridge, Mass., 1968). The most important literary version of cat lore to appear in Contat's time was *Les Chats* (Rotterdam, 1728) by François Augustin Paradis de Moncrif. Although it was a mock treatise aimed at a sophisticated audience, it drew on a vast array of popular superstitions and proverbs, many of which appeared in the collections of folklorists a century and a half later.

28 C.S.L. Davies, *Peace, Print and Protestantism* (St. Albans, Herts, 1977). The other references come from the sources cited in note 14. Among the many dictionaries of proverbs and slang, see André-Joseph Panckoucke, *Dictionnaire des proverbs françois et des façons de parler comiques, burlesques, et familières* (Paris, 1748) and Gaston Esnault, *Dictionnaire historique des argots français* (Paris, 1965).

the point should be clear: there was nothing unusual about the ritual killing of cats. On the contrary, when Jerome and his fellow workers tried and hanged all the cats they could find in the rue Saint-Séverin, they drew on a common element in their culture. But what significance did that culture attribute to cats?

30   To get a grip on that question, one must rummage through collections of folktales, superstitions, proverbs, and popular medicine. The material is rich, varied, and vast but extremely hard to handle. Although much of it goes back to the Middle Ages, little can be dated. It was gathered for the most part by folklorists in the late nineteenth and early twentieth centuries, when sturdy strains of folklore still resisted the influence of the printed word. But the collections do not make it possible to claim that this or that practice existed in the printing houses of mid-eighteenth-century Paris. One can only assert that printers lived and breathed in an atmosphere of traditional customs and beliefs which permeated everything. It was not everywhere the same—France remained a patchwork of *pays* rather than a unified nation until late in the nineteenth century—but everywhere some common motifs could be found. The commonest were attached to cats. Early modern Frenchmen probably made more symbolic use of cats than of any other animal, and they used them in distinct ways, which can be grouped together for the purposes of discussion, despite the regional peculiarities.

First and foremost, cats suggested witchcraft. To cross one at night in virtually any corner of France was to risk running into the devil or one of his agents or a witch abroad on an evil errand. White cats could be as satanic as the black, in the daytime as well as at night. In a typical encounter, a peasant woman of Bigorre met a pretty white house cat who had strayed in the fields. She carried it back to the village in her apron, and just as they came to the house of a woman suspected of witchcraft, the cat jumped out, saying "Merci, Jeanne."[29] Witches transformed themselves into cats in order to cast spells on their victims. Sometimes, especially on Mardi Gras, they gathered for hideous Sabbaths at night. They howled, fought, and copulated horribly under the direction of the devil himself in the form of a huge tomcat. To protect yourself from sorcery by cats there was one, classic remedy: maim it. Cut its tail, clip its ears, smash one of its legs, tear or burn its fur, and you would break its malevolent power. A maimed

---

29   Rolland, *Faune populaire*, p. 118. See note 14 for the other sources on which this account is based.

cat could not attend a Sabbath or wander abroad to cast spells. Peasants frequently cudgeled cats who crossed their paths at night and discovered the next day that bruises had appeared on women believed to be witches— or so it was said in the lore of their village. Villagers also told stories of farmers who found strange cats in barns and broke their limbs to save the cattle. Invariably a broken limb would appear on a suspicious woman the following morning.

Cats possessed occult power independently of their association with witchcraft and deviltry. They could prevent the bread from rising if they entered bakeries in Anjou. They could spoil the catch if they crossed the path of fishermen in Brittany. If buried alive in Béarn, they could clear a field of weeds. They figured as staple ingredients in all kinds of folk medicine aside from witches' brews. To recover from a bad fall, you sucked the blood out of a freshly amputated tail of a tomcat. To cure yourself from pneumonia, you drank blood from a cat's ear in red wine. To get over colic, you mixed your wine with cat excrement. You could even make yourself invisible, at least in Brittany, by eating the brain of a newly killed cat, provided it was still hot.

There was a specific field for the exercise of cat power: the household and particularly the person of the master or mistress of the house. Folktales like "Puss 'n Boots" emphasized the identification of master and cat, and so did superstitions such as the practice of tying a black ribbon around the neck of a cat whose mistress had died. To kill a cat was to bring misfortune upon its owner or its house. If a cat left a house or stopped jumping on the sickbed of its master or mistress, the person was likely to die. But a cat lying on the bed of a dying man might be the devil, waiting to carry his soul off to hell. According to a sixteenth-century tale, a girl from Quintin sold her soul to the devil in exchange for some pretty clothes. When she died, the pallbearers could not lift her coffin; they opened the lid, and a black cat jumped out. Cats could harm a house. They often smothered babies. They understood gossip and would repeat it out of doors. But their power could be contained or turned to your advantage if you followed the right procedures, such as greasing their paws with butter or maiming them when they first arrived. To protect a new house, Frenchmen enclosed live cats within its walls—a very old rite, judging from cat skeletons that have been exhumed from the walls of medieval buildings.

Finally, the power of cats was concentrated on the most intimate aspect of domestic life: sex. *Le chat, la chatte, le minet* mean the same thing in French slang as "pussy" does in English, and they have served as obscenities for centuries,[30] French folklore attaches special importance to the cat as a sexual metaphor or metonym. As far back as the fifteenth century, the petting of cats was recommended for success in courting women. Proverbial wisdom identified women with cats: "He who takes good care of cats will have a pretty wife." If a man loved cats, he would love women; and vice versa: "As he loves his cat, he loves his wife," went another proverb. If he did not care for his wife, you could say of him, "He has other cats to whip." A woman who wanted to get a man should avoid treading on a cat's tail. She might postpone marriage for a year—or for seven years in Quimper and for as many years as the cat meowed in parts of the Loire Valley. Cats connoted fertility and female sexuality everywhere. Girls were commonly said to be "in love like a cat"; and if they became pregnant, they had "let the cat go to the cheese." Eating cats could bring on pregnancy in itself. Girls who consumed them in stews gave birth to kittens in several folktales. Cats could even make diseased apple trees bear fruit, if buried in the correct manner in upper Brittany.

35   It was an easy jump from the sexuality of women to the cuckolding of men. Caterwauling could come from a satanic orgy, but it might just as well be toms howling defiance at each other when their mates were in heat. They did not call as cats, however. They issued challenges in their masters' names, along with sexual taunts about their mistresses: "Reno! Francois!" "Où allez-vous?—Voir la femme à vous.—Voir la femme à moi! Rouah!" (Where are you going?—To see your wife.—To see my wife! Ha!) Then the toms would fly at each other like the cats of Kilkenny, and their sabbath would end in a massacre. The dialogue differed according to the imaginations of the listeners and the onomatopoetic power of their dialect, but it usually emphasized predatory sexuality.[31] "At night all cats are gray," went the proverb, and the gloss in an eighteenth-century proverb collection made the sexual hint explicit: "That is to say that all women are beautiful

---

30   Emile Chautard, *La Vie étrange de l'argot* (Paris, 1931), pp. 367-68. The following expressions come from Panckoucke, *Dictionnaire des proverbs françois*; Esnault, *Dictionnaire historique des argots français*; and *Dictionnaire de l'Académie française* (Paris, 1762), which contains a surprising amount of polite cat lore. The impolite lore was transmitted in large measure by children's games and rhymes, some of them dating from the sixteenth century; Claude Gaignebet, *Le Folklore obscène des enfants* (Paris, 1980), p. 260.

31   Sébillot, *Le Folk-lore de France*, III, 93-94.

enough at night."[32] Enough for what? Seduction, rape, and murder echoed in the air when the cats howled at night in early modern France. Cat calls summoned up *Katzenmusik*, for charivaris often took the form of howling under a cuckold's window on the eve of Mardi Gras, the favorite time for cat sabbaths.

Witchcraft, orgy, cuckoldry, charivari, and massacre, the men of the Old Regime could hear a great deal in the wail of a cat. What the men of the rue Saint-Séverin actually heard is impossible to say. One can only assert that cats bore enormous symbolic weight in the folklore of France and that the lore was rich, ancient, and widespread enough to have penetrated the printing shop. In order to determine whether the printers actually drew on the ceremonial and symbolic themes available to them, it is necessary to take another look at Contat's text.

The text made the theme of sorcery explicit from the beginning. Jerome and Léveillé could not sleep because "some bedeviled cats make a sabbath all night long."[33] After Léveillé added his cat calls to the general caterwauling, "the whole neighborhood is alarmed. It is decided that the cats must be agents of someone casting a spell." The master and mistress considered summoning the curé to exorcise the place. In deciding instead to commission the cat hunt, they fell back on the classic remedy for witchcraft: maiming. The bourgeois—a superstitious, priest-ridden fool—took the whole business seriously. To the apprentices it was a joke. Léveillé in particular functioned as a joker, a mock "sorcerer" staging a fake "sabbath," according to the terms chosen by Contat. Not only did the apprentices exploit their master's superstition in order to run riot at his expense, but they also turned their rioting against their mistress. By bludgeoning her familiar, *la grise*, they in effect accused her of being the witch. The double joke would not be lost on anyone who could read the traditional language of gesture.

The theme of charivari provided an additional dimension to the fun. Although it never says so explicitly, the text indicates that the mistress was having an affair with her priest, a "lascivious youth," who had memorized obscene passages from the classics of pornography—Aretino and *L'Academie des dames*—and quoted them to her, while her husband droned on about his favorite subjects, money and religion. During a lavish dinner with the family, the priest defended the thesis "that it is a feat of wit to

---

32 Panckoucke, *Dictionnaire des proverbes françois*, p. 66.

33 This and the following quotations come from Contat's account of the cat massacre, *Anecdotes typographiques*, pp. 48-56.

cuckold one's husband and that cuckolding is not a vice." Later, he and the wife spent the night together in a country house. They fit perfectly into the typical triangle of printing shops: a doddering old master, a middle-aged mistress, and her youthful lover.[34] The intrigue cast the master in the role of a stock comic figure: the cuckold. So the revelry of the workers took the form of a charivari. The apprentices managed it, operating within the liminal area where novitiates traditionally mocked their superiors, and the journeymen responded to their antics in the traditional way, with rough music. A riotous, festival atmosphere runs through the whole episode, which Contat described as a *fête*: "Léveillé and his comrade Jerome preside over the *fête*," he wrote, as if they were kings of a carnival and the cat bashing corresponded to the torturing of cats on Mardi Gras or the *fête* of Saint John the Baptist.

As in many Mardi Gras, the carnival ended in a mock trial and execution. The burlesque legalism came naturally to the printers because they staged their own mock trials every year at the *fête* of Saint Martin, when the chapel squared accounts with its boss and succeeded spectacularly in getting his goat. The chapel could not condemn him explicitly without moving into open insubordination and risking dismissal. (All the sources, including the papers of the STN, indicate that masters often fired workers for insolence and misbehavior. Indeed, Léveillé was later fired for a prank that attacked the bourgeois more openly.) So the workers tried the bourgeois in absentia, using a symbol that would let their meaning show through without being explicit enough to justify retaliation. They tried and hanged the cats. It would be going too far to hang *la grise* under the master's nose after being ordered to spare it; but they made the favorite pet of the house their first victim, and in doing so they knew they were attacking the house itself, in accordance with the traditions of cat lore. When the mistress accused them of killing *la grise*, they replied with mock deference that "nobody would be capable of such an outrage and that they have too much respect for that house." By executing the cats with such elaborate ceremony, they

---

34 According to Giles Barber (ibid., pp. 7 and 60), the actual Jacques Vincent for whom Contat worked began his own apprenticeship in 1690; so he probably was born about 1675. His wife was born in 1684. Thus when Contat entered the shop, the master was about 62, the mistress about 53, and the bawdy young priest in his twenties. That pattern was common enough in the printing industry, where old masters often left their businesses to younger wives, who in turn took up with still younger journeymen. It was a classic pattern for charivaris, which often mocked disparities in age among newlyweds as well as humiliating cuckolds.

condemned the house and declared the bourgeois guilty—guilty of over-working and underfeeding his apprentices, guilty of living in luxury while his journeymen did all the work, guilty of withdrawing from the shop and swamping it with *alloués* instead of laboring and eating with the men, as masters were said to have done a generation or two earlier, or in the primitive "republic" that existed at the beginning of the printing industry. The guilt extended from the boss to the house to the whole system. Perhaps in trying, confessing, and hanging a collection of half-dead cats, the workers meant to ridicule the entire legal and social order.

They certainly felt debased and had accumulated enough resentment to explode in an orgy of killing. A half-century later, the artisans of Paris would run riot in a similar manner, combining indiscriminate slaughter with improvised popular tribunals.[35] It would be absurd to view the cat massacre as a dress rehearsal for the September Massacres of the French Revolution, but the earlier outburst of violence did suggest a popular rebellion, though it remained restricted to the level of symbolism.

Cats as symbols conjured up sex as well as violence, a combination perfectly suited for an attack on the mistress. The narrative identified her with *la grise*, her *chatte favorite*. In killing it, the boys struck at her: "It was a matter of consequence, a murder, which had to be hidden." The mistress reacted as if she had been assaulted: "They ravished from her a cat without an equal, a cat that she loved to madness." The text described her as lascivious and "impassioned for cats" as if she were a she-cat in heat during a wild cat's sabbath of howling, killing, and rape. An explicit reference to rape would violate the proprieties that were generally observed in eighteenth-century writing. Indeed, the symbolism would work only if it remained veiled—ambivalent enough to dupe the master and sharp enough to hit the mistress in the quick. But Contat used strong language. As soon as the mistress saw the cat execution she let out a scream. Then the scream was smothered in the realization that she had lost her *grise*. The workers assured her with feigned sincerity of their respect and the master arrived. "'Ah! the scoundrels,' he says. 'Instead of working they are killing cats.' Madame to Monsieur: 'These wicked men can't kill the masters; they have killed my cat.' ... It seems to her that all the blood of the workers would not be sufficient to redeem the insult."

It was metonymic insult, the eighteenth-century equivalent of the modern schoolboy's taunt: "Ah, your mother's girdle!" But it was stronger,

40

---

35 Pierre Caron, *Les Massacres de septembre* (Paris, 1935).

and more obscene. By assaulting her pet, the workers ravished the mistress symbolically. At the same time, they delivered the supreme insult to their master. His wife was his most precious possession, just as her *chatte* was hers. In killing the cat, the men violated the most intimate treasure of the bourgeois household and escaped unharmed. That was the beauty of it. The symbolism disguised the insult well enough for them to get away with it. While the bourgeois fumed over the loss of work, his wife, less obtuse, virtually told him that the workers had attacked her sexually and would like to murder him. Then both left the scene in humiliation and defeat. "Monsieur and Madame retire, leaving the workers in liberty. The printers, who love disorder, are in a state of great joy. Here is an ample subject for their laughter, a beautiful *copie*, which will keep them amused for a long time."

This was Rabelaisian laughter. The text insists upon its importance: "The printers know how to laugh, it is their sole occupation." Mikhail Bakhtin has shown how the laughter of Rabelais expressed a strain of popular culture in which the riotously funny could turn to riot, a carnival culture of sexuality and sedition in which the revolutionary element might be contained within symbols and metaphors or might explode in a general uprising, as in 1789. The question remains, however, what precisely was so funny about the cat massacre? There is no better way to ruin a joke than to analyze it or to overload it with social comment. But this joke cries out for commentary—not because one can use it to prove that artisans hated their bosses (a truism that may apply to all periods of labor history, although it has not been appreciated adequately by eighteenth-century historians), but because it can help one to see how workers made their experience meaning-ful by playing with themes of their culture.

The only version of the cat massacre available to us was put into writing, long after the fact, by Nicolas Contat. He selected details, ordered events, and framed the story in such a way as to bring out what was meaningful for him. But he derived his notions of meaning from his culture just as naturally as he drew in air from the atmosphere around him. And he wrote down what he had helped to enact with his mates. The subjective character of the writing does not vitiate its collective frame of reference, even though the written account must be thin compared with the action it describes. The workers' mode of expression was a kind of popular theater. It involved pan-tomime, rough music, and a dramatic "theater of violence" improvised in the work place, in the street, and on the rooftops. It included a play within a play, because Léveillé reenacted the whole farce several times as *copies* in the shop. In fact, the original massacre involved the burlesque of other ceremonies, such as trials and charivaris. So Contat wrote about a burlesque of a burlesque, and in reading it one should make allowances for the refraction of cultural forms across genres and over time.

Those allowances made, it seems clear that the workers found the massacre funny because it gave them a way to turn the tables on the bourgeois. By goading him with cat calls, they provoked him to authorize the massacre of cats, then they used the massacre to put him symbolically on trial for unjust management of the shop. They also used it as a witch hunt, which provided an excuse to kill his wife's familiar and to insinuate that she herself was the witch. Finally, they transformed it into a charivari, which served as a means to insult her sexually while mocking him as a cuckold. The bourgeois made an excellent butt of the joke. Not only did he become the victim of a procedure he himself had set in motion, he did not understand how badly he had been had. The men had subjected his wife to symbolic aggression of the most intimate kind, but he did not get it. He was too thick-headed, a classic cuckold. The printers ridiculed him in splendid Boccaccian style and got off scot-free. 45

The joke worked so well because the workers played so skillfully with a repertory of ceremonies and symbols. Cats suited their purposes perfectly. By smashing the spine of *la grise* they called the master's wife a witch and a slut, while at the same time making the master into a cuckold and a fool. It was metonymic insult, delivered by actions, not words, and it struck home because cats occupied a soft spot in the bourgeois way of life. Keeping pets was as alien to the workers as torturing animals was to the bourgeois. Trapped between incompatible sensitivities, the cats had the worst of both worlds.

The workers also punned with ceremonies. They made a roundup of cats into a witch hunt, a festival, a charivari, a mock trial, and a dirty joke. Then they redid the whole thing in pantomime. Whenever they got tired of working, they transformed the shop into a theater and produced *copies*— their kind of copy, not the authors'. Shop theater and ritual punning suited the traditions of their craft. Although printers made books, they did not use written words to convey their meaning. They used gestures, drawing on the culture of their craft to inscribe statements in the air.

Insubstantial as it may seem today, this joking was a risky business in the eighteenth century. The risk was part of the joke, as in many forms of humor, which toy with violence and tease repressed passions. The workers pushed their symbolic horseplay to the brink of reification, the point at which the killing of cats would turn into an open rebellion. They played on ambiguities, using symbols that would hide their full meaning while letting enough of it show through to make a fool of the bourgeois without giving him a pretext to fire them. They tweaked his nose and prevented him from protesting against it. To pull off such a feat required great dexterity. It showed that workers could manipulate symbols in their idiom as effectively as poets did in print.

The boundaries within which this jesting had to be contained suggest the limits to working-class militancy under the Old Regime. The printers identified with their craft rather than their class. Although they organized in chapels, staged strikes, and sometimes forced up wages, they remained subordinate to the bourgeois. The master hired and fired men as casually as he ordered paper, and he turned them out into the road when he sniffed insubordination. So until the onset of proletarianization in the late nineteenth century, they generally kept their protests on a symbolic level. A *copie*, like a carnival, helped to let off steam; but it also produced laughter, a vital ingredient in early artisanal culture and one that has been lost in labor history. By seeing the way a joke worked in the horseplay of a printing shop two centuries ago, we may be able to recapture that missing element—laughter, sheer laughter, the thigh-slapping, rib-cracking Rabelaisian kind, rather than the Voltairian smirk with which we are familiar.

APPENDIX: CONTAT'S ACCOUNT OF THE CAT MASSACRE

50   The following account comes from Nicolas Contat. *Anecdotes typographiques où l'on voit la description des coutumes, moeurs et usages singuliers des compagnons imprimeurs*, ed. Giles Barber (Oxford, 1980), pp. 51-53. After a day of exhausting work and disgusting food, the two apprentices retire to their bedroom, a damp and draughty lean-to in a corner of the courtyard. The episode is recounted in the third person, from the viewpoint of Jerome:

He is so tired and needs rest so desperately that the shack looks like a palace to him. At last the persecution and misery he has suffered throughout the day have come to an end, and he can relax. But no, some bedeviled cats celebrate a witches' sabbath all night long, making so much noise that they rob him of the brief period of rest allotted to the apprentices before the journeymen arrive for work early the next morning and demand admission by constant ringing of an infernal bell. Then the boys have to get up and cross the courtyard, shivering under their nightshirts, in order to open the door. Those journeymen never let up. No matter what you do, you always make them lose their time and they always treat you as a lazy good-for-nothing. They call for Léveillé. Light the fire under the cauldron! Fetch water for the dunking-troughs! True, those jobs are supposed to be done by the beginner apprentices, who live at home, but they don't arrive until six or seven. Thus everyone is soon at work—apprentices, journeymen, everyone but the master and the mistress: they alone enjoy the sweetness of sleep. That makes Jerome and Léveillé jealous. They resolve that they will not be the only ones to suffer; they want this master and mistress as associates. But how to turn the trick?

Léveillé has an extraordinary talent for imitating the voices and the smallest gestures of everyone around him. He is a perfect actor; that's the real profession that he has picked up in the printing shop. He also can produce perfect imitations of the cries of dogs and cats. He decides to climb from roof to roof until he reaches a gutter next to the bedroom of the bourgeois and the bourgeoise. From there he can ambush them with a volley of meows. It's an easy job for him: he is the son of a roofer and can scramble across roofs like a cat.

Our sniper succeeds so well that the whole neighborhood is alarmed. The word spreads that there is witchcraft afoot and that the cats must be the agents of someone casting a spell. It is a case for the curé, who is an intimate of the household and the confessor of Madame. No one can sleep any more.

Léveillé stages a sabbath the next night and the night after that. If you didn't know him, you would be convinced he was a witch. Finally, the master and the mistress cannot stand it any longer. "We'd better tell the boys to get rid of those malevolent animals," they declare. Madame gives them the order, exhorting them to avoid frightening la grise. That is the name of her pet pussy.

This lady is impassioned for cats. Many master printers are also. One of them has twenty-five. He has had their portraits painted and feeds them on roast fowl.

The hunt is soon organized. The apprentices resolve to make a clean sweep of it, and they are joined by the journeymen. The masters love cats, so consequently they must hate them. This man arms himself with the bar of a press, that one with a stick from the drying-room, others with broom handles. They hang sacks at the windows of the attic and the storerooms to catch the cats who attempt to escape by leaping outdoors. The beaters are

55

named, everything is organized. Léveillé and his comrade Jerome preside over the fête, each of them armed with an iron bar from the shop. The first thing they go for is la grise, Madame's pussy. Léveillé stuns it with a quick blow on the kidneys, and Jerome finishes it off. Then Léveillé stuffs the body in a gutter, for they don't want to get caught: it is a matter of consequence, a murder, which must be kept hidden. The men produce terror on the rooftops. Seized by panic, the cats throw themselves into the sacks. Some are killed on the spot. Others are condemned to be hanged for the amusement of the entire printing shop.

Printers know how to laugh; it is their sole occupation.

The execution is about to begin. They name a hangman, a troop of guards, even a confessor. Then they pronounce the sentence.

In the midst of it all, the mistress arrives. What is her surprise, when she sees the bloody execution! She lets out a scream; then her voice is cut, because she thinks she sees la grise, and she is certain that such a fate has been reserved for her favorite puss. The workers assure her that no one would be capable of such a crime: they have too much respect for the house.

60   The bourgeois arrives. "Ah! The scoundrels," he says. "Instead of working, they are killing cats." Madame to Monsieur: "These wicked men can't kill the masters, so they have killed my pussy. She can't be found. I have called la grise everywhere. They must have hanged her." It seems to her that all the workers' blood would not be sufficient to redeem the insult. The poor grise, a pussy without a peer!

Monsieur and Madame retire, leaving the workers in liberty. The printers delight in the disorder; they are beside themselves with joy.

What a splendid subject for their laughter, for a *belle copie*! They will amuse themselves with it for a long time. Léveillé will take the leading role and will stage the play at least twenty times. He will mime the master, the mistress, the whole house, heaping ridicule on them all. He will spare nothing in his satire. Among printers, those who excel in this entertainment are called *jobeurs*; they provide *joberie*.

Léveillé receives many rounds of applause.

It should be noted that all the workers are in league against the masters. It is enough to speak badly of them [the masters] to be esteemed by the whole assembly of typographers. Léveillé is one of those. In recognition of his merit, he will be pardoned for some previous satires against the workers.

(1985)

Questions

1. Summarize in your own words the various reasons for killing the cats, according to Darnton.

2. What do you feel is the author's own attitude to the sort of laughter the artisans produced?

3. Darnton describes the attack as a "metonymic insult" (paragraph 42, and again in paragraph 45). Explain in your own words what is meant by this.

4. What are some characteristics of the bourgeoisie in early eighteenth-century Paris insofar as you can infer them from this essay?

5. Though Darnton provides a remarkable range of explanatory detail for the apprentices' actions given a climate in which "cruelty to animals expressed a deep current of popular culture" (paragraph 29), he does not attempt to explain why or how it should have come to be such a deep cultural current. To what extent do you think it may be possible to explain certain core values of past cultures (attitudes towards slavery, for example, as much as attitudes towards animals) that have come to seem entirely repellent to us? To what extent do you feel it appropriate to condemn the presence of such attitudes in past civilizations?

6. Write a short essay attempting to explain the humor (in some people's eyes) of something that you are aware many people would regard as distinctly unfunny. (For example, you might discuss the "humorous" way in which killings are presented in certain violent movies, or the humor of ridicule practiced by Tom Green.)

7. In whatever form it takes in a particular culture, is "the humor of cruelty" usually highly gendered? (In other words, are men and women likely to not always find the same sorts of things funny?) Discuss this issue in relation both to Darnton's essay and to the world today.

ELAINE SHOWALTER

REPRESENTING OPHELIA:
WOMEN, MADNESS, AND
THE RESPONSIBILITIES
OF FEMINIST CRITICISM

*In this essay, Elaine Showalter discusses the character of
Ophelia in Shakespeare's* Hamlet *and offers an answer
to the question of how feminist criticism should
represent Ophelia in its own discourse.*

&

"**A**s a sort of a come-on, I announced that I would speak today about that piece of bait named Ophelia, and I'll be as good as my word." These are the words which begin the psychoanalytic seminar on *Hamlet* presented in Paris in 1959 by Jacques Lacan. But despite his promising come-on, Lacan was *not* as good as his word. He goes on for some 41 pages to speak about Hamlet, and when he does mention Ophelia, she is merely what Lacan calls "the object Ophelia"—that is, the object of Hamlet's male desire. The etymology of Ophelia, Lacan asserts, is "O-phallus," and her role in the drama can only be to function as the exteriorized figuration of what Lacan predictably and, in view of his own early work with psychotic women, disappointingly suggests is the phallus as transcendental signifier.[1]

---

1   Jacques Lacan, "Desire and the interpretation of desire in *Hamlet*," in *Literature and Psychoanalysis: The Question of Reading: Otherwise*, ed. Shoshana Felman (Baltimore, 1982), 11, 20, 23. Lacan is also wrong about the etymology of Ophelia, which probably derives from the Greek for "help" or "succor." Charlotte M. Yonge suggested a derivation from "ophis," "serpent." See her *History of Christian Names* (1884, republished Chicago, 1966), 346-7. I am indebted to Walter Jackson Bate for this reference. [Unless otherwise noted, all notes to this essay are from the author.]

To play such a part obviously makes Ophelia "essential," as Lacan admits; but only because, in his words, "she is linked forever, for centuries, to the figure of Hamlet."[2]

The bait-and-switch game that Lacan plays with Ophelia is a cynical but not unusual instance of her deployment in psychiatric and critical texts. For most critics of Shakespeare, Ophelia has been an insignificant minor character in the play, touching in her weakness and madness but chiefly interesting, of course, in what she tells us about Hamlet. And while female readers of Shakespeare have often attempted to champion Ophelia, even feminist critics have done so with a certain embarrassment. As Annette Kolodny ruefully admits: "it is after all, an imposition of high order to ask the viewer to attend to Ophelia's sufferings in a scene where, before, he's always so comfortably kept his eye fixed on Hamlet."

Yet when feminist criticism allows Ophelia to upstage Hamlet, it also brings to the foreground the issues in an ongoing theoretical debate about the cultural links between femininity, female sexuality, insanity, and representation. Though she is neglected in criticism, Ophelia is probably the most frequently illustrated and cited of Shakespeare's heroines. Her visibility as a subject in literature, popular culture, and painting, from Redon who paints her drowning, to Bob Dylan, who places her on Desolation Row, to Cannon Mills, which has named a flowery sheet pattern after her, is in inverse relation to her invisibility in Shakespearean critical texts. Why has she been such a potent and obsessive figure in our cultural mythology? Insofar as Hamlet names Ophelia as "woman" and "frailty," substituting an ideological view of femininity for a personal one, is she indeed representative of Woman, and does her madness stand for the oppression of women in society as well as in tragedy? Furthermore, since Laertes calls Ophelia a "document in madness," does she represent the textual archetype of woman *as* madness, or madness *as* woman? And finally, how should feminist criticism represent Ophelia in its own discourse? What is our responsibility towards her as character and as woman?

Feminist critics have offered a variety of responses to these questions. Some have maintained that we should represent Ophelia as a lawyer represents a client, that we should become her Horatia, in this harsh world reporting her and her cause aright to the unsatisfied. Carol Neely, for

---

2   Annette Kolodny, "Dancing through the minefield: some observations on the theory, practice, and politics of feminist literary criticism" (*Feminist Studies*, 6 (1980)), 7.

example, describes advocacy—speaking *for* Ophelia—as our proper role: "As a feminist critic," she writes, "I must 'tell' Ophelia's story."[3] But what can we mean by Ophelia's story? The story of her life? The story of her betrayal at the hands of her father, brother, lover, court, society? The story of her rejection and marginalization by male critics of Shakespeare? Shakespeare gives us very little information from which to imagine a past for Ophelia. She appears in only five of the play's twenty scenes; the pre-play course of her love story with Hamlet is known only by a few ambiguous flashbacks. Her tragedy is subordinated in the play; unlike Hamlet, she does not struggle with moral choices or alternatives. Thus another feminist critic, Lee Edwards, concludes that it is impossible to reconstruct Ophelia's biography from the text: "We can imagine Hamlet's story without Ophelia, but Ophelia literally has no story without Hamlet."[4]

5   If we turn from American to French feminist theory, Ophelia might confirm the impossibility of representing the feminine in patriarchal discourse as other than madness, incoherence, fluidity, or silence. In French theoretical criticism, the feminine or "Woman" is that which escapes representation in patriarchal language and symbolism; it remains on the side of negativity, absence, and lack. In comparison to Hamlet, Ophelia is certainly a creature of lack. "I think nothing, my lord," she tells him in the Mousetrap scene, and he cruelly twists her words:

> *Hamlet:* That's a fair thought to lie between maids' legs.
> *Ophelia:* What is, my lord?
> *Hamlet:* Nothing.

(III.ii.117-19)

In Elizabethan slang, "nothing" was a term for the female genitalia, as in *Much Ado About Nothing*. To Hamlet, then, "nothing" is what lies between maids' legs, for, in the male visual system of representation and desire, women's sexual organs, in the words of the French psychoanalyst Luce Irigaray, "represent the horror of having nothing to see."[5] When Ophelia is mad, Gertrude says that "Her speech is nothing," mere "unshaped

---

3   Carol Neely, "Feminist modes of Shakespearean criticism" (*Women's Studies*, 9 (1981)), 11.

4   Lee Edwards, "The labors of Psyche" (*Critical Inquiry*, 6 (1979)), 36.

5   Luce Irigaray: see *New French Feminisms*, ed. Elaine Marks and Isabelle de Courtivron (New York, 1982), 101. The quotation above, from III.ii, is taken from the

use." Ophelia's speech represents the horror of having nothing to say in the public terms defined by the court. Deprived of thought, sexuality, language, Ophelia's story becomes the story of O—the zero, the empty circle or mystery of feminine difference, the cipher of female sexuality to be deciphered by feminist interpretation.[6]

A third approach would be to read Ophelia's story as the female subtext of the tragedy, the repressed story of Hamlet. In this reading, Ophelia represents the strong emotions that the Elizabethans as well as the Freudians thought womanish and unmanly. When Laertes weeps for his dead sister he says of his tears that "When these are gone, / The woman will be out"—that is to say, that the feminine and shameful part of his nature will be purged. According to David Leverenz, in an important essay called "The Woman in *Hamlet*," Hamlet's disgust at the feminine passivity in himself is translated into violent revulsion against women, and into his brutal behavior towards Ophelia. Ophelia's suicide, Leverenz argues, then becomes "a microcosm of the male world's banishment of the female, because 'woman' represents everything denied by reasonable men."[7]

It is perhaps because Hamlet's emotional vulnerability can so readily be conceptualized as feminine that this is the only heroic male role in Shakespeare which has been regularly acted by women, in a tradition from Sarah Bernhardt to, most recently, Diane Venora, in a production directed by Joseph Papp. Leopold Bloom speculates on this tradition in *Ulysses*, musing on the Hamlet of the actress Mrs. Bandman Palmer: "Male impersonator. Perhaps he was a woman? Why Ophelia committed suicide?"[8]

While all of these approaches have much to recommend them, each also presents critical problems. To liberate Ophelia from the text, or to make her its tragic center, is to re-appropriate her for our own ends; to dissolve her into a female symbolism of absence is to endorse our own marginality; to make her Hamlet's anima is to reduce her to a metaphor of male experience. I would like to propose instead that Ophelia *does* have a story of her own

---

Arden Shakespeare, *Hamlet*, ed. Harold Jenkins (London and New York, 1982), 295. All quotations from *Hamlet* are from this text.

6   On images of negation and feminine enclosure, see David Wilbern, "Shakespeare's 'nothing,'" in *Representing Shakespeare: New Psychoanalytic Essays*, ed. Murray M. Schwartz and Coppélia Kahn (Baltimore, 1981).

7   David Leverenz, "The woman in *Hamlet*: an interpersonal view" (*Signs*, 4 (1978)), 303.

8   James Joyce, *Ulysses* (New York, 1961), 76.

that feminist criticism can tell; it is neither her life story, nor her love story, nor Lacan's story, but rather the *history* of her representation. This essay tries to bring together some of the categories of French feminist thought about the "feminine" with the empirical energies of American historical and critical research: to yoke French theory and Yankee knowhow.

Tracing the iconography of Ophelia in English and French painting, photography, psychiatry, and literature, as well as in theatrical production, I will be showing first of all the representational bonds between female insanity and female sexuality. Secondly, I want to demonstrate the two-way transaction between psychiatric theory and cultural representation. As one medical historian has observed, we could provide a manual of female insanity by chronicling the illustrations of Ophelia; this is so because the illustrations of Ophelia have played a major role in the theoretical construction of female insanity.[9] Finally, I want to suggest that the feminist revision of Ophelia comes as much from the actress's freedom as from the critic's interpretation.[10] When Shakespeare's heroines began to be played by women instead of boys, the presence of the female body and female voice, quite apart from details of interpretation, created new meanings and subversive tensions in these roles, and perhaps most importantly with Ophelia. Looking at Ophelia's history on and off the stage, I will point out the contest between male and female representations of Ophelia, cycles of critical repression and feminist reclamation of which contemporary feminist criticism is only the most recent phase. By beginning with these data from cultural history, instead of moving from the grid of literary theory, I hope to conclude with a fuller sense of the responsibilities of feminist criticism, as well as a new perspective on Ophelia.

"Of all the characters in *Hamlet*," Bridget Lyons has pointed out, "Ophelia is most persistently presented in terms of symbolic meanings."[11] Her behavior, her appearance, her gestures, her costume, her props, are freighted with emblematic significance, and for many generations of Shakespearean critics her part in the play has seemed to be primarily iconographic. Ophelia's symbolic meanings, moreover, are specifically feminine. Whereas for

---

9   Sander L. Gilman, *Seeing the Insane* (New York, 1981), 126.

10   See Michael Goldman, *The Actor's Freedom: Toward a Theory of Drama* (New York, 1975), for a stimulating discussion of the interpretative interaction between actor and audience.

11   Bridget Lyons, "The iconography of Ophelia" (*English Literary History*, 44 (1977)), 61.

Hamlet madness is metaphysical, linked with culture, for Ophelia it is a product of the female body and female nature, perhaps that nature's purest form. On the Elizabethan stage, the conventions of female insanity were sharply defined. Ophelia dresses in white, decks herself with "fantastical garlands" of wild flowers, and enters, according to the stage directions of the "Bad" Quarto, "distracted" playing on a lute with her "hair down singing." Her speeches are marked by extravagant metaphors, lyrical free associations, and "explosive sexual imagery."[12] She sings wistful and bawdy ballads, and ends her life by drowning.

All of these conventions carry specific messages about femininity and sexuality. Ophelia's virginal and vacant white is contrasted with Hamlet's scholar's garb, his "suits of solemn black." Her flowers suggest the discordant double images of female sexuality as both innocent blossoming and whorish contamination; she is the "green girl" of pastoral, the virginal "Rose of May" and the sexually explicit madwoman who, in giving away her wild flowers and herbs, is symbolically deflowering herself. The "weedy trophies" and phallic "long purples" which she wears to her death intimate an improper and discordant sexuality that Gertrude's lovely elegy cannot quite obscure.[13] In Elizabethan and Jacobean drama, the stage direction that a woman enters with disheveled hair indicates that she might either be mad or the victim of a rape; the disordered hair, her offense against decorum, suggests sensuality in each case.[14] The mad Ophelia's bawdy songs and verbal license, while they give her access to "an entirely different range of experience" from what she is allowed as the dutiful daughter, seem to be her one sanctioned form of self-assertion as a woman, quickly followed, as if in retribution, by her death.[15]

Drowning too was associated with the feminine, with female fluidity as opposed to masculine aridity. In his discussion of the "Ophelia complex,"

---

12 See Maurice and Hanna Charney, "The language of Shakespeare's madwomen" (*Signs*, 3 (1977)), 451, 457; and Carroll Camden, "On Ophelia's madness" (*Shakespeare Quarterly* (1964)), 254.

13 See Margery Garber, *Coming of Age in Shakespeare* (London, 1981), 155-7; and Lyons, op. cit., 65, 70-2.

14 On disheveled hair as a signifier of madness or rape, see Charney and Charney, op. cit., 452-3, 457; and Allan Dessen, *Elizabethan Stage Conventions and Modern Interpreters* (Cambridge, 1984), 36-8. Thanks to Allan Dessen for letting me see advance proofs of his book.

15 Charney and Charney, op. cit., 456.

the phenomenologist Gaston Bachelard traces the symbolic connections between women, water, and death. Drowning, he suggests, becomes the truly
feminine death in the dramas of literature and life, one which is a beautiful
immersion and submersion in the female element. Water is the profound
and organic symbol of the liquid woman whose eyes are so easily drowned
in tears, as her body is the repository of blood, amniotic fluid, and milk.
A man contemplating this feminine suicide understands it by reaching for
what is feminine in himself, like Laertes, by a temporary surrender to his
own fluidity—that is, his tears; and he becomes a man again in becoming
once more dry—when his tears are stopped.[16]

Clinically speaking, Ophelia's behavior and appearance are characteristic of the malady the Elizabethans would have diagnosed as female love-
melancholy, or erotomania. From about 1580, melancholy had become a
fashionable disease among young men, especially in London, and Hamlet
himself is a prototype of the melancholy hero. Yet the epidemic of melancholy associated with intellectual and imaginative genius "curiously by-
passed women." Women's melancholy was seen instead as biological, and
emotional in origins.[17]

15   On the stage, Ophelia's madness was presented as the predicable outcome of erotomania. From 1660, when women first appeared on the public
stage, to the beginnings of the eighteenth century, the most celebrated
of the actresses who played Ophelia were those whom rumor credited
with disappointments in love. The greatest triumph was reserved for Susan Mountfort, a former actress at Lincoln's Inn Fields who had gone
mad after her lover's betrayal. One night in 1720 she escaped from her
keeper, rushed to the theater, and just as the Ophelia of the evening was
to enter for her mad scene, "sprang forward in her place ... with wild eyes
and wavering motion."[18] As a contemporary reported, "she was in truth
Ophelia herself, to the amazement of the performers as well as of the audience—nature having made this last effort, her vital powers failed her and

---

16 Gaston Bachelard, *L'Eau et les rêves* (Paris, 1942), 109-25. See also Brigitte
Peucker, "Dröste-Hulshof's Ophelia and the recovery of voice" (*The Journal of English
and Germanic Philology* (1983)), 374-91.

17 Vieda Skultans, *English Madness: Ideas on Insanity 1580-1890* (London, 1977),
79-81. On historical cases of love-melancholy, see Michael MacDonald, *Mystical
Bedlam* (Cambridge, 1982).

18 C.E.L. Wingate, *Shakespeare's Heroines on the Stage* (New York, 1895), 283-4,
288-9.

she died soon after."[19] These theatrical legends reinforced the belief of the age that female madness was a part of female nature, less to be imitated by an actress than demonstrated by a deranged woman in a performance of her emotions.

The subversive or violent possibilities of the mad scene were nearly eliminated, however, on the eighteenth-century stage. Late Augustan stereotypes of female love-melancholy were sentimentalized versions which minimized the force of female sexuality, and made female insanity a pretty stimulant to male sensibility. Actresses such as Mrs. Lessingham in 1772, and Mary Bolton in 1811, played Ophelia in this decorous style, relying on the familiar images of the white dress, loose hair, and wild flowers to convey a polite feminine distraction, highly suitable for pictorial reproduction, and appropriate for Samuel Johnson's description of Ophelia as young, beautiful, harmless, and pious. Even Mrs. Siddons in 1785 played the mad scene with stately and classical dignity. For much of the period, in fact, Augustan objections to the levity and indecency of Ophelia's language and behavior led to censorship of the part. Her lines were frequently cut, and the role was often assigned to a singer instead of an actress, making the mode of representation musical rather than visual or verbal.

But whereas the Augustan response to madness was a denial, the romantic response was an embrace.[20] The figure of the madwoman permeates romantic literature, from the gothic novelists to Wordsworth and Scott in such texts as "The Thorn" and *The Heart of Midlothian*, where she stands for sexual victimization, bereavement, and thrilling emotional extremity. Romantic artists such as Thomas Barker and George Shepheard painted pathetically abandoned Crazy Kates and Crazy Anns, while Henry Fuseli's "Mad Kate" is almost demonically possessed, an orphan of the romantic storm.

In the Shakespearean theater, Ophelia's romantic revival began in France rather than England. When Charles Kemble made his Paris debut as Hamlet with an English troupe in 1827, his Ophelia was a young Irish ingénue named Harriet Smithson. Smithson used "her extensive command of mime to depict in precise gesture the state of Ophelia's confused mind."[21] In the mad scene, she entered in a long black veil, suggesting

---

19   Charles Hiatt, *Ellen Terry* (London, 1898), 11.

20   Max Byrd, *Visits to Bedlam: Madness and Literature in the Eighteenth Century* (Columbia, 1971), xiv.

21   Peter Raby, *Fair Ophelia: Harriet Smithson Berlioz* (Cambridge, 1982), 63.

the standard imagery of female sexual mystery in the gothic novel, with scattered bedlamish wisps of straw in her hair. Spreading the veil on the ground as she sang, she spread flowers upon it in the shape of a cross, as if to make her father's grave, and mimed a burial, a piece of stage business which remained in vogue for the rest of the century.

The French audiences were stunned. Dumas recalled that "it was the first time I saw in the theater real passions, giving life to men and women of flesh and blood."[22] The 23-year-old Hector Berlioz, who was in the audience on the first night, fell madly in love, and eventually married Harriet Smithson despite his family's frantic opposition. Her image as the mad Ophelia was represented in popular lithographs and exhibited in bookshop and printshop windows. Her costume was imitated by the fashionable, and a coiffure "à la folle," consisting of a "black veil with wisps of straw tastefully interwoven" in the hair, was widely copied by the Parisian beau monde, always on the lookout for something new.[23]

20   Although Smithson never acted Ophelia on the English stage, her intensely visual performance quickly influenced English productions as well; and indeed the romantic Ophelia—a young girl passionately and visibly driven to picturesque madness—became the dominant international acting style for the next 150 years, from Helena Modjeska in Poland in 1871, to the 18-year-old Jean Simmons in the Laurence Olivier film of 1948.

Whereas the romantic Hamlet, in Coleridge's famous dictum, thinks too much, has an "overbalance of the contemplative faculty" and an overactive intellect, the romantic Ophelia is a girl who *feels* too much, who drowns in feelings. The romantic critics seem to have felt that the less said about Ophelia the better; the point was to *look* at her. Hazlitt, for one, is speechless before her, calling her "a character almost too exquisitely touching to be dwelt upon."[24] While the Augustans represent Ophelia as music, the romantics transform her into an *objet d'art*, as if to take literally Claudius's lament, "poor Ophelia / Divided from herself and her fair judgment, / Without the which we are pictures."

Smithson's performance is best recaptured in a series of pictures done by Delacroix from 1830 to 1850, which show a strong romantic interest in

---

22   Ibid., 68.

23   Ibid., 72, 75.

24   Quoted in Camden, op. cit., 217.

the relation of female sexuality and insanity.[25] The most innovative and influential of Delacroix's lithographs is *La Mort d'Ophélie* of 1843, the first of three studies. Its sensual languor, with Ophelia half-suspended in the stream as her dress slips from her body, anticipated the fascination with the erotic trance of the hysteric as it would be studied by Jean-Martin Charcot and his students, including Janet and Freud. Delacroix's interest in the drowning Ophelia is also reproduced to the point of obsession in later nineteenth-century painting. The English Pre-Raphaelites painted her again and again, choosing the drowning which is only described in the play, and where no actress's image had preceded them or interfered with their imaginative supremacy.

In the Royal Academy show of 1852, Arthur Hughes's entry shows a tiny waif-like creature—a sort of Tinker Bell Ophelia—in a filmy white gown, perched on a tree trunk by the stream. The overall effect is softened, sexless, and hazy, although the straw in her hair resembles a crown of thorns. Hughes's juxtaposition of childlike femininity and Christian martyrdom was overpowered, however, by John Everett Millais's great painting of Ophelia in the same show. While Millais's Ophelia is sensuous siren as well as victim, the artist rather than the subject dominates the scene. The division of space between Ophelia and the natural details Millais had so painstakingly pursued reduces her to one more visual object; and the painting has such a hard surface, strangely flattened perspective, and brilliant light that it seems cruelly indifferent to the woman's death.

* * *

These Pre-Raphaelite images were part of a new and intricate traffic between images of women and madness in late nineteenth-century literature, psychiatry, drama, and art. First of all, superintendents of Victorian lunatic asylums were also enthusiasts of Shakespeare, who turned to his dramas for models of mental aberration that could be applied to their clinical practice. The case study of Ophelia was one that seemed particularly useful as an account of hysteria or mental breakdown in adolescence, a period of sexual instability which the Victorians regarded as risky for the women's mental health. As Dr. John Charles Buckmill, president of the Medico-Psychological Association, remarked in 1859, "Ophelia is the very type of a class of cases by no means uncommon. Every mental physician of moderately

---

25   Raby, op. cit., 182.

extensive experience must have seen many Ophelias. It is a copy from nature, after the fashion of the Pre-Raphaelite school."[26] Dr. John Conolly, the celebrated superintendent of the Hanwell Asylum, and founder of the committee to make Stratford a national trust, concurred. In his *Study of Hamlet* in 1863 he noted that even casual visitors to mental institutions could recognize an Ophelia in the wards: "the same young years, the same faded beauty, the same fantastic dress and interrupted song."[27] Medical textbooks illustrated their discussions of female patients with sketches of Ophelia-like maidens.

But Conolly also pointed out that the graceful Ophelias who dominated the Victorian stage were quite unlike the women who had become the majority of the inmate population in Victorian public asylums. "It seems to be supposed," he protested, "that it is an easy task to play the part of a crazy girl, and that it is chiefly composed of singing and prettiness. The habitual courtesy, the partial rudeness of mental disorder, are things to be witnessed.... An actress, ambitious of something beyond cold imitation, might find the contemplation of such cases a not unprofitable study."[28]

Yet when Ellen Terry took up Conolly's challenge, and went to an asylum to observe real madwomen, she found them "too *theatrical*" to teach her anything.[29] This was because the iconography of the romantic Ophelia had begun to infiltrate reality, to define a style for mad young women seeking to express and communicate their distress. And where the women themselves did not willingly throw themselves into Ophelia-like postures, asylum superintendents, armed with the new technology of photography, imposed the costume, gesture, props, and expression of Ophelia upon them. In England, the camera was introduced to asylum work in the 1850s by Dr. Hugh Welch Diamond, who photographed his female patients at the Surrey Asylum and at Bethlem. Diamond was heavily influenced by literary and visual models in his posing of the female subjects. His pictures of madwomen, posed in prayer, or decked with Ophelia-like garlands, were

---

26   J.C. Bucknill, *The Psychology of Shakespeare* (London, 1859, reprinted New York, 1979), 110. For more extensive discussions of Victorian psychiatry and Ophelia figures, see Elaine Showalter, *The Female Malady: Women, Madness and English Culture* (New York, 1986).

27   John Conolly, *Study of Hamlet* (London, 1863), 177.

28   Ibid., 177-8, 180.

29   Ellen Terry, *The Story of My Life* (London, 1908), 154.

copied for Victorian consumption as touched-up lithographs in professional journals.[30]

Reality, psychiatry, and representational convention were even more confused in the photographic records of hysteria produced in the 1870s by Jean-Martin Charcot. Charcot was the first clinician to install a fully equipped photographic atelier in his Paris hospital, La Salpêtrière, to record the performances of his hysterical stars. Charcot's clinic became, as he said, a "living theater" of female pathology; his women patients were coached in their performances for the camera, and, under hypnosis, were sometimes instructed to play heroines from Shakespeare. Among them, a 15-year-old girl named Augustine was featured in the published volumes called *Iconographies* in every posture of *la grande hystérie*. With her white hospital gown and flowing locks, Augustine frequently resembles the reproductions of Ophelia as icon and actress which had been in wide circulation.[31]

But if the Victorian madwoman looks mutely out from men's pictures, and acts a part men had staged and directed, she is very differently represented in the feminist revision of Ophelia initiated by newly powerful and respectable Victorian actresses, and by women critics of Shakespeare. In their efforts to defend Ophelia, they invent a story for her drawn from their own experiences, grievances, and desires.

Probably the most famous of the Victorian feminist revisions of the Ophelia story was Mary Cowden Clarke's *The Girlhood of Shakespeare's Heroines*, published in 1852. Unlike other Victorian moralizing and didactic studies of the female characters of Shakespeare's plays, Clarke's was specifically addressed to the wrongs of women, and especially to the sexual double standard. In a chapter on Ophelia called "The rose of Elsinore," Clarke tells how the child Ophelia was left behind in the care of a peasant couple when Polonius was called to the court at Paris, and raised in a cottage with a foster-sister and brother, Jutha and Ulf. Jutha is seduced and betrayed by a deceitful knight, and Ophelia discovers the bodies of Jutha and her still-born child, lying "white, frigid, and still" in the deserted parlor of the cottage in the middle of the night. Ulf, a "hairy loutish boy,"

---

30 Diamond's photographs are reproduced in Sander L. Gilman, *The Face of Madness: Hugh W. Diamond and the Origin of Psychiatric Photography* (New York, 1976).

31 See Georges Didi-Huberman, *L'Invention de l'hystérie* (Paris, 1982), and Stephen Heath, *The Sexual Fix* (London, 1983), 36.

likes to torture flies, to eat songbirds, and to rip the petals off roses, and he is also very eager to give little Ophelia what he calls a bear-hug. Both repelled and masochistically attracted by Ulf, Ophelia is repeatedly cornered by him as she grows up; once she escapes the hug by hitting him with a branch of wild roses; another time, he sneaks into her bedroom "in his brutish pertinacity to obtain the hug he had promised himself," but just as he bends over to her trembling body, Ophelia is saved by the reappearance of her real mother.

30   A few years later, back at the court, she discovers the hanged body of another friend, who has killed herself after being "victimized and deserted by the same evil seducer." Not surprisingly, Ophelia breaks down with brain fever—a staple mental illness of Victorian fiction—and has prophetic hallucinations of a brook beneath willow trees where something bad will happen to her. The warnings of Polonius and Laertes have little to add to this history of female sexual trauma.[32]

On the Victorian stage, it was Ellen Terry, daring and unconventional in her own life, who led the way in acting Ophelia in feminist terms as a consistent psychological study in sexual intimidation, a girl terrified of her father, of her lover, and of life itself. Terry's debut as Ophelia in Henry Irving's production in 1878 was a landmark. According to one reviewer, her Ophelia was "the terrible spectacle of a normal girl becoming hopelessly imbecile as the result of overwhelming mental agony. Hers was an insanity without wrath or rage, without exaltation or paroxysms."[33] Her "poetic and intellectual performance" also inspired other actresses to rebel against the conventions of invisibility and negation associated with the part.

Terry was the first to challenge the tradition of Ophelia's dressing in emblematic white. For the French poets, such as Rimbaud, Hugo, Musset, Mallarmé and Laforgue, whiteness was part of Ophelia's essential feminine symbolism; they call her "blanche Ophélia" and compare her to a lily, a cloud, or snow. Yet whiteness also made her a transparency, an absence that took on the colors of Hamlet's moods, and that, for the symbolists like Mallarmé, made her a blank page to be written over or on by the male imagination. Although Irving was able to prevent Terry from

---

32 Mary Cowden Clarke, *The Girlhood of Shakespeare's Heroines* (London, 1852). See also George C. Gross, "Mary Cowden Clarke, *The Girlhood of Shakespeare's Heroines*, and the sex education of Victorian women" (*Victorian Studies*, 16 (1972)), 37-58, and Nina Auerbach, *Woman and the Demon* (Cambridge, Mass., 1983), 210-15.

33 Hiatt, op. cit., 114. See also Wingate, op. cit., 304-5.

wearing black in the mad scene, exclaiming "My God, Madam, there must be only *one* black figure in this play, and that's Hamlet!" (Irving, of course, was playing Hamlet), nonetheless actresses such as Gertrude Eliot, Helen Maude, Nora de Silva, and in Russia Vera Komisarjevskaya, gradually won the right to intensify Ophelia's presence by clothing her in Hamlet's black.[34]

By the turn of the century, there was both a male and female discourse on Ophelia. A.C. Bradley spoke for the Victorian male tradition when he noted in *Shakespearean Tragedy* (1906) that "a large number of readers feel a kind of personal irritation against Ophelia; they seem unable to forgive her for not having been a heroine."[35] The feminist counterview was represented by actresses in such works as Helena Faucit's study of Shakespeare's female characters, and *The True Ophelia*, written by an anonymous actress in 1914, which protested against the "insipid little creature" of criticism, and advocated a strong and intelligent woman destroyed by the heartlessness of men.[36] In women's paintings of the *fin de siècle* as well, Ophelia is depicted as an inspiring, even sanctified emblem of righteousness.[37]

While the widely read and influential essays of Mary Cowden Clarke are now mocked as the epitome of naive criticism, these Victorian studies of the girlhood of Shakespeare's heroines are of course alive and well as psychoanalytic criticism, which has imagined its own prehistories of oedipal conflict and neurotic fixation; and I say this not to mock psychoanalytic criticism, but to suggest that Clarke's musings on Ophelia are a pre-Freudian speculation on the traumatic sources of a female sexual identity. The Freudian interpretation of *Hamlet* concentrated on the hero, but also had much to do with the re-sexualization of Ophelia. As early as 1900, Freud had traced Hamlet's irresolution to an Oedipus complex, and Ernest Jones, his leading British disciple, developed this view, influencing the performances of John Gielgud and Alec Guinness in the 1930s. In his final version of the study, *Hamlet and Oedipus*, published in 1949, Jones

---

34 Terry, op. cit., 155-6.

35 Andrew C. Bradley, *Shakespearean Tragedy* (London, 1906), 160.

36 Helena Faucit Martin, *On Some of Shakespeare's Female Characters* (Edinburgh and London, 1891), 4, 18; and *The True Ophelia* (New York, 1914), 15.

37 Among these paintings are the Ophelias of Henrietta Rae and Mrs. F. Littler. Sarah Bernhardt sculpted a bas relief of Ophelia for the Women's Pavilion at the Chicago World's Fair in 1893.

argued that "Ophelia should be unmistakably sensual, as she seldom is on stage. She may be 'innocent' and docile, but she is very aware of her body."[38]

35 In the theater and in criticism, this Freudian edict has produced such extreme readings as that Shakespeare intends us to see Ophelia as a loose woman, and that she has been sleeping with Hamlet. Rebecca West has argued that Ophelia is not "a correct and timid virgin of exquisite sensibilities," a view she attributes to the popularity of the Millais painting; but rather "a disreputable young woman."[39] In his delightful autobiography, Laurence Olivier, who made a special pilgrimage to Ernest Jones when he was preparing his *Hamlet* in the 1930s, recalls that one of his predecessors as actor-manager had said in response to the earnest question, "Did Hamlet sleep with Ophelia?"—"In my company, always."[40]

The most extreme Freudian interpretation reads *Hamlet* as two parallel male and female psychodramas, the counterpointed stories of the incestuous attachments of Hamlet and Ophelia. As Theodor Lidz presents this view, while Hamlet is neurotically attached to his mother, Ophelia has an unresolved oedipal attachment to her father. She has fantasies of a lover who will abduct her from or even kill her father, and when this actually happens, her reason is destroyed by guilt as well as by lingering incestuous feelings. According to Lidz, Ophelia breaks down because she fails in the female developmental task of shifting her sexual attachment from her father "to a man who can bring her fulfillment as a woman."[41] We see the effects of this Freudian Ophelia on stage productions since the 1950s, where directors have hinted at an incestuous link between Ophelia and her father, or more recently, because this staging conflicts with the usual ironic treatment of Polonius, between Ophelia and Laertes. Trevor Nunn's production with Helen Mirren in 1970, for example, made Ophelia and Laertes flirtatious doubles, almost twins in their matching fur-trimmed doublets, playing duets on the lute with Polonius looking on, like Peter, Paul, and Mary. In other productions of the same period, Marianne Faithfull was a haggard Ophelia equally attracted to Hamlet and Laertes, and, in one of the

---

38   Ernest Jones, *Hamlet and Oedipus* (New York, 1949), 139.

39   Rebecca West, *The Count and the Castle* (New Haven, 1958), 18.

40   Laurence Olivier, *Confessions of an Actor* (Harmondsworth, 1982), 102, 152.

41   Theodor Lidz, *Hamlet's Enemy: Madness and Myth in Hamlet* (New York, 1975), 88, 113.

few performances directed by a woman, Yvonne Nicholson sat on Laertes' lap in the advice scene, and played the part with "rough sexual bravado."[42]

Since the 1960s, the Freudian representation of Ophelia has been supplemented by an antipsychiatry that represents Ophelia's madness in more contemporary terms. In contrast to the psychoanalytic representation of Ophelia's sexual unconscious that connected her essential femininity to Freud's essays on female sexuality and hysteria, her madness is now seen in medical and biochemical terms, as schizophrenia. This is so in part because the schizophrenic woman has become the cultural icon of dualistic femininity in the mid-twentieth century as the erotomaniac was in the seventeenth and the hysteric in the nineteenth. It might also be traced to the work of R.D. Laing on female schizophrenia in the 1960s. Laing argued that schizophrenia was an intelligible response to the experience of invalidation within the family network, especially to the conflicting emotional messages and mystifying double binds experienced by daughters. Ophelia, he noted in *The Divided Self*, is an empty space. "In her madness there is no one there.... There is no integral selfhood expressed through her actions or utterances. Incomprehensible statements are said by nothing. She has already died. There is now only a vacuum where there was once a person."[43]

Despite his sympathy for Ophelia, Laing's readings silence her, equate her with "nothing," more completely than any since the Augustans; and they have been translated into performances which only make Ophelia a graphic study of mental pathology. The sickest Ophelias on the contemporary stage have been those in the productions of the pathologist-director Jonathan Miller. In 1974 at the Greenwich Theatre his Ophelia sucked her thumb; by 1981, at the Warehouse in London, she was played by an actress much taller and heavier than the Hamlet (perhaps punningly cast as the young actor Anton Lesser). She began the play with a set of nervous tics and tuggings of hair which by the mad scene had become a full set of schizophrenic routines—head banging, twitching, wincing, grimacing, and drooling.[44]

---

42 Richard David, *Shakespeare in the Theatre* (Cambridge, 1978), 75. This was the production directed by Buzz Goodbody, a brilliant young feminist radical who killed herself that year. See Colin Chambers, *Other Spaces: New Theatre and the RSC* (London, 1980), especially 63-7.

43 R.D. Laing, *The Divided Self* (Harmondsworth, 1965), 195n.

44 David, op. cit., 82-3; thanks to Marianne DeKoven, Rutgers University, for the description of the 1981 Warehouse production.

But since the 1970s too we have had a feminist discourse which has offered a new perspective on Ophelia's madness as protest and rebellion. For many feminist theorists, the madwoman is a heroine, a powerful figure who rebels against the family and the social order; and the hysteric who refuses to speak the language of the patriarchal order, who speaks otherwise, is a sister.[45] In terms of effect on the theater, the most radical application of these ideas was probably realized in Melissa Murray's agit-prop play *Ophelia*, written in 1979 for the English women's theater group "Hormone Imbalance." In this blank verse retelling of the Hamlet story, Ophelia becomes a lesbian and runs off with a woman servant to join a guerilla commune.[46]

40   While I've always regretted that I missed this production, I can't proclaim that this defiant ideological gesture, however effective politically or theatrically, is all that feminist criticism desires, or all to which it should aspire. When feminist criticism chooses to deal with representation, rather than with women's writing, it must aim for a maximum interdisciplinary contextualism, in which the complexity of attitudes towards the feminine can be analyzed in their fullest cultural and historical frame. The alternation of strong and weak Ophelias on the stage, virginal and seductive Ophelias in art, inadequate or oppressed Ophelias in criticism, tells us how these representations have overflowed the text, and how they have reflected the ideological character of their times, erupting as debates between dominant and feminist views in periods of gender crisis and redefinition. The representation of Ophelia changes independently of theories of the meaning of the play or the Prince, for it depends on attitudes towards women and madness. The decorous and pious Ophelia of the Augustan age and the postmodern schizophrenic heroine who might have stepped from the pages of Laing can be derived from the same figure; they are both contradictory and complementary images of female sexuality in which madness seems to act as the "switching-point, the concept which allows the co-existence of both sides of the representation."[47] There is no "true" Ophelia for whom

---

45   See, for example, Hélène Cixous and Catherine Clément, *La Jeune Née* (Paris, 1975).

46   For an account of this production, see Micheline Wandor, *Understudies: Theatre and Sexual Politics* (London, 1981), 47.

47   I am indebted for this formulation to a critique of my earlier draft of this paper by Carl Friedman, at the Wesleyan Center for the Humanities, April 1981.

feminist criticism must unambiguously speak, but perhaps only a Cubist Ophelia of multiple perspectives, more than the sum of all her parts.

But in exposing the ideology of representation, feminist critics have also the responsibility to acknowledge and to examine the boundaries of our own ideological positions as products of our gender and our time. A degree of humility in an age of critical hubris can be our greatest strength, for it is by occupying this position of historical self-consciousness in both feminism and criticism that we maintain our credibility in representing Ophelia, and that unlike Lacan, when we promise to speak about her, we make good on our word.

(1985)

Questions

1. According to Showalter's essay, what approach should feminist critics use in order to give the character of Ophelia "a story of her own"?

2. What are the component parts of Showalter's analysis? How does she organize her argument?

3. What is Showalter's thesis in this essay? Is there a thesis statement?

4. Describe Showalter's use of language in this essay. How does the language indicate the intended audience?

5. If you were directing a version of Hamlet for film or stage production, how would you represent Ophelia? Explain your choices.

STEPHEN JAY GOULD

ENTROPIC HOMOGENEITY ISN'T WHY NO ONE HITS .400 ANY MORE

*To hit .400 in baseball means that out of every 1000 chances
you hit fairly 400 times. To do this was once a remarkable but
by-no-means unheard of achievement. Since 1941, however,
no one has hit .400 over the course of a major league baseball
season. Scientist Stephen Jay Gould asks why.*

❧

Comparisons may be odious, but we cannot avoid them in a world that
prizes excellence and yearns to know whether current pathways lead
to progress or destruction. We are driven to contrast past with present and
use the result to predict an uncertain future. But how can we make fair
comparison since we gaze backward through the rose-colored lenses of our
most powerful myth—the idea of a former golden age?

Nostalgia for an unknown past can elevate hovels to castles, dung heaps
to snowclad peaks. I had always conceived Calvary, the site of Christ's
martyrdom, as a lofty mountain, covered with foliage and located far from
the hustle and bustle of Jerusalem. But I stood on its paltry peak last year.
Calvary lies inside the walls of old Jerusalem (just barely beyond the city
borders of Christ's time). The great hill is but one staircase high: its summit
lies *within* the Church of the Holy Sepulchre.

I had long read of Ragusa, the great maritime power of the medieval
Adriatic. I viewed it at grand scale in my mind's eye, a vast fleet balancing
the powers of Islam and Christendom, sending forth its élite to the vanguard of the "invincible" Spanish Armada. Medieval Ragusa has survived
intact—as Dubrovnik in Yugoslavia. No town (but Jerusalem) can match its
charm, but I circled the battlements of its city walls in 15 minutes. Ragusa,
by modern standards, is a modest village at most.

The world is so much bigger now, so much faster, so much more complex. Must our myths of ancient heroes expire on this altar of technological progress? We might dismiss our deep-seated tendency to aggrandize older heroes as mere sentimentalism—and plainly false by the argument just presented for Calvary and Ragusa. And yet, numbers proclaim a sense of truth in our persistent image of past giants as literally outstanding. Their legitimate claims are relative, not absolute. Great cities of the past may be villages today, and Goliath would barely qualify for the NBA. But, compared with modern counterparts, our legendary heroes often soar much farther above their own contemporaries. The distance between commonplace and extraordinary has contracted dramatically in field after field.

Baseball provides my favorite examples. Our national pastime may strike readers as an odd topic for this magazine, but few systems offer better data for a scientific problem that evokes as much interest, and sparks as much debate, as any other: the meaning of trends in history as expressed by measurable differences between past and present. This article uses baseball to address the general question of how we may compare an elusive past with a different present. How can we know whether past deeds matched or exceeded current prowess? In particular, was Moses right in his early pronouncement (Genesis 6:4): "There were giants in the earth in those days"?

Baseball has been a bastion of constancy in a tumultuously changing world, a contest waged to the same purpose and with the same basic rules for 100 years. It has also generated an unparalleled flood of hard numbers about achievement measured every which way that human cleverness can devise. Most other systems have changed so profoundly that we cannot meaningfully mix the numbers of past and present. How can we compare the antics of Larry Bird with basketball as played before the 24-second rule[1] or, going further back, the center jump after every basket, the two-hand dribble, and finally nine-man teams tossing a lopsided ball into Dr. Naismith's peach basket?[2] Yet while styles of play and dimensions of ball parks have altered substantially, baseball today is the same game that Wee Willie Keeler and Nap Lajoie played in the 1890s. Bill James, our premier guru of baseball stats, writes that "the rules attained essentially their

5

---

1   *24-second rule*   According to the rules of modern basketball, once a team has possession of the ball it must attempt a shot within twenty-four seconds.

2   *Dr. Naismith's peach basket*   Canadian James Naismith developed the game of basketball while working at the YMCA in Springfield, MA, in 1891; the first baskets were round fruit baskets with the bottoms cut out.

modern form after 1893" (when the pitching mound retreated to its current distance of 60 feet 6 inches). The numbers of baseball can be compared meaningfully for a century of play.

When we contrast these numbers of past and present, we encounter the well known and curious phenomenon that inspired this article: great players of the past often stand further apart from their teammates. Consider only the principal measures of hitting and pitching: batting average and earned run average. No one has hit .400 since Ted Williams reached .406 nearly half a century ago in 1941; yet eight players exceeded .410 in the 50 years before then. Bob Gibson had an earned run average of 1.12 in 1968. Ten other pitchers have achieved a single season E.R.A. below 1.30, but before Gibson we must go back a full 50 years to Walter Johnson's 1.27 in 1918. Could the myths be true after all? Were the old guys really better? Are we heading towards entropic homogeneity and robotic sameness?

These past achievements are paradoxical because we know perfectly well that all historical trends point to a near assurance that modern athletes must be better than their predecessors. Training has become an industry and obsession, an upscale profession filled with engineers of body and equipment, and a separate branch of medicine for the ills of excess zeal. Few men now make it to the majors just by tossing balls against a barn door during their youth. We live better, eat better, provide more opportunity across all social classes. Moreover, the pool of potential recruits has increased five-fold in 100 years by simple growth of the American population.

Numbers affirm this ineluctable improvement for sports that run against the absolute standard of a clock. The Olympian powers-that-be finally allowed women to run the marathon in 1984. Joan Benoit won it in 2:24:54. In 1896, Spiridon Loues had won in just a minute under three hours; Benoit ran faster than any male Olympic champion until Emil Zatopek's victory at 2:23:03 in 1952. Or consider two of America's greatest swimmers of the 1920s and '30s, men later recruited to play Tarzan (and faring far better than Mark Spitz in his abortive commercial career). Johnny Weissmuller won the 100-meter freestyle in 59.0 in 1924 and 58.6 in 1928. The women's record then stood at 1:12.4 and 1:11.0, but Jane had bested Tarzan by 1972 and the women's record has now been lowered to 54.79. Weissmuller also won the 400-meter freestyle in 5:04.2 in 1924, but Buster Crabbe had cut off more than 15 seconds by 1932 (4:48.4). Female champions in those years swam the distance in 6:02.2 and 5:28.5. The women beat Johnny in 1956, Buster in 1964, and have now (1984) reached 4:07.10, half a minute quicker than Crabbe.

Baseball, by comparison, pits batter against pitcher and neither against   10
a constant clock. If everyone improves as the general stature of athletes
rises, then why do we note any trends at all in baseball records? Why do
the best old-timers stand out above their modern counterparts? Why don't
hitting and pitching continue to balance?

The disappearance of .400 hitting becomes even more puzzling when
we recognize that *average* batting has remained relatively stable since the
beginning of modern baseball in 1876. The chart [below] displays the history of mean batting averages since 1876. (We only included men with an
average of at least two at-bats per game since we wish to gauge trends of
regular players. Nineteenth-century figures [National League only] include
80 to 100 players for most years [a low of 54 to a high of 147]. The American League began in 1901 and raised the average to 175 players or so during
the long reign of two eight-team leagues, and to above 300 for more recent
divisional play.) Note the constancy of mean values: the average ballplayer
hit about .260 in the 1870s, and he hits about .260 today. Moreover, this
stability has been actively promoted by judicious modifications in rules
whenever hitting or pitching threatened to gain the upper hand and provoke
a runaway trend of batting averages either up or down. Consider all the
major fluctuations:

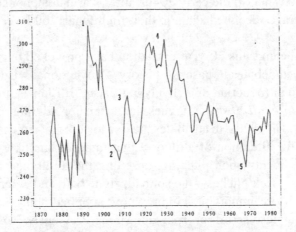

MEAN BATTING AVERAGE BY YEAR

*Averages rose after the pitching mound was moved back (1); declined after
adoption of the foul-strike rule (2); rose again after the invention of the
cork-center ball (3) and during the "lively ball" era (4). The dip in the '60s
(5) was corrected in 1969 by lowering the pitching mound and decreasing
the strike zone.*

After beginning around .260, averages began to drift downwards, reaching the .240s during the late 1880s and early 1890s. Then, during the 1893 season, the pitching mound was moved back to its current 60 feet 6 inches from home plate (it had begun at 45 feet, with pitchers delivering the ball underhand, and had moved steadily back during baseball's early days). The mean soared to its all-time high of .307 in 1894 and remained high (too high, by my argument) until 1901, when adoption of the foul-strike rule promoted a rapid down-turn. (Previously, foul balls hadn't influenced the count.)[3] But averages went down too far during the 1900s until the introduction of the cork-center ball sent them abruptly up in 1911. Pitchers accommodated, and within two years, averages returned to their .260 level—until Babe Ruth wreaked personal havoc upon the game by belting 29 homers in 1919 (more than entire teams had hit many times before). Threatened by the Black Sox scandal, and buoyed by the Babe's performance (and the public's obvious delight in his free-swinging style), the moguls introduced—whether by conscious collusion or simple acquiescence we do not know—the greatest of all changes in 1920. Scrappy one-run, savvy-baserunning, pitcher's baseball was out; big offense and swinging for the fences was in. Averages rose abruptly, and this time they stayed high for a full 20 years, even breaking .300 for the second (and only other) time in 1930. Then in the early 1940s, after war had siphoned off the best players, averages declined again to their traditional .260 level.

The causes behind this 20-year excursion have provoked one of the greatest unresolved debates in baseball history. Conventional wisdom attributes these rises to introduction of a "lively ball." But Bill James, in his masterly *Historical Baseball Abstract*, argues that no major fiddling with baseballs can be proved in 1920. He attributes the rise to coordinated changes in rules (and pervasive alteration of attitudes) that imposed multiple and simultaneous impediments upon pitching, upsetting the traditional balance for a full 20 years. Trick pitches—the spitball, shine ball, and emery ball—were all banned. More important, umpires now supplied shiny new balls any time the slightest scruff or spot appeared. Previously, soft, scratched, and darkened balls remained in play as long as possible (fans were even expected to throw back "souvenir" fouls). The replacement of discolored and scratched with shiny and new, according to James, would be just as

---

3   *Previously ... the count*   Since 1901, a foul ball has counted as a strike (except that a batter cannot go out on a foul).

effective for improving hitting as any mythical "lively ball." In any case averages returned to the .260s by the 1940s and remained quite stable until their marked decline in the mid-1960s. When Carl Yastrzemski won the American League batting title with a paltry .301 in 1968, the time for redress had come again. The moguls lowered the mound, restricted the strike zone, and averages promptly rose again—right back to their time-honored .260 level, where they have remained ever since.

This exegetical detail shows how baseball has been maintained, carefully and consistently, in unchanging balance since its inception. Is it not, then, all the more puzzling that downward trends in best performances go hand in hand with constancy of average achievement? Why, to choose the premier example, has .400 hitting disappeared, and what does this erasure teach us about the nature of trends and the differences between past and present?

We can now finally explicate the myth of ancient heroes—or, rather, we can understand its partial truth. Consider the two ingredients of our puzzle and paradox: (1) admitting the profound and general improvement of athletes (as measured in clock sports with absolute standards), star baseball players of the past probably didn't match today's leaders (or, at least, weren't notably better); (2) nonetheless, top baseball performances have declined while averages are actively maintained at a fairly constant level. In short, the old-timers did soar farther above their contemporaries, but must have been worse (or at least no better) than modern leaders. The .400 hitters of old were relatively better, but absolutely worse (or equal).

How can we get a numerical handle on this trend? I've argued several times in various articles for DISCOVER that students of biological evolution (I am one) approach the world with a vision different from time-honored Western perspectives. Our general culture still remains bound to its Platonic heritage of pigeonholes and essences. We divide the world into a set of definite "things" and view variation and subtle shadings as nuisances that block the distinctness of real entities. At best, variation becomes a device for calculating an average value seen as a proper estimate of the true thing itself. But variation *is* the irreducible reality; nature provides nothing else. Averages are often meaningless (mean height of a family with parents and young children). There is no quintessential human being—only black folks, white folks, skinny people, little people, Manute Bol and Eddie Gaedel. Copious and continuous variation is us.

But enough general pontification. The necessary item for this study is practical, not ideological. The tools for resolving the paradox of ancient heroes lie in the direct study of variation, not in exclusive attention to stellar

15

achievements. We've failed to grasp this simple solution because we don't view variation as reality itself, and therefore don't usually study it directly.

I can now state, in a few sentences, my theory about trends in general and .400 hitting in particular (sorry for the long cranking up, and the slow revving down to come, but simple ideas with unconventional contexts require some exposition if they hope to become reader-friendly). Athletes have gotten better (the world in general has become bigger, faster, and more efficient—this may not be a good thing at all; I merely point out that it has happened). We resist this evident trend by taking refuge in the myth of ancient heroes. The myth can be exploded directly for sports with absolute clock standards. In a system with relative standards (person against person)—especially when rules are subtly adjusted to maintain constancy in measures of average performance—this general improvement is masked and cannot be recovered when we follow our usual traditions and interpret figures for average performances as measures of real things. We can, however, grasp the general improvement of systems with relative standards by a direct study of variation—recognizing that variation itself is the irreducible reality. This improvement manifests itself as a *decline in variation*. Paradoxically, this decline produces a decrease in the difference between average and stellar performance. Therefore, modern leaders don't stand so far above their contemporaries. The "myth" of ancient heroes—the greater distance between average and best in the past—actually records the improvement of play through time.

Declining variation is the key to our puzzle. Hitting .400 isn't a thing in itself, but an extreme value in the distribution of batting averages (I shall present the data for this contention below). As variation shrinks around a constant mean batting average, .400 hitting disappears. It is, I think, as simple as that.

20   Reason One for Declining Variation: *Approach to the outer limits of human capacity*.

Well-off people in developed nations are getting taller and living longer, but the trend won't go on forever. All creatures have outer limits set by evolutionary histories. We're already witnessing the approach to limits in many areas. Maximum life span isn't increasing (although more and more people live long enough to get a crack at the unchanging heights). Racehorses have hardly speeded up, despite enormous efforts of breeders and the unparalleled economic incentive for shaving even a second off top performance (Kentucky Derby winners averaged 2:06.4 during the 1910s and 2:02.0 for the past ten years). Increase in human height has finally begun to level off (daughters of Radcliffe women are now no taller than their mothers). Women's sports records are declining rapidly as opportunity opens up, but some male records are stabilizing.

We can assess all these trends, and the inevitable decline in improvement as we reach the outer limits, because they're measured by absolute clock standards. Baseball players must also be improving, but the relative standard of batting averages, maintained at a mean of about .260, masks the advance. Let's assume that the wall at the right in the top diagram [below] represents the outer limit, and the bell-shaped curve well to its left marks variation in batting prowess 100 years ago. I suspect that all eras boast a few extraordinary individuals, people near the limits of body and endurance, however lower the general average. So, a few players resided near the right wall in 1880—but the average Joe stood far to their left, and variation among all players was great. Since then, everyone has improved. The best may have inched a bit towards the right wall, but average players have moved substantially in that direction. Meanwhile, increasing competition and higher standards have eliminated very weak hitters (once tolerated for their superior fielding and other skills).

THE EXTINCTION OF .400 HITTING

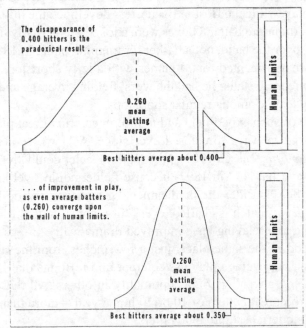

The disappearance of 0.400 hitters is the paradoxical result . . .

0.260 mean batting average

Best hitters average about 0.400

. . . of improvement in play, as even average batters (0.260) converge upon the wall of human limits.

0.260 mean batting average

Best hitters average about 0.350

Human Limits

So as average players approach the limiting right wall [previous page, bottom diagram], variation decreases strongly on both flanks—at the high end for simple decline in space between the average and the limit, and at the low end by decreasing tolerance as general play improves. The relative standards of baseball have masked this trend; hitting has greatly improved, but we still measure its average as .260 because pitching has gained in concert. We can, however, assess this improvement in a different way—by inevitable decline in variation as the average converges upon the limiting wall. Modern stars may be an inch or two closer to the wall—they're absolutely better (or at least no worse) than ancient heroes. But the average has moved several feet closer—and the distance between ordinary (kept at .260) and best has decreased. In short, no more .400 hitters. Ironically, the disappearance of .400 hitting is a sign of improvement, not decline.

Reason Two (really the same point stated differently): *Systems equilibrate as they improve.*

Baseball was feeling its way during the early days of major league play. Its rules were our rules, but scores of subtleties hadn't yet been developed or discovered; rough edges careered out in all directions from a stable center. To cite just a few examples (again from Bill James): pitchers began to cover first base in the 1890s; during the same decade, Brooklyn invented the cut-off play, while the Boston Beaneaters developed the hit-and-run and signals from runner to batter. Gloves were a joke in those early days—just a little leather over the hand, not a basket for trapping balls. In 1896 the Phillies actually experimented for 73 games with a lefty shortstop. Traditional wisdom applied. He stank; he had the worst fielding average and the fewest assists in the league among regular shortstops.

In an era of such experiment and indifference, truly great players could take advantage in ways foreclosed ever since. As I wrote in a previous article (*Vanity Fair*, March 1983), Wee Willie Keeler could "hit 'em where they ain't" (and bat .432 in 1897) because fielders didn't yet know where they should be. Consider the predicament of a modern Wade Boggs or a Rod Carew. Every pitch is charted, every hit mapped to the nearest square inch. Fielding and relaying have improved dramatically. Boggs and Keeler probably stood in the same place, just a few inches from the right wall of human limits, but average play has so crept up on Boggs that he lacks the space for taking advantage of suboptimality in others. All these improvements must rob great batters of 10 or 20 hits a year—more than enough to convert our modern best into .400 hitters.

To summarize, variation in batting averages must decrease as improving play eliminates the rough edges that great players could exploit, and as average performance moves towards the limits of human possibility and compresses great players into an ever decreasing space between average play and the unmovable right wall.

In my *Vanity Fair* article, I measured this decline of variation about a constant average on the cheap. I simply took the five highest and five lowest averages for regular players in each year and compared them with the league average. I found that differences between both average and highest and between average and lowest have decreased steadily through the years (*see chart, page 326*). The disappearance of .400 hitting—the most discussed and disputed trend in the history of baseball—isn't a reflection of generally higher averages in the past (for no one hit over .400 during the second decade of exalted averages, from 1931 to 1940, and most .400 hitting in our century occurred between 1900 and 1920, when averages stood at their canonical [and current] .260 level). Nor can this eclipse of high hitting be entirely attributed to the panoply of conventional explanations that view .400 averages as a former "thing" now extinct—more grueling schedules, too many night games, better fielding, invention of the slider and relief pitching. For .400 hitting isn't a thing to be extirpated, but an extreme value in a distribution of variation for batting averages. The reasons for declining variation, as presented above, are different from the causes for disappearance of an entity. Declining variation is a general property of systems that stabilize and improve while maintaining constant rules of performance through time. The extinction of .400 hitting is, paradoxically, a mark of increasingly *better* play.

We have now calculated the decline of variation properly, and at vastly more labor (with thanks to my research assistant Ned Young for weeks of work, and to Ed Purcell, Nobel laureate and one of the world's great physicists—but also just a fan with good ideas). The standard deviation is a statistician's basic measure of variation. To compute the standard deviation, you take (in this case) each individual batting average and subtract from it the league average for that year. You then square each value (multiply it by itself) in order to eliminate negative numbers for batting averages below the mean (a negative times a negative gives a positive number). You then add up all these values and divide them by the total number of players—giving an average squared deviation of individual players from the mean. Finally, you take the square root of this number to obtain the average, or standard, deviation itself. The higher the value, the more extensive, or spread out, the variation.

30   We calculated the standard deviation of batting averages for each year (an improvement from my former high and low five, but much more work). The chart on [this page] plots the trend of standard deviations in batting averages year by year. Our hypothesis is clearly confirmed. Standard deviations have been dropping steadily and irreversibly. The decline itself has decelerated over the years as baseball stabilizes—rapidly during the nineteenth century, more slowly through the twentieth, and reaching a stable plateau by about 1940.

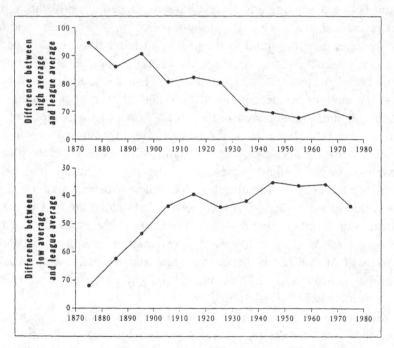

THE DECLINE IN EXTREMES

Batting averages are neither as high nor as low as they used to be.

    If I may make a personal and subjective comment. I was stunned and delighted (beyond all measure) by the elegance and clarity of this result. I pretty well knew what the general pattern would be because standard deviations are so strongly influenced by extreme values (a consequence of squaring each individual deviation in the calculation)—so my original cheap method of five highest and lowest produced a fair estimate. But I never dreamed that the decline would be so regular, so devoid of exception or anomaly for even a single year—so unvarying that we could even pick out such subtleties as the deceleration in decline. I've spent my entire professional career studying such statistical distributions, and I know how rarely one obtains such clean results in better behaved data of controlled experiments or natural growth in simple systems. We usually encounter some glitch, some anomaly, some funny years. But the decline of standard deviation for batting averages is so regular that it looks like a plot for a law of nature. I find this all the more remarkable because the graph of averages themselves through time (*page 328*) shows all the noise and fluctuation expected in natural systems. Yet mean batting averages have been constantly manipulated by the moguls of baseball to maintain a general constancy, while no one has tried to monkey with the standard deviation. Thus, while mean batting averages have gone up and down to follow the whims of history and the vagaries of invention, the standard deviation has marched steadily down at a decreasing pace, apparently perturbed by nothing of note. I regard this regularity of decline as further evidence that decreasing variation through time is the primary predictable feature of stabilizing systems

The details are impressive in their regularity. All four beginning years of the 1870s sport high values of standard deviation greater than 0.050, while the last reading in excess of 0.050 occurs in 1886. Values between 0.04 and 0.05 mark the rest of the nineteenth century, with three years just below, at 0.038 to 0.040. The last reading in excess of 0.040 occurs in 1911. Subsequently, decline within the 0.03 and 0.04 range shows the same precision of detail by even decrease with years. The last reading as high as 0.037 occurs in 1937, and of 0.035 in 1941. Only two years have exceeded 0.034 since 1957. Between 1942 and 1980, values remained entirely within the restricted range of 0.0285 to 0.0348. I'd thought that at least one unusual year would upset the pattern—that one nineteenth-century value would achieve late twentieth-century lows, or one more recent year soar to ancient highs—but we find no such thing. All measures from 1906 back to the beginning are higher than every reading from 1938 to 1980. We find no overlap at all. This—take it from an old trooper—is regularity with a vengeance. Something general is going on here, and I think I know what.

The decadal averages are listed on page 328, and show continuous decline before stabilization in the 1940s. (A note for statistically minded readers: standard deviations are expressed in their own units of measurement—mouse tails in millimeters, mountains in megatons. Thus, as mean values rise and fall, standard deviations may go up and down to track the mean rather than record exclusively the amount of spread. This poses no problem for most of our chart, because averages have been so stable through time at about .260. But the 20-point rise in averages during the 1920s and 1930s might entail artificially elevated standard deviations. We can correct for this effect by computing the coefficient of variation—100 times the standard deviation divided by the mean—for each year. Also listed are decadal averages for coefficients of variation—and we now see that apparent stabilization between the 1910s and 1920s was masking a continuing decline in coefficient of variation, as the 1920s rise in averages canceled out decline in variation when measured by the standard deviation.)

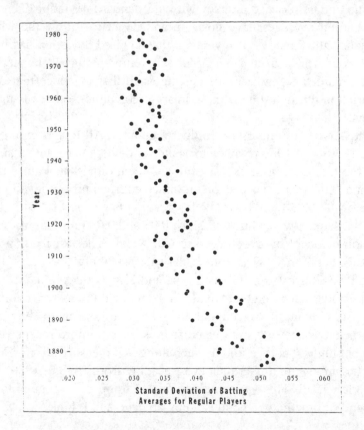

If my editors were more indulgent, I could wax at distressing length about more details and different measures. Just one final hint of more interesting pattern revealed by finer dissection: the chart above amalgamates the two leagues, but their trends are somewhat different. In the National

League, variation declined during the nineteenth century, but stabilized early in the twentieth. In the American League, founded in 1901, variation dropped steadily right through the 1940s. Thus, each league followed the same pattern—time of origin setting pattern of decline for decades to come. Can we use existence or stabilization of declining variation as a mark of maturity? Did the leagues differ fundamentally during the early years of our century—the National already mature, the American still facing a few decades of honing and trimming the edges?

No one has invested more time and energy in the study of numbers than baseball aficionados. We have measures and indices for everything imaginable—from simple lists of at-bats to number of times a black shortstop under six feet tall has been caught stealing third on pitchouts by righties to left-handed catchers. Yet I don't think that this most basic pattern in the standard deviation of batting averages has been properly noted, or its significance assessed. As I argued above, the biases of our upbringing force a focus on averages treated as things, and virtually preclude proper attention to variation considered as irreducible reality. The standard deviation is our base-level tool for studying variation—as fundamental as milk for babies and cockroaches for New York apartments. Yet, after decades of loving attention to minutiae of averages, we can still gain insights from an unexplored pattern in the very simplest kiddie measure of variation. What better illustration for my claim that our culture undervalues variation at its peril?

After this detail, I've earned the right to end with a bit of philosophical musing, ostensibly in the great decline-of-civilization tradition, but really a sneaky bit of optimism from the depth of my sanguine soul.

The message of this study in variation might seem glum, almost cosmically depressing in its paradox—that general improvement clips the wings of true greatness. No one soars above the commonplace any more. General advance brings declining variation in its wake; heroes are extinct. The small population of Europe yielded both a Bach and a Mozart in just 100 years; where shall we find such transcendent geniuses to guide (or at least enlighten) our uncertain and perilous present?

I wish to propose, in closing, a more general framework for understanding trends in time as an interaction between the location of bell-shaped curves in variation and the position (and potential for mobility) of the limiting right wall for human excellence. This theme transcends sports (or any particular example), and our model should include mind work as well as body work. I

35

suggest three rough categories, with a fundamental example for each, ranging from high to low potential for future accomplishment.

Consider science as a system of knowledge. In most areas, our ignorance is abysmal compared with our sense of what we might learn and
know. The curve of knowledge, in other words, stands far from the right
wall. Moreover, the wall itself (or at least our perception of it) seems flexible before the growth of knowledge, as new theories suggest pathways to
insight never considered previously. Science seems progressive since current ignorance provides so much space to its right, and since the wall itself
can be pushed back by the very process that signals our approach. Still, one
cannot avoid—with that special sadness reserved for recognizing a wonderful thing gone forever—the conviction that certain seminal discoveries
established truths so central and so broad in import that we cannot hope
to win insight in such great gulps again, for the right wall moves slowly
and with limits, and we may never again open up space for jumps so big.
Plate tectonics has revolutionized geology, but we cannot match the thrill
of those who discovered that time comes in billions, not thousands—for
deep time, once discovered, set the root of a profession forever. These are
exciting days for biology, but no one will taste the intellectual power of a
man alone at Downe—Charles Darwin reformulating all nature with the
passkey of evolution.

40   I would place most sports, as well as musical performance, in a second
category, where the best have long stood near an inflexible right wall. When
we remove impediments imposed by custom (women's sports) or technology (certain musical instruments), improvement may be rapid. But progress
comes in inches or milliseconds for goals long sought and unimpeded (I
doubt that Stern plays notably better than Paganini, Horowitz than Liszt,
E. Power Biggs than Bach—and neither horse nor human male is shaving
much off the mile run these days). The small contribution of this article lies
in this second domain—in showing that decline in variation will measure
improvement when relative standards mask progress measured against such
absolute criteria as clocks.

Lest we lament this second category for its limited licenses in improvement, consider the painful plight of a third domain where success in striving
depletes the system itself. The right wall of our first domain was far away
and somewhat flexible, near and rigid (but still stable) in our second. In this
third domain, success hits the wall and consumes it—as if the mile run had
disappeared as a competitive sport as soon as 100 people ran the distance
in less than four minutes. Given an ethic that exalts perennial originality

in artistic composition, the history of music (and many other arts) may fall into this domain. One composer may exploit a basic style for much of a career, but successors may not follow this style in much detail, or for very long. Such striving for newness may grant us joy forever if a limitless array of potential styles awaits discovery and exploitation. But perhaps the world is not so bounteous; perhaps we've already explored most of what even a highly sophisticated audience can deem accessible. Perhaps the wall of an intelligible vanguard has been largely consumed. Perhaps there is a simple solution to the paradox of why we now generate no Bach or Mozart in a world far larger, with musical training provided for millions more. Perhaps they reside among us, but we've consumed all styles of expression so deeply tuned to the human soul. If so, I might timidly advance a truly reactionary proposal. The death of Mozart at 35 may have been the deepest tragedy of our cultural history (great scientists have died even younger, but their work can be done by others). We perform his handful of operas over and over again. We might be enjoying a dozen more—some counted as the most sublime of all musical works—if he had survived even to 50. Suppose a composer now lived who could master his style and write every bit as well. The ethic of originality forbids it absolutely, but would the integrity of art collapse forever if this person wrote just a few more great pieces in that genre? Not a hundred, just three or four to supplement *Don Giovanni* and *Die Zauberflöte*. Would this not be esteemed a public service beyond all others?

Enough. I'm waxing lugubrious, despite promises to the contrary. For while I may yearn to hear Beethoven's tenth symphony, I don't lament a lost past or decry a soft present. In sports, and art, and science (how I wish it were so in politics as well), we live in the best world we've ever known, though not in the best of all possible worlds. So be it that improvement must bury in its wake the myth of ancient heroes. We've exposed the extinction of .400 hitting as a sign of progress, not degradation—the paradoxical effect of declining variation as play improves and stabilizes, and as average contestants also approach the right wall of human limits.

Do not lament the loss of literally outstanding performance (largely a figment, in any case, of failings among the ordinary, not a mark of greater prowess among the best). Celebrate instead the immense improvement of average play. (I rather suspect that we would regard most operatic performances of 1850, and most baseball games of 1900, as sloppy and amateurish—not to mention the village squabbles that enter history as epic battles.)

Do not lament our past ease in distinguishing the truly great. Celebrate instead the general excellence that makes professional sport so exciting today. And appreciate the need for subtlety and discernment that modern fans must develop to make proper assessments: we must all now be connoisseurs to appreciate our favorite games fully. Above all, remember that the possibility for transcendence never dies. We live for that moment, the truly unpredictable performance that shatters all expectation. We delight all the more in Dwight Gooden and Larry Bird because they stand out among a panoply of true stars. Besides, I really wrote this article only because I have a hunch that I want to share (and we professor types need to set context before we go out on a limb): Wade Boggs is gonna hit .400 this year.[4]

(1986)

Questions

1. In Gould's view, what *is* .400 hitting? Why is it important not to think of .400 hitting as an independent phenomenon in his view?

2. What effect does the introduction of gender have (paragraph 9)? Why is baseball a better context to explore issues of this sort than would be, say, basketball? Write a brief essay in which you use examples from either sports or other cultural activities (such as film or drama) to illustrate a much more general point.

3. Summarize in your own words in no more than two or three paragraphs Gould's argument as to why "no one hits .400 anymore."

4. Summarize in your own words Gould's argument about improvement (paragraph 27). Do you agree that this extension of his argument follows logically from the points he has already established?

5. Comment on Gould's diction. Why do you think he occasionally uses "big words" in an essay that is clearly aimed at the general reader as well as at an academic audience?

---

4   *Wade Boggs ... this year*   Wade Boggs hit .356 in 1986. The closest that a modern hitter has come to hitting .400 was Tony Gwynn of the San Diego Padres hitting .394 in the strike-shortened season of 1994.

Ngugi wa Thiong'o

from Decolonising the Mind

In this essay one of Africa's most distinguished
novelists discusses some of the connections
between language and culture.

❧

III

I was born into a large peasant family: father, four wives and about twenty-eight children. I also belonged, as we all did in those days, to a wider extended family and to the community as a whole.

We spoke Gĩkũyũ as we worked in the fields. We spoke Gĩkũyũ in and outside the home. I can vividly recall those evenings of storytelling around the fireside. It was mostly the grown-ups telling the children but everybody was interested and involved. We children would re-tell the stories the following day to other children who worked in the fields picking the pyrethrum flowers, tea-leaves or coffee beans of our European and African landlords.

The stories, with mostly animals as the main characters, were all told in Gĩkũyũ. Hare, being small, weak but full of innovative wit and cunning, was our hero. We identified with him as he struggled against the brutes of prey like lion, leopard, hyena. His victories were our victories and we learnt that the apparently weak can outwit the strong. We followed the animals in their struggle against hostile nature—drought, rain, sun, wind—a confrontation often forcing them to search for forms of co-operation. But we were also interested in their struggles amongst themselves, and particularly between the beasts and the victims of prey. These twin struggles, against nature and other animals, reflected real-life struggles in the human world.

Not that we neglected stories with human beings as the main characters. There were two types of characters in such human-centered narratives: the species of truly human beings with qualities of courage, kindness, mercy, hatred of evil, concern for others; and a man-eat-man two-mouthed species with qualities of greed, selfishness, individualism and hatred of what was good for the larger co-operative community. Co-operation as the ultimate good in a community was a constant theme. It could unite human beings with animals against ogres and beasts of prey, as in the story of how dove, after being fed with castor-oil seeds, was sent to fetch a smith working far away from home and whose pregnant wife was being threatened by these man-eating two-mouthed ogres.

5   There were good and bad story-tellers. A good one could tell the same story over and over again, and it would always be fresh to us, the listeners. He or she could tell a story told by someone else and make it more alive and dramatic. The differences really were in the use of words and images and the inflexion of voices to effect different tones.

We therefore learnt to value words for their meaning and nuances. Language was not a mere string of words. It had a suggestive power well beyond the immediate and lexical meaning. Our appreciation of the suggestive magical power of language was reinforced by the games we played with words through riddles, proverbs, transpositions of syllables, or through nonsensical but musically arranged words. So we learnt the music of our language on top of the content. The language, through images and symbols, gave us a view of the world, but it had a beauty of its own. The home and the field were then our pre-primary school but what is important, for this discussion, is that the language of our evening teach-ins, and the language of our immediate and wider community, and the language of our work in the fields were one.

And then I went to school, a colonial school, and this harmony was broken. The language of my education was no longer the language of my culture. I first went to Kamaandura, missionary run, and then to another called Maanguuū run by nationalists grouped around the Gīkūyū Independent and Karinga Schools Association. Our language of education was still Gīkūyū. The very first time I was ever given an ovation for my writing was over a composition in Gīkūyū. So for my first four years there was still harmony between the language of my formal education and that of the Limuru peasant community.

It was after the declaration of a state of emergency over Kenya in 1952 that all the schools run by patriotic nationalists were taken over by the colonial regime and were placed under District Education Boards chaired by Englishmen. English became the language of my formal education. In Kenya, English became more than a language: it was *the* language, and all the others had to bow before it in deference.

Thus one of the most humiliating experiences was to be caught speaking Gĩkũyũ in the vicinity of the school. The culprit was given corporal punishment—three to five strokes of the cane on bare buttocks—or was made to carry a metal plate around the neck with inscriptions such as I AM STUPID or I AM A DONKEY. Sometimes the culprits were fined money they could hardly afford. And how did the teachers catch the culprits? A button was initially given to one pupil who was supposed to hand it over to whoever was caught speaking his mother tongue. Whoever had the button at the end of the day would sing who had given it to him and the ensuing process would bring out all the culprits of the day. Thus children were turned into witch-hunters and in the process were being taught the lucrative value of being a traitor to one's immediate community.

The attitude to English was the exact opposite: any achievement in spoken or written English was highly rewarded; prizes, prestige, applause; the ticket to higher realms. English became the measure of intelligence and ability in the arts, the sciences, and all the other branches of learning. English became *the* main determinant of a child's progress up the ladder of formal education.

As you may know, the colonial system of education in addition to its apartheid racial demarcation had the structure of a pyramid: a broad primary base, a narrowing secondary middle, and an even narrower university apex. Selections from primary into secondary were through an examination, in my time called Kenya African Preliminary Examination, in which one had to pass six subjects ranging from Maths to Nature Study and Kiswahili. All the papers were written in English. Nobody could pass the exam who failed the English language paper no matter how brilliantly he had done in the other subjects. I remember one boy in my class of 1954 who had distinctions in all subjects except English, which he had failed. He was made to fail the entire exam. He went on to become a turn boy in a bus company. I who had only passes but a credit in English got a place at the Alliance High School, one of the most elitist institutions for Africans in colonial Kenya. The requirements for a place at the University, Makerere University College, were broadly the same: nobody could go on to wear the undergraduate red gown, no matter how brilliantly they had performed in all the other subjects unless they had a credit—not even a simple pass!—in English. Thus the most coveted place in the pyramid and in the system was only available to the holder of an English language credit card. English was the official vehicle and the magic formula to colonial elitedom.

Literary education was now determined by the dominant language while also reinforcing that dominance. Orature (oral literature) in Kenyan languages stopped. In primary school I now read simplified Dickens and Stevenson alongside Rider Haggard. Jim Hawkins, Oliver Twist, Tom Brown—not Hare, Leopard and Lion—were now my daily companions in the world of imagination. In secondary school, Scott and G.B. Shaw vied with more Rider Haggard, John Buchan, Alan Paton, Captain W.E. Johns. At Makerere I read English: from Chaucer to T.S. Eliot with a touch of Grahame Greene.

Thus language and literature were taking us further and further from ourselves to other selves, from our world to other worlds.

What was the colonial system doing to us Kenyan children? What were the consequences of, on the one hand, this systematic suppression of our languages and the literature they carried, and on the other the elevation of English and the literature it carried? To answer those questions, let me first examine the relationship of language to human experience, human culture, and the human perception of reality.

IV

15　Language, any language, has a dual character: it is both a means of communication and a carrier of culture. Take English. It is spoken in Britain and in Sweden and Denmark. But for Swedish and Danish people English is only a means of communication with non-Scandinavians. It is not a carrier of their culture. For the British, and particularly the English, it is additionally, and inseparably from its use as a tool of communication, a carrier of their culture and history. Or take Swahili in East and Central Africa. It is widely used as a means of communication across many nationalities. But it is not the carrier of a culture and history of many of those nationalities. However in parts of Kenya and Tanzania, and particularly in Zanzibar, Swahili is inseparably both a means of communication and a carrier of the culture of those people to whom it is a mother-tongue.

Language as communication has three aspects or elements. There is first what Karl Marx once called the language of real life, the element basic to the whole notion of language, its origins and development: that is, the relations people enter into with one another in the labor process, the links they necessarily establish among themselves in the act of a people, a community of human beings, producing wealth or means of life like food, clothing, houses. A human community really starts its historical being as a community of co-operation in production through the division of labor; the simplest is between man, woman and child within a household; the more complex divisions are between branches of production such as those who are sole hunters, sole gatherers of fruits or sole workers in metal. Then there are the most complex divisions such as those in modern factories where a single product, say a shirt or a shoe, is the result of many hands and minds. Production is co-operation, is communication, is language, is expression of a relation between human beings and it is specifically human.

The second aspect of language as communication is speech and it imitates the language of real life, that is communication in production. The verbal signposts both reflect and aid communication or the relation established between human beings in the production of their means of life. Language as a system of verbal signposts makes that production possible. The spoken word is to relations between human beings what the hand is to the relations between human beings and nature. The hand through tools mediates between human beings and nature and forms the language of real life: spoken words mediate between human beings and form the language of speech.

The third aspect is the written signs. The written word imitates the spoken. Where the first two aspects of language as communication through the hand and the spoken word historically evolved more or less simultaneously, the written aspect is a much later historical development. Writing is representation of sounds with visual symbols, from the simplest knot among shepherds to tell the number in a herd or the hieroglyphics among the Agīkūyū gicaandi singers and poets of Kenya, to the most complicated and different letter and picture writing systems of the world today.

In most societies the written and the spoken languages are the same, in that they represent each other: what is on paper can be read to another person and be received as that language, which the recipient has grown up speaking. In such a society there is broad harmony for a child between the three aspects of language as communication. His interaction with nature and with other men is expressed in written and spoken symbols or signs which are both a result of that double interaction and a reflection of it. The association of the child's sensibility is with the language of his experience of life.

But there is more to it: communication between human beings is also the basis and process of evolving culture. In doing similar kinds of things and actions over and over again under similar circumstances, similar even in their mutability, certain patterns, moves, rhythms, habits, attitudes, experiences and knowledge emerge. Those experiences are handed over to

20

the next generation and become the inherited basis for their further actions on nature and on themselves. There is a gradual accumulation of values which in time become almost self-evident truths governing their conception of what is right and wrong, good and bad, beautiful and ugly, courageous and cowardly, generous and mean in their internal and external relations. Over a time this becomes a way of life distinguishable from other ways of life. They develop a distinctive culture and history. Culture embodies those moral, ethical and aesthetic values, the set of spiritual eyeglasses, through which they come to view themselves and their place in the universe. Values are the basis of a people's identity, their sense of particularity as members of the human race. All this is carried by language. Language as culture is the collective memory bank of a people's experience in history. Culture is almost indistinguishable from the language that makes possible its genesis, growth, banking, articulation and indeed its transmission from one genera- tion to the next.

Language as culture also has three important aspects. Culture is a product of the history which it in turn reflects. Culture in other words is a product and a reflection of human beings communicating with one another in the very struggle to create wealth and to control it. But culture does not merely reflect that history, or rather it does so by actually forming images or pictures of the world of nature and nurture. Thus the second aspect of language as culture is as an image-forming agent in the mind of a child. Our whole conception of ourselves as a people, individually and collectively, is based on those pictures and images which may or may not correctly correspond to the actual reality of the struggles with nature and nurture which produced them in the first place. But our capacity to confront the world creatively is dependent on how those images correspond or not to that reality, how they distort or clarify the reality of our struggles. Language as culture is thus mediating between me and my own self; between my own self and other selves; between me and nature. Language is mediating in my very being. And this brings us to the third aspect of language as culture. Culture transmits or imparts those images of the world and reality through the spoken and the written language, that is through a specific language. In other words, the capacity to speak, the capacity to order sounds in a manner that makes for mutual comprehension between human beings is universal. This is the universality of language, a quality specific to human beings. It corresponds to the universality of the struggle against nature and that between human beings. But the particularity of the sounds, the words, the word order into phrases and sentences, and the specific manner, or laws, of their ordering is what distinguishes one language from another. Thus a specific culture is not transmitted through language in its universality but in its particularity as the language of a specific community with a specific history. Written literature and orature are the main means by which a particular language transmits the images of the world contained in the culture it carries.

Language as communication and as culture are then products of each other. Communication creates culture: culture is a means of communication. Language carries culture, and culture carries, particularly through orature and literature, the entire body of values by which we come to perceive ourselves and our place in the world. How people perceive themselves affects how they look at their culture, at their politics and at the social production of wealth, at their entire relationship to nature and to other beings. Language is thus inseparable from ourselves as a community of human beings with a specific form and character, a specific history, a specific relationship to the world.

v

So what was the colonialist imposition of a foreign language doing to us children?

The real aim of colonialism was to control the people's wealth: what they produced, how they produced it, and how it was distributed; to control, in other words, the entire realm of the language of real life. Colonialism imposed its control of the social production of wealth through military conquest and subsequent political dictatorship. But its most important area of domination was the mental universe of the colonized, the control, through culture, of how people perceived themselves and their relationship to the world. Economic and political control can never be complete or effective without mental control. To control a people's culture is to control their tools of self-definition in relationship to others.

For colonialism this involved two aspects of the same process: the destruction or the deliberate undervaluing of a people's culture, their art, dances, religions, history, geography, education, orature and literature, and the conscious elevation of the language of the colonizer. The domination of a people's language by the languages of the colonizing nations was crucial to the domination of the mental universe of the colonized.

Take language as communication. Imposing a foreign language, and suppressing the native languages as spoken and written, were already breaking the harmony previously existing between the African child and the three

25

aspects of language. Since the new language as a means of communication was a product of and was reflecting the "real language of life" elsewhere, it could never as spoken or written properly reflect or imitate the real life of that community. This may in part explain why technology always appears to us as slightly external, *their* product and not *ours*. The word "missile" used to hold an alien far-away sound until I recently learnt its equivalent in Gĩkũyũ, *ngurukuhĩ* and it made me apprehend it differently. Learning, for a colonial child, became a cerebral activity and not an emotionally felt experience.

But since the new, imposed languages could never completely break the native languages as spoken, their most effective area of domination was the third aspect of language as communication, the written. The language of an African child's formal education was foreign. The language of the books he read was foreign. The language of his conceptualization was foreign. Thought, in him, took the visible form of a foreign language. So the written language of a child's upbringing in the school (even his spoken language within the school compound) became divorced from his spoken language at home. There was often not the slightest relationship between the child's written world, which was also the language of his schooling, and the world of his immediate environment in the family and the community. For a co-lonial child, the harmony existing between the three aspects of language as communication was irrevocably broken. This resulted in the disassociation of the sensibility of that child from his natural and social environment, what we might call colonial alienation. The alienation became reinforced in the teaching of history, geography, music, where bourgeois Europe was always the center of the universe.

This disassociation, divorce, or alienation from the immediate environ-ment becomes clearer when you look at colonial language as a carrier of culture.

Since culture is a product of the history of a people which it in turn reflects, the child was now being exposed exclusively to a culture that was a product of a world external to himself. He was being made to stand out-side himself to look at himself. *Catching Them Young* is the title of a book on racism, class, sex, and politics in children's literature by Bob Dixon. "Catching them young" as an aim was even more true of a colonial child. The images of his world and his place in it implanted in a child take years to eradicate, if they ever can be.

30   Since culture does not just reflect the world in images but actually, through those images, conditions a child to see that world a certain way, the

colonial child was made to see the world and where he stands in it as seen and defined by or reflected in the culture of the language of imposition.

And since those images are mostly passed on through orature and literature it meant the child would now only see the world as seen in the literature of his language of adoption. From the point of view of alienation, that is of seeing oneself from outside oneself as if one was another self, it does not matter that the imported literature carried the great humanist tradition of the best in Shakespeare, Goethe, Balzac, Tolstoy, Gorky, Brecht, Sholokhov, Dickens. The location of this great mirror of imagination was necessarily Europe and its history and culture and the rest of the universe was seen from that center.

But obviously it was worse when the colonial child was exposed to images of his world as mirrored in the written languages of his colonizer. Where his own native languages were associated in his impressionable mind with low status, humiliation, corporal punishment, slow-footed intelligence and ability or downright stupidity, non-intelligibility and barbarism, this was reinforced by the world he met in the works of such geniuses of racism as a Rider Haggard or a Nicholas Monsarrat; not to mention the pronouncement of some of the giants of western intellectual and political establishment, such as Hume ("... The negro is naturally inferior to the whites ..."), Thomas Jefferson ("... The blacks ... are inferior to the whites on the endowments of both body and mind ..."), or Hegel with his Africa comparable to a land of childhood still enveloped in the dark mantle of the night as far as the development of self-conscious history was concerned. Hegel's statement that there was nothing harmonious with humanity to be found in the African character is representative of the racist images of Africans and Africa such a colonial child was bound to encounter in the literature of the colonial languages. The results could be disastrous.

(1986)

Questions

1. What is the rhetorical purpose of paragraph 14? Is it effective?

2. In paragraph 15, Ngugi argues that a language has a communication function for all people who speak that language, but that it also serves as a carrier of culture for all those for whom that language is the mother-tongue. If you speak two or more languages, does this assertion meet with your own experience?

3. Discuss how the imposition of a foreign language breaks "the harmony previously existing between the African child and the three aspects of language" (paragraph 26).

4. Toward the end of his essay, Ngugi makes reference to the European-based writers of literature he was forced to study as a child, and how these stories did not match his own experiences. How well do the poems, essays, plays, and novels you are being asked to read in this course reflect your experiences? If you were the instructor of this course, how would you go about selecting a reading list?

INTOXICATED BY MY ILLNESS

In one of Anatole Broyard's last essays, the author
describes how he was affected by the discovery
of his own terminal illness.

❧

So much of a writer's life consists of assumed suffering, rhetorical suffering, that I felt something like relief, even elation, when the doctor told me that I had cancer of the prostate. Suddenly there was in the air a rich sense of crisis, real crisis, yet one that also contained echoes of ideas like the crisis of language, the crisis of literature, or of personality. It seemed to me that my existence, whatever I thought, felt or did, had taken on a kind of meter, as in poetry, or in taxis.

When you learn that your life is threatened, you can turn toward this knowledge or away from it. I turned toward it. It was not a choice, but an automatic shifting of gears, a tacit agreement between my body and my brain. I thought that time had tapped me on the shoulder, that I had been given a real deadline at last. It wasn't that I believed the cancer was going to kill me, even though it had spread beyond the prostate—it could probably be controlled, either by radiation or hormonal manipulation. No, what struck me was the startled awareness that one day something, whatever it might be, was going to interrupt my leisurely progress. It sounds trite, yet I can only say that I realized for the first time that I don't have forever.

Time was no longer innocuous, nothing was casual any more. I understood that living itself had a deadline. Like the book I had been working on—how sheepish I would feel if I couldn't finish it. I had promised it to myself and to my friends. Though I wouldn't say this out loud, I had promised it to the world. All writers privately think this way.

When my friends heard I had cancer, they found me surprisingly cheerful and talked about my courage. But it has nothing to do with courage, at least not for me. As far as I can tell, it's a question of desire. I'm filled with desire—to live, to write, to do everything. Desire itself is a kind of immortality. While I've always had trouble concentrating, I now feel as concentrated as a diamond, or a microchip.

5   I remember a time in the 1950s when I tried to talk a friend of mine named Jules out of committing suicide. He had already made one attempt and when I went to see him he said "Give me a good reason to go on living." He was 30 years old.

I saw what I had to do. I started to sell life to him, like a real estate agent. Just look at the world, I said. How can you not be curious about it? The streets, the houses, the trees, the shops, the people, the movement and the stillness. Look at the women, so appealing, each in her own way. Think of all the things you can do with them, the places you can go together. Think of books, paintings, music. Think of your friends.

While I was talking I wondered, am I telling Jules the truth? He didn't think so, because he put his head in the oven a week later. As for me, I don't know whether I believed what I said or not, because I just went on behaving like everybody else. But I believe it now. When my wife made me a hamburger the other day I thought it was the most fabulous hamburger in the history of the world.

With this illness one of my recurrent dreams has finally come true. Several times in the past I've dreamed that I had committed a crime—or perhaps I was only accused of a crime, it's not clear. When brought to trial I refused to have a lawyer—I got up instead and made an impassioned speech in my own defense. This speech was so moving that I could feel myself tingling with it. It was inconceivable that the jury would not acquit me—only each time I woke before the verdict. Now cancer is the crime I may or may not have committed and the eloquence of being alive, the fervor of the survivor, is my best defense.

The way my friends have rallied around me is wonderful. They remind me of a flock of birds rising from a body of water into the sunset. If that image seems a bit extravagant, or tinged with satire, it's because I can't help thinking there's something comical about my friends' behavior, all these witty men suddenly saying pious, inspirational things.

10   They are not intoxicated as I am by my illness, but sobered. Since I refused to, they've taken on the responsibility of being serious. They appear abashed, or chagrined, in their sobriety. Stripped of their playfulness these pals of mine seem plainer, homelier—even older. It's as if they had all gone bald overnight.

Yet one of the effects of their fussing over me is that I feel vivid, multicolored, sharply drawn. On the other hand—and this is ungrateful—I remain outside of their solicitude, their love and best wishes. I'm isolated from them by the grandiose conviction that I am the healthy person and they are the sick ones. Like an existential hero, I have been cured by the truth while they still suffer the nausea of the uninitiated.

I've had eight-inch needles thrust into my belly where I could feel them tickling my metaphysics. I've worn Pampers. I've been licked by the flames and my sense of self has been singed. Sartre was right: you have to live each moment as if you're prepared to die.

Now at last I understand the conditional nature of the human condition. Yet, unlike Kierkegaard and Sartre, I'm not interested in the irony of my position. Cancer cures you of irony. Perhaps my irony was all in my prostate. A dangerous illness fills you with adrenaline and makes you feel very smart. I can afford now, I said to myself, to draw conclusions. All those grand generalizations toward which I have been building for so many years are finally taking shape. As I look back at how I used to be, it seems to me that an intellectual is a person who thinks that the classical clichés don't apply to him, that he is immune to homely truths. I know better now. I see everything with a summarizing eye. Nature is a terrific editor.

In the first stages of my illness, I couldn't sleep, urinate or defecate—the word ordeal comes to mind. Then when my doctor changed all this and everything worked again, what a voluptuous pleasure it was. With a cry of joy I realized how marvelous it is simply to function. My body, which in the last decade or two had become a familiar, no longer thrilling old flame, was reborn as a brand-new infatuation.

I realize of course that this elation I feel is just a phase, just a rush of consciousness, a splash of perspective, a hot flash of ontological alertness. But I'll take it, I'll use it. I'll use everything I can while I wait for the next phase. Illness is primarily a drama and it should be possible to enjoy it as well as to suffer it. I see now why the romantics were so fond of illness—the sick man sees everything as a metaphor. In this phase I'm infatuated with my cancer. It stinks of revelation.

As I look ahead, I feel like a man who has awakened from a long afternoon nap to find the evening stretched out before me. I'm reminded of D'Annunzio, the Italian poet, who said to a duchess he had just met at a party in Paris, "Come, we will have a profound evening." Why not? I see the balance of my life—everything comes in images now—as a beautiful paisley shawl thrown over a grand piano.

15

Why a paisley shawl, precisely? Why a grand piano? I have no idea. That's the way the situation presents itself to me. I have to take my imagery along with my medicine.

(1989)

Questions

1. What is the meaning of the title of the essay?

2. Why does Broyard say, "Desire itself is a kind of immortality"?

3. Broyard uses a continual stream of imagery and metaphors in this essay. Describe some of them, and their effects.

4. Who is Broyard talking to in this essay? What is his ultimate point?

5. How does stress affect you? Describe a period in your life when you were under extreme stress and how you dealt with it. What, if any, lasting effect did it have on your life? How did it change you?

EMILY MARTIN

THE EGG AND THE SPERM:

HOW SCIENCE HAS CONSTRUCTED A ROMANCE BASED ON STEREOTYPICAL MALE-FEMALE ROLES

In this 1991 scholarly article, anthropologist Emily Martin points out how our society has portrayed the story of male reproductive biology as one of "remarkable feats" and that of female reproductive biology as one of "passivity and decay."

ଐ

The theory of the human body is always a part of a world-picture ...
The theory of the human body is always a part of a fantasy.
[James Hillman, *The Myth of Analysis*][1]

As an anthropologist, I am intrigued by the possibility that culture shapes how biological scientists describe what they discover about the natural world. If this were so, we would be learning about more than the natural world in high school biology class; we would be learning about cultural beliefs and practices as if they were part of nature. In the course of my research I realized that the picture of egg and sperm drawn in popular as well as scientific accounts of reproductive biology relies on stereotypes central to our cultural definitions of male and female. The stereotypes imply not only that female biological processes are less worthy than their male counterparts but also that women are less worthy than men. Part of my goal in writing this article is to shine a bright light on the gender stereotypes hidden within the scientific language of biology. Exposed in such a light, I hope they will lose much of their power to harm us.

---

1   James Hillman, *The Myth of Analysis* (Evanston, Ill.: Northwestern University Press, 1972), 220. [Unless otherwise noted, all notes to this essay are from the author.]

EGG AND SPERM: A SCIENTIFIC FAIRY TALE

At a fundamental level, all major scientific textbooks depict male and female reproductive organs as systems for the production of valuable substances, such as eggs and sperm.[2] In the case of women, the monthly cycle is described as being designed to produce eggs and prepare a suitable place for them to be fertilized and grown—all to the end of making babies. But the enthusiasm ends there. By extolling the female cycle as a productive enterprise, menstruation must necessarily be viewed as a failure. Medical texts describe menstruation as the "debris" of the uterine lining, the result of necrosis, or death of tissue. The descriptions imply that a system has gone awry, making products of no use, not to specification, unsalable, wasted, scrap. An illustration in a widely used medical text shows menstruation as a chaotic disintegration of form, complementing the many texts that describe it as "ceasing," "dying," "losing," "denuding," "expelling."[3]

Male reproductive physiology is evaluated quite differently. One of the texts that sees menstruation as failed production employs a sort of breathless prose when it describes the maturation of sperm: "The mechanisms which guide the remarkable cellular transformation from spermatid to mature sperm remain uncertain.... Perhaps the most amazing characteristic of spermatogenesis is its sheer magnitude: the normal human male may manufacture several hundred million sperm per day."[4] In the classic text *Medical Physiology*, edited by Vernon Mountcastle, the male/female, productive/destructive comparison is more explicit: "Whereas the female *sheds* only a single gamete each month, the seminiferous tubules *produce* hundreds of millions of sperm each day" (emphasis mine).[5] The female author of another text marvels at the length of the microscopic seminiferous tubules, which, if uncoiled and placed end to end, "would span almost

2   The textbooks I consulted are the main ones used in classes for undergraduate premedical students or medical students (or those held on reserve in the library for these classes) during the past few years at Johns Hopkins University. These texts are widely used at other universities in the country as well.

3   Arthur C. Guyton, *Physiology of the Human Body*, 6th ed. (Philadelphia: Saunders College Publishing, 1984), 624.

4   Arthur J. Vander, James H. Sherman, and Dorothy S. Luciano, *Human Physiology: The Mechanisms of Body Function*, 3rd ed. (New York: McGraw Hill, 1980), 483-84.

5   Vernon B. Mountcastle, *Medical Physiology*, 14th ed. (London: Mosby, 1980), 2:1624.

one-third of a mile!" She writes, "In an adult male these structures produce millions of sperm cells each day." Later she asks, "How is this feat accomplished?"[6] None of these texts expresses such intense enthusiasm for any female processes. It is surely no accident that the "remarkable" process of making sperm involves precisely what, in the medical view, menstruation does not: production of something deemed valuable.[7]

One could argue that menstruation and spermatogenesis are not analogous processes and, therefore, should not be expected to elicit the same kind of response. The proper female analogy to spermatogenesis, biologically, is ovulation. Yet ovulation does not merit enthusiasm in these texts either. Textbook descriptions stress that all of the ovarian follicles containing ova are already present at birth. Far from being *produced*, as sperm are, they merely sit on the shelf, slowly degenerating and aging like overstocked inventory: "At birth, normal human ovaries contain an estimated one million follicles [each], and no new ones appear after birth. Thus, in marked contrast to the male, the newborn female already has all the germ cells she will ever have. Only a few, perhaps 400, are destined to reach full maturity during her active productive life. All the others degenerate at some point in their development so that few, if any remain by the time she reaches menopause at approximately 50 years of age."[8] Note the "marked contrast" that this description sets up between male and female, who has stockpiled germ cells by birth and is faced with their degeneration.

Nor are the female organs spared such vivid descriptions. One scientist writes in a newspaper article that a woman's ovaries become old and worn out from ripening eggs every month, even though the woman herself is still relatively young: "When you look through a laparoscope ... at an ovary that has been through hundreds of cycles, even in a superbly healthy American female, you see a scarred, battered organ."[9]

To avoid the negative connotations that some people associate with the female reproductive system, scientists could begin to describe male and female processes as homologous. They might credit females with "producing"

5

---

6   Eldra Pearl Solomon, *Human Anatomy and Physiology* (New York: CBS College Publishing, 1983), 678.

7   For elaboration, see Emily Martin, *The Woman in the Body: A Cultural Analysis of Reproduction* (Boston: Beacon, 1987), 27-53.

8   Vander, Sherman, and Luciano, 568.

9   Melvin Konner, "Childbearing and Age," *New York Times Magazine* (December 27, 1987), 22-23, esp. 22.

mature ova one at a time, as they're needed each month, and describe males as having to face problems of degenerating germ cells. This degeneration would occur throughout life among spermatogonia, the undifferentiated germ cells in the testes that are the long-lived, dormant precursors of sperm.

But the texts have an almost dogged insistence on casting female processes in a negative light. The texts celebrate sperm production because it is continuous from puberty to senescence, while they portray egg production as inferior because it is finished at birth. This makes the female seem unproductive, but some texts will also insist that it is she who is wasteful.[10] In a section heading for *Molecular Biology of the Cell*, a best-selling text, we are told that "Oogenesis is wasteful." The text goes on to emphasize that of the seven million oogonia, or egg germ cells, in the female embryo, most degenerate in the ovary. Of those that do go on to become oocytes, or eggs, many also degenerate, so that at birth only two million eggs remain in the ovaries. Degeneration continues throughout a woman's life: by puberty 300,000 eggs remain, and only a few are present by menopause. "During the 40 or so years of a woman's reproductive life only 400 to 500 eggs will have been released," the authors write. "All the rest will have degenerated. It is still a mystery why so many eggs are formed only to die in the ovaries."[11]

The real mystery is why the male's vast production of sperm is not seen as wasteful.[12] Assuming that a man "produces" 100 million (10^8) sperm

---

10   I have found but one exception to the opinion that the female is wasteful: "Smallpox being the nasty disease it is, one might expect nature to have designed antibody molecules with combining sites that specifically recognize the epitopes on smallpox virus. Nature differs from technology, however: it thinks nothing of wastefulness. (For example, rather than improving the chance that a spermatozoon will meet an egg cell, nature finds it easier to produce millions of spermatozoa.)" (Niels Kaj Jerne, "The Immune System," *Scientific American* 229, no. 1 [July 1973]: 53). Thanks to a *Signs* reviewer for bringing this reference to my attention.

11   Bruce Alberts et al., *Molecular Biology of the Cell* (New York: Garland, 1983), 795.

12   In her essay "Have Only Men Evolved?" (in *Discovering Reality: Feminist Perspectives on Epistemology, Metaphysics, Methodology, and Philosophy of Science*, ed. Sandra Harding and Merrill B. Hintikka [Dordrecht: Reidel, 1983], 45-69, esp. 60-61), Ruth Hubbard points out that sociobiologists have said the female invests more energy than the male in the production of her large gametes, claiming that this explains why the female provides parental care. Hubbard questions whether it "really takes more 'energy' to generate the one or relatively few eggs than the large excess of sperms required to

per day (a conservative estimate) during an average reproductive life of sixty years, he would produce well over two trillion sperm in his lifetime. Assuming that a woman "ripens" one egg per lunar month, or thirteen per year, over the course of her forty-year reproductive life, she would total five hundred eggs in her lifetime. But the word "waste" implies an excess, too much produced. Assuming two or three offspring, for every baby a woman produces, she wastes only around two hundred eggs. For every baby a man produces, he wastes more than one trillion (10^{12}) sperm.

How is it that positive images are denied to the bodies of women? A look at language—in this case, scientific language—provides the first clue. Take the egg and the sperm.[13] It is remarkable how "femininely" the egg behaves and how "masculinely" the sperm.[14] The egg is seen as large and passive.[15] It does not *move* or *journey*, but passively "is transported," "is swept,"[16] or even "drifts"[17] along the fallopian tube. In utter contrast, sperm are small, "streamlined,"[18] and invariably active. They "deliver" their genes to the egg, "activate the developmental program of

---

achieve fertilization." For further critique of how the greater size of eggs is interpreted in sociobiology, see Donna Haraway, "Investment Strategies for the Evolving Portfolio of Primate Females," in *Body/Politics*, ed. Mary Jacobus, Evelyn Fox Keller, and Sally Shuttleworth (New York: Routledge, 1990), 155-56.

13   The sources I used for this article provide compelling information on interactions among sperm. Lack of space prevents me from taking up this theme here, but the elements include competition, hierarchy, and sacrifice. For a newspaper report, see Malcolm W. Browne, "Some Thoughts on Self Sacrifice," *New York Times* (July 5, 1988), C6. For a literary rendition, see John Barth, "Night-Sea Journey," in his *Lost in the Funhouse* (Garden City, NY: Doubleday, 1968), 3-13.

14   See Carol Delaney, "The Meaning of Paternity and the Virgin Birth Debate," *Man* 21, no. 3 (September 1986): 494-513. She discusses the difference between this scientific view that women contribute genetic material to the fetus and the claim of long-standing Western folk theories that the origin and identity of the fetus comes from the male, as in the metaphor of planting a seed in soil.

15   For a suggested direct link between human behavior and purportedly passive eggs and active sperm, see Erik H. Erikson, "Inner and Outer Space: Reflections on Womanhood," *Daedalus* 93, no. 2 (Spring 1964): 582-606, esp. 591.

16   Guyton (n. 3 above), 619; and Mountcastle (n. 5 above), 1609.

17   Jonathan Miller and David Pelham, *The Facts of Life* (New York: Viking Penguin, 1984), 5.

18   Alberts et al., 796.

the egg,"[19] and have a "velocity" that is often remarked upon.[20] Their tails are "strong" and efficiently powered.[21] Together with the forces of ejaculation, they can "propel the semen into the deepest recesses of the vagina."[22] For this they need "energy," "fuel,"[23] so that with a "whip-lashlike motion and strong lurches"[24] they can "burrow through the egg coat"[25] and "penetrate" it.[26]

10   At its extreme, the age-old relationship of the egg and the sperm takes on a royal or religious patina. The egg coat, its protective barrier, is some-times called its "vestments," a term usually reserved for sacred, religious dress. The egg is said to have a "corona,"[27] a crown, and to be accompa-nied by "attendant cells."[28] It is holy, set apart and above, the queen to the sperm's king. The egg is also passive, which means it must depend on sperm for rescue. Gerald Schatten and Helen Schatten liken the egg's role to that of Sleeping Beauty: "a dormant bride awaiting her mate's magic kiss, which instills the spirit that brings her to life."[29] Sperm, by contrast, have a "mission,"[30] which is to "move through the female genital tract in quest of the ovum."[31] One popular account has it that the sperm carry out a "perilous journey" into the "warm darkness," where some fall away "exhausted." "Survivors" "assault" the egg, the successful candidates "sur-rounding the prize."[32] Part of the urgency of this journey, in more scientific

---

19 Ibid., 796.

20 See, e.g., William F. Ganong, *Review of Medical Physiology*, 7th ed. (Los Altos, Calif.: Lange Medical Publications, 1975), 322.

21 Alberts et al. (n. 11 above), 796.

22 Guyton, 615.

23 Solomon (n. 6 above), 683.

24 Vander, Sherman, and Luciano (n. 4 above), 4th ed. (1985), 580.

25 Alberts et al., 796.

26 All biology texts quoted above use the word "penetrate."

27 Solomon, 700.

28 A. Beldecos et al., "The Importance of Feminist Critique for Contemporary Cell Biology," *Hypatia* 3, no. 1 (Spring 1988): 61-76.

29 Gerald Schatten and Helen Schatten, "The Energetic Egg," *Medical World News* 23 (January 23, 1984): 51-53, esp. 51.

30 Alberts et al., 796.

31 Guyton (n. 3 above), 613.

32 Miller and Pelham (n. 17 above), 7.

terms, is that "once released from the supportive environment of the ovary, an egg will die within hours unless rescued by a sperm."[33] The wording stresses the fragility and dependency of the egg, even though the same text acknowledges elsewhere that sperm also live for only a few hours.[34]

In 1948, in a book remarkable for its early insights into these matters, Ruth Herschberger argued that female reproductive organs are seen as biologically interdependent, while male organs are viewed as autonomous, operating independently and in isolation:

> At present the functional is stressed only in connection with women: it is in them that ovaries, tubes, uterus, and vagina have endless interdependence. In the male, reproduction would seem to involve "organs" only.
>
> Yet the sperm, just as much as the egg, is dependent on a great many related processes. There are secretions which mitigate the urine in the urethra before ejaculation, to protect the sperm. There is the reflex shutting off of the bladder connection, the provision of prostatic secretions, and various types of muscular propulsion. The sperm is no more independent of its milieu than the egg, and yet from a wish that it were, biologists have lent their support to the notion that the human female, beginning with the egg, is congenitally more dependent than the male.[35]

Bringing out another aspect of the sperm's autonomy, an article in the journal *Cell* has the sperm making an "existential decision" to penetrate the egg: "Sperm are cells with a limited behavioral repertoire, one that is directed toward fertilizing eggs. To execute the decision to abandon the haploid state, sperm swim to an egg and there acquire the ability to effect membrane fusion."[36] Is this a corporate manager's version of the sperm's activities—"executing decisions" while fraught with dismay over difficult options that bring with them very high risk?

33 Alberts et al. (n. 11 above), 804.

34 Ibid., 801.

35 Ruth Herschberger, *Adam's Rib* (New York: Pelligrini & Cudaby, 1948), esp. 84. I am indebted to Ruth Hubbard for telling me about Herschberger's work, although at a point when this paper was already in draft form.

36 Bennett M. Shapiro. "The Existential Decision of a Sperm," *Cell* 49, no. 3 (May 1987): 293-94, esp. 293.

There is another way that sperm, despite their small size, can be made to loom in importance over the egg. In a collection of scientific papers, an electron micrograph of an enormous egg and tiny sperm is titled "A Portrait of the Sperm."[37] This is a little like showing a photo of a dog and calling it a picture of the fleas. Granted, microscopic sperm are harder to photograph than eggs, which are just large enough to see with the naked eye. But surely the use of the term "portrait," a word associated with the powerful and wealthy, is significant. Eggs have only micrographs or pictures, not portraits.

One depiction of sperm as weak and timid, instead of strong and powerful—the only such representation in western civilization, so far as I know—occurs in Woody Allen's movie *Everything You Always Wanted To Know About Sex* *But Were Afraid to Ask*. Allen, playing the part of an apprehensive sperm inside a man's testicles, is scared of the man's approaching orgasm. He is reluctant to launch himself into the darkness, afraid of contraceptive devices, afraid of winding up on the ceiling if the man masturbates.

15   The more common picture—egg as damsel in distress, shielded only by her sacred garments; sperm as heroic warrior to the rescue—cannot be proved to be dictated by the biology of these events. While the "facts" of biology may not *always* be constructed in cultural terms, I would argue that in this case they are. The degree of metaphorical content in these descriptions, the extent to which differences between egg and sperm are emphasized, and the parallels between cultural stereotypes of male and female behavior and the character of egg and sperm all point to this conclusion.

NEW RESEARCH, OLD IMAGERY

As new understandings of egg and sperm emerge, textbook gender imagery is being revised. But the new research, far from escaping the stereotypical representations of egg and sperm, simply replicates elements of textbook gender imagery in a different form. The persistence of this imagery calls to mind what Ludwig Fleck termed "the self-contained" nature of scientific thought. As he described it, "the interaction between what is already known, what remains to be learned, and those who are to apprehend it, go to ensure harmony within the system. But at the same time they

---

37 Lennart Nilsson, "A Portrait of the Sperm," in *The Functional Anatomy of the Spermatozoan*, ed. Bjorn A. Afzelius (New York: Pergamon, 1975), 79-82.

also preserve the harmony of illusions, which is quite secure within the confines of a given thought style."[38] We need to understand the way in which the cultural content in scientific descriptions changes as biological discoveries unfold, and whether that cultural content is solidly entrenched or easily changed.

In all of the texts quoted above, sperm are described as penetrating the egg, and specific substances on a sperm's head are described as binding to the egg. Recently, this description of events was rewritten in a biophysics lab at Johns Hopkins University—transforming the egg from the passive to the active party.[39]

Prior to this research, it was thought that the zona, the inner vestments of the egg, formed an impenetrable barrier. Sperm overcame the barrier by mechanically burrowing through, thrashing their tails and slowly working their way along. Later research showed that the sperm released digestive enzymes that chemically broke down the zona; thus, scientists presumed that the sperm used mechanical and chemical means to get through to the egg.

In this recent investigation, the researchers began to ask questions about the mechanical force of the sperm's tail. (The lab's goal was to develop a contraceptive that worked topically on sperm.) They discovered, to their great surprise, that the forward thrust of sperm is extremely weak, which contradicts the assumption that sperm are forceful penetrators.[40] Rather than thrusting forward, the sperm's head was now seen to move mostly back and forth. The sideways motion of the sperm's tail makes the head move sideways with a force that is ten times stronger than its forward movement. So even if the overall force of the sperm were strong enough to mechanically break the zona, most of its force would be directed sideways rather than forward. In fact, its strongest tendency, by tenfold, is to *escape* by attempting to pry itself off the egg. Sperm, then,

---

38 Ludwig Fleck, *Genesis and Development of a Scientific Fact*, ed. Thaddeus J. Trenn and Robert K. Merton (Chicago: University of Chicago Press, 1979), 38.

39 Jay M. Baltz carried out the research I describe when he was a graduate student in the Thomas C. Jenkins Department of Biophysics at Johns Hopkins University.

40 Far less is known about the physiology of sperm than comparable female substances, which some feminists claim is no accident. Greater scientific scrutiny of female reproduction has long enabled the burden of birth control to be placed on women. In this case, the researchers' discovery did not depend on development of any new technology: The experiments made use of glass pipettes, a manometer, and a simple microscope, all of which have been available for more than one hundred years.

must be exceptionally efficient at escaping from any cell surface they contact. And the surface of the egg must be designed to trap the sperm and prevent their escape. Otherwise, few if any sperm would reach the egg.

20   The researchers at Johns Hopkins concluded that the sperm and egg stick together because of adhesive molecules on the surfaces of each. The egg traps the sperm and adheres to it so tightly that the sperm's head is forced to lie flat against the surface of the zona, a little bit, they told me, "like Br'er Rabbit getting more and more stuck to tar baby the more he wriggles." The trapped sperm continues to wiggle ineffectually side to side. The mechanical force of its tail is so weak that a sperm cannot break even one chemical bond. This is where the digestive enzymes released by the sperm come in. If they start to soften the zona just at the tip of the sperm and the sides remain stuck, then the weak, flailing sperm can get oriented in the right direction and make it through the zona—provided that its bonds to the zona dissolve as it moves in.

Although this new version of the saga of the egg and the sperm broke through cultural expectations, the researchers who made the discovery continued to write papers and abstracts as if the sperm were the active party who attacks, binds, penetrates, and enters the egg. The only difference was that the sperm were now seen as performing these actions weakly.[41] Not until August 1987, more than three years after the findings described above, did these researchers reconceptualize the process to give the egg a more active role. They began to describe the zona as an aggressive sperm catcher, covered with adhesive molecules that can capture a sperm with a single bond and clasp it to the zona's surface.[42] In the words of their published account: "The innermost vestment, the *zona pellucida*, is a

41 Jay Baltz and Richard A. Cone, "What Force Is Needed to Tether a Sperm?" (abstract for Society for the Study of Reproduction, 1985), and "Flagellar Torque on the Head Determines the Force Needed to Tether a Sperm" (abstract for Biophysical Society, 1986).

42 Jay M. Baltz, David F. Katz, and Richard A. Cone, "The Mechanics of the Sperm-Egg Interaction at the Zona Pellucida," *Biophysical Journal* 54, no. 4 (October 1988): 643-54. Lab members were somewhat familiar with work on metaphors in the biology of female reproduction. Richard Cone, who runs the lab, is my husband, and he talked with them about my earlier research on the subject from time to time. Even though my current research focuses on biological imagery and I heard about the lab's work from my husband every day, I myself did not recognize the role of imagery in the sperm research until many weeks after the period of research and writing I describe.

glycoprotein shell, which captures and tethers the sperm before they pen-etrate it.... The sperm is captured at the initial contact between the sperm tip and the *zona*.... Since the thrust [of the sperm] is much smaller than the force needed to break a single affinity bond, the first bond made upon the tip-first meeting of the sperm and *zona* can result in the capture of the sperm."[43]

Experiments in another lab reveal similar patterns of data interpreta-tion. Gerald Schatten and Helen Schatten set out to show that, contrary to conventional wisdom, the "egg is not merely a large, yolk-filled sphere into which the sperm burrows to endow new life. Rather, recent research suggests the almost heretical view that sperm and egg are mutually active partners."[44] This sounds like a departure from the stereotypical textbook view, but further reading reveals Schatten and Schatten's conformity to the aggressive-sperm metaphor. They describe how "the sperm and egg first touch when, from the tip of the sperm's triangular head, a long, thin fila-ment shoots out and harpoons the egg." Then we learn that "remarkably, the harpoon is not so much fired as assembled at great speed, molecule by molecule, from a pool of protein stored in a specialized region called the acrosome. The filament may grow as much as twenty times longer than the sperm head itself before its tip reaches the egg and sticks."[45] Why not call this "making a bridge" or "throwing out a line" rather than firing a harpoon? Harpoons pierce prey and injure or kill them, while this filament only sticks. And why not focus, as the Hopkins lab did, on the stickiness of the egg, rather than the stickiness of the sperm?[46] Later in the article, the Schattens replicate the common view of the sperm's perilous journey into the warm darkness of the vagina, this time for the purpose of explaining its journey into the egg itself: "[The sperm] still has an arduous journey ahead. It must penetrate farther into the egg's huge sphere of cytoplasm and somehow locate the nucleus, so that the two cells' chromosomes can fuse. The sperm dives down into the cytoplasm, its tail beating. But it is

---

Therefore, I assume that any awareness the lab members may have had about how underlying metaphor might be guiding this particular research was fairly inchoate.

43   Ibid., 643, 650.

44   Schatten and Schatten (n. 29 above), 51.

45   Ibid., 52.

46   Surprisingly, in an article intended for a general audience, the authors do not point out that these are sea urchin sperm and note that human sperm do not shoot out fila-ments at all.

soon interrupted by the sudden and swift migration of the egg nucleus, which rushes toward the sperm with a velocity triple that of the movement of chromosomes during cell division, crossing the entire egg in about a minute."[47]

Like Schatten and Schatten and the biophysicists at Johns Hopkins, another researcher has recently made discoveries that seem to point to a more interactive view of the relationship of egg and sperm. This work, which Paul Wassarman conducted on the sperm and eggs of mice, focuses on identifying the specific molecules in the egg coat (the zona pellucida) that are involved in egg-sperm interaction. At first glance, his descriptions seem to fit the model of an egalitarian relationship. Male and female gametes "recognize one another," and "interactions ... take place between sperm and egg."[48] But the article in *Scientific American* in which those descriptions appear begins with a vignette that presages the dominant motif of their presentation: "It has been more than a century since Hermann Fol, a Swiss zoologist, peered into his microscope and became the first person to see a sperm penetrate an egg, fertilize it and form the first cell of a new embryo."[49] This portrayal of the sperm as the active party—the one that *penetrates* and *fertilizes* the egg and *produces* the embryo—is not cited as an example of an earlier, now outmoded view. In fact, the author reiterates the point later in the article: "Many sperm can bind to and penetrate the zona pellucida, or outer coat, of an unfertilized mouse egg, but only one sperm will eventually fuse with the thin plasma membrane surrounding the egg proper (*inner sphere*), *fertilizing the egg and giving rise to a new embryo.*"[50]

The imagery of sperm as aggressor is particularly startling in this case: the main discovery being reported is isolation of a particular molecule *on the egg coat* that plays an important role in fertilization! Wassarman's choice of language sustains the picture. He calls the molecule that has been isolated, ZP3, a "sperm receptor." By allocating the passive, waiting role to the egg, Wassarman can continue to describe the sperm as the actor, the one that makes it all happen: "The basic process begins when many sperm first attach loosely and then bind tenaciously to receptors on

47   Schatten and Schatten, 53.

48   Paul M. Wassarman, "Fertilization in Mammals," *Scientific American* 259, no. 6 (December 1988): 78-84, esp. 78, 84.

49   Ibid., 78.

50   Ibid., 79.

the surface of the egg's thick outer coat, the zona pellucida. Each sperm, which has a large number of egg-binding proteins on its surface, binds to many sperm receptors on the egg. More specifically, a site on each of the egg-binding proteins fits a complementary site on a sperm receptor, much as a key fits a lock."[51] With the sperm designated as the "key" and the egg the "lock," it is obvious which one acts and which one is acted upon. Could this imagery not be reversed, letting the sperm (the lock) wait until the egg produces the key? Or could we speak of two halves of a locket matching, and regard the matching itself as the action that initiates the fertilization?

It is as if Wassarman were determined to make the egg the receiving partner. Usually in biological research, the protein member of the pair of binding molecules is called the receptor, and physically it has a pocket in it rather like a lock. As the diagrams that illustrate Wassarman's article show, the molecules on the sperm are proteins and have "pockets." The small, mobile molecules that fit into these pockets are called ligands. As shown in the diagrams, ZP3 on the egg is a polymer of "keys"; many small knobs stick out. Typically, molecules in the sperm would be called receptors and molecules on the egg would be called ligands. But Wassarman chose to name ZP3 on the egg the receptor and to create a new term, "the egg-binding protein," for the molecule on the sperm that otherwise would have been called the receptor.[52]

Wassarman does credit the egg coat with having more functions than those of a sperm receptor. While he notes that "the zona pellucida has at times been viewed by investigators as a nuisance, a barrier to sperm and hence an impediment to fertilization," his new research reveals that the egg coat "serves as a sophisticated biological security system that screens incoming sperm, selects only those compatible with fertilization and development, prepares sperm for fusion with the egg and later protects the resulting embryo from polyspermy [a lethal condition caused by fusion of more than one sperm with a single egg]."[53] Although this description gives the egg an active role, that role is drawn in stereotypically feminine terms. The egg

25

---

51   Ibid., 78.

52   Since receptor molecules are relatively *immotile* and the ligands that bind to them relatively *motile*, one might imagine the egg being called the receptor and the sperm the ligand. But the molecules in question on egg and sperm are immotile molecules. It is the sperm as a *cell* that has motility, and the egg as a cell that has relative immotility.

53   Wassarman, 78-79.

selects an appropriate mate, *prepares* him for fusion, and then *protects* the resulting offspring from harm. This is courtship and mating behavior as seen through the eyes of a sociobiologist: woman as the hard-to-get prize, who, following union with the chosen one, becomes woman as servant and mother.

And Wassarman does not quit there. In a review article for *Science*, he outlines the "chronology of fertilization."[54] Near the end of the article are two subject headings. One is "Sperm Penetration," in which Wassarman describes how the chemical dissolving of the zona pellucida combines with the "substantial propulsive force generated by sperm." The next heading is "Sperm-Egg Fusion." This section details what happens inside the zona after a sperm "penetrates" it. Sperm "can make contact with, adhere to, and fuse with (that is, fertilize) an egg."[55] Wassarman's word choice, again, is astonishingly skewed in favor of the sperm's activity, for in the next breath he says that sperm *lose* all motility upon fusion with the egg's surface. In mouse and sea urchin eggs, the sperm enters at the *egg's* volition, according to Wassarman's description: "Once fused with egg plasma membrane [the surface of the egg], how does a sperm enter the egg? The surface of both mouse and sea urchin eggs is covered with thousands of plasma membrane-bound projections, called microvilli [tiny 'hairs']. Evidence in sea urchins suggests that, after membrane fusion, a group of elongated microvilli cluster tightly around and interdigitate over the sperm head. As these microvilli are resorbed, the sperm is drawn into the egg. Therefore, sperm motility, which ceases at the time of fusion in both sea urchins and mice, is not required for sperm entry."[56] The section called "Sperm Penetration" more logically would be followed by a section called "The Egg Envelopes," rather than "Sperm-Egg Fusion." This would give a parallel—and more accurate—sense that both the egg and the sperm initiate action.

Another way that Wassarman makes less of the egg's activity is by describing components of the egg but referring to the sperm as a whole entity. Deborah Gordon has described such an approach as "atomism" ("the part is independent of and primordial to the whole") and identified it

---

54   Paul M. Wassarman, "The Biology and Chemistry of Fertilization," *Science* 235, no. 4788 (January 30, 1987): 553-60, esp. 554.

55   Ibid., 557.

56   Ibid., 557-58. This finding throws into question Schatten and Schatten's description (n. 29 above) of the sperm, its tail beating, diving down into the egg.

as one of the "tenacious assumptions" of Western science and medicine.[57] Wassarman employs atomism to his advantage. When he refers to processes going on within sperm, he consistently returns to descriptions that remind us from whence these activities came: they are part of sperm that penetrate an egg or generate propulsive force. When he refers to processes going on within eggs, he stops there. As a result, any active role he grants them appears to be assigned to the parts of the egg, and not to the egg itself. In the quote above, it is the microvilli that actively cluster around the sperm. In another example, "the driving force for engulfment of a fused sperm comes from a region of cytoplasm just beneath an egg's plasma membrane."[58]

SOCIAL IMPLICATIONS

All three of these revisionist accounts of egg and sperm cannot seem to escape the hierarchical imagery of older accounts. Even though each new account gives the egg a larger and more active role, taken together they bring into play another cultural stereotype: woman as a dangerous and aggressive threat. In the Johns Hopkins lab's revised model, the egg ends up as the female aggressor who "captures and tethers" the sperm with her sticky zona, rather like a spider lying in wait in her web.[59] The Schatten lab has the egg's nucleus "interrupt" the sperm's dive with a "sudden and swift" rush by which she "clasps the sperm and guides its nucleus to the center."[60] Wassarman's description of the surface of the egg "covered with thousands of plasma membrane-bound projections, called microvilli" that reach out and clasp the sperm adds to the spiderlike imagery.[61]

These images grant the egg an active role but at the cost of appearing disturbingly aggressive. Images of woman as dangerous and aggressive, the femme fatale who victimizes men, are widespread in Western literature

30

---

57 Deborah R. Gordon, "Tenacious Assumptions in Western Medicine," in *Bio-medicine Examined*, ed. Margaret Lock and Deborah Gordon (Dordrecht: Kluwer, 1988), 19-56, esp. 26.

58 Wassarman, "The Biology and Chemistry of Fertilization," 558.

59 Baltz, Katz, and Cone (n. 42 above), 643, 650.

60 Schatten and Schatten, 53.

61 Wassarman, "The Biology and Chemistry of Fertilization," 557.

and culture.[62] More specific is the connection of spider imagery with the idea of an engulfing, devouring mother.[63] New data did not lead scientists to eliminate gender stereotypes in their descriptions of egg and sperm. Instead, scientists simply began to describe egg and sperm in different, but no less damaging, terms.

Can we envision a less stereotypical view? Biology itself provides another model that could be applied to the egg and the sperm. The cybernetic model—with its feedback loops, flexible adaptation to change, coordination of the parts within a whole, evolution over time, and changing response to the environment—is common in genetics, endocrinology, and ecology and has a growing influence in medicine in general.[64] This model has the potential to shift our imagery from the negative, in which the female reproductive system is castigated both for not producing eggs after birth and for producing (and thus wasting) too many eggs overall, to something more positive. The female reproductive system could be seen as responding to the environment (pregnancy or menopause), adjusting to monthly changes (menstruation), and flexibly changing from reproductivity after puberty to nonreproductivity later in life. The sperm and egg's interaction could also be described in cybernetic terms. J.F. Hartman's research in reproductive biology demonstrated fifteen years ago that if an egg is killed by being pricked with a needle, live sperm cannot get through the zona.[65] Clearly, this evidence shows that the egg and sperm do interact on more mutual terms, making biology's refusal to portray them that way all the more disturbing.

We would do well to be aware, however, that cybernetic imagery is hardly neutral. In the past, cybernetic models have played an important part in the imposition of social control. These models inherently provide a way of thinking about a "field" of interacting components. Once the field can be

---

62   Mary Ellman, *Thinking about Women* (New York: Harcourt Brace Jovanovich, 1968), 140; Nina Auerbach, *Woman and the Demon* (Cambridge, Mass.: Harvard University Press, 1982), esp. 186.

63   Kenneth Alan Adams, "Arachnophobia: Love American Style," *Journal of Psychoanalytic Anthropology* 4, no. 2 (1981): 157-97.

64   William Ray Arney and Bernard Bergen, *Medicine and the Management of Living* (Chicago: University of Chicago Press, 1984).

65   J.F. Hartman, R.B. Gwatkin, and C.F. Hutchison, "Early Contact Interactions between Mammalian Gametes In Vitro," *Proceedings of the National Academy of Sciences* (US) 69, no. 10 (1972): 2767-69.

seen, it can become the object of new forms of knowledge, which in turn can allow new forms of social control to be exerted over the components of the field. During the 1950s, for example, medicine began to recognize the psychosocial *environment* of the patient: the patient's family and its psychodynamics. Professions such as social work began to focus on this new environment, and the resulting knowledge became one way to further control the patient. Patients began to be seen not as isolated, individual bodies, but as psychosocial entities located in an "ecological" system: management of "the patient's psychology was a new entrée to patient control."[66]

The models that biologists use to describe their data can have important social effects. During the nineteenth century, the social and natural sciences strongly influenced each other: the social ideas of Malthus about how to avoid the natural increase of the poor inspired Darwin's *Origin of Species*.[67] Once the *Origin* stood as a description of the natural world, complete with competition and market struggles, it could be reimported into social science as social Darwinism, in order to justify the social order of the time. What we are seeing now is similar: the importation of cultural ideas about passive females and heroic males into the "personalities" of gametes. This amounts to the "implanting of social imagery on representations of nature so as to lay a firm basis for reimporting exactly that same imagery as natural explanations of social phenomena."[68]

Further research would show us exactly what social effects are being wrought from the biological imagery of egg and sperm. At the very least, the imagery keeps alive some of the hoariest old stereotypes about weak damsels in distress and their strong male rescuers. That these stereotypes are now being written in at the level of the cell constitutes a powerful move to make them seem so natural as to be beyond alteration.

The stereotypical imagery might also encourage people to imagine that what results from the interaction of egg and sperm—a fertilized egg—is the result of deliberate "human" action at the cellular level. Whatever the intentions of the human couple, in this microscopic "culture" a cellular "bride" (or femme fatale) and a cellular "groom" (her victim) make a cellular baby. Rosalind Petchesky points out that through visual representations such as sonograms, we are given "*images* of younger and younger, and tinier and tinier, fetuses being 'saved.'" This leads to "the point of visibility being

35

---

66 Arney and Bergen, 68.

67 Ruth Hubbard, "Have Only Men Evolved?" (n. 12 above), 51-52.

68 David Harvey, personal communication, November 1989.

'pushed back' *indefinitely*."[69] Endowing egg and sperm with intentional action, a key aspect of personhood in our culture, lays the foundation for the point of viability being pushed back to the moment of fertilization. This will likely lead to greater acceptance of technological developments and new forms of scrutiny and manipulation, for the benefit of these inner "persons": court-ordered restrictions on a pregnant woman's activities in order to protect her fetus, fetal surgery, amniocentesis, and rescinding of abortion rights, to name but a few examples.[70]

Even if we succeed in substituting more egalitarian, interactive metaphors to describe the activities of egg and sperm, and manage to avoid the pitfalls of cybernetic models, we would still be guilty of endowing cellular entities with personhood. More crucial, then, than what *kinds* of personalities we bestow on cells is the very fact that we are doing it at all. This process could ultimately have the most disturbing social consequences.

One clear feminist challenge is to wake up sleeping metaphors in science, particularly those involved in descriptions of the egg and the sperm. Although the literary convention is to call such metaphors "dead," they are not so much dead as sleeping, hidden within the scientific content of texts—and all the more powerful for it.[71] Waking up such metaphors, by becoming aware of when we are projecting cultural imagery onto what we study, will improve our ability to investigate and understand nature. Waking up such metaphors, by becoming aware of their implications, will rob them of their power to naturalize our social conventions about gender.

(1991)

---

69   Rosalind Petchesky, "Fetal Images: The Power of Visual Culture in the Politics of Reproduction," *Feminist Studies* 13, no. 2 (Summer 1987): 263-92, esp. 272.

70   Rita Arditti, Renate Klein, and Shelley Minden, *Test-Tube Women* (London: Pandora, 1984); Ellen Goodman, "Whose Right to Life?" *Baltimore Sun* (November 17, 1987); Tamar Lewin, "Courts Acting to Force Care of the Unborn," *New York Times* (November 23, 1987), A1 and B10; Susan Irwin and Brigitte Jordon, "Knowledge, Practice, and Power: Court Ordered Cesarean Sections," *Medical Anthropology Quarterly* 1, no. 3 (September 1987): 319-34.

71   Thanks to Elizabeth Fee and David Spain, who in February 1989 and April 1989, respectively, made points related to this.

Questions

1. We tend to think of metaphor as the province of literary writing; by contrast, we think of scientific writing as purely descriptive. Is metaphor in fact a useful mode of description for scientific matters? Is it to some extent necessary to resort to metaphor in order to explain scientific processes adequately?

2. Why in Martin's view are the Johns Hopkins researchers (not named in the body of the article, but identified in the references as J.M. Baltz, David F. Catz, and Richard A. Cone) who carried out the work she discusses in paragraphs 17-21 not more deserving of praise for their ground-breaking research?

3. What effect might the use of the active or the passive voice have when used in scientific research to describe gendered processes or behaviors? Select (or make up) a sentence on this sort of topic written in the active voice, and then re-write the sentence in the passive voice.

4. Discuss the organization of Martin's essay. Is there an overall progression in the ideas she presents?

JAMAICA KINCAID

ON SEEING ENGLAND FOR THE FIRST TIME

*An Antiguan-born American novelist reflects on
her experience of colonialism.*

&

When I saw England for the first time, I was a child in school sitting at a desk. The England I was looking at was laid out on a map gently, beautifully, delicately, a very special jewel; it lay on a bed of sky blue—the background of the map—its yellow form mysterious, because though it looked like a leg of mutton, it could not really look like anything so familiar as a leg of mutton because it was England—with shadings of pink and green, unlike any shadings of pink and green I had seen before, squiggly veins of red running in every direction. England was a special jewel all right, and only special people got to wear it. The people who got to wear England were English people. They wore it well and they wore it everywhere: in jungles, in deserts, on plains, on top of the highest mountains, on all the oceans, on all the seas. When my teacher had pinned this map up on the blackboard, she said, "This is England"—and she said it with authority, seriousness, and adoration, and we all sat up. It was as if she had said, "This is Jerusalem, the place you will go to when you die but only if you have been good." We understood then—we were meant to understand then—that England was to be our source of myth and the source from which we got our sense of reality, our sense of what was meaningful, our sense of what was meaningless—and much about our own lives and much about the very idea of us headed that last list.

At the time I was a child sitting at my desk seeing England for the first time, I was already very familiar with the greatness of it. Each morning before I left for school, I ate a breakfast of half a grapefruit, an egg, bread and butter and a slice of cheese, and a cup of cocoa; or half a grapefruit, a bowl

366

of oat porridge, bread and butter and a slice of cheese, and a cup of cocoa. The can of cocoa was often left on the table in front of me. It had written on it the name of the company, the year the company was established, and the words "Made in England." Those words, "Made in England," were written on the box the oats came in too. They would also have been written on the box the shoes I was wearing came in; the bolt of gray linen cloth lying on the shelf of a store from which my mother had bought three yards to make the uniform that I was wearing had written along its edge those three words. The shoes I wore were made in England; so were my socks and cotton undergarments and the satin ribbons I wore tied at the end of two plaits of my hair. My father, who might have sat next to me at breakfast, was a carpenter and cabinetmaker. The shoes he wore to work would have been made in England, as were his khaki shirt and trousers, his underpants and undershirt, his socks and brown felt hat. Felt was not the proper material from which a hat that was expected to provide shade from the hot sun should have been made, but my father must have seen and admired a picture of an Englishman wearing such a hat in England, and this picture that he saw must have been so compelling that it caused him to wear the wrong hat for a hot climate most of his long life. And this hat—a brown felt hat—became so central to his character that it was the first thing he put on in the morning as he stepped out of bed and the last thing he took off before he stepped back into bed at night. As we sat at breakfast, a car might go by. The car, a Hillman or a Zephyr, was made in England. The very idea of the meal itself, breakfast, and its substantial quality and quantity, was an idea from England; we somehow knew that in England they began the day with this meal called breakfast, and a proper breakfast was a big breakfast. No one I knew liked eating so much food so early in the day; it made us feel sleepy, tired. But this breakfast business was "Made in England" like almost everything else that surrounded us, the exceptions being the sea, the sky, and the air we breathed.

At the time I saw this map—seeing England for the first time—I did not say to myself, "Ah, so that's what it looks like," because there was no longing in me to put a shape to those three words that ran through every part of my life no matter how small; for me to have had such a longing would have meant that I lived in a certain atmosphere, an atmosphere in which those three words were felt as a burden. But I did not live in such an atmosphere. When my teacher showed us the map, she asked us to study it carefully, because no test we would ever take would be complete without this statement: "Draw a map of England." I did not know then that the statement "Draw a map of England" was something far worse than a declaration of war, for a flat-out declaration of war would have put me on alert. In fact, there was no need for war—I had long ago been conquered. I did not know then that this statement was part of a process that would result in my erasure—not my physical erasure, but my erasure all the same. I did not know then that this statement was meant to make me feel awe and small whenever I heard the word "England": awe at the power of its existence, small because I was not from it.

After that there were many times of seeing England for the first time. I saw England in history. I knew the names of all the kings of England. I knew the names of their children, their wives, their disappointments, their triumphs, the names of people who betrayed them. I knew the dates on which they were born and the dates they died. I knew their conquests and was made to feel good if I figured in them; I knew their defeats.

5   This view—the naming of the kings, their deeds, their disappointments—was the vivid view, the forceful view. There were other views, subtler ones, softer, almost not there—but these softer views were the ones that made the most lasting impression on me, the ones that made me really feel like nothing. "When morning touched the sky" was one phrase, for no morning touched the sky where I lived. The morning where I lived came on abruptly, with a shock of heat and loud noises. "Evening approaches" was another. But the evenings where I lived did not approach; in fact, I had no evening—I had night and I had day, and they came and went in a mechanical way: on, off, on, off. And then there were gentle mountains and low blue skies and moors over which people took walks for nothing but pleasure, when where I lived a walk was an act of labor, a burden, something only death or the automobile could relieve. And the weather there was so remarkable because the rain fell gently always, and the wind blew in gusts that were sometimes deep, and the air was various shades of gray, each an appealing shade for a dress to be worn when a portrait was being painted; and when it rained at twilight, wonderful things happened: People bumped into each other unexpectedly and that would lead to all sorts of turns of events—a plot, the mere weather caused plots.

The reality of my life, the life I led at the time I was being shown these views of England for the first time, for the second time, for the one hundred millionth time, was this: The sun shone with what sometimes seemed to be a deliberate cruelty; we must have done something to deserve that. My dresses did not rustle in the evening air as I strolled to the theater (I had no evening, I had no theater; my dresses were made of a cheap cotton, the weave of which would give way after not too many washings). I got up in the morning, I did my chores (fetched water from the public pipe for my mother, swept the yard), I washed myself, I went to a woman to have my hair combed freshly every day (because before we were allowed into our classroom our teachers would inspect us, and children who had not bathed that day, or had dirt under their fingernails, or whose hair had not been combed anew that day might not be allowed to attend class). I ate that breakfast. I walked to school. At school we gathered in an auditorium and sang a hymn, "All Things Bright and Beautiful," and looking down on us as we sang were portraits of the queen of England and her husband; they wore jewels and medals and they smiled. I was a Brownie. At each meeting we would form a little group around a flagpole, and after raising the Union Jack, we would say, "I promise to do my best, to do my duty to God and the queen, to help other people every day and obey the scouts' law."

But who were these people and why had I never seen them? I mean, really seen them, in the place where they lived? I had never been to England. England! I had seen England's representatives. I had seen the governor-general at the public grounds at a ceremony celebrating the queen's birthday. I had seen an old princess and I had seen a young princess. They had both been extremely not beautiful, but who among us would have told them that? I had never seen England, really seen it. I had only met a representative, seen a picture, read books, memorized its history. I had never set foot, my own foot, in it.

The space between the idea of something and its reality is always wide and deep and dark. The longer they are kept apart—idea of thing, reality of thing—the wider the width, the deeper the depth, the thicker and darker the darkness. This space starts out empty, there is nothing in it, but it rapidly becomes filled up with obsession or desire or hatred or love—sometimes all of these things, sometimes some of these things. That the idea of something and its reality are often two completely different things is something no one ever remembers; and so when they meet and find that they are not compatible, the weaker of the two, idea or reality, dies.

And so finally, when I was a grown-up woman, the mother of two children, the wife of someone, a person who resides in a powerful country that takes up more than its fair share of a continent, the owner of a house with many rooms in it and of two automobiles, with the desire and will (which I very much act upon) to take from the world more than I give back to it, more than I deserve, more than I need, finally then, I saw England, the real England, not a picture, not a painting, not through a story in a book, but

England, for the first time. In me, the space between the idea of it and its reality had become filled with hatred, and so when at last I saw it I wanted to take it into my hands and tear it into little pieces and then crumble it up as if it were clay, child's clay. That was impossible, and so I could only indulge in not-favorable opinions.

10   If I had told an English person what I thought, that I find England ugly, that I hate England; the weather is like a jail sentence; the English are a very ugly people; the food in England is like a jail sentence; the hair of English people is so straight, so dead-looking; the English have an unbearable smell so different from the smell of people I know, real people, of course, I would have been told that I was a person full of prejudice. Apart from the fact that it is I—that is, the people who look like me—who would make that English person aware of the unpleasantness of such a thing, the idea of such a thing, prejudice, that person would have been only partly right, sort of right: I may be capable of prejudice, but my prejudices have no weight to them, my prejudices have no force behind them, my prejudices remain opinions, my prejudices remain my personal opinion. And a great feeling of rage and disappointment came over me as I looked at England, my head full of personal opinions that could not have public, my public, approval. The people I come from are powerless to do evil on a grand scale.

    The moment I wished every sentence, everything I knew, that began with England would end with "and then it all died, we don't know how, it just all died" was when I saw the white cliffs of Dover. I had sung hymns and recited poems that were about a longing to see the white cliffs of Dover again. At the time I sang the hymns and recited the poems, I could really long to see them again because I had never seen them at all, nor had anyone around me at the time. But there we were, groups of people longing for something we had never seen. And so there they were, the white cliffs, but they were not that pearly, majestic thing I used to sing about, that thing that created such a feeling in these people that when they died in the place where I lived they had themselves buried facing a direction that would allow them to see the white cliffs of Dover when they were resurrected, as surely they would be. The white cliffs of Dover, when finally I saw them, were cliffs, but they were not white; you could only call them that if the word "white" meant something special to you; they were steep; they were so steep, the correct height from which all my views of England, starting with the map before me in my classroom and ending with the trip I had just taken, should jump and die and disappear forever.

(1991)

Questions

1. Define the following rhetorical devices and find an example from Kincaid's essay: anaphora, litotes, paradox, synecdoche, and metaphor. Explain the effect of the rhetorical device in each example.

2. Explain the significance of the felt hat that Kincaid's father wears.

3. Why do the cliffs of Dover in particular inspire such hatred for Kincaid?

4. How would you describe the emotional tone of this piece? How is it achieved? How does it affect your response to the ideas in the essay?

5. Kincaid often constructs sentences with words or phrases placed in apposition. Discuss this stylistic trait with particular references to paragraph 9.

6. By the end of the narrative, to what extent has Kincaid freed herself from colonialism's hold on her mind?

7. Read George Orwell's essay "Shooting an Elephant" (elsewhere in this anthology). How does Kincaid's experience of colonialism compare with Orwell's?

DIONNE BRAND

ON POETRY

*In this short piece a prominent poet and activist writes
about the nature and importance of poetry.*

❧

Every word turns on itself, every word falls after it is said. None of the
answers that I've given over the years is the truth. Those answers have
all been given like a guerrilla with her face in a handkerchief, her eyes
still. She is still, poised for quick movement, but still. Her boots sturdy,
the gravel under them dislodges and dusts. But her eyes are still. And I've
answered like the captive giving answers in an interrogation, telling just
enough to appease the interrogator and just enough to trace the story so she
could repeat it without giving anything away and without contradiction the
next time she has to tell it. I've told them the same things over and over
again, and I'll tell them again when they ask because they only ask certain
questions, like where I'm from and do I hate them.

But if I can give myself a moment, I would say it's been relief to write
poetry, it's been just room to live.

I've had moments when the life of my people has been so overwhelming to bear that poetry seemed useless, and I cannot say that there is any
moment that I do not think that now. At times it has been more crucial to
wield a scythe over high grass in a field in Marigot; at times it has been
more important to figure out how a woman without papers in Toronto can
have a baby and not be caught and deported; at times it has been more
helpful to organize a demonstration in front of the police station at Bay and
College Streets. Often there's been no reason whatsoever to write poetry.
There are days when I cannot think of a single reason to write this life
down.

There's a photograph of me when I was four. I'm standing next to my
little sister and my cousin. My big sister is in the picture, too. I do not

resemble myself except for my legs, which were bowed and still are. My little sister is crying, her fingers in her mouth, and my cousin looks stunned, as if she's been thrown into the picture. My big sister is tall and slender, heading for the glamour which will describe her life. She looks like Nancy Wilson. Black patent-leather shoes, white boat-necked dress. I am looking at the camera, my mouth open. I am holding a shac-shac, blurring in the picture, so that my little sister would stop crying. I look as if I'm trying to make this picture work. I remember the moment of consciously getting set, holding the shac-shac, being called upon to act, saying to my little sister don't cry, see, don't cry. My eyes in the picture are not those of a little girl; they seem knowledgeable, still. My little sister's eyes look teary, my cousin's, frightened, my big sister's, sad. Mine, still. Watching. I remember watching. Knowing that this was an occasion to watch out of ourselves and saying I'd hold the shac-shac so my little sister would not cry. I only recognize my legs and the eyes. Still. Watching out.

If I can take a second. Shaking the gravel from my shoes. Poetry is 5 here, just *here*. Something wrestling with how we live, something dangerous, something honest.

(1994)

Questions

1. What is the relation between Brand's political activism and the role of poetry in her life?

2. What does Brand mean when she writes, "Poetry is here, just *here*?"

3. Explain Brand's extended metaphor comparing herself to a guerrilla.

4. Identify the phrases that Brand repeats in this short article and speculate on why she does so.

5. Brand's older sister looks glamorous in the childhood photo, and she grows up to be glamorous. Why does Brand make this connection?

URSULA FRANKLIN

SILENCE AND THE NOTION OF THE COMMONS

*In this essay a leading physicist discusses the implications of
two changes technology has wrought: separating sound from its
source, and making the sound permanent.*

❧

In a technological world, where the acoustic environment is largely artificial, silence takes on new dimensions, be it in terms of the human need
for silence (perhaps a person's right to be free from acoustic assault), of
communication, or of intentional modification of the environment.

This article is based on the text of a lecture given at the Banff Centre
in August of 1993 as part of "The Tuning of the World" conference on
acoustic ecology. It consists of two separate but interrelated parts: silence
as spiritual experience (drawing largely, but not exclusively, on the Quaker
tradition of religious worship) and silence as a common good. Silence is
examined in terms of the general patterns of the social impact of modern
technology. Silence possesses striking similarities with such aspects of life
and community as unpolluted water, air, or soil, which once were taken for
granted, but which have become special and precious in technologically
mediated environments. The threat of a privatization of the soundscape is
discussed and some immediate measures suggested.

I would like to thank everyone involved in this conference, and the
organizers in particular, for inviting me to deliver this talk. I am very obviously an outsider and wish to come to this group to talk about something
that is central to all the work that you people are doing. And so I come
in a way as a friend and colleague, in a field where I am fully aware that
silence has been the subject of many publications. It is the subject of more
than a chapter in R. Murray Schafer's *The Tuning of the World* and John
Cage and others have written books on it. I would like to examine how our

concept—as well as our practice—of silence has been influenced by all the other things that have changed as our world has become what Jacques Ellul calls a "technological milieu," a world that is, in all its facets, increasingly mediated by technology.

Before we had a technologically mediated society, before we had electronics and electro-magnetic devices, sound was rightly seen as being ephemeral, sound was coupled to its source, and lasted only a very short time. This is very different from what we see in a landscape: however much we feel that the landscape might be modified, however much we feel that there is a horrible building somewhere in front of a beautiful mountain, on the scale of the soundscape, the landscape is permanent. What is put up is there. That's very different from the traditional soundscape. What modern technology has brought to sound is the possibility of doing two things: to separate the sound from the source and to make the sound permanent. In addition, modern devices make it possible to decompose, recompose, analyze and mix sounds, to change the initial magnitude and sustainability of sound, as well as to change all the characteristics that link the sound with its source. R. Murray Schafer called this "schizophonia," separating the sound from the source. We now have easy access to the multitude of opportunities that result from overcoming that coupling.

The social impact of this technology is significant. Prior to these developments there was a limitation to sound and sound penetration. If you heard a bagpipe band there was a limit to the amount of time it would play; if you found it displeasing you could patiently wait until the players got exhausted. But with a recording of a bagpipe band, you are out of luck. It's never going to be exhausted. Electronics, then, have altered the modern soundscape. While modern technology is a source of joy in modern composition, through the opening of many doors for expression, it is also the source of a good number of problems related to the soundscape, problems which society as a whole must adjust to, cope with, and possibly ameliorate.

But then there is not only sound, there is silence. Silence is affected by these same technological developments, the same means of separating sound from source and overcoming the ephemeral nature of a soundscape. I have attempted to define silence and to analyze the attributes that make it valuable. Defining silence as the absence of external or artificially generated sound is fine, but it's a little bit shallow, because silence in many ways is very much more than the absence of sound. Absence of sound is a condition necessary to silence but it is not sufficient in itself to define what we mean by silence. When one thinks about the concept of silence, one notices that there has to be somebody who listens before you can say there is silence. Silence, in addition to being an absence of sound, is defined by a listener, by hearing.

A further attribute, or parameter of silence, from my point of view, comes out of the question: *why is it that we worry about silence?* I feel that one comes to the root of the meaning and practice of silence only when one asks; *why is it that we value and try to establish silence?* Because silence is an enabling environment. This is the domain that we have traditionally associated with silence, the enabling condition in which unprogrammed and unprogrammable events can take place. That is the silence of contemplation; it is the silence when people get in touch with themselves; it is the silence of meditation and worship. The distinctive character of this domain of silence is that it is an enabling condition that opens up the possibility of unprogrammed, unplanned and unprogrammable happenings.

In this light we understand why, as Christians, traditional Quakers found it necessary in the seventeenth century, when they were surrounded by all the pomp and circumstance of the church of England, to reject it. We understand why they felt any ritual, in the sense of its programmed nature and predictability, to be a straitjacket rather than a comfort, and why they said to the amazement of their contemporaries: *we worship God in silence.* Their justification for the practice of silence was that they required it to hear God's voice. Beyond the individual's centering, beyond the individual effort of meditation, there was the need for *collective* silence. Collective silence is an enormously powerful event. There are contemporaneous accounts of Quaker meetings under heavy persecution in England, when thousands of people met silently on a hillside. Then out of the silence, one person— unappointed, unordained, unexpected, and unprogrammed—might speak, to say: *Out of the silence there can come a ministry.* The message is not essentially within that person, constructed in their intellect, but comes out of the silence to them. This isn't just history and theory. I think that if any one of you attended Quaker meetings, particularly on a regular basis, you would find that, suddenly, out of the silence, somebody speaks about something that had just entered *your* mind. It's an uncanny thing. The strength of collective silence is probably one of the most powerful spiritual forces.

Now, in order for something like this to happen, a lot of things are required. There is what Quakers call: *to be with heart and mind prepared.* But there is also the collective decision to be silent. And to be silent in order to let unforeseen, unforeseeable, and unprogrammed things happen. Such silence, I repeat, is the environment that enables the unprogrammed. I feel it is very much at risk.

I will elaborate on this, but first I want to say: there is another silence. There is the silence that enables a programmed, a planned, event to take place. There is the silence in which you courteously engage so that I might be heard: in order for one to be heard all the others have to be silent. But in many cases silence is not taken on voluntarily and it is this false silence of which I am afraid. It is not the silence only of the padded cell, or of solitary confinement; it is the silence that is enforced by the megaphone, the boom box, the PA system, and any other device that stifles other sounds and voices in order that a planned event can take place.

There is a critical juncture between the planned and the unplanned, the programmed and the unplannable that must be kept in mind. I feel very strongly that our present technological trends drive us toward a decrease in the space—be it in the soundscape, the landscape, or the mindscape— in which the unplanned and unplannable can happen. Yet silence has to remain available in the soundscape, the landscape, and the mindscape. Allowing openness to the unplannable, to the unprogrammed, is the core of the strength of silence. It is also the core of our individual and collective sanity. I extend that to the collectivity because, as a community, as a people, we are threatened just as much, if not more, by the impingement of the pro-grammed over the silent, over that which enables the unprogrammed. Much of the impingement goes unnoticed, uncommented upon, since it is much less obvious than the intrusion of a structure into the landscape. While we may not win all the battles at City Hall to preserve our trees, at least there is now a semi-consciousness that this type of struggle is important.

Where can one go to get away from the dangers of even the gentle pres-ence of programmed music, or Muzak, in our public buildings? Where do I protest that upon entering any place, from the shoe store to the restaurant, I am deprived of the opportunity to be quiet? Who has asked my permission to put that slop into the elevator I may have to use umpteen times every day? Many such "background" activities are intentionally manipulative. This is not merely "noise" that can be dealt with in terms of noise abate-ment. There are two aspects to be stressed in this context. One is that the elimination of silence is being done without anybody's consent. The other is that one really has to stop and think and analyze in order to see just how manipulative these interventions can be.

For instance, in the Toronto Skydome, friends tell me that the sound environment is coupled and geared to the game: if the home team misses, there are mournful and distressing sounds over the PA; when the home team scores there is a sort of athletic equivalent of the Hallelujah Chorus. Again, the visitor has no choice; the programmed soundscape is part of the event. You cannot be present at the game without being subjected to that mood manipulation. I wonder if music will soon be piped into the voter's booth, maybe an upbeat, slightly military tune: "*Get on with it. Get the votes in.*" Joking aside, soundscape manipulation is a serious issue. Who on earth has given anybody the right to manipulate the sound environment?

Now, I want to come back to the definition of silence and introduce the notion of the commons, because the soundscape essentially doesn't belong to anyone in particular. What we are hearing, I feel, is very much the privatization of the soundscape, in the same manner in which the enclosure laws in Britain destroyed the commons of old. There was a time when in fact every community had what was called "the commons," an area that belonged to everybody and where sheep could graze—a place important to all, belonging to all. The notion of the commons is deeply embedded in our social mind as something that all share. There are many "commons" that we take for granted and for millennia, clean air and clean water were the norm. Because of the ephemeral nature of sound in the past, silence was not considered part of the commons. Today, the technology to preserve and multiply sound and separate it from its source has resulted in our sudden awareness that silence, too, is a common good. Silence, which we need in order that unprogrammed and unprogrammable things can take place, is being removed from common access without much fuss and civic bother. It is being privatized.

15   This is another illustration of an often-observed occurrence related to the impact of technology: that things considered in the past to be normal or ordinary become rare or extraordinary, while those things once considered rare and unusual become normal and routine. Flying is no longer a big deal, but a handmade dress or a home-cooked meal may well be special. We essentially consider polluted water as normal now, and people who can afford it drink bottled water. It is hard to have bottled silence. But money still can buy distance from sound. Today, when there is civic anger, it is with respect to "noise"—like airport noise, etc. There is not yet such anger with respect to the manipulative elimination of silence from the soundscape.

There are those of us who have acknowledged and seen the deterioration of the commons as far as silence is concerned, who have seen that the soundscape is not only polluted by noise—so that one has to look for laws related to noise abatement—but also that the soundscape has become increasingly polluted through the private use of sound in the manipulative dimension of setting and programming moods and conditions. There is a desperate need for awareness of this, and for awareness of it in terms of the collectivity, rather than just individual needs. I feel very much that this is a time for civic anger. This is a time when one has to say: *town planning is constrained by by-laws on height, density, and other features; what are town planning's constraints in relation to silence?*

You may ask, what would I suggest? First of all, we must insist that, as human beings in a society, we have a right to silence. Just as we feel we have the right to walk down the street without being physically assaulted by people and preferably without being visually assaulted by ugly outdoor advertising, we also have the right not to be assaulted by sound, and in particular, not to be assaulted by sound that is there solely for the purpose of profit. Now is the time for civic rage, as well as civic education, but also for some action.

Think of the amount of care that goes into the regulation of parking, so that our good, precious, and necessary cars have a place to be well and safe. That's very important to society. I have yet to see, beyond hospitals, a public building that has a quiet room. Is not our sanity at least as important as the safety of our cars? One should begin to think: are there places, even in conferences like this, that are hassle-free, quiet spaces, where people can go? There were times when one could say to a kid: *"Where did you go?"*—*"Out."*—*"What did you do?"*—*"Nothing."* That sort of blessed time is past. The kid is programmed. We are programmed. And we don't even ask for a quiet space anymore.

One possible measure, relatively close at hand, is to set aside, as a normal matter of human rights, in those buildings over which we have some influence, a quiet room. Further, I highly recommend starting committee meetings with two minutes of silence, and ending them with a few minutes of silence, too. I sit on committees that have this practice, and find that it not only can expedite the business before the committee, but also contributes to a certain amount of peacefulness and sanity. One can start a lecture with a few minutes of silence, and can close it the same way. There can be a few minutes of silence before a shared meal. Such things help, even if they help only in small ways. I do think even small initiatives make silence "visible" as an ever-present part of life. I now invite you to have two minutes of silence before we go on into the question period. Let us be quiet together.

(1994)

Questions

1. This article appeared in a journal (*Musicworks: The Journal of Sound Exploration*) that might appropriately be described as semi-scholarly; its audience consists primarily either of academics in music departments or those well-versed in the technical aspects of music and sound. How does Franklin position herself in paragraph 3 in relationship to this audience? In the remainder of the article, does Franklin invite a wider audience?

2. Using paragraph 6 of this essay as an example, comment on why it is often necessary to go beyond dictionary definitions in defining a term for technical or academic purposes.

3. How strong are the connections between silence and religion? Discuss with relation both to Franklin's argument in paragraph 8 and to whatever evidence you are able to assemble from outside this article about religious attitudes and practices.

4. How in Franklin's view is silence often "enforced" (paragraph 10)?

5. Explain in your own words the notion of "the commons" (paragraph 14).

6. Write up a plan of Franklin's argument, with a phrase or two summarizing each paragraph, and using headings and/or connector arrows as you feel appropriate.

7. Do technological developments inevitably tend towards a reduction in the level of silence in society?

8. Write a brief essay arguing for or against increased regulation in your community of the soundscape.

ROBERT D. PUTNAM

BOWLING ALONE: AMERICA'S DECLINING SOCIAL CAPITAL

*This article by a prominent social scientist has had
a significant impact on American public policy
debates. In 2000 Putnam published an expanded
version of these ideas in a book of the same title.*

❧

Many students of the new democracies that have emerged over the past decade and a half have emphasized the importance of a strong and active civil society to the consolidation of democracy. Especially with regard to the postcommunist countries, scholars and democratic activists alike have lamented the absence or obliteration of traditions of independent civic engagement and a widespread tendency toward passive reliance on the state. To those concerned with the weakness of civil societies in the developing or postcommunist world, the advanced Western democracies and above all the United States have typically been taken as models to be emulated. There is striking evidence, however, that the vibrancy of American civil society has notably declined over the past several decades.

Ever since the publication of Alexis de Tocqueville's *Democracy in America*, the United States has played a central role in systematic studies of the links between democracy and civil society. Although this is in part because trends in American life are often regarded as harbingers of social modernization, it is also because America has traditionally been considered unusually "civic" (a reputation that, as we shall later see, has not been entirely unjustified).

When Tocqueville visited the United States in the 1830s, it was the Americans' propensity for civic association that most impressed him as the key to their unprecedented ability to make democracy work. "Americans of all ages, all stations in life, and all types of disposition," he observed, "are forever forming associations. There are not only commercial and industrial associations in which all take part, but others of a thousand different types—religious, moral, serious, futile, very general and very limited, immensely large and very minute.... Nothing, in my view, deserves more attention than the intellectual and moral associations in America."[1]

Recently, American social scientists of a neo-Tocquevillean bent have unearthed a wide range of empirical evidence that the quality of public life and the performance of social institutions (and not only in America) are indeed powerfully influenced by norms and networks of civic engagement. Researchers in such fields as education, urban poverty, unemployment, the control of crime and drug abuse, and even health have discovered that successful outcomes are more likely in civically engaged communities. Similarly, research on the varying economic attainments of different ethnic groups in the United States has demonstrated the importance of social bonds within each group. These results are consistent with research in a wide range of settings that demonstrates the vital importance of social networks for job placement and many other economic outcomes.

5   Meanwhile, a seemingly unrelated body of research on the sociology of economic development has also focused attention on the role of social networks. Some of this work is situated in the developing countries, and some of it elucidates the peculiarly successful "network capitalism" of East Asia.[2] Even in less exotic Western economies, however, researchers

1   Alexis de Tocqueville, *Democracy in America*, ed. J.P. Maier, trans. George Lawrence (Garden City, NY: Anchor Books, 1969), 513-17. [Unless otherwise noted, all notes to this essay are from the author.]

2   On social networks and economic growth in the developing world, see Milton J. Esman and Norman Uphoff, *Local Organizations: Intermediaries in Rural Development* (Ithaca: Cornell University Press, 1984), esp. 15-42 and 99-180; and Albert O. Hirschman, *Getting Ahead Collectively: Grassroots Experiences in Latin America* (Elmsford, NY: Pergamon Press, 1984), esp. 42-77. On East Asia, see Gustav Papanek, "The New Asian Capitalism: An Economic Portrait," in Peter L. Berger and Hsin-Huang Michael Hsiao, eds., *In Search of an East Asian Development Model* (New Brunswick, NJ: Transaction, 1987), 27-80; Peter B. Evans, "The State as Problem and Solution: Predation, Embedded Autonomy and Structural Change," in Stephan Haggard and Robert R. Kaufman, eds., *The Politics of Economic Adjustment* (Princeton: Princeton University Press, 1992), 139-81; and Gary G. Hamilton, William Zeile, and Wan-Jin Kim, "Network Structure of East Asian Economies," in Stewart R. Clegg and S. Gordon Redding, eds., *Capitalism in Contrasting Cultures* (Hawthorne, NY: De Gruyter, 1990), 105-29. See also Gary G. Hamilton and Nicole Woolsey Biggart, "Market, Culture, and Authority: A Comparative Analysis of Management and Organization in the Far

have discovered highly efficient, highly flexible "industrial districts" based on networks of collaboration among workers and small entrepreneurs. Far from being paleoindustrial anachronisms, these dense interpersonal and interorganizational networks undergird ultramodern industries, from the high tech of Silicon Valley to the high fashion of Benetton.

The norms and networks of civic engagement also powerfully affect the performance of representative government. That, at least, was the central conclusion of my own 20-year, quasi-experimental study of subnational governments in different regions of Italy.[3] Although all these regional governments seemed identical on paper, their levels of effectiveness varied dramatically. Systematic inquiry showed that the quality of governance was determined by longstanding traditions of civic engagement (or its absence). Voter turnout, newspaper readership, membership in choral societies and football clubs—these were the hallmarks of a successful region. In fact, historical analysis suggested that these networks of organized reciprocity and civic solidarity, far from being an epiphenomenon of socioeconomic modernization, were a precondition for it.

No doubt the mechanisms through which civic engagement and social connectedness produce such results—better schools, faster economic development, lower crime, and more effective government—are multiple and complex. While these briefly recounted findings require further confirmation and perhaps qualification, the parallels across hundreds of empirical studies in a dozen disparate disciplines and subfields are striking. Social scientists in several fields have recently suggested a common framework for understanding these phenomena, a framework that rests on the concept of *social capital*.[4] By analogy with notions of physical capital and human capital—tools

East," *American Journal of Sociology* (Supplement) 94 (1988): S52-S94; and Susan Greenhalgh, "Families and Networks in Taiwan's Economic Development," in Edwin Winckler and Susan Greenhalgh, eds., *Contending Approaches to the Political Economy of Taiwan* (Armonk, NY: M.E. Sharpe, 1987), 224-45.

3   Robert D. Putnam, *Making Democracy Work: Civic Traditions in Modern Italy* (Princeton: Princeton University Press, 1993).

4   James S. Coleman deserves primary credit for developing the "social capital" theoretical framework. See his "Social Capital in the Creation of Human Capital," *American Journal of Sociology* (Supplement) 94 (1988): S95-S120, as well as his *The Foundations of Social Theory* (Cambridge: Harvard University Press, 1990), 300-21. See also Mark Granovetter, "Economic Action and Social Structure: The Problem of Embeddedness," *American Journal of Sociology* 91 (1985): 481-510; Glenn C. Loury, "Why Should We Care About Group Inequality?" *Social Philosophy and Policy* 5   (continued)

and training that enhance individual productivity—"social capital" refers to features of social organization such as networks, norms, and social trust that facilitate coordination and cooperation for mutual benefit.

For a variety of reasons, life is easier in a community blessed with a substantial stock of social capital. In the first place, networks of civic engagement foster sturdy norms of generalized reciprocity and encourage the emergence of social trust. Such networks facilitate coordination and communication, amplify reputations, and thus allow dilemmas of collective action to be resolved. When economic and political negotiation is embedded in dense networks of social interaction, incentives for opportunism are reduced. At the same time, networks of civic engagement embody past success at collaboration, which can serve as a cultural template for future collaboration. Finally, dense networks of interaction probably broaden the participants' sense of self, developing the "I" into the "we," or (in the language of rational-choice theorists) enhancing the participants' "taste" for collective benefits.

I do not intend here to survey (much less contribute to) the development of the theory of social capital. Instead, I use the central premise of that rapidly growing body of work—that social connections and civic engagement pervasively influence our public life, as well as our private prospects—as the starting point for an empirical survey of trends in social capital in contemporary America. I concentrate here entirely on the American case, although the developments I portray may in some measure characterize many contemporary societies.

WHATEVER HAPPENED TO CIVIC ENGAGEMENT?

10 We begin with familiar evidence on changing patterns of political participation, not least because it is immediately relevant to issues of democracy in the narrow sense. Consider the well-known decline in turnout in national elections over the last three decades. From a relative high point in the early 1960s, voter turnout had by 1990 declined by nearly a quarter; tens of millions of Americans had forsaken their parents' habitual readiness to engage in the simplest act of citizenship. Broadly similar trends also characterize participation in state and local elections.

(1987): 249-71; and Robert D. Putnam, "The Prosperous Community: Social Capital and Public Life," *American Prospect* 13 (1993): 35-42. To my knowledge, the first scholar to use the term "social capital" in its current sense was Jane Jacobs, in *The Death and Life of Great American Cities* (New York: Random House, 1961), 138.

It is not just the voting booth that has been increasingly deserted by Americans. A series of identical questions posed by the Roper Organization to national samples ten times each year over the last two decades reveals that since 1973 the number of Americans who report that "in the past year" they have "attended a public meeting on town or school affairs" has fallen by more than a third (from 22 per cent in 1973 to 13 per cent in 1993). Similar (or even greater) relative declines are evident in responses to questions about attending a political rally or speech, serving on a committee of some local organization, and working for a political party. By almost every measure, Americans' direct engagement in politics and government has fallen steadily and sharply over the last generation, despite the fact that average levels of education—the best individual-level predictor of political participation—have risen sharply throughout this period. Every year over the last decade or two, millions more have withdrawn from the affairs of their communities.

Not coincidentally, Americans have also disengaged psychologically from politics and government over this era. The proportion of Americans who reply that they "trust the government in Washington" only "some of the time" or "almost never" has risen steadily from 30 per cent in 1966 to 75 per cent in 1992.

These trends are well known, of course, and taken by themselves would seem amenable to a strictly political explanation. Perhaps the long litany of political tragedies and scandals since the 1960s (assassinations, Vietnam, Watergate, Irangate, and so on) has triggered an understandable disgust for politics and government among Americans, and that in turn has motivated their withdrawal. I do not doubt that this common interpretation has some merit, but its limitations become plain when we examine trends in civic engagement of a wider sort.

Our survey of organizational membership among Americans can usefully begin with a glance at the aggregate results of the General Social Survey, a scientifically conducted, national-sample survey that has been repeated 14 times over the last two decades. Church-related groups constitute the most common type of organization joined by Americans; they are especially popular with women. Other types of organizations frequently joined by women include school-service groups (mostly parent-teacher associations), sports groups, professional societies, and literary societies. Among men, sports clubs, labor unions, professional societies, fraternal groups, veterans' groups, and service clubs are all relatively popular.

15   Religious affiliation is by far the most common associational membership among Americans. Indeed, by many measures America continues to
be (even more than in Tocqueville's time) an astonishingly "churched"
society. For example, the United States has more houses of worship per
capita than any other nation on Earth. Yet religious sentiment in America seems to be becoming somewhat less tied to institutions and more
self-defined.

How have these complex crosscurrents played out over the last three or
four decades in terms of Americans' engagement with organized religion?
The general pattern is clear: The 1960s witnessed a significant drop in
reported weekly churchgoing—from roughly 48 per cent in the late 1950s
to roughly 41 per cent in the early 1970s. Since then, it has stagnated or
(according to some surveys) declined still further. Meanwhile, data from
the General Social Survey show a modest decline in membership in all
"church-related groups" over the last 20 years. It would seem, then, that net
participation by Americans, both in religious services and in church-related
groups, has declined modestly (by perhaps a sixth) since the 1960s.

For many years, labor unions provided one of the most common organizational affiliations among American workers. Yet union membership
has been falling for nearly four decades, with the steepest decline occurring
between 1975 and 1985. Since the mid-1950s, when union membership
peaked, the unionized portion of the nonagricultural work force in America
has dropped by more than half, falling from 32.5 per cent in 1953 to 15.8
per cent in 1992. By now, virtually all of the explosive growth in union
membership that was associated with the New Deal has been erased. The
solidarity of union halls is now mostly a fading memory of aging men.[5]

The parent-teacher association (PTA) has been an especially important
form of civic engagement in twentieth-century America because parental
involvement in the educational process represents a particularly productive
form of social capital. It is, therefore, dismaying to discover that participation in parent-teacher organizations has dropped drastically over the last
generation, from more than 12 million in 1964 to barely 5 million in 1982
before recovering to approximately 7 million now.

---

5   Any simplistically political interpretation of the collapse of American unionism
would need to confront the fact that the steepest decline began more than six years before the Reagan administration's attack on PATCO. Data from the General Social Survey
show a roughly 40-per cent decline in reported union membership between 1975 and
1991.

Next, we turn to evidence on membership in (and volunteering for) civic and fraternal organizations. These data show some striking patterns. First, membership in traditional women's groups has declined more or less steadily since the mid-1960s. For example, membership in the national Federation of Women's Clubs is down by more than half (59 per cent) since 1964, while membership in the League of Women Voters (LWV) is off 42 per cent since 1969.[6]

Similar reductions are apparent in the numbers of volunteers for mainline civic organizations, such as the Boy Scouts (off by 26 per cent since 1970) and the Red Cross (off by 61 per cent since 1970). But what about the possibility that volunteers have simply switched their loyalties to other organizations? Evidence on "regular" (as opposed to occasional or "drop by") volunteering is available from the Labor Department's Current Population Surveys of 1974 and 1989. These estimates suggest that serious volunteering declined by roughly one-sixth over these 15 years, from 24 per cent of adults in 1974 to 20 per cent in 1989. The multitudes of Red Cross aides and Boy Scout troop leaders now missing in action have apparently not been offset by equal numbers of new recruits elsewhere.

Fraternal organizations have also witnessed a substantial drop in membership during the 1980s and 1990s. Membership is down significantly in such groups as the Lions (off 12 per cent since 1983), the Elks (off 18 per cent since 1979), the Shriners (off 27 per cent since 1979), the Jaycees (off 44 per cent since 1979), and the Masons (down 39 per cent since 1959). In sum, after expanding steadily throughout most of this century, many major civic organizations have experienced a sudden, substantial, and nearly simultaneous decline in membership over the last decade or two.

The most whimsical yet discomfiting bit of evidence of social disengagement in contemporary America that I have discovered is this: more Americans are bowling today than ever before, but bowling in organized leagues has plummeted in the last decade or so. Between 1980 and 1993 the total number of bowlers in America increased by 10 per cent, while

20

---

6   Data for the LWV are available over a longer time span and show an interesting pattern: a sharp slump during the Depression, a strong and sustained rise after World War II that more than tripled membership between 1945 and 1969, and then the post-1969 decline, which has already erased virtually all the postwar gains and continues still. This same historical pattern applies to those men's fraternal organizations for which comparable data are available—steady increases for the first seven decades of the century, interrupted only by the Great Depression, followed by a collapse in the 1970s and 1980s that has already wiped out most of the postwar expansion and continues apace.

league bowling decreased by 40 per cent. (Lest this be thought a wholly trivial example, I should note that nearly 80 million Americans went bowling at least once during 1993, *nearly a third more than voted in the 1994 congressional elections* and roughly the same number as claim to attend church regularly. Even after the 1980s' plunge in league bowling, nearly 3 per cent of American adults regularly bowl in leagues.) The rise of solo bowling threatens the livelihood of bowling-lane proprietors because those who bowl as members of leagues consume three times as much beer and pizza as solo bowlers, and the money in bowling is in the beer and pizza, not the balls and shoes. The broader social significance, however, lies in the social interaction and even occasionally civic conversations over beer and pizza that solo bowlers forgo. Whether or not bowling beats balloting in the eyes of most Americans, bowling teams illustrate yet another vanishing form of social capital.

Countertrends

At this point, however, we must confront a serious counterargument. Perhaps the traditional forms of civic organization whose decay we have been tracing have been replaced by vibrant new organizations. For example, national environmental organizations (like the Sierra Club) and feminist groups (like the National Organization for Women) grew rapidly during the 1970s and 1980s and now count hundreds of thousands of dues-paying members. An even more dramatic example is the American Association of Retired Persons (AARP), which grew exponentially from 400,000 card-carrying members in 1960 to 33 million in 1993, becoming (after the Catholic Church) the largest private organization in the world. The national administrators of these organizations are among the most feared lobbyists in Washington, in large part because of their massive mailing lists of presumably loyal members.

These new mass-membership organizations are plainly of great political importance. From the point of view of social connectedness, however, they are sufficiently different from classic "secondary associations" that we need to invent a new label—perhaps "tertiary associations." For the vast majority of their members, the only act of membership consists in writing a check for dues or perhaps occasionally reading a newsletter. Few ever attend any meetings of such organizations, and most are unlikely ever (knowingly) to encounter any other member. The bond between any two members of the Sierra Club is less like the bond between any two members of a gardening club and more like the bond between any two Red Sox fans (or perhaps any two devoted Honda owners): they root for the same team and they share some of the same interests, but they are unaware of each other's existence. Their ties, in short, are to common symbols, common leaders, and perhaps common ideals, but not to one another. The theory of social capital argues that associational membership should, for example, increase social trust, but this prediction is much less straightforward with regard to membership in tertiary associations. From the point of view of social connectedness, the Environmental Defense Fund and a bowling league are just not in the same category.

If the growth of tertiary organizations represents one potential (but probably not real) counterexample to my thesis, a second countertrend is represented by the growing prominence of nonprofit organizations, especially nonprofit service agencies. This so-called third sector includes everything from Oxfam and the Metropolitan Museum of Art to the Ford Foundation and the Mayo Clinic. In other words, although most secondary associations are nonprofits, most nonprofit agencies are not secondary associations. To identify trends in the size of the nonprofit sector with trends in social connectedness would be another fundamental conceptual mistake.[7]

A third potential countertrend is much more relevant to an assessment of social capital and civic engagement. Some able researchers have argued that the last few decades have witnessed a rapid expansion in "support groups" of various sorts. Robert Wuthnow reports that fully 40 per cent of all Americans claim to be "currently involved in [a] small group that meets regularly and provides support or caring for those who participate in it."[8] Many of these groups are religiously affiliated, but many others are not. For example, nearly 5 per cent of Wuthnow's national sample claim to participate regularly in a "self-help" group, such as Alcoholics Anonymous, and nearly as many say they belong to book-discussion groups and hobby clubs.

25

---

7   Cf. Lester M. Salamon, "The Rise of the Nonprofit Sector," *Foreign Affairs* 73 (July-August 1994): 109-22. See also Salamon, "Partners in Public Service: The Scope and Theory of Government-Nonprofit Relations," in Walter W. Powell, ed., *The Nonprofit Sector: A Research Handbook* (New Haven: Yale University Press, 1987), 99-117. Salamon's empirical evidence does not sustain his broad claims about a global "associational revolution" comparable in significance to the rise of the nation-state several centuries ago.

8   Robert Wuthnow, *Sharing the Journey: Support Groups and America's New Quest for Community* (New York: The Free Press, 1994), 45.

The groups described by Wuthnow's respondents unquestionably represent an important form of social capital, and they need to be accounted for in any serious reckoning of trends in social connectedness. On the other hand, they do not typically play the same role as traditional civic associations. As Wuthnow emphasizes,

> Small groups may not be fostering community as effectively as many of their proponents would like. Some small groups merely provide occasions for individuals to focus on themselves in the presence of others. The social contract binding members together asserts only the weakest of obligations. Come if you have time. Talk if you feel like it. Respect everyone's opinion. Never criticize. Leave quietly if you become dissatisfied.... We can imagine that [these small groups] really substitute for families, neighborhoods, and broader community attachments that may demand lifelong commitments, when, in fact, they do not.[9]

All three of these potential countertrends—tertiary organizations, nonprofit organizations, and support groups—need somehow to be weighed against the erosion of conventional civic organizations. One way of doing so is to consult the General Social Survey.

Within all educational categories, total associational membership declined significantly between 1967 and 1993. Among the college-educated, the average number of group memberships per person fell from 2.8 to 2.0 (a 26-per cent decline); among high-school graduates, the number fell from 1.8 to 1.2 (32 per cent); and among those with fewer than 12 years of education, the number fell from 1.4 to 1.1 (25 per cent). In other words, at *all* educational (and hence social) levels of American society, and counting *all* sorts of group memberships, *the average number of associational memberships has fallen by about a fourth over the last quarter-century*. Without controls for educational levels, the trend is not nearly so clear, but the central point is this: *more Americans than ever before are in social circumstances that foster associational involvement (higher education, middle age, and so on), but nevertheless aggregate associational membership appears to be stagnant or declining*.

Broken down by type of group, the downward trend is most marked for church-related groups, for labor unions, for fraternal and veterans'

---

9   Ibid., 3-6.

organizations, and for school-service groups. Conversely, membership in professional associations has risen over these years, although less than might have been predicted, given sharply rising educational and occupational levels. Essentially the same trends are evident for both men and women in the sample. In short, the available survey evidence confirms our earlier conclusion: American social capital in the form of civic associations has significantly eroded over the last generation.

GOOD NEIGHBORLINESS AND SOCIAL TRUST

I noted earlier that most readily available quantitative evidence on trends in social connectedness involves formal settings, such as the voting booth, the union hall, or the PTA. One glaring exception is so widely discussed as to require little comment here: the most fundamental form of social capital is the family, and the massive evidence of the loosening of bonds within the family (both extended and nuclear) is well known. This trend, of course, is quite consistent with—and may help to explain—our theme of social decapitalization.

A second aspect of informal social capital on which we happen to have reasonably reliable time-series data involves neighborliness. In each General Social Survey since 1974 respondents have been asked, "How often do you spend a social evening with a neighbor?" The proportion of Americans who socialize with their neighbors more than once a year has slowly but steadily declined over the last two decades, from 72 per cent in 1974 to 61 per cent in 1993. (On the other hand, socializing with "friends who do not live in your neighborhood" appears to be on the increase, a trend that may reflect the growth of workplace-based social connections.)

Americans are also less trusting. The proportion of Americans saying that most people can be trusted fell by more than a third between 1960, when 58 per cent chose that alternative, and 1993, when only 37 per cent did. The same trend is apparent in all educational groups; indeed, because social trust is also correlated with education and because educational levels have risen sharply, the overall decrease in social trust is even more apparent if we control for education.

Our discussion of trends in social connectedness and civic engagement has tacitly assumed that all the forms of social capital that we have discussed are themselves coherently correlated across individuals. This is in fact true. Members of associations are much more likely than nonmembers

30

to participate in politics, to spend time with neighbors, to express social trust and so on.

The close correlation between social trust and associational membership is true not only across time and across individuals, but also across countries. Evidence from the 1991 World Values Survey demonstrates the following:[10]

1. Across the 35 countries in this survey, social trust and civic engagement are strongly correlated; the greater the density of associational membership in a society, the more trusting its citizens. Trust and engagement are two facets of the same underlying factor—social capital.

2. America still ranks relatively high by cross-national standards on both these dimensions of social capital. Even in the 1990s, after several decades' erosion, Americans are more trusting and more engaged than people in most other countries of the world.

3. The trends of the past quarter-century, however, have apparently moved the United States significantly lower in the international rankings of social capital. The recent deterioration in American social capital has been sufficiently great that (if no other country changed its position in the meantime) another quarter-century of change at the same rate would bring the United States, roughly speaking, to the midpoint among all these countries, roughly equivalent to South Korea, Belgium, or Estonia today. Two generations' decline at the same rate would leave the United States at the level of today's Chile, Portugal, and Slovenia.

Why Is US Social Capital Eroding?

35   As we have seen, something has happened in America in the last two or three decades to diminish civic engagement and social connectedness. What could that "something" be? Here are several possible explanations, along with some initial evidence on each.

---

10   I am grateful to Ronald Inglehart, who directs this unique cross-national project, for sharing these highly useful data with me. See his "The Impact of Culture on Economic Development: Theory, Hypotheses, and Some Empirical Tests" (unpublished manuscript, University of Michigan, 1994).

The movement of women into the labor force. Over these same two or three decades, many millions of American women have moved out of the home into paid employment. This is the primary, though not the sole, reason why the weekly working hours of the average American have increased significantly during these years. It seems highly plausible that this social revolution should have reduced the time and energy available for building social capital. For certain organizations, such as the PTA, the League of Women Voters, the Federation of Women's Clubs, and the Red Cross, this is almost certainly an important part of the story. The sharpest decline in women's civic participation seems to have come in the 1970s; membership in such "women's" organizations as these has been virtually halved since the late 1960s. By contrast, most of the decline in participation in men's organizations occurred about ten years later; the total decline to date has been approximately 25 per cent for the typical organization. On the other hand, the survey data imply that the aggregate declines for men are virtually as great as those for women. It is logically possible, of course, that the male declines might represent the knock-on effect of women's liberation, as dishwashing crowded out the lodge, but time-budget studies suggest that most husbands of working wives have assumed only a minor part of the housework. In short, something besides the women's revolution seems to lie behind the erosion of social capital.

Mobility: The "re-potting" hypothesis. Numerous studies of organizational involvement have shown that residential stability and such related phenomena as home ownership are clearly associated with greater civic engagement. Mobility, like frequent re-potting of plants, tends to disrupt root systems, and it takes time for an uprooted individual to put down new roots. It seems plausible that the automobile, suburbanization, and the movement to the Sun Belt have reduced the social rootedness of the average American, but one fundamental difficulty with this hypothesis is apparent: the best evidence shows that residential stability and homeownership in America have risen modestly since 1965, and are surely higher now than during the 1950s, when civic engagement and social connectedness by our measures was definitely higher.

Other demographic transformations. A range of additional changes have transformed the American family since the 1960s—fewer marriages, more divorces, fewer children, lower real wages, and so on. Each of these changes might account for some of the slackening of civic engagement, since married, middle-class parents are generally more socially involved than other people. Moreover, the changes in scale that have swept over the

American economy in these years—illustrated by the replacement of the corner grocery by the supermarket and now perhaps of the supermarket by electronic shopping at home, or the replacement of community-based enterprises by outposts of distant multinational firms—may perhaps have undermined the material and even physical basis for civic engagement.

The technological transformation of leisure. There is reason to believe that deep-seated technological trends are radically "privatizing" or "individualizing" our use of leisure time and thus disrupting many opportunities for social-capital formation. The most obvious and probably the most powerful instrument of this revolution is television. Time-budget studies in the 1960s showed that the growth in time spent watching television dwarfed all other changes in the way Americans passed their days and nights. Television has made our communities (or, rather, what we experience as our communities) wider and shallower. In the language of economics, electronic technology enables individual tastes to be satisfied more fully, but at the cost of the positive social externalities associated with more primitive forms of entertainment. The same logic applies to the replacement of vaudeville by the movies and now of movies by the VCR. The new "virtual reality" helmets that we will soon don to be entertained in total isolation are merely the latest extension of this trend. Is technology thus driving a wedge between our individual interests and our collective interests? It is a question that seems worth exploring more systematically.

What Is to Be Done?

40   The last refuge of a social-scientific scoundrel is to call for more research. Nevertheless, I cannot forbear from suggesting some further lines of inquiry.

- We must sort out the dimensions of social capital, which clearly is not a unidimensional concept, despite language (even in this essay) that implies the contrary. What types of organizations and networks most effectively embody—or generate—social capital, in the sense of mutual reciprocity, the resolution of dilemmas of collective action, and the broadening of social identities? In this essay I have emphasized the density of associational life. In earlier work I stressed the structure of networks, arguing that "horizontal" ties represented more productive social capital than vertical ties.[11]

---

11 See my *Making Democracy Work*, esp. ch. 6.

- Another set of important issues involves macrosociological cross-currents that might intersect with the trends described here. What will be the impact, for example, of electronic networks on social capital? My hunch is that meeting in an electronic forum is not the equivalent of meeting in a bowling alley—or even in a saloon—but hard empirical research is needed. What about the development of social capital in the workplace? Is it growing in counterpoint to the decline of civic engagement, reflecting some social analogue of the first law of thermodynamics—social capital is neither created nor destroyed, merely redistributed? Or do the trends described in this essay represent a deadweight loss?

- A rounded assessment of changes in American social capital over the last quarter-century needs to count the costs as well as the benefits of community engagement. We must not romanticize small-town, middle-class civic life in the America of the 1950s. In addition to the deleterious trends emphasized in this essay, recent decades have witnessed a substantial decline in intolerance and probably also in overt discrimination, and those beneficent trends may be related in complex ways to the erosion of traditional social capital. Moreover, a balanced accounting of the social-capital books would need to reconcile the insights of this approach with the undoubted insights offered by Mancur Olson and others who stress that closely knit social, economic, and political organizations are prone to inefficient cartelization and to what political economists term "rent seeking" and ordinary men and women call corruption.[12]

- Finally, and perhaps most urgently, we need to explore creatively how public policy impinges on (or might impinge on) social-capital formation. In some well-known instances, public policy has destroyed highly effective social networks and norms. American slum-clearance policy of the 1950s and 1960s, for example, renovated physical capital, but at a very high cost to existing social capital. The consolidation of country post offices and small school districts has promised administrative and financial efficiencies, but full-cost accounting for the effects of these policies on social capital might produce a more negative verdict. On the

---

12   See Mancur Olson, *The Rise and Decline of Nations: Economic Growth, Stagflation, and Social Rigidities* (New Haven: Yale University Press, 1982), 2.

other hand, such past initiatives as the county agricultural-agent system, community colleges, and tax deductions for charitable contributions illustrate that government can encourage social-capital formation. Even a recent proposal in San Luis Obispo, California, to require that all new houses have front porches illustrates the power of government to influence where and how networks are formed.

The concept of "civil society" has played a central role in the recent global debate about the preconditions for democracy and democratization. In the newer democracies this phrase has properly focused attention on the need to foster a vibrant civic life in soils traditionally inhospitable to self-government. In the established democracies, ironically, growing numbers of citizens are questioning the effectiveness of their public institutions at the very moment when liberal democracy has swept the battlefield, both ideologically and geopolitically. In America, at least, there is reason to suspect that this democratic disarray may be linked to a broad and continuing erosion of civic engagement that began a quarter-century ago. High on our scholarly agenda should be the question of whether a comparable erosion of social capital may be under way in other advanced democracies, perhaps in different institutional and behavioral guises. High on America's agenda should be the question of how to reverse these adverse trends in social connectedness, thus restoring civic engagement and civic trust.

COMMENTARY AND WRITINGS ON RELATED TOPICS:

Nicholas Lemann, "Kicking in Groups," *The Atlantic Monthly* (April 1996). Mary Ann Zehr, "Getting Involved in Civic Life," *Foundation News and Commentary* (May/June 1996). *The* Foundation News and Commentary *is a publication of The Council on Foundations.*

(1995)

Questions

1. Putnam argues that "social capital" is greater in groups such as the PTA than it is for groups such as Alcoholics Anonymous. Note his reasons for this distinction and then argue for or against his position.

2. What rhetorical function does the "Countertrends" section play in the strength of Putnam's argument?

3. Under the heading "Why Is US Social Capital Eroding?" Putnam lists four possible reasons. Which of these four would you argue is the most significant? Can you think of other reasons that Putnam does not list?

4. Who do you think Putnam's intended audience is? What clues lead you to draw this conclusion? Pick another plausible audience and discuss how Putnam would need to alter his style in addressing it.

5. Discuss the importance of "social trust" to a democracy.

6. In what ways do you feel the Internet is increasing or decreasing social capital?

7. The ideas Putnam first presented here were revised and greatly expanded in the book published in 2000, *Bowling Alone: The Collapse and Revival of American Community*. Look up the book in your library and write two or three paragraphs discussing some of the respects in which the arguments as presented in the book have been extended and revised. Comment as well on the tone and the style of Putnam's writing in the book. How does it differ from that of the article?

ALICE BECK KEHOE

TRANSCRIBING INSIMA, A BLACKFOOT "OLD LADY"[1]

In this long essay, a well-known anthropologist recovers a lost voice in Native American History.

☙

Sue Sommers[2] had completed only one year of graduate work in anthropology at New York's Columbia University when she arrived in

---

1   David Reed Miller and Susan Miller introduced me to Sue Sommers Dietrich. After procrastinating for a couple of years I telephoned her home in south-suburban Chicago in August 1993 and made an appointment to interview her about the 1939 Blackfoot project. Sue was a delightful interviewee and a gracious hostess. She lent me three folders of her typed interviews with Insima so that the fragile sheets could be copied and archived by Mark Thiel, Marquette University archivist, and she invited me to return. Less than two months later, Sue Dietrich was killed by a car near her home.

The estate of Susan Dietrich has consented to the use of these interviews for this volume. [Unless otherwise noted, all notes to this essay are from the author.]

2   Sylvia Sue Roma Sommers, named after the women's rights activist Sylvia Pankhurst and Susan B. Anthony, was born in 1914 in Trenton, New Jersey, where her parents had immigrated from Russia. She earned a Bachelor of Arts in sociology from Hunter College in 1936, worked as a social worker in Harlem, and in 1938 enrolled in Columbia University's graduate program in anthropology. The following summer, at Ruth Benedict's invitation, she joined the Laboratory project on the Blackfeet Reservation.

Sommers served in World War II and afterward married Donald Dietrich, a psychoanalyst who, in 1948 and 1949, accompanied by Sue, did comparative psychology field research on three Plains reservations (one of them the Blackfeet). Sue Dietrich devoted herself to activities related to Quaker missions to promote peace, particularly a series of trips to Viet Nam and China. She visited the Blackfeet Reservation several times after the 1949 fieldwork with her husband, remaining in contact with the Yellow Kidney family.

Browning, Montana, on the Blackfeet Indian Reservation early in the summer of 1939. Ruth Benedict, her professor and organizer of the Columbia University Laboratory for ethnography, was already there, living in a tent. Sommers recalled that Professor Benedict had her sleeping bag on the ground, and was grateful when the young woman lent her an air mattress. Several other graduate students enrolled in the Laboratory project later became well-known anthropologists, including Oscar and Ruth Lewis, Esther Goldfrank, and Lucien Hanks and Jane Richardson, who later married (Goldfrank 1978:128). Benedict planned that they would divide and cover the four Blackfoot reserves, the North Blackfoot, Blood, and North Piegan in Alberta, Canada, and the Blackfeet (South Piegan[3]) in Montana, comparing the four societies and investigating their histories. Sue Sommers joined fellow student Gitel Steed and her painter husband, Bob, at Two Medicine River on the Montana reservation. Benedict gave the inexperienced students the simplest of instructions: "See if you can establish contact with a family and live with them."

Sommers arrived on the reservation during the South Piegans' annual reunion, the North American Indian Days powwow. She dressed in jeans and commercial moccasins, twisted her long, thick hair into two braids, and went into the campground. A group of women, noticing her, exclaimed over her braids. A middle-aged man, Jim Little Plume, came over and escorted Sommers to the tipi of Yellow Kidney, then about 70 years old, where she was invited to sit beside the fire hospitably burning in the tipi. A tourist from Connecticut came in with his two sons, saying that he wanted his boys adopted into the tribe and given Indian names. The tourist took out a notebook and asked each person's name, writing down the replies. When he came to Sommers, Jim Little Plume spoke up, "She is Long Braids, she is my wife." As soon as the man departed, everyone in the tipi laughed heartily at the joke. Little Plume showed up daily to escort Sommers around the reservation, and every morning he placed a bouquet of wildflowers at her tent.

Yellow Kidney and his wife Insima (*I'nssimaa*, "Gardener, Planter") agreed to set up a large tipi next to their house for the Steeds and Sommers. Tipis are often erected in the summer to shelter a family's guests, and this tipi was so comfortable that Benedict preferred it to the accommodations of the other students on the Canadian reserves. In the evenings, the Steeds and

---

3   Piegan and Peigan are variants of Pikuni, the closest English spelling for the Blackfoot term *Piikani*. The South Piegan in Montana are the *Aamsskaapipiikani*.

Sommers often joined the Yellow Kidney family in their home. Officially, Yellow Kidney spoke only Blackfoot and required anthropologists to hire interpreters at 25 cents an hour, but after hours, his English proved adequate if not fluent, and he would comment on the day's interpreter. Yellow Kidney's neighbor and long-time comrade (*itakkaa*, "buddy," "partner") was Jappy Takes Gun On Top, who had been stepfather to D.C. Duvall, the half-Piegan collaborator with Clark Wissler on the American Museum series of ethnographies of the Blackfoot (Wissler and Duvall 1908). Yellow Kidney was half-brother to Jim's deceased father, the original Little Plume, and their families had been neighbors on Two Medicine River early in the century. Cuts Different, widow of that Little Plume, remained close to her brother-in-law.

Sommers wanted to interview the three women in the family: Insima, her daughter Agnes Chief All Over, and Cuts Different. Although she obediently recorded extended interviews with Yellow Kidney, Philip Wells, and other respected older men throughout July, in mid-August she began interviewing Agnes Chief All Over and her fascinating mother. Jim Little Plume had interpreted at first, but he was killed on 9 July when Bob Steed's roadster, in which he was a passenger, overturned rounding a dangerous curve. Agnes took over the task of interpreting, and gave Sommers pages of her own life history as well.

5   Insima was 72, the same age as her husband Yellow Kidney, and had the Christian name Cecile. She had formerly been married to Yellow Wolf, more than 20 years her senior, who died at 82 about ten years before the Laboratory project. Insima was listed as "Cecile" in the 1907-08 Allotment Census, where her father is given as Isadore Sanderville, son of a non-Indian supposedly of the same name and a Piegan woman called Catch For Nothing. He had married Margaret, daughter of the Piegans Red Bird Tail and Twice Success. Cecile had two older brothers, Oliver and Richard (Dick), and a sister Louise (Mrs. John Crow in 1908). Dick Sanderville served on the Blackfeet Tribal Council as early as 1909.

Sue Sommers found Insima captivating. "Five by five feet," energetic and funny, and "really controlling, of the men, of everybody," Sommers recalled her. (One day, Insima picked up Sommers and threw her down, just in fun.) Insima much enjoyed imitating men, putting a pillow under her skirt to appear as a man's big paunch belly (see Appendix for one story of her joking). Her serious side was as a midwife and herb doctor. Sommers remembered her "running up and down the hills" picking medicinal herbs on one occasion while Sommers labored to get a car out of a stream crossing. Told of his wife's energy, Yellow Kidney remarked, "That's how she keeps in shape for when she wants to chase after men."

Ruth Benedict expected Sommers to take down Indians' life histories. Yellow Kidney's was an obvious choice, since he was a prominent elder in the community. Sue learned that as a young man Yellow Kidney had been in a circus, doing stunts on a horse, but the thick folder of typescript from days of interviews with him mentions nothing of this; instead, the practiced informant retold a list of Piegan bands, details of the All-comrades' societies, of the Sun Dance, of bison hunting. Trying to take a life history, Sommers found that Yellow Kidney veered off into what she called "folktales," well-known stories of battles and the foundation myths for medicine bundles and their rituals (Wissler 1912). Yellow Kidney had become familiar with what anthropologists wanted, from George Bird Grinnell (e.g., 1892, 1901) in the late 1880s through Walter McClintock, Clark Wissler and Duvall (1908), and James Willard Schultz, who married into Yellow Kidney's community. Salvage ethnography was the task, recording from the last generation to have lived as independent nations, experiencing the bison hunting, ceremonies, and warfare they lost when they settled upon the reservation in 1884. Personal histories were considered idiosyncratic, unscientific in the effort to obtain *the* culture of *the* tribe, and Yellow Kidney's circus exploits were definitely not subjects for a respected elder's recorded life history (cf. DeMallie 1984).

In accordance with the classic ethnographers' expectations that each "primitive" society had "a culture," whose tribal members hewed unthinking to a tradition passed on by their forebears over thousands of years,[4] Yellow Kidney told how it was supposed to have been. For example, "In buffalo days [there was] never a woman who vowed [the Sun Dance] and wasn't pure. Have that just lately. Only being very bad to family" (8-4-39:33). The technical word for Yellow Kidney's accounts is "normative." Wissler (1971 [1938]:206) understood that Indians collaborated, for their own reasons, with their ethnographers in this skewed model: "The old people I knew came to adult life before reservation days and so saw the breakdown of tribal life and independence. Some of them were discouraged as to the future, but by living in the past and capitalizing their ancestral pride, they carried on."

---

4   One might term this the Holiday Fruitcake paradigm: firmly molded, dark, studded with traits, infused with spirits, ritually bestowed and hardly nibbled at until, at last, Civilization came and, by the hand of Acculturation, discarded it.

Men's and Women's Business

Yellow Kidney and Insima were each requested to dictate life histories to young "Long Braids." Sommers collected her interview material into one thick folder labeled "Yellow Kidney," another labeled "Insema," and thinner transcripts from other Piegans. With one small exception, the July interviews were all with men. On 1 August 1939, Sommers got five pages of typescript from Short Chief (Good Leader Woman?), identified only as a woman over 80 whose first husband had been Heavy Gun. After another week with Yellow Kidney, on 11 August Sommers interviewed Agnes Chief All Over. At last, from 16 to 18 August, she could work with Insima, Agnes Chief All Over interpreting.

10   In contrast to her husband's didactic presentations of "Plains Indian culture," Insima said nothing of battles and myths. Her reminiscences focused on who married whom, and how good, or bad, the husbands were. Both she and her daughter Agnes recalled their childhoods and especially their relationships to women and girls. Notably absent from Insima's interviews are data on midwifery or herb doctoring, the specialties for which she was well known in her community, or on how she managed her professional and familial commitments. Insima seems to have offered "women's business," that is, marital concerns and childrearing (Goldfrank 1978:140), in complement to the "men's business" of warfare and ritual performance presented by her husband.

     "Insema Interviews" is the heading on the folder of typescripts. Immediately we are engrossed in a woman's account of coping with the actuality of reservation life. Men recited the glories of the "buffalo days"; for Insima, the real battles lay in surviving her nation's economic and political collapse. Sommers, if she had followed other mid-century anthropologists, might have labeled her recording of Insima's history a study of "acculturation," or how the Indian adopted a more Western style of life. Perhaps one factor in Sommers's neglect of publishing these field data was her inchoate understanding that the popular term was a biased, ethnocentric distortion of the indigenous nations' protracted contests with the invaders. From a First Nations' perspective, the Blackfoot adopted substitutes for their principal economic resource, the bison, and accepted opportunities to learn English, reading, and other means of dealing with the conquerors. To call these strategies "acculturation"—that is, moving *toward* Western culture—misses the essential point that indigenous people were struggling to *retain* as much of their heritage as possible under the much altered circumstances of the reservation.

Sommers's informants were members of a community formed out of the Grease Melters (translated "Fries" by Agnes Chief All Over; Mc-Clintock [1910:57] gives it as *Ich-poch-semo*), a band that dispersed onto farms around 1896, in Yellow Kidney's recollection (7/7/39:1). Sets of brothers formed its core: Yellow Kidney's father was a brother of the Three Suns (Big Nose), respected chief of the Grease Melters at the formation of the reservation in 1884. Yellow Kidney's half-brother was Little Plume, and Yellow Kidney had brought up his brother's son, Jim Little Plume, who became "Long Braids's" friend and guide. A young boy Sommers met, Buster Yellow Kidney, said to be *minipoka*, favorite child, to his maternal grandfather Yellow Kidney, today occupies the place of knowledgeable elder once held by that grandfather.

Insima's notion of a life history was a history of lives. She began the first lengthy interview with stories about her neighbor Running Owl (born 1859). Running Owl's daughter Susie and Insima's Agnes were close friends and they got married at the same time:

When Agnes was 15 she wanted to get married and she did [to Sam Middle Calf]. Gave her a house. Had a bed on the floor. At same time Susie married [John] Calf Tail. Running Owl didn't like to see this. Running Owl would follow both girls. First night they went to bed he went in and sat and smoked and smoked. Had lamp lit and watched them all night for several nights. Johnny [Calf Tail] told Susie, "Since your Father doesn't want you to marry me, I'm going to leave you," and he did. Not long after that Susie was killed by Jim Little Plume. Agnes' husband left her also.

This is both personal and social history, documenting the early age and instability of marriage among the Blackfoot of the early reservation period. Sommers's experience as a social worker in Harlem had prepared her to listen to accounts of lives quite different from those of most Columbia University students. Sommers's kind, gentle and attentive friend, Jim Little Plume, had, she was told at his funeral that July, "got up drunk one morning and shot his wife, child, and seven other people. He had been in prison for twenty years [but] he had gotten out before [Sommers] arrived and no one spoke of it to her; [she] was impressed at how accepting Indians are" (interview, 8/29/93). Sommers recalled, in 1993, that she and the Steeds attended Jim Little Plume's funeral, conducted by a priest. Two hundred people were there, she estimated, and Insima and Yellow Kidney "went over and gave prayers" in addition to the priest's service. Sommers went with a man named Yellow Owl to dig Jim's grave along the Two Medicine river (interview, 8/29/93). Half a century later, Sommers remembered Jim Little Plume fondly, and like the Indians, in our interview preferred not to dwell on the tragedies of his life. She had said to Insima at his wake, "Why hadn't you told me about his past?" Insima answered, "Would it have made a difference?" "That was one of the most important lessons I had ever learned," Sommers believed, "of great importance to my life."

INSIMA'S REMINISCENCES

15 Sommers's typescript for 16 August 1939 launched into "Indian's [Insima's] life." (Apparently Sommers initially misheard *I'nssimaa* as "Indian.") The young woman's transcription style of writing as rapidly as she could in English has the virtue of recording the stream of tale-telling. Sommers did not realize the importance of including her own queries in the text, so we can only guess where she asked for clarification or more information. Minor problems arise from Sommers's unfamiliarity with the dramatis personae of the Reservation, and from Agnes's occasional tendency to give a literal but inappropriate translation: for example, saying "daughter" for what Insima likely termed *itan*. As Sommers's fellow students Hanks and Richardson [1945:31] noted for the North Blackfoot, the term *itan* also includes "(female speaker) daughter of sister; daughter of comrade ... first generation female descendant of husband's senior," and extends to *otanimm*, "emotionally attached as to a daughter, adopted as a daughter." Her linguistic naiveté led Sommers to write (8/16/39, p. 28) that Fine Shield Woman, Pikuni first wife of James Willard Schultz, was Agnes's "daughter," although elsewhere Insima noted that Agnes was a year younger than Fine Shield Woman's son Hart; in English terminology, Fine Shield Woman was Agnes's first cousin. Occasionally, Agnes was careless using "he" versus "she," a common slip stemming from the fact that gender in the Blackfoot language distinguishes animate from inanimate, but not masculine from feminine.

Here is part of Insima's response—translated as she spoke by Agnes Chief All Over—to the ethnographer's request for her life history:

> Yellow Wolf [Insima's first husband] told father that he was going
> to Browning's Willow Creek to see if it was a good place to build a
> home. Moved with another family.

Moved. Camped right where Browning is now.[5] Rode and looked Willow Creek over and decided on a place on which they can settle down, and soon to get cattle and cut hay.[6]

Next day, moved to mountains to cut house logs ... and poles for corrals. When through, hauled them down as far as Browning on wagons. Build houses there. Finished. From there used to go to Old Agency for rations. Yellow Wolf got mowing machine, rake, and grindstone from government. Bear Paw joined them and asked, Why they didn't let them know they were going to move. Yellow Wolf thought, I wouldn't want to move. After [he] bought machinery a white man came—Mr. Stuart, he married an Indian woman. Told Yellow Wolf, "I heard about this place and you're going to have a lot of hay. Come to put it up for you so you can give me some." Agreed. First time [that] they learned how to cut hay and put it up. When through, put up corral and barn. Then heard some cattle was to be issued to them.

Black Bear said, they should winter cattle at Cut Bank because here, there isn't much shelter. "We'll take hay down there."

Yellow Wolf went to Old Agency. Each family got four cows and four calves regardless of size of families. They told him about milk and he knew how to milk and so did it right away, but didn't know how to make butter.

North of Browning, they found a place [to winter cattle]—thick trees for good shelter. All three—yet—Black Bear and Bear Paw had hayracks and in no time had half the hay there. Sometimes made 3 trips a day. When enough hay there, they moved there. Made house there of cotton[wood] trees.

[Insima] left Agnes because grandmother took Agnes and would[n't] let her go. Father agreed to let her stay and they go ahead. Will build house for them and then send for them.

Yellow Wolf went to agency and when he returned told wife to tell Mother [mother-in-law and son-in-law traditionally did not speak directly to one another] he wanted Agnes to go to school.

---

5 The Blackfeet Agency was transferred to Willow Creek, near Joe Kipp's trading post, in 1895, and the town of Browning grew up around Kipp's by 1900 (Farr 1984:40-42).

6 Cattle were issued to the Piegans beginning in 1890, as part of the 1886 treaty negotiations (Ewers 1958:307; Farr 1984:98).

Grandmother had Agnes—same story as for daughter. Didn't even know when she was brought to school. Policemen come around and collect children. Finally caught. Crying but taken to the school. Told that all children under six had to go to school, even if they were five or three—if older, whites claimed they were younger than they were.

When it occurred to Insima that Sommers would be unfamiliar with Blackfoot custom, she interjected explanations. For example, after mentioning how closely her second pregnancy followed Agnes's birth, she described methods of avoiding too-frequent pregnancies:

> Usually don't have intercourse with husband a month or six weeks after that [childbirth]. Afraid of husband then—don't want to have another child right away but they usually do have a child every two years. After tenth day [after childbirth], going to get out of bed, they put entirely new clothes on. Mother gets any old lady [telling her] that her girl is getting out of bed and to go help her put them on. When old lady gets there, takes all the clothes off. Makes sweet smoke—blankets, moccasins, stocking, etc., and hold them over smoke and then puts the clothes on her. Paints girl's face. Not paid for this. This lady must be old enough to no longer have children. Take all the girl's old clothes that she wore in bed, blanket, and she keeps these. This is to keep the girl from being caught [pregnant] right away.
>
> Agnes's "daughter" [that is, her *nitan. 'a*, Fine Shield Woman] was married to Mr. Schultz [James Willard Schultz]. Almost died when she gave birth to Hart Schultz. Potato [Fine Shield Woman's mother] went to Mother and asked her to help her daughter so she wouldn't have any more children. We almost lost her. Father agreed that something should be done. There was a round copper bracelet with a hole—put a buckskin string through it and put it on the woman's neck. Told her, if a dog has puppies don't pick up or take one (it's all right if they're older and running around) or you'll be caught then. Never did have another child.
>
> [Insima's] Mother also fixed up Louis Champagne's wife for birth control. Mother didn't like to do it anymore—only helped—felt it was killing. Doesn't know where she learned how. She only had one child.

Later in the interviews, Insima indulged in reminiscences of her childhood:

Insema went hunting when she was very small. In winter went with Boy Chief and Louis Champagne [Yellow Wolf's nephews] and her far away husband [the term for sister's husband (Hanks and Richardson 1945:31)], Morning Plume. A far away husband never says anything out of the way before girl marries and girl does not know how to treat a far away husband.

It was a cold but a nice day. Before she knew how to ride, her Mother used to tie her on the horse. Boy Chief and Morning Plume and Yellow Wolf chased a buffalo. The sky was clear—not a cloud. After each killed a buffalo, they started to cut them up. Then the clouds started to come up like a smoke. Hurried because it looked bad. Insema had an extra horse with her and Morning Plume had four extra horses and so did Yellow Wolf. She had just followed Morning Plume to the hunt. As fast as they cut meat and packed on horses, the cloud was traveling fast. We started back, Blizzard came and it sure was cold. Many had gone buffalo hunting but in all different directions.

While going, her moccasin ripped on heel—all at once felt a sting—didn't know but her heel had frozen. Got lost and way above the camps and stood around and heard dogs barking down below. When they came home—they—Mother and Father—were sure mad at her. When I got off horse I just fell backwards. They had told me not to go but I wanted to go and pick out my own meat. When I go inside tipi, my heel started to thaw and burn badly but I was ashamed to say anything. Went to another old lady and told her, my heel froze. She took a dried gut, cooked it in a fire until brown. Chewed it and put it on the frozen heel. Didn't sting anymore. Next morning, my heel blistered. Put more gut on. Blisters broke—put more gut on.

Next day, heard one boy missing, never returned and many men went on hunt. Blizzard was over. It was the equinox and storm. Boy had frozen to death. His blanket coat was raggy and leggings torn. Horse was right by him.

[Insima] got a lot of meat from men, hind legs, ribs, heart, liver, kidney, and some guts and ribs. Men didn't mind that she had come. Many times she went in the summer—followed the men.

Never went with Father. He would never get chance to go because he had two fast buffalo horses and some one would ask to borrow them and they would bring him meat.

Remembering hunting brought to mind the early reservation period when the bison herds disappeared:

People claimed they were being starved.... That was when they first learned to make a garden. Potatoes, rutabagas and carrots—about 57 years ago [1882]. Men plowed and women put in seeds. When first issued rations—flour, meat, bacon, rice, crackers, coffee, tobacco—big long plug, salt, tapioca—called it fish eggs. In fall when garden ready, issued it to them like rations. Have a great big slab of bacon. Scared of the flour because they found bones in it. Claim it was ghost bones—bones from human skeleton.[7] Had to use it but would pick bones out. When we started to eat it, two or three died every morning complaining of their stomachs. White man there [at Old Agency] with Indian wife who talked English and acted as interpreter [probably Malenda Wren (Farr 1984:29)].

Woman would tell them what husband dreamt last night, that he made two or three coffins and sure enough next morning he have to make that many coffins. Then buffalo all gone—no other way to live—not permitted to roam—had to stay right there. Think flour poisoned them. Didn't like smell of cows and so didn't like to eat them and didn't like so many different colored animals.

At Old Agency, women did all the work. Agent, Grey Beard, put out two saws and two axes and when he'd open up tool house all the women rush over. Hand out saw and tallest would grab, and same with rest. Pick out best friend to help her with the saw. Be 4 women with 2 axes. Usual to pay them paper money and white paper. The white paper was for sugar. Saw and axes would put up a cordwood and get $4 for one cordwood. Green paper—a dollar. Each get $4, and $1 for sugar.

---

7   Rodent bones may have occurred in the flour. The necessity of shipping food long distances without refrigeration, the government practice of accepting the lowest bids, and chicanery from suppliers all contributed to the likelihood of contamination in flour and other rations.

Men would go up to mountains and haul timber for the agency. One with big load—get $7—way up to mountains. In those days wagons very scarce. Build little log houses. Wouldn't stand long and roofs broke in. Took men a long time to [learn how to] guide a team and how to put harness on. Put harness on up side down. An old man when first learning how to cut hay—didn't know he had to oil it [the machine]. Started to get hot and smoke. Had wife follow with a bucket of water to pour on it. Stand awhile till wife returned with water.

Horses and cattle increased fast. Had over 510 heads of cattle. Father have over 480 horses; he had no cattle. Agency didn't issue cattle to old people. Insema had 22 head of horses.

Insema's fourth daughter was Molly. Molly was born one year after Yellow Wolf's fourth wife had left the family. Katie was the fifth child. She was born three years later. A third daughter had died when she was nine years. (Couldn't remember her name—she had no Indian name.) She had died of pneumonia. Her clothes and toys were buried with her. Molly died when Fannie [Molly's daughter] was very small and Insema raised her. Fannie went to school, staying in dormitory, [and got pregnant by] the principal. Blamed it on young Indian man because she didn't want to get the principal in trouble. He sent Fannie to Minot, ND and he paid all expenses and hospital fees there.

Husband [Yellow Wolf] got a salary as a policeman, but the amount was forgotten. He was paid every month. He never actually quit, nor was he fired, but he just didn't return to work. He wasn't paid after he failed to return to work. The salary was stopped after they had moved to Willow Creek. They were living at Willow Creek when Yellow Wolf died. At the time of Yellow Wolf's death, they had both a house and a tent. Yellow Wolf and Insema lived in the tent. Emma and her husband John Little Plume [not related to Yellow Wolf's brother] lived in the house, with Emma's husband's father and mother. Katie and her husband ([Paul] Home Gun), Agnes, her second husband James Big Top and her daughter Mary, lived in Yellow Wolf's tent.

Everyone was there because Yellow Wolf was very rich, and he knew he was going to die. Those who lived there all the time were Insema, Yellow Wolf and Mary, with Emma and her husband in their own house. (No one lived in Yellow Wolf's house throughout the summer.) Yellow Wolf died at 82 [c. 1927]. He did not die of any illness. He had been shot in war, a little below the shoulder, and the bullet had never been removed. It had swelled and finally burst inside. He [Insima?] cut her hair.[8]

She kept everything. All Yellow Wolf's clothes were put in a sack and buried with him, together with all his little things, pipe, tobacco, matches. He had given his saddle away while he was still alive, and had refused to ride again. Insema gave it to her father. Mrs. Powell—a white woman married to a fullblood—took her to Browning. She stayed with the woman less than a year. She did nothing at all. The woman's daughter-in-law did all the cooking and called them when food was ready. Her other two daughters came after them to eat. Insema did not pay anything for her keep during the time she was there. When father was living, Insema did a lot of work for her, beading and making repairs for her. This woman asked to take Insema home with her because she was older and felt Insema would be happier with her than with her children, who were young and often went out. Insema took only [her grand-daughter] Mary with her.

When Agnes had her baby, Insema was nearby but not present. Every time Agnes suffered, she had to run out and cry. Thus she was constantly running in and out. However, she was present at the second birth. (It is always like this—mothers hate to be present at the first birth their daughter has. Mother might stay if she felt others are not helping enough and she can do more for her daughter, everyone thinks she is brave in such a case.) There was no medicine smoke at that time, it had been stopped by the [blank: agent or priest?]. If the girl suffers for two or three days, they make a [blank] to bring child right away. Medicine man and wife called on Agnes to change clothes and make medicine so that she does not have another child soon. His wife took care of changing her clothes, and he painted her face yellow. Gave her no medicine or anything to wear. Told her that if she let no one wear her shawl she would not have another baby right away. He lied, for she had one three years later, and she so informed him. He was paid with a work horse.

---

8   It was Blackfoot custom that close family members, particularly widows, cut off their hair as a sign of grief and mourning. (Note Agnes's slip in choosing the English pronoun, since Blackfoot uses one animate form for both masculine and feminine.)

Insema adopted Mary after Agnes left her husband. She left in the summer and remarried in the fall. Agnes's new husband told Agnes to let Mother and Father keep Mary since they already had her. "Sometimes we'll take her home with us." Mary got used to her grandparents. Agnes got her clothes and shoes. Insema cared very little when Agnes left her first husband, because she knew he drank and gambled away the cattle and horses; he would never gather wood or go to work. Glad to be rid of him.

If grandparents love their grandchildren and feel that they can take better care of them than their parents, the mother cannot object. Nowadays, it is not necessary to go to court in order to adopt grandchildren. However, to adopt an unrelated orphan, it is necessary to go to court and pay $25.00. The child is then registered in your name and when you die, your property goes to adopted children.

Glad she picked out second husband because he was known as a good man. Agnes knew the second husband [James Big Top] when he was married to Minnie. They would come and stay several nights. Minnie's mother came down for a week. Minnie used to say he was good to her, but his mother was mean to her. Agnes didn't speak much to him. Heard later that Minnie had quit him.

Agnes met him in town, Browning, one day and he asked if she was going back to her husband. When she told him she was not, he asked her to marry him. She said nothing. He asked her again every time he met her. Told mother first time he asked. She finally said yes but said she had heard his mother was mean. He said she acted that way to Minnie because Minnie was running around with his brothers.

When Agnes married her second husband, Insema stopped the taboo [against mother- and son-in-law speaking]. Agnes and husband would visit her, but son-in-law and mother-in-law never spoke to each other. Agnes told her, "You should stop avoiding your son-in-law, it's unusual, you should think of your son-in-law as your son." She was glad not to have to avoid her son-in-law because now he could visit her. She thought of how she had had to avoid her first son-in-law and she would have to go out—only one place in tipi and both couldn't be present. Liked the new arrangement.

Mary [Middle Calf, Agnes's daughter, born 1902] got married that year. Agnes's first husband picked the man for her. Agnes knew nothing about it. She lived quite a distance from Mary. Nobody told Insema about it—she found out about it from others. When Yellow Wolf died, Mary's father came and took her home, and it was during that time that she was married.

Jack, Mary's husband, had given no gifts when he married. (That is not done anymore, Mary got nothing from anyone until later on. Insema started getting bedding, furnishing and tent for her.) Mary did not know Jack before they were married. They were both young.

Six years after Yellow Wolf died, Yellow Kidney's wife died. Insema had not known Yellow Kidney before she married him. His wife was the same age as Insema. Insema went to Browning and while there went to visit an old lady, Mrs. Bird. While she was visiting, Walter McGee and John Mountain Chief, policemen, came in and told her she was wanted at the Indian Agency. She wondered whether she had done something wrong and was under arrest. Decided to go and find out what it was about. Mrs. Bird told her that she would go there with her when Mrs. Bird had finished her cooking. They both went. They found a place, a small room, and Yellow Kidney waiting there. Yellow Kidney didn't know either what they wanted with him. They had just brought them together there.[9] "Wonder if they came after me over that man." They gave me a chair and told me to sit down. They placed her on one side of the desk and Yellow Kidney on the other.

Another policeman, Mr. Tevenus, started to talk to her. He said, "We sent for you because you are going to marry that man." She didn't wish to marry him—she had never known him before (she was very young at the time of her first marriage, and hadn't known any better). They said she wouldn't have to be rustling for herself, and she'd have someone to help her and do things for her. She didn't answer. Walter McGee started to talk kindly to her. Asked her if she had made up her mind. She told them, "The reason I am saying nothing is that I have children and grandchildren and Yellow Kidney might not like them." They said, "The reason we

---

9   This passage shows the paternalism of the reservation Agent, treating mature widowed men and women as if they were too feckless to make suitable living arrangements.

brought you together was that we thought you two would get along together. You are both good workers and will have a nice home soon." They wouldn't let her go until she said yes. Yellow Kidney had been listening to all this. His wife had died only two weeks before.

She said, "It's up to him to say whether he wants to marry me." They started to talk to him. Yellow Kidney said he'd marry her.

I went home but not with him. After I went out they told him to go where I was staying. He came there in a rig. He brought lots of grub, dress goods, a blanket and a shawl. When she got home she explained to Mary and Jack. They told her to marry him.

"I'd like to marry him but he's stranger and I feel ashamed."

Yellow Kidney: "I have some things for you and you can take all that's in the rig." When Yellow Kidney's wife had died they had taken everything that belonged to his wife. Mary Little Plume took all the cooking utensils. Stayed with Mary and Jack quite a while, when finally Yellow Kidney suggested they fix up his place for their own. They came here and cleaned up the place.

We can leave Insima here. She went on to tell of the marriage of her youngest daughter Katie to Paul Home Gun, "a good worker" who "never drinks or gambles," and Agnes's marriage to George Chief All Over after Agnes's second husband died. She also told stories of jealous husbands, and of the adventure of a mistreated Blackfoot youth and his orphaned comrade, who went over the mountains to the Flathead Valley and returned with two Salish Flathead women escaping from cruel husbands. This story resembles men's standard tales of war exploits, except that Insima emphasized the Salish women's active participation in the escape.

Insima's reminiscences are first-hand accounts of the early reservation period that in recent years has increasingly drawn historians' interest. Because scholars during that time were engaged in salvage ethnography, there was little contemporary description outside official documents and newspapers, and particularly little directly and candidly from Indians. The memoir Sommers transcribed is doubly rare because it is from a woman speaking freely and at length.

How valid is this document? Discourse analysis, formerly confined to linguistics, has entered general anthropology and made us more sensitive to the parameters of ethnographic work, to "issues of power and perspective, questions of how authoritative knowledge is legitimated, of self-awareness and authenticity of voice in the presentation of data, and of the constraints of the historical and cultural contexts within which knowledge develops" (Rubinstein 1991:12-13). In 1939, these issues were stuff for the researcher to grapple with before reaching the final draft of a monograph: it was unseemly to expose one's struggles. The persona one presented in print, to the public, was the aloof observer before whose magisterial gaze the events of the field fell into orderly categories. Sommers, who had been a social worker before entering graduate school, could not maintain such an objective analytical stance. World War II pre-empted her personal crisis over a career decision, and after the war she engaged herself in international social activism. Her 1939 typescripts remained raw data.

Rubinstein identifies a "folktale" (as Sommers would have called it) told within the profession of American anthropology, about naive graduate students supposedly cast into the field with only a blank notebook, to flounder about, shiver and shake, until a kind Native adopted them and taught them what they ought to know. Fifty years later, Sommers remembered herself as such a stereotypical innocent. But as Rubinstein points out (1991:14), all those graduate students who *felt*, as they arrived in a strange land, like babes cast adrift, had in fact been prepared by years of academic study of scientific observation and social analysis. They had all read the classics of ethnography *and* heard their professors informally tell their own field experiences. Benedict's instruction, as Sommers recalled it, seemed maddeningly simplistic, yet Sommers knew, from the seminars she took, what an ethnographer was expected to do once he or she "establishes contact with a family and lives with them." Her professor was on the reservation, ready to listen to her students' experiences and suggest how they might proceed. Sommers's fellow student Jane Richardson recalled that they

> sought out the tribal elders to obtain their recollections of Blackfoot life in more free-spirited times. The old ones liked to talk for hours about war deeds, or the sadly vanishing religion of the medicine bundles (Hoffman 1988:118).

This was, Richardson explained, "the formal method of anthropological research [she] had learned ... at Columbia" (Hoffman 1988:118).

In Sommers's typescripts we have admired a Blackfoot's matron's *story*, in every sense of that word, told to a young woman who showed herself respectful, empathetic, and fascinated by the lively "Old Lady." Insima, who had listened for too many years to men's stories of war and prescriptions of correct ritual, wanted young Long Braids to hear and record the affairs of real life, how Blackfoot people *lived*. *I'nssimaa*, the Gardener, would plant, would cultivate, a text on women's business—the business of maintaining life. Sommers had paid her dues for more than a month, dutifully recording the standard accounts of men; now, the feminist consciousness nourished in her childhood could resonate with her hostess's Blackfoot pride in womanly accomplishments. Sommers's transcript is perhaps naive in that she made no effort to learn the Blackfoot language (which is difficult for English speakers), she put on paper only the translated formal interviews with no minutiae of context, and she left out her own presence, her queries, her reactions.

As a straightforward narrative, however, Sommers's "Insema" folder documents both Blackfoot history and women's history. Its particulars reverberate against dry official archives and sweeping summaries. It is only *a* text, one woman's selected memories, but we owe gratitude to Ruth Benedict who let her student work in a much less-traveled way; to Sue Sommers who persisted; and especially to Insima and her daughter Agnes who wanted their stories to be history.

Conclusion

Insima's narratives convey the spirit with which the Piegans adapted to the new economy, carefully selecting ranch land and moving into cabins once they could no longer obtain sturdy bison skins for tipis. Insima partnered her husband in hauling wood and ranching while her mother, according to Blackfoot custom, cared for Insima's young child. It was hard for Insima's mother to see the granddaughter constrained by dresses, shoes, school buildings, kept from the outdoor exercise and work that make women strong. The older woman's fears of sickness were well founded, for mortality rates, especially among children, were appalling in the early reservation period. Yet, in spite of the terrible toll taken by malnutrition and diseases after the collapse of their indigenous economy, the Piegans maintained their communities throughout the radical step of becoming ranchers in widely separated hamlets along the prairie streams.

Clark Wissler (1971[1938]:239) remarked, "so far as I could see, the morale of the women was far less shattered [by reservation life] and it was they who saved tribal life from complete collapse." Wissler may very well have met Insima; his collaborator Duvall commissioned her in 1904 to make a cradleboard for the American Museum collections.[10] His evaluation of women's business on the reservation seems well borne out by Sommers's transcript of her interviews with Insima.

APPENDIX: INSIMA PLAYS THE DIRTY WHITE MAN

[Interview of 8-17-39 or 8-18-39, Insima speaking, Agnes Chief All Over interpreting]

> She [Insima] was picking [choke]cherries. There was an old lady "Steals Good" heard that another old lady had almost been raped. She got mad and said "I wish I had been there with my butcher knife." She was grinding cherries as she spoke. As she spoke she shook her big butcher knife. Insima thought "I'll see what you can do." Mary and Jack were camping there too. Told Mary "I'm going to play a trick on her. When you see me go to her out of the brush you tell her you're going to the house to put the baby to sleep." Insima went in the tent and put Yellow Kidney's pants on. Cut the fur off a pair of old chaps. Rubbed syrup all over her chin and pasted the fur all over chin and cheeks. Put coat on and dish towel around her head. Put her hair up under an old hat.
>
> Went way around and from east walked up to camp. When Mary saw her she said her piece. She [Steals Good] was facing the grinding. Insima said "Hello." She looked up and said "Hello." Made signs "Eat some of these cherries, they're good." Took some and spit them out and said "No good."
>
> "They're good." Stopped grinding and started backing away. She moved near her and drew her near and said "Lot of fat, lot of fat." "No, no, I haven't any meat." Insima grabbed her any place—kept yelling, "No good, no good." She kept hollering for Insima to come—half crying. She kept calling for Mary. Insima had her around the waist and reached under her dress and she cried out. She hollered and hollered. Insima held her tight and pushed her. She cried. Mary finally came running. Insima had an old axe over her

---

10 Duvall wrote Wissler, "Mrs. Yellow Wolf is making the Baby Board and her mother is making the dog travois" (letter of 12 October 1904), then on 10 November "Mrs. Yellow Wolf, and Boy, also failed to make some of the things" (Wissler papers, American Museum of Natural History).

shoulder and had dropped it. Insima was holding her under one leg to lift her. Mary was pushing them apart, talking English.

She grabbed the axe and said to Mary "Here's his axe—that dirty white man. I'm going to give it to Jack so he'll know."

Insima circled around to her tent and washed and changed. "What's wrong? I was picking cherries across the river and heard you screaming." Steals Good bawled her out. Asked her which way did white man go? Mary said "Down that way?"

Insima: "Why didn't you grab your knife?" "Well, right from the start he grabbed me and threw me down, and I never thought of my knife. There's his axe, I'm going to give it to my son."

"It was me. I wanted to see if you'd use your knife."

Old lady took after her and did grab her.

References

Benedict, Ruth
   1939 Letter to Oscar and Ruth Lewis. Unpublished, in possession of Ruth M. Lewis, Urbana, IL.

DeMallie, Raymond J., ed.
   1984 *The Sixth Grandfather: Black Elk's Teachings Given to John G. Neihardt*. Lincoln: University of Nebraska Press.

Dietrich, Sue Sommers
   1939 Field Notes, Blackfeet Indian Reservation, Montana. Typescript in author's possession.
   1993 Interview with Alice B. Kehoe, 29 August 1993, in Dietrich's home in Olympia Fields, IL.

Ewers, John C.
   1958 *The Blackfeet: Raiders on the Northwestern Plains*. Norman: University of Oklahoma Press.

Farr, William E.
   1984 *The Reservation Blackfeet, 1882-1945*. Seattle: University of Washington Press.

Goldfrank, Esther S.
   1978 *Notes on an Undirected Life*. Flushing, NY: Queens College Publications in Anthropology, no. 3.

Grinnell, George Bird
   1892 *Blackfoot Lodge Tales*. New York: Charles Scribner's Sons. See *American Anthropologist* o.s., 1896, 9:286-87; n.s. 1899, 1:194-96; 1901, 3:650-68 ("The Lodges of the Blackfoot").

Hanks, Lucien M., Jr., and Jane Richardson

1945 *Observations on Northern Blackfoot Kinship*. Monograph 9, American Ethnological Society. Seattle: University of Washington Press.

Hoffman, Edward

1988 *The Right to be Human: A Biography of Abraham Maslow*. Los Angeles: Jeremy P. Tarcher.

McClintock, Walter

1910 *The Old North Trail*. Lincoln: University of Nebraska Press (1968 Bison Book facsimile reprint).

Rubinstein, Robert A.

1991 *Introduction. In Fieldwork: The Correspondence of Robert Redfield & Sol Tax*. Boulder, CO: Westview Press.

Schultz, James Willard (Apikuni)

1907 *My Life as an Indian*. New York: Forest and Stream.

1962 *Blackfeet and Buffalo*. Keith C. Seele, ed. Norman: University of Oklahoma Press.

1974 *Why Gone Those Times? Blackfoot Tales*. Eugene Lee Silliman, ed. Norman: University of Oklahoma Press.

Wissler, Clark

1911 *The Social Life of the Blackfoot Indians*. Anthropological Papers, vol. 7, pt. 1, 1-64. New York: American Museum of Natural History.

1912 *Ceremonial Bundles of the Blackfoot Indians*. Anthropological Papers, vol. 7, pt. 2, 65-289. New York: American Museum of Natural History.

1971 [1938] *Red Man Reservations*. New York: Collier. (Originally published 1938 as *Indian Cavalcade or Life on the Old-Time Indian Reservations* by Sheridan House.)

Wissler, Clark, and D.C. Duvall

1908 *Mythology of the Blackfoot Indians*. Anthropological Papers, vol. 2, pt. 1, 1-163. New York: American Museum of Natural History.

(1996)

Questions

1. Kehoe presents a series of long excerpts from Sommers's transcription of Insima's account. Is this a more appropriate way of presenting the material than shaping it for the reader and presenting it in much shorter snippets?

2. Why were researchers at the time of the 1939 Blackfoot project not very interested in personal narratives of this sort? What were their priorities? In what way does Kehoe suggest that the priorities of the researchers dovetailed with the desires of the Blackfoot at the time?

3. For what reasons does Kehoe suggest that Sommers's transcription is a relatively reliable document?

4. Summarize in a paragraph the story of how Insima married Yellow Kidney.

5. What is suggested about the relative importance of men and women in Blackfoot society? What evidence can you point to in Insima's account itself that supports the generalizations made by Kehoe in the section "Men's and Women's Business," and by Wissler (quoted in the final paragraph of the essay)?

6. In their introduction to the volume in which this essay first appeared, Jennifer S.H. Brown and Elizabeth Vibert suggest that Insima's account of her life "counters the 'braves and buffalo' stereotypes of classic plains anthropology and imagery." What are some of the ways in which these stereotypes are undermined in Insima's account? To what extent might this be the result of Insima herself being an extraordinary individual (as opposed to being the result of a failure on the part of historians and anthropologists to take the point of view of women adequately into consideration)?

Thomas Hurka

Philosophy, Morality, and *The English Patient*

*In this article, a leading philosopher compares the
moral perspective implicit in the film* The English Patient
with that implied in Casablanca, *and argues that
each reflects the spirit of its time.*

❧

The movie *The English Patient*, based on the novel by Michael Ondaatje,
won nine Academy Awards this year, including Best Picture. This last
award normally goes only to serious movies, ones that address important
themes. But looked at this way, *The English Patient* is a disturbing choice.
It has a moral perspective on the events it describes, but it is a me-centered
and immoral one. Philosophy can help explain why.

In saying this, I don't assume that all art is subject to moral critique, a
common view in the nineteenth century. At that time, people believed that
even landscape painting and instrumental music have as their main function
to morally improve their audience, and should be evaluated for how well
they do so. I think it's obvious that many works of art have no moral content,
so a moral commentary on them is irrelevant. But other works, especially of
literature and drama, raise and explore moral issues. And when they do, we
can ask how well they do so.

The English Patient has a moral issue at the center of its plot. In an
Italian villa at the end of the Second World War, a burn victim is slowly
dying. His face is scarred beyond recognition, and he claims not to know
his own identity. But one character, Caravaggio, has figured out who the
patient is. He is Count Laszlo de Almasy, a Hungarian desert explorer who
just before the war gave the German army crucial desert maps that enabled
them to attack Tobruk and almost win the war in North Africa. Caravaggio
himself was captured and tortured in that offensive. He thinks Almasy is

guilty of betrayal and wants to bring him to account. Caravaggio has killed everyone else responsible for his capture and torture, and he now wants to kill Almasy. So a key question is: *did Almasy act wrongly in handing over the maps?* The rest of the movie addresses this question by showing what led to his choice.

Before the war Almasy was deeply in love with a married woman, Katherine Clifton. Much of the movie describes their passionate and all-consuming affair. But just before the outbreak of hostilities, Katherine was seriously injured in a desert plane crash that also killed her husband. Almasy, who was present, carried her to shelter in a cave and promised to return with help. His first attempt to get that help, from the British army, was rebuffed. Confronted by someone with no identification papers and a foreign accent, they instead arrested him as a spy. After escaping from the British, Almasy went to the German army. But to get their help he needed to offer them something in return. As the only way to keep his promise to Katherine, and from profound love for her, he gave the Germans the maps.

When he hears this story Caravaggio says he no longer has any desire to punish Almasy. The "poison," he says, has left him. And the movie's treatment of Almasy is now overwhelmingly sympathetic. Its emotional high point comes when Almasy, finding he has returned to Katherine too late, emerges from the cave carrying her dead body. Tears stream down his face; the photography is lush and gorgeous; the background music swells. As portrayed here Almasy is an entirely romantic figure. There is an equally sympathetic treatment as Almasy, having requested a morphine overdose, dies at the movie's end. Again both the camera and his nurse surround him with unqualified love.

After his escape from the British, Almasy faced a choice between a political end, resisting Nazism or at least not colluding with it, and a personal end, keeping his promise to Katherine. And the movie's treatment implies that his preference for the personal end was understandable and even right. This is implicit in the movie's most important line, a remark of Katherine's that it emphasizes by repeating: "Betrayals in war are childlike compared to our betrayals in peace." Loyalty in love, this line says, is more important than loyalty to political ends such as those fought for in war. Whatever its consequences for politics, any action done from love is right.

It is this utter denigration of the political that makes *The English Patient* immoral. There was not just some political end at stake in the Second World War; there was resistance to Nazism, a movement threatening millions of innocent people. Yet the movie treats even this end as morally

5

inconsequential. Its attitude is therefore the opposite of that taken in *Casablanca*, a movie likewise set in North Africa in the Second World War. In *Casablanca* Humphrey Bogart's character Rick sacrifices his love for Ilsa in order to join the fight against Nazism. As he tells her and her husband, "The problems of three little people don't amount to a hill of beans in this crazy world." In *The English Patient*, by contrast, the fight against Nazism is blithely sacrificed for love. The problems of the world, the movie says, and of the millions of people threatened by Nazism don't amount to a hill of beans beside those of two love-crazed people.

This critique of *The English Patient* is most compelling given a certain assumption about its plot; that given the time it took Almasy to reach the British army, escape from them, and reach the Germans, he should have known there was no chance Katherine would be alive when he reached the cave. He was keeping a promise to someone dead, and however romantic that may be, it has little moral weight beside a duty not to collude with Nazism.

This assumption may be challenged, however. Maybe Almasy got to the Germans fast enough that he did have a reasonable chance of saving Katherine. Then his choice was fraught in a way that Rick's in *Casablanca* is not. Whatever Rick does, he knows Ilsa will be safe. But for Almasy to honor the political demand is to consign his loved one to death. Given this circumstance, is his choice so obviously wrong?

10   *The English Patient*, revealingly, doesn't bother to settle this morally crucial detail of plot. But let's grant that Katherine might still have been alive. A movie could then portray Almasy as caught between two powerful but conflicting moral demands, one personal and one political, with some horrible violation inevitable whichever choice he makes. If he resists Nazism he fails the woman he loves; if he saves her he colludes with moral evil. This possible movie has the structure some find in classical Greek tragedies such as Aeschylus's *Agamemnon*, where the protagonist faces a tragic conflict between two competing moral duties and cannot avoid doing something morally wrong. Whichever duty he chooses, he is guilty of violating the other and must pay for that guilt. But this possible movie is not *The English Patient*, which gives Almasy's political duty no serious attention at all. Here, when love is at stake, its demands not only outweigh the competing demands of politics but render them trivial.

This is certainly Almasy's view. Before the war he thought the coming conflict was just one between silly nationalisms. In the Italian villa, after his story has been told, he thinks his choice about the maps was not just right but obviously so. Told that his explorer friend Madox killed himself when he learned of Almasy's betrayal, he is simply and entirely surprised: *why would anyone react like that?* And he offers excuses for his choice that are morally pathetic. One is that his action did not mean that any extra people were killed; it only changed which people were killed. But even if this is true (and how does Almasy know it?), he couldn't have known it at the time. His transfer of the maps could easily have led to a Nazi victory in North Africa, with incalculable effects on the future course of the war. And doesn't it matter whether the people killed in war are guilty Nazi aggressors or morally innocent defenders?

Almasy's view is also the movie's. As I have said, its treatment of him, especially in its most emotionally loaded scenes, is entirely sympathetic. And this sympathy is almost inevitable given the way the movie frames the moral issue Almasy faces.

In a recent moral defense of the movie, Ondaatje has borrowed from that central line of Katherine's. Its theme, he says, is "love, desire, betrayals in war and betrayals in peace." This is indeed how the movie presents Almasy's choice, as one between conflicting loyalties and different possible betrayals. But the concepts of loyalty and betrayal are essentially personalized or me-centered: *I can be loyal to a person I love or to the nation I belong to or to a group of people specially connected to ME. But I can't be loyal to a stranger, and I can't betray a stranger.* In framing the moral issue as it does, the movie frames it in an essentially me-centered way. Almasy is to ask himself which of the people specially connected to him he should care most about, or which attachment to him, that of his lover or of his nation, is morally most important.

But this approach entirely ignores a more impersonal type of moral demand. This demand is impersonal not in the sense that it is not about people but in that it is about people independently of any special connection to oneself, or just as human beings. Other people matter morally in themselves and we have duties to care about them whatever their relation to us. This impersonal type of duty was utterly central in the Second World War. Nazism threatened the lives of millions of innocent people and regardless of their nationality those people needed protection. This is clearly recognized in *Casablanca*. In that movie Rick has no reason of loyalty to join the fight against Nazism; he is an American and the U.S. is not yet in the war. But he sees that, loyalties aside, Nazism is an evil that must be resisted. His reason for fighting is therefore not me-centered but in the sense I am using impersonal. And this kind of reason is given no place in *The English Patient*. By recognizing only the concepts of loyalty and betrayal, that movie leaves no room for a demand to care about people only as people.

15　　That is why the movie inevitably sympathizes with Almasy's choice. If the alternatives are loyalty to a particular person one loves and loyalty to something as abstract as a nation, of course the former is more important. It's the same with E.M. Forster's famous remark that if he had to choose between betraying his country and betraying his friend, he hoped he would have the guts to betray his country. As described, that choice again seems correct. But in each case this is only because the choice is described in a tendentiously incomplete way, one leaving out impersonal considerations. And those considerations are often morally decisive. Consider: if you had to choose between betraying your friend and colluding in the murder of millions of innocent people, would you hope you had the guts to murder those people?

This is the central immorality of *The English Patient*: its reduction of all moral demands to me-centered demands, those based on other people's relationships to oneself. The reduction appears in many places in the movie.

One is its taking seriously another of Almasy's pathetic excuses. He wasn't guilty of betrayal in handing over the maps, he says, because the British betrayed him first in refusing him help to save Katherine. Set aside the question of whether the British really did mistreat Almasy at all. With the world on the brink of war, he was in disputed territory with no papers; he was abusive in his manners and gave no satisfactory explanation for his request. But that aside, why should one little betrayal by the British license him to collude with Nazis? That conclusion would only follow if the coming war were, as Almasy thought, just another conflict between silly nationalisms. But of course in this war one side, whatever the other's failings, was incomparably morally worse. That is why Elizabeth Pathy Salett was entirely correct to say, in the *Washington Post* article to which Ondaatje responded, that the movie's "presentation of a moral equivalency between the Germans and Allies trivializes the significance of the choices men like Almasy made."

Even the voice against Almasy in the movie speaks in me-centered terms. That voice is Caravaggio, and what does Caravaggio want? He above all wants revenge, and revenge is again a personalized concept: *I can want revenge only for a wrong done to me or someone closely connected to me, and I get revenge only if I inflict it myself.* In both respects a desire for revenge contrasts with a desire for justice, which can be aroused by wrong-doing against anyone and can be satisfied when punishment is imposed by anyone, including the impersonal state. But expressing the moral challenge to Almasy in terms of revenge again has a trivializing effect. It reduces that challenge to a "poison" that can be easily extracted when Almasy's story is told. And it utterly underdescribes the subject of that challenge. As part of his torture Caravaggio had his thumbs cut off. This means that he can no longer do sleight of hand tricks—when he tries one with an egg he drops it—and can no longer ply his former trade as a pickpocket. It is hard to think of a less adequate representation of the threat posed by Nazism.

Here are, then, three levels of moral critique of *The English Patient*. First, the movie sympathizes with a choice that is simply morally wrong. Second, it sees nothing at all problematic about a choice that, even if not simply wrong, violates an important political duty. Third, the movie casts its moral considerations entirely in the me-centered terms of loyalty and betrayal, never recognizing the impersonal demands that were so central in its setting of the Second World War. Of these critiques the second and especially the third are philosophical. Moral philosophy does not consider issues that are completely different from those of ordinary moral thought. It considers the same issues but at a higher level of abstraction, identifying the principles and structures of principles that underlie and explain particular moral judgments. In this, as in many cases, it is the most philosophical critique that is most important. It is because it recognizes only me-centered and no impersonal moral duties that *The English Patient* sees nothing troubling in and even sympathizes with a highly questionable choice.

Casablanca was very much a product of its time. Its impersonal moral vision expresses the experience of people who were fighting to resist aggression on another continent. *The English Patient* is, unfortunately, also a product of its time, one in which many people have abandoned concern for those in other countries or even for less fortunate members of their own society. It is a time of withdrawal from the impersonal concerns of politics into a smaller realm focused on the self and its few chosen intimates. It is no surprise that *The English Patient* won its Academy Awards. The movie has the kind of high-minded tone that Academy voters find impressive. And its substance fits the depressing tenor of our time.

20

(1997)

Questions

1. Hurka concludes that *The English Patient* is "a product of its time, one in which many people have abandoned concern for those in other countries or even for less fortunate members of their own society." To what extent do you believe this to be true? Do you think it was any more or less true in 1997 when this article appeared than it is today?

2. This article is unusual in that it was written in two different versions. Hurka originally published a newspaper column on this topic in *The Globe and Mail*; that piece is posted on the website for *The Broadview Anthology of Expository Prose*. The column ignited a storm of controversy, and in the wake of many letters to the editor Hurka was asked by *Queen's Quarterly* to write a longer version for publication in that journal (an academic publication, but one that aims for an audience outside the academy as well as within it). After reading the original newspaper version, compare the two. What elements in particular does Hurka expand on in writing the longer version?

3. Comment on the difference in paragraphing between the two versions. Are there indications in the writing style that a somewhat different audience is being addressed? (Note in answering that the same individuals may constitute a different audience when glancing at a morning newspaper and when reading a semi-scholarly journal.)

4. What if any grounds do you feel may justify intervention by a nation or a group of nations in the affairs of another country? What practical or pragmatic considerations (if any) should also be taken into consideration? Write a brief essay on this topic, either in the abstract or using a particular current issue as your focus.

5. A key principle that Hurka espouses when he talks about writing is that the writer should devote space in an essay to the different ideas being presented that is commensurate with the importance placed by the writer on each of those ideas. On those grounds, what can be said about which of Hurka's ideas he feels to be most important?

JUDITH RICH HARRIS

WHERE IS THE CHILD'S ENVIRONMENT? A GROUP SOCIALIZATION THEORY OF DEVELOPMENT[1]

This article is one of the most controversial and influential
academic research papers of its time. In it, Harris calls into
question both the prevailing theory on which much
of modern parenting has been based and the ground on
which the nature/nurture debate has been conducted.

❧

In 1983, after many dozens of pages spent reviewing the literature on the effects parents have on children, Eleanor Maccoby and John Martin paused for a critical overview of the field of socialization research. They questioned the size and robustness of the effects they had just summarized; they wondered whether the number of significant correlations was greater than that expected by chance. They cited other research indicating that biological or adoptive siblings do not develop similar personalities as a result of being reared in the same household. This was their conclusion:

> These findings imply strongly that there is very little impact of the physical environment that parents provide for children and very little impact of parental characteristics that must be essentially the same for all children in a family ... Indeed, the implications

1   I thank the following people, who do not necessarily agree with the views presented here, for their helpful comments on earlier versions of this work: William A. Corsaro, Judith L. Gibbons, Charles S. Harris, Neil J. Salkind, Sandra Scarr, and Naomi Weisstein. [Unless otherwise noted, all notes to this essay are from the author.]

are either that parental behaviors have no effect, or that the only effective aspects of parenting must vary greatly from one child to another within the same family. (Maccoby & Martin, 1983, p. 82)

Since 1983, many developmental psychologists have focused on the second of Maccoby and Martin's two possible implications, "that the only effective aspects of parenting must vary greatly from one child to another." The other possibility, "that parental behaviors have no effect," has never been considered as a serious alternative.

This article examines both alternatives. I begin by showing why "must vary greatly from one child to another" cannot explain the results that puzzled Maccoby and Martin. Then I consider the possibility "that parental behaviors have no effect." The conclusion reached is that, within the range of families that have been studied, parental behaviors have no effect on the psychological characteristics their children will have as adults. To explain this outcome, I propose a theory of group socialization (GS theory), based on the findings of behavioral genetics, on sociological views of intra- and intergroup processes, on psychological research showing that learning is highly context-specific, and on evolutionary considerations.

DOES THE FAMILY ENVIRONMENT MATTER?

By the time they are adults, adoptive siblings who were reared in the same home will, on average, bear no resemblance to each other in personality. Biological siblings who were reared in the same home will be somewhat more alike, but still not very similar. Even identical (monozygotic) twins reared in the same home will not be identical in personality. They will not be noticeably more alike than identical twins reared in separate homes (Bouchard, Lykken, McGue, Segal, & Tellegen, 1990; Plomin & Daniels, 1987; Scarr, 1992).

5   These are some of the findings of the field of developmental behavioral genetics. The data on which they are based consist of correlations between pairs of people who share all, some, or none of their genes, and who did or did not grow up in the same home. Two conclusions—one surprising and the other not—emerged from the analysis of such data. The unsurprising conclusion was that about half of the variance in the measured psychological characteristics was due to differences in heredity. The surprising conclusion involved the other half of the variance: Very little of it could be attributed to differences in the home environments in which the participants

in these studies were reared (Loehlin & Nichols, 1976; Plomin, Chipuer, & Neiderhiser, 1994; Plomin & Daniels, 1987; Scarr, 1992).

Behavioral Genetic Methods and Results

Behavioral genetic studies begin by collecting data—for example, scores on personality or intelligence tests—from pairs of people. Ideally, data from two or more types of subject pairs, such as twins and adoptive siblings, are combined in the data analysis. That makes it possible to test different mathematical models, based on slightly different assumptions, to see which provides the best fit for the data. The winning model is then used to divide up the variance calculated from the test scores—the individual differences among the subjects—into three, or sometimes four, sectors.

The first sector consists of variance that can be attributed to shared genes; this is called *heritability*. Heritability generally accounts for 40% to 50% of the variance in personality characteristics, if the measurements are made in adulthood (McGue, Bouchard, Iacono, & Lykken, 1993; N.L. Pedersen, Plomin, Nesselroade, & McClearn, 1992; Plomin, Owen, & McGuffin, 1994).

The second sector consists of variance that can be attributed to *shared environmental influence*—the home in which a given pair of people were reared. This sector is very small if the measurements are made in adulthood: from 0 to 10% in most studies (Bouchard, 1994; Lochlin, 1992; Plomin & Daniels, 1987). The implication of this finding is that resemblances between siblings are due almost entirely to shared genes. Their shared environment has not made them more alike.

The third sector consists of measurement error, which is around 20% for personality tests (Plomin, 1990). Some analyses do not produce an estimate for this component of the variance, in which case it is included in the last sector, which consists of variance that can be attributed neither to shared genes nor to shared rearing environment (Goldsmith, 1993a). This sector of the variance is usually referred to as *nonshared environmental influence*, but a more accurate label for it is *unexplained environmental variance*. On the average, from 40% to 50% of the variance in adult personality characteristics falls into the unexplained or nonshared sector.

If heredity can account for only about half of the reliable variation among adults, then environmental influences must account for the rest. The challenge is to find the source of these influences. Behavioral genetic studies have demonstrated which aspects of the environment are *not* likely to be important. The aspects that are not likely to be important are all those

10

that are shared by children who grow up in the same home: the parents' personalities and philosophies of child rearing, their presence or absence in the home, the number of books or TV sets or guns the home contains, and so on. In short, almost all of the factors previously associated with the term *environment*, and associated even more closely with the term *nurture*, appear to be ineffective in shaping children's personalities.

Within-Family Environmental Differences

This outcome went against the deeply held beliefs of many developmental psychologists. But, unlike the socialization research that was judged by Maccoby and Martin (1983) to be lacking in robustness, the findings of behavioral genetics are quite reliable. The results are consistent within and between studies and cannot readily be explained away (Scarr, 1993). Children reared in the same home by the same parents do not, on average, turn out to be similar unless they share genes, and even if they share all of their genes, they are not as similar as one might expect. For identical twins reared in the same home, correlations of personality characteristics are seldom above .50, which leaves at least 30% of the variance unexplained by shared genes plus a shared home environment.[2]

Faced with these results, most behavioral geneticists and many socialization theorists turned to Maccoby and Martin's (1983) second alternative, "that the only effective aspects of parenting must vary greatly from one child to another within the same family" (p. 82). The unexplained variance was attributed to *within-family environmental differences* (Daniels and Plomin, 1985; Dunn, 1992; Hoffman, 1991). According to this concept, each child in a family inhabits his or her unique niche in the ecology of the family, and it is within these niches, or *microenvironments* (Braungart, Plomin, DeFries, & Fulker, 1992; Dunn & Plomin, 1990), that the formative aspects of development are presumed to occur.

In the past decade, much attention has been focused on these microenvironments. That they exist is unquestionable; the question is whether they can account for almost half the variance in personality characteristics. The next section summarizes the evidence that has led one

---

2   A correlation of .50 between twins means that .50 of the variance covaries between them; therefore the correlation accounts for 50% of the variance in that measure (for a detailed explanation, see Plomin, 1990). Allowing 20% for measurement error leaves 30% of the variance unaccounted for.

behavioral geneticist to admit that the matter "remains largely a mystery" (Bouchard, 1994, p. 1701) and another to conclude that the family environment (macro- and micro-) may, in fact, "exert little influence on personality development over the life course" (Rowe, 1994, p. 1).

* * *

WHO SOCIALIZES THE CHILD?

In the days when psychoanalytic theory was an influential force in developmental psychology, a child learned how to behave by identifying with his father or her mother. Identification, around age 4 or 5, led to the formation of a superego; good behavior was then enforced by the superego. Fraiberg (1959) used this theory to account for the fact that most children learn family rules and become less likely to violate them as they get older. As an illustration she offered the story of Julia and the eggs:

> Thirty-month-old Julia finds herself alone in the kitchen while her mother is on the telephone. A bowl of eggs is on the table. An urge is experienced by Julia to make scrambled eggs....When Julia's mother returns to the kitchen, she finds her daughter cheerfully plopping eggs on the linoleum and scolding herself sharply for each plop, "NoNoNo. Mustn't dood it. NoNoNo. *Mustn't* dood it!" (Fraiberg, 1959, p. 135)

Fraiberg attributed this lapse to the fact that Julia had not yet acquired a superego, presumably because she had not yet identified with her mother. But notice what Julia was doing: By making "scrambled eggs" and yelling "NoNoNo!" she was behaving exactly like her mother. What Julia must learn is that she is not allowed to behave like her mother. Children in our society spend their early years discovering that they cannot do most of the things they see their parents doing—making messes, telling other people how to behave, and engaging in many other activities that look like fun to those who are not allowed to do them.

Cross-Cultural Considerations

Julia's dilemma is not unique to our society; there are many societies in which the distinction between acceptable adult behavior and acceptable child behavior is greater than in our own. In the Marquesas Islands

15

of Polynesia, children must learn two different sets of rules for social behavior: one for interacting with other children, the other for interacting with parents and other adults. The adult is expected to initiate and control interactions; the child is expected to be restrained and compliant (Martini, 1994). Polynesian children cannot learn the rules of social interaction by observing their parents' behavior. Furthermore, in most traditional societies, parents do not act either as playmates or as teachers to their children. The kind of parental instruction we take for granted in the United States is by no means universal. The Kaluli of Papua, New Guinea do not help children learn language by rephrasing a toddler's poorly formed sentence into proper grammar; they believe it is the responsibility of the child to make the listener understand what she or he wants to say (Snow, 1991). In the Embu District of Kenya, parents and toddlers have few verbal interactions of any sort: "Almost all sustained social interactions and most verbal interchanges of toddlers in this culture involve other children" (McDonald, Sigman, Espinosa, & Neumann, 1994, p. 411).

Fortunately, children can learn things in a variety of ways; even a creature as simple as a honeybee has more than one mechanism for getting to a flower (Gould, 1992). Many kinds of learning do not require the presence of a model, and for those that do, such as language learning, every society provides some kind of a model. In most traditional societies, the models are older children, especially siblings (Zukow, 1989). A common pattern in such societies is that toddlers are given over to the care of an older sister or brother when they are 2 or 2½, and the older sibling—who may be no more than 4 or 5—carries the younger one along to the children's play group. There the toddler might be allowed to participate as a sort of living doll or be left to watch or to whine on the sidelines (Martini, 1994; Whiting & Edwards, 1988). Thus, siblings are a part—often a major part—of the young child's social group. Outside-the-home socialization begins, according to GS theory, in this mixed-age, mixed-sex group. By preadolescence, children in most present-day societies are able to form age- and sex-segregated groups (Edwards, 1992).

Is the Family a Group?

In urbanized societies, school-age children spend most of their time outside the home in age- and sex-segregated groups that do not ordinarily include a sibling. Most of their interactions with their siblings and parents occur within the home. Does the family function like a group? Does the child identify with this group?

In some societies—particularly Asian societies—the answer appears to be yes. Chinese, Japanese, and Indian cultures emphasize the importance of the family group or social group and deemphasize the importance of the individual; independence and autonomy are not considered virtues in a child (Cole, 1992; Guisinger & Blatt, 1994; Miller, 1987; H.W. Stevenson, Chen, & Lee, 1992). In precolonial China, if a man committed a serious crime, his siblings, parents, and children were executed along with him, the idea being that the whole family shared in the responsibility (Heckathorn, 1992).

In contrast, Western culture puts the emphasis on the individual rather than the group (Guisinger & Blatt, 1994; Miller, 1987). Only in certain situations—for example, when they are traveling together in an unfamiliar area—are the members of North American or European families likely to function as a group. When they are at home together, I believe that they function as individuals, each with her own agenda, his own patch of turf to defend. They are not a group because the social category *our family* is not salient. It is not salient because no other social categories are present, either actually or symbolically (Turner, 1987), in the privacy of the contemporary Western home.

Within-Family Effects

When group identity is not salient, differentiation is likely to predominate over assimilation. If siblings see themselves as separate individuals rather than as part of the family group, status hierarchies and social comparisons may increase the differences among them. Dominance hierarchies would tend to make older siblings dominant over younger ones, which happens as a matter of course in most societies and which North American parents try very hard, and not very successfully, to prevent (Whiting & Edwards, 1988). However, there is little or no resemblance between children's relationships with their siblings and their relationships with their peers (Abramovitch et al., 1986; Stocker & Dunn, 1990), which is consistent with the finding that birth order has no reliable effects on personality (Ernst & Angst, 1983; Reiss et al., 1994).

Social comparisons between siblings may have more interesting consequences. Tesser's (1988) self-evaluation maintenance theory predicts that siblings should each develop specialties of their own—areas that they consider important to their self-definition and in which they are willing to compete. If one sibling is an excellent pianist, for example, the other sibling may avoid playing the piano for fear of being bested in the comparison. Note that this "niche-picking" process does not require any parental intervention or labeling: it involves only the two individuals in question. Nor is there need to postulate a special motivator; within-group jockeying for status, found in most human and nonhuman primate groups, is sufficient to do the job.

Within-family social comparisons should also widen personality differences between siblings—a within-family contrast effect. If this effect occurs, it must be small in magnitude. Schachter (1982) asked college students to judge how similar they were to their siblings and found a tendency toward polarization of personality attributes that was significant only between firstborns and secondborns. Loehlin (1992) investigated the possibility that a contrast effect might occur between twins who are reared together; he assumed that if such an effect existed, it would make twins reared together less similar in personality than twins reared apart. He found that twins reared together were somewhat *more* similar than those reared apart[3] and concluded that no contrast effect had occurred. However, twins reared together also share an environment outside the home; they go to the same school and often belong to the same peer group. According to GS theory, the shared outside-the-home environment should make twins reared together more alike than twins reared apart; thus, if they are not more alike, a within-family contrast effect may be reducing their similarity. Notice that this prediction—that inside-the-family effects will make twins more different and outside-the-family effects will make them more alike—is exactly the opposite of the assumption made by behavioral geneticists.

Parental Influence Versus Peer Influence

In a number of studies, researchers have asked children and adolescents questions of the form, "What would you do if your friends wanted you to do something that your parents told you not to do?" (e.g., Berndt, 1979; Bowerman & Kinch, 1969). Depending on the precise wording of the question, the results generally show that parents' influence is high during the early school years and then gradually declines, and that peers' influence is low at first and gradually increases, reaching a peak in early adolescence.

Such experiments are misleading or irrelevant for several reasons. First, the questions are asked by a researcher who is an adult. Given the context-sensitivity of social behavior, the replies might be different if the questioner

25

---

3   Although Loehlin found that identical twins reared together were more similar in personality than those reared apart, other researchers (e.g., Bouchard et al., 1990) have found reared-apart and reared-together identical twins to be equally similar.

were a child. Second, replies to questions of the type "What would you do if ...?" have low validity, as shown by the lack of correspondence between tests of moral judgment and tests of moral behavior (see Perry & Bussey, 1984). Third, the questions tend to focus on emotionally charged relationships, rather than on behavior; in effect, the child is being asked, "Whom do you love more, your parents or your friends?" Finally, children generally belong to peer groups that share their attitudes and, in many cases, their parents' attitudes. They may know that their friends would not ask them to do something dangerous or illegal.

When researchers observe, rather than ask questions, peer influence is found to be potent, even at ages and in circumstances where parental influence would be expected to have priority. For example, it is well known that preschoolers are loath to eat certain foods, despite much favorable propaganda or forceful urging from their parents. As Birch (1987) discovered, the best way to induce children of this age to eat a disliked food is to put them at a table with a group of children who like it.

Absence of Parents Versus Absence of Peers

No one can question the fact that, without parents, babies and young children are bitterly unhappy (Bowlby, 1969); in fact, an early attachment to a caregiver appears to be a requirement for normal social development (Rutter, 1979), just as early exposure to light and pattern is a requirement for normal development of the visual system (Mitchell, 1980). However, case studies involving deprivation of one kind or another suggest that the absence of peers may have more serious long-term consequences than the absence of parents. Rhesus monkeys reared without peers are more abnormal as adults than those reared without a mother (Harlow & Harlow, 1962/1975). The case of the Jewish children who spent their first 3 years together in a Nazi concentration camp (Freud & Dann, 1951) suggests that the same may be true for humans. The six children had been cared for in the concentration camp by an everchanging series of adults, none of whom survived. When the children arrived in England and came to the attention of Anna Freud, they were found to be completely indifferent—if not hostile—to all adults; they cared only about each other. According to Hartup (1983), these children grew up to become normal adults and at last report were leading "effective lives" (pp. 157-158).

Cases like Victor, the wild boy of Aveyron (Lane, 1976), and Genie, the locked-up girl of California (Curtiss, 1977), do not have happy endings.

Note, though, that these children were deprived not only of normal parent-child relationships but of normal peer relationships as well. There is a case in which two children—twins—were isolated but were locked up together; these children were completely rehabilitated after a few years in which they lived with a foster family and attended school (Koluchová, 1972, 1976).

Dyadic Relationships Versus Group Processes

The view that early relationships with parents are of central importance in personality development is a legacy from psychoanalytic psychology. Among the modern adherents to this view are the attachment theorists (Ainsworth, Blehar, Waters, & Wall, 1978; Bowlby, 1969). According to attachment theory, infants whose mothers care for them in a sensitive, responsive way are likely to become securely attached to their mothers; secure attachments increase the chances of success in later undertakings, especially those that are social in nature. Security of attachment is assessed by observing a child's behavior, generally at age 12 or 13 months, when the mother leaves the child in an unfamiliar laboratory room and then returns a short time later. Children who greet their mothers with unalloyed joy are adjudged securely attached (Ainsworth et al., 1978; Belsky, Rovine, & Taylor, 1984; Sroufe, 1985).

30 There are two major problems that make most socialization research, including the attachment literature, difficult to interpret. First is the nature-or-nurture problem. Behavioral geneticists have pointed out clearly and repeatedly (e.g., Plomin & Daniels, 1987; Scarr, 1993) that most socialization studies lack an essential control: If all the pairs of research participants share 50% of their genes, as do mothers and their biological children, there is no way of factoring out the effects of heredity from those of environment. There is no way of telling whether the observed resemblances between the mothers and their children (in friendliness, nervousness, competence, etc.) are due to heredity, environment, or both.

Second is the cause-or-effect problem. A mother-child relationship, like all dyadic relationships, involves two people who each play a role in the success of the relationship (Hartup & Laursen, 1991; Hinde & Stevenson-Hinde, 1986). Just as some adults are better than others at caring for infants, some infants are better than others at evoking sensitive, responsive parenting. Because infants who are particularly appealing to their mothers are also likely to be appealing to other people, a child who does well in one relationship is likely to do well in others (Jacobson & Wille, 1986).

Thus, it is surprising to discover that the correlations among a child's various relationships are actually quite low. A child who is securely attached to Mother is not necessarily securely attached to Father (Fox, Kimmerly, & Schafer, 1991; Main & Weston, 1981) or to other caregivers (Goossens & van Ijzendoorn, 1990). Efforts to link parent-child relationships with child-peer relationships have had inconsistent results; some studies (Pastor, 1981; Waters, Wippman, & Sroufe, 1979) find a correlation, others do not (Howes, Matheson, & Hamilton, 1994). Sometimes correlations are found that are "counterintuitive" (Youngblade, Park, & Belsky, 1993, p. 564). As mentioned previously, there is also little or no correlation between the nature of children's sibling relationships and their relationships with their peers (Abramovitch et al., 1986; Stocker & Dunn, 1990). These findings are surprising because it is the same child, with the same genes, who participates in all of these relationships.

The most reasonable explanation of why these correlations are so low is that behaviors, emotions, and cognitions acquired in a dyadic relationship are specific to that relationship (Hinde & Stevenson-Hinde, 1986; MacKinnon-Lewis et al., 1994). There may be, as Bowlby (1969) proposed, a "working model" of the mother-child relationship in the child's mind, but if so, it is trotted out only when Mother is around. A child discovers very early in life that learning what to expect from Mother is of limited usefulness for dealing with Father or Sister. A child who has learned through hard experience to avoid the school bully does not avoid all of the other children on the playground (Asendorpf & van Aken, 1994).

Evolutionary considerations discussed earlier led to the view that dyadic relationships and group affiliation are driven by separate adaptive mechanisms. Consistent with this view is the finding that children's group relationships are to a large extent independent of their dyadic relationships. Although there are children who get along poorly in every social context, many children who have low status in the group are able to form successful friendships (Bukowski & Hoza, 1989; Parker & Asher, 1993a, 1993b).

According to GS theory, identification with a group, not participation in dyadic relationships, is responsible for environmental modifications of personality characteristics. If two people are a dyad and three are a group, this distinction may appear to be splitting hairs. However, the difference between group processes and dyadic relationships is not just a matter of number. The important point about human groups is that they are social categories. When children categorize themselves as members of a group, they take on its norms of behavior (Turner, 1987). A child who says, "Oh

35

Mom, I can't wear that, the kids will laugh at me," is not worrying about the reaction of her best friend—she is worried about the consequences of violating group norms.

In dyadic relationships, children learn how to behave with Person A, with Person B, and with Person C. In the peer group they learn how to behave in public.

The Transient Effects of the Home Environment

Behavioral genetic data indicate that any transient effect of the home environment on personality fades by adulthood—shared environment accounts for little or no variance in adult characteristics. According to GS theory, the reason the home environment has no lasting effects is that children are predisposed to favor the outside-the-home behavioral system over the one they acquired at home. Children who learn one language at home and a different one outside the home become increasingly reluctant to speak the home language, even at home (Baron, 1992). The language they speak with their peers will become their "native language" when they are adults (Bickerton, 1983).

Some researchers have claimed that the reason the immigrant child drops the home language is that it lacks economic and cultural prestige; it is not valued by the community (Umbel, Pearson, Fernandez, & Oller, 1992). Evidence against this view comes from deaf children born to hearing parents during the era when sign language was not valued by the community—in fact, the community tried hard to suppress it. This misguided effort failed. When these children went to schools where, for the first time, they met other deaf children, they picked up sign language in the dormitories. Sign language was brought into the schools by the deaf children of deaf parents, and all the children used it surreptitiously to converse among themselves (Meier, 1991; Newport, 1990). It became their "native language" despite earnest efforts by their teachers to give them a language that had greater economic and cultural prestige.

There are good evolutionary reasons why children might be biologically predisposed to discard what they learned in their first few years of life. First, their parental home is not where they are likely to spend their future. As Erikson (1963) noted about the school-age child, "There is no workable future within the womb of his family" (p. 259). In order to survive and reproduce, children must be able to function successfully in the world outside their home. They must form alliances that go beyond the nuclear family.

Second, children are already similar to their parents for genetic reasons—the 40% or 50% of the variance that is attributable to heritability. If environmental influences added to and increased these similarities, children would be so much like their parents and siblings that the family might lack sufficient variability. This would decrease the number and variety of ecological niches the members of the family could fit into and reduce the likelihood that at least one child would survive.

There is a biological mechanism that reduces the chances of incest: In humans and other animals, the sex drive tends to be dampened by stimuli that are too familiar. Members of the opposite sex who are familiar from infancy and early childhood are generally not regarded as sexually stimulating (Tooby & Cosmides, 1990; Wilson & Daly, 1992). I suggest that a similar mechanism may operate in regard to socialization: When there is a choice, children do not choose what they learned in infancy and early childhood.

REFERENCES

Abramovitch, R., Corter, C., Pepler, D.J., & Stanhope, L. (1986). Sibling and peer interaction: A final follow-up and a comparison. *Child Development, 57*, 217-229.

Ainsworth, M.D.S., Blehar, M.C., Waters, E., & Wall, S. (1978). *Patterns of attachment: A psychological study of the Strange Situation*. Hillsdale, NJ: Erlbaum.

Asendorpf, J.B., & van Aken, M.A.G. (1994). Traits and relationship status: Stranger versus peer group inhibition and test intelligence versus peer group competence as early predictors of later self-esteem. *Child Development, 65*, 1786-1798.

Baron, N.S. (1992). *Growing up with language: How children learn to talk*. Reading, MA: Addison-Wesley.

Belsky, J., Rovine, M., & Taylor, D.G. (1984). The Pennsylvania Infant and Family Development Project: III. The origins of individual differences in infant-mother attachment: Maternal and infant contributions. *Child Development, 55*, 718-728.

Berndt, T.J. (1979). Developmental changes in conformity to peers and parents. *Developmental Psychology, 15*, 606-616.

Bickerton, D. (1983, July). Creole languages. *Scientific American, 249*, 116–122.

Birch, L.L. (1987). Children's food preferences: Developmental patterns and environmental influences. *Annals of Child Development*, *4*, 171-208.

Bouchard, T.J., Jr. (1994, June 17). Genes, environment, and personality. *Science*, *264*, 1700-1701.

Bouchard, T.J., Jr., Lykken, D.T., McGue, M., Segal, N.L., & Tellegen, A. (1990, October 12). Sources of human psychological differences: The Minnesota Study of Twins Reared Apart. *Science*, *250*, 223-228.

Bowerman, C.E., & Kinch, J.W. (1969). Changes in family and peer orientation of children between the fourth and tenth grades. In M. Gold & E. Douvan (Eds.), *Adolescent development* (pp. 137-141). Boston: Allyn & Bacon.

Bowlby, J. (1969). *Attachment and loss: Vol. 1. Attachment.* New York: Basic Books.

Braungart, J.M., Plomin, R., DeFries, J.C., & Fulker, D.W. (1992). Genetic influence on tester–rated infant temperament as assessed by Bayley's Infant Behavior Record: Nonadoptive and adoptive siblings and twins. *Developmental Psychology*, *28*, 40-47.

Bukowski, W.M., & Hoza, B. (1989). Popularity and friendship: Issues in theory, measurement, and outcome. In T.J. Berndt & G.W. Ladd (Eds.), *Peer relationships in child development* (pp. 15-45). New York: Wiley.

Cole, M. (1992). Culture in development. In M.H. Bornstein & M.E. Lamb (Eds.), *Developmental psychology: An advanced textbook* (pp. 731-789). Hillsdale, NJ: Erlbaum.

Curtiss, S.R. (1977). *Genie: A linguistic study of a modern day "wild child."* New York: Academic Press.

Daniels, D., & Plomin, R. (1985). Differential experience of siblings in the same family. *Developmental Psychology*, *21*, 747-760.

Dunn, J. (1992). Siblings and development. *Current Directions in Psychological Science*, *1*, 6-9.

Dunn, J., & Plomin, R. (1990). *Separate lives: Why siblings are so different.* New York: Basic Books.

Edwards, C.P. (1992). Cross-cultural perspectives on family-peer relations. In R.D. Parke & G.W. Ladd (Eds.), *Family-peer relationships: Modes of linkage* (pp. 285-316). Hillsdale, NJ: Erlbaum.

Erikson, E.H. (1963). *Childhood and society* (2nd ed.). New York: Norton.

Ernst, C., & Angst, J. (1983). *Birth order: Its influence on personality.* Berlin, Germany: Springer-Verlag.

Fox, N.A., Kimmerly, N.L., & Schafer, W.D. (1991). Attachment to mother/attachment to father: A meta-analysis. *Child Development*, *62*, 210-225.

Fraiberg, S. (1959). *The magic years*. New York: Scribner's.

Freud, A., & Dann, S. (1951). An experiment in group upbringing. *Psychoanalytic Study of the Child*, *6*, 127-168.

Goldsmith, H.H. (1993a). Nature-nurture issues in the behavioral genetics context: Overcoming barriers to communication. In R. Plomin & G.E. McClearn (Eds.), *Nature, nurture, and psychology* (pp. 325-339). Washington, DC: American Psychological Association.

Goossens, F.A., & van Ijzendoorn, M.H. (1990). Quality of infants' attachments to professional caregivers: Relation to infant-parent attachment and day-care characteristics. *Child Development*, *61*, 550-567.

Gould, J.L. (1992). Interpreting the honeybee's dance. *American Scientist*, *80*, 278-279.

Guisinger, S., & Blatt, S.J. (1994). Individuality and relatedness: Evolution of a fundamental dialectic. *American Psychologist*, *49*, 104-111.

Harlow, H.F., & Harlow, M.K. (1975). Social deprivation in monkeys. In R.C. Atkinson (Ed.), *Readings from Scientific American: Psychology in progress* (pp. 225-233). San Francisco: Freeman. (Original work published 1962).

Hartup, W.W. (1983). Peer relations. In P.H. Mussen (Series Ed.) & E.M. Hetherington (Vol. Ed.), *Handbook of child psychology: Vol. 4. Socialization, personality, and social development* (4th ed., pp. 103-196). New York: Wiley.

Hartup, W.W., & Laursen, B. (1991). Relationships as developmental contexts. In R. Cohen & A.W. Siegel (Eds.), *Context and development* (pp. 253-279). Hillsdale, NJ: Erlbaum.

Heckathorn, D.D. (1992). Collective sanctions and group heterogeneity: Cohesion and polarization in normative systems. In E.J. Lawler, B. Markovsky, C. Ridgeway, & H.A. Walker (Eds.), *Advances in group processes* (Vol. 9, pp. 41-63). Greenwich, CT: JAI Press.

Hinde, R.A., & Stevenson-Hinde, J. (1986). Relating childhood relationships to individual characteristics. In W.W. Hartup & Z. Rubin (Eds.), *Relationships and development* (pp. 27-50). Hillsdale, NJ: Erlbaum.

Hoffman, L.W. (1991). The influence of the family environment on personality: Accounting for sibling differences. *Psychological Bulletin*, *110*, 187-203.

Howes, C., Matheson, C.C., & Hamilton, C.E. (1994). Maternal, teacher, and child care history correlates of children's relationships with peers. *Child Development*, *65*, 264-273.

Jacobson, J.L., & Wille, D.E. (1986). The influence of attachment pattern on developmental changes in peer interaction from the toddler to the preschool period. *Child Development, 57*, 338-347.

Koluchová, J. (1972). Severe deprivation in twins: A case study. *Journal of Child Psychology and Psychiatry, 13*, 107-114.

Koluchová, J. (1976). The further development of twins after severe and prolonged deprivation: A second report. *Journal of Child Psychology and Psychiatry, 17*, 181-188.

Lane, H. (1976). *The wild boy of Aveyron.* Cambridge, MA: Harvard University Press.

Loehlin, J.C. (1992). *Genes and environment in personality development.* Newbury Park, CA: Sage.

Loehlin, J.C., & Nichols, R.C. (1976). *Heredity, environment, and personality.* Austin: University of Texas Press.

Maccoby, E.E., & Martin, J.A. (1983). Socialization in the context of the family: Parent-child interaction. In P.H. Mussen (Series Ed.) & E.M. Hetherington (Vol. Ed.), *Handbook of child psychology: Vol. 4. Socialization, personality, and social development* (4th ed., pp. 1-101). New York: Wiley.

MacKinnon-Lewis, C., Volling, B.L., Lamb, M.E., Dechman, K., Rabiner, D., & Curtner, M.E. (1994). A cross-contextual analysis of boys' social competence from family to school. *Developmental Psychology, 30*, 325-333.

Main, M., & Weston, D.R. (1981). The quality of the toddler's relationship to mother and to father: Related to conflict behavior and the readiness to establish new relationships. *Child Development, 52*, 932-940.

Martini, M. (1994). Peer interactions in Polynesia: A view from the Marquesas. In J.L. Roopnarine & J.E. Johnson (Eds.), *Children's play in diverse cultures* (pp. 73-103). Albany: State University of New York Press.

McDonald, M.A., Sigman, M., Espinosa, M.P., & Neumann, C.G. (1994). Impact of a temporary food shortage on children and their mothers. *Child Development, 65*, 404-415.

McGue, M., Bouchard, T.J., Jr., Iacono, W.G., & Lykken, D.T. (1993). Behavioral genetics of cognitive ability: A life-span perspective. In R. Plomin & G.E. McClearn (Eds.), *Nature, nurture, and psychology* (pp. 59-76). Washington, DC: American Psychological Association.

Meier, R.P. (1991). Language acquisition by deaf children. *American Scientist, 79*, 60-70.

Miller, J.G. (1987). Cultural influences on the development of conceptual differentiation in person description. *British Journal of Developmental Psychology, 5*, 309-319.

Mitchell, D.E. (1980). The influence of early visual experience on visual perception. In C.S. Harris (Ed.), *Visual coding and adaptability* (pp. 1-50). Hillsdale, NJ: Erlbaum.

Newport, E.L. (1990). Maturational constraints on language learning. *Cognitive Science, 14*, 11-28.

Parker, J.G., & Asher, S.R. (1993a). Beyond group acceptance: Friendship and friendship quality as distinct dimensions of children's peer adjustment. In D. Perlman and W.H. Jones (Eds.), *Advances in personal relationships* (Vol. 4, pp. 261-294). London: Jessica Kingsley Publishers.

Parker, J.G., & Asher, S.R. (1993b). Friendship and friendship quality in middle childhood: Links with peer group acceptance and feelings of loneliness and social dissatisfaction. *Developmental Psychology, 29*, 611-621.

Pastor, D. (1981). The quality of mother-infant attachment and its relationship to toddlers' initial sociability with peers. *Developmental Psychology, 17*, 326-335.

Pedersen, N.L., Plomin, R., Nesselroade, J.R., & McClearn, G.E. (1992). A quantitative genetic analysis of cognitive abilities during the second half of the life span. *Psychological Science, 3*, 346-353.

Perry, D.G., & Bussey, K. (1984). *Social development.* Englewood Cliffs, NJ: Prentice-Hall.

Plomin, R. (1990). *Nature and nurture: An introduction to human behavioral genetics.* Pacific Grove, CA: Brooks/Cole.

Plomin, R., Chipuer, H.M., & Neiderhiser, J.M. (1994). Behavioral genetic evidence for the importance of nonshared environment. In E.M. Hetherington, D. Reiss, & R. Plomin (Eds.), *Separate social worlds of siblings: The impact of nonshared environment on development* (pp. 1-31). Hillsdale, NJ: Erlbaum.

Plomin, R., & Daniels, D. (1987). Why are children in the same family so different from one another? *Behavioral and Brain Sciences, 10*, 1-60.

Plomin, R., Owen, M.J., & McGuffin, P. (1994, June 17). The genetic basis of complex human behaviors. *Science, 264*, 1733-1739.

Reiss, D., Plomin, R., Hetherington, E.M., Howe, G.W., Rovine, M., Tryon, A., & Hagan, M.S. (1994). The separate worlds of teenage siblings: An introduction to the study of the nonshared environment and adolescent development. In E.M. Hetherington, D. Reiss, & R. Plomin (Eds.),

Separate social worlds of siblings: The impact of nonshared environment on development (pp. 63-109). Hillsdale, NJ: Erlbaum.

Rowe, D.C. (1994). *The limits of family influence: Genes, experience, and behavior*. New York: Guilford Press.

Rutter, M. (1979). Maternal deprivation, 1972-1978: New findings, new concepts, new approaches. *Child Development, 50*, 283-305.

Scarr, S. (1992). Developmental theories for the 1990s: Development and individual differences. *Child Development, 63*, 1-19.

Scarr, S. (1993). Biological and cultural diversity: The legacy of Darwin for development. *Child Development, 64*, 1333-1353.

Schachter, F.F. (1982). Sibling deidentification and split-parent identification: A family tetrad. In M.E. Lamb & B. Sutton-Smith (Eds.), *Sibling relationships: Their nature and significance across the life-span* (pp. 123-151). Hillsdale, NJ: Erlbaum.

Snow, C. (1991). A new environmentalism for child language acquisition. *Harvard Graduate School of Education Bulletin, 36* (1), 15-16.

Sroufe, L.A. (1985). Attachment classification from the perspective of infant-caregiver relationships and infant temperament. *Child Development, 56*, 1-14.

Stevenson, H.W., Chen, C., & Lee, S. (1992). Chinese families. In J.L. Roopnarine & B. Carter (Eds.), *Parent-child relations in diverse cultures* (pp. 17-33). Norwood, NJ: Ablex.

Stocker, C., & Dunn, J. (1990). Sibling relationships in childhood: Links with friendships and peer relationships. *British Journal of Developmental Psychology, 8*, 227-244.

Tesser, A. (1988). Toward a self-evaluation maintenance model of social behavior. In L. Berkowitz (Ed.), *Advances in experimental social psychology* (Vol. 21, pp. 81-227). San Diego, CA: Academic Press.

Tooby, J., & Cosmides, L. (1990). The past explains the present: Emotional adaptations and the structure of ancestral environments. *Ethology and Sociobiology, 11*, 375-424.

Turner, J.C., (with Hogg, M.A., Oakes, P.J., Reicher, S.D., & Wetherell, M.S.). (1987). *Rediscovering the social group: A self-categorization theory*. Oxford, England: Basil Blackwell.

Umbel, V.M., Pearson, B.Z., Fernández, M.C., & Oller, D.K. (1992). Measuring bilingual children's receptive vocabulary. *Child Development, 63*, 1012-1020.

Waters, E., Wippman, J., & Sroufe, L.A. (1979). Attachment, positive affect, and competence in the peer group: Two studies in construct validation. *Child Development, 50*, 821-829.

Whiting, B.B., & Edwards, C.P. (1988). *Children of different worlds: The formation of social behavior.* Cambridge, MA: Harvard University Press.

Wilson, M., & Daly, M. (1992). The man who mistook his wife for a chattel. In J. Barkow, L. Cosmides, & J. Tooby (Eds.), *The adapted mind: Evolutionary psychology and the generation of culture* (pp. 289-322). New York: Oxford University Press.

Youngblade, L.M., Park, K.A., & Belsky, J. (1993). Measurement of young children's close friendship: A comparison of two independent assessment systems and their associations with attachment security. *International Journal of Behavioral Development, 16*, 563-587.

Zukow, P.G. (1989). Siblings as effective socializing agents: Evidence from Central Mexico. In P.G. Zukow (Ed.), *Sibling interaction across cultures: Theoretical and methodological issues* (pp. 79-104). New York: Springer-Verlag.

(1997)

Questions

1. As Harris points out, as soon as one casts the debate as to the respective influence of heredity and environment in terms of "nature/ nurture" one has already implicitly concluded that the one important element in a child's environment is the "nurture" of parents. What evidence is presented here to suggest that the influence of environmental factors other than style of parenting are more important?

2. What implications for parenting do Harris's arguments have?

3. Explain in your own words the difference between correlation and cause.

4. Are there elements of Harris's argument that to you seem counterintuitive? To what extent does your own experience and knowledge support Harris's line of argument?

5. Why are studies involving twins important to issues of the sort that Harris is discussing?

Philip Gourevitch

from We Wish to Inform You That Tomorrow We Will Be Killed with Our Families

Surprised by his own conflicting responses to the genocidal horrors he has witnessed in Rwanda, the author inquires into how ordinary people can be capable of extraordinary crimes.

❧

In the Province of Kibungo, in eastern Rwanda, in the swamp- and pastureland near the Tanzanian border, there's a rocky hill called Nyarubuye with a church where many Tutsis were slaughtered in mid-April of 1994. A year after the killing I went to Nyarubuye with two Canadian military officers. We flew in a United Nations helicopter, traveling low over the hills in the morning mists, with the banana trees like green starbursts dense over the slopes. The uncut grass blew back as we dropped into the center of the parish schoolyard. A lone soldier materialized with his Kalashnikov, and shook our hands with stiff, shy formality. The Canadians presented the paperwork for our visit, and I stepped up into the open doorway of a classroom.

At least fifty mostly decomposed cadavers covered the floor, wadded in clothing, their belongings strewn about and smashed. Macheted skulls had rolled here and there.

The dead looked like pictures of the dead. They did not smell. They did not buzz with flies. They had been killed thirteen months earlier, and they hadn't been moved. Skin stuck here and there over the bones, many of which lay scattered away from the bodies, dismembered by the killers, or by scavengers—birds, dogs, bugs. The more complete figures looked a lot like people, which they were once. A woman in a cloth wrap printed with flowers lay near the door. Her fleshless hip bones were high and her legs slightly spread, and a child's skeleton extended between them. Her torso was hollowed out. Her ribs and spinal column poked through the rotting cloth. Her head was tipped back and her mouth was open: a strange image—half agony, half repose.

I had never been among the dead before. What to do? Look? Yes. I wanted to see them, I suppose; I had come to see them—the dead had been left unburied at Nyarubuye for memorial purposes—and there they were, so intimately exposed. I didn't need to see them. I already knew, and believed, what had happened in Rwanda. Yet looking at the buildings and the bodies, and hearing the silence of the place, with the grand Italianate basilica standing there deserted, and beds of exquisite, decadent, death-fertilized flowers blooming over the corpses, it was still strangely unimaginable. I mean one still had to imagine it.

Those dead Rwandans will be with me forever, I expect. That was why   5
I had felt compelled to come to Nyarubuye: to be stuck with them—not with their experience, but with the experience of looking at them. They had been killed there, and they were dead there. What else could you really see at first? The Bible bloated with rain lying on top of one corpse or, littered about, the little woven wreaths of thatch which Rwandan women wear as crowns to balance the enormous loads they carry on their heads, and the water gourds, and the Converse tennis sneaker stuck somehow in a pelvis.

The soldier with the Kalashnikov—Sergeant Francis of the Rwandese Patriotic Army, a Tutsi whose parents had fled to Uganda with him when he was a boy, after similar but less extensive massacres in the early 1960s, and who had fought his way home in 1994 and found it like this—said that the dead in this room were mostly women who had been raped before being murdered. Sergeant Francis had high, rolling girlish hips, and he walked and stood with his butt stuck out behind him, an oddly purposeful posture, tipped forward, driven. He was, at once, candid and briskly official. His English had the punctilious clip of military drill, and after he told me what I was looking at I looked instead at my feet. The rusty head of a hatchet lay beside them in the dirt.

A few weeks earlier, in Bukavu, Zaire, in the giant market of a refugee camp that was home to many Rwandan Hutu militiamen, I had watched a man butchering a cow with a machete. He was quite expert at his work, taking big precise strokes that made a sharp hacking noise. The rallying cry to the killers during the genocide was "Do your work!" And I saw that it *was* work, this butchery; hard work. It took many hacks—two, three, four, five hard hacks—to chop through the cow's leg. How many hacks to dismember a person?

Considering the enormity of the task, it is tempting to play with theories of collective madness, mob mania, a fever of hatred erupted into a mass crime of passion, and to imagine the blind orgy of the mob, with each member killing one or two people. But at Nyarubuye, and at thousands of other sites in this tiny country, on the same days of a few months in 1994, hundreds of thousands of Hutus had worked as killers in regular shifts. There was always the next victim, and the next. What sustained them, beyond the frenzy of the first attack, through the plain physical exhaustion and mess of it?

The pygmy in Gikongoro said that humanity is part of nature and that we must go against nature to get along and have peace. But mass violence, too, must be organized; it does not occur aimlessly. Even mobs and riots have a design, and great and sustained destruction requires great ambition. It must be conceived as the means toward achieving a new order, and although the idea behind that new order may be criminal and objectively very stupid, it must also be compellingly simple and at the same time absolute. The ideology of genocide is all of those things, and in Rwanda it went by the bald name of Hutu Power. For those who set about systematically exterminating an entire people—even a fairly small and unresisting subpopulation of perhaps a million and a quarter men, women, and children, like the Tutsis in Rwanda—blood lust surely helps. But the engineers and perpetrators of a slaughter like the one just inside the door where I stood need not enjoy killing, and they may even find it unpleasant. What is required above all is that they want their victims dead. They have to want it so badly that they consider it a necessity.

10   So I still had much to imagine as I entered the classroom and stepped carefully between the remains. These dead and their killers had been neighbors, schoolmates, colleagues, sometimes friends, even in-laws. The dead had seen their killers training as militias in the weeks before the end, and it was well known that they were training to kill Tutsis; it was announced on the radio, it was in the newspapers, people spoke of it openly. The week before the massacre at Nyarubuye, the killing began in Rwanda's capital, Kigali. Hutus who opposed the Hutu Power ideology were publicly denounced as "accomplices" of the Tutsis and were among the first to be killed as the extermination got under way. In Nyarubuye, when Tutsis asked the Hutu Power mayor how they might be spared, he suggested that they seek sanctuary at the church. They did, and a few days later the mayor came

to kill them. He came at the head of a pack of soldiers, policemen, militiamen, and villagers; he gave out arms and orders to complete the job well. No more was required of the mayor, but he was also said to have killed a few Tutsis himself.

The killers killed all day at Nyarubuye. At night they cut the Achilles tendons of survivors and went off to feast behind the church, roasting cattle looted from their victims in big fires, and drinking beer. (Bottled beer, banana beer—Rwandans may not drink more beer than other Africans, but they drink prodigious quantities of it around the clock.) And, in the morning, still drunk after whatever sleep they could find beneath the cries of their prey, the killers at Nyarubuye went back and killed again. Day after day, minute to minute, Tutsi by Tutsi: all across Rwanda, they worked like that. "It was a process," Sergeant Francis said. I can see that it happened, I can be told how, and after nearly three years of looking around Rwanda and listening to Rwandans, I can tell you how, and I will. But the horror of it—the idiocy, the waste, the sheer wrongness—remains uncircumscribable.

Like Leontius, the young Athenian in Plato, I presume that you are reading this because you desire a closer look, and that you, too, are properly disturbed by your curiosity. Perhaps, in examining this extremity with me, you hope for some understanding, some insight, some flicker of self-knowledge—a moral, or a lesson, or a clue about how to behave in this world: some such information. I don't discount the possibility, but when it comes to genocide, you already know right from wrong. The best reason I have come up with for looking closely into Rwanda's stories is that ignoring them makes me even more uncomfortable about existence and my place in it. The horror, as horror, interests me only insofar as a precise memory of the offense is necessary to understand its legacy.

The dead at Nyarubuye were, I'm afraid, beautiful. There was no getting around it. The skeleton is a beautiful thing. The randomness of the fallen forms, the strange tranquility of their rude exposure, the skull here, the arm bent in some uninterpretable gesture there—these things were beautiful, and their beauty only added to the affront of the place. I couldn't settle on any meaningful response: revulsion, alarm, sorrow, grief, shame, incomprehension, sure, but nothing truly meaningful. I just looked, and I took photographs, because I wondered whether I could really see what I was seeing while I saw it, and I wanted also an excuse to look a bit more closely.

We went on through the first room and out the far side. There was another room and another and another and another. They were all full of bodies, and more bodies were scattered in the grass and there were stray skulls in the grass, which was thick and wonderfully green. Standing outside, I heard a crunch. The old Canadian colonel stumbled in front of me, and I saw, though he did not notice, that his foot had rolled on a skull and broken it. For the first time at Nyarubuye my feelings focused, and what I felt was a small but keen anger at this man. Then I heard another crunch, and felt a vibration underfoot. I had stepped on one, too.

15 Rwanda is spectacular to behold. Throughout its center, a winding succession of steep, tightly terraced slopes radiates out from small roadside settlements and solitary compounds. Gashes of red clay and black loam mark fresh hoe work; eucalyptus trees flash silver against brilliant green tea plantations; banana trees are everywhere. On the theme of hills, Rwanda produces countless variations: jagged rain forests, round-shouldered buttes, undulating moors, broad swells of savanna, volcanic peaks sharp as filed teeth. During the rainy season, the clouds are huge and low and fast, mists cling in highland hollows, lightning flickers through the nights, and by day the land is lustrous. After the rains, the skies lift, the terrain takes on a ragged look beneath the flat unvarying haze of the dry season, and in the savannas of the Akagera Park wildlife blackens the hills.

One day, when I was returning to Kigali from the south, the car mounted a rise between two winding valleys, the windshield filled with purple-bellied clouds, and I asked Joseph, the man who was giving me a ride, whether Rwandans realize what a beautiful country they have. "Beautiful?" he said. "You think so? After the things that happened here? The people aren't good. If the people were good, the country might be OK." Joseph told me that his brother and sister had been killed, and he made a soft hissing click with his tongue against his teeth. "The country is empty," he said. "Empty!"

It was not just the dead who were missing. The genocide had been brought to a halt by the Rwandese Patriotic Front, a rebel army led by Tutsi refugees from past persecutions, and as the RPF advanced through the country in the summer of 1994, some two million Hutus had fled into exile at the behest of the same leaders who had urged them to kill. Yet except in some rural areas in the south, where the desertion of Hutus had left nothing but bush to reclaim the fields around crumbling adobe houses, I, as a newcomer, could not see the emptiness that blinded Joseph to Rwanda's beauty. Yes, there were grenade-flattened buildings, burnt homesteads, shot-up facades, and mortar-pitted roads. But these were the ravages of war, not of genocide, and by the summer of 1995, most of the dead had been buried. Fifteen months earlier, Rwanda had been the most densely populated country in Africa. Now the work of the killers looked just as they had intended: invisible.

From time to time, mass graves were discovered and excavated, and the remains would be transferred to new, properly consecrated mass graves. Yet even the occasionally exposed bones, the conspicuous number of amputees and people with deforming scars, and the superabundance of packed orphanages could not be taken as evidence that what had happened to Rwanda was an attempt to eliminate a people. There were only people's stories.

"Every survivor wonders why he is alive," Abbé Modeste, a priest at the cathedral in Butare, Rwanda's second-largest city, told me. Abbé Modeste had hidden for weeks in his sacristy, eating communion wafers, before moving under the desk in his study, and finally into the rafters at the home of some neighboring nuns. The obvious explanation of his survival was that the RPF had come to the rescue. But the RPF didn't reach Butare till early July, and roughly seventy-five percent of the Tutsis in Rwanda had been killed by early May. In this regard, at least, the genocide had been entirely successful: to those who were targeted, it was not death but life that seemed an accident of fate.

"I had eighteen people killed at my house," said Etienne Niyonzima, a former businessman who had become a deputy in the National Assembly. "Everything was totally destroyed—a place of fifty-five meters by fifty meters. In my neighborhood they killed six hundred and forty-seven people. They tortured them, too. You had to see how they killed them. They had the number of everyone's house, and they went through with red paint and marked the homes of all the Tutsis and of the Hutu moderates. My wife was at a friend's, shot with two bullets. She is still alive, only"—he fell quiet for a moment—"she has no arms. The others with her were killed. The militia left her for dead. Her whole family of sixty-five in Gitarama were killed." Niyonzima was in hiding at the time. Only after he had been separated from his wife for three months did he learn that she and four of their children had survived. "Well," he said, "one son was cut in the head with a machete. I don't know where he went." His voice weakened, and caught. "He disappeared." Niyonzima clicked his tongue, and said, "But the others are still alive. Quite honestly, I don't understand at all how I was saved."

Laurent Nkongoli attributed his survival to "Providence, and also good neighbors, an old woman who said, 'Run away, we don't want to see your

20

corpse.'" Nkongoli, a lawyer, who had become the vice president of the National Assembly after the genocide, was a robust man, with a taste for double-breasted suit jackets and lively ties, and he moved, as he spoke, with a brisk determination. But before taking his neighbor's advice, and fleeing Kigali in late April of 1994, he said, "I had accepted death. At a certain moment this happens. One hopes not to die cruelly, but one expects to die anyway. Not death by machete, one hopes, but with a bullet. If you were willing to pay for it, you could often ask for a bullet. Death was more or less normal, a resignation. You lose the will to fight. There were four thousand Tutsis killed here at Kacyiru"—a neighborhood of Kigali. "The soldiers brought them here, and told them to sit down because they were going to throw grenades. And they sat.

"Rwandan culture is a culture of fear," Nkongoli went on. "I remember what people said." He adopted a pipey voice, and his face took on a look of disgust: "'Just let us pray, then kill us,' or 'I don't want to die in the street, I want to die at home.'" He resumed his normal voice. "When you're that resigned and oppressed you're already dead. It shows the genocide was prepared for too long. I detest this fear. These victims of genocide had been psychologically prepared to expect death just for being Tutsi. They were being killed for so long that they were already dead."

I reminded Nkongoli that, for all his hatred of fear, he had himself accepted death before his neighbor urged him to run away. "Yes," he said. "I got tired in the genocide. You struggle so long, then you get tired."

Every Rwandan I spoke with seemed to have a favorite, unanswerable question. For Nkongoli, it was how so many Tutsis had allowed themselves to be killed. For François Xavier Nkurunziza, a Kigali lawyer, whose father was Hutu and whose mother and wife were Tutsi, the question was how so many Hutus had allowed themselves to kill. Nkurunziza had escaped death only by chance as he moved around the country from one hiding place to another, and he had lost many family members. "Conformity is very deep, very developed here," he told me. "In Rwandan history, everyone obeys authority. People revere power, and there isn't enough education. You take a poor, ignorant population, and give them arms, and say, 'It's yours. Kill.' They'll obey. The peasants, who were paid or forced to kill, were looking up to people of higher socio-economic standing to see how to behave. So the people of influence, or the big financiers, are often the big men in the genocide. They may think they didn't kill because they didn't take life with their own hands, but the people were looking to them for their orders. And, in Rwanda, an order can be given very quietly."

As I traveled around the country, collecting accounts of the killing, 25
it almost seemed as if, with the machete, the *masu*—a club studded with
nails—a few well-placed grenades, and a few bursts of automatic-rifle fire,
the quiet orders of Hutu Power had made the neutron bomb obsolete.

"Everyone was called to hunt the enemy," said Theodore Nyilink-
waya, a survivor of the massacres in his home village of Kimbogo, in the
southwestern province of Cyangugu. "But let's say someone is reluctant.
Say that guy comes with a stick. They tell him, 'No, get a *masu*.' So, OK,
he does, and he runs along with the rest, but he doesn't kill. They say, 'Hey,
he might denounce us later. He must kill. Everyone must help to kill at least
one person.' So this person who is not a killer is made to do it. And the next
day it's become a game for him. You don't need to keep pushing him."

At Nyarubuye, even the little terracotta votive statues in the sacristy
had been methodically decapitated. "They were associated with Tutsis,"
Sergeant Francis explained.

(1999)

Questions

1. What is the author's conclusion at the end of his journey? What mes-
    sage is Gourevitch trying to convey to us about Rwanda's experience,
    and how it may relate to us?

2. How does Gourevitch communicate the horror of the scene of the
    corpses in the schoolroom?

3. How can you explain Gourevitch's use of the word "beautiful" in
    reference to the massacred bodies he sees? Why does he use it, and
    what effect does it have on the reader?

4. The first part of the essay deals with how Gourevitch dealt personally
    with confronting the facts of the massacre. The second part deals in a
    more objective way with the politics underlying the massacre. How
    does the first part of the essay affect the reading of the second part?

LARISSA LAI

POLITICAL ANIMALS AND THE BODY OF HISTORY[1]

An accomplished young writer explores issues of politics,
literature and identity—including racial and sexual identity.

☙

Entranceways are the most difficult because you have to pass through them alone. I wanted to bring someone with me, someone who in this moment might function as a translator, not from some other language into English but from one English to another. Because I already know this entranceway is not where I come from, and yet I must say I do, in order for you to understand me.

Ashok Mathur, a writer, critic and activist, but mostly a trusted friend was here first, keeping watch over the literary/academic entranceway, asking the leading question. I did not want to come in the door like that. And yet it seemed to be the main entrance. He thought it was important that I enter the dialogue, and so asked the question—a door-opening kind of question, a come-right-this-way sort of question to lead the sniff-sniffing fox out of her lair onto the green. Not to assume she'd be hunted, but no sense denying the possibility.

The question was this: How could you or would you describe your writing as coming from a racialized space?[2]

A question from the middle of a conversation, begun in some other place, long ago and far away. Which is to say right here and now, but of another root, another wellspring. An awkward question because it demands

---

1   This piece was originally produced for the conference *Making History, Constructing Race* at the University of Victoria, October 23-25, 1998. [author's note]

2   E-mail interview with Ashok Mathur, July 1998. Available at http://www.acs.ucalgary.ca/~amathur/. [author's note]

a starting point apart from the self. A question that assumes one already knows how she is looked at from someplace that is by definition outside of her, and yet familiar at the same time.

It took me a long time to answer. I kept turning the question around in my head, asking myself what he meant when he asked it, and how he perceived his own work in that regard. We'd talked about the question before, so I knew he understood my ambivalence. How can a person write from a place constructed for her, pejoratively, by someone else? Why would she want to? But then, does she have a choice? My racialization is a historical fact, begun in Europe centuries before I was born, and perpetuated in a sometimes friendly Canadian sort of way through the social, bureaucratic and corporate structures of this society. I still live with the hope that the body exists prior to race, that experience exists prior to race. Living in a country that could not and does not exist without the concept of race, and for that matter, why be polite, white superiority, it is often hard to maintain this hope. When I say pejorative, I mean, you know, I didn't *ask* for this. And when Ashok asks me how I see my work coming from a racialized space, he is implicitly acknowledging that we both know this. He is asking me, faced with this recognition, what I intend to do about the injustice of it. He is asking me whether I see this othering of my body and my work by the mainstream as my responsibility to undo. If it is not my responsibility, are there reasons why I would choose to do it? He is asking me whether or not I think I have a choice. He is asking me because he faces similar questions.

These questions rise from the context this country has handed me. They are not the centre of my world. What I mean to say is, I didn't want to come in the door like this, nor dressed in these clothes, these shackles. But would you, white or brown, content or discontent, have recognized me otherwise? Perhaps. But I am not yet a creature of great faith.

My work comes from many places at once. There is an aspect in recent years that has been about trying, Houdini-like to break from the box which allows only two possibilities—to understand and work from the racialized position this society allots to the likes of us, or to work from a "color-blind" liberal position which actively denies the way we have been racialized even as it perpetuates the very racial interests it claims not to see.

Growing up in Canada in the seventies, and eighties, I was very much crammed inside the racism-was-terrible-but-now-it's-over box—a quick-fix product of official Multiculturalism that did precious little materially except sweep the problem of white racism under the carpet. This liberal position, so seemingly loaded with good intentions, had a pale, clammy underside that merely masked existing power imbalances while doing little to rectify them. For those of us who grew up in that era, it meant knowing something was wrong but never being able to put your finger on it.

In the late eighties/early nineties, I was drawn to the anti-oppression movements, which, though they had been growing for years, were currently flowering on the West Coast and in other parts of the country. It was and continues to be incredibly empowering to embrace a confrontative politic that refuses to accept the historically rooted racism of this country and to call it into question wherever it rears its ugly head. I was and am very interested in questions of strategy—How can people of color and First Nations people empower ourselves and one another given the colonial and neo-colonial contexts we live with? In a collective sense, this means taking particular stands on issues such as appropriation and affirmative action as a means of pushing white liberals to look at the hypocrisies of color-blindness, multiculturalism and other stances that seemed so liberal in the seventies. It means forcing the hand of those who would like credit for a belief in equality without having to put that belief into practice by giving up the ill-gotten gains of racially endowed power.

10   I took a particular interest in questions of history for a number of reasons. I think part of what is so aggravating about the reactionary racism that is so often the knee-jerk response to an anti-racist critique is the way in which it denies this country's ugly histories—the histories of the residential schools, the Japanese Internment, the Chinese Exclusion Act, the Komagata Maru incident as well as larger international histories of colonialism and exploitation which shaped and continue to shape the globe. It was particularly empowering to be introduced to works by marginalized people that addressed these histories from our own points of view. There was an urgency around their production and reading which I still feel. Gloria Anzaldua and Cherie Moraga's *This Bridge Called My Back* was seminal, as much as a presence as a test. I remember being thrilled by the publication of *Piece of My Heart: A Lesbian of Colour Anthology* put out by Sister Vision Press in 1990. Trinh's *Woman, Native, Other* was also important, as was bell hooks' *Ain't I a Woman*. There were also numerous cultural projects and special issues of periodicals that while problematic in their tokenized status were, nonetheless, affirming and thought-provoking. Although very few of these things became institutionalized or regularized, each served as a form to move dialogue forward. In some ways the ad hoc nature of these projects was liberating in that they allowed various

communities different ways of entering the discussions and validated a variety of voices in a variety of media.

I began to take note, however, of how certain texts became rapidly fetishized by critics, academics and the general public in ways comparable to the way anthropologists and missionaries address field notes. I attended many readings and I can't count the number of times audience members have asked writers of color, referring to the main character of any particular writer's text: "Is that you?" Or of my own work, which at moments actively resists that question: "Did you get these stories from your grandmother?" The suggestion is, of course, that we are not creative agents capable of constructing nuanced fictions which address historical situations, but rather mere native informants reconstructing, as accurately as our second-rate minds allow, what actually happened. Not, I might add, that I am trying to create a hierarchy of genres that inadvertently favors narrative fiction—I think it is very important that those who remember "what actually happened" write about it, and I have faith that they have written and will continue to write it well. It is rather the reception of the work, and the assumptions around that reception, that I wish to critique.

I understand that these questions may well be addressed to novel writers across race, class, gender and sexuality lines; however, their anthropological resonance with regard to marginalized peoples can not be denied. (I betcha no one ever asked Dickens if he was really Tiny Tim.) I feel a certain ambivalence here. My authority as an author is of no great importance or interest to me. My one great wish for readers is that they understand writing as a practice rather than as the production of an inert, consumable text. In some ways, the question "Is that you?" affirms this wish.

There are other genres that have a tradition of foregrounding within the body of their texts questions about how we read, that have a history of resisting readings that would consume them. These are the same texts that within many circles, both progressive and conservative, get labeled as too intellectual, too academic, incomprehensible. They are circulated within certain small if thoughtful circles, but do not reach the audiences which novels reach. I do not wish to address the question of whether their "elitism" is inherent or constructed. I am conscious of my choice to write fiction as a strategy chosen because it reaches people. On the other hand, in this age of steroid-enhanced capitalism, the tension between engaging those technologies which enable one to reach large numbers of people, and opening oneself and one's work to quick fix consumption, is no easy thing to resolve. Indeed, the quick fix consumptive scrutiny itself is all too easily transmuted into a kind of surveillance which generates new stereotypes, dangerous ones if their sources can be traced to a semblance of native reportage. This is the editorial power of capital.

And yet the fact remains that narrative compels me. What is history, after all, but narrative? And she who inhabits that narrative truly has ground to stand on. That grounding is necessary when her belonging to the land she lives on is so contested.

15   My second interest in the question of history is a more personal one, tied to my own historical situation. It is also very much caught up in questions of strategy: How do we diasporized types make a homespace for ourselves given all the disjunctures and discontinuities of our histories, and for that matter, the co-temporalities of some of them? It is also about the second box, if you were following my Houdini metaphor. The paradox of claiming a racialized space as a space from which to work is an uncomfortable one. To claim a racialized space is empowering in that it demands acknowledgement of a history of racism to which the mainstream does not want to admit. It demands acknowledgement of the continued perpetuation of that racism often, though not always, in new forms in the present. On the other hand, to claim that space also confirms and validates that eurocentric racist stance by placing ourselves in opposition to it, enforcing a binarism which itself is a Western social construct. So how to break from the second box without falling back into the first one, the one which denies a history or race and racialization as shaping our lives?

My strategy in recent years has been to make a project of constructing a consciously artificial history for myself and others like me—a history with women identified women of Chinese descent living in the West at its center. (I eschew the term "lesbian" because of its eurocentric roots, and because it does not necessarily connote community or social interdependence.) It must be artificial because our history is so disparate, and also because it has been so historically rare for women to have control over the means of recording and dissemination. The writing and rewriting of history has always been the prerogative of men and of the upper classes. I have the added disadvantage—the result of an unfortunate combination of my own childhood foolishness and the pressures of assimilation—of not being able to read Chinese. So my readings of history are bleached not only by the ideological interests of gender and class but also of race and culture.

As a quick example, my research into the life of Yu Hsuan-chi, the courtesan and poet on whom the "Poetess" character in *When Fox is a Thousand* is based, turned up two records of her. One described her as a woman with many lovers, hence lascivious, hence immoral, hence capable of murder. The second suggested she might have been framed for the murder of a young maidservant by an official who did not like her strong ideas about the role of women in Chinese society. Although she is supposed to have left a sizable body of poetry, very little of it appears in anthologies of Chinese poetry in translation, which tend to favor sanctioned male heavyweights.

The history I'm going to write, I told myself, may be ideologically interested, but no more so than what's already out there.

Several queer Asian theorists caution against projecting the needs and contexts of the present onto the past (see Shah, Lee). How can we understand, for instance, temple images in South Asia in the same terms that the makers of those images understood them, regardless of what we think we see? At the same time, without claiming those histories what are we? Shah suggests that the fact that we are here now in the present should be enough. But it isn't. In the everyday discussions of politically active people of color, lesbian, gay or straight, I hear this nostalgic referring back to a homeland that no longer exists, indeed, one that never did. I don't think this practice originates so much with naiveté as with a burning desire for that past; that it should have form, that it should have a body. Sometimes I feel our very survival in this country depends on the articulation of this form, the construction and affirmation of this body.

Animals at last. The myth and the tall tale. The secret and the subterranean. The dark, the feminine, the yin. All allies in this task. For, if diaspora cultures in the West are to be living breathing things they must change. We must have the power of construction, as long, of course, as we behave as responsibly as we know how in the act of construction. (By "responsibly" I mean that the ideas I have discussed above do matter. I do not hold the ideal of freedom of speech, or freedom of the imagination above other freedoms and other ideals, especially at a historical moment when these freedoms are regularly invoked in order to justify the reproduction of tired stereotypes and the perpetuation of historically unjust power imbalances. I do not believe in censorship, because I think it solves nothing. I do believe in integrity, and expect it of myself and of other writers.) This project obviously can not be one of creating a totalizing history; it is rather one of uninhibited, zany invention for the sheer joy of it.

My interest in the archetype of the fox began with my stumbling across Pu Songling's *Strange Tales of Liaozhai*, a well-known text of the sixteenth century. Pu is supposed to have collected these various tales of the supernatural

20

from ordinary people and compiled them into this anthology. The preface to one translation (which comes out of the PRC) talks about these tales as proto-socialist in their critiques of class structure, corruption and abuse of power. A reason to love them—or is this merely a pretext to circulate an old text that has been such a pleasurable read for so many years? There are stories in the compilation which are obviously allegorical in their intentions. And then there are the fox stories, which certainly have their allegorical aspects, but I like to think that there is more to them than that. Some are not so politically palatable at all, such as the one about a wily supernatural fox woman who leads an innocent man from his pious life into debauchery, sickness and death. There is another about an unsavory young man who leers at a beautiful woman; the woman turns out to be a fox, and the fox trounces him. There is yet another about how a fox and a young man fall in love—star-crossed love, of course, because the human and the divine are not supposed to have carnal dealings with one another. I suppose this one could be read as a comment on class or a critique of the repression of romantic love.

But what is more compelling in many ways is the figure of the fox herself, as a creature of darkness, death, germination and sexuality. The fox has the power to travel both above the earth and below it. In order to work her mischief she needs human form, which she achieves by entering the graveyard late at night and finding the corpse of some poor young girl who has died before her time. She breathes life into it. In this form, her power over men (and perhaps women too?) is the power of seduction. I find these stories very rich and very visceral. They are also politically compelling for a number of reasons. The first is contemporary feminism's struggle with questions of sexual representation. What does it mean for a feminist to embrace the power of seduction? And am I a feminist, or is that also a colonized space? The second is the question of how to deal with sexual representations of Asians in the West where we have been so much exoticized and/or de-sexualized in a society which insists on pathologizing the sexuality of the other. I was compelled to find out what kind of warrior the fox could be in that battle. The third is the possibility of employing the fox as a new trope of lesbian representation, or, if that term and its history reeks too much of its Western origins, then as a trope of Asian women's community and power.

I have been much influenced by the work of the Vancouver collective Kiss and Tell, and by much of the sex-positive work that has come out of Canada and the United States in recent years. The work is valuable in that it makes sex a site of resistance as well as a site of pleasure. I can't help thinking, however, that much as using one's racialization as a point of entry into political and philosophical discussions shapes what one can say and learn, so using sex as a point of departure shapes the way one thinks about women's community, and how one goes about looking for echoes of it in the past. My concern here, I hope, is not one of prudery or reaction, but one of wanting a little more give in the technologies we use to tap history. Elsewhere I have spoken about my interest in a tradition of spinsterhood, which became radicalized in Shundak (my father's long-ago county of origin, in Guandong Province) at the turn of the last century. Although my sources on this tradition are entirely and problematically anthropological, I was struck by the argument (see Sankar) that the act that clinched this practice for women was not sex but the acceptance of the idea that younger generations of spinsters could feed, through ancestral worship, the souls of the older generation. This practice is normally reserved for the members of patriarchal families only.

That said, I must also add that it is extremely difficult to find historical materials on Chinese lesbians. I suspect this is not because they did not exist, but because for a long time sexual practice was not considered as a focal point for identity. It could be argued, in fact, that the notion of identity arose from Western philosophical traditions, and from the needs of Western colonial practices. Later, the absence of such texts could be ascribed to the fact that women's lives were not deemed important enough to write about, or if worthy of writing, not deemed worthy of translation. The only scholarship on lesbian history in China that I could find in English was an appendix to a book called *Passions of the Cut Sleeve*, which dealt in its main body with the history of gay men. That appendix, perhaps ten pages long, focused exclusively on the question of sexual practice, which felt empty and unsatisfying in its narrowness.

Insofar as *When Fox is a Thousand* concerns anti-racism—and it does, although I think it also goes much further than that—I think issues of the body are primary. There are the obvious metaphors—the Fox breathing life into the bodies of the dead is like an Asian woman trying to breathe life into the assimilated almost-white self required by the social pressures of liberalism. She can never do it perfectly. There are always moments where the synapses don't connect, where there are understandings missing. But for the Fox, these moments of breathing life into the dead are also moments of passion. This is something she is compelled to do. It is her nature. The work of Calgary writer Yasmin Ladha is compelling in that it talks about colonialism and its effect in terms of romance. A very messy and dangerous romance, rife with

25

the abuse of power, but also tinged with hope. I think in doing so she takes a great risk, particularly as the specters of Pocahontas, Suzy Wong, Madame Butterfly and their ilk loom above us. But to engage in this way also opens up possibilities for living here that might not otherwise exist.

It did not occur to me until well after completing the book that the notion of transformation through breath is both a Taoist and a Buddhist notion. Or perhaps, indeed, it is a remnant of some earlier indigenous religion that has since disappeared or become subsumed by these more organized forms. Breath, like writing, is stilling and insistent. It moves and it sustains life. To engage the breath is to disrupt the binary opposition of Houdini's two boxes, to break from what Judith Butler refers to as "the discursive site of injury." What happens for me in the process of writing, at certain electric moments, is a contacting of the past that resonates with something akin to truth and belonging. A bit metaphysical perhaps but in a country built on denial, I am used to ghosts and not frightened of things that are only half apparent. These are not moments that sing of hurt but rather compel my interest in Taoist and pre-Taoist cosmologies. Here again, there are dangers. My compunction towards home-making belongs to the realm of the feminine in a way of which some branches of feminism might not approve. I think it is important to remember, to get back to the question of racialization, that there are entire knowledge systems and ways of living in our historical pasts that pre-date white racist modes of identification and their reclamations. How to touch those systems and practices may not be obvious, and the dangers of naïve idealization are far from negligible. For me, the consciously artificial narrative construction of history that acknowledges the desires of the present but also resonates with the past, seems a very useful possibility.

Thanks to Rita Wong, Ashok Mathur and Debora O for their support and feedback on this piece.

WORKS CITED

Butler, Judith. "Subjection, Resistance, Resignification: Between Freud and Foucault." *Psychic Life of Power: Theories on Subjection*. Stanford: Stanford UP, 1997. 83-105.

Eng, David L. and Alice Y. Hom, ed. *Q&A: Queer in Asian America*. Philadelphia: Temple UP, 1998.

Hinsch, Bret. *Passions of the Cut Sleeve: The Male Homosexual Tradition in China*. Los Angeles: U of California P, 1992.

Ladha, Yasmin. *Lion's Granddaughter and Other Stories*. Edmonton: NeWest Press, 1992.

Lai, Larissa. "The Heart of the Matter: Interview with Yasmin Ladha," *Kinesis*. Vancouver, February 1993. 15.

____. *When Fox is a Thousand*. Vancouver: Press Gang, 1995.

Lee, JeeYeun. "Toward a Queer Korean American Diasporic History." Eng and Hom. 185-209.

Sankar, Andrea. "Sisters and brothers, lovers and enemies: marriage resistance in southern Kwangtung." *Journal of Homosexuality*. 11.3/4 (1985): 69-81.

Pu, Songling, *Selected Tales of Liaozhai*. Trans. Yang Xianyi and Gladys Yang. Beijing: Panda Books, 1981.

____. *Strange Tales of Liaozhai*. Trans. Lu Yunzhong et al. Hong Kong: The Commercial Press, 1988.

P'u Sung-ling. *Strange Stories from a Chinese Studio*. Trans. Herbert A. Giles. Hong Kong: Kelly and Walsh, 1968.

Shah, Nayan. "Sexuality, Identity and the Uses of History." Eng and Hom. 141-56.

(1999)

Questions

1. What does Lai mean in paragraph 5 when she writes, "I still live with the hope that the body exists prior to race, that experience exists prior to race"?

2. Why does Lai wish to construct a consciously artificial history in her writing?

3. In paragraph 9, Lai refers to "pushing white liberals to look at the hypocrisies of color-blindness." According to Lai, how has racism in Canada changed over the decades?

4. The article was originally published in *Canadian Literature*, a scholarly journal. Discuss the ways in which Lai has geared her article toward this particular audience.

5. In what ways is publishing an essay such as this one effective in the fight against racism? Compare the effect of such an essay with that of writing an article in a popular magazine, demonstrating in an anti-racism rally, or standing up to racism when you see it in practice.

WITOLD RYBCZYNSKI

ONE GOOD TURN

WHY THE ROBERTSON SCREWDRIVER IS THE BIGGEST LITTLE INVENTION OF THE TWENTIETH CENTURY

A leading writer on cultural and architectural history addresses the unlikely topic of the screwdriver.

❧

Take a close look at a modern screw. It is a remarkable little object. The thread begins at the gimlet point, sharp as a pin. This point gently tapers into the body of the screw, whose core is cylindrical. At the top, the core tapers into a smooth shank, the thread running out to nothing.

From the time of their invention in the Middle Ages until the beginning of the twentieth century, all screws had either square or octagonal heads, or slots. The former were turned by a wrench, the latter by a screwdriver. There is no mystery as to the origin of the slot. A square head had to be accurate to fit the wrench; a slot was a shape that could be roughly filed or cut by hand. Screws with slotted heads could also be countersunk so that they would not protrude beyond the surface.

Yet a slotted screw has several drawbacks. It is easy to "cam out," that is, to push the screwdriver out of the slot; the result is often damage to the material that is being fastened or injury to one's fingers—or both. The slot offers a tenuous purchase on the screw, and it is not uncommon to strip the slot when trying to tighten a new screw or loosen an old one. Finally, there are awkward situations—balancing on a stepladder, for example, or working in confined quarters—when one has to drive the screw with one hand. This is almost impossible to do with a slotted screw. The screw wobbles, the screwdriver slips, the screw falls to the ground and rolls away, the handyman curses—not for the first time—the inventor of this maddening device.

American screw manufacturers were well aware of these shortcomings. Between 1860 and 1890, there was a flurry of patents for magnetic screwdrivers, screw-holding gadgets, slots that did not extend across the face of the screw, double slots, and a variety of square, triangular, and hexagonal sockets or recesses. The last held the most promise. Replacing the slot by a socket held the screwdriver snugly and prevented cam-out. The difficulty—once more—lay in manufacturing. Screw heads are formed by mechanically stamping a cold-steel rod; punching a socket sufficiently deep to hold the screwdriver tended to either weaken the screw or deform the head.

The solution was discovered by a twenty-seven-year-old Canadian, Peter L. Robertson. Robertson was a so-called "high-pitch man" for a Philadelphia tool company, a traveling salesman who plied his wares on street corners and at country fairs in eastern Canada. He spent his spare time in his workshop, dabbling in mechanical inventions. He invented and promoted "Robertson's 20th Century Wrench-Brace," a combination tool that could be used as a brace, a monkey wrench, a screwdriver, a bench vise, and a rivet maker. He vainly patented an improved corkscrew, a new type of cufflink, even a better mousetrap. Then, in 1906, he applied for a patent for a socket-head screw.

Robertson later said that he got the idea for the socket head while demonstrating a spring-loaded screwdriver to a group of sidewalk hawkers in Montreal—the blade slipped out of the slot and injured his hand. The secret of his invention was the exact shape of the recess, which was square with chamfered edges, slightly tapering sides, and a pyramidal bottom. Later, he rather grandly explained his invention: "It was discovered early by the use of this form of punch, constructed with the exact angles indicated, cold metal would flow to the sides, and not be driven ahead of the tools, resulting beneficially in knitting the atoms into greater strength, and also assisting in the work of lateral extension, and without a waste or cutting away of any of the metal so treated, as is the case in the manufacture of the ordinary slotted head screw."

An enthusiastic promoter, Robertson found financial backers, talked a small Ontario town, Milton, into giving him a loan and other concessions, and established his own screw factory. "The big fortunes are in the small inventions," he trumpeted to prospective investors. "This is considered by many as the biggest little invention of the twentieth century so far." In truth, the square socket really was a big improvement. The special square-headed screwdriver fitted snugly—Robertson claimed an accuracy within one

5

one-thousandth of an inch—and never cammed out. Craftsmen, especially furniture-makers and boat builders, appreciated the convenience of screws that were self-centering and could be driven with one hand. Industry liked socket-head screws, too, since they reduced product damage and speeded up production. The Fisher Body Company, which made wood bodies in Canada for Ford cars, became a large Robertson customer; so did the new Ford Model T plant in Windsor, Ontario, which soon accounted for a third of Robertson's output. Within five years, he was employing seventy-five workers and had built his own powerhouse and a plant to draw the cold-steel rod used in making the screws.

In 1913, Robertson decided to expand his business outside Canada. His father had been a Scottish immigrant, so Robertson turned his attention to Britain. He established an independent English company to serve as a base for exporting to Germany and Russia. The venture was not a success. He was thwarted by a combination of undercapitalization, the First World War, the defeat of Germany, and the Russian Revolution. Moreover, it proved difficult to run businesses on two continents. After seven years, unhappy English shareholders replaced Robertson as managing director. The English company struggled along until it was liquidated in 1926.

Meanwhile, Robertson turned to the United States. Negotiations with a large screw manufacturer in Buffalo broke down after it became clear that Robertson was unwilling to share control over production decisions. Henry Ford was interested, since his Canadian plants were reputedly saving as much as $2.60 per car using Robertson screws. However, Ford, too, wanted a measure of control that the stubborn Robertson was unwilling to grant. They met, but no deal was struck. It was Robertson's last attempt to export his product. A life-long bachelor, he spent the rest of his life in Milton, a big fish in a decidedly small pond.

10   Meanwhile, American automobile manufacturers followed Ford's lead and stuck to slotted screws. Yet the success of the new Robertson screw did not go unnoticed. In 1936 alone, there were more than twenty American patents for improved screws and screwdrivers.

Several of these were granted to Henry F. Phillips, a forty-six-year-old businessman in Portland, Oregon. Like Robertson, Phillips had been a traveling salesman. He was also a promoter of new inventions and acquired patents from a Portland inventor, John P. Thompson, for a socket screw. Thompson's socket was too deep to be practicable, but Phillips incorporated its distinctive shape—a cruciform—into an improved design of his own. Like Robertson, Phillips claimed that the socket was "particularly adapted for firm engagement with a correspondingly shaped driving tool or screwdriver, and in such a way that there will be no tendency of the driver to cam out of the recess." Unlike Robertson, however, Phillips did not start his own company but planned to license his patent to screw manufacturers.

All the major screw companies turned him down. "The manufacture and marketing of these articles do not promise sufficient commercial success," was a typical response. Phillips did not give up. Several years later the president of the giant American Screw Company agreed to undertake the industrial development of the innovative socket screw. In his patents, Phillips emphasized that the screw was particularly suited to power-driven operations, which at the time chiefly meant automobile assembly lines. The American Screw Company convinced General Motors to test the new screw; it was first used in the 1936 Cadillac. The trial proved so effective that within two years all automobile companies save one had switched to socket screws, and by 1939 most screw manufacturers produced what were now called Phillips screws.

The Phillips screw has many of the same benefits as the Robertson screw (and the added advantage that it can be driven with a slotted screwdriver if necessary). "We estimate that our operators save between thirty and sixty percent of their time by using Phillips screws," wrote a satisfied builder of boats and gliders. "Our men claim they can accomplish at least seventy-five percent more work than with the old-fashioned type," maintained a manufacturer of garden furniture. Phillips screws—and the familiar cross-tipped screwdrivers—were now everywhere. The First World War had stymied Robertson; the Second World War ensured that the Phillips screw became an industry standard as it was widely adopted by wartime manufacturers. By the mid-1960s, when Phillip's patents expired, there were more than 160 domestic, and eighty foreign, licensees.

The Phillips screw became the international socket screw; the Robertson screw is used only in Canada and by a select number of American woodworkers. (Starting in the 1950s, Robertson screws began to be used by some American furniture manufacturers, by the mobile-home industry, and eventually by a growing number of craftsmen and hobbyists. The Robertson company itself was purchased by an American conglomerate in 1968.) A few years ago, *Consumer Reports* tested Robertson and Phillips screwdrivers. "After driving hundreds of screws by hand and with a cordless drill fitted with a Robertson tip, we're convinced. Compared with slotted and Phillips-head screwdrivers, the Robertson worked faster, with less cam-out."

15   The explanation is simple. Although Phillips designed his screw to have "firm engagement" with the screwdriver, in fact a cruciform recess is a less perfect fit than a square socket. Paradoxically, this very quality is what attracted automobile manufacturers to the Phillips screw; the point of an automated driver turning the screw with increasing force would pop out of the recess when the screw was fully set, preventing overscrewing. Thus, a certain degree of cam-out was incorporated into the design from the beginning. However, what worked on the assembly line has bedeviled handymen ever since. Phillips screws are notorious for slippage, cam-out, and stripped sockets (especially if the screw or the screwdriver is improperly made).

Here I must confess myself to be a confirmed Robertson user. The square-headed screwdriver sits snugly in the socket; you can shake a Robertson screwdriver, and the screw on the end will not fall off; drive a Robertson screw with a power drill and the fully set screw simply stops the drill dead; no matter how old, rusty, or painted over, a Robertson screw can always be unscrewed. The "biggest little invention of the twentieth century"? Why not.

(2000)

Questions

1. Although the author purports the Robertson to be a superior screw to the Phillips, it has not had the commercial success of the Phillips. What role did the differing business philosophies of the two inventors play in this result?

2. This article is an excerpt from a book rather than a self-contained essay. How is the effectiveness of the article limited because of this? With this in mind, what changes would you make to the article to strengthen it?

3. In the final sentence of paragraph 9, why does the author reveal that Robertson was a life-long bachelor? Why does he choose this moment to do so? Why does he then employ an often used metaphor instead of simply stating that Robertson was an important man in an otherwise unimportant town? Other than the bare facts, what, if anything, is the author trying to infer in this sentence?

4. Rybczynski is often described as an "engaging" writer. Through what means does he effectively engage the interest of his readers?

TIM DEVLIN

DOES WORKING FOR WELFARE WORK?

In this article from a general interest magazine,
an Alberta writer evaluates a government program
of which he has personal experience.

ℰ

"I've led an interesting life, in the Chinese sense of the word inter-
esting. I was almost 42 when I returned to Canada penniless and
applied for welfare for the first time in my life—after spending 18
months in a Bangkok prison. I have no trade skills, so Calgary's
booming construction industry was not an option for me. I began
applying for simple laboring positions, unloading trucks, factory
production lines—jobs I would have had no trouble getting 20
years earlier. Nobody wanted to hire me, and after years of drug
addiction and a trip through a surreal Third World death camp,
I was terrified of life in all of its jangling chords. I fully accept
responsibility for the situation I found myself in, but it was frighten-
ing nevertheless, and I eagerly grasped at the hope that Alberta
Job Corps purported to represent."

Marianne (all names have been changed) is a single mother of two teen-
age children. After a serious illness she lost her job and became a sta-
tistic on the provincial welfare rolls. She was drafted into Alberta Job Corps,
the Alberta government's work-for-welfare program, and has since found an
office job—a "stepping stone." She says the program provided motivation at
the "right time" in her life. Marianne is a true success story, but she looked
decidedly out of place at Alberta Job Corps. An intelligent and well-read
41-year-old, she was hardly a typical recruit. Given the mandate of the program it's difficult to understand why she was drafted in the first place.

Alberta Job Corps (AJC), or "the Corps" as some of the troops laugh-
ingly refer to it, was ostensibly set up to get the chronically unemployed

back to work. The program was launched in 1995 with plenty of fanfare. It is administered by Supports for Independence (SFI), which falls under the Ministry of Human Resources and Employment.

According to internal SFI documents, the Job Corps is intended for welfare recipients who are poor candidates for "academic upgrading or formal skill development." They have "issues" ruling them out of other government programs because "they would not be hired or would drop out of jobs after short stints." These "issues" include alcoholism, drug addiction and mental illness. While acknowledging the client group in question is unsuitable for "pre-employment training" or "training on the job," the document warns they are in danger of being cut off financial support: "For these clients Alberta Job Corps is the last opportunity."

Cecelia is in her early 40s and she wants to work, but has been diagnosed as suffering from bipolar disorder. Mathew is 32 years old and able bodied, but he was in a car crash in 1994, suffers from severe brain scarring, seizures, alcoholism and serious anger management issues. Subsisting on welfare since the crash, living in a seedy downtown hotel, Mathew says when he was referred to AJC, he was interested "right off the bat."

5   After interviews, Cecelia and Mathew were asked to sign documents and congratulated as new recruits making $5.65 an hour, the minimum wage at the time. Both were told they would be learning marketable skills directly transferable into the workplace, supplemented with training courses including the handling of dangerous goods and first aid. If they had the right stuff for the Corps they would move into lead hand positions and receive $7.50 an hour. They were also told that 80 per cent of the people in the AJC program were off financial assistance one year later. "She (the employment development worker) glorified it and made it sound like I was going to come out with something, and it sounded like a real good program," says Mathew. But instead, he discovered "it's a joke."

He says all he did during his time at AJC was paint, and "not very well." Mathew complains he found the experience, "very, very disorganized" and "confusing," and says he learned very little in the way of marketable skills. Mathew "flipped out" on several occasions and says his anger problems grew worse because of the frustration he felt. He was taking an expensive medication to control seizures. Before AJC, Mathew's prescriptions were covered by SFI. He maintains he couldn't afford to buy his medication working at minimum wage, and he quit after SFI refused to help pay for it. Mathew didn't have enough hours for Employment Insurance benefits and was refused welfare because he had quit AJC. He later approached the

Southern Alberta Brain Injury Society, which is helping him with a claim under the Assured Income for the Severely Handicapped program. Mathew adds that paying minimum wage to people who have been trapped in the system is not enough incentive to motivate anyone. He feels that raising the wage "even a dollar" would be enough to stimulate people to "get something going with their life."

Cecelia has also found it hard to pay for her medication at minimum wage and no benefits. "It's a catch 22" Cecelia sighs, "I'm so fed up." She has stopped taking one medication, which costs $150 per month.

Alberta Job Corps operates in Calgary, Edmonton and the two northern corners of the province. According to a government spokesman the program cost $8.8-million last year. Province-wide, 938 welfare clients were hired. The Regional Income and Employment Program Management Committee, composed of the managers from district SFI offices, meets monthly. Attached to the minutes from a meeting held in 1999 are statistics circulated by Donna Daniluck, the manager of Alberta Job Corps. The numbers show that even with pressure to keep the program supplied with bodies, it was only operating at "about 60 per cent of capacity." Highlights from a study by the Social Research and Demonstration Corporation were also attached to the minutes. The study notes that while successfully enforcing a work-for-benefits approach, "workfare programs have not reduced caseloads or led to unsubsidized employment." More disturbing is another "key lesson" the document identifies: "Welfare-to-work programs have not usually increased the overall incomes to families," because "increased earnings have largely been offset by reductions in benefits."

A confidential source who works for Supports for Independence explains that the province's galloping economy and tightened eligibility requirements have led to a big drop in the number of welfare recipients in recent years. He says that while AJC draws its employees from a diminished client base, pressure at the district welfare offices ensures clients are referred to AJC. Social workers try to screen those who are obviously unsuitable, but others are directed to the program simply to find out what is wrong. He agrees it's an expensive way to weed out the unemployable and says part of the screening problem lies in the fact the provincial government has "de-skilled" the profession. He points out that in the last few years, people with no training, some with "nothing more than Grade 10," were promoted from secretarial jobs into front line positions as financial benefit workers.

Single mothers make up a significant percentage of recruits at AJC. Many have children under school age; some have children under the age of

10

one. The SFI source explains that once a baby is six months old, mothers are required to look for work, some type of job preparation program or school "even if the woman is breastfeeding." In some cases he says, women are forced into low paying jobs, and the daycare bill, which SFI picks up, means the government actually loses money on the deal. He calls the guidelines a "harsh, harsh policy," and describes as hypocritical the cries of "family values" from members of the Klein government. He feels that women "should not be referred to Job Corps because the chance of their being able to support their families is slim to none."

In Calgary AJC operates out of a building in a busy northeast warehouse district. The comprehensive program claims to develop basic plumbing, electrical, automotive, carpentry and painting skills. The schedule is laid out in week-by-week modules which combine training with on-site work experience. In the last weeks of what is supposed to be a six-month program, the emphasis shifts and participants begin actively searching for a full-time job.

Eight Employment Development Workers (EDWs) oversee the clients daily. Four of them are social workers. The rest are skilled tradesmen or journeymen who have abandoned the volatile construction industry for the questionably more secure bosom of the Alberta government. Ministry spokesman Tom Neufeld says that to qualify to work at AJC tradesmen have to possess proven supervisory experience. He says they are encouraged to take "human services training" but that is not a mandatory requirement.

Serious ethical questions arise when construction workers are placed in charge of welfare clients. Three women interviewed say they saw inappropriate behavior that would not have been tolerated in the private sector, let alone in a situation where "vulnerable people" are involved. One AJC trades supervisor was suspended for two weeks after complaints about his behavior, but returned to work with no explanation offered, not even to the woman who laid the complaint.

Emily was recently referred to Alberta Job Corps. She is in her 50s and entered the job market a few years ago following a marriage breakdown. Although she has upgraded her clerical skills, and is intelligent and warm, Emily continues to have difficulty finding full-time, continuous employment because of her age. You would be hard pressed to find anyone more ill suited to the Job Corps experience. An AJC employee who painted on various projects with Emily says it was "like trying to work on a construction site with your mom." Of the initial referral, Emily says "I didn't want to go; I just went because I had to." How appropriate is it to refer women like Emily and mothers with babies to Job Corps? The trades are seasonal. Women usually don't work out in the trades and they can run into a lot of discrimination.

The universal complaint from people attending AJC is that while they are initially told they will be learning a variety of construction skills, nearly all of the projects are painting jobs. Despite that, everyone interviewed (more than 20 people) maintains that no one really has any idea of how to paint to a professional standard. For the most part crews are dropped off at job sites in the morning and the supervisor doesn't return until the end of the day. "We weren't taught anything," according to Emily, "the trades people were not out there." Mathew didn't find the supervisors much help either: "They just dropped you off and you had your lead hands come and show you what to do."

15

Lead hands don't necessarily lead. Emily says it didn't matter if people had the necessary skills or leadership ability. Lead hand appointments were "based on attendance and being on time." Emily relates how four lead hands, working together because hardly anyone else showed up that day, were suspended after they were caught drinking. Another employee became the poster boy for new recruits, even though he freely admits to drinking on the job. Jerry agrees he has a serious alcohol problem but he was able to drag himself to work in the morning and that was all it took to advance at AJC. He was appointed lead hand and was twice lauded for his flawless attendance—at an awards presentation held each month when new clients join the program. During his time as lead hand Jerry was in charge of a crew painting a Government of Alberta office. He says that was his favorite project because the place was like "a maze. You could disappear and nobody knew where you were. And there was a liquor store across the street."

Marianne had no experience with addiction. She immediately noticed that most of the people had alcohol or other drug problems, but trained social workers seemed blind to the fact. Marianne was "quite surprised they were not helping these people in that way," and says the root problem, addiction, was ignored except in the most obvious cases.

Alberta Job Corps attempts to educate clients in a number of life skills areas, but Emily calls the one-day seminars on topics like household budgeting a waste of time, "just information." She observes that other people didn't pay much attention in class, nor did they apply any of the lessons offered. "They still would have no money. They still were doing the things they were doing before." Attendance at morning muster is usually lowest after payday (sometimes half the workforce stays home) and Emily says there are "suspensions constantly, letters, written warnings." Emily believes that most of the people cannot survive in the real world because "they're having a hard time in a place where they are given so many chances. A real employer is not going to take that."

Employees at AJC attend abbreviated courses in a number of areas including the transportation of dangerous goods, first aid and bobcat training. Marianne says none of the workshops offered at the Corps were "long enough or in-depth enough." She feels not enough attention is paid to individual needs and likens it to a "school where there's not enough teachers compared to kids."

20   From a practical point of view, the most valuable training offered at Alberta Job Corps is the St. John's Ambulance First Aid course. Marianne says the teacher was professional and helpful, but she estimates only half the people in her class of 10 would be competent in an emergency. When asked how she would feel about someone from AJC performing first aid on her, Emily laughs, "Thanks but no thanks."

Despite taking minimal certification courses in the handling and transport of dangerous goods, and passing, Emily still doesn't feel confident about working with toxic substances. She believes there should be more supervision on the projects because there has been carelessness and the supervisors don't really inspect the job sites at the end of the day. She says that job is often left up to the lead hand and "God only knows what kind of mind frame the lead hand is in."

The bobcat course at AJC is an example of wasted dollars. A small skid-steer front-end loader, a bobcat is expensive to maintain and transport. Three hours are spent on classroom instruction, followed by a short written test. Each person operates the bobcat for roughly ten minutes, sometimes simply driving up and down the back alley behind AJC headquarters. Everyone who passes the written exam (and people are given more than one chance) is issued a meaningless certificate. In the real working world it takes 300 hours of training and practice before someone is considered proficient in operating a bobcat.

An African immigrant, who calls himself a "citizen of the world," says that the social workers at AJC are totally out of touch. Frank, who instantly passes from street-smart wise guy into charming offbeat philosopher, feels the staff doesn't understand the people directed to Job Corps. He grins as he describes how one individual told him she knew what it was like to be a visible minority because she'd been to Barbados on a two-week vacation. The EDW couldn't understand why Frank found her comments so amusing.

Although Frank received the training and accompanying certificates provided by AJC, he says the "pieces of paper" haven't helped him get a job, because "in the real world nobody wanted to see them." He is collecting Employment Insurance and points to his list of employer contacts as evidence he is still looking for a job. "I played the game the way they wanted me to play it," Frank laughs ruefully.

In literature distributed to potential employers, mostly church and community groups, AJC is described as an "effective program" which broadens job skills and allows welfare clients to break free from government assistance. It promises "hands-on" skill development that approximates "actual work" situations. On an average day, however, less than five hours is actually spent on the job. Mathew says that sometimes crews sat around at the rear of the building until 9:30, and after driving to the job site, in some cases 40 minutes traveling time, it was nearly coffee time. "You work a bit till coffee time. Then by the time you figure out what you're supposed to be doing again, there's more time wasted. It's almost lunchtime." Emily says with another coffee break, cleanup and a pickup time around 3:30, on a good day there was four hours of "actual work."

The SFI source says sometimes people hang onto low paying seasonal jobs for a few months, but for the most part "it's a revolving door." For a majority of the clients, all that is accomplished is a temporary shift from the welfare rolls over to the federal Employment Insurance program. He says attending AJC takes individuals out of the Alberta system briefly but it never relieves the pressure on the public purse.

Nonetheless, Clint Dunford, the minister responsible, says that overall he is happy with AJC, claiming he has had nothing but positive feedback and has no knowledge of any problems. Dunford has toured a couple of AJC work sites and says, "actually we're pretty proud of the program. I've just been moving merrily along, saying OK, of all the things that I'm responsible for I guess I don't have to worry about that one."

Dunford caused a flap when he took over as Minister of Human Resources and Employment last spring. Asked at the time to comment on statistics that indicate a large number of working families in Alberta were forced to rely on food banks, the Lethbridge West MLA implied that those people were taking advantage of the system.

When asked if tradespeople at AJC had received training that would prepare them to work with SFI clients, many of whom are emotionally damaged and easily manipulated, the minister laughed. Dunford said the working world isn't "a cocoon," and that the program is set up that way.

"Clients have to have some sort of mentor and somebody with some skills so who should it be but a tradesman?"

Dunford says that roughly 70 per cent of the people initially hired by AJC are off social assistance one year later. He did not know how many people that figure represented, the cost per individual or the total cost of the program. According to ministry statistics, on a year-to-year basis, the number is closer to 65 per cent. By any standard the figures quoted are a poor measure of true success. Although the program is nearly five years old, no reliable follow-up studies have been done. Ministry spokesman Tom Neufeld says that after clients leave they are never contacted directly. Instead, results are measured by checking the SFI rolls six months after a person leaves Job Corps and again at the one-year mark. If someone is not receiving welfare benefits at that point they are considered a success story. Most telling, in fact, is that the ministry stops monitoring clients after one year. No figures are available at the two-year mark, when an individual's Employment Insurance benefits would be exhausted and the program could be more accurately assessed.

30   Forcing people with serious psychiatric and emotional problems, often combined with crippling addictions, to participate in a program that neither improves their lot in life nor saves money seems pointless. Many of the clients at Alberta Job Corps are frankly unsympathetic characters, but they are still people. If conservative ideology demands that individuals considered unemployable in the private sector work for a subsistence existence, perhaps the Klein government should fully and honestly embrace the concept. A percentage of the clients, and the non-profit groups that make use of free labor provided by AJC, benefit from the program. Perhaps an ongoing workfare system could be developed that accepts the failings of these people and offers them continuous employment, to say nothing of a raise and some basic medical benefits.

What brings individuals to the brink of the abyss? In every case the reasons are different, but one thing is certain: no one chooses the streets or the welfare shuffle or the food bank because the experiences are fun, invigorating or financially rewarding. The human beings in question are damaged, and if there is a time in history and a place on the planet where we can afford to take care of such lost souls in a meaningful way, surely it is Alberta.

"Both the minister and a senior government official have suggested I am simply someone with a 'grudge' because I'd had a 'bad experience' in a program. In fact, I enjoyed my time at AJC and I liked

most of the people I met there. The social workers and the majority of the trades-people are trying to make a difference, and there is a much different attitude than I've encountered at most welfare offices. Unfortunately the program is fatally flawed. Except for first aid, I did not learn anything of value and I would suggest, given my background and education, I had a better chance than most of the clients directed to AJC.

"Alberta Job Corps did help restore my confidence, and in an ironic twist the AJC experience got me back into the field of journalism. It also filled me with disgust that the government of the province I was born in would use damaged people to make a political point."

(2000)

Questions

1   This essay relies on personal anecdote for much of its effect. To what extent do you think an anecdotal approach is helpful in exploring public policy issues?

2.   Though this article addresses the specific situation in the province of Alberta, it has relevance to many other geographical areas; "workfare" has been a popular concept throughout much of North America at times. Does this essay alter in any way your own opinions about "workfare"?

3.   The quotations appearing at the beginning and the end of this article recount the author's own experiences—though they are not identified as being by the author. Do you find that they help to set the article in an appropriate context? Or do they seem to you largely irrelevant to the article itself? Do you think it would have been more appropriate for the author to have made clear who is speaking?

4.   In the nineteenth century it was commonly believed that if someone was poor it was their own fault rather than a matter of bad luck or of the structure of society. That view had almost died out by the late 1970s, but is now again held by significant numbers of people. Is it in fact possible to generalize on such matters? Make a list of as many possible causes of individual poverty and individual wealth as you can think of. Compare your list with those of others, and then write a brief essay on the topic.

Naomi Klein

The Swoosh

In this selection from her enormously influential bestseller No
Logo: Taking Aim at the Brand Bullies, *a leading social activist
discusses "the most inflated of all the balloon brands."*

❧

Nike CEO Phil Knight has long been a hero of the business schools.
Prestigious academic publications such as *The Harvard Business Review* have lauded his pioneering marketing techniques, his understanding
of branding and his early use of outsourcing. Countless MBA candidates
and other students of marketing and communications have studied the Nike
formula of "brands, not products." So when Phil Knight was invited to be
a guest speaker at the Stanford University Business School—Knight's own
alma mater—in May 1997, the visit was expected to be one in a long line
of Nike love-ins. Instead, Knight was greeted by a crowd of picketing students, and when he approached the microphone he was taunted with chants
of "Hey Phil, off the stage. Pay your workers a living wage." The Nike
honeymoon had come to a grinding halt.

No story illustrates the growing distrust of the culture of corporate
branding more than the international anti-Nike movement—the most publicized and tenacious of the brand-based campaigns. Nike's sweatshop scandals have been the subject of over 1,500 news articles and opinion columns.
Its Asian factories have been probed by cameras from nearly every major
media organization, from CBS to Disney's sports station, ESPN. On top of
all that, it has been the subject of a series of Doonesbury cartoon strips and
the butt of Michael Moore's documentary *The Big One*. As a result, several
people in Nike's PR department work full time dealing with the sweatshop
controversy—fielding complaints, meeting with local groups and developing Nike's response—and the company has created a new executive position: vice president for corporate responsibility. Nike has received hundreds

and thousands of letters of protest, faced hundreds of both small and large groups of demonstrators, and is the target of a dozen critical Web sites.

For the last two years, anti-Nike forces in North America and Europe have attempted to focus all the scattered swoosh bashing on a single day. Every six months they have declared an International Nike Day of Action, and brought their demands for fair wages and independent monitoring directly to Nike's customers, shoppers at flagship Nike Towns in urban centers or the less glamorous Foot Locker outlets in suburban malls. According to Campaign for Labor Rights, the largest anti-Nike event so far took place on October 18, 1997: eighty-five cities in thirteen countries participated. Not all the protests have attracted large crowds, but since the movement is so decentralized, the sheer number of individual anti-Nike events has left the company's public-relations department scrambling to get its spin onto dozens of local newscasts. Though you'd never know it from its branding ubiquity, even Nike can't be everywhere at once.

Since so many of the stores that sell Nike products are located in malls, protests often end with a security guard escorting participants into the parking lot. Jeff Smith, an activist from Grand Rapids, Michigan, reported that "when we asked if private property rights ruled over free speech rights, the [security] officer hesitated and then emphatically said YES!" (Though in the economically depressed city of St. John's, Newfoundland, anti-Nike campaigners reported that after being thrown out of a mall, "they were approached by a security guard who asked to sign their petition.")[1] But there's plenty that can be done on the sidewalk or in the mall parking lot. Campaigners have dramatized Nike's labor practices through what they call "sweatshop fashion shows," and "The Transnational Capital Auction: A Game of Survival" (the lowest bidder wins), and a global economy treadmill (run fast, stay in the same place). In Australia, anti-Nike protestors have been known to parade around in calico bags painted with the slogan "Rather wear a bag than Nike." Students at the University of Colorado in Boulder dramatized the difference between the legal minimum wage and a living wage by holding a fundraising run in which "participants pay an entrance fee of $1.60 (daily wages for a Nike worker in Vietnam) and the winner will receive $2.10 (the price of three square meals in Vietnam)."[2]

---

1   Memo, 4 May 1998, from Maquila Solidarity Network, "Nike Day of Action Canada Report & Task Force Update." [Unless otherwise noted, all notes to this essay are from the author.]

2   "Nike protest update," *Labour Alerts*, 18 October 1997.

Meanwhile, activists in Austin, Texas, made a giant papier-mâché Nike sneaker piñata, and a protest outside a Regina, Saskatchewan, shopping center featured a deface-the-swoosh booth. The last stunt is something of a running theme in all the anti-Nike actions: Nike's logo and slogan have been jammed so many times—on T-shirts, stickers, placards, banners and pins—that the semiotic bruises have turned them black and blue.

5 Tellingly, the anti-Nike movement is at its strongest inside the company's home state of Oregon, even though the area has reaped substantial economic benefits from Nike's success (Nike is the largest employer in Portland and a significant local philanthropist). Phil Knight's neighbors, nonetheless, have not all rushed to his defense in his hour of need. In fact, since the *Life* magazine soccer-ball story broke, many Oregonians have been out for blood. The demonstrations outside the Portland Nike Town are among the largest and most militant in the country, sometimes sporting a menacing giant Phil Knight puppet with dollar signs for eyes or a twelve-foot Nike swoosh dragged by small children (to dramatize child labor). And in contravention of the principles of nonviolence that govern the anti-Nike movement, one protest in Eugene, Oregon, led to acts of vandalism including the tearing-down of a fence surrounding the construction of a new Nike Town, gear pulled off shelves at an existing Nike store and, according to one eyewitness, "an entire rack of clothes ... dumped off a balcony into a fountain below."[3]

Local papers in Oregon have aggressively (sometimes gleefully) followed Knight's sweatshop scandals, and the daily paper *The Oregonian* sent a reporter to Southeast Asia to do its own lengthy investigation of the factories. Mark Zusman, editor of the Oregon newspaper *The Willamette Week*, publicly admonished Knight in a 1996 "memo": "Frankly, Phil, it's time to get a little more sophisticated about this media orgy ... Oregonians already have suffered through the shame of Tonya Harding, Bob Packwood and Wes Cooley. Spare us the added humiliation of being known as the home of the most exploitative capitalist in the free world."[4]

Even Nike's charitable donations have become controversial. In the midst of a critical fundraising drive to try to address a $15 million shortfall, the Portland School Board was torn apart by a debate about whether to accept Nike's gift of $500,000 in cash and swooshed athletic gear. The board

---

3   "Nike Mobilization: Local Reports," *Labor Alerts*, Campaign for Labor Rights, 26 October 1998.

4   Mark L. Zusman, "Editor's Notebook," *Willamette Week*, 12 June 1996.

ended up accepting the donation, but not before looking their gift horse publicly in the mouth. "I asked myself," school board trustee Joseph Tam told *The Oregonian*, "Nike contributed this money so my children can have a better education, but at whose expense? At the expense of children who work for six cents an hour? ... As an immigrant and as an Asian I have to face this moral and ethical dilemma."[5]

Nike's sponsorship scandals have reached far beyond the company's home state. In Edmonton, Alberta, teachers, parents and some students tried to block Nike from sponsoring a children's street hockey program because "a company which profits from child labor in Pakistan ought not to be held up as a hero to Edmonton children."[6] At least one school involved in the city-wide program sent back its swooshed equipment to Nike headquarters. And when Nike approached the City of Ottawa Council in March 1998 to suggest building one of its swooshed gymnasium floors in a local community center, it faced questions about "blood money." Nike withdrew its offer and gave the court to a more grateful center, run by the Boys and Girls Clubs. The dilemma of accepting Nike sponsorship money has also exploded on university campuses.

At first, much of the outrage stemmed from the fact that when the sweat-shop scandal hit the papers, Nike wasn't really acting all that sorry about it. While Kathie Lee Gifford and the Gap had at least displayed contrition when they got caught with their sweatshops showing, Phil Knight had practically stonewalled: denying responsibility, attacking journalists, blaming rogue contractors and sending out flacks to speak for the company. While Kathie Lee was crying on TV, Michael Jordan was shrugging his shoulders and saying that his job was to shoot hoop, not play politics. And while the Gap agreed to allow a particularly controversial factory in El Salvador to be monitored by local human-rights groups, Nike was paying lip service to a code of conduct that its Asian workers, when interviewed, had never heard of.

But there was a critical difference between Nike and the Gap at this 10 stage. Nike didn't panic when its scandals hit the middle-American mall, because the mall, while it is indeed where most Nike products are sold, is not where Nike's image was made. Unlike the Gap, Nike has drawn on the inner cities, merging, as we've seen, with the styles of poor black and Latino

5   *Oregonian*, 16 June 1996.

6   Campaign for Labor Rights Web site, regional reports.

youth to load up on imagery and attitude. Nike's branding power is thoroughly intertwined with the African-American heroes who have endorsed its products since the mid-eighties: Michael Jordan, Charles Barkley, Scottie Pippen, Michael Johnson, Spike Lee, Tiger Woods, Bo Jackson—not to mention the rappers who wear Nike gear on stage. While hip-hop style was the major influence at the mall, Phil Knight must have known that as long as Nike was King Brand with Jordan fans in Compton and the Bronx, he could be stirred but not shaken. Sure, their parents, teachers and church leaders might be tut-tutting over sweatshops, but as far as Nike's core demographic of thirteen- to seventeen-year-old kids was concerned, the swoosh was still made of Teflon.

By 1997, it had become clear to Nike's critics that if they were serious about taking on the swoosh in an image war, they would have to get at the source of the brand's cachet—and as Nick Alexander of the multicultural *Third Force* magazine wrote in the summer of that year, they weren't even close. "Nobody has figured out how to make Nike break down and cry. The reason is that nobody has engaged African Americans in the fight.... To gain significant support from communities of color, corporate campaigns need to make connections between Nike's overseas operations and conditions here at home."[7]

The connections were there to be made. It is the cruelest irony of Nike's "brands, not products" formula that the people who have done the most to infuse the swoosh with cutting-edge meaning are the very people most hurt by the company's pumped-up prices and nonexistent manufacturing base. It is inner-city youth who have most directly felt the impact of Nike's decision to manufacture its products outside the US, both in high unemployment rates and in the erosion of the community tax base (which sets the stage for the deterioration of local public schools).

Instead of jobs for their parents, what the inner-city kids get from Nike is the occasional visit from its marketers and designers on "bro-ing" pilgrimages. "Hey, bro, what do you think of these new Jordans—are they fresh or what?" The effect of high-priced cool hunters whipping up brand frenzy on the cracked asphalt basketball courts of Harlem, the Bronx and Compton has already been discussed: kids incorporate the brands into gang-wear uniforms; some want the gear so badly they are willing to sell drugs, steal, mug, even kill for it. Jessie Collins, executive director of the

---

7   Nick Alexander, "Sweatshop Activism: Missing Pieces," *Z Magazine*, September 1997, 14-17.

Edenwald-Gun Hill Neighborhood Center in the northeast Bronx, tells me that it's sometimes drug or gang money, but more often it's the mothers' minimum-wage salary or welfare checks that are spent on disposable status wear. When I asked her about the media reports of kids stabbing each other for their $150 Air Jordans she said dryly, "It's enough to beat up on your mother for ... $150 is a hell of a lot of money."[8]

Shoe-store owners like Steven Roth of Essex House of Fashion are often uncomfortable with the way so-called street fashions play out for real on the postindustrial streets of Newark, New Jersey, where his store is located:

> I do get weary and worn down from it all. I'm always forced to face the fact that I make my money from poor people. A lot of them are on welfare. Sometimes a mother will come in here with a kid, and the kid is dirty and poorly dressed. But the kid wants a hundred-twenty-buck pair of shoes and that stupid mother buys them for him. I can feel that kid's inner need—this desire to own these things and have the feelings that go with them—but it hurts me that this is the way things are.[9]

It's easy to blame the parents for giving in, but that "deep inner need" for designer gear has grown so intense that it has confounded everyone from community leaders to the police. Everyone pretty much agrees that brands like Nike are playing a powerful surrogate role in the ghetto, subbing for everything from self-esteem to African-American cultural history to political power. What they are far less sure about is how to fill that need with empowerment and a sense of self-worth that does not necessarily come with a logo attached. Even broaching the subject of brand fetishism to these kids is risky. With so much emotion invested in celebrity consumer goods, many kids take criticism of Nike or Tommy as a personal attack, as grave a transgression as insulting someone's mother to his face.

Not surprisingly, Nike sees its appeal among disadvantaged kids differently. By supporting sports programs in Boys and Girls Clubs, by paying to repave urban basketball courts and by turning high-performance sports gear into street fashions, the company claims it is sending out the inspirational message that even poor kids can "Just Do It." In its press material and ads, 15

---

8   Personal interview, 6 October 1997.

9   Katz, *Just Do It*, 271.

there is an almost messianic quality to Nike's portrayal of its role in the inner cities: troubled kids will have higher self-esteem, fewer unwanted pregnancies and more ambition—all because at Nike "We see them as athletes." For Nike, its $150 Air Jordans are not a shoe but a kind of talisman with which poor kids can run out of the ghetto and better their lives. Nike's magic slippers will help them fly—just as they made Michael Jordan fly.

A remarkable, subversive accomplishment? Maybe. But one can't help thinking that one of the main reasons black urban youth can get out of the ghetto only by rapping or shooting hoops is that Nike and the other multinationals are reinforcing stereotypical images of black youth and simultaneously taking all the jobs away. As US Congressman Bernie Sanders and Congresswoman Marcy Kaptur stated in a letter to the company, Nike has played a pivotal part in the industrial exodus from urban centers. "Nike has led the way in abandoning the manufacturing workers of the United States and their families.... Apparently, Nike believes that workers in the United States are good enough to purchase your shoe products, but are no longer worthy enough to manufacture them."[10]

And when the company's urban branding strategy is taken in conjunction with this employment record, Nike ceases to be the savior of the inner city and turns into the guy who steals your job, then sells you a pair of overpriced sneakers and yells, "Run like hell!" Hey, it's the only way out of the ghetto, kid. Just do it.

That's what Mike Gitelson thought, anyway. A social worker at the Bronx's Edenwald-Gun Hill Neighborhood Center, he was unimpressed with the swoosh's powers as a self-help guru in the projects and "sick of seeing kids wearing sneakers they couldn't afford and which their parents couldn't afford."[11] Nike's critics on college campuses and in the labor movement may be fueled largely by moral outrage, but Mike Gitelson and his colleagues simply feel ripped off. So rather than lecturing the kids on the virtues of frugality, they began telling them about how Nike made the shoes that they wanted so badly. Gitelson told them about the workers in Indonesia who earned $2 a day, he told them that it cost Nike only $5 to make the shoes they bought for between $100 and $180, and he told them about how Nike didn't make any of its shoes in the US—which was part of the reason their parents had such a tough time finding work. "We got really angry,"

10 Letter dated 24 October 1997.

11 Personal interview.

says Gitelson, "because they were taking so much money from us here and then going to other countries and exploiting people even worse.... We want our kids to see how it affects them here on the streets, but also how here on the streets affects people in Southeast Asia." His colleague at the center, youth worker Leo Johnson, lays out the issue using the kids' own lingo. "Yo, dude," he tells his preteen audiences, "you're being suckered if you pay $100 for a sneaker that costs $5 to make. If somebody did that to you on the block, you know where it's going."[12]

The kids at the center were upset to learn about the sweatshops but they were clearly most pissed off that Phil Knight and Michael Jordan were playing them for chumps. They sent Phil Knight a hundred letters about how much money they had spent on Nike gear over the years—and how, the way they figured it, Nike owed them big time. "I just bought a pair of Nikes for $100," one kid wrote. "It's not right what you're doing. A fair price would have been $30. Could you please send me back $70?" When the company answered the kids with a form letter, "That's when we got really angry and started putting together the protest," Gitelson says.

They decided the protest would take the form of a "shoe-in" at the Nike Town at Fifth Avenue and Fifty-seventh Street. Since most of the kids at the center are full-fledged swooshaholics, their closets are jam-packed with old Air Jordans and Air Carnivores that they would no longer even consider wearing. To put the obsolete shoes to practical use, they decided to gather them together in garbage bags and dump them on the doorstep of Nike Town.

When Nike executives got wind that a bunch of black and Latino kids from the Bronx were planning to publicly diss their company, the form letters came to an abrupt halt. Up to that point, Nike had met most criticism by attacking its critics as members of "fringe groups," but this was different: if a backlash took root in the inner cities, it could sink the brand at the mall. As Gitelson puts it, "Our kids are exactly who Nike depends upon to set the trends for them so that the rest of the country buys their sneakers. White middle-class adults who are fighting them, well, it's almost okay. But when youth of color start speaking out against Nike, they start getting scared."[13]

---

12 David Gonzalez, "Youthful Foes Go Toe to Toe with Nike," *New York Times*, 27 September 1997, B1.

13 Personal interview.

The executives in Oregon also knew, no doubt, that Edenwald was only the tip of the iceberg. For the past couple of years, debates have been raging in hip-hop scenes about rappers "label whoring for Nike and Tommy" instead of supporting black-owned clothing companies like FUBU (For Us By Us). And rapper KRS-One planned to launch the Temple of Hip Hop, a project that promised to wrest the culture of African-American youth away from white record and clothing labels and return it to the communities that built it. It was against this backdrop that, on September 10, 1997—two weeks before the shoe-in protest was scheduled to take place—Nike's chief of public relations, Vada Manager, made the unprecedented move of flying in from Oregon with a colleague to try to convince the center that the swoosh was a friend of the projects.

"He was working overtime to put the spins on us," says Gitelson. It didn't work. At the meeting, the center laid out three very concrete demands:

1. Those who work for Nike overseas should be paid a living wage, with independent monitoring to ensure that it is happening.
2. Nike sneakers should be sold less expensively here in America with no concessions to American workforce (i.e. no downsizing, or loss of benefits).
3. Nike should seriously re-invest in the inner city in America, especially New York City since we have been the subject of much of their advertising.[14]

Gitelson may have recognized that Nike was scared—but not *that* scared. Once it became clear that the two parties were at an impasse, the meeting turned into a scolding session as the two Nike executives were required to listen to Edenwald director Jessie Collins comparing the company's Asian sweatshops with her experience as a young girl picking cotton in the sharecropping South. Back in Alabama, she told Manager, she earned $2 a day, just like the Indonesians. "And maybe a lot of Americans can't identify with those workers' situation, but I certainly can."[15]

Vada Manager returned to Oregon defeated and the protest went off as planned, with two hundred participants from eleven community centers

---

14 Minutes from 10 September meeting between Nike executives and the Edenwald-Gun Hill Neighborhood Center.

15 Personal interview.

around New York. The kids—most of whom were between eleven and thirteen years old—hooted and hollered and dumped several clear garbage bags of smelly old Nikes at the feet of a line of security guards who had been brought in on special assignment to protect the sacred Nike premises. Vada Manager again flew to New York to run damage control, but there was little he could do. Local TV crews covered the event, as did an ABC news team and *The New York Times*.

In a harsh bit of bad timing for the company, the *Times* piece ran on a page facing another story about Nike. Graphically underlining the urgency of the protest, this story reported that a fourteen-year-old boy from Crown Heights had just been murdered by a fifteen-year-old boy who beat him and left him on the subway tracks with a train approaching. "Police Say Teenager Died for His Sneakers and Beeper," the headline read. And the brand of his sneakers? Air Jordans. The article quoted the killer's mother saying that her son had got mixed up with gangs because he wanted to "have nice things." A friend of the victim explained that wearing designer clothes and carrying a beeper had become a way for poor kids to "feel important." 25

The African-American and Latino kids outside Nike Town on Fifth Avenue—the ones swarmed by cameras and surrounded by curious onlookers—were feeling pretty important, too. Taking on Nike "toe to toe," as they said, turned out to be even more fun than wearing Nikes. With the Fox News camera pointed in his face, one of the young activists—a thirteen-year-old boy from the Bronx—stared into the lens and delivered a message to Phil Knight: "Nike, we made you. We can break you."

What is perhaps most remarkable about the Nike backlash is its durability. After four solid years in the public eye, the Nike story still has legs (so too, of course, does the Nike brand). Still, most corporate scandals are successfully faced down with a statement of "regret" and a few glossy ads of children playing happily under the offending logo. Not with Nike. The news reports, labor studies and academic research documenting the sweat behind the swoosh have yet to slow down, and Nike critics remain tireless at dissecting the steady stream of materials churned out by Nike's PR machine. They were unmoved by Phil Knight's presence on the White House Task Force on Sweatshops—despite his priceless photo op standing beside President Clinton at the Rose Garden press conference. They sliced and diced the report Nike commissioned from civil-rights leader Andrew Young, pointing out that Young completely dodged the question of whether Nike's factory wages are inhumanely exploitative, and attacking him for relying on translators provided by Nike itself when he visited the factories in Indonesia and Vietnam. As for Nike's other study-for-hire—this one by a group of Dartmouth business students who concluded that workers in Vietnam were living the good life on less than $2 a day—well, everyone pretty much ignored that one altogether.

Finally, in May 1998, Phil Knight stepped out from behind the curtain of spin doctors and called a press conference in Washington to address his critics directly. Knight began by saying that he had been painted as a "corporate crook, the perfect corporate villain for these times." He acknowledged that his shoes "have become synonymous with slave wages, forced overtime and arbitrary abuse." Then, to much fanfare, he unveiled a plan to improve working conditions in Asia. It contained some tough new regulations on factory air quality and the use of petroleum-based chemicals. It promised to provide classes inside some Indonesian factories and promised not to hire anyone under eighteen years old in the shoe factories. But there was still nothing substantial in the plan about allowing independent outside monitors to inspect the factories, and there were no wage raises for the workers. Knight did promise, however, that Nike's contractors would no longer be permitted to appeal to the Indonesian government for a waiver on the minimum wage.

It wasn't enough. That September the San Francisco human-rights group Global Exchange, one of the company's harshest critics, released an alarming report on the status of Nike's Indonesian workers in the midst of the country's economic and political crisis. "While workers producing Nike shoes were low paid before their currency, the rupiah, began plummeting in late 1997, the dollar value of their wages has dropped from $2.47/day in 1997 to 80 cents/day in 1998." Meanwhile, the report noted that with soaring commodity prices, workers "estimated that their cost of living had gone up anywhere from 100 to 300 per cent."[16] Global Exchange called on Nike to double the ages of its Indonesian workforce, an exercise that would cost it $20 million a year—exactly what Michael Jordan is paid annually to endorse the company.

30   Not surprisingly, Nike did not double the wages, but it did, three weeks later, give 30 per cent of the Indonesian workforce a 25 per cent raise.[17] That, too, failed to silence the crowds outside the superstores, and five

16 "Wages and Living Expense for Nike Workers in Indonesia," report released by Global Exchange, 23 September 1998.

17 "Nike Raises Wages for Indonesian Workers," *Oregonian*, 16 October 1998.

months later Nike came forward again, this time with what vice president of corporate responsibility Maria Eitel called "an aggressive corporate responsibility agenda at Nike."[18] As of April 1, 1999, workers would get another 6 per cent raise. The company had also opened up a Vietnamese factory near Ho Chi Minh City to outside health and safety monitors, who found conditions much improved. Dara O'Rourke of the University of California at Berkeley reported that the factory had "implemented important changes over the past 18 months which appear to have significantly reduced worker exposures to toxic solvents, adhesives and other chemicals." What made the report all the more remarkable was that O'Rourke's inspection was a genuinely independent one: in fact, less than two years earlier, he had enraged the company by leaking a report conducted by Ernst & Young that showed that Nike was ignoring widespread violations at that same factory.

O'Rourke's findings weren't all glowing. There were still persistent problems with air quality, factory overheating and safety gear—and he had visited only the one factory.[19] As well, Nike's much-heralded 6 per cent pay raise for Indonesian workers still left much to be desired; it amounted to an increase of one cent an hour and, with inflation and currency fluctuation, only brought wages to about half of what Nike paychecks were worth before the economic crisis. Even so, these were significant gestures coming from a company that two years earlier was playing the role of the powerless global shopper, claiming that contractors alone had the authority to set wages and make the rules.

The resilience of the Nike campaign in the face of the public-relations onslaught is persuasive evidence that invasive marketing, coupled with worker abandonment, strikes a wide range of people from different walks of life as grossly unfair and unsustainable. Moreover, many of those people are not interested in letting Nike off the hook simply because this formula has become the standard one for capitalism-as-usual. On the contrary, there seems to be a part of the public psyche that likes kicking the most macho and extreme of all the sporting-goods companies in the shins—I mean *really* likes it. Nike's critics have shown that they don't want this story to be

---

18 "Nike to Improve Minimum Monthly Wage Package for Indonesian Workers," Nike press release, 19 March 1999.

19 Steven Greenhouse, "Nike Critic Praises Gains in Air Quality at Vietnam Factory," *New York Times*, 12 March 1999.

brushed under the rug with a reassuring bit of corporate PR; they want it out in the open, where they can keep a close eye on it.

In large part, this is because Nike's critics know the company's sweat-shop scandals are not the result of a series of freak accidents: they know that the criticisms leveled at Nike apply to all the brand-based shoe companies contracting out to a global maze of firms. But rather than this serving as a justification, Nike—as the market leader—has become a lightning rod for this broader resentment. It has been latched on to as the essential story of the extremes of the current global economy: the disparities between those who profit from Nike's success and those who are exploited by it are so gaping that a child could understand what is wrong with this picture and indeed it is children and teenagers who most readily do.

So, when does the total boycott of Nike products begin? Not soon, appar-ently. A cursory glance around any city in the world shows that the swoosh is still ubiquitous; some athletes still tattoo it on their navels, and plenty of high-school students still deck themselves out in the coveted gear. But at the same time, there can be little doubt that the millions of dollars that Nike has saved in labor costs over the years are beginning to bite back, and take a toll on its bottom line. "We didn't think that the Nike situation would be as bad as it seems to be," said Nikko stock analyst Tim Finucane in *The Wall Street Journal* in March 1998.[20] Wall Street really had no choice but to turn on the company that had been its darling for so many years. Despite the fact that Asia's plummeting currencies meant that Nike's labor costs in Indo-nesia, for instance, were a quarter of what they were before the crash, the company was still suffering. Nike's profits were down, orders were down, stock prices were *way* down, and after an average annual growth of 34 per cent since 1995, quarterly earnings were suddenly down by 70 per cent. By the third quarter, which ended in February 1999, Nike's profits were once again up 70 per cent—but by the company's own account, the recovery was not the result of rebounding sales but rather of Nike's decision to cut jobs and contracts. In fact, Nike's revenues and future orders were down in 1999 for the second year in a row.[21]

---

20 Shanthi Kalathil, "Being Tied to Nike Affects Share Price of Yue Yuen," *Wall Street Journal*, 25 March 1998.

21 "Third quarter brings 70 per cent increase in net income for sneaker giant," Associ-ated Press, 19 March 1999.

Nike has blamed its financial problems on everything *but* the human-rights campaign. The Asian currency crisis was the reason Nikes weren't selling well in Japan and South Korea; or it was because Americans were buying "brown shoes" (walking shoes and hiking boots) as opposed to big white sneakers. But the brown-shoe excuse rang hollow. Nike makes plenty of brown shoes—it has a line of hiking boots, and it owns Cole Haan (and recently saved millions by closing down the Cole Haan factory in Portland, Maine, and moving production to Mexico and Brazil).[22] More to the point, Adidas staged a massive comeback during the very year that Nike was free-falling. In the quarter when Nike nose-dived, Adidas sales were up 42 per cent, its net income was up 48 per cent, to $255 million, and its stock price had tripled in two years. The German company, as we have seen, turned its fortunes around by copying Nike's production structure and all but Xeroxing its approach to marketing and sponsorships. In 1997-98, Adidas even redesigned its basketball shoes so they looked just like Nikes: big, white and ultra high tech. But unlike Nikes, they sold briskly. So much for the brown-shoe theory.

Over the years Nike has tried dozens of tactics to silence the cries of its critics, but the most ironic by far has been the company's desperate attempt to hide behind its product. "We're not political activists. We are a footwear manufacturer," said Nike spokeswoman Donna Gibbs, when the sweatshop scandal first began to erupt.[23] A footwear manufacturer? This from the company that made a concerted decision in the mid-eighties not to be about boring corporeal stuff like footwear—and certainly nothing as crass as manufacturing. Nike wanted to be about sports, Knight told us, it wanted to be about the idea of sports, then the idea of transcendence through sports; then it wanted to be about self-empowerment, women's rights, racial equality. It wanted its stores to be temples, its ads a religion, its customers a nation, its workers a tribe. After taking us all on such a branded ride, to turn around and say, "Don't look at us, we just make shoes" rings laughably hollow.

Nike was the most inflated of all the balloon brands, and the bigger it grew, the louder it popped.

(2000)

35

---

22   "Cole Haan Joins Ranks of Shoe Companies Leaving Maine," Associated Press, 23 April 1999.

23   Zusman, "Editor's Notebook."

Questions

1. What is a "balloon brand"?

2. Summarize in no more than two paragraphs the case against Nike as Klein presents it.

3. In Klein's view, why is it particularly pernicious for Nike to have drawn on the ethos of black inner-city culture in shaping the image of its brand?

4. To what extent does it trouble you to buy products that were made under exploitive conditions? To what degree are your purchasing decisions likely to be altered by information such as that provided by Klein?

5. Legible clothing makes a statement about the values and self-image of the wearer. But it also provides free advertising. Do you wear legible clothing? Why?

6. How would you describe the tone of Klein's writing? With particular reference to paragraphs 26-28, comment on how this tone is created.

7. Klein refers elsewhere in her book to the loss of "unmarketed space" in modern Western society. Comment on this phenomenon as you perceive it.

Margaret Atwood

First Job

In this short piece written for The New Yorker, *a famous poet and novelist tells the story of her first "real job."*

❧

I'll pass over the mini-jobs of adolescence—the summer-camp stints that were more like getting paid for having fun. I'll pass over, too, the self-created pin-money generators—the puppet shows put on for kids at office parties, the serigraph posters turned out on the Ping-Pong table—and turn to my first real job. By "real job," I mean one that had nothing to do with friends of my parents or parents of my friends but was obtained in the adult manner, by looking through the ads in newspapers and going in to be interviewed—one for which I was entirely unsuited, and that I wouldn't have done except for the money. I was surprised when I got it, underpaid while doing it, and frustrated in the performance of it, and these qualities have remained linked, for me, to the ominous word "job."

The year was 1962, the place was Toronto. It was summer, and I was faced with the necessity of earning the difference between my scholarship for the next year and what it would cost me to live. The job was in the coffee shop of a small hotel on Avenue Road; it is now in the process of being torn down, but at that time it was a clean, well-lighted place, with booths along one side and a counter—possibly marble—down the other. The booths were served by a waitressing pro who lipsticked outside the lines, and who thought I was a mutant. My job would be serving things at the counter—coffee I would pour, toast I would create from bread, milkshakes I would whip up in the obstetrical stainless-steel device provided. ("Easy as pie," I was told.) I would also be running the customers' money through the cash register—an opaque machine with buttons to be pushed, little drawers that shot in and out, and a neurotic system of locks.

I said I had never worked a cash register before. This delighted the manager, a plump, unctuous character out of some novel I hadn't yet read.

493

He said the cash register, too, was easy as pie, and I would catch on to it in no time, as I was a smart girl with an MA. He said I should go and get myself a white dress.

I didn't know what he meant by "white dress." I bought the first thing I could find on sale, a nylon afternoon number with daisies appliquéd onto the bodice. The waitress told me this would not do: I needed a dress like hers, a *uniform*. ("How dense can you be?" I overheard her saying.) I got the uniform, but I had to go through the first day in my nylon daisies.

5   This first humiliation set the tone. The coffee was easy enough—I just had to keep the Bunn filled—and the milkshakes were possible; few people wanted them anyway. The sandwiches and deep-fried shrimp were made at the back: all I had to do was order them over the intercom and bin the leftovers.

But the cash register was perverse. Its drawers would pop open for no reason, or it would ring eerily when I swore I was nowhere near it; or it would lock itself shut, and the queue of customers waiting to pay would lengthen and scowl as I wrestled and sweated. I kept expecting to be fired for incompetence, but the manager chortled more than ever. Occasionally, he would bring some man in a suit to view me. "She's got an MA," he would say, in a proud but pitying voice, and the two of them would stare at me and shake their heads.

An ex-boyfriend discovered my place of employment, and would also come to stare and shake his head, ordering a single coffee, taking an hour to drink it, leaving me a sardonic nickel tip. The Greek short-order cook decided I would be the perfect up-front woman for the restaurant he wanted to open: he would marry me and do the cooking, I would speak English to the clientele and work—was he mad?—the cash register. He divulged his bank balance, and demanded to meet my father so the two of them could close the deal. When I declined, he took to phoning me over the intercom to whisper blandishments, and to plying me with deep-fried shrimp. A girl as scrawny as myself, he pointed out, was unlikely to get such a good offer again.

Then the Shriners hit town, took over the hotel, and began calling for buckets of ice, or for doctors because they'd had heart attacks: too much tricycle-riding in the hot sun was felling them in herds. I couldn't handle the responsibility, the cash register had betrayed me once too often, and the short-order cook was beginning to sing Frank Sinatra songs to me. I gave notice.

Only when I'd quit did the manager reveal his true stratagem: they'd wanted someone inept as me because they suspected their real cashier of skimming the accounts, a procedure I was obviously too ignorant to ever figure out. "Too stunned," as the waitress put it. She was on the cashier's side, and had me fingered as a stoolie all along.

(2001)

Questions

1. Describe as concisely as you can Atwood's tone in this essay.

2. What are some of the sources of humor in this piece? To what extent do you think it would be amusing to readers unfamiliar with North American culture?

3. Say as much as you can about the unusual use of words in the following phrases in paragraph 2; what is going on in each case, and what effect does it have on the reader?

   "lipsticked outside the lines"

   "toast I would create from bread"

   "an opaque machine"

4. Comment on the choice of the verb "pointed out" in the last sentence of paragraph 7.

5. Write a short and light-hearted essay about a job you have worked at; in writing it try out some of the same stylistic devices that Atwood employs.

Mark Beeman, Edward M. Bowden, Jason
Haberman, Jennifer L. Stevenson, Stella
Arambel-Liu, Richard Greenblatt,
Paul J. Reber, and John Kounios

Neural Activity When People Solve Verbal Problems with Insight

*In this scholarly article, Mark Beeman, John Kounios, et al.
present their findings on the neurological processes of insight.*

❧

Abstract

People sometimes solve problems with a unique process called insight, accompanied by an "Aha!" experience. It has long been unclear whether different cognitive and neural processes lead to insight versus noninsight solutions, or if solutions differ only in subsequent subjective feeling. Recent behavioral studies indicate distinct patterns of performance and suggest differential hemispheric involvement for insight and noninsight solutions. Subjects solved verbal problems, and after each correct solution indicated whether they solved with or without insight. We observed two objective neural correlates of insight. Functional magnetic resonance imaging[1] (Experiment 1) revealed increased activity in the right hemisphere anterior superior temporal gyrus[2] for insight relative to noninsight solutions. The same region was active during initial solving efforts. Scalp

---

1 *Functional magnetic resonance imaging* A specialized scan that measures neural activity through changes in blood flow in the brain.

2 *superior temporal gyrus* A ridge on the cerebral cortex with functions including the processing of speech and the recognition of facial expressions.

electroencephalogram[3] recordings (Experiment 2) revealed a sudden burst of high-frequency (gamma-band) neural activity in the same area beginning 0.3 s prior to insight solutions. This right anterior temporal area is associated with making connections across distantly related information during comprehension. Although all problem solving relies on a largely shared cortical[4] network, the sudden flash of insight occurs when solvers engage distinct neural and cognitive processes that allow them to see connections that previously eluded them.

INTRODUCTION

According to legend, Archimedes shouted "Eureka!" ("I have found it!") when he suddenly discovered that water displacement could be used to calculate density. Since then, "Eureka!," or "Aha!," has often been used to express the feeling one gets when solving a problem with *insight*. Insight is pervasive in human (and possibly animal [Epstein et al. 1984]) cognition, occurring in perception, memory retrieval, language comprehension, problem solving, and various forms of practical, artistic, and scientific creativity (Sternberg and Davidson 1995). The Archimedes legend has persisted over two millennia in part because it illustrates some of the key ways in which insight solutions differ from solutions achieved through more straightforward problem solving. We examine the neural bases of these different problem-solving methods.

Although many processes are shared by most types of problem solving, insight solutions appear to differ from noninsight solutions in several important ways. The clearest defining characteristic of insight problem solving is the subjective "Aha!" or "Eureka!" experience that follows insight solutions (Schooler et al. 1993). This subjective experience can lead to a strong emotional response—according to legend, Archimedes ran home from the baths shouting "Eureka!" without donning his clothes first. In addition, problem solving with insight is characterized by the following features. (1) Solvers first come to an impasse, no longer progressing toward a solution (Duncker 1945). Archimedes, for example, was stymied by King Hiero's challenge to determine whether his new crown was pure gold

---

3   *electroencephalogram* A recording of neural activity through the electricity produced by neurons firing in the brain.

4   *cortical* Relating to the outer areas of the brain, which are associated with higher brain functions.

without damaging the crown. (2) Solvers usually cannot report the processing that enables them to reinterpret the problem and overcome the impasse (Maier 1931). Insight often occurs when people are not even aware they are thinking of the problem, as reportedly happened to Archimedes while in the baths. (3) Solvers experience their solutions as arising suddenly (Metcalfe and Wiebe 1987; Smith and Kounios 1996) and immediately recognize the correctness of the solution (or solution path). (4) Performance on insight problems is associated with creative thinking and other cognitive abilities different from those associated with performance on noninsight problems (Schooler and Melcher 1997). Some researchers have argued that all these characteristics of insight solutions are essentially epiphenomenal, that insight and noninsight solutions vary only in emotional intensity, and that they are attained with precisely the same cognitive (hence neural) mechanisms (Weisberg and Alba 1981; Weisberg 1986; Perkins 2000).

Persistent questions about insight concern whether unconscious processing precedes reinterpretation and solution, whether distinct cognitive and neural mechanisms beyond a common problem-solving network are involved in insight, and whether the apparent suddenness of insight solutions reflects truly sudden changes in cognitive processing and neural activity. Recent work suggests that people are thinking—at an unconscious level—about the solution prior to solving problems with insight. Specifically, while working on a verbal problem they have yet to solve, people presented with a potential solution word read the actual solution word faster than they read an unrelated word (Bowden and Beeman 1998). This "solution priming" effect is greater—and in fact people make solution decisions about presented words more quickly—when words are presented to the left visual hemifield,[5] which projects directly to the right hemisphere (RH), than when words are presented to the right visual hemifield, which projects to the left hemisphere (LH). This suggests that RH semantic processing[6] is more likely than LH semantic processing to produce lexical or semantic information that leads to the solution. These RH advantages occur only when solvers experience insight—the "Aha!" or "Eureka!" feeling that comes with insight solutions (Bowden and Beeman 2003a). Moreover, when subjects try to solve classic insight problems, they benefit more from hints presented to the left visual field (i.e., the RH) than from hints presented to the right visual field (i.e., the LH) (Fiore and Schooler 1998).

---

5   *visual hemifield*   Half of the field of vision.

6   *semantic processing*   Brain function related to linguistic meaning.

Problem solving is a complex behavior that requires a network of [5] cortical areas for all types of solving strategies and solutions, so solving problems with and without insight likely invokes many shared cognitive processes and neural mechanisms. One critical cognitive process distinguishing insight solutions from noninsight solutions is that solving with insight requires solvers to recognize distant or novel semantic (or associative) relations; hence, insight-specific neural activity should reflect that process. The most likely area to contribute to this component of insight problem solving is the anterior superior temporal gyrus (aSTG) of the RH. Language comprehension studies demonstrate that the RH is particularly important for recognizing distant semantic relations (Chiarello et al. 1990; Beeman 1998), and bilateral aSTG is involved in semantic integration. For example, sentences and complex discourse increase neural activity in aSTG bilaterally (Mazoyer et al. 1993; Stowe et al. 1999), and discourse that places particular demands on recognizing or computing distant semantic relations specifically increases neural activity in RH temporal areas (St. George et al. 1999; Mason and Just 2004), especially aSTG (Meyer et al. 2000; Kircher et al. 2001). If this prediction of RH aSTG involvement is confirmed, it will help constrain neurocognitive theories of insight. Other cortical areas, such as prefrontal cortex[7] and the anterior cingulate[8] (AC) may also be differentially involved in producing insight and noninsight solutions.

We used functional magnetic resonance imaging (FMRI) in Experiment 1 and electroencephalogram (EEG) measurement in Experiment 2 to test the empirically and theoretically derived hypothesis that solving problems with insight requires engagement of (or increased emphasis on) distinct neural mechanisms, particularly in the RH anterior temporal lobe. Event-related experimental designs compared neural activity when people solved verbal problems with insight to neural activity when they solved problems (from the same problem set) without insight.

As in earlier behavioral work, we used a set of compound remote associate problems (Bowden and Beeman 2003b) adapted from a test of creative cognition (Mednick 1962).... Subjects saw three problem words (*pine*, *crab*, *sauce*) and attempted to produce a single solution word (*apple*) that can form a familiar compound word or phrase with each of the three

---

7   *prefrontal cortex*   The front part of the frontal lobes of the brain, associated with planning, decision making, and the coordination of thoughts and actions.

8   *anterior cingulate*   A segment of the outer layers of the brain, associated with decision making, reward anticipation, and some biological functions.

problem words (*pineapple*, *crab apple*, *applesauce*). We relied on solvers' reports to sort solutions into insight solutions and noninsight solutions, avoiding the complication that presumed insight problems can sometimes be solved without insight (Davidson 1995) and circumventing the use of different types of problems requiring different cognitive operations. Thus, we made use of the most important defining characteristic of insight problems: the subjective conscious experience—the "Aha!" A similar technique revealed distinct behavioral characteristics when people recognized solutions with insight (Bowden and Beeman 2003a). Note that this is a very "tight" comparison. In both conditions problems are solved using a network of processes common to both insight and noninsight solutions. If insight ratings reflect some distinct cognitive processes, this contrast will reveal the distinct underlying brain activity. In other words, within the cortical network for problem solving, different components will be engaged or emphasized for insight versus noninsight solutions. FMRI (Experiment 1) should reveal neuroanatomical locations of processes that are unique to insight solutions, and EEG (Experiment 2) should reveal the time course (e.g., whether insight really is sudden) and frequency characteristics of neurophysiological differences.

Sequence of Events for Each Trial

(A) The "Compound" prompt was presented for 0.5 s, then persisted for a variable amount of additional time (0-2 s) until a cue from the scanner indicated the beginning of a new whole brain acquisition. (B) A three-word problem appeared in the center of the screen and persisted until subjects indicated with a bimanual button press that they had solved the problem, or until the 30-s time limit elapsed. Thus, event timing and condition were completely dependent on subjects' responses. (C) Following the button press or time limit, subjects were prompted to verbalize the solution (or press the buttons and say "Don't know" if the time limit expired prior to solution) then (D) prompted to indicate (with a bimanual button press) whether they felt insight, as described prior to the experiment. (E) Next, subjects performed 9 s of an unrelated filler task (three line-matching trials, 3 s each), allowing BOLD[9] signal to return to baseline (in areas not involved in line matching).

---

9 *BOLD* Blood-oxygen-level dependence. "BOLD signal" refers to the changes in blood flow measured in an FMRI.

Results

Experiment 1.

Subjects solved 59% of the problems presented, and pressed buttons indicating "insight" for 56% (s.d.[10] = 18.2) of their solutions, "no insight" for 41% (s.d. = 18.9) of their solutions, and "other" for 2% of their solutions. We marked a point about 2 s (rounded to the nearest whole second) prior to each solution button press as the solution event, and examined a time window 4-9 s after this event (i.e., 2-7 s after the button press) to isolate the corresponding hemodynamic[11] response. Solving problems and responding to them required a strict sequence of events (reading of words, solving effort, solving, button press, verbalizing the solution, insight decision), but this sequence was identical whether subjects indicated solving with or without insight, so differences in FMRI signal resulted from the degree to which distinct cognitive processes and neural systems led to insight or noninsight solutions.

... The most robust insight effect [is that] as predicted, insight solutions were associated with greater neural activity in the RH aSTG than noninsight solutions. The active area was slightly anterior to primary auditory cortex, posterior to temporal pole, and along the medial aspect of the aSTG, extending down the lateral edge of the descending ramus of the Sylvian fissure to midway through the middle temporal gyrus (MTG). (This site is also close to the superior temporal sulcus, which has been implicated in language.) Across all 13 subjects, the peak signal difference at a single voxel[12] within the RH aSTG was 0.25% across the 6-s window, and 0.30% at a single time to repetition (TR), i.e., the time needed to repeat the image of the whole brain. Overall signal in this region was robust, reaching 96.8% of the brainwide average (after removing voxels in other brain areas with signal below a standard criterion)....

Several cortical areas showed strong solution-related FMRI signal, but approximately equally for insight and noninsight solutions. Some of these areas (e.g., motor cortex) relate to the response sequence rather than solution processes; other areas probably reflect component processes of a problem-solving network common to both insight and noninsight solving, such as retrieving potential solutions. Two areas that may be of interest

10

---

10 *s.d.* Standard deviation.

11 *hemodynamic* Relating to blood circulation.

12 *voxel* Unit of measure in medical scans.

for future studies are AC and posterior middle/superior temporal gyrus. Both these areas, in the RH only, showed strong, negative solution-related signal, approximately equal in the two solution types. AC is an area that might be predicted to be involved in reorienting attention as solvers overcome impasses, given its role in performance monitoring and cognitive control (MacDonald et al. 2000). RH posterior MTG is active when subjects "get" jokes (Goel and Dolan 2001) and when they attempt to solve problems with deductive reasoning (Parsons and Osherson 2001). However, in our experiment, only the RH aSTG showed a robust insight effect.

Experiment 2.

A separate group of subjects participated in fundamentally the same paradigm while we continuously recorded EEGs from the scalp. We then compared time-frequency analyses of the EEGs associated with insight solutions versus noninsight solutions. EEG provides temporal resolution greatly superior to that of FMRI and thus can better elucidate the time course and suddenness of the insight effect. Furthermore, complex EEG oscillations can be parsed into constituent frequency components, some of which have been linked to particular types of neural and cognitive processes (Ward 2003).

The high temporal resolution of EEG allows us to address one of the fundamental questions raised earlier: does insight really occur suddenly, as subjective experience suggests? For problems typically solved without insight, solvers report gradually increasing closeness to solution. In contrast, for problems typically solved with insight, solvers report little or no progress until shortly before they actually solve the problem (Metcalfe 1986; Metcalfe and Wiebe 1987). Similarly, quantitative analyses of the distributions of response times and accuracies during anagram solving (a task frequently eliciting the experience of insight) reveal that a solution becomes available in a discrete transition from a state of little or no information about the correct response directly to the final state of high accuracy. This contrasts with various language and memory tasks not associated with insight, which yield partial outputs before processing has been completed (Kounios and Smith 1995; Smith and Kounios 1996).

We predicted that a sudden change in neural activity associated with insight solutions would produce an EEG correlate. Specifically, we predicted that high-frequency EEG oscillations in the gamma band (i.e., greater than 30 Hz) would reflect this sudden activity, because prior research has associated gamma-band activity with the activation of perceptual, lexical, and semantic representations (Tallon-Baudry and Bertrand 1999; Pulvermüller 2001). Gamma-band electrical activity correlates with the blood oxygenation level-dependent (BOLD) response apparent in FMRI signal; lower-frequency EEG components do not seem to have direct correlates in FMRI signal (Foucher et al. 2003; Laufs et al. 2003). Consequently, based on the language literature discussed earlier and on our FMRI results, we predicted a discrete insight-related increase in gamma-band activity at electrodes over the anterior temporal lobe of the RH.

Participants solved 46% (s.d. = 8.2) of the problems correctly within the time limit. Of correctly solved problems, subjects reported more insight solutions (56%, s.d. = 8.4) than noninsight solutions (42%, s.d. = 9.0), (t[18] = 3.47, p = 0.003); there was no difference in mean response times (insight solutions = 9.94 s, s.d. − 2.60; noninsight solutions = 9.25 s, s.d. = 3.06; t < 1.0).

There was a burst of gamma-band activity associated with correct insight solutions (but not noninsight solutions) beginning approximately 0.3 s before the button-press solution response at anterior right temporal electrodes ..., with no significant difference between insight and noninsight solutions over homologous LH sites. A repeated-measures analysis of variance (ANOVA) performed on log-transformed gamma-band (39 Hz) EEG power at left and right temporal electrode sites (T7 and T8, respectively) for insight and noninsight trials using two time windows (−1.52 to −0.36 s and −0.30 to −0.02 s, measured with respect to the solution response) yielded significant insight × time window (F[1,18] = 6.68, p = 0.019) and insight × time window × Hemisphere (F[1,18] = 8.11, p = 0.011) interactions. The overall interaction occurred because there was an insight × hemisphere interaction from −0.30 to −0.02 s (F[1,18] = 4.61, p = 0.046) but no effect in the −1.52 to −0.36 s time window. Within the −0.30 to −0.02 s interval for these two electrodes, there was a significant insight effect at the right temporal (T8) site (t[18] = 3.48, p = 0.003), but not at the homologous left temporal (T7) site or any other LH temporal electrode. Laplacian mapping of this effect ... is remarkably consistent with the FMRI signal in RH aSTG observed in Experiment 1....

DISCUSSION

Complex problem solving requires a complex cortical network to encode the problem information, search memory for relevant information,

15

evaluate this information, apply operators, and so forth. The FMRI and EEG results reported here conclusively demonstrate that solving verbal problems with insight requires at least one additional component to this cortical network, involving RH aSTG, that is less important to solving without insight. The insight effect in RH aSTG accords with the literature on integrating distant or novel semantic relations during language comprehension. When people comprehend (read or listen to) sentences or stories, neural activity increases in aSTG or temporal pole bilaterally more than when comprehending single words (Mazoyer et al. 1993; Bottini et al. 1994; Stowe et al. 1999; Humphries et al. 2001; Meyer et al. 2000). Neural activity increases in predominantly RH aSTG during tasks that emphasize integration across sentences to extract themes (St. George et al. 1999) or to form more coherent memories for stories (Mason and Just 2004). RH aSTG is also selectively active when subjects must generate the best ending to a sentence (Kircher et al. 2001) or mentally repair grammatically incorrect sentences (Meyer et al. 2000), both of which likely require intense semantic integration.

Like the results in language processing, the current results are predicted by the theory that the RH performs relatively coarse semantic coding (Beeman 1998; similarly, Chiarello et al. 1990). This theory contends that when people encounter words, semantic processing in several LH areas engages in relatively fine semantic coding which produces small semantic fields—i.e., this processing strongly focuses on a few concepts closely related to the input word in the given context. This is very effective for most straightforward language processing. In contrast, the homologous RH areas engage in relatively coarse semantic coding, which produces large and weak semantic fields—i.e., this processing includes many concepts, even concepts distantly related to the input words and context. This process is ineffective for rapid interpretation or selection but increases semantic overlap among multiple semantic fields (Beeman et al. 1994), which is useful when drawing together parts of a story or conversation that are only distantly related (Beeman 1993; Beeman et al. 2000). In this view, the coarseness of semantic coding is largely influenced by slight asymmetries in neural microcircuitry that produce more discrete, less redundant input fields in pyramidal neurons of the LH language cortex, and more overlapping input fields in corresponding neurons in the RH (for reviews see Beeman 1998; Hutsler and Galuske 2003).

We suggest that semantic integration, generally, is important for connecting various problem elements together and connecting the problem to the solution, and that coarsely coded semantic integration, computed in RH aSTG, is especially critical to insight solutions, at least for verbal problems (or problems that can be solved with verbal or semantic information). People come to an impasse on insight problems because their retrieval efforts are misdirected by ambiguous information in the problem or by their usual method for solving similar problems. Large semantic fields allowing for more overlap among distantly related concepts (or distantly associated lexical items) may help overcome this impasse. Because this semantic processing is weak, it may remain unconscious, perhaps overshadowed by stronger processing of the misdirected information (Schooler et al. 1993; Smith 1995), and solvers remain stuck at impasse. Eventually, solution-related information bursts into awareness "in a sudden flash." This can happen after misdirected processing decays or is suppressed, after solution-related processing grows, or after environmental cues occur—such as the water overflowing the bathtub when Archimedes got in. Archimedes had semantic and verbal knowledge about how to compute density from weight and volume, but struggled with measuring the volume of an irregularly shaped crown without harming the crown (e.g., melting it). His observation of water displacement allowed him to connect known concepts in new ways. This is the nature of many insights, the recognition of new connections across existing knowledge.

A persistent question has been whether the cognitive and neural events that lead to insight are as sudden as the subjective experience. The timing and frequency characteristics of the EEG results shed light on this question. We propose that the gamma-band insight effect in Experiment 2 reflects the sudden transition of solution-related cognitive processing from an unconscious to a conscious state. Recent research associates gamma-band oscillations with the ignition of neural cell assemblies supporting the transient feature binding necessary to activate a representation (Tallon-Baudry and Bertrand 1999; Pulvermüller 2001)—in this case, a phonological, lexical, or semantic representation corresponding to the solution word and its associations to the problem words. According to this hypothesis, greater synchronous gamma-band activity for insight than for noninsight solutions could reflect a more integrated or unitized solution representation. Furthermore, synchronous gamma-band activity has been hypothesized to play a critical role in the accessibility to consciousness of such representations (Engel and Singer 2001). The timing (with respect to the solution button press) of the insight gamma-band effect closely approximates estimates derived from cognitive behavioral studies of the amount of time required to access an available solution and generate a two-alternative, forced-choice button-press response (e.g., Kounios et al. 1987; Meyer et al. 1988; Smith and Kounios 1996). The present experiments had no response choice (i.e., always the same bimanual button press for solutions), so subjects could easily have responded 0.3 s after solving the problems. Thus, we infer that the observed gamma burst reflects the sudden conscious availability of a solution word resulting from an insight.

Suddenly recognizing new connections between problem elements is a hallmark of insight, but it is only one component of a large cortical network necessary for solving problems with insight, and recognizing new connections likely contributes to other tasks, such as understanding metaphors (Bottini et al. 1994) and deriving a story theme (St. George et al. 1999). Similar tasks may depend on related cortical networks. For example, appreciating semantic jokes (Goel and Dolan 2001) and engaging in deductive reasoning that sometimes involves insight (Parsons and Osherson 2001) both increase activity in RH posterior MTG. It is striking that the insight effect observed in the RH in our experiments occurred when people solved verbal problems, which traditional views suggest should involve mostly LH processing with little or no contribution from the RH. It is possible that insight solutions to nonverbal problems would require different cortical networks. However, the observed effect cannot be due simply to verbal retrieval, which must occur for both insight and noninsight solutions; it could be due to a type of verbal retrieval specific to insight solutions, but not involved in noninsight solutions.

We turn now to another result from the EEG time-frequency analysis, which was not predicted but nevertheless suggests a provocative interpretation. The gamma burst thought to reflect the transition of the insight solution from an unconscious to a conscious state was preceded by insight-specific activity in the alpha band (8-13 Hz). Specifically, there was a burst of alpha power (estimated at 9.8 Hz) associated with insight solutions detected over right posterior parietal cortex from approximately 1.4 s until approximately 0.4 s before the solution response, at which point insight alpha power decreased to the level of noninsight alpha power, or below....

Alpha rhythms are understood to reflect idling or inhibition of cortical areas (Pfurtscheller et al. 1996). Increased alpha power measured over parietal-occipital cortex indicates idling or inhibition of visual cortex. This has been attributed to gating of visual information flowing into the perceptual system in order to protect fragile or resource-intensive processes from interference from bottom-up stimulation (Ray and Cole 1985; Worden et al. 2001; Jensen et al. 2002; Cooper et al. 2003; Ward 2003). This interpretation assumes that brain areas are normally highly interactive, and that allowing one process to proceed relatively independently requires active attenuation of this interaction. For instance, when subjects attend to visual space in the hemifield projecting to one hemisphere, posterior alpha increases over the other hemisphere, which receives inputs from the unattended hemifield (Worden et al. 2001). Analogously, the present results suggest selective gating of visual inputs to the RH during the interval preceding the insight-related right temporal gamma burst.... Hypothetically, this allows weaker processing about more distant associations between the problem words and potential solutions to gain strength, by attenuating bottom-up activation or other neural activity not related to solution that would decrease the signal-to-noise ratio for the actual solution....

This interpretation of the early insight-specific alpha effect is consistent with previous behavioral research suggesting that, prior to an insight, the solution to a verbal problem can be weakly activated (Bowers et al. 1990), especially in the RH (Bowden and Beeman 1998; Bowden and Beeman 2003a). Thus insight solutions may be associated with early unconscious solution-related processing, followed by a sudden transition to full awareness of the solution. We suggest that, in Experiment 2, the early posterior alpha insight effect is an indirect correlate of the former, and the right temporal gamma effect is a direct correlate of the latter.

In sum, when people solve problems with insight, leading to an "Aha!" experience, their solutions are accompanied by a striking increase in neural activity in RH aSTG. Thus, within the network of cortical areas required for problem solving, different components are engaged or emphasized when solving with versus without insight. We propose that the RH aSTG facilitates integration of information across distant lexical or semantic relations, allowing solvers to see connections that had previously eluded them. In the two millennia since Archimedes shouted "Eureka!," it has seemed common knowledge that people sometimes solve problems— whether great scientific questions or trivial puzzles—by a seemingly distinct mechanism called insight. This mechanism involves suddenly seeing a problem in a new light, often without awareness of how that new light was switched on. We have demonstrated that insight solutions are indeed associated with a discrete, distinct pattern of neural activity, supporting unique cognitive processes.

25

MATERIALS AND METHODS

Subjects.

Ten men and eight women were paid to participate in Experiment 1; 19 new subjects (nine men, ten women) were paid to participate in Experiment 2. All were young (18-29) neurologically intact, right-handed, native English speakers; Experiment 1 participants met safety criteria for FMRI scanning. After hearing about all methods and risks and performing practice trials, they consented to participate. In Experiment 1, data from four men and one woman were excluded due to poor FMRI signal or because subjects provided fewer than ten insight or noninsight responses. This research was approved by the University of Pennsylvania Institutional Review Board.

Behavioral paradigm.

Following practice, subjects attempted 124 compound remote associate problems during FMRI scanning. These problems (Bowden and Beeman 2003b) can be solved quickly and evoke an "Aha!" experience, producing a distinct behavioral signature (Bowden and Beeman 2003a), roughly half the time they are solved. Figure 1 illustrates the sequence of events for each trial. Each trial began with the task label "Compound" presented on liquid crystal diode goggles for 0.5 to 2.5 s. A gating signal from the scanner triggered the central presentation of three problem words, which persisted until subjects solved the problem or 30 s elapsed. If subjects solved the problem, they made a bimanual button press, after which the word "Solution?" prompted them to verbalize their solution. After 2 s the word "Insight?" prompted subjects to press buttons indicating whether they solved the problem with insight.

Prior to the experiment subjects were told the following: "A feeling of insight is a kind of 'Aha!' characterized by suddenness and obviousness. You may not be sure how you came up with the answer, but are relatively confident that it is correct without having to mentally check it. It is as though the answer came into mind all at once—when you first thought of the word, you simply knew it was the answer. This feeling does not have to be overwhelming, but should resemble what was just described." The experimenter interacted with subjects until this description was clear. This subjective rating could be used differently across subjects (or even across trials), blurring condition boundaries; yet the distinct neural correlates of insight observed across the group demonstrate that there was some consistency.

If subjects failed to solve problems within 30 s, the "Solution?" prompt appeared, and subjects pressed the "no" buttons and verbalized "Don't Know." Then the "Insight?" prompt appeared, and subjects pressed the "no" buttons again. After the insight rating, subjects performed three line-matching trials (3 s each) to distract them from thinking about the problems, allowing the critical BOLD signal to return to baseline (Binder et al. 1999). The total time from the end of one problem to the onset of the next was 14.5-16.5 s. The condition (e.g., insight or noninsight solution) and time of events was determined by subjects' responses.

Image acquisition.
Imaging was performed at the Hospital of the University of Pennsylvania, on a 1.5 Tesla GE SIGNA scanner with a fast gradient system for echo-planar imaging and a standard head coil. Head motion was restricted with plastic braces and foam padding. Anatomical high-resolution T1-weighted axial and sagittal images were acquired while subjects performed practice trials. Functional images (21 slices, 5 mm thick; 3.75-mm $\times$ 3.75 mm in-plane resolution; TR = 2000 ms for 21 slices; time to echo = 40 ms) were acquired in the same axial plane as the anatomical images using gradient-echo echo-planar sequences sensitive to BOLD signal (Kwong et al. 1992; Ogawa et al. 1992). Each functional run was preceded by a 20-s saturation period. Subjects participated in four 15-min runs and a fifth run of varying length, depending on the number of remaining problems....

ACKNOWLEDGMENTS
The authors thank Zoe Clancy, Jamie Hanson, Claudia Maennel, Andrew Schutzbank, and Dan Kimberg for assistance with this project. This work was supported by the National Institute of Deafness and Other Communication Disorders, grants R01 DC-04052 (to MJ-B), and R01 DC-04818 (to JK).

AUTHOR CONTRIBUTIONS
MJ-B, EMB, and JK conceived and designed the experiments. MJ-B, JH, JLF, SA-L, and JK performed the experiments. MJ-B, JH, JLF, RG, PJR, and JK analyzed the data. MJ-B, EMB, and JK wrote the paper.

REFERENCES[13]

Beeman M (1993) Semantic processing in the right hemisphere may contribute to drawing inferences from discourse. Brain Lang 44: 80-120.

Beeman M (1998) Coarse semantic coding and discourse comprehension. In: Beeman M, Chiarello C, editors. Right hemisphere language comprehension: Perspectives from cognitive neuroscience. Mahwah (N.J.): Lawrence Erlbaum Associates. pp. 255-284.

Beeman MJ, Bowden EM, Gernsbacher MA (2000) Right and left hemisphere cooperation for drawing predictive and coherence inferences during normal story comprehension. Brain Lang 71: 310-336.

Beeman M, Friedman RB, Grafman J, Perez E, Diamond S, et al. (1994) Summation priming and coarse semantic coding in the right hemisphere. J Cogn Neurosci 6: 26-45.

Binder JR, Frost JA, Hammeke TA, Bellgowan PSF, Rao SM, et al. (1999) Conceptual processing during the conscious resting state: A functional MRI study. J Cogn Neurosci 11: 80-93.

Bottini G, Corcoran R, Sterzi R, Paulesu E, Schenone P, et al. (1994) The role of the right hemisphere in the interpretation of figurative aspects of language: A positron emission tomography activation study. Brain 117: 1241-1253.

Bowden EM, Beeman MJ (1998) Getting the right idea: Semantic activation in the right hemisphere may help solve insight problems. Psychol Sci 6: 435-440.

Bowden EM, Beeman M (2003a) Aha! Insight experience correlates with solution activation in the right hemisphere. Psychon Bull Rev 10: 730-737.

Bowden EM, Beeman M (2003b) Normative data for 144 compound remote associate problems. Behav Res Meth Instr Comput 35: 634-639.

Bowers KS, Regehr G, Balthazard C, Parker K (1990) Intuition in the context of discovery. Cognit Psychol 22: 72-110.

Chiarello C, Burgess C, Richards L, Pollock A (1990) Semantic and associative priming in the cerebral hemispheres: Some words do, some don't, ... sometimes, some places. Brain Lang 38: 75-104.

Cooper NR, Croft RJ, Dominey SJJ, Burgess AP, Gruzelier JH (2003) Paradox lost? Exploring the role of alpha oscillations during externally vs. internally directed attention and the implications for idling and inhibition hypotheses. Int J Psychophysiol 47: 65-74.

---

13 References have been excerpted to show only those cited in the included material.

Davidson JE (1995) The suddenness of insight. In: Sternberg RJ, Davidson JE, editors. The nature of insight. Cambridge (Mass.): MIT Press. pp. 125-155.

Duncker K (1945) On problem solving. Psychol Monogr. no 58: online.

Engel AK, Singer W (2001) Temporal binding and the neural correlates of sensory awareness. Trends Cognit Sci 5: 16-25.

Epstein R, Kirshnit CE, Lanza RP, Rubin LC (1984) 'Insight' in the pigeon: Antecedents and determinants of an intelligent performance. Nature 308: 61-62.

Fiore SM, Schooler JW (1998) Right hemisphere contributions to creative problem solving: Converging evidence for divergent thinking. In Beeman M, Chiarello C, editors. Right hemisphere language comprehension: Perspectives from cognitive neuroscience. Mahwah (N.J.): Lawrence Erlbaum Associates. pp. 349-371.

Foucher JR, Otzenberger H, Gounot D (2003) The BOLD response and the gamma oscillations respond differently than evoked potentials: An interleaved EEG-fMRI study. BMC Neurosci 4: 22.

Goel V, Dolan RJ (2001) The functional anatomy of humor: Segregating cognitive and affective components. Nat Neurosci 4(3): 237-238.

Humphries C, Willard K, Buchsbaum B, Hickok G (2001) Role of anterior temporal cortex in auditory sentence comprehension: An fMRI study. NeuroReport 12: 1749-1752.

Hutsler J, Galuske AW (2003) Hemispheric asymmetries in cerebral cortical networks. Trends Neurosci 26: 429-435.

Jensen O, Gelfand J, Kounios J, Lisman JE (2002) Posterior 9-12 Hz oscillations increase with memory load during retention in a short-term memory task. Cereb Cortex 12: 877-882.

Kircher TTJ, Brammer M, Andreu NT, Williams SCR, McGuire PK (2001) Engagement of right temporal cortex during linguistic context. Neuropsychologia 39: 798-809.

Kounios J, Smith RW (1995) Speed-accuracy decomposition yields a sudden insight into all-or-none information processing. Acta Psychol 90: 229-241.

Kounios J, Osman AM, Meyer DE (1987) Structure and process in semantic memory: New evidence based on speed-accuracy decomposition. J Exp Psychol Gen 116: 3-25.

Kwong KK, Belliveau JW, Chesler DA, Goldberg IE, Weisskoff RM, et al. (1992) Dynamic magnetic resonance imaging of human brain activity during primary sensory stimulation. Proc Natl Acad Sci U S A 89: 5675-5679.

Laufs H, Krakow K, Sterzer P, Eger E, Beyerle A, et al. (2003) Electroen-cephalographic signatures of attentional and cognitive default modes in spontaneous brain activity fluctuations at rest. Proc Natl Acad Sci U S A 100: 11053-11058.

MacDonald AW, Cohen JD, Stenger VA, Carter CS (2000) Dissociating the role of the dorsolateral prefrontal cortex and anterior cingulate cortex in cognitive control. Science 288: 1835-1838.

Maier NRF (1931) Reasoning in humans. II: The solution of a problem and its appearance in consciousness. J Comp Psychol 12: 181-194.

Mason R, Just M (2004) How the brain processes causal inferences in text: A theoretical account of generation and integration component processes utilizing both cerebral hemispheres. Psychol Sci 14: 1-7.

Mazoyer BM, Tzourio N, Frak V, Syrota A, Murayama N, et al. (1993) The cortical representation of speech. J Cognit Neurosci 5: 467-479.

Mednick SA (1962) The associative basis of the creative process. Psychol Rev 69: 220-232.

Metcalfe J (1986) Premonitions of insight predict impending error. J Exp Psychol Learn Mem Cogn 12: 623-634.

Metcalfe J, Wiebe D (1987) Intuition in insight and noninsight problem solving. Mem Cognit 15: 238-246.

Meyer M, Friederici AD, von Cramon Y (2000) Neurocognition of auditory sentence comprehension: Event related fMRI reveals sensitivity to syn-tactic violations and task demands. Brain Res Cogn Brain Res 9: 19-33.

Meyer DE, Irwin DE, Osman AM, Kounios J (1988) The dynamics of cognition and action: Mental processes inferred from speed-accuracy decomposition. Psychol Rev 95: 183-237.

Ogawa S, Tank DW, Menon R, Ellermann J, Kim S-G, et al. (1992) Intrin-sic signal changes accompanying sensory stimulation: Functional brain mapping with magnetic resonance imaging. Proc Natl Acad Sci U S A 89: 5951-5955.

Parsons LM, Osherson D (2001) New evidence for distinct right and left brain systems for deductive versus probabilistic reasoning. Cereb Cor-tex 11: 954-965.

Perkins D (2000) The eureka effect: The art and logic of breakthrough thinking. New York: W.W. Norton. 292 p.

Pfurtscheller G, Stancak A, Neuper C (1996) Event-related synchronization (ERS) in the alpha band—An electrophysiological correlate of cortical idling: A review. Int J Psychophysiol 24: 39-46.

Pulvermüller F (2001) Brain reflections of words and their meaning. Trends Cogn Sci 5: 517-524.

Ray WJ, Cole HW (1985) EEG alpha activity reflects attentional demands, and beta activity reflects emotional and cognitive processes. Science 228: 750-752.

Robertson DA, Gernsbacher MA, Guidotti SJ, Robertson RWR, Irwin W, et al. (2000) Functional neuroanatomy of the cognitive process of mapping during discourse comprehension. Psychol Sci 11: 255-260.

St. George M, Kutas M, Martinez A, Sereno MI (1999) Semantic integration in reading: Engagement of the right hemisphere during discourse processing. Brain 122: 1317-1325.

Schooler JW, Melcher J (1997) The ineffability of insight. In: Smith SM, Ward TB, Finke RA, editors. The creative cognition approach. Cambridge (Mass.): MIT Press. pp. 97-133.

Schooler JW, Ohlsson S, Brooks K (1993) Thoughts beyond words: When language overshadows insight. J Exp Psychol Gen 122: 166-183.

Smith RW, Kounios J (1996) Sudden insight: All-or-none processing revealed by speed-accuracy decomposition. J Exp Psychol Learn Mem Cogn 22: 1443-1462.

Smith SM (1995) Getting into and out of mental ruts: A theory of fixation, incubation, and insight. In: Sternberg RJ, Davidson JE, editors. The nature of insight. Cambridge (Mass.): MIT Press. pp. 229-252.

Sternberg RJ, Davidson JE, editors. (1995) The nature of insight. Cambridge (Mass.): MIT Press. 618 p.

Stowe LA, Paans AMJ, Wijers AA, Zwarts F, Mulder G, et al. (1999) Sentence comprehension and word repetition: A positron emission tomography investigation. Psychophysiology 36: 786-801.

Tallon-Baudry C, Bertrand O (1999) Oscillatory gamma activity in humans and its role in object representation. Trends Cogn Sci 3: 151-162.

Waltz JA, Knowlton BJ, Holyoak KJ, Boone KB, Mishkin FS, et al. (1999) A system for relational reasoning in human prefrontal cortex. Psychol Sci 10: 119-125.

Ward LM (2003) Synchronous neural oscillations and cognitive processes. Trends Cogn Sci 7: 553-558.

Weisberg RW (1986) Creativity: Genius and other myths. New York: WH Freeman and Company. 169 p.

Weisberg RW, Alba J (1981) An examination of the alleged role of "fixation" in the solution of several "insight" problems. J Exp Psychol Gen 110: 169-192.

Worden MS, Foxe JJ, Wang N, Simpson GV (2001) Anticipatory biasing of visuospatial attention indexed by retinotopically specific alpha-band electroencephalography increases over occipital cortex. J Neurosci 20(RC63): 61-66.

(2004)

Questions

1. What is significant about the role of the right hemisphere in insight?

2. What do Beeman, Kounios, et al. accomplish by doing two separate experiments?

3. Presenting only Beeman, Kounios, et al.'s observations, describe what happens in the brain leading up to an insight. Separately, summarize Beeman, Kounios, et al.'s interpretation of these physical occurrences. Is the interpretation they give reasonable? Why or why not?

4. How closely did Beeman et al.'s findings match their predictions?

5. What reasons do Beeman et al. give to justify their choice to administer word problems that can be solved through either insight or conscious reasoning? Are there any limitations to this method?

Questions on connections between this article and the following essay, "The Eureka Hunt," can be found at the end of that essay.

JONAH LEHRER

THE EUREKA HUNT

In this New Yorker *article, a science writer
discusses recent responses to the question
"Why do good ideas come to us when they do?"*

❧

The summer of 1949 was long and dry in Montana. On the afternoon of
August 5th—the hottest day ever recorded in the state—a lightning fire
was spotted in a remote area of pine forest. A parachute brigade of fifteen
firefighters known as smoke jumpers was dispatched to put out the blaze;
the man in charge was named Wag Dodge. When the jumpers left Missoula,
in a C-47 cargo plane, they were told that the fire was small, just a few
burning acres in the Mann Gulch.

Mann Gulch, nearly three miles long, is a site of geological transition,
where the Great Plains meet the Rocky Mountains, pine trees give way to
tall grasses, and steep cliffs loom over the steppes of the Midwest. The fire
began in the trees on one side of the gulch. By the time the firefighters arrived, the blaze was already out of control. Dodge moved his men along the
other side of the gulch and told them to head downhill, toward the water.

When the smoke jumpers started down the gulch, a breeze was blowing the flames away from them. Suddenly, the wind reversed, and Dodge
watched the fire leap across the gulch and spark the grass on his side. He
and his men were only a quarter mile uphill. An updraft began, and fierce
winds howled through the canyon as the fire sucked in the surrounding
air. Dodge was suddenly staring at a wall of flame fifty feet tall and three
hundred feet deep. In a matter of seconds, the fire began to devour the grass,
hurtling toward the smoke jumpers at seven hundred feet a minute.

Dodge screamed at his men to retreat. They dropped their gear and
started running up the steep canyon walls, trying to reach the top of the
ridge. After a few minutes, Dodge glanced over his shoulder and saw that

515

the fire was less than fifty yards away. He realized that the blaze couldn't be outrun; the gulch was too steep, the flames too fast.

5   So Dodge stopped running. The decision wasn't as suicidal as it appeared: in a moment of desperate insight, he had devised an escape plan. He lit a match and ignited the ground in front of him, the flames quickly moving up the grassy slope. Then Dodge stepped into the shadow of his fire, so that he was surrounded by a buffer of burned land. He wet his handkerchief with water from his canteen, clutched the cloth to his mouth, and lay down on the smoldering embers. He closed his eyes and tried to inhale the thin layer of oxygen clinging to the ground. Then he waited for the fire to pass over him.

Thirteen smoke jumpers died in the Mann Gulch fire. White crosses below the ridge still mark the spots where the men died. But after several terrifying minutes Dodge emerged from the ashes, virtually unscathed.

There is something inherently mysterious about moments of insight. Wag Dodge, for instance, could never explain where his idea for the escape fire came from. ("It just seemed the logical thing to do" was all he could muster.) His improbable survival has become one of those legendary stories of insight, like Archimedes shouting "Eureka!" when he saw his bathwater rise, or Isaac Newton watching an apple fall from a tree and then formulating his theory of gravity. Such tales all share a few essential features, which psychologists and neuroscientists use to define "the insight experience." The first of these is the impasse: before there can be a breakthrough, there has to be a mental block. Wag Dodge spent minutes running from the fire, although he was convinced that doing so was futile. Then, when the insight arrived, Dodge immediately realized that the problem was solved. This is another key feature of insight: the feeling of certainty that accompanies the idea. Dodge didn't have time to think about whether his plan would work. He simply knew that it would.

Mark Jung-Beeman, a cognitive neuroscientist at Northwestern University, has spent the past fifteen years trying to figure out what happens inside the brain when people have an insight. "It's one of those defining features of the human mind, and yet we have no idea how or why it happens," he told me. Insights have often been attributed to divine intervention, but, by mapping the epiphany as a journey between cortical circuits, Jung-Beeman wants to purge the insight experience of its mystery. Jung-Beeman has a tense smile, a receding hairline, and the wiry build of a long-distance runner. He qualified for the 1988 and 1992 Olympic trials in the fifteen hundred meters, although he gave up competitive running after, as he puts it, "everything below the hips started to fall apart." He now subsists on long walks and manic foot tapping. When Jung-Beeman gets excited about an idea—be it the cellular properties of pyramidal neurons or his new tread-mill—his speech accelerates, and he starts to draw pictures on whatever paper is nearby. It's as if his mind were sprinting ahead of his mouth.

Jung-Beeman became interested in the nature of insight in the early nineteen-nineties, while researching the right hemisphere of the brain. At the time, he was studying patients who had peculiar patterns of brain dam-age. "We had a number of patients with impaired right hemispheres," he said. "And the doctors would always say, 'Wow, you're lucky—it got the right hemisphere. That's the minor hemisphere. It doesn't do much, and it doesn't do anything with language.'" But it gradually became clear to Jung-Beeman that these patients did have serious cognitive problems after all, particularly with understanding linguistic nuance, and he began to suspect that the talents of the right hemisphere had been overlooked. If the left hemisphere excelled at denotation—storing the primary meaning of a word—Jung-Beeman suspected that the right hemisphere dealt with connotation, everything that gets left out of a dictionary definition, such as the emotional charge in a sentence or a metaphor. "Language is so complex that the brain has to process it in two different ways at the same time," he said. "It needs to see the forest and the trees. The right hemisphere is what helps you see the forest."

It wasn't clear how to pinpoint these nuanced aspects of cognition, because the results of right-hemisphere damage were harder to spot than those of left hemisphere damage. But in 1993 Jung-Beeman heard a talk by the psychologist Jonathan Schooler on moments of insight. Schooler had demonstrated that it was possible to interfere with insight by making people explain their thought process while trying to solve a puzzle—a phenom-enon he called "verbal overshadowing." This made sense to Jung-Beeman, since the act of verbal explanation would naturally shift activity to the left hemisphere, causing people to ignore the more subtle associations coming from the right side of the brain. "That's when I realized that insight could be a really interesting way to look at all these skills the right hemisphere excelled at," he said. "I guess I had an insight about insight."

Jung-Beeman began searching in the right hemisphere for the source of insight in the brain. He decided to compare puzzles solved in moments of insight with those solved by methodical testing of potential solutions, in which people could accurately trace their thought process and had no sense

10

of surprise when the answer came. Unfortunately, all the classic puzzles developed by scientists to study insight required insight; if subjects didn't solve them in a sudden "Aha!" moment, they didn't solve them at all. In a popular puzzle known as "the candle problem," for instance, subjects are given a cardboard box containing a few thumbtacks, a book of matches, and a candle. They are told to attach the candle to a piece of corkboard so that it can burn properly. Nearly ninety per cent of people pursue the same two strategies. They try to tack the candle directly to the board, which causes the candle wax to shatter. Or they try melting the candle with the matches, so that it sticks to the board; but the wax doesn't hold and the candle falls. Only four per cent of people manage to come up with the solution, which involves attaching the candle to the cardboard box and tacking the cardboard box to the corkboard.

To isolate the brain activity that defined the insight process, Jung-Beeman needed to develop a set of puzzles that could be solved either by insight or by analysis. Doing so was a puzzle in itself. "It can get pretty frustrating trying to find an experimentally valid brainteaser," Jung-Beeman said. "The puzzles can't be too hard or too easy, and you need to be able to generate lots of them." He eventually settled on a series of verbal puzzles, based on ones used by a psychologist in the early nineteen-sixties, which he named the Compound Remote Associate Problems, or CRAP. (The joke is beginning to get old, and in his scientific papers Jung-Beeman decorously leaves off the final "P.")

In a C.R.A. word puzzle, a subject is given three words, such as "pine," "crab," and "sauce," and asked to think of a word that can be combined with all three—in this case, "apple" ("pineapple," "crab apple," "apple sauce"). The subjects have up to thirty seconds to solve the puzzle. If they come up with an answer, they press the space bar on the keyboard and say whether the answer arrived via insight or analysis. When I participated in the experiment in Jung-Beeman's lab, I found that it was surprisingly easy to differentiate between the two cognitive paths. When I solved puzzles with analysis, I tended to sound out each possible word combination, cycling through all the words that went with "pine" and then seeing if they also worked with "crab" or "sauce." If I worked toward a solution, I always double-checked it before pressing the space bar. An insight, on the other hand, felt instantaneous: the answer arrived like a revelation.

Jung-Beeman initially asked his subjects to solve the puzzles while inside an fMRI machine, a brain scanner that monitors neural activity by tracking changes in blood flow. But fMRI has a three-to-five-second delay, as the blood diffuses across the cortex. "Insights happen too fast for fMRI," Jung-Beeman said. "The data was just too messy." Around this time, he teamed up with John Kounios, a cognitive neuroscientist at Drexel University, who was interested in insight largely because it seemed to contradict the classic model of learning, in which the learning process was assumed to be gradual. Kounios, a man with a shock of unruly wavy hair and an affinity for rumpled button-up vests, had been working with electroencephalography, or EEG, which measures the waves of electricity produced by the brain by means of a nylon hat filled with greased electrodes. (The device looks like a bulky shower cap.) Because there is no time delay with EEG, Kounios thought it could be useful for investigating the fleeting process of insight. Unfortunately, the waves of electricity can't be traced back to their precise source, but Kounios and Jung-Beeman saw that combining EEG with fMRI might allow them to construct a precise map, both in time and space, of the insight process.

The resulting studies, published in 2004 and 2006, found that people who solved puzzles with insight activated a specific subset of cortical areas. Although the answer seemed to appear out of nowhere, the mind was carefully preparing itself for the breakthrough. The first areas activated during the problem solving process were those involved with executive control, like the prefrontal cortex and the anterior cingulate cortex. The scientists refer to this as the "preparatory phase," since the brain is devoting its considerable computational power to the problem. The various sensory areas, like the visual cortex, go silent as the brain suppresses possible distractions. "The cortex does this for the same reason we close our eyes when we're trying to think," Jung-Beeman said. "Focus is all about blocking stuff out."

What happens next is the "search phase," as the brain starts looking for answers in all the relevant places. Because Jung-Beeman and Kounios were giving people word puzzles, they saw additional activity in areas related to speech and language. The search can quickly get frustrating, and it takes only a few seconds before people say that they've reached an impasse, that they can't think of the right word. "Almost all of the possibilities your brain comes up with are going to be wrong," Jung-Beeman said. "And it's up to the executive control areas to keep on searching or, if necessary, change strategies and start searching somewhere else."

But sometimes, just when the brain is about to give up, an insight appears. "You'll see people bolt up in their chair and their eyes go all wide," Ezra Wegbreit, a graduate student in the Jung-Beeman lab who often administers the C.R.A. test, said. "Sometimes they even say 'Aha!' before

15

they blurt out the answer." The suddenness of the insight comes with a burst of brain activity. Three hundred milliseconds before a participant communicates the answer, the EEG registers a spike of gamma rhythm, which is the highest electrical frequency generated by the brain. Gamma rhythm is thought to come from the "binding" of neurons, as cells distributed across the cortex draw themselves together into a new network, which is then able to enter consciousness. It's as if the insight had gone incandescent.

Jung-Beeman and Kounios went back and analyzed the information from the fMRI experiment to see what was happening inside the brain in the seconds before the gamma burst. "My biggest worry was that we would find nothing," Kounios said. "I thought there was a good possibility that whatever we found on the EEG wouldn't show up on the brain imaging." When the scientists looked at the data, however, they saw that a small fold of tissue on the surface of the right hemisphere, the anterior superior temporal gyrus (aSTG), became unusually active in the second before the insight. The activation was sudden and intense, a surge of electricity leading to a rush of blood. Although the function of the aSTG remains mostly a mystery—the brain is stuffed with obscurities—Jung-Beeman wasn't surprised to see it involved with the insight process. A few previous studies had linked the area to aspects of language comprehension, such as the detection of literary themes and the interpretation of metaphors. (A related area was implicated in the processing of jokes.) Jung-Beeman argues that these linguistic skills, like insight, require the brain to make a set of distant and unprecedented connections. He cites studies showing that cells in the right hemisphere are more "broadly tuned" than cells in the left hemisphere, with longer branches and more dendritic spines. "What this means is that neurons in the right hemisphere are collecting information from a larger area of cortical space," Jung-Beeman said. "They are less precise but better connected." When the brain is searching for an insight, these are the cells that are most likely to produce it.

The insight process, as sketched by Jung-Beeman and Kounios, is a delicate mental balancing act. At first, the brain lavishes the scarce resource of attention on a single problem. But, once the brain is sufficiently focused, the cortex needs relax in order to seek out the more remote association in the right hemisphere, which will provide the insight. "The relaxation phase is crucial," Jung-Beeman said. "That's why so many insights happen during warm showers." Another ideal moment for insights, according to the scientists, is the early morning, right after we wake up. The drowsy brain is unwound and disorganized, open to all sorts of unconventional ideas. The right hemisphere is also unusually active. Jung-Beeman said, "The problem with the morning, though, is that we're always so rushed. We've got to get the kids ready for school, so we leap out of bed and never give ourselves a chance to think." He recommends that, if we're stuck on a difficult problem, it's better to set the alarm clock a few minutes early so that we have time to lie in bed and ruminate. We do some of our best thinking when we're still half asleep.

As Jung-Beeman and Kounios see it, the insight process is an act of cognitive deliberation—the brain must be focused on the task at hand—transformed by accidental, serendipitous connections. We must concentrate, but we must concentrate on letting the mind wander. The patterns of brain activity that define this particular style of thought have recently been studied by Joy Bhattacharya, a psychologist at Goldsmiths, University of London. Using EEG, he has found that he can tell which subjects will solve insight puzzles up to eight seconds before the insight actually arrives. One of the key predictive signals is a steady rhythm of alpha waves emanating from the right hemisphere. Alpha waves typically correlate with a state of relaxation, and Bhattacharya believes that such activity makes the brain more receptive to new and unusual ideas. He has also found that unless subjects have sufficient alpha-wave activity they won't be able to make use of hints the researchers give them. 20

One of the surprising lessons of this research is that trying to force an insight can actually prevent the insight. While it's commonly assumed that the best way to solve a difficult problem is to focus, minimize distractions, and pay attention only to the relevant details, this clenched state of mind may inhibit the sort of creative connections that lead to sudden breakthroughs. We suppress the very type of brain activity that we should be encouraging. Jonathan Schooler has recently demonstrated that making people focus on the details of a visual scene, as opposed to the big picture, can significantly disrupt the insight process. "It doesn't take much to shift the brain into left-hemisphere mode," he said. "That's when you stop paying attention to those more holistic associations coming in from the right hemisphere." Meanwhile, in a study published last year, German researchers found that people with schizotypy—a mental condition that resembles schizophrenia, albeit with far less severe symptoms—were significantly better at solving insight problems than a control group. Schizotypal subjects have enhanced right-hemisphere function and tend to score above average on measures of creativity and associative thinking.

Schooler's research has also led him to reconsider the bad reputation of letting one's mind wander. Although we often complain that the brain is too easily distracted, Schooler believes that letting the mind wander is essential. "Just look at the history of science," he said. "The big ideas seem to always come when people are sidetracked, when they're doing something that has nothing to do with their research." He cites the example of Henri Poincaré, the nineteenth-century mathematician, whose seminal insight into non-Euclidean geometry arrived while he was boarding a bus. "At the moment when I put my foot on the step," Poincaré wrote, "the idea came to me, without anything in my former thoughts seeming to have paved the way for it.... I did not verify the idea; I should not have had the time, as, upon taking my seat in the omnibus, I went on with the conversation already commenced, but I felt a perfect certainty." Poincaré credited his sudden mathematical insight to "unconscious work," an ability to mull over the mathematics while he was preoccupied with unrelated activities, like talking to a friend on the bus. In his 1908 essay "Mathematical Creation," Poincaré insisted that the best way to think about complex problems is to immerse yourself in the problem until you hit an impasse. Then, when it seems that "nothing good is accomplished," you should find a way to distract yourself, preferably by going on a "walk or a journey." The answer will arrive when you least expect it. Richard Feynman, the Nobel Prize-winning physicist, preferred the relaxed atmosphere of a topless bar, where he would sip 7 UP, "watch the entertainment," and, if inspiration struck, scribble equations on cocktail napkins.

Kounios and Jung-Beeman aren't quite ready to offer extensive practical advice, but, when pressed, they often sound like Poincaré. "You've got to know when to step back," Kounios said. "If you're in an environment that forces you to produce and produce, and you feel very stressed, then you're not going to have any insights." Many stimulants, like caffeine, Adderall, and Ritalin, are taken to increase focus—one recent poll found that nearly twenty per cent of scientists and researchers regularly took prescription drugs to "enhance concentration"—but, according to Jung-Beeman and Kounios, drugs may actually make insights less likely, by sharpening the spotlight of attention and discouraging mental rambles. Concentration, it seems, comes with the hidden cost of diminished creativity. "There's a good reason Google puts Ping-Pong tables in their headquarters," Kounios said. "If you want to encourage insights, then you've got to also encourage people to relax." Jung-Beeman's latest paper investigates why people who are in a good mood are so much better at solving insight puzzles. (On average, they solve nearly twenty per cent more C.R.A. problems.)

Last year, Kounios and Jung-Beeman were invited to present their findings to DARPA, the central research agency of the Department of Defense. ("It was quite strange," Kounios recalls. "I never thought I'd be talking about creativity to national security officials.") DARPA was interested in finding ways to encourage insights amid the stress of war, fostering creativity on the battlefield. The scientists are convinced that it's only a matter of time before it becomes possible to "up-regulate" insight. "This could be a drug or technology or just a new way to structure our environment," Jung-Beeman said. "I think we'll soon get to the point where we can do more than tell people to take lots of showers."

For now, though, the science of promoting insight remains rooted in anecdote, in stories of people, like Poincaré, who were able to consistently induce the necessary state of mind. Kounios tells a story about an expert Zen meditator who took part in one of the C.R.A. insight experiments. At first, the meditator couldn't solve any of the insight problems. "This Zen guy went through thirty or so of the verbal puzzles and just drew a blank," Kounios said. "He was used to being very focused, but you can't solve these problems if you're too focused." Then, just as he was about to give up, he started solving one puzzle after another, until, by the end of the experiment, he was getting them all right. It was an unprecedented streak. "Normally, people don't get better as the task goes along," Kounios said. "If anything, they get a little bored." Kounios believes that the dramatic improvement of the Zen meditator came from his paradoxical ability to focus on not being focused, so that he could pay attention to those remote associations in the right hemisphere. "He had the cognitive control to let go," Kounios said. "He became an insight machine."

The most mysterious aspect of insight is not the revelation itself but what happens next. The brain is an infinite library of associations, a cacophony of competing ideas, and yet, as soon as the right association appears, we know. The new thought, which is represented by that rush of gamma waves in the right hemisphere, immediately grabs our attention. There is something paradoxical and bizarre about this. On the one hand, an epiphany is a surprising event; we are startled by what we've just discovered. Some part of our brain, however, clearly isn't surprised at all, which is why we are able to instantly recognize the insight. "As soon as the insight happens, it just seems so obvious," Schooler said. "People can't believe they didn't see it before."

25

The brain area responsible for this act of recognition is the prefrontal cortex, which lights up whenever people are shown the right answer—even if they haven't come up with the answer themselves. Pressed tight against the bones of the forehead, the prefrontal cortex has undergone a dramatic expansion during human evolution, so that it now represents nearly a third of the brain. While this area is often associated with the most specialized aspects of human cognition, such as abstract reasoning, it also plays a critical role in the insight process. Hallucinogenic drugs are thought to work largely by modulating the prefrontal cortex, tricking the brain into believing that its sensory delusions are revelations. People have the feeling of an insight but without the content. Understanding how this happens—how a circuit of cells can identify an idea as an insight, even if the idea has yet to enter awareness—requires an extremely precise level of investigation. The rhythms of brain waves and the properties of blood can't answer the question. Instead, it's necessary to study the brain at its most basic level, as a loom of electrical cells.

Earl Miller is a neuroscientist at M.I.T. who has devoted his career to understanding the prefrontal cortex. He has a shiny shaved head and a silver goatee. His corner office in the gleaming Picower Institute is cantilevered over a railroad track, and every afternoon the quiet hum of the lab is interrupted by the rattle of a freight train. Miller's favorite word is "exactly"— it's the adverb that modifies everything, so that a hypothesis is "exactly right," or an experiment was "exactly done"—and that emphasis on precision has defined his career. His first major scientific advance was a by-product of necessity. It was 1995, and Miller had just started his lab at M.I.T. His research involved recording directly from neurons in the monkey brain, monitoring the flux of voltage within an individual cell as the animals performed various tasks. "There were machines that allowed you to record from eight or nine at the same time, but they were very expensive," Miller said. "I still had no grants, and there was no way I could afford one." So Miller began inventing his own apparatus in his spare time. After a few months of patient tinkering, he constructed a messy tangle of wires, steel screws, and electrodes that could simultaneously record from numerous cells, distributed across the brain. "It worked even better than the expensive machine," Miller said.

This methodological advance—it's known as multiple electrode recording—allowed Miller to ask a completely new kind of scientific question. For the first time, it was possible to see how cells in different brain areas interacted. Miller was most interested in the interactions of the prefrontal cortex. "You name the brain area, and the prefrontal cortex is almost certainly linked to it," he said. It took more than five years of painstaking probing, as Miller recorded from cells in the monkey brain, but he was eventually able to show that the prefrontal cortex wasn't simply an aggregator of information. Instead, it was like the conductor of an orchestra, waving its baton and directing the players. This is known as "top-down processing," since the prefrontal cortex (the "top" of the brain) is directly modulating the activity of other areas. This is why, during the focusing phase of the insight process, Jung-Beeman and Kounios saw activity in the prefrontal cortex and the neighboring anterior cingulate cortex. They were watching the conductor at work.

In 2001, Miller and Jonathan Cohen, a neuroscientist at Princeton, published an influential paper that laid out their theory of how, exactly, the prefrontal cortex controls the rest of the brain. According to Miller and Cohen, this brain area is responsible not only for focusing on the task at hand but for figuring out what other areas need to be engaged in order to solve a problem. One implication of this is that if we're trying to solve a verbal puzzle the prefrontal cortex will selectively activate the specific brain areas involved with verbal processing. If it decides to turn on parts of the right hemisphere, then we might end up with an insight; if it decides to restrict its search to the left hemisphere, we'll probably arrive at a solution incrementally or not at all.

This "integrative" theory of the prefrontal cortex suggests why we can instantly recognize the insight, even when it seems surprising: the brain has been concertedly pursuing the answer; we just didn't know it. "Your consciousness is very limited in capacity," Miller said, "and that's why your prefrontal cortex makes all these plans without telling you about it." When that obscure circuit in the right hemisphere finally generates the necessary association, the prefrontal cortex is able to identify it instantly, and the insight erupts into awareness. We suddenly notice the music that has been playing all along.

Because Miller can eavesdrop on neurons, he's been able to see how these insights operate at the cellular level. One of his current experiments involves showing monkeys different arrangements of dots and asking them to sort the arrangements into various categories that they have been taught. The monkeys guess randomly at first, learning from trial and error. "But then, at a certain point, the monkey just gets it," Miller said. "They just start being able to categorize arrangements of dots that they've never seen before. That's the moment of categorical insight." This primate epiphany

30

registers as a new pattern of neural activity in the prefrontal cortex. The brain cells have been altered by the breakthrough. "An insight is a restructuring of information—it's seeing the same old thing in a completely new way," Miller said. "Once that restructuring occurs, you never go back."

And yet even this detailed explanation doesn't fully demystify insight. It remains unclear how simple cells recognize what the conscious mind cannot, or how they are able to filter through the chaos of bad ideas to produce the epiphany. "This mental process will always be a little unknowable, which is why it's so interesting to study," Jung-Beeman said. "At a certain point, you just have to admit that your brain knows much more than you do." An insight is a fleeting glimpse of the brain's huge store of unknown knowledge. The cortex is sharing one of its secrets.

So it was for Wag Dodge. After the fire crossed the river, all the other smoke jumpers were fixated on reaching the ridge. Panic had narrowed their thoughts, so that beating the flames up the slope was their sole goal. But, because Dodge realized that the fire would beat them to the top, his prefrontal cortex started frantically searching for an alternative. It was able to look past his fear and expand the possibilities of his thought process, as he considered remote mental associations that he'd never contemplated before. (As Miller says, "That Dodge guy had some really high prefrontal function.") And then, just as the blaze started to suck the oxygen out of the air, some remote bit of his brain realized that he could cheat death by starting his own fire. This unprecedented idea, a flicker of electricity somewhere in the right hemisphere, was immediately recognized as the solution the prefrontal cortex had been searching for. And so Dodge stopped running. He stood still as the wall of flame raced toward him. Then he lit the match.

(2008)

Questions

1. In your own words, describe the difference between insight and analysis. How can you tell them apart in experience, and what happens differently in the brain?

2. What does the prefrontal cortex do?

3. Why did Jung-Beeman and Kounios conduct tests using both fMRI and EEG?

4. Discuss the strategies Lehrer uses in this article to make scientific findings interesting and understandable to a layperson audience.

5. How completely do you think science can "demystify" insight and other conscious experiences?

6. To what extent do the findings outlined in this article reflect common sense notions of how people think? To what extent do they contradict them?

Questions on "Neural Activity When People Solve Verbal Problems with Insight" and "The Eureka Hunt"

1. Compare and contrast the tone, diction, and sentence structure of the two articles. How does each article reflect its intended audience?

2. How accurately does Lehrer represent the research conducted by Beeman (referred to by Lehrer as Jung-Beeman), Kounios, et al.? Is this level of accuracy satisfactory?

3. Find a component of Beeman, Kounios, et al.'s article that is not represented in Lehrer's. Why might Lehrer have chosen not to include this element?

4. In "The Eureka Hunt," Lehrer uses simile and metaphor to illustrate scientific concepts. Following his example, rewrite a paragraph from Beeman, Kounios, et al.'s article, replacing technical language with metaphorical language.

5. Lehrer quotes Joy Bhattacharya, who provides a different interpretation of the role of alpha waves in insight than Beeman, Kounios, et al. provide in their article. Explain their reasoning. Does one interpretation seem more likely?

BINYAVANGA WAINAINA

HOW TO WRITE ABOUT AFRICA

*In this biting piece, author and journalist Binyavanga
Wainaina provides instructions to foreigners
aspiring to write about his home continent.*

℮

Always use the word "Africa" or "Darkness" or "Safari" in your title. Subtitles may include the words "Zanzibar," "Masai," "Zulu," "Zambezi," "Congo," "Nile," "Big," "Sky," "Shadow," "Drum," "Sun" or "Bygone." Also useful are words such as "Guerrillas," "Timeless," "Primordial" and "Tribal." Note that "People" means Africans who are not black, while "The People" means black Africans.

Never have a picture of a well-adjusted African on the cover of your book, or in it, unless that African has won the Nobel Prize. An AK-47, prominent ribs, naked breasts: use these. If you must include an African, make sure you get one in Masai or Zulu or Dogon dress.

In your text, treat Africa as if it were one country. It is hot and dusty with rolling grasslands and huge herds of animals and tall, thin people who are starving. Or it is hot and steamy with very short people who eat primates. Don't get bogged down with precise descriptions. Africa is big: fifty-four countries, 900 million people who are too busy starving and dying and warring and emigrating to read your book. The continent is full of deserts, jungles, highlands, savannahs and many other things, but your reader doesn't care about all that, so keep your descriptions romantic and evocative and unparticular.

Make sure you show how Africans have music and rhythm deep in their souls, and eat things no other humans eat. Do not mention rice and beef and wheat; monkey-brain is an African's cuisine of choice, along with goat, snake, worms and grubs and all manner of game meat. Make sure you show that you are able to eat such food without flinching, and describe how you learn to enjoy it—because you care.

528

Taboo subjects: ordinary domestic scenes, love between Africans   5
(unless a death is involved), references to African writers or intellectuals,
mention of school-going children who are not suffering from yaws or Ebola
fever or female genital mutilation.

Throughout the book, adopt a *sotto* voice, in conspiracy with the reader,
and a sad *I-expected-so-much* tone. Establish early on that your liberalism
is impeccable, and mention near the beginning how much you love Africa,
how you fell in love with the place and can't live without her. Africa is
the only continent you can love—take advantage of this. If you are a man,
thrust yourself into her warm virgin forests. If you are a woman, treat Africa
as a man who wears a bush jacket and disappears off into the sunset. Africa
is to be pitied, worshipped or dominated. Whichever angle you take, be
sure to leave the strong impression that without your intervention and your
important book, Africa is doomed.

Your African characters may include naked warriors, loyal servants,
diviners and seers, ancient wise men living in hermitic splendor. Or corrupt
politicians, inept polygamous travel-guides, and prostitutes you have slept
with. The Loyal Servant always behaves like a seven-year-old and needs a
firm hand; he is scared of snakes, good with children, and always involving
you in his complex domestic dramas. The Ancient Wise Man always comes
from a noble tribe (not the money-grubbing tribes like the Gikuyu, the Igbo
or the Shona). He has rheumy eyes and is close to the Earth. The Modern
African is a fat man who steals and works in the visa office, refusing to
give work permits to qualified Westerners who really care about Africa.
He is an enemy of development, always using his government job to make
it difficult for pragmatic and good-hearted expats to set up NGOs or Legal Conservation Areas. Or he is an Oxford-educated intellectual turned
serial-killing politician in a Savile Row suit. He is a cannibal who likes
Cristal champagne, and his mother is a rich witch-doctor who really runs
the country.

Among your characters you must always include The Starving African,
who wanders the refugee camp nearly naked, and waits for the benevolence
of the West. Her children have flies on their eyelids and pot bellies, and her
breasts are flat and empty. She must look utterly helpless. She can have
no past, no history; such diversions ruin the dramatic moment. Moans are
good. She must never say anything about herself in the dialogue except
to speak of her (unspeakable) suffering. Also be sure to include a warm
and motherly woman who has a rolling laugh and who is concerned for
your well-being. Just call her Mama. Her children are all delinquent. These

characters should buzz around your main hero, making him look good. Your hero can teach them, bathe them, feed them; he carries lots of babies and has seen Death. Your hero is you (if reportage), or a beautiful, tragic international celebrity/aristocrat who now cares for animals (if fiction).

Bad Western characters may include children of Tory cabinet ministers, Afrikaners, employees of the World Bank. When talking about exploitation by foreigners mention the Chinese and Indian traders. Blame the West for Africa's situation. But do not be too specific.

Broad brushstrokes throughout are good. Avoid having the African characters laugh, or struggle to educate their kids, or just make do in mundane circumstances. Have them illuminate something about Europe or America in Africa. African characters should be colorful, exotic, larger than life—but empty inside, with no dialogue, no conflicts or resolutions in their stories, no depth or quirks to confuse the cause.

10 Describe, in detail, naked breasts (young, old, conservative, recently raped, big, small) or mutilated genitals, or enhanced genitals. Or any kind of genitals. And dead bodies. Or, better, naked dead bodies. And especially rotting naked dead bodies. Remember, any work you submit in which people look filthy and miserable will be referred to as the "real Africa," and you want that on your dust jacket. Do not feel queasy about this: you are trying to help them to get aid from the West. The biggest taboo in writing about Africa is to describe or show dead or suffering white people.

Animals, on the other hand, must be treated as well rounded, complex characters. They speak (or grunt while tossing their manes proudly) and have names, ambitions and desires. They also have family values: *see how lions teach their children?* Elephants are caring, and are good feminists or dignified patriarchs. So are gorillas. Never, ever say anything negative about an elephant or a gorilla. Elephants may attack people's property, destroy their crops, and even kill them. Always take the side of the elephant. Big cats have public-school accents. Hyenas are fair game and have vaguely Middle Eastern accents. Any short Africans who live in the jungle or desert may be portrayed with good humor (unless they are in conflict with an elephant or chimpanzee or gorilla, in which case they are pure evil).

After celebrity activists and aid workers, conservationists are Africa's most important people. Do not offend them. You need them to invite you to their 30,000-acre game ranch or "conservation area," and this is the only way you will get to interview the celebrity activist. Often a book cover with a heroic-looking conservationist on it works magic for sales. Anybody white, tanned and wearing khaki who once had a pet antelope or a farm is a conservationist, one who is preserving Africa's rich heritage. When interviewing him or her, do not ask how much funding they have; do not ask how much money they make off their game. Never ask how much they pay their employees.

Readers will be put off if you don't mention the light in Africa. And sunsets, the African sunset is a must. It is always big and red. There is always a big sky. Wide empty spaces and game are critical—Africa is the Land of Wide Empty Spaces. When writing about the plight of flora and fauna, make sure you mention that Africa is overpopulated. When your main character is in a desert or jungle living with indigenous peoples (anybody short) it is okay to mention that Africa has been severely depopulated by Aids and War (use caps).

You'll also need a nightclub called Tropicana, where mercenaries, evil nouveau riche Africans and prostitutes and guerrillas and expats hang out.

Always end your book with Nelson Mandela saying something about rainbows or renaissances. Because you care.   15

(2005)

Questions

1. Summarize in your own words what mistakes Wainaina observes Western writers making when they write about Africa. Are his accusations fair?

2. Comment on Wainaina's use of satire. How else might he have written this piece? Would other ways have been more effective, or less?

3. Choose a group that you feel is widely misrepresented in the media (e.g. youth, protesters, people on welfare, disabled people) and write a piece on "How to Write about" that group in the style of this article.

4. Look in your library or on the Internet and find some examples of recent writing about Africa. To what extent does "How to Write about Africa" describe the writing you find?

5. In this piece, Wainaina gives us a clear picture of what bad writing about Africa looks like. How much can we learn from the essay about what good writing about Africa should look like?

Questions on connections between this essay and the following speech, "On Not Winning the Nobel Prize," can be found at the end of that speech.

DORIS LESSING

ON NOT WINNING THE NOBEL PRIZE

*Doris Lessing is a British author renowned for her novels
exploring human psychology and social issues. Lessing spent
much of her childhood in the British colony of Southern
Rhodesia, now Zimbabwe. She delivered this lecture when she
was awarded the Nobel Prize for Literature in 2007.*

❧

Iam standing in a doorway looking through clouds of blowing dust to where I am told there is still uncut forest. Yesterday I drove through miles of stumps, and charred remains of fires where, in '56, there was the most wonderful forest I have ever seen, all now destroyed. People have to eat. They have to get fuel for fires.

This is north-west Zimbabwe in the early eighties, and I am visiting a friend who was a teacher in a school in London. He is here "to help Africa," as we put it. He is a gently idealistic soul and what he found in this school shocked him into a depression, from which it was hard to recover. This school is like every other built after Independence. It consists of four large brick rooms side by side, put straight into the dust, one two three four, with a half room at one end, which is the library. In these classrooms are blackboards, but my friend keeps the chalks in his pocket, as otherwise they would be stolen. There is no atlas or globe in the school, no textbooks, no exercise books, or biros. In the library there are no books of the kind the pupils would like to read, but only tomes from American universities, hard even to lift, rejects from white libraries, or novels with titles like *Weekend in Paris* and *Felicity Finds Love*.

There is a goat trying to find sustenance in some aged grass. The headmaster has embezzled the school funds and is suspended, arousing the question familiar to all of us but usually in more august contexts: How is it these people behave like this when they must know everyone is watching them?

My friend doesn't have any money because everyone, pupils and teachers, borrow from him when he is paid and will probably never pay him back. The pupils range from six to twenty-six, because some who did not get schooling as children are here to make it up. Some pupils walk many miles every morning, rain or shine and across rivers. They cannot do homework because there is no electricity in the villages, and you can't study easily by the light of a burning log. The girls have to fetch water and cook before they set off for school and when they get back.

As I sit with my friend in his room, people drop in shyly, and everyone   5
begs for books. "Please send us books when you get back to London," one man says. "They taught us to read but we have no books." Everybody I met, everyone, begged for books.

I was there some days. The dust blew. The pumps had broken and the women were having to fetch water from the river. Another idealistic teacher from England was rather ill after seeing what this "school" was like.

On the last day they slaughtered the goat. They cut it into bits and cooked it in a great tin. This was the much anticipated end-of-term feast: boiled goat and porridge. I drove away while it was still going on, back through the charred remains and stumps of the forest.

I do not think many of the pupils of this school will get prizes.

The next day I am to give a talk at a school in North London, a very good school, whose name we all know. It is a school for boys, with beautiful buildings and gardens.

These children here have a visit from some well known person every   10
week, and it is in the nature of things that these may be fathers, relatives, even mothers of the pupils. A visit from a celebrity is not unusual for them.

As I talk to them, the school in the blowing dust of north-west Zimbabwe is in my mind, and I look at the mildly expectant English faces in front of me and try to tell them about what I have seen in the last week. Classrooms without books, without textbooks, or an atlas, or even a map pinned to a wall. A school where the teachers beg to be sent books to tell them how to teach, they being only eighteen or nineteen themselves. I tell these English boys how everybody begs for books: "Please send us books." I am sure that anyone who has ever given a speech will know that moment when the faces you are looking at are blank. Your listeners cannot hear what you are saying, there are no images in their minds to match what you are telling them—in this case the story of a school standing in dust clouds, where water is short, and where the end of term treat is a just-killed goat cooked in a great pot.

Is it really so impossible for these privileged students to imagine such bare poverty?

I do my best. They are polite.

I'm sure that some of them will one day win prizes.

15   Then, the talk is over. Afterwards I ask the teachers how the library is, and if the pupils read. In this privileged school, I hear what I always hear when I go to such schools and even universities.

"You know how it is," one of the teachers says. "A lot of the boys have never read at all, and the library is only half used."

Yes, indeed we do know how it is. All of us.

We are in a fragmenting culture, where our certainties of even a few decades ago are questioned and where it is common for young men and women, who have had years of education, to know nothing of the world, to have read nothing, knowing only some speciality or other, for instance, computers.

What has happened to us is an amazing invention—computers and the Internet and TV. It is a revolution. This is not the first revolution the human race has dealt with. The printing revolution, which did not take place in a matter of a few decades, but took much longer, transformed our minds and ways of thinking. A foolhardy lot, we accepted it all, as we always do, never asked, What is going to happen to us now, with this invention of print? In the same way, we never thought to ask, How will our lives, our way of thinking, be changed by this Internet, which has seduced a whole generation with its inanities so that even quite reasonable people will confess that once they are hooked, it is hard to cut free, and they may find a whole day has passed in blogging etc.

20   Very recently, anyone even mildly educated would respect learning, education, and our great store of literature. Of course, we all know that when this happy state was with us, people would pretend to read, would pretend respect for learning. But it is on record that working men and women longed for books, and this is evidenced by the founding of working men's libraries and institutes, the colleges of the 18th and 19th centuries.

Reading, books, used to be part of a general education.

Older people, talking to young ones, must understand just how much of an education reading was, because the young ones know so much less. And if children cannot read, it is because they have not read.

We all know this sad story.

But we do not know the end of it.

We think of the old adage, "Reading maketh a full man"—and forget-   25
ting about jokes to do with over-eating—reading makes a woman and a
man full of information, of history, of all kinds of knowledge.

But we in the West are not the only people in the world. Not long ago a
friend who had been in Zimbabwe told me about a village where people had
not eaten for three days, but they were still talking about books and how to
get them, about education.

I belong to an organization which started out with the intention of getting books into the villages. There was a group of people who in another
connection had traveled Zimbabwe at its grass roots. They told me that
the villages, unlike what is reported, are full of intelligent people, teachers retired, teachers on leave, children on holidays, old people. I myself
paid for a little survey to discover what people in Zimbabwe want to read,
and found the results were the same as those of a Swedish survey I had
not known about. People want to read the same kinds of books that we in
Europe want to read—novels of all kinds, science fiction, poetry, detective
stories, plays, and do-it-yourself books, like how to open a bank account.
All of Shakespeare too. A problem with finding books for villagers is that
they don't know what is available, so a set book, like the *Mayor of Caster-
bridge*, becomes popular simply because it just happens to be there. *Animal
Farm*, for obvious reasons, is the most popular of all novels.

Our organization was helped from the very start by Norway, and then
by Sweden. Without this kind of support our supplies of books would have
dried up. We got books from wherever we could. Remember, a good paperback from England costs a month's wages in Zimbabwe: that was *before*
Mugabe's reign of terror. Now with inflation, it would cost several years'
wages. But having taken a box of books out to a village—and remember
there is a terrible shortage of petrol—I can tell you that the box was greeted
with tears. The library may be a plank on bricks under a tree. And within
a week there will be literacy classes—people who can read teaching those
who can't, citizenship classes—and in one remote village, since there were
no novels written in the language Tonga, a couple of lads sat down to write
novels in Tonga. There are six or so main languages in Zimbabwe and there
are novels in all of them: violent, incestuous, full of crime and murder.

It is said that a people gets the government it deserves, but I do not think
it is true of Zimbabwe. And we must remember that this respect and hunger
for books comes, not from Mugabe's regime, but from the one before it, the
whites. It is an astonishing phenomenon, this hunger for books, and it can
be seen everywhere from Kenya down to the Cape of Good Hope.

30   This links improbably with a fact: I was brought up in what was virtually a mud hut, thatched. This kind of house has been built always, everywhere there are reeds or grass, suitable mud, poles for walls. Saxon England for example. The one I was brought up in had four rooms, one beside another, and it was full of books. Not only did my parents take books from England to Africa, but my mother ordered books by post from England for her children. Books arrived in great brown paper parcels, and they were the joy of my young life. A mud hut, but full of books.

Even today I get letters from people living in a village that might not have electricity or running water, just like our family in our elongated mud hut. "I shall be a writer too," they say, "because I've the same kind of house you lived in."

But here is the difficulty, no?

Writing, writers, do not come out of houses without books.

There is the gap. There is the difficulty.

35   I have been looking at the speeches by some of your recent prizewinners. Take the magnificent Pamuk. He said his father had 500 books. His talent did not come out of the air, he was connected with the great tradition.

Take V.S. Naipaul. He mentions that the Indian Vedas were close behind the memory of his family. His father encouraged him to write, and when he got to England he would visit the British Library. So he was close to the great tradition.

Let us take John Coetzee. He was not only close to the great tradition, he was the tradition: he taught literature in Cape Town. And how sorry I am that I was never in one of his classes, taught by that wonderfully brave, bold mind.

In order to write, in order to make literature, there must be a close connection with libraries, books, with the Tradition.

I have a friend from Zimbabwe, a Black writer. He taught himself to read from the labels on jam jars, the labels on preserved fruit cans. He was brought up in an area I have driven through, an area for rural blacks. The earth is grit and gravel, there are low sparse bushes. The huts are poor, nothing like the well cared-for huts of the better off. A school—but like one I have described. He found a discarded children's encyclopedia on a rubbish heap and taught himself from that.

40   On Independence in 1980 there was a group of good writers in Zimbabwe, truly a nest of singing birds. They were bred in old Southern Rhodesia,

under the whites—the mission schools, the better schools. Writers are not made in Zimbabwe. Not easily, not under Mugabe.

All the writers traveled a difficult road to literacy, let alone to becoming writers. I would say learning to read from the printed labels on jam jars and discarded encyclopedias was not uncommon. And we are talking about people hungering for standards of education beyond them, living in huts with many children—an overworked mother, a fight for food and clothing.

Yet despite these difficulties, writers came into being. And we should also remember that this was Zimbabwe, conquered less than a hundred years before. The grandparents of these people might have been storytellers working in the oral tradition. In one or two generations there was the transition from stories remembered and passed on, to print, to books. What an achievement.

Books, literally wrested from rubbish heaps and the detritus of the white man's world. But a sheaf of paper is one thing, a published book quite another. I have had several accounts sent to me of the publishing scene in Africa. Even in more privileged places like North Africa, with its different tradition, to talk of a publishing scene is a dream of possibilities.

Here I am talking about books never written, writers that could not make it because the publishers are not there. Voices unheard. It is not possible to estimate this great waste of talent, of potential. But even before that stage of a book's creation which demands a publisher, an advance, encouragement, there is something else lacking.

Writers are often asked, How do you write? With a wordprocessor? an electric typewriter? a quill? longhand? But the essential question is, "Have you found a space, that empty space, which should surround you when you write?" Into that space, which is like a form of listening, of attention, will come the words, the words your characters will speak, ideas—inspiration. 45

If a writer cannot find this space, then poems and stories may be stillborn.

When writers talk to each other, what they discuss is always to do with this imaginative space, this other time. "Have you found it? Are you holding it fast?"

Let us now jump to an apparently very different scene. We are in London, one of the big cities. There is a new writer. We cynically enquire, Is she good-looking? If this is a man, charismatic? Handsome? We joke but it is not a joke.

This new find is acclaimed, possibly given a lot of money. The buzzing of paparazzi begins in their poor ears. They are feted, lauded, whisked about the world. Us old ones, who have seen it all, are sorry for this neophyte, who has no idea of what is really happening.

50 He, she, is flattered, pleased.

But ask in a year's time what he or she is thinking—I've heard them: "This is the worst thing that could have happened to me," they say.

Some much publicized new writers haven't written again, or haven't written what they wanted to, meant to.

And we, the old ones, want to whisper into those innocent ears. "Have you still got your space? Your soul, your own and necessary place where your own voices may speak to you, you alone, where you may dream. Oh, hold onto it, don't let it go."

My mind is full of splendid memories of Africa which I can revive and look at whenever I want. How about those sunsets, gold and purple and orange, spreading across the sky at evening. How about butterflies and moths and bees on the aromatic bushes of the Kalahari? Or, sitting on the pale grassy banks of the Zambesi, the water dark and glossy, with all the birds of Africa darting about. Yes, elephants, giraffes, lions and the rest, there were plenty of those, but how about the sky at night, still unpolluted, black and wonderful, full of restless stars.

55 There are other memories too. A young African man, eighteen perhaps, in tears, standing in what he hopes will be his "library." A visiting American seeing that his library had no books, had sent a crate of them. The young man had taken each one out, reverently, and wrapped them in plastic. "But," we say, "these books were sent to be read, surely?" "No," he replies, "they will get dirty, and where will I get any more?"

This young man wants us to send him books from England to use as teaching guides.

"I only did four years in senior school," he says, "but they never taught me to teach."

I have seen a teacher in a school where there were no textbooks, not even a chalk for the blackboard. He taught his class of six to eighteen year olds by moving stones in the dust, chanting "Two times two is ..." and so on. I have seen a girl, perhaps not more than twenty, also lacking textbooks, exercise books, biros, seen her teach the A B C by scratching the letters in the dirt with a stick, while the sun beat down and the dust swirled.

We are witnessing here that great hunger for education in Africa, any-where in the Third World, or whatever we call parts of the world where parents long to get an education for their children which will take them out of poverty.

I would like you to imagine yourselves somewhere in Southern Africa, standing in an Indian store, in a poor area, in a time of bad drought. There is a line of people, mostly women, with every kind of container for water. This store gets a bowser of precious water every afternoon from the town, and here the people wait.

The Indian is standing with the heels of his hands pressed down on the counter, and he is watching a black woman, who is bending over a wadge of paper that looks as if it has been torn from a book. She is reading *Anna Karenin*.

She is reading slowly, mouthing the words. It looks a difficult book. This is a young woman with two little children clutching at her legs. She is pregnant. The Indian is distressed, because the young woman's headscarf, which should be white, is yellow with dust. Dust lies between her breasts and on her arms. This man is distressed because of the lines of people, all thirsty. He doesn't have enough water for them. He is angry because he knows there are people dying out there, beyond the dust clouds. His older brother had been here holding the fort, but he had said he needed a break, had gone into town, really rather ill, because of the drought.

This man is curious. He says to the young woman, "What are you reading?"

"It is about Russia," says the girl.

"Do you know where Russia is?" He hardly knows himself.

The young woman looks straight at him, full of dignity, though her eyes are red from dust, "I was best in the class. My teacher said I was best."

The young woman resumes her reading. She wants to get to the end of the paragraph.

The Indian looks at the two little children and reaches for some Fanta, but the mother says, "Fanta makes them thirstier."

The Indian knows he shouldn't do this but he reaches down to a great plastic container beside him, behind the counter, and pours out two mugs of water, which he hands to the children. He watches while the girl looks at her children drinking, her mouth moving. He gives her a mug of water. It hurts him to see her drinking it, so painfully thirsty is she.

Now she hands him her own plastic water container, which he fills. The young woman and the children watch him closely so that he doesn't spill any.

She is bending again over the book. She reads slowly. The paragraph fascinates her and she reads it again.

"Varenka, with her white kerchief over her black hair, surrounded by the children and gaily and good-humoredly busy with them, and at the same visibly excited at the possibility of an offer of marriage from a man she cared for, looked very attractive. Koznyshev walked by her side and kept casting admiring glances at her. Looking at her, he recalled all the delightful things he had heard from her lips, all the good he knew about her, and became more and more conscious that the feeling he had for her was something rare, something he had felt but once before, long, long ago, in his early youth. The joy of being near her increased step by step, and at last reached such a point that, as he put a huge birch mushroom with a slender stalk and up-curling top into her basket, he looked into her eyes and, noting the flush of glad and frightened agitation that suffused her face, he was confused himself, and in silence gave her a smile that said too much."

This lump of print is lying on the counter, together with some old copies of magazines, some pages of newspapers with pictures of girls in bikinis.

It is time for the woman to leave the haven of the Indian store, and set off back along the four miles to her village. Outside, the lines of waiting women clamor and complain. But still the Indian lingers. He knows what it will cost this girl—going back home, with the two clinging children. He would give her the piece of prose that so fascinates her, but he cannot really believe this splinter of a girl with her great belly can really understand it.

75 Why is perhaps a third of *Anna Karenin* here on this counter in a remote Indian store? It is like this.

A certain high official, from the United Nations as it happens, bought a copy of this novel in a bookshop before he set out on his journey to cross several oceans and seas. On the plane, settled in his business class seat, he tore the book into three parts. He looked around his fellow passengers as he did this, knowing he would see looks of shock, curiosity, but some of amusement. When he was settled, his seat belt tight, he said aloud to whomever could hear, "I always do this when I've a long trip. You don't want to have to hold up some heavy great book." The novel was a paperback, but, true, it is a long book. This man is well used to people listening when he spoke. "I always do this, traveling," he confided. "Traveling at all these days, is hard enough." And as soon as people were settling down, he opened his part of *Anna Karenin*, and read. When people looked his way, curiously or not, he confided in them. "No, it really is the only way to travel." He knew the novel, liked it, and this original mode of reading did add spice to what was after all a well known book.

When he reached the end of a section of the book, he called the air hostess, and sent the chapters back to his secretary, traveling in the cheaper seats. This caused much interest, condemnation, certainly curiosity, every time a section of the great Russian novel arrived, mutilated but readable, in the back part of the plane. Altogether, this clever way of reading *Anna Karenin* makes an impression, and probably no one there would forget it.

Meanwhile, in the Indian store, the young woman is holding on to the counter, her little children clinging to her skirts. She wears jeans, since she is a modern woman, but over them she has put on the heavy woolen skirt, part of the traditional dress of her people: her children can easily cling onto its thick folds.

She sends a thankful look to the Indian, whom she knew liked her and was sorry for her, and she steps out into the blowing clouds.

The children are past crying, and their throats are full of dust. 80

This was hard, oh yes, it was hard, this stepping, one foot after another, through the dust that lay in soft deceiving mounds under her feet. Hard, but she was used to hardship, was she not? Her mind was on the story she had been reading. She was thinking, She is just like me, in her white headscarf, and she is looking after children, too. I could be her, that Russian girl. And the man there, he loves her and will ask her to marry him. She had not finished more than that one paragraph. Yes, she thinks, a man will come for me, and take me away from all this, take me and the children, yes, he will love me and look after me.

She steps on. The can of water is heavy on her shoulders. On she goes. The children can hear the water slopping about. Half way she stops, sets down the can.

Her children are whimpering and touching it. She thinks that she cannot open it, because dust would blow in. There is no way she can open the can until she gets home.

"Wait," she tells her children, "wait."

She has to pull herself together and go on. 85

She thinks, My teacher said there is a library, bigger than the supermarket, a big building and it is full of books. The young woman is smiling as she moves on, the dust blowing in her face. I am clever, she thinks. Teacher said I am clever. The cleverest in the school—she said I was. My children will be clever, like me. I will take them to the library, the place full of books, and they will go to school, and they will be teachers—my teacher told me I could be a teacher. My children will live far from here, earning money. They will live near the big library and enjoy a good life.

You may ask how that piece of the Russian novel ever ended up on that counter in the Indian store?

It would make a pretty story. Perhaps someone will tell it.

On goes that poor girl, held upright by thoughts of the water she will give her children once home, and drink a little of herself. On she goes, through the dreaded dusts of an African drought.

90   We are a jaded lot, we in our threatened world. We are good for irony and even cynicism. Some words and ideas we hardly use, so worn out have they become. But we may want to restore some words that have lost their potency.

We have a treasure-house of literature, going back to the Egyptians, the Greeks, the Romans. It is all there, this wealth of literature, to be discovered again and again by whoever is lucky enough to come upon it. A treasure. Suppose it did not exist. How impoverished, how empty we would be.

We own a legacy of languages, poems, histories, and it is not one that will ever be exhausted. It is there, always.

We have a bequest of stories, tales from the old storytellers, some of whose names we know, but some not. The storytellers go back and back, to a clearing in the forest where a great fire burns, and the old shamans dance and sing, for our heritage of stories began in fire, magic, the spirit world. And that is where it is held, today.

Ask any modern storyteller and they will say there is always a moment when they are touched with fire, with what we like to call inspiration, and this goes back and back to the beginning of our race, to the great winds that shaped us and our world.

95   The storyteller is deep inside every one of us. The story-maker is always with us. Let us suppose our world is ravaged by war, by the horrors that we all of us easily imagine. Let us suppose floods wash through our cities, the seas rise. But the storyteller will be there, for it is our imaginations which shape us, keep us, create us—for good and for ill. It is our stories that will recreate us, when we are torn, hurt, even destroyed. It is the storyteller, the dream-maker, the myth-maker, that is our phoenix, that represents us at our best, and at our most creative.

That poor girl trudging through the dust, dreaming of an education for her children, do we think that we are better than she is—we, stuffed full of food, our cupboards full of clothes, stifling in our superfluities?

I think it is that girl, and the women who were talking about books and an education when they had not eaten for three days, that may yet define us.

(2007)

Questions

1. Why, according to Lessing, is literature important?
2. According to Lessing, what kind of impact have Western education and literature had on Southern Africa? Is this an accurate representation?
3. What does the story of the young woman reading *Anna Karenin* illustrate in the context of the speech?
4. How does Lessing portray the attitude toward books adopted by most young Western people? Is this fair?
5. Why does Lessing deliberately leave out an explanation of how the piece of *Anna Karenin* ended up in the Indian store?
6. Why does Lessing begin her speech with the mention of the destroyed forest?

Questions on "How to Write about Africa" and "On Not Winning the Nobel Prize"

1. What elements that Wainaina identifies in his essay do you find in Lessing's speech?
2. To what extent, if at all, does Lessing go beyond the simplistic representation of Africa that Wainaina criticizes?
3. Lessing is a white British person who spent much of her youth in Southern Rhodesia (now Zimbabwe), while Wainaina is a black person born in Kenya who now lives in the United States. Do their respective backgrounds make you see their writing differently? Should they? Why or why not?

MALCOLM GLADWELL

NONE OF THE ABOVE: WHAT I.Q. DOESN'T TELL YOU ABOUT RACE

*Is I.Q. genetically determined? A noted journalist explores the
meaning of I.Q. and its relationship to race, class, and culture.*

❧

One Saturday in November of 1984, James Flynn, a social scientist at
the University of Otago, in New Zealand, received a large package
in the mail. It was from a colleague in Utrecht, and it contained the results
of I.Q. tests given to two generations of Dutch eighteen-year-olds. When
Flynn looked through the data, he found something puzzling. The Dutch
eighteen-year-olds from the nineteen-eighties scored better than those who
took the same tests in the nineteen-fifties—and not just slightly better, *much*
better.

Curious, Flynn sent out some letters. He collected intelligence-test
results from Europe, from North America, from Asia, and from the developing world, until he had data for almost thirty countries. In every case,
the story was pretty much the same. I.Q.s around the world appeared to be
rising by 0.3 points per year, or three points per decade, for as far back as
the tests had been administered. For some reason, human beings seemed to
be getting smarter.

Flynn has been writing about the implications of his findings—now
known as the Flynn effect—for almost twenty-five years. His books consist
of a series of plainly stated statistical observations, in support of deceptively
modest conclusions, and the evidence in support of his original observation
is now so overwhelming that the Flynn effect has moved from theory to
fact. What remains uncertain is how to make sense of the Flynn effect. If
an American born in the nineteen-thirties has an I.Q. of 100, the Flynn effect says that his children will have I.Q.s of 108, and his grandchildren
I.Q.s of close to 120—more than a standard deviation higher. If we work in

544

the opposite direction, the typical teen-ager of today, with an I.Q. of 100, would have had grandparents with average I.Q.s of 82—seemingly below the threshold necessary to graduate from high school. And, if we go back even farther, the Flynn effect puts the average I.Q.s of the schoolchildren of 1900 at around 70, which is to suggest, bizarrely, that a century ago the United States was populated largely by people who today would be considered mentally retarded.

For almost as long as there have been I.Q. tests, there have been I.Q. fundamentalists. H.H. Goddard, in the early years of the past century, established the idea that intelligence could be measured along a single, linear scale. One of his particular contributions was to coin the word "moron." "The people who are doing the drudgery are, as a rule, in their proper places," he wrote. Goddard was followed by Lewis Terman, in the nineteen-twenties, who rounded up the California children with the highest I.Q.s, and confidently predicted that they would sit at the top of every profession. In 1969, the psychometrician Arthur Jensen argued that programs like Head Start, which tried to boost the academic performance of minority children, were doomed to failure, because I.Q. was so heavily genetic; and in 1994 Richard Herrnstein and Charles Murray, in "The Bell Curve," notoriously proposed that Americans with the lowest I.Q.s be sequestered in a "high-tech" version of an Indian reservation, "while the rest of America tries to go about its business."[1] To the I.Q. fundamentalist, two things are beyond dispute: first, that I.Q. tests measure some hard and identifiable trait that predicts the quality of our thinking; and, second, that this trait is stable—that is, it is determined by our genes and largely impervious to environmental influences.

This is what James Watson, the co-discoverer of DNA, meant when he told an English newspaper recently that he was "inherently gloomy" about the prospects for Africa. From the perspective of an I.Q. fundamentalist, the fact that Africans score lower than Europeans on I.Q. tests suggests an ineradicable cognitive disability. In the controversy that followed, Watson was defended by the journalist William Saletan, in a three-part series for the online magazine *Slate*. Drawing heavily on the work of J. Philippe Rushton— a psychologist who specializes in comparing the circumference of what he calls the Negroid brain with the length of the Negroid penis—Saletan took

5

---

1   *The New Yorker* posted the following correction to this statement: "In fact, Herrnstein and Murray deplored the prospect of such 'custodialism' and recommended that steps be taken to avert it. We regret the error."

the fundamentalist position to its logical conclusion. To erase the difference between blacks and whites, Saletan wrote, would probably require vigorous interbreeding between the races, or some kind of corrective genetic engineering aimed at upgrading African stock. "Economic and cultural theories have failed to explain most of the pattern," Saletan declared, claiming to have been "soaking [his] head in each side's computations and arguments." One argument that Saletan never soaked his head in, however, was Flynn's, because what Flynn discovered in his mailbox upsets the certainties upon which I.Q. fundamentalism rests. If whatever the thing is that I.Q. tests measure can jump so much in a generation, it can't be all that immutable and it doesn't look all that innate.

The very fact that average I.Q.s shift over time ought to create a "crisis of confidence," Flynn writes in "What Is Intelligence?," his latest attempt to puzzle through the implications of his discovery. "How could such huge gains be intelligence gains? Either the children of today were far brighter than their parents or, at least in some circumstances, I.Q. tests were not good measures of intelligence."

The best way to understand why I.Q.s rise, Flynn argues, is to look at one of the most widely used I.Q. tests, the so-called WISC (for Wechsler Intelligence Scale for Children). The WISC is composed of ten subtests, each of which measures a different aspect of I.Q. Flynn points out that scores in some of the categories—those measuring general knowledge, say, or vocabulary or the ability to do basic arithmetic—have risen only modestly over time. The big gains on the WISC are largely in the category known as "similarities," where you get questions such as "In what way are 'dogs' and 'rabbits' alike?" Today, we tend to give what, for the purposes of I.Q. tests, is the right answer: dogs and rabbits are both mammals. A nineteenth-century American would have said that "you use dogs to hunt rabbits."

"If the everyday world is your cognitive home, it is not natural to detach abstractions and logic and the hypothetical from their concrete referents," Flynn writes. Our great-grandparents may have been perfectly intelligent. But they would have done poorly on I.Q. tests because they did not participate in the twentieth century's great cognitive revolution, in which we learned to sort experience according to a new set of abstract categories. In Flynn's phrase, we have now had to put on "scientific spectacles," which enable us to make sense of the WISC questions about similarities. To say that Dutch I.Q. scores rose substantially between 1952 and 1982 was another way of saying that the Netherlands in 1982 was, in at least certain respects, much more cognitively demanding than the Netherlands in 1952. An I.Q., in other words, measures not so much how smart we are as how *modern* we are.

This is a critical distinction. When the children of Southern Italian immigrants were given I.Q. tests in the early part of the past century, for example, they recorded median scores in the high seventies and low eighties, a full standard deviation below their American and Western European counterparts. Southern Italians did as poorly on I.Q. tests as Hispanics and blacks did. As you can imagine, there was much concerned talk at the time about the genetic inferiority of Italian stock, of the inadvisability of letting so many second-class immigrants into the United States, and of the squalor that seemed endemic to Italian urban neighborhoods. Sound familiar? These days, when talk turns to the supposed genetic differences in the intelligence of certain races, Southern Italians have disappeared from the discussion. "Did their genes begin to mutate somewhere in the 1930s?" the psychologists Seymour Sarason and John Doris ask, in their account of the Italian experience. "Or is it possible that somewhere in the 1920s, if not earlier, the sociocultural history of Italo-Americans took a turn from the blacks and the Spanish Americans which permitted their assimilation into the general undifferentiated mass of Americans?"

The psychologist Michael Cole and some colleagues once gave members of the Kpelle tribe, in Liberia, a version of the WISC similarities test: they took a basket of food, tools, containers, and clothing and asked the tribesmen to sort them into appropriate categories. To the frustration of the researchers, the Kpelle chose functional pairings. They put a potato and a knife together because a knife is used to cut a potato. "A wise man could only do such-and-such," they explained. Finally, the researchers asked, "How would a fool do it?" The tribesmen immediately re-sorted the items into the "right" categories. It can be argued that taxonomical categories are a developmental improvement—that is, that the Kpelle would be more likely to advance, technologically and scientifically, if they started to see the world that way. But to label them less intelligent than Westerners, on the basis of their performance on that test, is merely to state that they have different cognitive preferences and habits. And if I.Q. varies with habits of mind, which can be adopted or discarded in a generation, what, exactly, is all the fuss about?

When I was growing up, my family would sometimes play Twenty Questions on long car trips. My father was one of those people who insist that the standard categories of animal, vegetable, and mineral be

10

supplemented with a fourth category: "abstract." Abstract could mean something like "whatever it was that was going through my mind when we drove past the water tower fifty miles back." That abstract category sounds absurdly difficult, but it wasn't: it merely required that we ask a slightly different set of questions and grasp a slightly different set of conventions, and, after two or three rounds of practice, guessing the contents of someone's mind fifty miles ago becomes as easy as guessing Winston Churchill. (There is one exception. That was the trip on which my old roommate Tom Connell chose, as an abstraction, "the Unknown Soldier"—which allowed him legitimately and gleefully to answer "I have no idea" to almost every question. There were four of us playing. We gave up after an hour.) Flynn would say that my father was teaching his three sons how to put on scientific spectacles, and that extra practice probably bumped up all of our I.Q.s a few notches. But let's be clear about what this means. There's a world of difference between an I.Q. advantage that's genetic and one that depends on extended car time with Graham Gladwell.

Flynn is a cautious and careful writer. Unlike many others in the I.Q. debates, he resists grand philosophizing. He comes back again and again to the fact that I.Q. scores are generated by paper-and-pencil tests—and making sense of those scores, he tells us, is a messy and complicated business that requires something closer to the skills of an accountant than to those of a philosopher.

For instance, Flynn shows what happens when we recognize that I.Q. is not a freestanding number but a value attached to a specific time and a specific test. When an I.Q. test is created, he reminds us, it is calibrated or "normed" so that the test-takers in the fiftieth percentile—those exactly at the median—are assigned a score of 100. But since I.Q.s are always rising, the only way to keep that hundred-point benchmark is periodically to make the tests more difficult—to "renorm" them. The original WISC was normed in the late nineteen-forties. It was then renormed in the early nineteen-seventies, as the WISC-R; renormed a third time in the late eighties, as the WISC III; and renormed again a few years ago, as the WISC IV—with each version just a little harder than its predecessor. The notion that anyone "has" an I.Q. of a certain number, then, is meaningless unless you know which WISC he took, and when he took it, since there's a substantial difference between getting a 130 on the WISC IV and getting a 130 on the much easier WISC.

This is not a trivial issue. I.Q. tests are used to diagnose people as mentally retarded, with a score of 70 generally taken to be the cutoff. You can imagine how the Flynn effect plays havoc with that system. In the nineteen-seventies and eighties, most states used the WISC-R to make their mental-retardation diagnoses. But since kids—even kids with disabilities—score a little higher every year, the number of children whose scores fell below 70 declined steadily through the end of the eighties. Then, in 1991, the WISC III was introduced, and suddenly the percentage of kids labeled retarded went up. The psychologists Tomoe Kanaya, Matthew Scullin, and Stephen Ceci estimated that, if every state had switched to the WISC III right away, the number of Americans labeled mentally retarded should have doubled.

That is an extraordinary number. The diagnosis of mental disability is one of the most stigmatizing of all educational and occupational classifications—and yet, apparently, the chances of being burdened with that label are in no small degree a function of the point, in the life cycle of the WISC, at which a child happens to sit for his evaluation. "As far as I can determine, no clinical or school psychologists using the WISC over the relevant 25 years noticed that its criterion of mental retardation became more lenient over time," Flynn wrote, in a 2000 paper. "Yet no one drew the obvious moral about psychologists in the field: They simply were not making any systematic assessment of the I.Q. criterion for mental retardation."

Flynn brings a similar precision to the question of whether Asians have a genetic advantage in I.Q., a possibility that has led to great excitement among I.Q. fundamentalists in recent years. Data showing that the Japanese had higher I.Q.s than people of European descent, for example, prompted the British psychometrician and eugenicist Richard Lynn to concoct an elaborate evolutionary explanation involving the Himalayas, really cold weather, premodern hunting practices, brain size, and specialized vowel sounds. The fact that the I.Q.s of Chinese-Americans also seemed to be elevated has led I.Q. fundamentalists to posit the existence of an international I.Q. pyramid, with Asians at the top, European whites next, and Hispanics and blacks at the bottom.

Here was a question tailor-made for James Flynn's accounting skills. He looked first at Lynn's data, and realized that the comparison was skewed. Lynn was comparing American I.Q. estimates based on a representative sample of schoolchildren with Japanese estimates based on an upper-income, heavily urban sample. Recalculated, the Japanese average came in not at 106.6 but at 99.2. Then Flynn turned his attention to the Chinese-American estimates. They turned out to be based on a 1975 study in San Francisco's Chinatown using something called the Lorge-Thorndike Intelligence Test. But the Lorge-Thorndike test was normed in the

15

nineteen-fifties. For children in the nineteen-seventies, it would have been a piece of cake. When the Chinese-American scores were reassessed using up-to-date intelligence metrics, Flynn found, they came in at 97 verbal and 100 nonverbal. Chinese-Americans had slightly lower I.Q.s than white Americans.

The Asian-American success story had suddenly been turned on its head. The numbers now suggested, Flynn said, that they had succeeded not because of their *higher* I.Q.s. but despite their *lower* I.Q.s. Asians were overachievers. In a nifty piece of statistical analysis, Flynn then worked out just how great that overachievement was. Among whites, virtually everyone who joins the ranks of the managerial, professional, and technical occupations has an I.Q. of 97 or above. Among Chinese-Americans, that threshold is 90. A Chinese-American with an I.Q. of 90, it would appear, does as much with it as a white American with an I.Q. of 97.

There should be no great mystery about Asian achievement. It has to do with hard work and dedication to higher education, and belonging to a culture that stresses professional success. But Flynn makes one more observation. The children of that first successful wave of Asian-Americans really did have I.Q.s that were higher than everyone else's—coming in somewhere around 103. Having worked their way into the upper reaches of the occupational scale, and taken note of how much the professions value abstract thinking, Asian-American parents have evidently made sure that their own children wore scientific spectacles. "Chinese Americans are an ethnic group for whom high achievement preceded high I.Q. rather than the reverse," Flynn concludes, reminding us that in our discussions of the relationship between I.Q. and success we often confuse causes and effects. "It is not easy to view the history of their achievements without emotion," he writes. That is exactly right. To ascribe Asian success to some abstract number is to trivialize it.

20   Two weeks ago, Flynn came to Manhattan to debate Charles Murray at a forum sponsored by the Manhattan Institute. Their subject was the black-white I.Q. gap in America. During the twenty-five years after the Second World War, that gap closed considerably. The I.Q.s of white Americans rose, as part of the general worldwide Flynn effect, but the I.Q.s of black Americans rose faster. Then, for about a period of twenty-five years, that trend stalled—and the question was why.

Murray showed a series of PowerPoint slides, each representing different statistical formulations of the I.Q. gap. He appeared to be pessimistic that the racial difference would narrow in the future. "By the nineteen-seventies,

you had gotten most of the juice out of the environment that you were going to get," he said. That gap, he seemed to think, reflected some inherent
difference between the races. "Starting in the nineteen-seventies, to put it
very crudely, you had a higher proportion of black kids being born to really
dumb mothers," he said. When the debate's moderator, Jane Waldfogel,
informed him that the most recent data showed that the race gap had begun
to close again, Murray seemed unimpressed, as if the possibility that blacks
could ever make further progress was inconceivable.

Flynn took a different approach. The black-white gap, he pointed out,
differs dramatically by age. He noted that the tests we have for measuring
the cognitive functioning of infants, though admittedly crude, show the
races to be almost the same. By age four, the average black I.Q. is 95.4—
only four and a half points behind the average white I.Q. Then the real
gap emerges: from age four through twenty-four, blacks lose six-tenths of a
point a year, until their scores settle at 83.4.

That steady decline, Flynn said, did not resemble the usual pattern of
genetic influence. Instead, it was exactly what you would expect, given
the disparate cognitive environments that whites and blacks encounter
as they grow older. Black children are more likely to be raised in single-
parent homes than are white children—and single-parent homes are less
cognitively complex than two-parent homes. The average I.Q. of first-grade
students in schools that blacks attend is 95, which means that "kids who
want to be above average don't have to aim as high." There were possibly
adverse differences between black teen-age culture and white teen-age
culture, and an enormous number of young black men are in jail—which
is hardly the kind of environment in which someone would learn to put on
scientific spectacles.

Flynn then talked about what we've learned from studies of adoption
and mixed-race children—and that evidence didn't fit a genetic model,
either. If I.Q. is innate, it shouldn't make a difference whether it's a mixed-
race child's mother or father who is black. But it does: children with a white
mother and a black father have an eight-point I.Q. advantage over those
with a black mother and a white father. And it shouldn't make much of a
difference where a mixed-race child is born. But, again, it does: the children
fathered by black American G.I.s in postwar Germany and brought up by
their German mothers have the same I.Q.s as the children of white American G.I.s and German mothers. The difference, in that case, was not the
fact of the children's blackness, as a fundamentalist would say. It was the
fact of their *Germanness*—of their being brought up in a different culture,

under different circumstances. "The mind is much more like a muscle than we've ever realized," Flynn said. "It needs to get cognitive exercise. It's not some piece of clay on which you put an indelible mark." The lesson to be drawn from black and white differences was the same as the lesson from the Netherlands years ago: I.Q. measures not just the quality of a person's mind but the quality of the world that person lives in.

(2007)

Questions

1. In your own words, summarize Gladwell's thesis. What evidence does he give to support his argument?

2. What does I.Q. actually measure? How important do you think this measurement is?

3. Considering the information given in this article, do you think that I.Q. should be used in the diagnosis of mental disability? If so, why? If not, why not, and what method would be better?

4. In part, I.Q. tests measure one's ability to apply abstract taxonomical categories. Gladwell writes that "it can be argued" that the ability to apply these categories is "a developmental improvement" because it can lead to technological and scientific advancement. Do you agree? Is it good for I.Q. tests to emphasize the importance of this mode of thinking?

PRICED TO SELL: IS FREE THE FUTURE?

Gladwell responds to Chris Anderson's book
Free: The Future of a Radical Price *in a discussion
of the commercial future of ideas in the digital age.*

❧

At a hearing on Capitol Hill in May, James Moroney, the publisher of the Dallas *Morning News*, told Congress about negotiations he'd just had with the online retailer Amazon. The idea was to license his newspaper's content to the Kindle, Amazon's new electronic reader. "They want seventy per cent of the subscription revenue," Moroney testified. "I get thirty per cent, they get seventy per cent. On top of that, they have said we get the right to republish your intellectual property to any portable device." The idea was that if a Kindle subscription to the Dallas *Morning News* cost ten dollars a month, seven dollars of that belonged to Amazon, the provider of the gadget on which the news was read, and just three dollars belonged to the newspaper, the provider of an expensive and ever-changing variety of editorial content. The people at Amazon valued the newspaper's contribution so little, in fact, that they felt they ought then to be able to license it to anyone else they wanted. Another witness at the hearing, Arianna Huffington, of the *Huffington Post*, said that she thought the Kindle could provide a business model to save the beleaguered newspaper industry. Moroney disagreed. "I get thirty per cent and they get the right to license my content to any portable device—not just ones made by Amazon?" He was incredulous. "That, to me, is not a model."

Had James Moroney read Chris Anderson's new book, "Free: The Future of a Radical Price," Amazon's offer might not have seemed quite so surprising. Anderson is the editor of *Wired* and the author of the 2006 bestseller "The Long Tail," and "Free" is essentially an extended elaboration of Stewart Brand's famous declaration that "information wants to be free." The digital age, Anderson argues, is exerting an inexorable downward pressure on the prices of all things "made of ideas." Anderson does not consider this a passing trend. Rather, he seems to think of it as an iron law: "In the digital realm you can try to keep Free at bay with laws and locks, but eventually the force of economic gravity will win." To musicians who believe that their music is being pirated, Anderson is blunt. They should stop complaining, and capitalize on the added exposure that piracy provides by making money through touring, merchandise sales, and "yes, the sale of some of [their] music to people who still want CDs or prefer to buy their music online." To the Dallas *Morning News*, he would say the same thing. Newspapers need to accept that content is never again going to be worth what they want it to be worth, and reinvent their business. "Out of the bloodbath will come a new role for professional journalists," he predicts, and he goes on:

> There may be more of them, not fewer, as the ability to participate in journalism extends beyond the credentialed halls of traditional media. But they may be paid far less, and for many it won't be a full time job at all. Journalism as a profession will share the stage with journalism as an avocation. Meanwhile, others may use their

skills to teach and organize amateurs to do a better job covering their own communities, becoming more editor/coach than writer. If so, leveraging the Free—paying people to get *other* people to write for non-monetary rewards—may not be the enemy of professional journalists. Instead, it may be their salvation.

Anderson is very good at paragraphs like this—with its reassuring arc from "bloodbath" to "salvation." His advice is pithy, his tone uncompromising, and his subject matter perfectly timed for a moment when old-line content providers are desperate for answers. That said, it is not entirely clear what distinction is being marked between "paying people to get *other* people to write" and paying people to write. If you can afford to pay someone to get other people to write, why can't you pay people to write? It would be nice to know, as well, just how a business goes about reorganizing itself around getting people to work for "non-monetary rewards." Does he mean that the New York *Times* should be staffed by volunteers, like Meals on Wheels? Anderson's reference to people who "prefer to buy their music online" carries the faint suggestion that refraining from theft should be considered a mere preference. And then there is his insistence that the relentless downward pressure on prices represents an iron law of the digital economy. Why is it a law? Free is just another price, and prices are set by individual actors, in accordance with the aggregated particulars of marketplace power. "Information wants to be free," Anderson tells us, "in the same way that life wants to spread and water wants to run downhill." But information can't actually want anything, can it? *Amazon* wants the information in the Dallas paper to be free, because that way Amazon makes more money. Why are the self-interested motives of powerful companies being elevated to a philosophical principle? But we are getting ahead of ourselves.

Anderson's argument begins with a technological trend. The cost of the building blocks of all electronic activity—storage, processing, and bandwidth—has fallen so far that it is now approaching zero. In 1961, Anderson says, a single transistor was ten dollars. In 1963, it was five dollars. By 1968, it was one dollar. Today, Intel will sell you two billion transistors for eleven hundred dollars meaning that the cost of a single transistor is now about .000055 cents.

5   Anderson's second point is that when prices hit zero extraordinary things happen. Anderson describes an experiment conducted by the M.I.T. behavioral economist Dan Ariely, the author of "Predictably Irrational." Ariely offered a group of subjects a choice between two kinds of

chocolate—Hershey's Kisses, for one cent, and Lindt truffles, for fifteen cents. Three-quarters of the subjects chose the truffles. Then he redid the experiment, reducing the price of both chocolates by one cent. The Kisses were now free. What happened? The order of preference was reversed. Sixty-nine per cent of the subjects chose the Kisses. The price difference between the two chocolates was exactly the same, but that magic word "free" has the power to create a consumer stampede. Amazon has had the same experience with its offer of free shipping for orders over twenty-five dollars. The idea is to induce you to buy a second book, if your first book comes in at less than the twenty-five-dollar threshold. And that's exactly what it does. In France, however, the offer was mistakenly set at the equivalent of twenty cents—and consumers didn't buy the second book. "From the consumer's perspective, there is a huge difference between cheap and free," Anderson writes. "Give a product away, and it can go viral. Charge a single cent for it and you're in an entirely different business.... The truth is that zero is one market and any other price is another."

Since the falling costs of digital technology let you make as much stuff as you want, Anderson argues, and the magic of the word "free" creates instant demand among consumers, then Free (Anderson honors it with a capital) represents an enormous business opportunity. Companies ought to be able to make huge amounts of money "around" the thing being given away—as Google gives away its search and e-mail and makes its money on advertising.

Anderson cautions that this philosophy of embracing the Free involves moving from a "scarcity" mind-set to an "abundance" mind-set. Giving something away means that a lot of it will be wasted. But because it costs almost nothing to make things, digitally, we can afford to be wasteful. The elaborate mechanisms we set up to monitor and judge the quality of content are, Anderson thinks, artifacts of an era of scarcity: we had to worry about how to allocate scarce resources like newsprint and shelf space and broadcast time. Not anymore. Look at YouTube, he says, the free video archive owned by Google. YouTube lets anyone post a video to its site free, and lets anyone watch a video on its site free, and it doesn't have to pass judgment on the quality of the videos it archives. "Nobody is deciding whether a video is good enough to justify the scarce channel space it takes, because there is no scarce channel space," he writes, and goes on:

Distribution is now close enough to free to round down. Today, it costs about $0.25 to stream one hour of video to one person. Next year, it will be $0.15. A year later it will be less than a dime. Which is why YouTube's founders decided to give it away.... The result is both messy and runs counter to every instinct of a television professional, but this is what abundance both requires and demands.

There are four strands of argument here: a technological claim (digital infrastructure is effectively Free), a psychological claim (consumers love Free), a procedural claim (Free means never having to make a judgment), and a commercial claim (the market created by the technological Free and the psychological Free can make you a lot of money). The only problem is that in the middle of laying out what he sees as the new business model of the digital age Anderson is forced to admit that one of his main case studies, YouTube, "has so far failed to make any money for Google."

Why is that? Because of the very principles of Free that Anderson so energetically celebrates. When you let people upload and download as many videos as they want, lots of them will take you up on the offer. That's the magic of Free psychology: an estimated seventy-five billion videos will be served up by YouTube this year. Although the magic of Free technology means that the cost of serving up each video is "close enough to free to round down," "close enough to free" multiplied by seventy-five billion is still a very large number. A recent report by Credit Suisse estimates that YouTube's bandwidth costs in 2009 will be three hundred and sixty million dollars. In the case of YouTube, the effects of technological Free and psychological Free work against each other.

So how does YouTube bring in revenue? Well, it tries to sell advertisements alongside its videos. The problem is that the videos attracted by psychological Free—pirated material, cat videos, and other forms of user-generated content—are not the sort of thing that advertisers want to be associated with. In order to sell advertising, YouTube has had to buy the rights to professionally produced content, such as television shows and movies. Credit Suisse put the cost of those licenses in 2009 at roughly two hundred and sixty million dollars. For Anderson, YouTube illustrates the principle that Free removes the necessity of aesthetic judgment. (As he puts it, YouTube proves that "crap is in the eye of the beholder.") But, in order to make money, YouTube has been obliged to pay for programs that *aren't* crap. To recap: YouTube is a great example of Free, except that Free technology ends up not being Free because of the way consumers respond to Free, fatally compromising YouTube's ability to make money around Free, and forcing it to retreat from the "abundance thinking" that lies at the heart of Free. Credit Suisse estimates that YouTube will lose close to half a billion dollars this year. If it were a bank, it would be eligible for TARP funds.

Anderson begins the second part of his book by quoting Lewis Strauss, the former head of the Atomic Energy Commission, who famously predicted in the mid-nineteen-fifties that "our children will enjoy in their homes electrical energy too cheap to meter."

"What if Strauss had been right?" Anderson wonders, and then diligently sorts through the implications: as much fresh water as you could want, no reliance on fossil fuels, no global warming, abundant agricultural production. Anderson wants to take "too cheap to meter" seriously, because he believes that we are on the cusp of our own "too cheap to meter" revolution with computer processing, storage, and bandwidth. But here is the second and broader problem with Anderson's argument: he is asking the wrong question. It is pointless to wonder what would have happened if Strauss's prediction *had* come true while rushing past the reasons that it could *not* have come true.

Strauss's optimism was driven by the fuel cost of nuclear energy which was so low compared with its fossil-fuel counterparts that he considered it (to borrow Anderson's phrase) close enough to free to round down. Generating and distributing electricity, however, requires a vast and expensive infrastructure of transmission lines and power plants—and it is this infrastructure that accounts for most of the cost of electricity. Fuel prices are only a small part of that. As Gordon Dean, Strauss's predecessor at the A.E.C., wrote, "Even if coal were mined and distributed free to electric generating plants today, the reduction in your monthly electricity bill would amount to but twenty per cent, so great is the cost of the plant itself and the distribution system."

This is the kind of error that technological utopians make. They assume that their particular scientific revolution will wipe away all traces of its predecessors—that if you change the fuel you change the whole system. Strauss went on to forecast "an age of peace," jumping from atoms to human hearts. "As the world of chips and glass fibers and wireless waves goes, so goes the rest of the world," Kevin Kelly, another *Wired* visionary, proclaimed at the start of his 1998 digital manifesto, "New Rules for the New Economy," offering up the same non sequitur. And now comes Anderson. "The more products are made of ideas, rather than stuff, the faster they can get cheap," he writes, and we know what's coming next: "However, this is not limited to digital products." Just look at the pharmaceutical industry, he

10

says. Genetic engineering means that drug development is poised to follow the same learning curve of the digital world, to "accelerate in performance while it drops in price."

But, like Strauss, he's forgotten about the plants and the power lines. The expensive part of making drugs has never been what happens in the laboratory. It's what happens after the laboratory, like the clinical testing, which can take years and cost hundreds of millions of dollars. In the pharmaceutical world, what's more, companies have chosen to use the potential of new technology to do something very different from their counterparts in Silicon Valley. They've been trying to find a way to serve smaller and smaller markets—to create medicines tailored to very specific subpopulations and strains of diseases—and smaller markets often mean higher prices. The biotechnology company Genzyme spent five hundred million dollars developing the drug Myozyme, which is intended for a condition, Pompe disease, that afflicts fewer than ten thousand people worldwide. That's the quintessential modern drug: a high-tech, targeted remedy that took a very long and costly path to market. Myozyme is priced at three hundred thousand dollars a year. Genzyme isn't a mining company: its real assets are intellectual property—information, not stuff. But, in this case, information does not want to be free. It wants to be really, really expensive.

15   And there's plenty of other information out there that has chosen to run in the opposite direction from Free. The *Times* gives away its content on its Web site. But the *Wall Street Journal* has found that more than a million subscribers are quite happy to pay for the privilege of reading online. Broadcast television—the original practitioner of Free—is struggling. But premium cable, with its stiff monthly charges for specialty content, is doing just fine. Apple may soon make more money selling iPhone downloads (ideas) than it does from the iPhone itself (stuff). The company could one day give away the iPhone to boost downloads; it could give away the downloads to boost iPhone sales; or it could continue to do what it does now, and charge for both. Who knows? The only iron law here is the one too obvious to write a book about, which is that the digital age has so transformed the ways in which things are made and sold that there are no iron laws.

(2009)

Questions

1. Explain the meaning of the claim that "information wants to be free."

2. Summarize in your own words three of Anderson's points from the article. What arguments does Gladwell make to refute each of these points? In each case, which side is more convincing and why?

3. Find places in the article where Gladwell draws attention to Anderson's persuasive rhetorical style. Why do you think Gladwell does this? Is it an effective strategy?

4. Should Internet piracy be illegal? Why or why not?

5. Gladwell points out that YouTube, a major case study in Anderson's research, lost almost half a billion dollars in 2009. Do you think it could be successful in the long term? If so, how? If not, why not?

6. What is "technological utopianism," and what argument does Gladwell make against it? Do you agree with him?

ADAM GOPNIK

THE CORRECTIONS

In this essay a noted New Yorker *writer discusses
"abridgment, enrichment, and the nature of art."*

❧

Our theme today is addition and subtraction, abridgment and expansion, and their effects on works of art and entertainment. (Sorry, what was that? No, the seminar on history of the cinema is in the next classroom.) What can be taken away from a book or a movie, what can be added to it, and what does it tell us about what we bring to both?

The first form to consider is subtraction, or what might more grandly be called the aesthetic of abridgment, as illustrated by a new and ambitious series of "compact editions" produced by the British publisher Orion. "The great classics contain passionate romance, thrilling adventure, arresting characters and unforgettable scenes and situations," an explanatory note tells us. "But finding time to read them can be a problem." So Orion has taken nineteenth-century classics—among them "Moby-Dick," "Anna Karenina," "Vanity Fair," and "The Mill on the Floss"—and cut them neatly in half, like Damien Hirst[1] animals, so that they can be taken in quickly and all the more admired.

Although the tone of the blurbs and the back matter is defiantly unapologetic, the names of the abridgers are mysteriously absent, suggesting that, with the shyness of old-fashioned pornographers, they don't want to be quite so openly associated with the project as their publisher's pride would suggest they ought. Who was the mohel of "Moby-Dick"; who took the vanity out of "Vanity Fair"; who threw Anna under the train a hundred pages sooner than before? Orion isn't telling. Yet the work had to be done with considerable tact and judgment. A good condensation of a hard book is

---

1   *Damien Hirst*   Artist best known for his works involving dissected animals preserved in formaldehyde.

hardly a crime; if Joseph Campbell and Henry Morton Robinson, an editor at *Reader's Digest*, hadn't labored over their "skeleton key" to "Finnegan's Wake," readers would still find Joyce's book not just difficult but unapproachable. The Orionites should be proud of their work; their abridgments are skillfully done.

Take "Moby-Dick," a book that, if every reader has not always wanted shorter, then certainly, as Dr. Johnson said about "Paradise Lost," no reader has ever wanted *longer*. The first chapter of the compact edition is typical of the Orion approach. Most of the famous first paragraph, most of the famous first chapter, is presented as Melville wrote it. No muscle is removed—unlike, say, A.L. Rowse's modernization of Shakespeare, no attempt is made to simplify or improve the author's vocabulary and knotty, convoluted syntax. Ishmael asks us to call him so, and the story proceeds.

What is cut in the first chapter is the two long passages that depart from   5 the Ishmaelian specifics: a reflection on people watching boats in Manhattan and the allure of the sea even in a city ("Posted like silent sentinels all around the town, stand thousands upon thousands of mortal men fixed in ocean reveries"), and Melville's invocation of the history of ocean worship ("Why did the old Persians hold the sea holy? Why did the Greeks give it a separate deity?"). These passages are, by modern critical standards, "showy" and "digressive," nervously intent to display stray learning and to make obscure allusion more powerful than inherent emotion. The same thing happens in the subsequent chapters. Melville's story is intact and immediate; it's just that the long bits about the technical details of whaling are gone, as are most of the mock Shakespearean interludes, the philosophical meanderings, and the metaphysical huffing and puffing. The entire chapter "The Whiteness of the Whale," where Melville tries to explain why white, the natural symbol of Good, is also somehow the natural symbol of Evil, is just, well, whited out.

All abridgments and additions are part of their period; we scoff at the eighteenth century for cutting the tragic end of "Lear" and tacking on a happy one, but the recent, much praised Royal Shakespeare production added a gratuitous Grand Guignol hanging of the poor Fool, on the shaky basis of a sideways reference to his death two acts later. By the same token, the Orion "Moby-Dick" is not defaced; it is, by conventional contemporary standards of good editing and critical judgment, *improved*. The compact edition adheres to a specific idea of what a good novel ought to be: the contemporary aesthetic of the realist psychological novel. This is not what a contemptuous philistine would do with the book. It is what a good editor, of the Maxwell Perkins variety, would do: cut out the self-indulgent stuff and present a clean story, inhabited by plausible characters—the "taut, spare, driving" narrative beloved of Sunday reviewers. You can pretty much read the soothing letter to the author that would have accompanied the suggested cuts, had he been alive to receive it. ("Herman: just a few small trims along the way; myself I find the whaling stuff fascinating, but I fear your reader wants to move along with the story—and frankly the tensile strength of the narrative is being undercut right now by a lot of stray material that takes us *way* off line. The 'slip' of your research is showing! Here's an idea someone here had the other day: why don't we do a 'readers' guide' where all of this rich, fascinating, miscellaneous whaling material can be made available to people who want it without interfering with the flow of the story?") What the Orion "Moby-Dick" says about the book is what a good critic or professional editor would say about the book. It's what they *did* say: there's too much digression and sticky stuff and extraneous learning. If he'd cut that out, it would be a better story.

Only years of careful inculcation in the masterpiece makes us hesitate. And rightly so. For when you come to the end of the compact "Moby-Dick" you don't think, What a betrayal; you think, Nice job—what were the missing bits again? And when you go back to find them you remember why the book isn't just a thrilling adventure with unforgettable characters but a great book. The subtraction does not turn good work into hackwork; it turns a hysterical, half-mad masterpiece into a sound, sane book. It still has its phallic reach and point, but lacks its flaccid, anxious self-consciousness: it is all Dick and no Moby.

Just as "'Moby-Dick' in half the time" dispenses with Melville's digressions and showy knowledge, the compact "Vanity Fair" relieves Thackeray of his "preciousness"—the discursive, interfering commentary on the action that charmed his Victorian readers. In a middle chapter called "In Which Amelia Invades the Low Countries," for instance, Thackeray's chatty, confidential tone is altered by his subtractors into the sparer narrative voice of good writing. The scene is set for Amelia's arrival in Brussels on the eve of Waterloo, and Thackeray's descriptive prose is kept mostly intact. ("This flat, flourishing, easy country never could have looked more rich and prosperous than in that summer of 1815.") In the original, though, Thackeray precedes that description with a loquacious paragraph:

But it may be said as a rule, that every Englishman in the Duke of Wellington's army paid his way. The remembrance of such a fact surely becomes a nation of shopkeepers. It was a blessing for a commerce-loving country to be over-run by such an army of customers; and to have such creditable warriors to feed. And the country which they came to protect is not military. For a long period of history they have let other people fight there. When the present writer went to survey with eagle glance the field of Waterloo, we asked the conductor of the diligence, a portly warlike-looking veteran, whether he had been at the battle. *"Pas si bête"*[2]—such an answer and sentiment as no Frenchman would own to—was his reply.

And so on, in a similarly intimate, letter-to-the-reader vein. This is, of course, not merely digressive but "sentimental," and, like a later aside about how foolish Napoleon was not to wait until the allies had fallen apart from their own internal differences, breaks up the flow and movement of the story.

Even as sympathetic a reader as Edmund Wilson hated Thackeray's rambling remarks and continual intrusions of mild ironies. But Thackeray without his little jokes and warm asides becomes another, duller writer—too constantly on message. Meaning resides in the margins; Thackeray wants to insinuate, not force, his way into the reader's confidence. Becky Sharp lives for us not just because her creator made her but because her creator couldn't leave her alone; he is always *there*, fussing over her shoulder, commenting on her behavior, the way we do with real people who obsess us. Transparent, objective lucidity is the last emotion we have about the actual; we fret, comment, editorialize, intrude, despair, laugh, and gossip.

The real lesson of the compact editions is not that vandals shouldn't be let loose on masterpieces but that masterpieces are inherently a little loony. They run on the engine of their own accumulated habits and weirdnesses and self-indulgent excesses. They have to, since originality is, necessarily, something still strange to us, rather than something that we already know about and approve. What makes writing matter is not a story, cleanly told, but a voice, however odd or ordinary, and a point of view, however strange or sentimental. Books can be snipped at, and made less melodically muddled, but they lose their overtones, their bass notes, their chesty resonance—the same thing that happens, come to think of it, to human castrati.

10

---

2   *Pas si bête*   French: (I'm) not that stupid.

Novelists have always seen their work cut—by the interfering editor or the posthumous abridger—but they almost never see it expanded. Henry James's New York Edition did add late-James lace to mid-James linen, but the sewing always shows. (There are those who think that the late long First Folio "Hamlet" is a messy author's expansion of the short, stern early quarto, but they are a minority.) On the whole, once authors get the words out, they may have to settle for less, but they don't come back for more. For the aesthetic of addition, we need to turn to the movies. We can study it in the "director's cuts" provided on those special-feature-laden DVDs which are by now the actual quanta of the movies—the form in which they really get seen. The director's cut, after all, is not a cut (the sole exception I've seen is the Coen brothers' revamped "Blood Simple," which is roughly five minutes leaner than the version that enjoyed theatrical release) but an expansion, the bitter putting-back-in of all that the assembled execs and idiots forced the director to take out.

Yet what gets put back in is often stifling and slowing. Francis Ford Coppola's near-masterpiece "Apocalypse Now" is, in its expanded and presumably perfected version, also long-winded and diffuse, escaping its relentless thematic concentration for side-lit erotic encounters with *Playboy* Playmates and mysterious French colonial women, pleasing but a little pointless. And no amount of putting back in can redeem the silliness of the heavy symbolism at the movie's close (or make a heavy actor look any lighter). What one feels in most director's cuts is not so much addition, new things brought in, as mere chest expansion, the same number of breaths taken more slowly.

The search for meaningful additions leads you, finally, to the director's *commentaries*, which can provide even mediocre films with depth, irony, and counterpoint. They reflect an organic genre; among people in the movie industry, the Angry-Apologetic Monologue is the most frequent form of shoptalk. There is nothing movie people like to talk about so much as how their movie was ruined by the studio or the star. These monologues are often more interesting than the films they superintend, more interesting even than the films they superintend might have been if they had been made as the narrator wishes they had been. They are fascinating in a way that your account of why you didn't get tenure or your book failed to sell is not, because all but the worst movies involve not just an aspiration toward success but a real confrontation of impulses: there's an idealist impulse toward art and a realist impulse toward commerce, and the clash of the two, however inevitable the ending, is the natural material of drama.

It is this real drama that the additive aesthetic of the DVD commentary supplies.

A fine example is the lurid, stylish psycho-thriller "The Cell." It is the tale of a serial killer who kidnaps women and imprisons them in a tank, slowly drowning them, and who is undone by Jennifer Lopez, a psychotherapist able to enter his mind (don't ask). It was directed by Tarsem Singh, an Indian-born music video veteran, and the reason for the odd emotionlessness of a film about the attempted murder of a young girl soon becomes apparent. "She couldn't go underwater without holding her nose!" Singh says angrily, a few minutes after the main victim-to-be appears suspended in the killing tank. He punished the actress, he explains, who, having promised to swim desperately in the grim tank, turned out to be unable to do so, by denying her closeups. "I just needed to get in with her," he says in a tone of regret. "I couldn't bring myself—I was so hurt."

Or, at a higher level, take Allen Coulter's somber "Hollywoodland," the intelligent, brilliantly acted (particularly by Diane Lane and Bob Hoskins and Ben Affleck), yet unbelievably dull story of how the fifties television Superman, George Reeves, killed himself or was killed in a very minor Hollywood scandal. The source of the film's strange tone—"Hollywood Babylon" retold as a Ph.D. thesis—becomes apparent when you watch the film with Coulter's commentary. Coulter turns out to be an immensely serious, erudite craftsman, highly self-conscious about his effects. "I was thinking about the Japanese Noh theatre, which begins with a clacking on the side of a drum," he says of the otherwise routine opening shot of his film; and each effect thereafter is registered and calculated to a degree that would have shamed Henry James himself. Adrien Brody plays a detective investigating the death, and the height of his hair is discussed with aggrieved indignation; it seems that people have compared Brody's hair to Eddie Cochran's hair, whereas, in fact, "his hair is *exactly* the same height as James Dean's." Barely audible sound clues are minutely parsed for their implied significance; it turns out that the extras, looped in post-production, were allowed to murmur only about timely subjects from 1959. Every moment in the mix, every change of light (from the "fading Kodachrome" look of the Brody story to the saturated look of the Affleck bits), every discreet genuflection to another movie is lovingly catalogued. ("Just a bit of an homage to a great cut in 'Chinatown,' one of my favorite edits in all film.") We learn that the longest lens in the Adrien Brody sequence is the same length as the shortest lens in the Ben Affleck sequences. We learn that the director drew up a "flow chart" of gum-chewing, marking the dramatic

15

trajectory on which the Brody character does and does not chew gum, and thereby revealing his moral growth.

The attention to detail is amazing—Coulter will make a great movie someday—but the accumulated effect of all this passionate perfectionism is to suggest a form of self-delusion, the artist having lost sight of the thing most obvious to the viewer, which is that the story he has to tell is too insignificant to hold one's attention for the time required to tell it. The tale of how the guy who played Superman on a cheap, forgotten TV series shot himself lacks the grip of tragedy, even pop tragedy, which demands, after all, that the hero once counted. (Joe Orton's life can be made ugly and tragic because the scale of his gifts implies both conditions; but George Reeves's death is merely sad and a little sordid.) The enormous care lavished on material that would never be worthy of the effort is more moving than the film; the addition adds pathos to inertia. The will to believe, without which a popular artist has to give up even trying, does not just turn sows' ears into silk purses; more often, it makes silk ears, beautifully surfaced and yet still attached to the same old animal.

To dig still deeper into the strange pathos of respective narration, take the late-Brosnan-period James Bond movie "The World Is Not Enough." It was directed by the British documentarian Michael Apted, a man of genuine accomplishment, whose "Seven Up" series, tracing the development of a group of British schoolkids of various class backgrounds from childhood to, by now, middle age, will be recalled as one of the classics of our time. (His "Coal Miner's Daughter" remains a very good thing, too.) Now, the Bond film he agreed to shoot contains, within its frames, the single most sublimely silly conception in modern cinema: Denise Richards as a nuclear physicist in hot pants named Christmas Jones. You might think this would be a hard movie to render dull, yet dull and confused it is, leaving even Denise Richards almost sexless and undistracting. The reason becomes apparent in Apted's commentary. Apted, who has a respect for actors and a feeling for the real, could not—cannot now—adequately subsume himself into the kind of dumb but deadpan, yet on its own terms serious, stylishness that a Bond film demands. "Blood-curdling action," he announces quietly before some early action sequences, "tires an audience out"—surely a dubious motto for the director of a Bond film. And then, "Gunfire can get extremely tedious, noisy and tedious."

He was brought in, we soon realize, to give some "weight" to the performances, with the result that the action sequences stop abruptly, interrupted by heavy-breathing dramatic acting, up and down the piano, by Sophie Marceau as the heroine and the game Pierce Brosnan as Bond. Apted broods intelligently on "the developing dynamic of the Elektra-Bond relationship," and says sapient things about the "vulnerability" of the villain. When Denise makes her appearance, he says gently that she has "perhaps a less developed role than some of the others," though "undeveloped" might seem to be the last word one would use for Denise Richards. The trouble is that he kept trying to make the movie good in the wrong way. When a babe is brought out for Bond to sleep with, Apted says nice things about what a fine actress she is. But do we want a Bond babe to be a fine actress? A director who is thinking of her as a full-fledged thespian may be a better man than the one who is thinking of her as a full-bosomed ornament. But he is a worse Bond director. By the time we come to a tedious and nearly indecipherable sequence with a submarine, which ends the film, Apted is almost as dispirited as the viewer. He says, feebly, "I did a lot of little inserts of buttons and flashing lights and whatever." And there they are, full of oogah horns and bright-red things that flick on and off, signifying nothing.

The net effect is like that of a funny Malcolm Bradbury novel about the tormented inner life of a documentary-film director, serious and much admired, who finds himself directing a Bond film. This—the sensitive commentary and the cynical film together—makes something that is close to being a work of art in itself, the tale of a man with a tangled conscience and a submarine to sink. The commentary provides the film with the complicated point of view, the detachment, the alienation, the odd play of foreground and background, the sad tone of attentive unease and retrospective remorse that we associate with, well, the classic modern novel. With this film—with so many films, I've come to believe—the life and variety, the sincerity of purpose, the surprising point of view, the humanity and life leach through more strongly when the creator is contemplating his ragtag and jury-rigged and compromised creation than when the creation is left to lumber and stoop and speak for itself. Dr. Frankenstein and his monster together are the subject of art; the doctor alone is mere science journalism, and the monster alone mere horror.

What these commentaries reveal to us is this: the movies we see are the already abridged versions of longer novels of ambition and intelligence, thwarted and rewarded. The augmented film teaches us the same lesson as the subtracted book: art is a business not of clear narratives but of troubled narrators. Western literature begins not with the Trojan War but with the poet's announcement that he is going to tell a story *about* the Trojan War. It is self-consciousness of purpose, not transparency of action, that ignites a

20

poem. The trouble with popular entertainment is perhaps not that we don't have enough strong stories but that there are not enough weak narrators— not enough Ishmaels, whose slack and troubled attentiveness, accumulated sighs and second thoughts make the Ahabs live. Movies need their Thompsons as much as their Kanes. (Thompson? He's the roving reporter who makes the story go for Welles; nobody remembers his name, but without him there's no Rosebud, and no movie.) The insertion of that second nettling watching presence is what separates the merely crafty from the artful, the compact from the achieved, and guarantees that, no matter how the maker's hand may add and subtract, the viewer's mind will continue to divide, and multiply.

(2007)

Questions

1. Who is Gopnik's intended audience? How do you know?

2. What does Gopnik mean when he says that "Dr. Frankenstein and his monster together are the subject of art; the doctor alone is mere science journalism, and the monster alone mere horror"?

3. Outline the structure of this essay. What is Gopnik's thesis and where does he state it?

4. Describe the tone of this piece, giving examples to support your claim. In particular, what attitude does Gopnik express toward the works of film and literature he discusses?

5. Why does Gopnik say that a film and its commentary combine to create "something that is close to being a work of art in itself"? Do you agree?

6. Choose a film, novel, or short story that you believe to be an example of great art. Discuss the role of narrative voice in the work you have chosen.

Eric Schlosser

Penny Foolish:

Why Does Burger King Insist on Shortchanging Tomato Pickers?

*Investigative journalist Eric Schlosser questions the treatment
of migrant tomato pickers in this editorial piece.*

❧

The migrant farm workers who harvest tomatoes in South Florida have one of the nation's most backbreaking jobs. For 10 to 12 hours a day, they pick tomatoes by hand, earning a piece-rate of about 45 cents for every 32-pound bucket. During a typical day each migrant picks, carries and unloads two tons of tomatoes. For their efforts, this holiday season many of them are about to get a 40 per cent pay cut.

Florida's tomato growers have long faced pressure to reduce operating costs; one way to do that is to keep migrant wages as low as possible. Although some of the pressure has come from increased competition with Mexican growers, most of it has been forcefully applied by the largest purchaser of Florida tomatoes: American fast food chains that want millions of pounds of cheap tomatoes as a garnish for their hamburgers, tacos and salads.

In 2005, Florida tomato pickers gained their first significant pay raise since the late 1970s when Taco Bell ended a consumer boycott by agreeing to pay an extra penny per pound for its tomatoes, with the extra cent going directly to the farm workers. Last April, McDonald's agreed to a similar arrangement, increasing the wages of its tomato pickers to about 77 cents per bucket. But Burger King, whose headquarters are in Florida, has adamantly refused to pay the extra penny—and its refusal has encouraged tomato growers to cancel the deals already struck with Taco Bell and McDonald's.

This month the Florida Tomato Growers Exchange, representing 90 per cent of the state's growers, announced that it will not allow any of its members to collect the extra penny for farm workers. Reggie Brown, the executive vice president of the group, described the surcharge for poor migrants as "pretty much near un-American."

5   Migrant farm laborers have long been among America's most impoverished workers. Perhaps 80 per cent of the migrants in Florida are illegal immigrants and thus especially vulnerable to abuse. During the past decade, the United States Justice Department has prosecuted half a dozen cases of slavery among farm workers in Florida. Migrants have been driven into debt, forced to work for nothing and kept in chained trailers at night. The Coalition of Immokalee Workers—a farm worker alliance based in Immokalee, Fla.—has done a heroic job improving the lives of migrants in the state, investigating slavery cases and negotiating the penny-per-pound surcharge with fast food chains.

Now the Florida Tomato Growers Exchange has threatened a fine of $100,000 for any grower who accepts an extra penny per pound for migrant wages. The organization claims that such a surcharge would violate "federal and state laws related to antitrust, labor and racketeering." It has not explained how that extra penny would break those laws; nor has it explained why other surcharges routinely imposed by the growers (for things like higher fuel costs) are perfectly legal.

The prominent role that Burger King has played in rescinding the pay raise offers a spectacle of yuletide greed worthy of Charles Dickens. Burger King has justified its behavior by claiming that it has no control over the labor practices of its suppliers. "Florida growers have a right to run their businesses how they see fit," a Burger King spokesman told *The St. Petersburg Times*.

Yet the company has adopted a far more activist approach when the issue is the well-being of livestock. In March, Burger King announced strict new rules on how its meatpacking suppliers should treat chickens and hogs. As for human rights abuses, Burger King has suggested that if the poor farm workers of southern Florida need more money, they should apply for jobs at its restaurants.

Three private equity firms—Bain Capital, the Texas Pacific Group and Goldman Sachs Capital Partners—control most of Burger King's stock. Last year, the chief executive of Goldman Sachs, Lloyd C. Blankfein, earned the largest annual bonus in Wall Street history, and this year he stands to receive an even larger one. Goldman Sachs has served its investors well lately, avoiding the subprime mortgage meltdown and, according to Business Week, doubling the value of its Burger King investment within three years.

Telling Burger King to pay an extra penny for tomatoes and provide a decent wage to migrant workers would hardly bankrupt the company. Indeed, it would cost Burger King only $250,000 a year. At Goldman Sachs, that sort of money shouldn't be too hard to find. In 2006, the bonuses of the top 12 Goldman Sachs executives exceeded $200 million—more than twice as much money as all of the roughly 10,000 tomato pickers in southern Florida earned that year. Now Mr. Blankfein should find a way to share some of his company's good fortune with the workers at the bottom of the food chain.

10

(2007)

Questions

1. According to Schlosser's article, who is responsible for the plight of migrant farm workers? What should those responsible be doing differently?

2. Schlosser reports that Reggie Brown of the Florida Tomato Growers Exchange described the surcharge to increase tomato pickers' wages as "'pretty much near un-American.'" What does Brown mean by this? How reasonable is this objection?

3. Will this article influence your decision to buy from Burger King and other large fast food companies? Why or why not?

4. To what extent is Schlosser's presentation of the information in this article biased?

Margaret Wente

The Charitable and the Cheap: Which One Are You?

In this op-ed piece, Globe and Mail *columnist Margaret Wente reveals that "the most generous people of all are probably not who you think they are."*

❧

A friend of mine in Chicago puts in a lot of time raising money for the theater. Chicago, she told me, has more than 150 professional or semi-professional theater companies, all of which depend at least partly on private donations to keep them afloat. I was stunned. Here in Toronto, the theater capital of Canada, there are maybe a couple of dozen.

Why the huge difference? Chicago is bigger and richer than Toronto, but not that much bigger and richer. It's no more highbrow either, or at least I like to think not.

The difference, I've concluded, is that Chicagoans are far more generous. They have a thriving culture of giving. They figure that if they like the theater, then they'd better write the checks. Here in Toronto we figure that somebody else—maybe the government—should write the checks.

On the generosity scale, the Americans lead the world. They make us look pretty chintzy. They give twice as much of their income to charity as we do. If we gave the same percentage of our incomes to charity as the Americans do, the Canadian charitable sector would be richer by more than $9-billion every year.

5   ·Fortunately, we do a whole lot better than the Europeans. They're the world's worst cheapskates. (Only four per cent of Swedes give to charity at all.) What explains the generosity gap? The standard answer is that people who expect the state to pay for more (through higher taxes) give less, and vice versa. Social attitudes about the importance of philanthropy

572

are directly related to the value people place on individual initiative and the role of the state.

But the most generous people of all are probably not who you think they are. They aren't the rich. They aren't my well-heeled liberal neighbors in latte-land (the ones who complain about cutbacks to the arts), and they aren't the urban cyclists who hold rallies for the homeless and vote NDP.

The most generous people in North America are the small-town folks who go to church, drive pick-up trucks, are very family-oriented, have average jobs, and probably hate the gun registry. They give away more of their income—by far—than anybody else.

The charity gap is driven not by economics but by values. And those values are old-fashioned ones. In the US, the value that correlates most highly with giving is religious faith. "Religious people don't give only to the church," says Arthur C. Brooks, an economist at Syracuse University who is an expert on who gives, and how much. "They also make more gifts to secular causes." The people who give away the most of all (3.7 per cent of their income) live in Utah.

These days, people who are religious are also far more likely to be politically conservative. They're the red-state Bushies, or the Albertans who vote Tory blue. Mr. Brooks's new book, *Who Really Cares*, proves without a doubt that while godless liberals talk the talk, churchgoing conservatives walk the walk. People in the top five Bush states give three times more of their income to charity than people in the top five Kerry states. Conservatives give away more money and volunteer more time to help the poor. They even give more blood. Liberals talk about how we must do more to help the environment and the homeless; conservatives actually help them.

These findings are a little rattling for people who think "compassion-ate conservatism" is a joke. They are also a little humbling for secular people (such as me) who write a check now and then and congratulate ourselves. And they came as a surprise to Mr. Brooks (who is that rare creature in the US, an independent voter). "I came into this thinking that people who say they're compassionate, are compassionate," he says. "I found that's not the case."

Mr. Brooks believes that giving isn't just a civic duty, but a spiritual need. Whether you support a theater or put time in at a soup kitchen, charity helps us connect with something bigger than ourselves. The people who make him angry are the ones who think charity is bad. Yes, there are quite a few. Many of them lurk in major universities. They argue that

10

if something is truly important, the government should do it. Charity, they say, just lets the government off the hook, and therefore should be discouraged. Don't count on them to pick you up if you're run over on a downtown street. They'd rather blame the government for letting too many cars on the road.

Here in Canada the correlation between charity and faith is not quite as strong as in the US. But the correlation with other traditional values is. Our most generous province is Manitoba, where 1 per cent of people's income is donated to charity. The most generous place in Canada may well be a town like Brandon, where life revolves around family and kids and virtually everybody volunteers for something. "This town has a wonderful ability to pull together," says Debbie Arsenault, who runs the local United Way. "All the charities that operate in this community would tell you the same thing."

Recently, a major American TV show decided to subject Mr. Brooks's findings to a real-world test. It got the Salvation Army to station a bell-ringer in Sioux Falls, South Dakota, just outside the Wal-Mart. The Sally Ann put another bell-ringer in San Francisco, just outside Saks. The average income in San Francisco is twice as much as in Sioux Falls. The San Francisco bell-ringer, who encountered twice as many people, collected only half as much money as the one in Sioux Falls. As one city official explained to Mr. Brooks, "We were taught to tithe here, sir."

So what's the least charitable place in Canada? That would be Quebec, where people donate only 0.3 per cent of their income. Quebeckers are far more European in their expectations of the state, and are also the most secular. You want real compassion? Go to Utah. You want lots of theater? Go to Chicago. You want to get something back? Try giving. It's a good thing.

(2007)

Questions

1. According to Wente, who are the most generous people? Who are the least? Why is this so?

2. Who is Wente's ideal audience for this article? What values and preconceived beliefs would a member of this audience have? How can you tell?

3. What does Wente say about those who argue that "charity is bad"? Is this part of her argument convincing?

4. What stereotypes does Wente allude to? Comment on the role of stereotypes in the article.

5. Albert Camus is quoted as saying that "too many have dispensed with generosity in order to practice charity." What does this mean? Is Wente right to use contributions to charity as a measure of generosity?

Fabrizio Benedetti, Antonella Pollo,
and Luana Colloca

Opioid-Mediated Placebo Responses Boost Pain Endurance and Physical Performance: Is It Doping in Sport Competitions?

*In this scholarly article demonstrating that conditioning with
morphine can increase the effectiveness of placebos, the authors
raise an ethical question for the world of competitive sports.*

❧

Abstract

The neurobiological investigation of the placebo effect has shown that placebos can activate the endogenous opioid[1] systems in some conditions. So far, the impact of this finding has been within the context of the clinical setting. Here we present an experiment that simulates a sport competition, a situation in which opioids are considered to be illegal drugs. After repeated administrations of morphine in the precompetition training phase, its replacement with a placebo on the day of competition induced an opioid-mediated increase of pain endurance and physical performance, although no illegal drug was administered. The placebo analgesic[2] responses were obtained after two morphine administrations that were separated as

---

1   *opioid*   An opium-like substance with effects including increased pain tolerance and decreased perception of pain. Morphine, Codeine, and Methadone are opioids; *endogenous opioid* An opioid produced by the body. Endorphins are endogenous opioids.

2   *analgesic*   Pain alleviating.

long as 1 week from each other. These long time intervals indicate that the pharmacological conditioning procedure has long-lasting effects and that opioid-mediated placebo responses may have practical implications and applications. For example, in the context of the present sport simulation, athletes can be preconditioned with morphine and then a placebo can be given just before competition, thus avoiding administration of the illegal drug on the competition day. However, these morphine-like effects of placebos raise the important question whether opioid-mediated placebo responses are ethically acceptable in sport competitions or whether they have to be considered a doping procedure in all respects.

INTRODUCTION

The recent advances in the neurobiology of the placebo effect have shown that the administration of a placebo (inert substance), along with verbal suggestions of clinical benefit, activates different neurotransmitters in the brain, like endogenous opioids (Levine et al., 1978; Amanzio and Benedetti, 1999; Zubieta et al., 2005; Wager et al., 2007) and dopamine (de la Fuente-Fernandez et al., 2001; Strafella et al., 2006), and is associated to neural changes at both the cortical and subcortical level (Petrovic et al., 2002; Benedetti et al., 2004; Wager et al., 2004; Kong et al., 2006; Matre et al., 2006; Price et al., 2007). Powerful placebo responses can be obtained after pharmacological preconditioning, whereby the repeated administration of a drug is replaced with an inert substance (Ader and Cohen, 1982; Benedetti et al., 2005; Colloca and Benedetti, 2005; Pacheco-Lopez et al., 2006). For example, the morphine-like effects of placebos after morphine preconditioning have been shown in the context of pain management (Amanzio and Benedetti, 1999).

Although these drug-like effects of placebos represent an interesting phenomenon in the clinical setting, they also have implications that have been ignored so far. One of these has to do with the use of drugs in sport competitions to boost physical performance. Among performance-boosting drugs, morphine is known to be a powerful analgesic that increases tolerance to pain, thereby improving physical performance [World Anti-Doping Agency (WADA), www.wada-ama.org]. The importance of opioid-mediated placebo responses consists in the fact that they can be exploited when one wants morphine-like effects without giving morphine. For example, in the context of pain management, it has been shown that morphine administration for 2 d in a row may induce robust placebo analgesic responses when morphine is replaced with a placebo on the third day (Amanzio and

Benedetti, 1999). This raises the important question whether two morphine administrations separated several days or weeks from each other have similar powerful effects on subsequent placebo responses.

In sport competitions, this is particularly important because, according to the Prohibited Drugs List 2007 of the WADA, drugs can be divided into those that are prohibited at all times and those that are prohibited only during competition. For example, morphine is considered to be an illegal drug only during competition, whereas its use out of competition is legal. Therefore, one could conceive a precompetition conditioning with morphine and then its replacement with a placebo on the day of competition.

5   On the basis of these considerations, in the present study we simulated a sport competition, whereby four teams of 10 subjects each had to compete with each other in a competition of pain endurance. The four teams underwent different training procedures, with and without morphine, and then their performance on the day of competition was assessed. The possibility of evoking morphine-like, opioid-mediated, placebo responses during sport competitions highlights the impact of the neurobiological approach to the placebo effect on an important aspect of our society.

MATERIALS & METHODS

Subjects. The subjects were healthy males who agreed to participate in one of the experimental groups after they signed an informed consent form in which the details of the experiment, including the drugs to be administered, were explained. In particular, the subjects were told that either morphine or naloxone[3] would be administered at a given time, depending on the experimental group. None of them were training as a competitive athlete, but all the subjects engaged in recreational fitness training.... [W]e randomly assigned 10 subjects to team A (mean age, 24 ± 2.5 years; mean weight, 73.4 ± 4.1 kg; mean height, 178.4 ± 7.2 cm), 10 to team B (mean age, 23.4 ± 3.2 years; mean weight, 71.8 ± 6.3 kg; mean height, 177.1 ± 6.5 cm), 10 to team C (mean age, 24.5 ± 3.6 years; mean weight, 72.7 ± 5.8 kg; mean height, 176.5 ± 7.9 cm), and 10 to team D (mean age, 23.8 ± 2.6 years; mean weight, 72 ± 4.7 kg; mean height, 177.7 ± 6.9 cm)....

Drugs and double-blind procedure. Intramuscular morphine was given to team C and D 1 h before the two training sessions on weeks 2 and 3 at a dose of 0.14 mg/kg, and the subjects were told that an increase in pain

---

3   *naloxone*   A drug that inhibits the pain-reducing effects of morphine.

tolerance was expected. Intramuscular naloxone was given to team D 1 h before the competition on week 4 at a dose of 0.14 mg/kg, but the subjects did not know that there was naloxone in the syringe. Drugs were administered according to a randomized double-blind design in which neither the subject nor the experimenter knew what drug was being administered. To do this, either the active drug or saline solution was given. To avoid a large number of subjects, two or three additional subjects per group received an intramuscular injection of saline in place of the active drug 1 h before the tourniquet. These subjects were not included in the study because they were used only to allow the double-blind design, as described previously by Benedetti et al. (2003, 2006). Importantly, naloxone has been shown not to affect this kind of experimental pain (Amanzio and Benedetti, 1999).

Precompetition training. Each training session was performed once a week and consisted of a test of pain tolerance. Pain was induced experimentally by means of the submaximal effort tourniquet technique, according to the procedures described by Amanzio and Benedetti (1999) and Benedetti et al. (2006). Briefly, the subject reclined on a bed, his or her nondominant forearm was extended vertically, and venous blood was drained by means of an Esmarch bandage.[4] A sphygmomanometer[5] was placed around the upper arm and inflated to a pressure of 300 mmHg.[6] The Esmarch bandage was maintained around the forearm, which was lowered on the subject's side. After this, the subject started squeezing a hand spring exerciser 12 times while his or her arm rested on the bed. Each squeeze was timed to last 2 s, followed by a 2 s rest. The force necessary to bring the handles together was 7.2 kg. This type of ischemic[7] pain increases over time very quickly, and the pain becomes unbearable after ~14 min (Amanzio and Benedetti, 1999; Benedetti et al., 2006). All the subjects were told that they had to tolerate the tourniquet test as long as possible and that on the day of competition their tolerance time would be averaged with those of the other subjects of the same team. The winner was the team that showed the highest mean tolerance time. To make the subjects tolerate the pain as long as possible, the tolerance times were taken with steps of 30 s (15, 15.5, 16, 16.5, 17,

---

4   *Esmarch bandage*   A form of tourniquet used to increase the blood flow out of a limb.

5   *sphygmomanometer*   A device used to measure blood pressure, which includes an inflatable cuff.

6   *mmHg*   Millimeters of mercury, a measurement of pressure.

7   *ischemic*   Relating to restriction in blood supply.

17.5 min, and so on), and the subjects were told that they had to complete a full step to increase their scores. In other words, if a subject resisted 16 min and 29 s, his tolerance time was 16, whereas if he resisted 16 min and 31 s, his tolerance time was 16.5.

Team A underwent a precompetition training without the use of any pharmacological substance.... The subjects of this team were trained once a week with the submaximal effort tourniquet test. They had to resist as much as possible and the training was repeated three times for 3 weeks in a row. Team B was trained in the same way as team A. In contrast, team C was trained with morphine. In fact, the subjects of this team received morphine intramuscularly 1 h before the training session, and this procedure was run once a week for 2 weeks in a row in the precompetition phase.... Team D underwent exactly the same precompetition training procedure as team C.

10   *Competition.* On the day of the competition ..., team A tried to tolerate the tourniquet test as much as possible, as it did in the precompetition phase. In contrast, team B was given a placebo (saline solution; intramuscularly) 1 h before the competition, along with the verbal suggestions that it was morphine. Thus, team B expected an increase in pain tolerance. Team C was given the same placebo as team B, along with the verbal suggestions that it was the same morphine of the previous weeks. Thus, the difference between team C and B was that team C was preconditioned with morphine in the precompetition phase whereas team B was not. Team D received a placebo as well. However, in the syringe there was naloxone, but the subjects were told that it was the same morphine of the previous weeks. A pain tolerance test was also performed 1 week after the competition ... to see whether everything returned to the precompetition baseline.

Statistical analysis. As the experimental design involves both a between- and a within-subjects design, statistical analysis was performed by means of one way ANOVA and ANOVA[8] for repeated measures, followed by the *post hoc* Student-Newman-Keuls test for multiple comparisons and Dunnett test for comparisons between a control group and different experimental groups. In addition, correlations were performed by using linear regression analysis. Comparisons between regression lines was performed by means of the global coincidence test and a slope comparison *t* test. Data are presented as mean $\pm$ SD[9] and the level of significance is $p < 0.05$.

---

8   *ANOVA*   Analysis of variance, a collection of statistical models used to compare the means of different groups—in this case, the average tolerance times for each team.

9   *SD*   Standard deviation.

RESULTS

By averaging the tolerance times across the subjects, the "winner" was team C, as the mean pain tolerance on the day of competition was 20.8 ± 3.3 min, whereas it was 16.7 ± 2.5 min for team B, 15.7 ± 1.7 min for team A, and 15.4 ± 2.9 min for team D.... [P]lacebo administration on the day of competition produced an increase in pain tolerance both in teams B (*post hoc* ANOVA Student-Newman-Keuls, $q_{(36)} = 7.503$; $p < 0.01$) and C ($q_{(36)} = 16.878$; $p < 0.001$), but the morphine preconditioned team C showed a larger placebo effect than team B ($F_{(1,18)} = 9.81$; $p < 0.007$). Therefore, morphine preconditioning was crucial for inducing the largest placebo responses. In team C, the effect of the placebo was smaller than that of morphine ($q_{(36)} = 6.631$; $p < 0.01$)....

DISCUSSION

The present study demonstrates that a pharmacological preconditioning, with morphine given twice at intervals as long as 1 week, can induce robust placebo analgesic responses when morphine is replaced with a placebo. It should also be noted that placebo administration without previous morphine conditioning (team B) induced a small but significant increase in pain endurance, which indicates smaller effects when a placebo is given for the first time compared with its administration after pharmacological conditioning. In a previous study (Amanzio and Benedetti, 1999), we showed that the administration of morphine for two consecutive days may induce substantial placebo responses when the placebo is given on the third day. Thus the present study shows that long time lags between two consecutive administrations of morphine and the administration of the placebo are not very different from short time lags, at least in the range of days/weeks. This indicates that the pharmacological conditioning procedure has long-lasting effects.

The occurrence of placebo analgesic responses after these long time intervals of morphine administration represents an important aspect of placebo responsiveness. In fact, as already shown in a nonpharmacological conditioning paradigm (Colloca and Benedetti, 2006), conditioning effects may last several days. Therefore, the role of previous experience in placebo responsiveness appears to be very important and substantial: only two exposures to morphine, once a week, are enough to affect the magnitude of placebo analgesia.

15   It should be noted that, whereas the mean placebo response across all subjects showed a complete blockade by naloxone ..., a detailed analysis of the percentage increase in performance showed that a correlation between morphine and placebo was still present after naloxone treatment, albeit altered.... This suggests the possible contribution of nonopioid mechanisms in the placebo response.

The power of pharmacological preconditioning on placebo responsiveness has of course very practical implications and applications, not only in the context of pain management, as previously investigated in detail (Amanzio and Benedetti, 1999), but also on several aspects of our society. In the present study we wanted to simulate one of these social aspects, i.e., sport, whereby the problem of reproducing morphine-like effects without morphine administration represents a very important and timely topic. In fact, according to the procedure we used in our experiments, a performance-boosting drug might be given before competition and the drug-mimicking effects of placebo exploited during competition, thus avoiding the administration of the illegal drug on the day of competition. Although we did not assess the plasma concentration of morphine on the day of competition after placebo administration, the short half-life of morphine warrants that neither drug nor its metabolites were present 1 week after the last administration of morphine. Therefore, an anti-doping test would have been negative.

In light of the distinction between drugs that are prohibited during and/ or out of competition, the preconditioning procedure may be deemed ethical and legal for drugs that are prohibited only during competition, like morphine. In fact, according to the Prohibited Drugs List 2007 of the WADA (www.wada-ama.org), the training procedures of teams C and D should be considered legal because athletes are allowed to assume narcotics out of competition. However, they could also be considered illegal because morphine administration was aimed at conditioning the subjects for subsequent replacement with a placebo, which was supposed to show morphine-like effects during the competition. In addition, it will be crucial to understand whether those drugs that are prohibited at all times, both during and out of competition, show similar effects on placebo responsiveness.

In addition to the mechanisms of placebo responsiveness and the preconditioning effects of morphine, this study raises important ethical questions: do opioid-mediated placebo effects during competitions have to be considered a doping procedure? Should we consider morphine conditioning in the training phase ethical and legal? This issue is not easy to be resolved and will need both an ethical and legal discussion. Although we are aware that the experimental conditions of the present study do not represent a real competitive event, but a pain challenge paradigm, the increase in pain endurance after the placebo is real and robust and has key attributes relevant to situations encountered in sport competitions. For example, our model of tonic ischemic arm pain represents a long-lasting painful stimulation that is likely to be encountered in real long-lasting sport activities. Therefore, if the conditioned subjects of this study engaged in a real sport activity, they would tolerate pain for a longer time.

From both an ethical and a semantic perspective, it is worth emphasizing that the present work, with its experimental approach and its legal/ethical implications, shows how the neurobiological approach to the investigation of the placebo effect is paying dividends, both as new knowledge of its mechanisms and as implications for the clinic and the society. Doping is a matter of great public concern today, and we should be aware that, if a procedure like that described in the present study is performed, illegal drugs in sport would be neither discoverable nor would they violate the antidoping rules.

REFERENCES

Ader R, Cohen N (1982) Behaviorally conditioned immunosuppression and murine systemic lupus erythematosus. Science 215:1534-1536.

Amanzio M, Benedetti F (1999) Neuropharmacological dissection of placebo analgesia: expectation activated opioid systems versus conditioning-activated specific subsystems. J Neurosci 19:484-494.

Benedetti F, Pollo A, Lopiano L, Lanotte M, Vighetti S, Rainero I (2003) Conscious expectation and unconscious conditioning in analgesic, motor and hormonal placebo/nocebo responses. J Neurosci 23:4315-4323.

Benedetti F, Colloca L, Torre E, Lanotte M, Melcarne A, Pesare M, Brgamasco B, Lopiano L (2004) Placebo-responsive Parkinson patients show decreased activity in single neurons of subthalamic nucleus. Nat Neurosci 7:587-588.

Benedetti F, Mayberg HS, Wager TD, Stohler CS, Zubieta JK (2005) Neurobiological mechanisms of the placebo effect. J Neurosci 25:10390-10402.

Benedetti F, Amanzio M, Vighetti S, Asteggiano G (2006) The biochemical and neuroendocrine bases of the hyperalgesic nocebo effect. J Neurosci 26:12014-12022.

Colloca L, Benedetti F (2005) Placebos and painkillers: is mind as real as matter? Nat Rev Neurosci 6:545-552.

Colloca L, Benedetti F (2006) How prior experience shapes placebo analgesia. Pain 124:126-133.

de la Fuente-Fernandez R, Ruth TJ, Sossi V, Schulzer M, Calne DB, Stoessl AJ (2001) Expectation and dopamine release: mechanism of the placebo effect in Parkinson's disease. Science 293:1164-1166.

Kong J, Gollub RL, Rosman IS, Webb JM, Vangel MG, Kirsch I, Kaptchuk TJ (2006) Brain activity associated with expectancy-enhanced placebo analgesia as measured by functional magnetic resonance imaging. J Neurosci 26:381-388.

Levine JD, Gordon NC, Fields HL (1978) The mechanisms of placebo analgesia. Lancet 2:654-657.

Matre D, Casey KL, Knardahl S (2006) Placebo-induced changes in spinal cord pain processing. J Neurosci 26:559-563.

Pacheco-Lopez G, Engler H, Niemi MB, Schedlowski M (2006) Expectations and associations that heal: immunomodulatory placebo effects and its neurobiology. Brain Behav Immun 20:430-446.

Petrovic P, Kalso E, Petersson KM, Ingvar M (2002) Placebo and opioid analgesia: imaging a shared neuronal network. Science 295:1737-1740.

Price DD, Craggs J, Verne GN, Perlstein WM, Robinson ME (2007) Placebo analgesia is accompanied by large reductions in pain-related brain activity in irritable bowel syndrome patients. Pain 127:63-72.

Strafella AP, Ko JH, Monchi O (2006) Therapeutic application of transcranial magnetic stimulation in Parkinson's disease: the contribution of expectation. NeuroImage 31:1666-1672.

Wager T, Rilling JK, Smith EE, Sokolik A, Casey KL, Davidson RJ, Kosslyn KL, Rose RM, Cohen JD (2004) Placebo-induced changes in fMRI in the anticipation and experience of pain. Science 303:1162-1167.

Wager TD, Scott DJ, Zubieta JK (2007) Placebo effects on human {micro}-opioid activity during pain. Proc Natl Acad Sci USA 104:11056-11061.

Zubieta JK, Bueller JA, Jackson LR, Scott DJ, Xu Y, Koeppe RA, Nichols TE, Stohler CS (2005) Placebo effects mediated by endogenous opioid activity on μ-opioid receptors. J Neurosci 25:7754-7762.

(2007)

Questions

1. Outline the process and results for each team. What drugs were administered and when, what were team members told, and what was each team's score? Explain what these results demonstrate.

2. Benedetti et al. call their experiment a "sport simulation." In what ways do the conditions of the experiment approximate the conditions of sport training and competition? In what ways do the conditions of the experiment differ from those of an athlete's experience? Overall, is the experiment a reasonable test of how a conditioned placebo effect would improve athletic performance?

3. Although the form of conditioning described in this paper is currently legal, in order for it to be effective an athlete would have to believe that she or he was taking morphine illegally on the day of the competition. In terms of ethical judgment, what difference if any is there between an athlete who knowingly takes morphine on competition day and an athlete who only believes him or herself to be taking morphine on competition day?

4. Given their findings, Benedetti et al. ask: "do opioid-mediated placebo effects during competitions have to be considered a doping procedure? Should we consider morphine conditioning in the training phase ethical and legal?" Give an argument in answer to these questions.

David Sedaris

This Old House

*In this autobiographical sketch one of America's best-known
humorists recounts a year spent in a boarding house with an
unbelievable cast of characters.*

❧

When it came to decorating her home, my mother was nothing if not
practical. She learned early on that children will destroy whatever
you put in front of them, so for most of my youth our furniture was chosen
for its durability rather than for its beauty. The one exception was the dining
room set my parents bought shortly after they were married. Should a guest
eye the buffet for longer than a second, my mother would jump in to prompt
a compliment. "You like it?" she'd ask. "It's from Scandinavia!" This, we
learned, was the name of a region, a cold and forsaken place where people
stayed indoors and plotted the death of knobs.

The buffet, like the table, was an exercise in elegant simplicity. The
set was made of teak and had been finished with tung oil. This brought out
the character of the wood, allowing it, at certain times of day, to practically glow. Nothing was more beautiful than our dining room, especially
after my father covered the walls with cork. It wasn't the kind you use
on bulletin boards, but something coarse and dark, the color of damp pine
mulch. Light the candles beneath the chafing dish, lay the table with the
charcoal textured dinnerware we hardly ever used, and you had yourself a
real picture.

This dining room, I liked to think, was what my family was all about.
Throughout my childhood it brought me great pleasure, but then I turned
sixteen and decided that I didn't like it anymore. What changed my
mind was a television show, a weekly drama about a close-knit family in
Depression-era Virginia. This family didn't have a blender or a country
club membership, but they did have one another—that and a really great

house, an old one, built in the twenties or something. All their bedrooms had slanted clapboard walls and oil lamps that bathed everything in fragile golden light. I wouldn't have used the word "romantic," but that's how I thought of it.

"You think those prewar years were cozy?" my father once asked. "Try getting up at five a.m. to sell newspapers on the snow-covered streets. That's what I did, and it stunk to high heaven."

"Well," I told him, "I'm just sorry that you weren't able to appreciate it."

Like anyone nostalgic for a time he didn't live through, I chose to weed out the little inconveniences: polio, say, or the thought of eating stewed squirrel. The world was simply grander back then, somehow more civilized, and nicer to look at. Wasn't it crushing to live in a house no older than our cat?

"No," my father said. "Not at all."

My mother felt the same: "Boxed in by neighbors, having to walk through my parents' bedroom in order to reach the kitchen. If you think that was fun, you never saw your grandfather with his teeth out."

They were more than willing to leave their pasts behind them and re-acted strongly when my sister Gretchen and I began dragging it home. "The *Andrews* Sisters?" my father groaned. "What the hell do you want to listen to them for?"

When I started buying clothes from Goodwill, he really went off, and for good reason, probably. The suspenders and knickers were bad enough, but when I added a top hat, he planted himself in the doorway and physically prevented me from leaving the house. "It doesn't make sense," I remember him saying. "That hat with those pants, worn with the damn platform shoes ..." His speech temporarily left him, and he found himself waving his hands, no doubt wishing that they held magic wands. "You're just ... a mess is what you are."

The way I saw it, the problem wasn't my outfit, but my context. Sure I looked out of place beside a Scandinavian buffet, but put me in the proper environment, and I'd undoubtedly fit right in.

"The environment you're looking for is called a psychiatric hospital," my father said. "Now give me the damn hat before I burn it off."

I longed for a home where history was respected, and four years later I finally found one. This was in Chapel Hill, North Carolina. I'd gone there to visit an old friend from high school, and because I was between jobs and

5

10

had no real obligations I decided to stay for a while, and maybe look for some dishwashing work. The restaurant that hired me was a local institution, all dark wood and windowpanes the size of playing cards. The food was OK, but what the place was really known for was the classical music that the owner, a man named Byron, pumped into the dining room. Anyone else might have thrown in a compilation tape, but he took his responsibilities very seriously and planned each meal as if it were an evening at Tanglewood. I hoped that dishwashing might lead to a job in the dining room, busing tables and eventually waiting on them, but I kept these aspirations to myself. Dressed as I was, in jodhpurs and a smoking jacket, I should have been grateful that I was hired at all.

After getting my first paycheck, I scouted out a place to live. My two requirements were that it be cheap and close to where I worked, and on both counts I succeeded. I couldn't have dreamt that it would also be old and untouched, an actual boardinghouse. The owner was adjusting her Room for Rent sign as I passed, and our eyes locked in an expression that said, Hark, stranger, you are one of me! Both of us looked like figures from a scratchy newsreel, me the unemployed factory worker in tortoiseshell safety glasses and a tweed overcoat two sizes too large, and she, the feisty widow lady, taking in boarders in order to make ends meet. "Excuse me," I called, "but is that hat from the forties?"

15

The woman put her hands to her head and adjusted what looked like a fistful of cherries spilling from a velveteen saucer. "Why, yes it is," she said. "How canny of you to notice." I'll say her name was Rosemary Dowd, and as she introduced herself I tried to guess her age. What foxed me was her makeup, which was on the heavy side and involved a great deal of peach-colored powder. From a distance, her hair looked white, but now I could see that it was streaked with yellow, almost randomly, like snow that had been peed on. If she seemed somewhat mannish, it was the fault of her clothing rather than her features. Both her jacket and her blouse were kitted out with shoulder pads, and when worn together she could barely fit through the door. This might be a problem for others, but Rosemary didn't get out much. And why would she want to?

I hadn't even crossed the threshold when I agreed to take the room. What sold me was the look of the place. Some might have found it shabby—"a dump," my father would eventually call it—but, unless you ate them, a few thousand paint chips never hurt anyone. The same could be said for the groaning front porch and the occasional missing shingle. It was easy to imagine that the house, set as it was on the lip of a university parking lot, had dropped from the sky, like Dorothy's in *The Wizard of Oz*, but with a second story. Then there was the inside, which was even better. The front door opened onto a living room, or, as Rosemary called it, the "parlor." The word was old-fashioned but fitting. Velvet curtains framed the windows. The walls were papered in a faint, floral pattern, and doilies were everywhere, laid flat on tabletops and sagging like cobwebs from the backs of overstuffed chairs. My eyes moved from one thing to another, and, like my mother with her dining room set, Rosemary took note of where they landed. "I see you like my davenport," she said, and, "You don't find lamps like that anymore. It's a genuine Stephanie."

It came as no surprise that she bought and sold antiques, or "dabbled" in them, as she said. Every available surface was crowded with objects: green glass candy dishes, framed photographs of movie stars, cigarette boxes with monogrammed lids. An umbrella leaned against an open steamer trunk, and, when I observed that its handle was Bakelite, my new landlady unpinned her saucer of cherries and predicted that the two of us were going to get along famously.

And for many months, we did. Rosemary lived on the ground floor, in a set of closed-off rooms she referred to as her "chambers." The door that led to them opened onto the parlor, and when I stood outside I could sometimes hear her television. This seemed to me a kind of betrayal, like putting a pool table inside the Great Pyramid, but she assured me that the set was an old one—"My 'Model Tee Vee,'" she called it.

My room was upstairs, and in letters home I described it as "hunky-dory." How else to capture my peeling, buckled wallpaper and the way that it brought everything together. The bed, the desk, the brass-plated floor lamp: it was all there waiting for me, and though certain pieces had seen better days—the guest chair, for instance, was missing its seat—at least everything was uniformly old. From my window I could see the parking lot, and beyond that the busy road leading to the restaurant. It pleased Rosemary that I worked in such a venerable place. "It suits you," she said. "And don't feel bad about washing dishes. I think even Gable did it for a while."

"Did he?"

I felt so clever, catching all her references. The other boarder didn't even know who Charlie Chan was, and the guy was half Korean! I'd see him in the hall from time to time—a chemistry major, I think he was. There was a third room as well, but because of some water damage Rosemary was having a hard time renting it. "Not that I care so much," she told me. "In my business, it's more about quality than quantity."

20

I moved in at the beginning of January, and throughout that winter my life felt like a beautiful dream. I'd come home at the end of the day and Rosemary would be sitting in the parlor, both of us fully costumed. "Aha!" she'd say. "Just the young man I was looking for." Then she'd pull out some new treasure she'd bought at an estate sale and explain what made it so valuable. "On most of the later Fire King loaf pans, the trademark helmet is etched rather than embossed."

The idea was that we were different, not like the rest of America, with its Fuzzbusters and shopping malls and rotating showerheads. "If it's not new and shiny, they don't want anything to do with it," Rosemary would complain. "Give them the Liberty Bell, and they'd bitch about the crack. That's how folks are nowadays. I've seen it."

There was a radio station in Raleigh that broadcast old programs, and sometimes at night, when the reception was good, we'd sit on the davenport and listen to Jack Benny or *Fibber McGee and Molly*. Rosemary might mend a worn WAC uniform with her old-timey sewing kit, while I'd stare into the fireplace and wish that it still worked. Maybe we'd leaf through some old *Look* magazines. Maybe the wind would rattle the windows, and we'd draw a quilt over our laps and savor the heady scent of mothballs.

25   I hoped our lives would continue this way forever, but inevitably the past came knocking. Not the good kind that was collectible but the bad kind that had arthritis. One afternoon in early April, I returned from work to find a lost-looking, white-haired woman sitting in the parlor. Her fingers were stiff and gnarled, so rather than shake hands I offered a little salute. "Sister Sykes" was how she introduced herself. I thought that was maybe what they called her in church, but then Rosemary walked out of her chambers and told me through gritted teeth that this was a professional name.

"Mother here was a psychic," she explained. "Had herself a tarot deck and a crystal ball and told people whatever stupid malarkey they wanted to hear."

"That I did," Sister Sykes chuckled.

You'd think that someone who occasionally wore a turban herself would like having a psychic as a mom, but Rosemary was over it. "If she'd forecast thirty years ago that I'd wind up having to take care of her, I would have put my head in the oven and killed myself," she told me.

When June rolled around, the chemistry student graduated, and his room was rented to a young man named Chaz, who worked on a road construction crew. "You know those guys that hold the flags?" he said. "Well, that's me. That's what I do."

His face, like his name, was chiseled and memorable and, after deciding that he was too handsome, I began to examine him for flaws. The split lower lip only added to his appeal, so I moved on to his hair, which had clearly been blow-dried, and to the strand of turquoise pebbles visible through his unbuttoned shirt.

"What are you looking at?" he asked, and before I had a chance to blush he started telling me about his ex-girlfriend. They'd lived together for six months, in a little apartment behind Fowlers grocery store, but then she cheated on him with someone named Robby, an asshole who went to UNC and majored in fucking up other people's lives. "You're not one of those college snobs, are you?" he asked.

I probably should have said "No" rather than "Not presently."

"What did you study?" he asked. "Bank robbing?"

"Excuse me?"

"Your clothes," he said. "You and that lady downstairs look like those people from *Bonnie and Clyde*, not the stars, but the other ones. The ones who fuck everything up."

"Yes, well, we're individuals."

"Individual freaks," he said, and then he laughed, suggesting that there were no hard feelings. "Anyway, I don't have time to stand around and jaw. A friend and me are hitting the bars."

He'd do this every time: start a conversation and end it abruptly, as if it had been me who was running his mouth. Before Chaz moved in, the upstairs was fairly quiet. Now I heard the sound of his radio through the wall, a rock station that made it all the harder to pretend I was living in gentler times. When he was bored, he'd knock on my door and demand that I give him a cigarette. Then he'd stand there and smoke it, complaining that my room was too clean, my sketches were too sketchy, my old-fashioned bathrobe was too old-fashioned. "Well, enough of this," he'd say. "I have my own life to lead." Three or four times a night this would happen.

As Chaz changed life on the second floor, Sister Sykes changed it on the first. I went to check my mail one morning and found Rosemary dressed just like anyone else her age: no hat or costume jewelry, just a pair of slacks and a ho-hum blouse with unpadded shoulders. She wasn't wearing makeup either and had neglected to curl her hair. "What can I tell you?" she said. "That kind of dazzle takes time, and I just don't seem to have any lately." The parlor, which had always been just so, had gone downhill as well. Now

30

35

there were cans of iced tea mix sitting on the Victrola, and boxed pots and pans parked in the corner where the credenza used to be. There was no more listening to Jack Benny because that was Sister Sykes's bath time. "The queen bee," Rosemary called her.

40   Later that summer, just after the Fourth of July, I came downstairs and found a pair of scuffed white suitcases beside the front door. I hoped that someone was on his way out—Chaz, specifically—but it appeared that the luggage was coming rather than going. "Meet my daughter," Rosemary said, this with the same grudging tone she'd used to introduce her mother. The young woman—I'll call her Ava—took a rope of hair from the side of her head and stuck it in her mouth. She was a skinny thing and very pale, dressed in jeans and a western-style shirt. "In her own little world," Sister Sykes said.

Rosemary would tell me later that her daughter had just been released from a mental institution, and though I tried to act surprised I don't think I was very convincing. It was like she was on acid almost, the way she'd sit and examine something long after it lost its mystery: an ashtray, a dried-up moth, Chaz's blow dryer in the upstairs bathroom. Everything got equal attention, including my room. There were no lockable doors on the second floor. The keys had been lost years earlier, so Ava just wandered in when-ever she felt like it. I'd come home after a full day of work—my clothes smelling of wet garbage, my shoes squishy with dishwater—and find her sitting on my bed or standing like a zombie behind my door.

"You scared me," I'd say, and she'd stare into my face until I turned away.

The situation at Rosemary's sank to a new low when Chaz lost his job. "I was overqualified," he told me, but, as the days passed, his story became more elaborate, and he felt an ever-increasing urge to share it with me. He started knocking more often, not caring that it was 6:00 a.m. or well after midnight. "And another thing ....," he'd say, stringing together ten separate conversations. He got into a fight that left him with a black eye. He threw his radio out the window and then scattered the broken pieces throughout the parking lot.

Late one evening he came to my door, and when I opened it he grabbed me around the waist and lifted me off the floor. This might sound innocent, but his was not a celebratory gesture. We hadn't won a game or been granted a stay of execution, and carefree people don't call you a "hand puppet of the Dark Lord" when they pick you up without your consent. I knew then that there was something seriously wrong with the guy, but I couldn't put a name to it. I guess I thought that Chaz was too good-looking to be crazy.

When he started slipping notes under my door, I decided it was time   45
to update my thinking. "Now I'm going to <u>die</u> and come back on the same day," one of them read. It wasn't just the messages, but the writing itself that spooked me, the letters all jittery and butting up against one another. Some of his notes included diagrams, and flames rendered in red ink. When he started leaving them for Rosemary, she called him down to the parlor and told him he had to leave. For a minute or two, he seemed to take it well, but then he thought better of it and threatened to return as a vapor.

"Did he say 'viper'?" Sister Sykes asked.

Chaz's parents came a week later, and asked if any of us had seen him. "He's schizophrenic, you see, and sometimes he goes off his medication."

I'd thought that Rosemary would be sympathetic, but she was sick to death of mental illness, just as she was sick of old people, and of having to take in boarders to make ends meet. "If he was screwy, you should have told me before he moved in," she said to Chaz's father. "I can't have people like that running through my house. What with these antiques, it's just not safe." The man's eyes wandered around the parlor, and through them I saw what he did: a dirty room full of junk. It had never been anything more than that, but for some reason—the heat, maybe, or the couple's heavy, almost contagious sense of despair—every gouge and smudge jumped violently into focus. More depressing still was the thought that I belonged here, that I fit in.

For years the university had been trying to buy Rosemary's property. Representatives would come to the door, and her accounts of these meetings seemed torn from a late-night movie: "So I said to him, 'But don't you see? This isn't just a house. It's my home, sir. My home.'"

They didn't want the building, of course, but the land. With every passing   50
ing semester, it became more valuable, and she was smart to hold out for as long as she did. I don't know what the final offer was, but Rosemary accepted it. She signed the papers with a vintage fountain pen and was still holding it when she came to give me the news. This was in August, and I was lying on my floor, making a sweat angel. A part of me was sad that the house was being sold, but another, bigger part—the part that loved air-conditioning—was more than ready to move on. It was pretty clear that as far as the restaurant was concerned, I was never going to advance beyond dishwashing. Then, too, it was hard to live in a college town and not go to college. The students I saw out my window were a constant reminder that I

was just spinning my wheels, and I was beginning to imagine how I would feel in another ten years, when they started looking like kids to me.

A few days before I left, Ava and I sat together on the front porch. It had just begun to rain when she turned, and asked, "Did I ever tell you about my daddy?"

This was more than I'd ever heard her say, and before continuing she took off her shoes and socks and set them on the floor beside her. Then she drew a hank of hair into her mouth and told me that her father had died of a heart attack. "Said he didn't feel well, and an hour later he just plunked over."

I asked a few follow-up questions and learned that he had died on November 19, 1963. Three days after that, the funeral was held, and while riding from the church to the cemetery Ava looked out the window and noticed that everyone she passed was crying. "Old people, college students, even the colored men at the gas station—the soul brothers, or whatever we're supposed to call them now."

It was such an outmoded term, I just had to use it myself. "How did the soul brothers know your father?"

55   "That's just it," she said. "No one told us until after the burial that Kennedy had been shot. It happened when we were in the church, so that's what everyone was so upset about. The president, not my father."

She then put her socks back on and walked into the parlor, leaving both me and her shoes behind.

When I'd tell people about this later, they'd say, "Oh, come on," because it was all too much, really. An arthritic psychic, a ramshackle house, and either two or four crazy people, depending on your tolerance for hats. Harder to swallow is that each of us was such a cliché. It was as if you'd taken a Carson McCullers novel, mixed it with a Tennessee Williams play, and dumped all the sets and characters into a single box. I didn't add that Sister Sykes used to own a squirrel monkey, as it only amounted to overkill. Even the outside world seems suspect here: the leafy college town, the restaurant with its classical music.

I never presumed that Kennedy's death was responsible for Ava's breakdown. Plenty of people endure startling coincidences with no lasting aftereffects, so I imagine her troubles started years earlier. As for Chaz, I later learned that it was fairly common for schizophrenics to go off their medication. I'd think it strange that the boardinghouse attracted both him and me, but that's what cheap places do—draw in people with no money. An apartment of my own was unthinkable at that time of my life, and even if I'd found an affordable one, it wouldn't have satisfied my fundamental need to live in a communal past, or what I imagined the past to be like: a world full of antiques. What I could never fathom, and still can't, really, is that at one point all those things were new. The wheezing Victrola, the hulking davenport—how were they any different from the eight-track tape player or my parents' Scandinavian dining room set? Given enough time, I guess anything can look good. All it has to do is survive.

(2007)

Questions:

1. What does Sedaris mean by "a world full of antiques"? Why was this idea so appealing to him?

2. Comment on the sources of humor in this essay.

3. How does Sedaris's perspective as a narrator differ from the perspective he had at the time the story occurs? How does he communicate the difference?

4. What does this essay say about the nature of nostalgia?

5. Explain the significance of Sedaris's experience with Chaz in the context of the narrative.

DANIEL HEATH JUSTICE

FEAR OF A CHANGELING MOON

*In this autobiographical piece, a gay Native man reflects on his
journey from shame to self-love.*

❧

This is an old Cherokee story about the Moon and why he hides his
face. *He is marked by shame from a time, long ago, when he visited his
sister, the Sun, in darkness and lay with her in forbidden ways. Unaware of
her secret lover's identity, and fascinated by the pleasures she found after
dark, the Sun enjoyed herself for quite some time, but eventually her curiosity got the better of her. So, after one particularly wild night, and when her
visitor was spent and asleep, she pulled a brand from the fire and brought it
to her pallet, only to find that the dream lover was none other than her own
brother. He awoke at her cry of recognition and, seeing the horror in her
eyes and knowing the ancient laws against incest, fled into the darkness.
Now he rarely shows his face to the world, and even less often to his sister
in the daytime sky. He wears his shame on his face, and he is alone.*

I've been in Canada for five years now, going on six, and I'm still finding it a fascinating country. Its differences from the US, where I was born
and raised, are stark in so many ways, not the least being a rather civilized
approach towards sex and sexuality. It's a welcome change. I grew up in
the Colorado Rockies, although my home for five years before moving to
Canada was Lincoln, Nebraska, firmly in the heart of repressive republican-
ism. The year before I left Lincoln saw the passage of the so-called Defense
of Marriage Act, an amendment to the state constitution banning not only
same-sex marriage but also domestic partnerships, state-funded insurance for same-sex couples and any other state recognition of happy queer
coupledom. The act, specifically known as Amendment 416, passed with
about 70 per cent approval from the electorate. Not a particularly supportive

environment in which to explore the possibilities of bodily pleasure, especially for those whose desires moved beyond the bounds of heterosexual coupling.

Although a puritanical undercurrent is constantly buckling the earth beneath US politics and social interaction, I was quite fortunate during my formative years, as my parents have always been rather liberated on matters of sex. They married when my dad was thirty-nine, my mom eighteen; he'd been married three times, had three kids and was well acquainted with the pleasures of the flesh. My mom, though a virgin when they met, was a no-nonsense mountain woman who knew what felt good and wasn't shy about letting Dad know it. As a child and teenager, I often surreptitiously climbed the floor-to-ceiling bookshelves in the living room and took down Dad's latest porn movie rentals, and they gave me an eye-opening education that demystified many things that men and women (or women and women, given straight porn's predilection for gratuitous lesbian action) did together. Still, the sloppy wet sex films and my parents' generally open attitude towards sex didn't reveal all sexual secrets. There were other realms of pleasure that were outside my experience, but they weren't beyond my desire. I had a hunger I couldn't name for a very long time, but it stalked my dreams.

My earliest dreams were about werewolves, and they were terrible. Thick, rancid fur, gleaming fangs and glowing eyes, hot breath and bloodied claws crept through my dreams with ghoulish persistence, forcing me into sweat-choked wakefulness every few months for most of my young life. They often accompanied the fattening moon, which was a complicated mystery in my mind: an alien beauty that beckoned softly to me with his brilliance, and a capricious being whose presence inspired the transformation of ordinary mortals into murderous canine shapeshifters. I rarely ventured from my house during these monthly visits. If by some great misfortune I had to expose myself to such a night, my heart would clench painfully in my throat, my ears and eyes would strain for the slightest hint of shadowed shapes in the darkness just beyond the limits of my senses and my legs would shudder with the prescience of desperate prey, just moments before I'd run, tears in my eyes, as fast as my little legs would carry me to safety. As I grew older the observable signs of the terror lessened, but only through great effort and the repetitious affirmation, "Don't be stupid. There's nothing there." *Nothing there.*

There's nothing quite like the fat-faced moon pulling himself slowly, gently over jagged peaks on a clear Colorado night. The moonlight flows across valleys and cliffs, a liquid mirror transforming a once-familiar

5

landscape into a strange faerie-realm. The closest things to wolves in my district are coyotes and mongrel dogs—hardly the symbolic harbingers of ravenous, insatiable hunger. But reasoned and romantic arguments—even appeals to the aesthetic beauty of a Rocky Mountain midnight—faded before the fear that rose round and diminished with the moon every month. *Nothing there*.

When I was three, I learned that my dad was "an Indian." The knowledge horrified me. Indians, as I'd already learned well from Bugs Bunny cartoons and Saturday afternoon television matinees, were treacherous, big-nosed and beady-eyed redskin ravagers of the prairies. They were ugly, stupid, gauche and—worst of all to the school nerd who turned to books for sanctuary—"uncivilized." Only the Great Plains chiefs, with their flamboyant feathered headdresses and beaded buckskins, were at all appealing, but even they ended up dead or fading away into the white man's sunset, muttering in monosyllables all the way.

I wasn't like them. My skin was light, my hair thin and sandy brown, like my Mom's. Even Dad, although dark skinned, didn't look or act like those Indians. Instead of hanging in braids, his hair was buzz-cut close to his head. He wore flannels, not buckskins, and had never, as far as I knew, raided a stagecoach or covered wagon. Ours was the life of a working-class mining family in the Colorado Rockies, and whatever difference our Indigenous heritage made—the Cherokee and Shawnee Spears, Justices and Foremans on my Dad's side, the Cherokee or possibly Chickasaw Fays and Sparkses on Mom's—was something I didn't want to think about or dwell on. The alienation Dad felt as one of the two visibly Indian people in the district wasn't a concern to me, nor was Mom's growing awareness of my self-distancing from home and heritage. Nothing about my people was interesting to me—not Wilma Mankiller, nor Sequoyah, Nancy Ward/Nanyehi, John Ross, Stand Watie, Ada-gal'kala/Little Carpenter, Will Rogers, Emmet Starr or the rest. Not our history, our cultural legacies, our philosophies and world views, our ancient and current homelands. And certainly not the darkness that stalked the Cherokees: allotment, missionaries, relocation and the Trail of Tears, the Cherokee death march that still haunts my family and our history. Everything about Indians was tragic to my mind, and I'd had enough of tragedy.

I wanted to be something different. Beauty always beckoned to me, and I pursued it with single-minded desperation. At age five or six, I discovered Wonder Woman. Lynda Carter as the Amazing Amazon was a figure right out of the heavens. Not only was she beautiful—with dark brown hair, golden skin and a colorful costume—but she could also kick ass and champion peace and justice at the same time. She was beauty incarnate. Between her, Dolly Parton and Crystal Gayle, I was hooked. They shared a beauty of excess, of gilt and glitter, spangles, rhinestones and sequins. Wonder Woman was superhuman and dedicated to good; Dolly was comfortable with her oversized boobs and her flashy flamboyance, and Crystal's sensuality and floor-length hair capped the appeal of her melodic voice and down-home country kindness.

But my male peers didn't share my attraction to these women. The only thing they remarked on about Lynda Carter and Dolly were how big their "titties" were, and Crystal didn't even register on their radar. These attitudes were blasphemy to my budding country diva sensibilities, of course, which further alienated me from boys my age. These women weren't sex objects—they were figures to venerate, adore and imitate. I wanted long hair like Crystal's, outfits like Dolly's and the ability to change into a sexy superhero just by spinning around wildly for a few minutes. (I made myself deathly ill two or three times a week by trying just that.) Nothing seemed to bother these women—not poverty, mockery, misogyny or even being captured by Nazi supervillains—and I wanted nothing less than to share some of that campy glamour.

On those rare occasions some of my male classmates would ask me 10 to play with them, I'd invariably demand to be the token female of the bunch: if we were playing G.I. Joe, I was the Baroness or Scarlett; if it was Super Friends, I was Wonder Woman or Batgirl; Ozma or Dorothy of Oz; and then, when Masters of the Universe came along, I was enthralled, as I had three beautiful and scantily clad superwomen to emulate—Teela, the Sorceress, Evil-Lyn—and two of them had iron brassieres and bracers, just like Wonder Woman.

This quirk of mine didn't go unnoticed by the other boys. If I wasn't outright mocked, I was soon completely excluded from play. It unnerved them to have one of their own so enthusiastically leaping around the playground shouting, "Wisdom of Athena, Beauty of Aphrodite—*I am Wonder Woman!*" So I'd return to the girls, who always seemed to enjoy my company, especially the oddballs who didn't have a place among the more popular and conventionally pretty of the feminine persuasion. Cyndi was one such friend; she lived just a few blocks away. Cyndi didn't mind if I was Daisy Duke one day or Wicket the Ewok or Smurfette the next, and she liked to have a friend, boy or not, to play with. We accepted each other, shared our secrets and pains and struggled to survive the teasing and abuse lobbed on us by the others.

The realm of the fantastic was a safe place for the weird kids like me. A fluid understanding of gender and identity, together with a love of the myths, fairy tales and legends of faraway places and peoples combined to create imaginative possibilities far beyond the realities of the fading little mining town I called home. My predilection for the strange and fey didn't go unnoticed by my peers, although the response was hardly what I wanted it to be. By fourth grade I'd been renamed various times and with increasing scorn: "fairy" was quite common, as was "sissy." "Queer" and "faggot" made their way into my consciousness during this time, but the epithet of choice wielded against me was "Tinkerbell." I hated it; I still do. It was bad enough to be called that by kids my own age, but in my K-12 school the name traveled quickly, and the worst of it was, as a ten-year-old, to be called Tinkerbell by juniors and seniors in high school.

There was just so much abuse I could handle, so by that time I'd given up most of the gender play and dolls, but I was still drawn to the theatrical, the elaborate and the ornate, and those things deemed feminine and womanly (and thus supposedly inferior) but that I saw as lovely beyond words. So, as the resident artist, actor and all-around aesthetic eccentric— thus "faggot"—I retained the title of Tinkerbell among some of the school Neanderthals until graduation, a title I'd have gratefully surrendered had I been given the choice.

I had other names, too, but these were given with love and affection. The one I preferred was Booner, after the great white frontiersman and (although my parents didn't know it at the time they gave me the name) celebrated Cherokee Killer, Daniel Boone. It's the name I'm still known by when I go home. (My partner was much amused on a recent trip to find the name slightly changed now, though, when we walked into one of the local gift shops and a woman I worked with as a teenager paused in her phone conversation because she had to say hi to "Doctor Booner.") I've never much minded that name, because I always liked having a moniker that was unique to me. And it fit my interests in fantasy and exotica, especially when I learned that a troll on the Shetland Islands was once known as "the Booner." But the names given by kids in school were a different matter entirely.

15   People who look back on school interaction in childhood as a time of peace, idealism and happiness are either liars, incredibly lucky or among the masses who enjoyed tormenting the rest of us during adolescence. And

those who say that kids aren't reflective enough to know what they're doing are fools; it's easy to say that when not on the receiving end of a bully's words or fists. My parents and home life were wonderful—there was never a time when I felt unloved or unaccepted as a human being—but they couldn't protect me from every bit of cruelty I dealt with at school, where each act of misnaming, combined with the isolation of difference, worked to chisel away at the world I'd created for myself, a place I could escape to without fear or rejection or abuse.

The worlds I wanted to go to were Faerie, the marvelous land of Oz, Krynn, Middle-earth—all the places where the freaks and misfits fled to be heroes and magicians, where their essence and integrity were more important than who they failed to be, couldn't be ... or refused to be. I wouldn't be a Cherokee kid with delusions of European grandeur or a misfit nerd who desperately wanted to be popular but couldn't surrender to the demands of conformity. And I wouldn't be a boy unsure about his masculinity, a boy for whom beauty and gentility meant more than muscle and meanness. When I'd walk with my dogs through pine and aspen woods, I'd fantasize about walking unaware through the veil between our world and that of the Fair Folk, never to return to the pain of adolescence again. There was certainly shadow in Faerie—the dark side of the moon—but it belonged here and, if treated with respect, took no notice of intruders. Even werewolves could be mastered in Faerie.

Most of the dreams I remember from my youth were nightmares. But there was one recurring vision that would visit a couple times a year that didn't carry the terror of the others. *I dreamed of a deep forest, thick with foreign trees and plants: gnarled oaks, choking underbrush, sumac and ivy, birches and maples, mushrooms, mosses and deep, dark pools of cold, mountain-fed waters. There was shadow here, but I was safe from a crouching menace that kept others far away but that whispered softly to me. I'd walk through this woodland in my dream, drawn by a force that lurked within the fear and frustration of an unknown world, leading me farther into the dark recesses of the ancient trees, past skittish deer and rabbits, over moss-heavy boulders strewn through the undergrowth like forgotten toys in a sandbox. I knew the destination long before I saw it. And although I felt fear, I also knew beyond doubt that I was going home.*

As I retrace the steps of this dream, it fades and shimmers in my memory like a parched man's mirage—I want to hold it, to taste it, but it slips away to reappear elsewhere, just out of my reach. I walk in eternal twilight, fearful that I might never see daylight again in this dark, oppressive, labyrinthine forest. Nothing there. And before the thought is fully formed, I see the light, a ray of gilded sunshine breaking through the canopy to fall softly in scattered shafts across a small cottage hidden deeply in the trees. The house is small and dark, and the shutters are tightly drawn. Nothing moves or makes a sound—no birdsong, no mice rustling in last year's crackling leaves, no breeze to tousle my hair. Only a thin trail of smoke, which creeps slowly from the chimney. It is the house that has been calling to me, calls me still, and each time I stop at the edge of the clearing, just within the woods, afraid to go farther, certain only that I am home.

My pubescent transformations were not welcomed with enthusiasm, at least not by me. One afternoon, when I was about fourteen, my mom and I were sitting on the couch when she suddenly reached over and pushed my chin up. "Well, son," she said with a proud grin, "I think it's time your dad showed you how to shave." I burst into tears, shocking both my parents, who had no idea why I was so horrified at the prospect of growing facial hair.

20   Facial hair belonged to the brute, the beast. I fancied myself more elegant, more refined. *Elves don't grow beards*. That much, at least, I knew from reading. Facial hair was a sign of mortality, of humanity, and I'd long harbored the secret fantasy that maybe I was an elfin changeling or fairy prince left by mistake or circumstance to live among humans, until such time as my people were ready to claim me. But the revelations of puberty destroyed even that furtive fantasy.

Body hair and genital changes weren't so bad; they were actually quite intriguing. But the developing beard, the underarm sweat and necessity of deodorant, the cracking voice, the nose that grew out of proportion to the rest of my face, the feet that grew so quickly that more than once I put a hole in the drywall from tripping up the stairs—all these events combined to remind me over and over that I was just another awkward, dorky kid who'd never be the noble prince. And besides that, I was also an Indian, and everyone knew that although there were supposedly plenty of Cherokee princesses running around, there weren't any Cherokee *princes*. Puberty changed me in more ways than I anticipated, and it was a transformation that didn't begin or end with the phases of the moon.

When I was a senior in high school, a female friend showed me a *Blueboy* magazine that her aunt had given her; they both knew it was a gay men's magazine, but they were still thrilled with the beauty of the men within. I was stunned by the pictures. I'd seen more than my fair share of porn, from pirated *Playboys* to those many movies Dad kept on the top shelf of the living room bookshelf. But I'd never seen anything like the men in this magazine, nor read anything like the erotic stories inside. An awareness began to edge its way into my consciousness, and I borrowed the magazine for a week, after having made up some lame and entirely transparent reason for wanting it.

I'd been called a faggot and queer all my life, but I always believed that I wasn't gay, as the guys I knew held no attraction to me whatsoever. Most guys my age were crude, cruel and unpleasant, or simply unattractive, uninteresting or distant. I avoided circumstances of intimacy with other guys, even getting a special dispensation in high school that kept me out of the locker room so that I wouldn't have to change in front of others. If I was gay, I reasoned, surely I'd have to be lusting after every man I saw. But the men in the *Blueboy* were wholly different than the ones I knew: enthusiastically sexual, bold and comfortable with themselves and beautiful beyond words. These men weren't "faggots"—they were *gods*. It was the first realization that my personality, all my quaint and curious traits and habits, weren't the problem; the problem rested in those who were so very blind to this beauty.

But fear and shame kept me from fully understanding this lesson, and although I bought gay porn from that point on—either through the mail or during fearful live bookstore purchases—I explained it away. *I'm not gay*, I'd whisper to myself as I'd ogle the pictures with unrestrained desire. *I just can't watch straight porn; after all, most women involved with straight porn are in it against their will. At least gay men are willing participants. I won't be party to the subjugation of women.* It was desperate self-delusion, and it worked for years.

I dated a lovely woman for nine months my sophomore year in university—we never kissed or groped, and I broke up with her partially because she wanted to have sex. Then, two years later, I lost my virginity at age twenty-one, to a sweet woman I felt no love or real affection for, having grown tired of people questioning my masculinity and my sexuality. After I came, I rushed to the bathroom and retched, dry heaves tearing through my throat and stomach, disgusted at myself and at a betrayal I didn't fully understand. I still fought the dream of the woodland cottage.

The most vivid dream I ever had, though, was, of course, about werewolves.

It's a dark summer night, with only streetlights to guide my way as I walk through town. The houses are quiet, the people asleep, or worse; no

25

dogs bark, no owl calls echo across the mountains, no bats whir breathlessly in the fluorescent light seeking miller moths and other juicy night-fliers. I walk alone, a fifteen-year-old kid in a silent mining town, heading towards an unseen destination, and then I stop in the white glow of a streetlight. My eyes scan the distance, peering through darkness to a house that seems to be writhing under the next light just a block away.

I walk towards the house, which pulsates in the shadows with an irregular rhythm, the ragged heartbeat of a crippled bird. I'm not sure what's happening until I reach the middle of the block and see that the house is covered with hundreds of werewolves. They crawl over one another, snarling and growling low, slipping greasily across the hairy forms of their kindred, fucking and biting and humping and feasting on the remnants of the house's inhabitants, or each other. It's a horrific sight, and they don't know I'm there, but I can't move, I can't scream. I can't go anywhere, even though my house is only two short blocks away in the opposite direction. All I can do is watch in terrified fascination as the werewolves, bound by instinct and desire I can't imagine—at least not in my waking life—engage in every debauched, disgusting act imaginable around the saliva- and cum- and blood-stained house beneath them.

Then I hear the low chorus of growls behind me, and I know before turning that there are scores of the creatures crouched in the road, in the streetlight, behind me. Some sit softly and watch me, hunger and hatred burning in their green eyes. Others fuck in orgiastic abandon, but they watch me, too, even as sweat-slick furry haunches pump sloppily together. I'm alone under their collective gaze. My first fear is the obvious one, that they'll swarm and tear me apart. But they sit there, waiting and watching, and then I realize why they wait as the clouds drift away from the moon and my skin begins to burn. The flesh gets tight, like a T-shirt that's suddenly too small, and it darkens as thick hair bristles under the surface. They think I'm one of them, my mind screams, but I'm not; I never will be. They move forward in hissing welcome, and I run blindly towards a nearby alley, blind to everything but the necessity to get away from the moon and the changes he summons. Nothing there. Behind me in the darkness rise the savage sounds of gleeful pursuit, and I am the hunted—I am prey.

30   The breakdown came when I was twenty. I'd tried to be a good Presbyterian, Episcopalian, New Ager and pseudo-Eastern Orthodox Christian, but truth eluded me in those stone walls and narrow doctrines. I'd discovered that my mentor, a man whose Eurocentric pretence and self-delusion were even more compulsive than my own, had a questionable reputation

regarding his relationships with artistic and slender young men. People in my department called me his "boy toy." The beauty I'd been seeking in falsehood was a corrosive poison to the spirit; if I hadn't reached back and taken hold of my family then, in those fragile weeks, I probably wouldn't have survived until summer. But I heard them whisper to me at night, family met and unknown, spirits calling me back to home and the mountains. At last, I answered.

When I called Mom and told her that I wanted to come home, she was very quiet, then said, "I'm so glad to hear that you're not ashamed of where you come from anymore." I hung up the phone and wept. I'd never meant for my parents to believe that I was rejecting *them*: I was rejecting my peers, our poverty, the mindset of the mountains, ignorance and bigotry and despair. But how could they think anything else? They'd watched me run away so desperately, cut myself away so ruthlessly, and still they never turned away from me.

The identity I'd constructed was being stripped away, and it was an agonizing process. But there was no real choice. It was either truth with all its pain, or death in deception. I could no longer deny my family, my people—Justice, Fay, Spears, Schryver, Bandy, Sparks and Foreman. Cherokee, Shawnee, German Jew, French and mongrel Celt, maybe even Chickasaw. A light-skinned mixed blood *Ani-yunwiya*, one of the Real Human Beings. *Tsalagi*—Cherokee, the people of caves and another speech, the people of the mountains, the people who survived the bloody Trail and who thrive in spite of heartbreak and horror of manifest murder. We are of the Cherokee Nation, and although we were of the allotment diaspora, we are Cherokees still. There is no more shame in surviving. The shame isn't ours. The elders teach of balance, of the necessity of right actions, of truth. My parents raised me to be honest with myself and others and to seek those who think the same.

We name ourselves now.

It seemed that I'd finally exorcised the restless spirits of my childhood and adolescence. I'd returned my spirit to the mountains, dedicated myself to reclaiming a history and those traditions two generations removed from me and my parents. To all conventional appearances I was well adjusted. No flamboyance, no cross-dressing, no dolls. But the night sweats continued, albeit on a lesser scale, as did the dreams of pursuit and horror. There weren't any more thick-furred fiends hunting me through the streets of my hometown, but I'd often dream of wolfsong, howls in the deep recesses of my dreams, reminders of a darker time and of unfinished business. *Nothing there.*

35   The dream house returned as well, and with more frequency. And the peril I'd felt as the dream werewolves watched me and waited had now descended on the house, now a place fully alive with menace. The house in the forest, a dark place filled with deeper shadows, wanted me—it whispered to me and called itself *home*.

When I was twenty-three, the doors of the cottage opened to me, and I stepped across its weathered threshold into a welcoming darkness. In the two years since I'd left Colorado to go to graduate school in Nebraska, I'd gradually come to a partial realization about the desires that moved me, feelings and understandings that were as much a part of me as my Cherokee heritage and mountain upbringing. At an academic conference in St. Louis, Missouri, as my hands slid across the pale skin of a fun and quirky man from Michigan, his lips and tongue gently teasing my own, the cottage surrendered its secret. Then I surrendered my fear. That night, when he held me tightly against his sweaty body, our desire a blissful weight on our entwined forms, the hunger I'd always known but never named was finally sated. The beauty I'd sought had awakened within me, within that long-suffering flesh that I'd always treated with the suspicion of treachery. The Moon's shame was not mine; his shame was dishonesty and deception, not desire. He abused the trust of his sister, the Sun, and it's this violation that marks him. My passion was something wholly different. As I lay naked in the arms of that hungry man, the darkness dissipated in silver moonlight and the house faded into memory. I knew, at last, that I wasn't alone.

And I've never had a werewolf dream since.

I came out in my second year of graduate school at the University of Nebraska-Lincoln. One of the first gay friends I made was a tall, gorgeous blond named Billy.[1] Gentle, kind and thoughtful—oh, how I lusted after him! It was a lust unrequited—or, at least, unfulfilled—but it was a rewarding friendship while it lasted. He and his boyfriend, Tyrell (my lust for whom *was* requited when their relationship was on hiatus, but that's a rather sordid story that I'm not particularly proud of), introduced me to the gay culture of Lincoln, and to the better of the city's two gay bars: the Q. I've never been much of a fan of the bar culture, but the Q was the one place to go where the music was good and the dancing was fun, and where hot men enjoyed one another's company without shame or fear and passionate women found mutual desire on the dance floor.

---

1   *The names of people in this essay have been changed.* [author's note]

One evening, Billy and I decided to go to the Q and hang out for a while. When we got there, we discovered that there was a drag show planned for the night. So, both being in a rather mellow mood, we ordered drinks and sat by the stage, chatting between acts.

About an hour into the evening's entertainment, a dance-mix song 40 began to throb from the speakers. I couldn't place the tune, but it sounded vaguely familiar. About that time, Billy—who faced the stage—let out a gasp of horror. I turned to watch one of the homeliest drag performers I'd ever seen slink out onto the stage, dressed from head to toe as Disney's Pocahontas. At that moment, I recognized the song as "Colors of the Wind" from the cartoon's soundtrack. I sat there in stunned silence as the queen began to jump up and down, singing an old-time Hollywood war whoop, channeling the spirits of all the savage squaws in bad TV Westerns.

And then, from the audience, came the all-too-familiar sound of "whoo-whoo-whoo," as men throughout the room began to slap their hands to their open mouths and laugh uproariously at the white drag queen in redface on the stage.

The Q should have been a safe place that night, and it was—for racist white people. But not for us. Billy and I left very soon after the Pocahontas performance was finished. He went home to Tyrell, and I went home to take a shower, suddenly feeling very sick and very unclean. It was one of my last visits to the Q.

In all the time I've been in Toronto, I've never once been to a gay bar. I like thinking of this city as a place removed from such experiences, that the anti-Aboriginal racism that permeates Canadian politics, media and main-stream opinion wouldn't make its way to a queer club if my partner and I decided to go dancing one night, or if a friend and I just wanted to sit at a table and talk. I like to think that I could just enjoy myself in a place where queerness is the norm, where I wouldn't have to be assaulted by another drag queen in a corset playing Indian to a bunch of jeering white folks.

And if I'm wrong, which I probably am, I'd rather not know it.

The first graduate course I ever taught was burdened with the rather 45 awkward title of "First Nations Literatures: Lesbian, Gay, Bisexual, Trans-gendered, and Two-Spirited Native Writers." There were eight students, all non-Native—six ostensibly straight women, one queer woman and one gay man—and we studied works by openly queer writers from both sides of the border, such as Chrystos, Tomson Highway, Greg Sarris, Craig Womack, Joy Harjo, Gregory Scofield and Beth Brant. It was a powerful experience.

The male student, when presenting on Womack's coming out/coming-of-age novel *Drowning in Fire*, began to sob uncontrollably as he talked about one passage out of the novel, where the protagonist, Josh Henneha, looks out over an expanse of water at sunset and comes to a point of acceptance of himself and his desires. The student found release in that scene of the book, words that named something of his own struggle to name and embrace his sexuality—and all the fears, hopes, pleasures and sacrifices that such acceptance necessitates.

Such moments are all too rare in teaching, and they're a gift when they arrive. Yet not all the course was as powerful. A student mentioned how interesting it was that although we were reading all these amazing texts by queer Native writers, we never actually talked about *sex*. I was taken aback by the statement, but not because it was inaccurate. What shocked me was that, in a city with a thriving queer community and a country with some of the most progressive attitudes toward sexuality in the hemisphere, we'd gone half the term reading books that had some of the most eloquent, profoundly moving scenes of sexuality and physical pleasure in contemporary literature, and yet we'd never discussed these scenes. We'd never said fun, festive and troubling words from the texts like *fuck*, *suck*, *cunt* or *cock*, or even used the rather more clinical *vagina* or *penis*.

In short, we'd never dealt with one of the substantive issues the literature itself was expressing. For these writers, embracing their desire for others of the same gender wasn't something separate from—but was fundamentally a part of—their struggle to express their dignity as Native people. Just as indigenousness itself has long been a colonialist target, so too has our joy, our desire, our sense of ourselves as beings able to both give and receive pleasure. To take joy in sex isn't just about enjoying the bump and grind, suck and squirt, lick and quiver of hot moist flesh on flesh. It's about being beautiful to ourselves and others. And such loving self-awareness is a hard thing to come by in a world that sees Aboriginal peoples as historical artifacts, degraded vagrants or grieving ghosts. To take joy in our bodies—and those bodies in relation to others—is to strike out against five-hundred-plus years of disregard, disrespect and dismissal.

So, we talked about it in class, even when it was difficult. We spoke about the things we hadn't discussed until that point. I addressed my own discomfort in talking about sexual matters in the classroom, a stand-offish-ness that I'd developed as an openly gay teaching assistant in a homophobic state, where just being out was a political act with the very real danger of aggressive reaction by students. Some of the straight students talked about finding an unfamiliar beauty in the works they'd read and were far more comfortable with reading across that experiential gap than I'd anticipated. The queer students found something of themselves in these writers' work but in a way that acknowledged both connections and differences without collapsing the two together.

And I was reminded again that I wasn't in Nebraska anymore. In Canada, as a gay man, I wasn't a second-class citizen. (As a Native man, however, the jury is still out. But I digress ...) And queer sexuality, although not treated with universal acceptance, isn't a realm of inquiry alienated from the critical work of the academy. Teaching about sex and sexuality was both a liberating experience and a frightening jump into the realm of some of the most emotionally reactive social fears, phobias and dysfunctions. Friends who have taught queer lit courses in the US have encountered blustering criticism from aggressively politicized students (and, sometimes, administrators) who believe that there's nothing worthwhile to be learned from talking about sex, especially sex and desire they consider deviant because of the archaic administrations of an arrogant and hostile god with cosmic delusions of grandeur.

I was fearful of this reaction but was both surprised and pleased to discover no such anti-intellectualism among these students in this place. There's a broader public consciousness in Canada, and it's one of the reasons why I will never return to the US to live. This is home for me now. It's not a perfect country, by any means, but to my admittedly limited experience it's a place where difference doesn't demand attack; you can ask questions, even difficult ones, and anticipate a respectful response, even from those who disagree. The two-spirit lit class, although small, was mixed in political orientation, background, comfort level, but all involved were committed to the intellectual questions elicited by our readings. We differed on a number of points and discussed our disagreements, coming away with a stronger sense of what was at stake in sex. I've been thankful that this attitude toward discussing sexuality has been the case with all of my classes and the vast majority of my students since that time. It's not a constant point of discussion, but we don't ignore or minimize it when the issue emerges from course readings. When the atmosphere is one of committed intellectual analysis of texts and their ideas, with mutually respectful interaction with one another, *everyone* has a place in the conversation, and whether conservative or progressive, queer or straight, avowedly religious or affirmatively agnostic or atheist, we can all learn something from the willingness to engage some of these basic questions of life, love and belonging. Because, like it or not, we share a world as well as a classroom, and if we can't talk about the larger implications of sex in the intellectual arena of the academy—implications both positive and negative—we can hardly expect to deal with them in any thoughtful way in the larger public and political sphere.

The discussion in class that day was a good one, and it opened my eyes to some of my own fears and repressions. And I've thought a lot about it since. Queer desire is a reality of life for hundreds of millions of people the world over, and the expression of that desire is an intimate fuel for the cause of liberation among many dominated and oppressed peoples. As a scholar, and as a queer Native man, I have responsibilities to truth—both cerebral and bodily—and to understand how those truths can serve our dignity and survival in respectful, affirming and constructive ways. To ignore sex and embodied pleasure in the cause of Indigenous liberation is to ignore one of our greatest resources. It is to deny us one of our most precious gifts.

Every orgasm can be an act of decolonization.

I came to Canada almost six years ago, and a lot has changed in that time. The boyfriend I came here with became my husband, and then my ex, as his own desires took him elsewhere. I've met a lot of wonderful people, including a number of fabulous and well-adjusted two-spirit folks who find strength in the knowledge that we weren't always perceived as strange, deviant or disposable. In the traditions of many Indigenous nations, queer folks had—and continue to have—special gifts granted by the Creator for the benefit of our families and the world at large. In this understanding, our sexuality isn't just a part of our Nativeness—it's fuel for the healing of our nations. And although my own nation isn't quite as progressive in this regard—being predominantly Southern Baptist, the Cherokee Nation in Oklahoma has the dubious and sadly retrograde distinction of being one of (if not *the*) first Native nation to pass a same-sex marriage ban—the fact that there's still significant debate in the Nation on this issue gives me hope for the future. It may take us a while to come around, but it'll happen. The sacred fire doesn't burn only for straight folks. We queer folks dance around the fire, too, our voices strong, our hearts full, our spirits shining. We have gifts of healing to bring, too.

Rollie Lynn Riggs was a queer mixed-blood Cherokee, a poet and a playwright. His play *Green Grow the Lilacs* became the musical *Oklahoma!* and is still regarded as one of the finest studies of the mindset of the people of that state. It's also devoid of Indians. Their absence is palpable, a visible erasure from a man who proudly claimed his Cherokee heritage but left the land of his people because of his sexuality. Oklahoma lingered in his mind, wandering through the red dusk of his imagination until he died of cancer in a New York City hospital. Throughout his life he explored in the shadows what it was to be Indian and gay in a world that had no use for either. And he died alone.

Riggs and I share much in our love of language, our connection to the land and the people and our struggles with understanding our desires. But his rich and artistically inspiring life is also an object lesson in the corrosive consequences of accepting the world's bigotry as a measure of your own worth. He's a much-honored queer Cherokee forefather, but I don't want to be like him. I want to continue to live the life and celebrate the love he couldn't. And if the spirits are willing, I will.

It's been over eleven years now since I began the long walk back to Cherokee pride and wholeness, and about nine since I came out. I'm now with a beautiful, blue-eyed, big-hearted Scots-Canadian man who has taught me more about love, passion and tenderness that I'd ever thought to know in all the years of self-hatred and shame that came before. In his gentle eyes I am lovely and desired, not for what I can give to him alone but for what we can give one another. It helps that he's also more than happy to help me make a horizontal stand against colonization whenever I'm in the mood—and, being the committed and passionate activist that I am, I am often in the mood.

I think back on this continuing journey, all the unexpected twists and double-backs along the trail, where fragile flesh has hungered for human touch and all too often come away unfulfilled. Would awkward and insecure eighteen-year-old Booner recognize the relatively confident and self-assured thirty-two-year-old Daniel? In those days I thought I'd be a perfectly "civilized," tweed-bound Oxford don and High Church Christian apologist by this point, not a balding, goateed Cherokee nationalist and proud son of the Rockies with multiple tattoos and piercings, a queer Native lit professor living and loving in the semi-socialist wilds of Canada. Booner had expected to have a wife and children, although he had no physical desire for women, nor any significant need to be a father. Although he had furtive dreams of sex with men, he certainly never imagined finding a deep and abiding love with a same-sex partner. Would that shy, scared and ashamed young man have faced all the mingled fears of the flesh earlier if he'd known that surrendering to the wolfsong and the moonlit shadows of the night would have brought such a healing balm to the spirit of his older self?

55

I'm not at all sure that he'd have understood or approved if he could see the man who would one day type these words. But maybe, when walking his dogs on a cold, clear winter's night, as he stood looking to the lonely moon's scarred face in the Colorado darkness, he might have known that his hunger was anything but a curse, that his desire was fundamentally different from that of the shame-marked Moon, that the howls in the dark dreams were a kinship cry drawing him towards all the primal power and beauty that passion could offer. Wolves aren't monsters; the monsters abide in deception, fear and self-loathing, not in truthful joy. We all hunger; we long to be loved and to love in return. That, at least, he might have found comforting as he trudged through the moonlit snow towards the warming lights of home.

(2008)

Questions

1. Describing how he felt about being Native when he was a child, Justice writes, "Nothing about my people was interesting to me." What does he mean, and why did he feel this way? How does he later reinterpret his heritage?

2. Trace the appearance through this essay of one of the following images: werewolves, the moon, or the land of Faerie. What is the significance of this image? Does Justice's orientation to the image change in the course of the narrative?

3. Comment on the significance of names and naming in this essay.

4. How does Justice's Native identity affect his experience of homosexuality? How does his homosexuality affect his experience of Nativeness?

5. What does Justice argue about the political importance of sex? Do you agree?

6. How does Justice describe the difference between the political environments in Canada and in the US? In your experience, how accurate is his description of the country you are in?

BARACK OBAMA

A MORE PERFECT UNION

This speech on race relations in the United States
is widely considered a turning point in
Obama's 2008 Presidential campaign.

℮

"We the people, in order to form a more perfect union."

Two hundred and twenty one years ago, in a hall that still stands across the street, a group of men gathered and, with these simple words, launched America's improbable experiment in democracy. Farmers and scholars; statesmen and patriots who had traveled across an ocean to escape tyranny and persecution finally made real their declaration of independence at a Philadelphia convention that lasted through the spring of 1787.

The document they produced was eventually signed but ultimately unfinished. It was stained by this nation's original sin of slavery, a question that divided the colonies and brought the convention to a stalemate until the founders chose to allow the slave trade to continue for at least twenty more years, and to leave any final resolution to future generations.

Of course, the answer to the slavery question was already embedded within our Constitution—a Constitution that had at is very core the ideal of equal citizenship under the law; a Constitution that promised its people liberty, and justice, and a union that could be and should be perfected over time.

And yet words on a parchment would not be enough to deliver slaves 5 from bondage, or provide men and women of every color and creed their full rights and obligations as citizens of the United States. What would be needed were Americans in successive generations who were willing to do their part—through protests and struggle, on the streets and in the courts, through a civil war and civil disobedience and always at great risk—to narrow that gap between the promise of our ideals and the reality of their time.

613

This was one of the tasks we set forth at the beginning of this campaign—to continue the long march of those who came before us, a march for a more just, more equal, more free, more caring and more prosperous America. I chose to run for the presidency at this moment in history because I believe deeply that we cannot solve the challenges of our time unless we solve them together—unless we perfect our union by understanding that we may have different stories, but we hold common hopes; that we may not look the same and we may not have come from the same place, but we all want to move in the same direction—towards a better future for our children and our grandchildren.

This belief comes from my unyielding faith in the decency and generosity of the American people. But it also comes from my own American story.

I am the son of a black man from Kenya and a white woman from Kansas. I was raised with the help of a white grandfather who survived a Depression to serve in Patton's Army during World War II and a white grandmother who worked on a bomber assembly line at Fort Leavenworth while he was overseas. I've gone to some of the best schools in America and lived in one of the world's poorest nations. I am married to a black American who carries within her the blood of slaves and slaveowners—an inheritance we pass on to our two precious daughters. I have brothers, sisters, nieces, nephews, uncles and cousins, of every race and every hue, scattered across three continents, and for as long as I live, I will never forget that in no other country on Earth is my story even possible.

It's a story that hasn't made me the most conventional candidate. But it is a story that has seared into my genetic makeup the idea that this nation is more than the sum of its parts—that out of many, we are truly one.

10 Throughout the first year of this campaign, against all predictions to the contrary, we saw how hungry the American people were for this message of unity. Despite the temptation to view my candidacy through a purely racial lens, we won commanding victories in states with some of the whitest populations in the country. In South Carolina, where the Confederate Flag still flies, we built a powerful coalition of African Americans and white Americans.

This is not to say that race has not been an issue in the campaign. At various stages in the campaign, some commentators have deemed me either "too black" or "not black enough." We saw racial tensions bubble to the surface during the week before the South Carolina primary. The press has scoured every exit poll for the latest evidence of racial polarization, not just in terms of white and black, but black and brown as well.

And yet, it has only been in the last couple of weeks that the discussion of race in this campaign has taken a particularly divisive turn.

On one end of the spectrum, we've heard the implication that my candidacy is somehow an exercise in affirmative action; that it's based solely on the desire of wide-eyed liberals to purchase racial reconciliation on the cheap. On the other end, we've heard my former pastor, Reverend Jeremiah Wright, use incendiary language to express views that have the potential not only to widen the racial divide, but views that denigrate both the greatness and the goodness of our nation; that rightly offend white and black alike.

I have already condemned, in unequivocal terms, the statements of Reverend Wright that have caused such controversy.[1] For some, nagging questions remain. Did I know him to be an occasionally fierce critic of American domestic and foreign policy? Of course. Did I ever hear him make remarks that could be considered controversial while I sat in church? Yes. Did I strongly disagree with many of his political views? Absolutely— just as I'm sure many of you have heard remarks from your pastors, priests, or rabbis with which you strongly disagreed.

But the remarks that have caused this recent firestorm weren't simply controversial. They weren't simply a religious leader's effort to speak out against perceived injustice. Instead, they expressed a profoundly distorted view of this country—a view that sees white racism as endemic, and that elevates what is wrong with America above all that we know is right with America; a view that sees the conflicts in the Middle East as rooted primarily in the actions of stalwart allies like Israel, instead of emanating from the perverse and hateful ideologies of radical Islam.

As such, Reverend Wright's comments were not only wrong but divisive, divisive at a time when we need unity; racially charged at a time when we need to come together to solve a set of monumental problems—two wars, a terrorist threat, a falling economy, a chronic health care crisis and potentially devastating climate change; problems that are neither black or white or Latino or Asian, but rather problems that confront us all.

Given my background, my politics, and my professed values and ideals, there will no doubt be those for whom my statements of condemnation are not enough. Why associate myself with Reverend Wright in the first place,

15

---

1   *statements of ... such controversy*   At the time this speech was delivered, there was a major controversy in the media over statements that Obama's pastor Jeremiah Wright had made during sermons, including an assertion that the American government had "failed" black people.

they may ask? Why not join another church? And I confess that if all that I knew of Reverend Wright were the snippets of those sermons that have run in an endless loop on the television and YouTube, or if Trinity United Church of Christ conformed to the caricatures being peddled by some commentators, there is no doubt that I would react in much the same way.

But the truth is, that isn't all that I know of the man. The man I met more than twenty years ago is a man who helped introduce me to my Christian faith, a man who spoke to me about our obligations to love one another; to care for the sick and lift up the poor. He is a man who served his country as a US Marine; who has studied and lectured at some of the finest universities and seminaries in the country, and who for over thirty years led a church that serves the community by doing God's work here on Earth—by housing the homeless, ministering to the needy, providing day care services and scholarships and prison ministries, and reaching out to those suffering from HIV/AIDS.

In my first book, *Dreams From My Father*, I described the experience of my first service at Trinity:

20   "People began to shout, to rise from their seats and clap and cry out, a forceful wind carrying the reverend's voice up into the rafters.... And in that single note—hope!—I heard something else; at the foot of that cross, inside the thousands of churches across the city, I imagined the stories of ordinary black people merging with the stories of David and Goliath, Moses and Pharaoh, the Christians in the lion's den, Ezekiel's field of dry bones. Those stories—of survival, and freedom, and hope—became our story, my story; the blood that had spilled was our blood, the tears our tears; until this black church, on this bright day, seemed once more a vessel carrying the story of a people into future generations and into a larger world. Our trials and triumphs became at once unique and universal, black and more than black; in chronicling our journey, the stories and songs gave us a means to reclaim memories that we didn't need to feel shame about ... memories that all people might study and cherish—and with which we could start to rebuild."

That has been my experience at Trinity. Like other predominantly black churches across the country, Trinity embodies the black community in its entirety—the doctor and the welfare mom, the model student and the former gang-banger. Like other black churches, Trinity's services are full of raucous laughter and sometimes bawdy humor. They are full of dancing, clapping, screaming and shouting that may seem jarring to the untrained ear. The church contains in full the kindness and cruelty, the fierce intelligence and the shocking ignorance, the struggles and successes, the love and yes, the bitterness and bias that make up the black experience in America.

And this helps explain, perhaps, my relationship with Reverend Wright. As imperfect as he may be, he has been like family to me. He strengthened my faith, officiated my wedding, and baptized my children. Not once in my conversations with him have I heard him talk about any ethnic group in derogatory terms, or treat whites with whom he interacted with anything but courtesy and respect. He contains within him the contradictions—the good and the bad—of the community that he has served diligently for so many years.

I can no more disown him than I can disown the black community. I can no more disown him than I can my white grandmother—a woman who helped raise me, a woman who sacrificed again and again for me, a woman who loves me as much as she loves anything in this world, but a woman who once confessed her fear of black men who passed by her on the street, and who on more than one occasion has uttered racial or ethnic stereotypes that made me cringe.

These people are a part of me. And they are a part of America, this country that I love.

Some will see this as an attempt to justify or excuse comments that are simply inexcusable. I can assure you it is not. I suppose the politically safe thing would be to move on from this episode and just hope that it fades into the woodwork. We can dismiss Reverend Wright as a crank or a dema-gogue, just as some have dismissed Geraldine Ferraro, in the aftermath of her recent statements, as harboring some deep-seated racial bias.

But race is an issue that I believe this nation cannot afford to ignore right now. We would be making the same mistake that Reverend Wright made in his offending sermons about America—to simplify and stereotype and amplify the negative to the point that it distorts reality.

The fact is that the comments that have been made and the issues that have surfaced over the last few weeks reflect the complexities of race in this country that we've never really worked through—a part of our union that we have yet to perfect. And if we walk away now, if we simply retreat into our respective corners, we will never be able to come together and solve challenges like health care, or education, or the need to find good jobs for every American.

Understanding this reality requires a reminder of how we arrived at this point. As William Faulkner once wrote, "The past isn't dead and buried. In fact, it isn't even past." We do not need to recite here the history of racial

25

injustice in this country. But we do need to remind ourselves that so many of the disparities that exist in the African-American community today can be directly traced to inequalities passed on from an earlier generation that suffered under the brutal legacy of slavery and Jim Crow.

Segregated schools were, and are, inferior schools; we still haven't fixed them, fifty years after Brown v. Board of Education, and the inferior education they provided, then and now, helps explain the pervasive achievement gap between today's black and white students.

30 Legalized discrimination—where blacks were prevented, often through violence, from owning property, or loans were not granted to African-American business owners, or black homeowners could not access FHA mortgages, or blacks were excluded from unions, or the police force, or fire departments—meant that black families could not amass any meaningful wealth to bequeath to future generations. That history helps explain the wealth and income gap between black and white, and the concentrated pockets of poverty that persists in so many of today's urban and rural communities.

A lack of economic opportunity among black men, and the shame and frustration that came from not being able to provide for one's family, contributed to the erosion of black families—a problem that welfare policies for many years may have worsened. And the lack of basic services in so many urban black neighborhoods—parks for kids to play in, police walking the beat, regular garbage pick-up and building code enforcement—all helped create a cycle of violence, blight and neglect that continue to haunt us.

This is the reality in which Reverend Wright and other African-Americans of his generation grew up. They came of age in the late fifties and early sixties, a time when segregation was still the law of the land and opportunity was systematically constricted. What's remarkable is not how many failed in the face of discrimination, but rather how many men and women overcame the odds; how many were able to make a way out of no way for those like me who would come after them.

But for all those who scratched and clawed their way to get a piece of the American Dream, there were many who didn't make it—those who were ultimately defeated, in one way or another, by discrimination. That legacy of defeat was passed on to future generations—those young men and increasingly young women who we see standing on street corners or languishing in our prisons, without hope or prospects for the future. Even for those blacks who did make it, questions of race, and racism, continue to define their worldview in fundamental ways. For the men and women of Reverend Wright's generation, the memories of humiliation and doubt and fear have not gone away; nor has the anger and the bitterness of those years. That anger may not get expressed in public, in front of white co-workers or white friends. But it does find voice in the barbershop or around the kitchen table. At times, that anger is exploited by politicians, to gin up votes along racial lines, or to make up for a politician's own failings.

And occasionally it finds voice in the church on Sunday morning, in the pulpit and in the pews. The fact that so many people are surprised to hear that anger in some of Reverend Wright's sermons simply reminds us of the old truism that the most segregated hour in American life occurs on Sunday morning. That anger is not always productive; indeed, all too often it distracts attention from solving real problems; it keeps us from squarely facing our own complicity in our condition, and prevents the African-American community from forging the alliances it needs to bring about real change. But the anger is real; it is powerful; and to simply wish it away, to condemn it without understanding its roots, only serves to widen the chasm of misunderstanding that exists between the races.

In fact, a similar anger exists within segments of the white community. 35 Most working- and middle-class white Americans don't feel that they have been particularly privileged by their race. Their experience is the immigrant experience—as far as they're concerned, no one's handed them anything, they've built it from scratch. They've worked hard all their lives, many times only to see their jobs shipped overseas or their pension dumped after a lifetime of labor. They are anxious about their futures, and feel their dreams slipping away; in an era of stagnant wages and global competition, opportunity comes to be seen as a zero sum game, in which your dreams come at my expense. So when they are told to bus their children to a school across town; when they hear that an African American is getting an advantage in landing a good job or a spot in a good college because of an injustice that they themselves never committed; when they're told that their fears about crime in urban neighborhoods are somehow prejudiced, resentment builds over time.

Like the anger within the black community, these resentments aren't always expressed in polite company. But they have helped shape the political landscape for at least a generation. Anger over welfare and affirmative action helped forge the Reagan Coalition. Politicians routinely exploited fears of crime for their own electoral ends. Talk show hosts and conservative commentators built entire careers unmasking bogus claims of racism while dismissing legitimate discussions of racial injustice and inequality as mere political correctness or reverse racism.

Just as black anger often proved counterproductive, so have these white resentments distracted attention from the real culprits of the middle class squeeze—a corporate culture rife with inside dealing, questionable accounting practices, and short-term greed; a Washington dominated by lobbyists and special interests; economic policies that favor the few over the many. And yet, to wish away the resentments of white Americans, to label them as misguided or even racist, without recognizing they are grounded in legitimate concerns—this too widens the racial divide, and blocks the path to understanding.

This is where we are right now. It's a racial stalemate we've been stuck in for years. Contrary to the claims of some of my critics, black and white, I have never been so naïve as to believe that we can get beyond our racial divisions in a single election cycle, or with a single candidacy—particularly a candidacy as imperfect as my own.

But I have asserted a firm conviction—a conviction rooted in my faith in God and my faith in the American people—that working together we can move beyond some of our old racial wounds, and that in fact we have no choice if we are to continue on the path of a more perfect union.

40   For the African-American community, that path means embracing the burdens of our past without becoming victims of our past. It means continuing to insist on a full measure of justice in every aspect of American life. But it also means binding our particular grievances—for better health care, and better schools, and better jobs—to the larger aspirations of all Americans—the white woman struggling to break the glass ceiling, the white man who's been laid off, the immigrant trying to feed his family. And it means taking full responsibility for our own lives—by demanding more from our fathers, and spending more time with our children, and reading to them, and teaching them that while they may face challenges and discrimination in their own lives, they must never succumb to despair or cynicism; they must always believe that they can write their own destiny.

Ironically, this quintessentially American—and yes, conservative—notion of self-help found frequent expression in Reverend Wright's sermons. But what my former pastor too often failed to understand is that embarking on a program of self-help also requires a belief that society can change.

The profound mistake of Reverend Wright's sermons is not that he spoke about racism in our society. It's that he spoke as if our society was static; as if no progress has been made; as if this country—a country that has made it possible for one of his own members to run for the highest of-fice in the land and build a coalition of white and black; Latino and Asian, rich and poor, young and old—is still irrevocably bound to a tragic past. But what we know—what we have seen—is that America can change. That is the true genius of this nation. What we have already achieved gives us hope—the audacity to hope—for what we can and must achieve tomorrow.

In the white community, the path to a more perfect union means ac-knowledging that what ails the African-American community does not just exist in the minds of black people; that the legacy of discrimination—and current incidents of discrimination, while less overt than in the past—are real and must be addressed. Not just with words, but with deeds—by in-vesting in our schools and our communities; by enforcing our civil rights laws and ensuring fairness in our criminal justice system; by providing this generation with ladders of opportunity that were unavailable for previous generations. It requires all Americans to realize that your dreams do not have to come at the expense of my dreams; that investing in the health, wel-fare, and education of black and brown and white children will ultimately help all of America prosper.

In the end, then, what is called for is nothing more, and nothing less, than what all the world's great religions demand—that we do unto others as we would have them do unto us. Let us be our brother's keeper, Scripture tells us. Let us be our sister's keeper. Let us find that common stake we all have in one another, and let our politics reflect that spirit as well.

For we have a choice in this country. We can accept a politics that breeds division, and conflict, and cynicism. We can tackle race only as spectacle—as we did in the OJ trial—or in the wake of tragedy, as we did in the aftermath of Katrina—or as fodder for the nightly news. We can play Reverend Wright's sermons on every channel, every day and talk about them from now until the election, and make the only question in this cam-paign whether or not the American people think that I somehow believe or sympathize with his most offensive words. We can pounce on some gaffe by a Hillary supporter as evidence that she's playing the race card, or we can speculate on whether white men will all flock to John McCain in the general election regardless of his policies.

We can do that.

But if we do, I can tell you that in the next election, we'll be talking about some other distraction. And then another one. And then another one. And nothing will change.

45

That is one option. Or, at this moment, in this election, we can come together and say, "Not this time." This time we want to talk about the crumbling schools that are stealing the future of black children and white children and Asian children and Hispanic children and Native American children. This time we want to reject the cynicism that tells us that these kids can't learn; that those kids who don't look like us are somebody else's problem. The children of America are not those kids, they are our kids, and we will not let them fall behind in a 21st-century economy. Not this time.

This time we want to talk about how the lines in the Emergency Room are filled with whites and blacks and Hispanics who do not have health care; who don't have the power on their own to overcome the special interests in Washington, but who can take them on if we do it together.

50   This time we want to talk about the shuttered mills that once provided a decent life for men and women of every race, and the homes for sale that once belonged to Americans from every religion, every region, every walk of life. This time we want to talk about the fact that the real problem is not that someone who doesn't look like you might take your job; it's that the corporation you work for will ship it overseas for nothing more than a profit.

This time we want to talk about the men and women of every color and creed who serve together, and fight together, and bleed together under the same proud flag. We want to talk about how to bring them home from a war that never should've been authorized and never should've been waged, and we want to talk about how we'll show our patriotism by caring for them, and their families, and giving them the benefits they have earned.

I would not be running for President if I didn't believe with all my heart that this is what the vast majority of Americans want for this country. This union may never be perfect, but generation after generation has shown that it can always be perfected. And today, whenever I find myself feeling doubtful or cynical about this possibility, what gives me the most hope is the next generation—the young people whose attitudes and beliefs and openness to change have already made history in this election.

There is one story in particularly that I'd like to leave you with today— a story I told when I had the great honor of speaking on Dr. King's birthday at his home church, Ebenezer Baptist, in Atlanta.

There is a young, twenty-three year old white woman named Ashley Baia who organized for our campaign in Florence, South Carolina. She had been working to organize a mostly African-American community since the beginning of this campaign, and one day she was at a roundtable discussion where everyone went around telling their story and why they were there.

And Ashley said that when she was nine years old, her mother got cancer. And because she had to miss days of work, she was let go and lost her health care. They had to file for bankruptcy, and that's when Ashley decided that she had to do something to help her mom.

She knew that food was one of their most expensive costs, and so Ashley convinced her mother that what she really liked and really wanted to eat more than anything else was mustard and relish sandwiches. Because that was the cheapest way to eat.

She did this for a year until her mom got better, and she told everyone at the roundtable that the reason she joined our campaign was so that she could help the millions of other children in the country who want and need to help their parents too.

Now Ashley might have made a different choice. Perhaps somebody told her along the way that the source of her mother's problems were blacks who were on welfare and too lazy to work, or Hispanics who were coming into the country illegally. But she didn't. She sought out allies in her fight against injustice.

Anyway, Ashley finishes her story and then goes around the room and asks everyone else why they're supporting the campaign. They all have different stories and reasons. Many bring up a specific issue. And finally they come to this elderly black man who's been sitting there quietly the entire time. And Ashley asks him why he's there. And he does not bring up a specific issue. He does not say health care or the economy. He does not say education or the war. He does not say that he was there because of Barack Obama. He simply says to everyone in the room, "I am here because of Ashley."

"I'm here because of Ashley." By itself, that single moment of recognition between that young white girl and that old black man is not enough. It is not enough to give health care to the sick, or jobs to the jobless, or education to our children.

But it is where we start. It is where our union grows stronger. And as so many generations have come to realize over the course of the two-hundred and twenty one years since a band of patriots signed that document in Philadelphia, that is where the perfection begins.

(2008)

Questions

1. Who is Obama's audience? How does he appeal to different segments of the audience throughout his speech?

2. Define the following rhetorical devices and find an example from Obama's speech: anaphora, alliteration, metonymy, polysyndeton. Explain the effect of the rhetorical device in each example.

3. What does the old man who says he has come to the roundtable discussion "'because of Ashley'" represent in the context of the speech?

4. How does Obama appeal to American patriotism in this speech?

5. Comment on the role of religion in Obama's rhetoric and argument.

6. How does Obama address the issue of unity? In doing so, does he pay enough attention to diverse backgrounds and concerns?

IRENE PEPPERBERG, JENNIFER VICINAY,
AND PATRICK CAVANAGH

PROCESSING OF THE MÜLLER-LYER ILLUSION BY A GREY PARROT (*PSITTACUS ERITHACUS*)

Scientist Irene Pepperberg is known for her work with the remarkable Grey parrot Alex, whose linguistic and cognitive abilities helped change scientific perspective on animal intelligence. In this scholarly article, Pepperberg takes advantage of Alex's communication skills to reveal a possible similarity between human and parrot visual processing.

❧

ABSTRACT

Alex, a Grey parrot (*Psittacus erithacus*) who identifies the bigger or smaller of two objects by reporting its color or matter using a vocal English label and who states "none" if they do not differ in size, was presented with two-dimensional Müller-Lyer figures (Brentano form) in which the central lines were of contrasting colors. His responses to "What color bigger/smaller?" demonstrated that he saw the standard length illusion in the Müller-Lyer figures in 32 of 50 tests where human observers would also see the illusion and reported the reverse direction only twice. He did not report the illusion when (a) arrows on the shafts were perpendicular to the shafts or closely approached perpendicularity, (b) shafts were 6 times thicker than the arrows, or (c) after being tested with multiple exposures—conditions that also lessen or eliminate the illusion for human observers. These data suggest that parrot and human visual systems process the Müller-Lyer figure in analogous ways despite a 175-fold difference in the respective sizes of their brain volumes. The similarity in results also indicates that parrots with vocal abilities like Alex's can be reliably tested on visual illusions with paradigms similar to those used on human subjects.

1. INTRODUCTION

Given that the goal of the visual system is to process information accurately—as a matter of survival—the ability of the human brain to be fooled by optical illusions attracts considerable empirical and theoretical interest. The study of optical illusions in birds, small prey-animals with the capacity for flight and thus likely an even greater need for visual accuracy, would provide important insights into the processing strategies of the avian visual system. Some perceptual tasks, such as occlusion on non-optical-illusion visual object recognition, recognition-by-component (e.g., DiPietro et al 2002; van Hamme et al 1992; also Cook 2001) or detecting patterns of non-random perceptual structure (e.g., Cook et al 2005) have been examined in birds, but only a few conclusive studies on optical illusions have been performed on subjects with a visual system markedly different from those of primates (e.g., Fujita et al 1993; Nakamura et al 2006). How might non-mammalian brains process such information?

The avian brain is anatomically distinct from that of mammals but, at least for birds such as corvids and psittacids,[1] differs quantitatively rather than qualitatively from mammals when processing certain cognitive tasks (e.g., Emery and Clayton 2004; Jarvis et al 2005; Pepperberg 1999, 2006); for tasks that primarily involve visual processing, however, differences may be more striking....

No illusion experiments have been performed on parrots, larger-brained and longer-lived birds whose visual systems have not, with the exception of studies on UV sensitivity (e.g., Bowmaker et al 1994, 1996; Cuthill et al 2000; Goldsmith and Butler 2005; Wilkie et al 1998), been examined as extensively as that of pigeons or chickens. Behavioral similarities between chickens and parrots, and differences between parrots and pigeons, on tasks such as object permanence that require amodal completion (see review in Regolin et al 2004; note Aust and Huber 2006) merely suggest that parrot visual systems more closely resemble those of chickens than pigeons.[2]

---

1   *corvids and psittacids*   Notably intelligent families of birds, colloquially known as the crow family and parrot family, respectively.

2   An avian veterinarian, Dr Greg Harrison (personal communication, 4-14-06), also suggested that the parrot system was more like that of a chicken than a pigeon. [author's note]

Furthermore, no studies have been performed on an avian subject that, without any training on the actual task, could simply state vocally whether or not an optical illusion had been observed. Determining whether a parrot could respond in such a manner would provide comparative behavioral data and a basis for future comparative studies on more complex types of visual processing; such data might also stimulate neurobiological studies on parrot visual systems.

The Müller-Lyer illusion was chosen as the initial task because it is well-represented in the scientific literature. Müller-Lyer (1889/1981) first described how humans either underestimated or overestimated the length of a line that had arrows attached, respectively, either inwardly < > or outwardly > <. Researchers suggest that the illusion can result from "... several factors interacting at different levels of visual processing, ranging from low-level mechanisms such as optical blur and retinal inhibition, to high-level mechanisms, such as cognitive contrast and visual attention" (Predebon 2004, page 916); Sekuler and Erlebacher (1971) argue that the arrows-in and arrows-out Müller-Lyer illusions are functionally distinct. A human with visual agnosia[3] failed to detect the illusion, suggesting that it depends on pictorial-depth cues (Gregory 1968; Turnbull et al 2004), but the illusion is preserved in patients with visuospatial neglect[4] (e.g., Vallar et al 2000). Changizi and Widders (2002) claim that the illusion is based on a prediction of where an observer would be moving in space [i.e., also a three-dimensional (3-D) cue], but other data (e.g., experiments and review in Zanker and Abdullah 2004) suggest that filtering in the early visual system leads to confusion about the location of line endings. Weidner and Fink (2007) argue that the Müller-Lyer illusion depends on integrating bottom-up visual and top-down cognitive processes. How would a Grey parrot, with a non-primate brain and visual system, respond to this illusion? ... [S]ome evidence exists for the illusion in ring doves (Warden and Baar 1929), pigeons (Nakamura et al 2005, 2006), and chickens (Winslow 1933);[5] these studies suggest that, whatever neurobiological systems are involved, mammalian vision may not be critical for seeing the illusion (Otto-deHaart et al 1999).

5

---

3   *visual agnosia*   Inability of the brain to interpret some kinds of visual stimulus; symptoms vary depending on the cause.

4   *visuospatial neglect*   Inability to respond to stimuli on one side of the visual field.

5   ... [S]ome of these studies involved memory rather than direct choice. [author's note]

The subject in this study was Alex, a Grey parrot with previous training on relative size judgments for 3-D objects (Pepperberg and Brezinsky 1991). Using a vocal color or material label, he could identify the larger or smaller object within a set, or state "none" if they did not differ in size. Before being tested on Müller-Lyer figures, he was given familiarization trials to enable transfer of his relative size judgments to two-dimensional (2-D) figures. Once he began to respond appropriately, he was given various versions of the Müller-Lyer figure.... The experiments were designed to answer the following queries: Does a Grey parrot (a) see the Müller-Lyer illusion at all?; (b) see the illusion under varying conditions of angle and size contrast between the central line and the arrows (e.g., Gardner and Long 1961; note Predebon 2004)?; (c) respond appropriately under control conditions when arrows are replaced by vertical bars? and (d) habituate over time as do some humans (e.g., Mountjoy 1958)?

2. EXPERIMENT

2.1 Subject

Alex, a 30-year-old male Grey parrot (*Psittacus erithacus* ...), had been the subject of numerous cognitive and communicative studies for 29 years (e.g., Pepperberg 1999). Testing locations and living conditions when neither testing nor training were in progress are described in Pepperberg and Wilkes (2004). Food and water were available at his vocal request at all times. In this study he used previously documented abilities [Pepperberg (1999), colors (rose {red}, green, purple, blue, yellow, orange, grey)], and to understand the concept of relative size and absence of size difference (Pepperberg and Brezinsky 1991).

2.2 Procedure

2.2.1 *Familiarization*. Because Alex's prior training on size difference had involved 3-D objects (Pepperberg and Brezinsky 1991) and his ability to label 2-D representations of 3-D objects was still under study, he was first shown sets of two differently colored 2-D horizontal lines and asked to identify the bigger or smaller one or to state "none" if they were equally sized. The two horizontal lines, without arrows, 4 mm in width and of differing colors and lengths (varying between 5 and 15 cm), were drawn 5 cm apart on a standard white 365 index card; each card had different colored pairs and different size variations, including lines of equal size.

A randomly chosen card was placed on a felt-covered tray used for other tasks (e.g., number studies, object permanence—Pepperberg 1999,

2006). Initially, the tray was held horizontally, approximately 20 cm from one of Alex's eyes, with the experimenter compensating as much as possible for Alex's head movement so as to maintain presentation in front of a single eye. Subsequently, the tray was held vertically, approximately 15 cm from one of his eyes, to increase his attentiveness. The experimenter again compensated, as much as possible, for Alex's head movements to maintain presentation in front of one eye. Because no one has determined the extent of binocular overlap in a Grey parrot (either the angular overlap or, given the fairly large thick beak, the distance at which binocular overlap begins) nor the acuity of vision in the area of binocular overlap,[6] we opted to constrain presentation to what was likely to be monocular observation. (Note: Alex will not tolerate even a stray feather near his eye; thus using an eye patch to ensure monocular vision is not an option.) The distances of the stimuli from Alex's eye in this study were roughly the same as in all previous projects (e.g., Pepperberg 1999, 2006).

Figure 1. Alex viewing one of the stimuli. During trials, the stimulus was centered on Alex's eye; for this figure, the stimulus was positioned so that it would be visible to the reader.

When Alex made contact with the questioner with the other eye, he was asked "What color bigger/smaller?" He could respond with either color or "none." He received one or two familiarization sessions (~20 min/session) each week for about 6 months with breaks for trainer vacations; sessions continued until he attended to the cards consistently. Such training was necessary to direct his focus to the 2-D stimuli; his initial responses were to label the cards themselves (correctly) as 'paper' or 'four-corner paper', attempt to chew them, or, most commonly, to ignore the trainer and cards

10

---

6   Walls (1942) states that most parrots have a binocular overlap of 6%-10%, but does not specify which species were studied. No data exist concerning the foveae of Grey parrots nor concerning their areas of highest visual acuity. [author's note]

and either state colors that were not on the cards or begin to preen. We were not concerned with his accuracy because he had previously demonstrated his understanding of bigger/smaller (Pepperberg and Brezinsky 1991) and the familiarization procedure was carried out only to ensure that he would respond to the 2-D stimuli. We specifically did not wish to train him on the task by rewarding and thus reinforcing particular responses to these queries, so as to avoid cuing him about tests to follow....

2.3 *Test Procedure*

... Test situations included specific precautions to avoid cuing. One control was a design such that each test session was, as noted above, presented intermittently during free periods or work on unrelated topics. An examiner who, for example, poses a series of similar questions may come to expect a particular answer and unconsciously accept an indistinct (and by our criteria incorrect) response of, for example, "gree" (a mix of "green" and "three") for "green." ... Alex's responses had to be chosen from his entire repertoire and from among numerous possible topics during each session. Second, in general, a human other than the one presenting the tray (one of three possible individuals in these studies), who did not know what was on the tray, confirmed the answer; his/her interpretation of Alex's response was thus unlikely to be influenced by expectation of a certain label. Only after his/her confirmation was Alex rewarded (Pepperberg 1981). Third, this evaluator was unlikely to be influenced by hearing the type of question posed: in a previous study, transcriptions of contextless tapes of Alex's responses in a session agreed 98.2% with original evaluations (Pepperberg 1992).[7] Fourth, because Alex had not been trained on this task, no overlap occurred between training and testing situations and, because training on color labels had occurred years before, by students no longer present, he could not have picked up on trainer-induced cues specific to a given label (Pepperberg 1981).

Any direct cuing or training of Alex as to the correct answer by the presenter was highly unlikely for four reasons. First, in a previous two-item relative-size test in which the presenter was blind to the task (items were

---

7   This percentage represented 106 matches of 108 vocalizations. As an additional control, the principal investigator made two transcriptions of a student, new to the lab, as he responded to the same type of questions as Alex. The first transcription was live; the second, made several days later, was of a tape from which all questions had been edited. The two transcriptions of the student's vocalizations matched to within 95.8% (68 of 71 vocalizations). [author's note]

hidden in a cigar box) and the evaluator was out of Alex's view, Alex's accuracy of 78.7% (Pepperberg and Brezinsky 1991) was equivalent to his usual ~80% rate (Pepperberg 1999); tests, however, took twice as long because of difficulty of maintaining Alex's attention to the task. Here, in four a-posteriori control trials in which the experimenter could not see the stimuli ... and the evaluator was again out of Alex's view, the only effect was that trials took almost 15 min each because Alex could now use one of his eyes to focus on, and be distracted by, other events in the lab; he reported the illusion in the expected direction on three of the four trials, obviating the issue of cuing.[8] Second, unlike figure 1, which is posed as noted, the stimulus was centered on one of Alex's eyes such that his head blocked most of the stimulus from the experimenter, and the experimenter's eyes were focused entirely on Alex's other eye and maintained that focus during questioning. Thus, the experimenter's eye gaze could not cue Alex as to which side (the 'bigger' or 'smaller') was correct in a given trial. Moreover, if he were indeed cuing into an experimenter's gaze to determine which color to label, he would not have made so many responses of "none" when the illusion was seen by the experimenter. Third, because the stimulus direction varied and questions varied between targeting bigger or smaller (i.e., questions were neither massed nor did not necessarily alternate, but could be either the same or different on a given day, and often only one question was asked on a given day), Alex could not learn to respond, for example, only to colors associated with arrows pointing in a particular direction, or to the right or left side. Also, because the specific response (one of six colors or 'none') varied from trial to trial, Alex could not be trained or cued as to one proper response, and the experimenter would praise him equally well no matter what he said (unless the response was ... irrelevant). Fourth, he was unlikely to have been trained or been cued as to the association between arrow direction and size, because his first actual error (giving a response in the incorrect direction) did not occur until trial 22.

As in previous studies (e.g., Pepperberg 2006), a small percentage of sessions was videotaped and subsequently analyzed to ensure interobserver reliability. If interobserver reliability with a blind, naive coder was high, we could be assured of the validity of other trials. Given that Alex was more interested in the student performing the taping and the video camera rather than the objects to be labeled, such trials were difficult to execute and kept

---

8   Fisher's exact test on Alex's results for [these] trials during the experiment and after it showed no significant differences ($p = 0.154$, one-tailed). [author's note]

to a minimum. Four trials were digitized and presented to observers who had never interacted with Alex....

3. Results

Alex's data were scored as 'illusion reported' if he named the color of the shaft that human observers would report, as 'no illusion' if he reported "none," and 'opposite the illusion' if he reported the color opposite to the illusion response.... The test procedure also allowed a question to be repeated (up to four times) until Alex named one of the two shaft colors or, in one control, the arrow color, or stated (and stuck with) "none." In general, Alex's first report was one of these appropriate responses. In about 10% of the trials, however, Alex initially stated colors that were not present but when queried a second time, gave one color that was present. Given that his accuracy in labeling colors is 80%-85% (errors occur either because of lack of attention to the stimuli or because stimuli that appear as one color to humans may appear as a different color to parrots—Pepperberg 1999), the second responses were used for these trials.

3.1 *Longitudinal responses*

15 ... [Alex] reported the illusion in about 65% of the trials where human observers would have shown the classic illusion ... and he showed a lessened or absent illusion in control trials where humans would not have shown the illusion....

3.6 *Interobserver reliability*
4 trials were videotaped, digitized, and presented auditorially to four different observers (two female, two male) who were completely naïve with respect to Alex's speech patterns; they could not see the stimuli Alex was being shown. All four agreed on their responses to all four samples. If we collapse all trials over all listeners, interobserver reliability is 100%.

3.7 *Visual acuity*
Alex's acuity was tested with three sets of digits of different sizes (6.3, 12.7, and 25.4 mm in height). The letters were arranged on a background at a viewing distance of 10 to 15 cm and Alex had to name the color of a probed digit ("What color 5?"). Performance was quite good (for the small number of trials) down to the smallest size tested. For the larger digits, Alex had 2 of 2 trials correct, for the 12.7 mm digits, 3 of 4 correct, and for

the 6.3 mm digits, 4 of 5 correct. Because the Müller-Lyer figures were 10 cm or more in length, an order of magnitude larger than the small digits, there is little evidence that Alex would suffer any substantive blurring of the figure or even of the details where the central shaft met the arrows.

4. DISCUSSION

Alex can, under a variety of conditions, perceive the Müller-Lyer illusion, thus demonstrating that neither human neuroanatomy and processing nor human binocular vision are required for such perception. Attention likely plays some role in the strength of the illusion as might visual experience …

4.4 *Visual experience*
A separate but equally intriguing issue involves the effect of environmental stimuli on visual processing abilities. Specifically, humans living in what is often called a 'non-carpentered world'—i.e., an environment without significant examples of right-angled, parallel-perpendicular intersections—experience some optical illusions differently from humans in carpentered societies; in fact, some do not see the Müller-Lyer illusion at all (Segall et al 1966). Interestingly, in some non-carpentered societies children do see the Müller-Lyer illusions and adults do not whereas the opposite is true in other societies[9] although few subjects of any age in non-carpentered societies see the illusion to the same extent as do Westerners (e.g., Segall et al 1966). Thus, for humans, the illusion is not likely innately specified but develops or degrades after interaction with the environment. One would expect wild parrots—likely lacking evolutionary pressures that would favor an adaptation for sensitivity to right-angled, parallel-perpendicular stimuli—to react as do humans in a non-carpentered society. Any captive-born parrot would, however, have the same experience as humans in carpentered societies, but would process these experiences with a non-primate visual system. Demonstrating that even one captive Grey parrot responds to the Müller-Lyer illusion somewhat as do humans in carpentered societies strengthens the argument for the effects of visual input on the processing of the Müller-Lyer illusion (note McCauley and Henrich 2006), although comparisons with wild-caught parrots would be required for conclusive evidence.

---

9   Note work by Brosvic et al (2002) suggesting that 13-15 years seems to be the age at which Western children's decreasing sensitivity to the Müller-Lyer illusion reaches an asymptote. [author's note]

5. Conclusion

20 At least one Grey parrot, Alex, reports the Müller-Lyer illusion under certain conditions. We recognize that our comparisons between parrots and humans, and even parrots and other avian species, are speculative, and are presented in order to generate further interest in cross-species comparisons. Our data suggest that this parrot would provide interesting information on other optical illusions and be an appropriate subject for other comparative studies of visual processing.

Acknowledgments

Research was supported by donors to The Alex Foundation, with special thanks to The Pearl Family Foundation, Alex and Michael Shulman, Greg LaMorte, William Lipton, Kathryn and Walter McAdams, Megumi Oka and the Makioka Foundation, Janice Boyd, Nancy Chambers, Mary Ogg, John Paton, Jan Hartley, Nancy Clark and Bill Broach, the Andrew De Mar Family Foundation, Noriko and Soshi Matsumoto, Hitomi Okumura, Jay Sugarman, Debby and Michael Smith, Janet and Kip Trumbule, Deborah Rivel and Robert Goodale, Mark Hagen, the Canadian Parrot Society, Mercedes Lackey, Mary Long, Ann Arbor Cage Bird Club, Great Lakes Avicultural Society, Kay Fewell, Deborah Thrasher, Tree Top Bird Center, Lisa Fortin Jackson, Paula Geheb, JamieWhittaker, ABC Pets, 2luvbirds, Nancy Marbach, Georgia Hayes, Bird Paradise, Tracy Hylka/Bella Embroidery, Grey Feather Toy Creations, the Medwick Foundation, Featherlust Farms, Tammy Carreiro, Debbie Rijnders/Tinley Advies & Producties BV, Vanessa Rolfe, LeighAnn and Carl Hartsfield, the Harrison family for Harrison's Bird Diet, Fowl Play, Gourmet Pet Supply, and Avian Naturals for treats, Carol D'Arezzo for Alex's perch, and Avian Adventures for cages and additional financial support.

References[10]

Aust J, Huber L, 2006 "Does the use of natural stimuli facilitate amodal completion in pigeons?" *Perception* 35 333-349

Bowmaker J K, Heath L A, Das D, Hunt D M, 1994 "Spectral sensitivity and opsin structure of avian rod and cone visual pigments" *Investigative Ophthamology and Visual Science* 35 1708

---

10 References have been excerpted to show only those cited in the included material.

Bowmaker J K, Heath L A, Wilkie S E, Das D, Hunt D M, 1996 "Middle-wave cone and rod visual pigments in birds: Spectral sensitivity and opsin structure" *Investigative Ophthamology and Visual Science* 37 S804

Brosvic G M, Dihoff R E, Fama J, 2002 "Age-related susceptibility to the Müller-Lyer and the Horizontal-Vertical illusions" *Perceptual and Motor Skills* 94 229-234

Changizi M A, Widders D M, 2002 "Latency correction explains the classical geometric illusions" *Perception* 31 1241-1262

Cook R G, 2001 *Avian Visual Cognition* [online: www.pigeon.tufts.edu/avc]

Cook R G, Goto K, Brooks D I, 2005 "Avian detection and identification of perceptual organization in random noise" *Behavioural Processes* 69 79-95

Cuthill I C, Hart N S, Partridge J C, Bennett A T D, Hunt S, Church S C, 2000 "Avian color vision and avian color playback experiments" *Acta Ethologica* 3 29-37

DiPietro N T, Wasserman E A, Young M E, 2002 "Effects of occlusion on pigeons' visual object recognition" *Perception* 31 1299-1312

Emery N J, Clayton N S, 2004 "The mentality of crows: convergent evolution of intelligence in corvids and apes" *Science* 306 1903-1907

Fujita K, Blough D S, Blough P M, 1993 "Effects of the inclination of context lines on perception of the Ponzo illusion by pigeons" *Animal Learning & Behavior* 21 29-34

Gardner R W, Long R I, 1961 "Selective attention and the Müller-Lyer illusion" *Psychological Record* 11 317-320

Goldsmith T, Butler B K, 2005 "Color vision of the budgerigar (*Melopsittacus undulates*): hue matches, tetrachromacy, and intensity discrimination" *Journal of Comparative Physiology A, Neuroethology, Sensory, Neural, and Behavioral Physiology* 191 933-951

Gregory R L, 1968 "Perceptual illusions and brain models" *Proceedings of the Royal Society of London, Series B* 171 279-296

Jarvis E D, Güntürkün O, Bruce L, Csillag A, Karten H, Kuenzel W, Medina L, et al (there are 22 further authors), 2005 "Avian brains and a new understanding of vertebrate evolution" *Nature Reviews Neuroscience* 6 151-159

McCauley R N, Henrich J, 2006 "Susceptibility to the Müller-Lyer illusion, theory-neutral observation, and the diachronic penetrability of the visual system" *Philosophical Psychology* 19 79-101

Mountjoy P T, 1958 "Effects of exposure time and intertrial interval upon decrement to the Müller-Lyer illusion" *Journal of Experimental Psychology* 56 97-102

Müller-Lyer F C, 1889/1981 "Optische Urtheilstäuschungen" *Archiv für Anatomie und Physiologie*, "The contributions of F.C. Müller-Lyer" *Perception* 10 126-146

Nakamura N N, Fujita K F, Ushitani T U, Miyata H M, 2005 "Perception of the Müller-Lyer illusion in pigeons and humans", paper presented at the International Ethological Congress, Budapest, August

Nakamura N, Fujita K, Ushitani T, Miyatat H, 2006 "Perception of the standard and the reversed Müller-Lyer figures in pigeons (*Columbia livia*) and humans (*Homo sapiens*)" *Journal of Comparative Psychology* 120 252-261

Otto-deHaart G, Carey D P, Milne A B, 1999 "More thoughts on perceiving and grasping the Müller-Lyer illusion" *Neuropsychologia* 37 1437-1444

Pepperberg I M, 1981 "Functional vocalizations by an African Grey parrot (*Psittacus erithacus*)" *Zeitschrift für Tierpsychologie* 55 139-160

Pepperberg I M, 1992 "Proficient performance of a conjunctive, recursive task by an African Grey parrot (*Psittacus erithacus*)" *Journal of Comparative Psychology* 108 36-44

Pepperberg I M, 1999 The Alex Studies: Cognitive and Communicative Abilities of Grey Parrots (Cambridge, MA: Harvard University Press)

Pepperberg I M, 2006 "Addition of a Grey Parrot (*Psittacus erithacus*) including absence of quantity" *Journal of Comparative Psychology* 120 1-11

Pepperberg I M, Brezinsky M V, 1991 "Acquisition of a relative class concept by an African Grey Parrot (*Psittacus erithacus*): Discriminations based on relative size" *Journal of Comparative Psychology* 105 286-294

Pepperberg I M, Wilkes S R, 2004 "Lack of referential vocal learning from LCD video by Grey parrots (*Psittacus erithacus*)" *Interaction Studies* 5 75-97

Predebon J, 2004 "Selective attention and asymmetry in the Müller-Lyer illusion" *Psychonomic Bulletin Review* 11 916-920

Regolin L, Marconato F, Vallortigara G, 2004 "Hemispheric differences in the recognition of partly occluded objects by newly hatched domestic chicks (*Gallus gallus*)" *Animal Cognition* 7 162-170

Segall M, Campbell D, Herskovitz M J, 1966 *The Influence of Culture on Visual Perception* (New York: Bobs-Merrill)

Sekuler R, Erlebacher A, 1971 "The two illusions of Müller-Lyer: Confusion theory re-examined" *American Journal of Psychology* 84 477-486

Turnbull O H, Driver J, McCarthy R A, 2004 "2D but not 3D: Pictorial deficits in a case of visual agnosia" *Cortex* 40 723-738

Vallar G, Daini R, Antonucci G, 2000 "Processing of an illusion of length in spatial hemineglect: study of bisection" *Neuropsychologia* 38 1087-1097

van Hamme L J, Wasserman E A, Biederman I, 1992 "Discrimination of contour-deleted images by pigeons" *Journal of Experimental Psychology: Animal Behavior Processes* 18 387-399

Walls G L, 1942 *The Vertebrate Eye and Its Adaptive Radiation* (Bloomfield Hills, MI: Cranbrook Institute of Science) page 295

Warden D J, Baar J, 1929 "The Müller-Lyer illusion in the ring dove, *Turtur risorius*" *Journal of Comparative Psychology* 9 275-292

Weidner R, Fink G R, 2007 "The neural mechanisms underlying the Müller-Lyer illusion and its interaction with visuospatial judgments" *Cerebral Cortex* 17 878-884

Wilkie S E, Vissers P M A M, Das D, DeGrip W J, Bowmaker J K, Hunt D M, 1998 "The molecular basis for UV vision in birds: spectral characteristics, cDNA sequence and retinal localization of the UV-sensitive visual pigment of the budgerigar (*Melopsittacus undulates*)" *Biochemical Journal* 330 541-547

Winslow C N, 1933 "Visual illusions in the chick" *Archives of Psychology* 153 1-83

Zanker J M, Abdullah A K, 2004 "Are size illusions in simple line drawings affected by shading" *Perception* 33 1475-1482

(2008)

Questions

1. In what respects does Alex experience the illusion in the same way as human beings? What do these similarities suggest?

2. Why do Pepperberg et al. choose to focus on optical illusion, and why do they choose the Müller-Lyer illusion in particular?

3. What are the advantages of using a single trained animal such as Alex in an experiment? What are the disadvantages?

Questions on connections between this article and the following selection from Pepperberg's book Alex & Me *can be found at the end of that selection.*

Irene Pepperberg

from ALEX & ME:

HOW A SCIENTIST AND A PARROT UNCOVERED A HIDDEN WORLD OF ANIMAL INTELLIGENCE—AND FORMED A DEEP BOND IN THE PROCESS

In Alex & Me, *Irene Pepperberg recounts the thirty years she spent as a researcher conducting experiments with Alex, a Grey parrot. Alex could communicate with a vocabulary of over one hundred words, apply concepts, and count and add as well as a young child.*

☙

I had been thinking about doing work on optical illusions with Alex ever since I was at the Media Lab. In the summer of 2005, I teamed up with Patrick Cavanagh, a psychology professor at Harvard, to put the idea into practice. The human brain plays many tricks on us, so we sometimes see things not as they are. Patrick and I planned to ask a simple but profound question: does Alex *literally* see the world as we do? That is, does his brain experience the optical illusions just as our brains do?

I envisaged this work as the next horizon in my journey with Alex, beyond naming objects or categories or numbers. Bird and human brains diverged evolutionarily some 280 million years ago. Does that mean that bird and mammalian brains are so different structurally that they operate very differently, too?

Until a landmark paper by Eric Jarvis and colleagues in 2005, the answer to this question had been a resounding *yes!* Look at a mammalian brain and you are struck by the multiple folds of the massive cerebral cortex. Bird brains, it was said, don't have such a cortex. Hence, their cognitive capacity should be extremely limited. This, essentially, was the argument I had faced through three decades of work with Alex. He was not supposed to be able to name objects and categories, understand "bigger" and "smaller," "same" and "different," because his was a bird brain. But, of course, Alex did do such things. I knew that Alex was proving a profound truth: brains may look different, and there may be a spectrum of ability that is determined by anatomical details, but brains and intelligence are a universally shared trait in nature—the capacity varies, but the building blocks are the same.

By the turn of the millennium, my argument was beginning to gain ground. It wasn't just my work with Alex but others' work, too. Animals were being granted a greater degree of intelligence than had been previously allowed. One sign of this was that I was asked to co-chair a symposium at the 2002 annual meeting of the American Association for the Advancement of Science, called "Avian Cognition: When Being Called 'Bird Brain' Is a Compliment." The preamble read as follows: "This symposium demonstrates that many avian species, despite brain architectures that lack much cortical structure and evolutionary histories and that differ so greatly from those of humans, equal and sometimes surpass humans with respect to various cognitive tasks." Even five years earlier, such a symposium would have been a difficult sell. That was progress. Jarvis's paper three years later effectively said that bird and mammalian brains are not so very structurally different after all. More progress.

When Patrick and I submitted our grant proposal to the National Science Foundation in July 2006, we were expecting that, in some respects at least, Alex would see the world as we do. We didn't wait to hear whether we would be funded before we embarked on some preliminary work. We chose a well-known illusion as the first test. You have probably seen it in psychology textbooks and popular articles: two parallel lines of equal length, both with arrows at the ends, one with the arrows pointing out, the other with the arrows pointing in. Despite being the same length, the line with the arrows pointing in looks longer to human eyes. That's the illusion. We had to modify the test a little so as to use Alex's unique abilities; we varied the color of the two lines, keeping the arrows black. We then asked, "What color bigger/smaller?" Right away, and repeatedly, Alex selected the one that you or I would choose. He did see the world as we do, at least with this illusion. That was a very promising step.

By June 2007, Patrick and I were pretty sure that we would get our grant, and by the end of August we learned that it would start on September 1, a Saturday. We would have money for a year. The following Monday we

5

threw a party to celebrate, on the seventh floor of Harvard's William James Hall. I was especially happy, and relieved to see my financial woes lessen.

I'd been teaching part-time at Harvard's Extension School since 2006 and in the psychology department beginning in 2007. I survived with a little extra income from The Alex Foundation, but it still had meant tofu and a 57-degree thermostat setting for me. The new grant would change all that. I would become a regular research associate, with a small but decent salary and benefits. And 35 percent of the lab costs would be covered. That was $35,000 less I would have to raise for that year. I could not have been happier. It wasn't a tenured professorship, but it was quite an improvement.

Alex was a little subdued that week, though nothing out of the ordinary. The birds had had some kind of infection the previous month, but they were now fine. The vet had given them all a clean bill of health. On the afternoon of Wednesday the fifth, Adena Schachner joined me and Alex in the lab. She is a graduate student in the psychology department at Harvard, researching in the origins of musical abilities. We thought it would be interesting to do some work with Alex. That evening, we wanted to see what types of music engaged him. Adena played some eighties disco, and Alex had a good time, bobbing his head in time with the beat. Adena and I danced to some of the songs while Alex bobbed along with us. Next time, we promised ourselves, we would get more serious about the music work.

The following day, Thursday the sixth, Alex wasn't much interested in working on phonemes with two of the students during the morning session. "Alex very uncooperative in the task. Turned around," they wrote in Alex's work log. By midafternoon he was much more engaged, this time with a simple task of correctly suggesting a colored cup, underneath which was a nut. I arrived at five o'clock, as usual. Arlene had left for the day. She and the students had already moved the floor mats to one side for the regular Friday morning cleaning by the maintenance crew. Shannon Cabell, a student, was with me. We sat at the computer, with Alex between us on his perch, looking at the screen. I was working on new optical illusion tests, trying to get the colors and shapes right—nothing demanding, just fiddling with things. Alex was affectionate and chatty as usual.

10   At six forty-five the supplemental lights went on, as usual, a signal that we had a few minutes left to clean up. Then the main lights went off, and it was time to put the birds in their cages: Wart first, then Alex, then the always reluctant Griffin.

"You be good. I love you," Alex said to me.

"I love you too," I replied.

"You'll be in tomorrow?"

"Yes," I said, "I'll be in tomorrow." That was our usual parting exchange. Griffin and Wart said nothing, as usual.

I left and drove forty minutes to my home in Swampscott, on the North   15
Shore. I went through email, had a bite to eat and a glass of wine, and went to bed.

(2008)

Questions

1. Why would research into optical illusions represent "the next horizon" in Pepperberg's work with Alex?

2. The morning after this excerpt concludes, Alex is unexpectedly found dead in his cage. How is this piece of the book written to shape the later emotional impact of Alex's death?

3. Is Pepperberg's treatment of Alex ethical? Why or why not?

Questions on "Processing of the Müller-Lyer Illusion by a Grey Parrot" and Alex & Me

1. In *Alex & Me*, Pepperberg mentions the experiment discussed in the article. Compare and contrast her abstract of the article with her recounting of the experiment in the book, discussing both the content and the tone.

2. Pepperberg devotes more attention to Alex's personality in *Alex & Me* than she does in her scholarly article. Is this appropriate? Why or why not? Having read both, can you see evidence of Alex's personality in the article?

3. a)   Pepperberg writes elsewhere in *Alex & Me* that the "single greatest lesson" her experiments with Alex revealed is that "animal minds are a great deal more like human minds than the vast majority of behavioral scientists believed." "This insight," she writes, "has profound implications, philosophically, sociologically, and practically." What are some of these implications?

b) In Peter Singer's article "Speciesism and the Equality of Animals," reprinted elsewhere in this anthology, he argues that the capacity to suffer must replace intelligence as our primary measure of how to treat animals ethically. Which is more important in defining the relationship between (and moral value of) human and non-human animals—intelligence or the capacity for suffering? Give an argument in support of each, and then explain what you believe.

WILLIAM F. BAKER, D. STANTON KORISTA,
AND LAWRENCE C. NOVAK

ENGINEERING THE WORLD'S TALLEST—BURJ DUBAI

Burj Dubai, renamed Burj Khalifa since the publication of this article, was the world's tallest human-made structure when it was completed in 2010. Here, Baker, Stanton, and Novak describe the innovations that made the building possible.

☙

ABSTRACT

The goal of the Burj Dubai Tower is not simply to be the world's highest building; it is to embody the world's highest aspirations. The super-structure is currently under construction and as of fall 2007 has reached over 150 stories. The final height of the building is a "well-guarded secret." The height of the multi-use skyscraper will "comfortably" exceed the current record holder, the 509 meter (1671 ft) tall Taipei 101. The 280,000 m² (3,000,000 ft²) reinforced concrete multi-use Burj Dubai tower is utilized for retail, a Giorgio Armani Hotel, residential and office.

As with all super-tall projects, difficult structural engineering problems needed to be addressed and resolved. This paper presents the structural system for the Burj Dubai Tower.

STRUCTURAL SYSTEM DESCRIPTION

Designers purposely shaped the structural concrete Burj Dubai—"Y" shaped in plan—to reduce the wind forces on the tower, as well as to keep the structure simple and foster constructability. The structural system can be described as a "buttressed" core (Figur[e] 1 ...). Each wing, with its

643

own high performance concrete corridor walls and perimeter columns, buttresses[1] the others via a six-sided central core, or hexagonal hub. The result is a tower that is extremely stiff laterally and torsionally.[2] SOM[3] applied a rigorous geometry to the tower that aligned all the common central core, wall, and column elements.

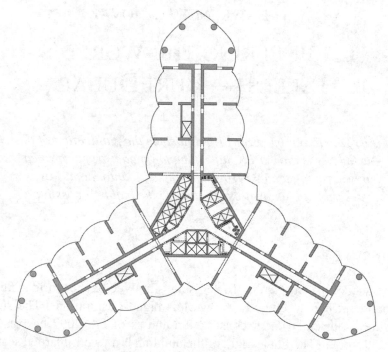

Figure 1—Typical Floor Plan.

Each tier of the building sets back in a spiral stepping pattern up the building. The setbacks are organized with the Tower's grid, such that the building stepping is accomplished by aligning columns above with walls below to provide a smooth load path.[4] This allows the construction to proceed without the normal difficulties associated with column transfers.

The setbacks are organized such that the Tower's width changes at each setback. The advantage of the stepping and shaping is to "confuse the

5

---

1   *buttresses*   I.e., supports.

2   *stiff … torsionally*   I.e., resistant to pressure from the side and to twisting.

3   *SOM*   Skidmore, Owings & Merrill, the firm that developed the structural design.

4   *load path*   Transfer of force from one component of the structure to another.

wind." The wind vortices never get organized because at each new tier the wind encounters a different building shape.

The Tower and Podium structures are currently under construction ... and the project is scheduled for topping out in 2008.

DEFINITION OF WORLD'S TALLEST

From the outset, it has been intended that the Burj Dubai be the World's Tallest Building. The official arbiter of height is the Council on Tall Buildings and Urban Habitat (CTBUH) founded at Lehigh University in Bethlehem, Pennsylvania, and currently housed at the Illinois Institute of Chicago in Chicago, Illinois. The CTBUH measures the height of buildings using four categories (measured from sidewalk at the main entrance). The categories and current record holders are as follows:

1. Highest Occupied Floor:
    Taipei 101   439m
2. Top of Roof:
    Taipei 101   449m
3. Top of Structure:
    Taipei 101   509m
4. Top of Pinnacle, Mast, Antenna or Flagpole:
    Sears Tower   527m

Although not considered to be a "building" the Tallest Freestanding Structure is:
    CN Tower   553m

Although the final height of the Tower is a well-guarded secret, Burj Dubai will be the tallest by a significant amount in all the above categories.[5]

ARCHITECTURAL DESIGN

The context of Burj Dubai being located in the city of Dubai, UAE,[6] drove the inspiration for the building form to incorporate cultural and historical

10

---

5   *tallest by ... above categories*   At 828m high upon its completion, the tower, as predicted, surpassed the previous record holders in all of these categories.

6   *UAE*   United Arab Emirates.

[elements] particular to the region. The influences of the Middle Eastern domes and pointed arches in traditional buildings, spiral imagery in Middle Eastern architecture, resulted in the tri-axial geometry of the Burj Dubai and the tower's spiral reduction with height....

The Y-shaped plan is ideal for residential and hotel usage, with the wings allowing maximum outward views and inward natural light.

Figure 4—Construction Photo.

Structural Analysis and Design

The center hexagonal reinforced concrete core walls provide the torsional resistance of the structure similar to a closed tube or axle. The center hexagonal walls are buttressed by the wing walls and hammer head walls which behave as the webs and flanges[7] of a beam to resist the wind shears

---

7   *webs and flanges*   I.e., connecting and supporting elements.

and movements. Outriggers[8] at the mechanical floors allow the columns to participate in the lateral load resistance of the structure; hence, all of the vertical concrete is utilized to support both gravity and lateral loads. The wall concrete specified strengths ranged from C80 to C60 cube strength[9] and utilized Portland cement[10] and fly ash.[11] Local aggregates were utilized for the concrete mix design. The C80 concrete for the lower portion of the structure had a specified Young's Elastic Modulus[12] of 43,800 N/mm² (6,350ksi) at 90 days. The wall and column sizes were optimized using virtual work/LaGrange multiplier methodology[13] which results in a very efficient structure (Baker et al., 2000).

The wall thicknesses and column sizes were fine-tuned to reduce the effects of creep[14] and shrinkage[15] on the individual elements which compose the structure. To reduce the effects of differential column shortening, due to creep, between the perimeter columns and interior walls, the perimeter columns were sized such that the self-weight gravity stress on the perimeter columns matched the stress on the interior corridor walls. The five (5) sets of outriggers, distributed up the building, tie all the vertical load carrying elements together, further ensuring uniform gravity stresses; hence, reducing differential creep movements. Since the shrinkage of concrete occurs more quickly in thinner walls or columns, the perimeter column thickness of 600mm (24") matched the typical corridor wall thickness (similar volume to surface ratios) ... to ensure the columns and walls will generally shorten at the same rate due to concrete shrinkage....

---

8   *Outriggers*   Supports extending outward from the building.

9   *cube strength*   The load per unit area at which a cube of Portland cement fails when tested in a standardized manner.

10   *Portland cement*   A commonly-used water-resistant cement.

11   *fly ash*   A residue generated when coal is burned, which is often used in combination with Portland cement.

12   *Young's Elastic Modulus*   The stiffness of a material, indicated by a ratio of stress to strain. It is measured in units of pressure: here, either milli-pascals (N/mm²) or kilopounds of force per square inch (ksi).

13   *LaGrange multiplier methodology*   A mathematical strategy, used in this case to determine the most efficient measurements for the building.

14   *creep*   The gradual deformation of a structure due to stress.

15   *shrinkage*   The decrease in volume of concrete due to drying and chemical changes over time.

Foundations and Site Conditions

The Tower foundations consist of a pile supported raft.[16] The solid reinforced concrete raft is 3.7 meters (12 ft) thick and was poured utilizing C50 (cube strength) self consolidating concrete (SCC). The raft was constructed in four (4) separate pours (three wings and the center core). Each raft pour occurred over at least a 24 hour period. Reinforcement was typically at 300mm spacing in the raft, and arranged such that every 10th bar in each direction was omitted, resulting in a series of "pour enhancement strips" throughout the raft at which 600mm x 600mm openings at regular intervals facilitated access and concrete placement....

The groundwater in which the Burj Dubai substructure is constructed is particularly severe, with chloride concentrations of up to 4.5%, and sulphates of up to 0.6%. The chloride and sulfate concentrations found in the ground water are even higher than the concentrations in sea water. Due to the aggressive conditions present due to the extremely corrosive groundwater, a rigorous program of measures was required to ensure the durability of the foundations. Measures implemented include specialized waterproofing systems, increased concrete cover,[17] the addition of corrosion inhibitors to the concrete mix, stringent crack control design criteria and an impressed current cathodic[18] protection system utilizing titanium mesh.... A controlled permeability formwork liner was utilized for the Tower raft which results in a higher strength/lower permeable concrete cover to the rebar. Furthermore, a specially designed concrete mix was formulated to resist attack from the ground water. The concrete mix for the piles was a 60 MPa[19] mix based on a triple blend with 25% fly ash, 7% silica fume,[20] and a water to cement ratio of 0.32. The concrete was also designed as fully self consolidating concrete, incorporating a viscosity modifying admixture with a slump flow[21] of 675 +/- 75mm to limit the possibility of defects during construction.

---

16   *raft*   A type of foundation designed to prevent settlement.

17   *concrete cover*   Distance between the embedded reinforcement and surface of the concrete.

18   *cathodic*   Using polarized electrodes.

19   *MPa*   Milli-pascals.

20   *silica fume*   A substance that is commonly added to Portland cement to increase its strength and resistance to corrosion.

21   *slump flow*   A measure of consistency.

WIND ENGINEERING

For a building of this height and slenderness, wind forces and the result-ing motions in the upper levels become dominant factors in the structural design. An extensive program of wind tunnel tests and other studies were undertaken under the direction of Dr. Peter Irwin of Rowan Williams Davies and Irwin Inc.'s (RWDI) boundary layer wind tunnels in Guelph, Ontario.... The wind tunnel program included rigid-model force balance tests,[22] a full multi degree of freedom aeroelastic model studies,[23] mea-surements of localized pressures, pedestrian wind environment studies and wind climatic studies. Wind tunnel models account for the cross wind effects of wind induced vortex shedding on the building.... The aeroelastic and force balance studies used models mostly at 1:500 scale. The RWDI wind engineering was peer reviewed by Dr. Nick Isyumov of the University of Western Ontario Boundary Layer Wind Tunnel Laboratory.

In addition to the structural loading tests, the Burj Dubai tower was studied by RWDI for cladding,[24] pedestrian level, and stack effect[25] (Irwin et al., 2006)

To determine the wind loading on the main structure wind tunnel tests were undertaken early in the design using the high-frequency-force-balance technique.[26] The wind tunnel data were then combined with the dynamic properties of the tower in order to compute the tower's dynamic response and the overall effective wind force distributions at full scale. For the Burj Dubai the results of the force balance tests were used as early input for the structural design and detailed shape of the Tower and allowed parametric studies to be undertaken on the effects of varying the tower's stiffness and mass distribution....

Several rounds of force balance tests were undertaken as the geom-etry of the tower evolved and was refined. The three wings set back in a clockwise sequence with the A wing setting back first. After each round of wind tunnel testing, the data was analyzed and the building was reshaped

---

22 *rigid-model ... tests* Tests which estimate the overall effects of wind forces by measuring the movements at the base of a lightweight model.

23 *aeroelastic model studies* Studies mapping deformity due to aerodynamic forces.

24 *cladding* Exterior covering.

25 *stack effect* Movement of air into and out of the building.

26 *high ... technique* Wind-tunnel method involving a model mounted on a highly sensitive balance.

to minimize wind effects and accommodate unrelated changes in the Client's program. In general, the number and spacing of the set backs changed as did the shape of wings. This process resulted in a substantial reduction of wind forces on the tower by "confusing" the wind (Figur[e] 16 ...) by encouraging disorganized vortex shedding over the height of the tower.

Figure 16—Tower Massing.

Long-Term and Construction Sequence Analysis

Historically, engineers have typically determined the behavior of concrete [27] structures using linear-elastic finite element analysis[27] and/or summations of vertical column loads. As building height increases, the results of such conventional analysis may increasingly diverge from actual behavior. Long-term, time-dependant deformations in response to construction sequence, creep, and shrinkage can cause redistribution of forces and gravity induced sidesway that would not be detected by conventional methods. When the time-dependant effects of construction, creep, shrinkage, variation of concrete stiffness with time, sequential loading and foundation settlements are not considered, the predicted forces and deflections may be inaccurate. To account for these time-dependant concrete effects in the Burj Dubai Tower structure, a comprehensive construction sequence analysis incorporating the effects of creep and shrinkage was utilized to study the time-dependant behavior of the structure (Baker et al., 2007)....

20

Construction

The Burj Dubai utilizes the latest advancements in construction techniques and material technology. The walls are formed using Doka's SKE 100 automatic self-climbing formwork system.... The circular nose columns are formed with steel forms, and the floor slabs are poured on MevaDec formwork. Wall reinforcement is prefabricated on the ground in 8m sections to allow for fast placement.

The construction sequence for the structure has the central core and slabs being cast first, in three sections; the wing walls and slabs follow behind; and the wing nose columns and slabs follow behind these.... Concrete is distributed to each wing utilizing concrete booms which are attached to the jump form system. Due to the limitations of conventional surveying techniques, a special GPS monitoring system has been developed to monitor the verticality of the structure. The construction survey work is being supervised by Mr. Doug Hayes, Chief Surveyor for the Burj Dubai Tower, with the Samsung BeSix Arabtec Joint Venture.

---

27 *linear ... analysis* A form of structural analysis used to approximate the ways a building will deform over time due to internal stresses.

Conclusion

When completed, the Burj Dubai Tower will be the world's tallest structure. The architects and engineers worked hand in hand to develop the building form and the structural system, resulting in a tower which efficiently manages its response to the wind, while maintaining the integrity of the design concept.

It represents a significant achievement in terms of utilizing the latest design, materials, and construction technology and methods, in order to provide an efficient, rational structure to rise to heights never before seen.

Project Team

Owner: Emaar Properties PJSC
Project Manager: Turner Construction International
Architect/Structural Engineers/MEP Engineers: Skidmore, Owings & Merrill LLP
Adopting Architect & Engineer/Field Supervision: Hyder Consulting Ltd.
Independent Verification and Testing Agency: GHD Global Party Ltd.
General Contractor: Samsung/BeSix/Arabtec
Foundation Contractor: NASA Multiplex

References[28]

Baker, Korista, Novak, Pawlikowski & Young (2007), *"Creep & Shrinkage and the Design of Supertall Buildings—A Case Study: The Burj Dubai Tower"*, ACI SP-246: Structural Implications of Shrinkage and Creep of Concrete.

Baker, Novak, Sinn & Viise (2000), *"Structural Optimization of 2000-Foot Tall 7 South Dearborn Building"*, Proceedings of the ACSE Structures Congress 2000—Advanced Technology in Structural Engineering and 14th Analysis & Computational Conference.

Irwin, Baker, Korista, Weismantle & Novak (2006), *"The Burj Dubai Tower: Wind Tunnel Testing of Cladding and Pedestrian Level"*, Structure Magazine, published by NCSEA, November 2006, pp 47-50.

(2008)

---

28 References have been excerpted to show only those cited in the included material.

Questions

1. Baker et al. say that, in designing the tower, "difficult structural engineering problems needed to be addressed and resolved." What are some of the problems they discuss? How did they overcome these challenges?

2. The construction of the tower cost about $1.5 billion in US dollars. Do you think the cost was worthwhile? Why or why not?

3. This article is primarily intended for an expert audience. Using the information in the article, write a short piece that could appear in a newspaper or magazine for general readers. Explain how the tone and content of your piece differ from the original.

PEGGY ORENSTEIN

STOP YOUR SEARCH ENGINES

In this article for The New York Times Magazine,
*autobiographer Peggy Orenstein wonders if
"forcing ourselves offline may be the path to true knowledge."*

❧

Not long ago, I started an experiment in self-binding: intentionally creating an obstacle to behavior I was helpless to control, much the way Ulysses lashed himself to his ship's mast to avoid succumbing to the Sirens' song. In my case, though, the irresistible temptation was the Internet. But before I began, I wondered about the genesis of the term "self-binding." So I hopped online and found Jon Elster, a professor of political science at Columbia University, whose book "Ulysses Unbound" explores whether voluntarily restricting your choices enhances or curtails freedom.

That reminded me: I hadn't read "The Odyssey" since college, and because I was pretty sure that my copy was at the bottom of a carton of books in faraway Minneapolis, I Googled the original text. I browsed several versions before downloading what seemed like the best translation. Because my interest lay specifically with the Sirens (quick Web break to make sure that should be uppercase), I sifted through a variety of classicists' interpretations of their role. Then—and this seemed reasonable enough—I searched for the "Sirens" episode in James Joyce's "Ulysses." I can't quite recollect how I got to the video for the song "Sirens," by the alternative rock group AVA, but that put me in mind of Blink-182 (with whom AVA shares a frontman), so I clicked over to that band's site to check for any updates on the release of its new album, then watched its reunion performance from February's Grammy Awards.... When I looked up, three and a half hours had passed.

And that is why I need the mast. It came in the form of an app called Freedom, which blocks your Internet access for up to eight hours at a stretch.

The only way to get back online is to reboot your computer, which—though not as foolproof as, say, removing the modem entirely and overnighting it to yourself (another strategy I've contemplated)—is cumbersome and humiliating enough to be an effective deterrent. The program was developed by Fred Stutzman, a graduate student in information and library science, whose own failsafe self-binding technique—writing at a cafe without Internet access—came undone when the place went wireless. "We're moving toward this era where we'll never be able to escape from the cloud," he told me. "I realized the only way to fight back was at an individual, personal level."

Freedom, which runs only on Macs, is downloaded more than 4,000 times a month. Stutzman says this mass-erosion of our self-control was inevitable, as the instrument of our productivity merged with that of our distraction: since computers have expanded from mere business tools to full-service entertainment centers. But I think there's something deeper going on as well. Those mythical bird-women (look it up) didn't seduce with beauty or carnality—not with petty diversions—but with the promise of unending knowledge. "Over all the generous earth we know everything that happens," they crooned to passing ships, vowing that any sailor who heeded their voices would emerge a "wiser man." That is precisely the draw of the Internet.

It is heartening that the yearning for learning is the most powerful of all human cravings (though it applies equally to obtaining the wisdom of Zeus or the YouTube video on how to peel a banana like a monkey). Yet the sea surrounding the Sirens was littered with corpses. Can increased knowledge really destroy us? 5

Well, yes. According to Elster, there are certainly occasions when choosing ignorance could be smart. You might decline, for instance, to undergo testing for the genetic marker for Huntington's disease, which is fatal and incurable. Or say you were an East German after reunification: would you want to read files that may show that your spouse had informed against you? As a culture, we have banned research on reproductive cloning, fearing how future generations might use the results.

In my slightly less agonizing situation, the trap is more of a bait and switch: the promise is of infinite knowledge, but what's delivered is infinite information, and the two are hardly the same. In that sense, Homer may have been the original neuropsychologist: centuries after his death, brain studies show that true learning is largely an unconscious process. If we're inundated with data, our brains' synthesizing functions are overwhelmed by the effort to keep up. And the original purpose—deeper knowledge of a subject—is lost, as surely as the corpses surrounding Sirenum scopuli.[1]

It could be that sometimes our greatest freedom may be to choose freedom from freedom. I am still surprised by the relief that floods me whenever I bind myself from going online, when I have no option but to ignore the incessant tweets and e-mail messages and videos and news links and even the legitimate research.

I'm not wishing the Internet away. It has become so integral to my work—to my *life*—that I honestly can't recall what I did without it. But it has allowed us to reflexively indulge every passing interest, to expect answers to every fleeting question, to believe that if we search long enough, surf a little further, we can hit the dry land of knowing "everything that happens" and that such knowledge is both possible and desirable. In the end, though, there is just more sea, and as alluring as we can find the perpetual pursuit of little thoughts, the net result may only be to prevent us from forming the big ones.

(2009)

Questions

1. What does Orenstein say is the difference between knowledge and information?

2. What does Orenstein mean when she says that "sometimes our greatest freedom may be to choose freedom from freedom"? Is this true?

3. Discuss the role of the metaphor of the Sirens in this article.

4. In this article, Orenstein describes one way the Internet has changed our relationship to knowledge. Brainstorm other ways—both good and bad—the Internet might affect the way we think. Overall, do you think the impact of the Internet on thought is positive or negative?

---

1   *Sirenum scopuli*   Rocky island home of the Sirens.

Neal McLeod

Cree Poetic Discourse

*In this academic article an Indigenous poet advocates
a narrative-based approach to Cree scholarship.*

❧

Introduction

In many Indigenous Studies departments throughout Canada, the discipline has been put into the category of social science. Such an approach, while effective on some levels, does narrative violence to the integrity of Indigenous narrative knowing. By narrative violence, I mean that Indigenous narratives are sanitized and there is a conceptual shift that often takes the vitality away from Indigenous life-worlds. Within the United States, writers such as Robert Warrior, Paula Allen Gunn, and many others have encouraged the use of literary paradigms to examine Indigenous knowledge; they have also, in large part, resisted the narrative violence inflicted upon Indigenous knowing in the academic institutions within Canada.

Thinking poetically involves the movement away from the epistemological straitjacket and the colonial box that the social sciences have often placed on Indigenous narratives. Thinking poetically gives us a space to recreate, although imperfectly, the narrative thinking of the greatest of our kêhtê-ayak, Old Ones, and our storytellers. This metaphorical discourse, composed of symbolic and poetic descriptions of the world and our experiences, saturates and permeates Cree narrative memory. I call this way of understanding the world through sound Cree poetics: Cree poetics link human beings to the rest of the world through the process of mamâhtâwisiwin, the process of tapping into the Great Mystery, which, in turn, is mediated by historicity and wâhkôhtowin (kinship). Louise Halfe's poetic interpretation of the classical Cree story Cihcîpiscikwân (Rolling Head) exemplifies the idea of Cree poetics. Halfe's poetic discourse embodies and is part of what I call a "body poetic," which connects our living bodies to the living earth around us.

NARRATIVE VIOLENCE OF CONVENTIONAL ACADEMIC DISCOURSE

Academia has also, in many ways, become an extension of the process of the colonialism of Indigenous people and the subordination of Indigenous narrative knowing. This colonialism is done in a tacit manner, and many people who critique it are dismissed as "radicals." Consequently, these individuals are excluded from the old boys' academic clubs, which are often exceptionally incestuous. Many of the adherents to the conventional academic disciplines pretend to be leading experts on Indigenous cultural and knowledge ways, which has been a particular problem in fields such as history and anthropology.

Vine Deloria, Jr., perhaps more than anyone, radically questioned the epistemological and narrative violence inflicted upon Indigenous people. He radically critiques the racism and colonialism that exist in the academy, as well as the culture of tokenism. What made Vine Deloria, Jr.'s critique of Western representations of Indigenous knowing so radical and effective was the fact that he did not care about the manufacturing of Indigenous knowledge within the academy. Ironically, he was hired because he radically attacked the status quo and grounded his position as a lawyer and social activist. While Vine Deloria, Jr. broke a great deal of ground conceptually, his position was like all positions, fundamentally limited because he did not make many culturally specific references within his work. In many ways, his work was a "negative sculpting" of what Indigenous knowledge was not in relationship to Christianity, modernity, and colonialism. By negative sculpting, I mean the way in which Deloria defines what Indigenous knowledge is not, as opposed to what it is.

5   Our narratives have been guided and dissected by academia; what is needed now is a new wave of writing and a new wave of Indigenous scholarship. As contemporary Indigenous scholars, we need to ground our discourses in culturally specific metaphors and ground ourselves in the languages of the ancient pathways of Indigenous thinking. In essence, we need to build the "positive space" of Indigenous knowledge. Writers such as Vine Deloria, Jr. were and are important because they were grounded in their communities and cultures; however, contemporary Indigenous scholarship

must be one of cultural specificity. Nimosôm[1] (my grandfather), John R. McLeod, a pioneer in the development of Indian control of Indian education, once said that he wished for the "creation of an Indian-controlled institution where the finest Indian thinking could occur." He thought poetically about our traditions by immersing himself in the stories, languages, and ceremonies of the kêhtê-ayak [Old Ones]. Part of this attempt to think poetically involved radically rethinking Christianity—just as Deloria did before him.

Ê-ÂNISKO-ÂCIMOCIK: CONNECTING THROUGH STORYTELLING

Ê-ânisko-âcimocik, literally translated, means "they connect through telling stories." The central strand in which Cree poetic discourse flourishes and continues is through the connection of contemporary storytellers and poets to the ancient poetic pathways of our ancestors. By drawing upon the epic and traditional narratives of our people, we can ground ourselves in culturally specific references and linguistic anchors, allowing us, in turn, to resist the onslaught of modernity and colonialism, which while related, are not the same.

One of the key components of Indigenous Studies involves the use of names. Names define and articulate a place within society and the world. Indigenous names are absolutely essential for the description of Indigenous realities. In order to describe this reality, we need words to shape and interpret it. For instance, we need to be able to name the process of poetry. In Cree, I would say that this process could be described as mamâhtâwisiwin [the process of tapping into the Great Mystery], which is mediated by our historicity and wâhkôhtowin (kinship). Because of this connection to other generations, there emerges an ethical dimension to Cree poetic discourse, namely, the moral responsibility to remember.

One of the challenges of linking to the old narrative memory is to keep the language and understandings inherent therein. My great-grandfather, Kôkôcîs, Peter Vandall, noted the importance of language and the need to preserve it in order to maintain ties between generations:

---

1   Generally Cree does not use capitals, but the author chooses to use capitals when nouns are embedded in English text so as not to privilege the English language. Also, the author chooses not to use the convention of italicizing Cree so as to avoid the status of Cree as a "foreign language." [author's note]

êwako aya, tâpiskôc ôki anohc, namôya tâpsikoc kiskinahamâtowin ôki nêhiyâsisak, mitoni nitawêyihtamwak nêhiyawak kahkiyaw, tâpiskôt otawâsimisiwâwa môniyaw-kiskêyihtamowin kit-âyayit.

It is that, for instance, the young Crees of today do not seem to want education, all of the Crees really want their children to have White-Man's knowledge. (Vandall 36)

Nicâpan (my great-grandfather) contrasts the western and Cree modes of education, and laments the way in which many Crees have seemingly turned their back on our narrative traditions. He describes how many have absorbed the epistemological and narrative violence inflicted upon our rich traditions. The consequence of this absorption is that we often do not value our traditions, turning, instead, to Western models and frameworks. It is precisely this internalization of colonization that Vine Deloria, Jr. radically attacked as well. In contrast, Nicâpan notes the importance of having dignity and pride in our narrative traditions:

êkwa namôya êkosi ta-kî-itôtahkik osk-âyak. ka-kî-kiskêyihtahkik ôma ê-nêhiyâwicik, êkwa onêhiyâwiwiniwâw anima namôya kakêtihk ê-itêyihtâkwaniyik.

Now, the young people should not do that. They should know that they are Cree, and that their Creeness means a great deal. (Vandall 36)

It should be noted that Nicâpan uses terms such as "seems like" and "it appears" to describe the way in which many people, especially young people, have turned their backs on ancient Cree poetic pathways: the way in which kêhtê-ayak transmit culture through stories and narratives. Such a narrative strategy allows people to change their behavior yet still save their honor in the process. It also invokes the power of ancient Cree poetic pathways as a way of restoring the dignity of his people, especially the younger ones. Within this process, there is a struggle to preserve a narrative genealogy, which differs from the trajectories of English-speaking scholarship and mainstream literatures. Our ancient poetic pathways are not a mimicry of colonial narrative structures, but are rather grounded in our own traditions and worldviews.

MAMÂHTÂWISIWIN: CREE POETIC PROCESS

Poetic thinking involves dreaming, relying on the visceral, like a painter or jazz musician. A poetic way of thinking urges us to radically rethink the surface of things, like a dreamer. Such thinking allows us to bring back the words and the depth of the Great Mystery that the kêhtê-ayak have already charted out (Ermine). In a way, thinking poetically is radically historical and does not mean the "narrative space" is ordered chronologically. Poetic thinking involves the bending of time to a single point of consciousness. That is why Vine Deloria, Jr. in *God is Red* so aptly noted that much Indigenous thinking is in terms of space instead of time. Mamâhtâwisiwin, the Cree poetic process, is mediated by not only historicity but also wâhkohtowin, including our kinship to the land. The process of mamâhtâwisiwin involves spirituality and the belief that reality is more than what we understand on the surface.

The term ê-mamâhtâwisit, the verb form of mamâhtâwisiwin, means he or she is "spiritually gifted." It could also be translated perhaps as "they know something that you will never know." Once I asked my friend Edward Caisse from Green Lake, Saskatchewan, about a line from Pulp Fiction: "she is a funky dancer." He said, "ê-mamâhtâwisimot" or "she or he knows something that you will never know by the way she dances." Sometimes old Cree words become toys for anthropologists and other cultural tourists, but it should be noted that these terms and ideas have great relevance today. For instance, one Cree term for computer is "mamâhtâwisi-âpacihcikan," which could be rendered as "the powerful machine." 10

"Ê-mamâhtâwisit Wisâhkêcâhk" is a common expression within Cree stories. It means that Kistêsinâw, our elder brother, "has the ability to tap into the Great Mystery." Because of this ability, Kistêsinâw was the first ceremonialist, trying to link living beings in this dimension to the force of life beyond our conscious reality. In the process, Wîsahkêcâhk transformed the world, made it safe for humans, and gave names and shapes to creation.

In Louise Halfe's powerful book *The Crooked Good*, the narrator Ê-kwêskît ("Turn around woman") talks about the origin of stories and the source of poetic insight as "[t]he gifted people of long ago, *kayâs kî-mamâhtâwisiwak iyiniwak*" (Halfe 3). She adds:

They never died. They are scattered here, there, everywhere, somewhere. They know the language, the sleep, the dream, the laws, these singers, these healers, *âtayôhkanak*, these ancient story keepers. (Halfe 3)

Just like Nôhtokwêw Âtayôhkan (the Old Grandmother Spirit) keeps the stories, the mamâhtâwisiwak, the poetic dreamers, keep ancient poetic pathways.

In *The Crooked Good*, Halfe discusses the classic Cree narrative Rolling Head and reframes it by retrieving the feminine voice through the sound of colonial imagination. In this work, Cree poetic memory is essential to the process of retrieving the hidden and submerged female perspective.

Ê-kwêskît: she notes that she is a "dreamer" (Halfe 4). She adds, "I dream awake. Asleep ... the day was the story" (Halfe 4). Part of the process is tapping into the Great Mystery, creating pathways for other dreamers. "The story" is always open and always open to re-examination: "So, every day, I am born" (Halfe 4). What Halfe means by this statement is that she can always add more to her journey through life and to her poetic pathway.

EMBODIED UNDERSTANDING

15 All poetic pathways are "embodied understandings" and are the poet-dreamer's location in understanding the world and reality. In many ways, this idea is similar to Gadamer's notion of *Urteil* ("the original place"). Through an embodied sense of awareness, one is about to link one's own experiences with a larger narrative structure. Through this embodied understanding, one is able to expand one's own understanding and also, in a small way, the larger collective memory.

Often times, this embodied memory involves everyday experience and everyday events. Stories are not abstract and cut off from the living world around but rather are completely enmeshed in the concrete world of sensations and physical connections. Embodied memory is the connection to sensations of the body and also the connection to the sensations of the land.

Marilyn Dumont's poem "âcimowina" in *A Really Good Brown Girl* is an interesting example of this living memory. She does not describe the stories of her grandmother directly but rather the sensations that emerge from the concrete world around. She opens her poem by making the stories (âcimowina) of her grandmother embodied:

> my grandmother stories follow me,
> spill out of their bulging suitcases
> get left under beds
> hung on doorknobs (Dumont 70)

The stories exist within her living place, her house, and are around her in all of the daily sensations: "their stories smell of Noxzema, mothballs and dried meat" (Dumont 70). The sensation of smell is indeed one of the strongest forms of awareness that we have. She also describes the stories in terms of medicines that are found around her house:

> their Polident dentures in old cottage cheese containers,
> Absorbine Junior, Buckley's and "rat root" take over my bathroom
>   counters (Dumont 70)

By drawing upon Dumont's description and words, we can immerse ourselves in the embodied elements of her grandmother's stories. This poetics of embodiment, of wâhkôhtowin, is also found in various Treaty narratives wherein concepts such as forever (in terms of how long the Treaties would last), which sound very distant and abstract within the English narrative, are rendered poetically embodied through the discourse of traditional knowledge keepers. The well-respected Jim Kâ-Nîpitêhtêw recited the classical Cree phrasing of this:

> hâw, êkos êkwa, êkw ôma k-ês-âsotamâtakok, kâkikê, iskoyikohk pîsim ka-pimohtêt, iskoyikohk sîpiy ka-pimiciwahk, iskoyikohk maskosiya kê-sâkikihiki, êkospî isko ka-pimotêmakan ôma k-ês-âsotamâtân.

> Indeed, thus now the promises which I have made for you, forever, so long as the sun shall cross [walk- N.M.] the sky, so long as the rivers shall run, so long as the grass shall grow, that is how long these promises I have made to you will last. (Kâ-Nîpitêhtêw 113)

Forever, then, is understood in relation to the concrete, living earth, and we come to understand its meaning through our connection to these elements.

Central to an embodied, poetic understanding of the world is what I would call the "poetics of empathy," which could be translated into Cree by the term "wâhkôhtowin" (kinship/relationships). Through relations, we are able to create the web of understanding of our embodied locations and stretch it outwards to a wider context of collective historicity and through a poetics grounded in dialogue and an open-ended flow of narrative understanding. A poetics of wâhkôhtowin and empathy are key to a thorough engaging with history. These concepts are at the heart of Louise Halfe's *The Crooked Good*. In her book of poetry, Halfe radically questions the way in which Cihcîpiscikwân (Rolling Head) has been told and urges us to recover the hidden female voice that has been shattered and altered by colonialism and Christianity. Describing this re-imagining of the narrative mapping, she states, "The story gnawed, teased our infinite heavens" (Halfe 22).

In the disseminated versions, the Rolling Head is portrayed as a disembodied woman who has been unfaithful to her husband and who, in turn, has been beheaded. She is also portrayed as a mother who pursues her children and who scares them in her pursuit. What is missing in these accounts is the empathy that we could feel for the mother as well as the embodied understanding of her voice and position within the narrative.

20   Empathy to Cihcîpiscikwân dramatically enlarges our understanding of the narrative and also moves to correct some of the extreme distortions caused by Christianity, such as the limiting of the role of women, which has often accompanied the colonization of Indigenous women and peoples. Halfe's radical reinterpretation brings back lost elements through narrative imagination, while recreating and redrawing ancient themes and ancient poetic pathways. Cihcîpiscikwân, following and attempting to recover our sons, marks the land and sky in the same way that Wîsâhkêcâhk did. Thus, Cihcîpiscikwân is a dreamer and ancient Cree poet.

Halfe describes the loss of Cihcîpiscikwân and, in particular, the destruction of the home: "Their home eaten by fire" (Halfe 26). The home has been altered and destroyed by a series of factors, not simply because of Rolling Head's infidelity. Another key factor intimated by Halfe is the fact that the husband has been away a great deal because of hunting trips. Rolling Head, through the named narrator of Ê-kwêskît and Rib Woman, regains her character and her point of view. The reshaped narrative gives her position form and embodiment. Halfe notes that Cihcîpiscikwân "dig[s] through *okiskêyihtamawin*—her knowledge/sad and lonely/more than her bitter medicine" (Halfe 16). Cihcîpiscikwân is portrayed as having lost a great deal—the father has pushed things beyond livable limits. By presenting the narrative in this manner, the storyteller gives birth to understanding, and we are empathetic to Cihcîpiscikwân. We feel her pain, and we feel her sorrow.

CIHCÎPISCIKWÂN: THE ROLLING HEAD NARRATIVE

Central to understanding the innovative way in which Louise Halfe has opened the interpretation of the Rolling Head narrative, it would be helpful to examine the narrative in some detail through an intra-textual dialogue. Cree poetic consciousness rests on the notion that a narrative can never exhaust its possibilities, as there are always new embodiments and new interpretative locations. The conversation and dialogue between these interpretative locations and interpretative embodiments also enriches the conversation.

Each telling of a story is an embodiment—by telling I mean in both oral and written forms. Each understanding is, in turn, embodied. Thus, our understanding of poetic narrative pathways is an occasion of speaking and, in turn, an occasion of understanding. Each occasion of speaking/ telling accounts for variations within the narratives and helps to explain differences between different accounts. The versions of narratives that have been committed to writing in various forms do not represent the totality of the speaker/teller, nor do they represent the totality of the possibilities of any narrative within a larger context. The occasion of speaking/telling, the demands of the audience, and the time in which the story is communicated alter the way in which the story is presented and, indeed, understood.

An interesting element in the occasion of the speaking/telling of the various versions of the Cihcîpiscikwân âtayôhkêwin (sacred story) is that one can analyze the narratives in the light of Christian influence. By examining the most "complete" version of the narrative, namely that of Edward Ahenakew, we see that the existence of the snake as a lover of Wîsakêcâhk's mother is most striking. A superficial reading would make it appear that the snake is perhaps a Christian influence, especially because Edward Ahenakew was an Anglican priest. What makes this hypothesis more plausible is that the Alanson Skinner text, recorded earlier, does not have the Trickster's mother's lover as a snake. Instead, the lover is simply in human form. It should be noted that there is a profound measure of overlap between the Plains Cree and the Plains Ojibway.

Skinner's representation of the lover in human form is also questionable because the Rolling Head and the Flood narrative cycle is scattered throughout Skinner's collection in fragments. From this, we can presume, apart from many of the narratives being summaries, that the stories would have also been told during shorter sessions. Thus, one of the ways in which we can account for the differences between these two representations is

25

related to issues of transcription and also to the fact that Edward Ahenakew was a cultural insider, a Cree from the Sandy Lake reserve. He represented the narratives himself and not through the distorting lens of an outsider anthropologist.

Another argument that the snake is a pre-Christian element is that the Leonard Bloomfield version, which was recorded in the 1930s (a few years after the Ahenakew version), also has the lover as a snake. The decisive counter-evidence that the lover of Cihcîpiscikwân was not a human, but a snake, is in the Bloomfield version: the storyteller consciously juxtaposes his version of creation with the Christian creation story. This juxtaposition would seemingly imply that he was extremely conscious of any Christian influence that may have been operative in the Cree world at the time.

The motif of the snake figures strongly within Cree narrative traditions. Louise Halfe's interpretation of the narrative opens us to non-Christian interpretations of understanding this central figure within the narrative of Cihcîpiscikwân and of a return to older ways of understanding snakes. For instance, there is a story told to me by Charlie Burns of Kâ-Monakos, which is also the origin story for the place name of Maskihkiy Âstôtin (Medicine Hat). Within the narrative, the Crees are surrounded by the Blackfoot, and Kâ-Monakos calls upon his helper the snake to create a tunnel through which the Crees can escape. Thus, in this story, the snake is a helper and not an evil entity as in the Christian framework. Opening this understanding allows us to be more empathetic to Rolling Head's lover and also, in turn, to Rolling Head.

TOWARDS A CRITICAL CREE POETIC CONSCIOUSNESS

Cree narrative memory is essentially open-ended, and different elements of a story can be emphasized during a single performance, which can be characterized as the "occasion of speaking/telling." In other words, there can never be a "complete" authoritative performance of a narrative because the audience and the demands of the occasion will always vary. Furthermore, a narrative can never be fully exhausted because the dynamics between the teller and the listener will also vary: the story will always be understood in slightly different ways depending on the experiences of people in the group listening. Such open-endedness within Cree poetic consciousness is the foundation of critical thinking. I would argue that Cree poetics is a first order act of theory and critical thinking. The storytellers, kâ-mamâhtâwisiwak, engaged in this process open up new possibilities of narratives in a variety of ways: finding new ways of interpreting old narratives in light of new experiences, recovering old voice echoes lost due to colonialism, and discovering new understandings of narratives due to intra-narrative dialogue (âniskwâpitamâcimowin: "the act of inter-textual connecting"). This model of critical consciousness reframes the notion of theory. Instead of theory being abstract and detached from concrete experience, theory (critical poetic consciousness) emerges out of concrete situations and through conversation and storyteller. In this way, then, our Elders and storytellers could be thought of as theorists and critical thinkers.

It is important to remember that Indigenous poetic consciousness does not simply involve a glorification of tradition but rather a radical questioning of tradition, albeit one that is grounded in it. This is perhaps one of the most important contributions of Louise Halfe's book *The Crooked Good*. The title itself reminds me of another of the core elements of Cree poetic thinking. Good and evil are not binary opposites but exist in all possibilities, all moments, and all beings. As Derrida has pointed out, the West has done epistemological violence to itself by thinking in terms of binaries, which distort a more holistic understanding of reality. This epistemological and narrative violence has by extension through colonialism been inflicted upon Indigenous people and their narratives and texts. Interestingly, the old narrative of Cihcîpiscikwân is described as a "nightmare" (Halfe 20) or an embodiment of trauma, which has occurred collectively through colonization but also existentially through the choices that we make in our daily lives.

In *The Crooked Good*, Louise Halfe helps us move beyond an essentialized understanding of the narrative of Cihcîpiscikwân. She moves towards an organic understanding of the story, and links a contemporary understanding to a past understanding, as evidenced in the last page of the book where the narrator Ê-kwêskît's words exist side by side with those of Rolling Head (Halfe 124). Through this intra-narrative dialogue, the ancient story becomes saturated with new layers and organically grows through the activity of narrative imagination. Narrative imaginations expand the interpretative possibilities of the sacred story and, in turn, the interpretative possibilities of the present moment and present reality. The narrative layering of the story engages our state of being embodied in a collective poetic pathway, allowing us to think critically of this positioning and, finally, to think of possibilities to reshape this embodied present. The central character, Cihcîpiscikwân, embodies this state of critical poetic consciousness: "*cihcipistikwân* stretches through her watery sleep/Phantom arms. Feels ... where does the gathering of the self begin?" (Halfe 19).

30

Mistasiniy: Linking to Ancient Poetic Pathways in my Own Work

In my own writing as poet, I have drawn heavily upon older Cree narratives. In particular, I have learned a great deal from Charlie Burns, storyteller from Nîhtâikihcikanisihk ("where there is good growing"—my reserve, the James Smith Cree reserve in north-eastern Saskatchewan). In particular, I remember one story, the story of Mistasiniy, which I included in my book *Cree Narrative Memory*. In my upcoming book of poetry, I rendered the narrative in the following way in excerpted form:

Mistasiniy

a boy was in a travois
wood cut earth
makes marks
tâpiskoc nêhiyawâsinahikan
like Cree writing, syllabics
pulled from sun
paths opened up
no light, and lets sun fall
through new cracks
napêsis with kôhkom
passing through prairie
travois holding baby body
loses in the pathway
paths of heard voices

boy was found
by a mosâpêw
buffalo bull
old, body cut
paths across prairie
his old body
memories of clustered
sun's passing
he sheltered the boy
from the wind
sâpowâstan, blowing through

another bull
younger challenged him
did not want
the orphan boy in the camp
he came from those
killed the buffalo, he said
they fought, raced
and the old buffalo won
keep the boy, and sheltered him
like trees hiding the earth
from open suspicious sky

as time gathered
created words and lost others
the boy was told
that he had to go home
mosôm buffalo gave stories
like body held memory
his body moving
ê-waskâwît

people in the boys camp
knew he was coming back
awa ê-kî-kôsapahtat
performed the ceremony
opened ground and sang songs
he came back, came home
but as he left
grandfather turned into stone (McLeod 2008)

Mistasiniy (the Grandfather stone) was destroyed in 1966 because two major waterways were to be joined in Saskatchewan. There was, indeed, a great campaign by many to try to save the stone or move it, but regrettably these efforts did not reach fruition. The narrative embodies the notion of wâhkôhtowin, as the stone embodies the relationship that people have to the buffalo. In addition, the narrative also marks the importance of adoption and the way in which we can raise children, who may not be ours biologically.

I adopted my son, Cody McLeod, and made sense of my adoption through thinking about the Mistasiniy. I wrote a poem about my understanding of the older narrative and I linked the older story organically to my life:

MEDITATIONS ON PASKWA-MOSTOS AWÂSIS

Buffalo Child
I remember
when you came to me
vulnerable, shy
unprotected from prairie wind
sickly, dry pasty skin
tired of open spaces
valley loses shelter
trees wind
through the end

Buffalo Child, paskwa-mostos awâsis
wakes the prairie grass
promises of his grandfather
you give your hide
your house of being
sit on open prairie
heavy and old standing earth
broken by dynamite
tears the line of old relationship
but the ancient stone
becomes my body

Buffalo Child
paskwa-mostos awâsis
rock has fallen
clipped from valley's embrace
but the story lives through
this boy
his body becomes
this ancient stone

> I took a boy in
> like Old Buffalo Grandfather
> as I tried my best to guide him
> I thought of this story often
>
> our bodies tattooed
> with land's memories
> with land speak, askiwêwin
> even though the stone is gone
> the story lives on
> old stories give our bodies shape
> and guide the path of sound
> like trees guiding the wind (McLeod 2008)

I understood that my son Cody was a living embodiment of that story and that the kinship tie to him had been marked in the land by Mistasiniy. These old stories mark our bodies with meaning and live on within us, despite colonial encroachments such as the destruction of the stone. This poem is also an example of the organic nature in which old narratives become alive through our lives and experiences. Cree poetic consciousness radically questions the way in which the West has framed "history" in progressive and teleological terms. Rather, narratives are alive and are embodied in the moment and historicity of our understanding, never fixed and always changing organically, like the colors and shapes in the sky, like the folds and contours of water on lakes.

CONCLUSION

Cree poetic discourse is an old, ancient activity, stretching back to the beginning of Cree consciousness and ceremonies. Mamâhtâwisiwin, "tapping into the Great Mystery," describes this process within the Cree language. If we are to move towards Indigenous Studies as a unique discipline, with its own intellectual and narrative trajectories, we must draw upon conceptual frameworks within Indigenous languages and cultures. Cree poetic discourse connects to old voice echoes—to the stories and embodied experience of the ancestors. Through our dialogue with these older stories (âniskwâpitamâcimowin), pathways of understanding are retraveled and indeed expanded. These poetic pathways are embodied and emerge from a concrete, tactile engagement with the world.

Not only do the ancient, poetic pathways become embodied, they also, through the process of âniskwâpitamâcimowin, of inter-textual narrative interchange, allow us to see beyond the contingencies of the present. In turn, this critical Cree consciousness allows us to re-imagine narratives and to envision and imagine new possibilities for the future. Cree poetic discourse is profoundly grounded in land and territory and ancestral knowledge. At the same time, contemporary poets, writers, and contemporary storytellers extend Cree poetic discourse into the present.

WORKS CITED

Ahenakew, Edward. "Cree Trickster Tales." *The Journal of American Folklore*, 42.166 (1929): 309-53.

Bloomfield, Leonard. *Plains Cree Texts*. New York: G.E. Stechert, 1934.

Burns, Charlie. "*kâ-monakos*" told orally to author many times since 2000.

Deloria, Vine, Jr. *God is Red: A Native View of Religion*. 1972. Golden, CO: Fulcrum, 1994.

Dumont, Marilyn. *A Really Good Brown Girl*. London: Brick Books, 1996.

Ermine, Willie. "Aboriginal Epistemology." *First Nations Education in Canada: The Circle Unfolds*. Ed. Marie Battiste and Jean Barman. Vancouver: U British Columbia P, 1995. 101-12.

Gadamer, Hans-Georg. *Truth and Method*. 1960. New York: Seabury Press, 1975.

Halfe, Louise. *The Crooked Good*. Regina: Couteau Press, 2007.

Kâ-Nîpitêhtêw, Jim (*pimwêwêhahk*). "The Pipestem and the Making of Treaty Six." *ana kâ-pimwêwêhahk okakêskihkêmowina*. Ed. and trans. Freda Ahenakew and H.C. Wolfart. Winnipeg: U of Manitoba P, 1998. 106-19.

McLeod, Neal. *Gabriel's Beach*. Regina: Hagios Press, 2008.

Skinner, Alanson. "Plains Ojibway Tales." *The Journal of American Folklore* 32.124 (1919): 280-305.

Vandall, Peter (*kôkôcîs*). "Being Cree." *wâskahikaniwiyiniw-âcimowina: Stories of the House People*. Ed. and trans. Fred Ahenakew. Winnipeg: U of Manitoba P, 1987. 36-37.

(2010)

Questions

1. McLeod uses Cree language in his essay, and many of his key concepts are expressed as Cree words.

   a) Explain the following in terms of their importance in the article: kêhtê-ayak, ê-ânisko-âcimocik, mamâhtâwisiwin, and wâhkôhtowin.

   b) Why does McLeod use the Cree words instead of English translations?

2. According to McLeod, why are "all poetic pathways ... 'embodied understandings'"?

3. In what way can Cree "Elders and storytellers ... be thought of as theorists and critical thinkers"?

4. In his poem "meditations on paskwa-mostos awâsis," how does McLeod see the relationship between the ancient story of Mistasiniy and his own life?

5. McLeod argues against the colonialism associated with conventional academic discourse. In terms of writing style and intellectual approach, how does this article compare with other academic essays you have read?

6. The approach to capitalization by McLeod and by a number of other Indigenous writers is to some degree unconventional. Identify some words capitalized in this selection that most writing guides would advise against capitalizing. What ethical or political point do you think the author may be making through his approach to capitalization? More generally, discuss his approach in the context of the tendency of many contemporary writers to employ capital letters much more frequently than writers of previous generations have done.

7. What do you take McLeod to mean when he says that "there can never be a 'complete' authoritative performance of a [Cree] narrative"? What are the advantages of this approach to narrative?

8. McLeod writes that there is "an ethical dimension to Cree poetic discourse, namely, the moral responsibility to remember." What does he mean by this? To what extent do poets and thinkers from other cultures have a similar moral responsibility to their own heritage, and to what extent is this ethical dimension unique to Indigenous discourses?

MICHAEL HARRIS

THE UNREPENTANT WHORE

*A Canadian investigative journalist creates a portrait of activist
Jamie Lee Hamilton and the social issues that inform her life.*

☙

One day in the deep end of winter, 1998, it rained on Vancouver's City Hall. It rained on the 6.9 Mercedes that pulled up to the entrance a little before noon. It rained on Jamie Lee Hamilton's good swing coat as she emerged from the car and lugged out four bulging garbage bags. It rained on the fourteen media crews that watched her carry the bags up the steps, hair plastered to her face. It rained on all of them as she dumped sixty-seven pairs of stilettos at the city's feet—one for every woman who she believed had gone missing from the Downtown Eastside.

Nobody knew that this was the start of the largest serial killer case in Canada's history; nor that Robert Pickton was still, then, taking women back to his pig farm on the outskirts of the city to mutilate and murder them; nor that, more than a decade later, in 2009, a constitutional appeal would argue that our country had systematically imperiled the lives of these women with brutal laws that forced them to work in untenable conditions. All Hamilton knew was that women—sex workers—were disappearing and nothing was being done.

If missing women are silenced women, Hamilton has made it her mission to be fully present and accounted for. An aboriginal, transsexual sex worker from one of the country's poorest neighborhoods, she's a kind of activist polyglot, able to speak with whatever voice best suits the situation. She presents as insistently at ease, adding "dear" and "honey" to her sentences like dollops of crème fraîche. Still, mention her name, and journalists, politicos, and armchair commentators turtle in their heads with alternating fear and exasperation: she's infamous for her public and embarrassing arguments with anyone who crosses her. (Even one of her fiercest supporters told me, "You'd be safer writing a profile of a Mafia don.")

Perhaps that's why her letters requesting a meeting with the mayor had been ignored, leaving her no choice but to show up at City Hall in person—and her person can be as intimidating as her reputation. Her face is hearty and galvanized with energy, the strength of her shoulders set off against plunging necklines. When Mayor Philip Owen emerged, she picked up a red sequined stiletto to present to him, thinking she could ask for a meeting in front of rolling cameras. Owen bolted.

Following this initial embarrassment, she pitched a tent on the lawn of City Hall and slept there until, a few days later, it went missing. When she reported the theft from a phone inside the building, the police asked, "Do you have any suspects?" Yes, she said in her gravelly voice: Mayor Philip Owen. City Hall gave her back the tent. But still no meeting.

Her final stand was soon afterward, on February 3, when she walked into a council meeting (having neglected to proceed through the required channels) and demanded an audience. The room emptied. But she stood at the mike for hours, anyway, waiting for a response. Once the media caught a whiff of "Crazy Shoe Lady, Part Three," city manager Ken Dobell delivered the news: "Okay, you've got your meeting."

"You're just the top city bureaucrat," returned Hamilton. "You get the mayor in his seat, on-camera, telling me I've got a meeting." So Owen did, and the struggle of sexual outliers had a new poster child.

In 1969, while a team of drag queens and friends rioted against police at New York's Stonewall Inn, sparking the North American gay rights movement, Jimmy Hamilton was a confused thirteen-year-old living in a Downtown Eastside housing project. His father—a union man who had worked at a foundry until silicosis of the lungs forced him into part-time work as a janitor at a burger joint—was furious that his son had turned out to be a "sissy." His mother, the revered aboriginal rights activist Alice Hamilton, took him to the REACH Community Health Centre, where a doctor asked Jimmy, "Do you think you're homosexual?"

Blink. "What do you mean?"

"Well," he said, searching for some delicate definition, "do you feel like a girl?"

"Oh, yes," Jimmy said, and was sent out. His mother was called in. Fifteen minutes later, when the boy poked his head around the door again, he found her in tears.

It could have been worse. Homosexuality was legalized in Canada that year, so instead of undergoing therapeutic "cures" (the sexual equivalent of an exorcism, and about as useful) Jimmy rode the bus from his housing project out to the University of British Columbia, where his counseling sessions were videotaped for research purposes by Dr. William Maurice in a room next to a daycare for psychiatric patients. Looking around, Jimmy asked his doctor, "Am I crazy?"

"No," said Maurice, "and don't let anyone tell you it's wrong."

Jimmy became the first boy in Canada to be medically sanctioned with a female identity—not that it made any difference at school. He was called "fag," "fairy," and "freak" by his schoolmates; phys ed classes, where he was forced to shower with boys, were particularly painful and alien. Jimmy's solution was simply to stop going. He had heard there was a burgeoning gay scene on the Granville strip, in particular at the White Lunch cafeteria (supposedly thus named to assure customers they didn't use Chinese cooks). There, he met five co-conspirators, all about fifteen years old.

15   One of his new friends told him about turning tricks beneath the stately Birks clock at Granville and Georgia. When Jimmy hit the hot spot, a pleasant man in his fifties rolled up and offered to pay for a blow job. They did the deed in the nearby Drake Steam Baths. "Easiest money I had ever made," Hamilton says, and growing up in the projects, easy was something money had never been before. He started hustling regularly: he could score forty bucks for oral or a hand job dressed as a boy, and double that if he was dressed as a girl.

The six friends would pool their resources and rent a room at the Palms Hotel, where they could practice applying makeup and walking in high heels; then they'd head over to the White Lunch to flirt and pick up men. Because transsexual sex workers are rare, they become a coveted, precious commodity. They become, often for the first time in their lives, beloved for who they are. The manager of the White Lunch, Molly, was not such an admirer. "You girls are dressing far too slutty," she finally spat. "You can't come in here till you learn how to dress like proper ladies."

The kids bridled at being ousted from the tiny space they'd carved out for themselves. They retreated to the Palms to plot their revenge. Ambushing the White Lunch dressed in even sluttier clothes—fishnet stockings, micro-miniskirts, loudest possible makeup—they lined up at the counter, reached their hands past the sneeze guard like a team of ballerinas at rehearsal, and stuck their fingers into a corresponding line of pies.

Behind any individual life looms a whorl of politics. In 1972, the vagrancy law, outlawing pretty much all street life, was deemed a relic of ancient morality and replaced with what's called the soliciting law, which meant sex-oriented vagrants could still be shuffled along. Hunky-dory, said the police. Fine, said the residents of aspirational neighborhoods. Then, in 1978, the Supreme Court redefined soliciting as pressing or persistent behavior; simply saying, "Want a date?" didn't qualify.

This proved problematic, since the murder of a twelve-year-old shoe-shine boy in an apartment above a Yonge Street body rub parlor the year before had prompted raids of massage parlors in Toronto. (There had been similar campaigns in Vancouver even earlier.) Masses of sex workers were pushed onto the street. Needing a legal mechanism to shoo them, the government passed the communication law in 1985, which criminalized any communication for the purposes of prostitution in a public place (including cars).

It was the end of what Hamilton calls "the golden age of prostitution." 20 By night, she would dress up as Cher and perform "Gypsies, Tramps, and Thieves" for audiences at a downtown Vancouver gay bar called BJs. By late night, she would join hundreds of other sex workers strolling the West End, a pimp-free "drive-in brothel" where transsexuals, boys, and "fish" (biological women) could look out for one another and openly ply their trade.

Gordon Price, the director of the City Program at Simon Fraser University, was then leading CROWE (Concerned Residents of the West End) in the push to remove sex workers, and he remembers things differently. There were pimps, he says, dangerous ones, and everyone from schoolchildren to grandmothers was being solicited. Price becomes highly excitable when he discusses the past. "A new status quo, with sex workers working happily among residents, simply was not an option," he says. "It was us or them."

On the right side of Price's line in the sand: the West End's thriving gay community, which had moved with breathtaking speed toward empowerment since 1969. Fourteen years later, the gay bookstore Little Sister's and AIDS Vancouver, two totems of political will, came to life; by 1985, the city even had a gay newspaper. Homosexuals were real citizens, and capable of pushing other minorities around. Hamilton, who'd started on hormone therapy in 1977, thereby slowly and permanently distinguishing herself from the drag queens, remembers being barred from performing at one gay bar. Sex workers, meanwhile, were seen as "vermin that had to be exterminated," says Becki Ross, chair of the Women's and Gender Studies Department at UBC. "They had to be removed to give people a sense they were living in a 'contamination-free zone.'"

The pressure from residents grew to such a fever pitch that it finally resulted in a 1984 injunction by BC Supreme Court chief justice Allan McEachern; hundreds of sex workers were pushed out of the West End and, pursued by the communication law, into increasingly desolate spaces, until they were finally allowed to rest in the industrial no man's land of the Downtown Eastside. Since it had last been Hamilton's regular haunt, the city's central library, an Eaton's, and several offices had closed up shop, leaving a hole filled by deinstitutionalized psychiatric patients, whose presence encouraged a street-based drug trade, which in turn promoted theft and violent crime.

Pushing prostitutes there consolidated the city's undesirables into one messy (yet handily avoidable) package. "There was no precedent for this in Western jurisprudence," says Ross. And yet she points out that no one notable in the labor movement, the feminist movement, or the gay rights movement stepped forward to protect sex workers. Ross's research has led her to believe that their unchallenged relocation was the seedbed of the scores of Pickton murders that followed.

25 "I say the state created the killing fields of the Downtown Eastside," declares Hamilton, upping the ante, as ever. People tend to roll their eyes when she makes such accusations. But she never had the luxury of being politically neutral. When Expo came in 1986, she organized protests against the displacement of those in low-income housing; she founded a sub-local of the Canadian Union of Public Employees, as well as a hot meal program and food bank for transsexuals. She became a Native Princess, a Ms. Gay Vancouver, and, inevitably, an honorary member of the traveling cast of *A Chorus Line*.

In the fall of 1996, Hamilton entered the municipal election race, winning herself pride of place as the first transsexual person in Canada to run for public office. When she didn't win the seat, she used her connections to open a now-infamous safe space on Hastings Street called Grandma's House, where sex workers could stop in to warm up, grab a coffee and spare clothing, and use the Internet. Angel funding came from two society women, Jacqui Cohen (heiress of the Army & Navy discount chain) and Cynnie Woodward (of the department store family). Provincial and city governments backed her with "about $27,000" each year.

But not even the beleaguered DTES community would put up with what it perceived as sanctioned sex work in its front yard. The local business association drove the outfit to a nearby residential street, where it again incurred the wrath of locals. Someone started making anonymous death threats on the phone. (When Hamilton alerted the police, the officer who came by said, "If I had a place like this in my neighborhood, I don't think I'd be happy about it either.")

She was staffing Grandma's House one night when, at four in the morning, a slight aboriginal woman arrived with a pair of guys, drunk off their asses. A third was waiting in the car outside. "I've got nowhere to go," she said, eyes saucer wide. "Can I do this in one of the rooms here?" Hamilton was perfectly aware of the bawdy house law that made that an illegal option (it was introduced with the vagrancy law in the late nineteenth century). But she decided that sending this woman into a car with three overheated men wasn't an ethical option: "She'd have been violated. We knew by then there was a serial killer on the prowl, and I just couldn't send her away."

Over the next few months, at the height of Hamilton's celebrity (thanks to her antics at City Hall), rumors surfaced that other working girls were servicing johns at Grandma's House, and government funding was pulled in January of 2000. One day that August, Hamilton was stepping into a cab, en route to a radio interview with CKNW, when she was arrested on the sidewalk, charged with running a bawdy house. After eight hours, she was released on the condition that she shutter Grandma's House.

Hamilton is, famously, "an unrepentant whore." Is she also an unrepentant madam? Sitting with her recently, I ask point-blank, "So, were you running a bawdy house?" She looks nonplussed: "Well, *yeah*." A hand flicks at some imaginary dirt on a cushion. "But so is every five-star hotel in this country.

"And you know what I really resented? They called it a *common* bawdy house. Listen, there was nothing common about it."

30

If Hamilton gets her way, of course, bawdy houses *will* become common, and some wonder whether the sex trade will be hurt by the trappings of legitimacy, such as income tax and EI premiums. To some extent, minorities are ruined by their success; civil liberties denude civil righteousness. For better or worse, though, the long-distance destination for sex workers appears to be homogenization. The police, at least, are less interested in persecuting them. Between 1998 and 2008, total prostitution charges in Canada plummeted from 5,950 down to 2,535.

And Libby Davies, MP for Vancouver East, is among a small group of politicians who are starting to recognize this essentially useless voting demographic. "The laws we have are not protecting sex workers," she says.

(Indeed, Hamilton has a list of twenty-five women she claims have gone missing since Pickton was arrested; it's increasingly likely there are more killers like him.) "The key point is this: I don't believe the state should be involved in shutting down consensual sexual activities between adults, whether money is involved or not. The state should only be involved where there's violence or exploitation."

Leading the charge to keep the state out of prostitutes' bedrooms is Alan Young, the gregarious, mustachioed Toronto lawyer who argued before the Superior Court of Ontario last year that Canada's laws deny sex workers the safety they are entitled to under the Constitution. Grandma's House was front and center in his case. "Jamie created a safe house among the lowest of the low, and they shut 'em down," he says. "I needed to show the judge that even when you took measures to protect yourself, the law will sanction you. If the law prevents people from protecting themselves, that's not the law."

35   Whatever the outcome of Young's case, it will be appealed and appealed again. But it's the start of a multi-tiered approach, and after the preliminary fury of grassroots activism like Hamilton's it's only with the collaboration of suits like Young and Davies that real change can occur. Davies points to Vancouver's drug policy (which has pioneered safe injection sites) as a model for future work with the sex industry: "You've got academics, bureaucrats, elected people, drug users, West Side parents, and people in the media all in on the conversation. When they all converged on drug issues, it became something very powerful. The problem is that it's a much more fractious proposition once you start talking about sex."

You only have to look at the politically correct (and horribly cumbersome) string of letters that labels the LGBTTIQQ2S community to know she's right. And it's almost taken for granted that gay men would break away from so much baggage. Why would they be concerned that sex workers are being murdered, or that transsexuals are still not explicitly protected from discrimination anywhere in Canada except the Northwest Territories? Well, maybe because it's not just hypocritical to desert another minority after you've gained your own civil rights; it's impolitic, too.

We gay folk may consider ourselves beyond the struggles of a person like Jamie Lee Hamilton (happily consuming our *Will & Grace* and purchasing our same-sex wedding cards with pride). But consider that while we report feelings of safety to our friends at Statistics Canada, the numbers tell us homosexuals are still two to four times more likely to be victims of violent crime. Nor has the wholesale absorption of hetero-normative marriage rights taken place: in the last census, only 7,460 people nation-wide identified themselves as being part of a same-sex marriage. In the US, Maine's population recently approved a referendum overturning a same-sex marriage law; around the same time, New York and New Jersey both opted to disallow gay marriage. People change quickly (their minds, their genitals, whatever), but public opinion turns like a freighter.

When the New York State senate was preparing to vote on the rights of its gay constituents, straight senator Diane Savino—a supporter of same-sex marriage—said to her gay colleague, Senator Tom Dwayne, "My only hope, Tom, is that ... we can learn from you, and that you don't learn from us." What she may have been getting at is that there's value, irreplaceable value, in the minority experience. That the section of society that most discomfits the masses is precisely the one that can teach us something about the social hierarchy by which we all benefit and suffer to varying degrees.

The more time I spend with Hamilton, the more her multiple statuses (transsexual, sex worker, aboriginal, working class) appear to slip over my vision, like those successive lenses at the eye doctor's that finally bring the lowest letters into focus.

On Kingsway, the street that defies Vancouver's grid system and runs at a disruptive angle across town, Hamilton has furnished a second-floor space with all the accoutrement necessary to create her idea of a community center for trans women and their admirers. The door to Queens Cross is marked with the street address 1874½—a *Harry Potter*-esque nod to the unregulated spaces in between.

My eyes have to adjust to the dim lighting. Hamilton—a proud shop-keep—sits behind a cash register in a vestibule. Normally, men pay a $20 entrance fee to socialize here. She gives me a free pass (it's a weekday, and early in the evening, so we're alone anyway). We lounge by candlelight on overstuffed white leather sofas. Around us, there are numerous mannequin heads sporting wigs. At the rear, I see a room with a massage table, and there's a video room to the left. The space drips with makeshift sensuality, but "it operates within city guidelines," she assures me.

Hamilton is at ease in her boudoir, her legs curled beneath her. She's finally given up on a career in politics, after three further failed attempts at public office in 1999, 2000, and 2008. She tells me she won't run again, because her sex work will always be used against her. "They'd only want me if I said I was *reformed*. But I'm not reformed. Listen, I'm fifty-four and can still work in the sex industry. I'm *glad*." Her political will is too brazen, too tart, in any case, for her to serve in milquetoast council chambers. When a certain feminist group recently decided to inform Hamilton of her own safety interests, she told them the same thing she used to tell pimps who tried to work their way into the West End strolls: "If you really want to be an expert, you need to go home, put on a dress, and come suck some cock."

I ask her whether she considers herself lonely in her identity. Is she, hovering there at the multi-hued hub of her own Venn diagram, a minority among minorities? She studies the flame from a red candle, then starts to answer: "You know, I just live my life ..." It's no more complicated than that.

"Be a gentleman," she urges, "and walk me to my bus stop."

(2010)

Questions

1. Hamilton's activist career is marked by her uncompromising expression of her personality and political opinions; Harris writes that "[h]er political will is too brazen, too tart, in any case, for her to serve in milquetoast council chambers." In terms of her activism, what are the advantages of this "brazen" public image? What are the disadvantages?

2. Comment on the balance between formal and colloquial language in this piece. Is this balance successful?

3. Who is this article likely to appeal to? Who is less likely to find it appealing? Consider the tone of the writing as well as the underlying political assumptions.

4. What relationship does Harris see between gay rights and the rights of "sexual outliers" such as transsexuals and sex workers?

5. What laws, if any, do you think there should be regarding prostitution? Why?

6. Since the publication of this article, there have been changes in Canadian law regarding prostitution, and the laws in the US differ significantly from those in Canada. Research the current laws in your area. Are these laws just? Why or why not?

JAMES SALTER

THE ART OF THE DITCH

James Salter spent twelve years in the US Air Force before beginning his career as a writer. In this article for The New York Review of Books, *he reviews William Langewiesche's book* Fly by Wire: The Geese, the Glide, the Miracle on the Hudson, *an account of Chesley Sullenberger's remarkable emergency landing of US Airways Flight 1549.*

❧

Not long after takeoff from LaGuardia last January 15, as the Charlotte-bound US Airways flight was climbing out smoothly over the Bronx on a northerly heading, something hit the airplane. Something that seemed big. There was a loud noise and a collective gasp from the passengers. Some of them had seen something like a flash of brown going into the engines. The airplane began to wiggle a little and decelerate. The flight attendants were still strapped in their seats not near any windows, but they guessed what had happened. There was a smell of something burning. It had become completely quiet. There was no word from the cockpit. A woman would text her husband, "My flight is crashing."

The airplane was not crashing, but it was definitely headed down. At about 2,500 feet it had collided with a flock of Canada geese flying southwest; geese are not uncommon in the New York area, their ancient migratory routes passing over it. At least five birds had hit the plane, three or more going into and virtually destroying both engines. The copilot, Jeffrey Skiles, had been at the controls, and he and the pilot, Chesley Sullenberger, had suddenly seen, at the same time, the flock of geese slightly above and ahead.

"Birds!" Sullenberger cried just before they hit.

"Whoa!" Skiles said.

683

5   They were fortunate that a bird—Canada geese are large—hadn't crashed directly into the windshield, but the engines were already banging and winding down. Fire was coming from both of them, flames from one and fireballs from the other. Briefly, for some fifteen seconds, Sullenberger tried to restart the engines and also, more or less instinctively since it was not part of the procedure, he started an auxiliary power unit in the tail to maintain electrical power. His pulse rate must have been high, but he said calmly, "My aircraft," and took over the controls.

   Sullenberger was almost fifty-eight years old, an experienced and steady captain who had been flying since he was sixteen. He had learned to fly in high school in Denison, Texas, from a grass field and had gone on to the Air Force Academy and the beginnings of a career as a fighter pilot, during which he had flown a Vietnam-era fighter, the F-4 Phantom. He had never, in his long flying career, had an engine failure. It was hardly surprising since jet engines are simple in design and extremely reliable although subject to damage if anything reasonably substantial comes into the intake. He called New York Approach and said, "We lost thrust in both engines. We're turning back towards LaGuardia."

   As Sullenberger began a turn to the left to return to the field, Skiles began working on the checklist of air restarting procedures. They had slowed to a recommended gliding speed. In the cabin no one knew what was happening, although knowledgeable passengers could see that they were turning back and had some idea of the situation.

The pleasures of air travel, such as they once were, have long since vanished, the result of airline deregulation and the fierce competition that followed, along with the inconveniences of guarding against terrorism. Airline pilots and even flight attendants have seen their pay and prestige inexorably decline over the years.

   Of the people to whom you almost blindly entrust your life—surgeons and pilots come to mind—you may get some idea of a surgeon through references, former patients, affiliations, and perhaps from your own impressions during a consultation, but an airline pilot is a remote and unknown figure. He or she is, depending on the country and category of operator, presumably well-trained and capable, but there are, as William Langewiesche points out, more than 300,000 airline pilots in the world, not all of equal experience or ability. There is a low end and a high end and probably a bell curve. From the operating table you can only fall a few feet at the most or gently pass from profound sleep into oblivion, never knowing the difference. In an airplane, though statistically safer than in a car, you are existentially on the edge, and a mischance can send scores or even hundreds of terrified, otherwise unrelated people, as if in *The Bridge of San Luis Rey*, smashing into the ground. Or water.

Sullenberger had been quickly offered Runway 13 to land on at LaGuardia. He was just descending through 1,900 feet, and the field was still out of sight to the left. He was a precise, mature pilot. At this already crucial point he had two tasks and just one decision. The tasks were, first, to get one or both engines restarted. If he was successful, that would solve things. If not, or in any case, he had to land the airplane someplace. The question was: where? Runway 13 was seven thousand feet long. In a case like this, you might prefer ten thousand feet, but of equal importance was that the water of Flushing Bay came right to the threshold of the runway, there was no overrun or stretch of grass if you hit short. So it would have to work out almost perfectly. It was too risky. He called and said, regarding the offer of the runway, "We're unable. We may end up in the Hudson."

There are emergencies that come about slowly, with time to weigh all options—running low on fuel, for example—and emergencies that arrive suddenly, within seconds sometimes. What makes in-flight emergencies different is that the airplane cannot be parked in order to figure things out. Circumstances can be such as to cause confusion and even panic. In primary training, at the time when I went through it, a check flight was certain to include, although it was meant to be a surprise, the throttle being suddenly jerked back to idle and the check pilot announcing, "Forced landing." You had to look around, quickly judge alternatives, and, adjusting your course and glide, head for the best of them. The forced landing drill would almost never be given just after takeoff, since there was heavy traffic around the field, and we had no radios in the planes.

Fly by Wire is a story with two heroes, one of them the pilot of the stricken plane, and the other the man who had been responsible for the advanced control concepts of the airplane itself, an Airbus A320. This is Bernard Ziegler, the impressive engineer and pilot now in his late seventies and retired, who envisioned, championed, and oversaw the entire generation of airplanes for Airbus, and whose portrait is masterfully drawn. Langewiesche is a pilot himself and has written with an intimacy about flying. A good portion of *Fly by Wire* is given over to the Airbus A320, its characteristics, and its excellent design. Cables or hydraulic

10

lines to the control surfaces in airplanes had long since been replaced by electric wires and small motors. The addition of digital computers created what is known as fly-by-wire. It is not a robotic system; the pilot is still in control, although in the A320 the computers have been given great authority. Essentially they prevent the pilot from flying the airplane hazardously. They limit angles of bank and elevation and are programmed to prevent stalls by precisely trading off angle of attack and airspeed and even automatically increasing power if required. A good pilot can do this but perhaps not as invariably or finely as the computer. A less good pilot is definitely made safer.

This is not to say that the airplane cannot crash. The Air France Flight 447 out of Brazil that crashed in the Atlantic last June with 228 people aboard—the cause still unknown—was an Airbus 330. In 1988 one of the first A320s, with 136 passengers aboard, some of whom had never flown before, was part of an unforgettable air show at a small field near Mulhouse in France. The passengers did not know they were taking part in a show; they mainly knew that they would be circling Mont Blanc on the flight.

The pilot was an Airbus convert and enthusiast, forty-four years old with thousands of flying hours and an excellent reputation. There were to be two passes over the field, the first slow and the second at speed. The minimum altitude was to be one hundred feet. There were 15,000 spectators. You can see a film of it all on YouTube: Mulhouse, Airbus A320, mislabeled "during take-off." The airplane, wheels down, full flaps, nose high on the very edge of a stall, flies serenely along barely thirty feet above the ground. The pilot had disengaged the automatic throttle advancement, which presumably one should not be able to do, in order to hold the plane on the very knife edge a second or two longer than the computers would allow, and then to shove the throttles forward himself. He did it too late. The airplane, refusing to stall but without the power it needed to go higher, plowed into the trees, first the tail and then gradually, as if drawn into the forest, the rest:

> For the air show spectators, the sight was surreal. First the airplane sailed by them almost within reach, with some announcer finding things to say. Then they watched it sail away and, without the slightest urgency, continue smoothly into the trees. Lifted by its wings, and still largely under control, it sank slowly from sight with its nose held high, until only the nose was visible moving forward through the forest like the head of a swimmer refusing to drown.

A great burst of flame marks the end. Actions of the flight attendants   15
saved almost all lives. Langewiesche's descriptions of accidents in addition
to this one are particularly dramatic and convincing. Accident reports are
frequently like legal documents or autopsies, but, without being sensational,
he makes them compelling.

Sullenberger, in his Airbus A320, continued with Skiles to try to restart the
engines, and amid unnecessary and irrelevant voice alarms going off in the
cockpit, continued talking to the controller. Teterboro, an airport off to the
right in New Jersey and no closer than LaGuardia, was briefly considered,
but, like Newark, rejected. The decision had really been made. The best
choice was the Hudson.

Ditching is best done with power. The general assumption is that the
airplane will be going down in the ocean somewhere, perhaps in a bay. With
its landing gear up and at close to normal touchdown speed, the airplane is
flown parallel to any waves and between them, and the aft section is the first
to come into contact with the water. There have been only a few airliner
ditchings and apparently only one without power, in Java, just seven years
before Sullenberger's. That plane also ditched into a river (and one person,
a flight attendant, died).

The need for power is obvious: the pilot wants to be in complete control of the descent, holding it off just above a stall and allowing the tail to
touch and then smoothly setting the rest of the fuselage down like a boat
launched at more than a hundred miles an hour. The only ditching I know
about personally—they were, of course, commonplace during World War
II—happened just off Oahu in August 1947. I was a lieutenant in a Troop
Carrier squadron, and we were awakened in the middle of the night to help
search for a B-17 carrying the US ambassador to Japan that had gone down
only an hour or so earlier.

The B-17 was from MacArthur's flight section in Tokyo and was on
the way to Washington, DC, with the ambassador, who was carrying the
draft of the US-Japanese peace treaty in a lead-weighted briefcase. Crossing the Pacific in those days was done in long, slow stages, stopping to
refuel at Guam, Kwajalein, and Oahu. It turned out that the refueling at
Kwajalein had been careless, the gas tanks had not been "sticked"—their
contents visually checked with a calibrated stick, the normal procedure—
and the gauges on the instrument panel, more trustworthy in the lower
ranges, had suddenly gone down when the airplane was between Johnston
Island and Oahu, showing not enough fuel to reach either. The pilot,

hoping against hope that they were wrong, continued until one by one the engines quit.

20   The navigator of the flight, whom I knew, said that they sat listening as the engines went silent and then started down, the altimeter slowly and hesitantly unwinding. The lights were on in the main cabin that had been fitted up for travel, and the plane's landing lights were on. In their brightness, as they neared the water, the large black swells of the ocean could be seen. The plane started into a trough but then the wingtip hit a wave and, lights still on, as in the *Titanic*, the plane started up in a big cartwheel. They could hear the rivets singing as they tore from the metal of the wing, the navigator said, and over the plane went, plunging into darkness. He survived, in a life vest, floating with some others in the ocean until the next day, but the ambassador, George Atcheson, and the draft treaty did not.

Sullenberger's first announcement to the cabin, when the die had been cast and they were going to end up in the river, was "This is the captain. Brace for impact." Although three and a half minutes, the time that elapsed between hitting the geese and landing in the river, seems leisurely enough—a man can run close to a mile in that length of time—the pair in the cockpit were too occupied to explain, even in the briefest terms, what was going on.

> The order came as a surprise to nearly everyone. One man said out loud, "What does that mean?" Soon enough he figured it out.... The most astute passengers had known for a while that they were descending over the Hudson, and would not be returning to LaGuardia, but some had held out hope that they were headed for Newark instead. Now they knew that the airplane was going to crash into the river. The flight attendants did not know it, because ... they had no eye-level windows while seated in their positions, and were expected to rely on instructions from the cockpit.... They therefore reacted purely by rote, chanting, "Brace! Brace! Heads down! Stay down!" with no idea of how high they were, where they were, or what was going on.

A man in the back had the poise and presence of mind to call out, "Exit row people, get ready!" A woman mid-plane with a baby boy on her lap did not know what to do. The man next to her asked if he could brace her son for her, and she passed the child to him, and he did.

In the cockpit the ground warning alarm had begun, an automatic voice repeating that the plane was too low. Sullenberger called for the flaps on the wings to be extended in order to slow the plane for impact. At two hundred feet he began breaking his glide and ballooned a little. They were at 150 knots—about 180 miles an hour. He lowered the nose slightly and then, pulling back on the stick in the last few seconds before touching down, his airspeed spent, remarked coolly to Skiles, "Got any ideas?"

"Actually not," Skiles said.

They touched the water at an optimum angle, nose slightly high, 120 knots. The left engine tore away, the plane's belly ripped open toward the rear, and the aircraft skimmed to a stop. There was such heavy spray that the passengers near the windows thought they had gone entirely underwater.

The evacuation of the plane was all one could hope for. Water entered quickly. There was an eighty-five-year-old woman who needed a walker, plus several children aboard. In the rear, the floor had buckled and a beam had broken through. There was more water there; it rose to almost chest-high before everyone was out. The flight had been sold out only one empty seat. The flight attendants, three women all in their fifties, were exemplary. Doreen Welsh, the oldest, in the rear, had the greatest difficulties and was seriously injured. People tried to swim in the river, some slipped into the water and were pulled back, all ended up standing on the wings, some waist deep in water, or in the inflated slides and rafts. Sullenberger and Skiles had all along been moving through the cabin assisting and handing out life vests. In the end Sullenberger went through the deep water in the cabin one last time to make certain no one was left. The water was bone-chillingly cold, but within five minutes the first of the rescue boats was at the plane. There had been no casualties. All survived.

Chesley Sullenberger and his entire crew had performed admirably. The event was so spectacular, in full view of Manhattan and the New Jersey side of the Hudson, and it ended so happily that the public embraced it. It seemed a miracle, and Sullenberger, decent, conscientious, serious, was a hero. It was a life-changing event, he said in an interview, not only for himself but for everyone on the airplane and their families. It was also true that some of his passengers, having been rescued, simply went back to LaGuardia and caught a later plane, just as at Mulhouse twenty of the passengers had simply walked from the burning wreckage through the forest to the autoroute and hitchhiked home.

25

A "miracle." On examination it seems more like a bit of luck and a job perfectly done. Airline crashes normally produce so many fatalities that this was an unexpectedly nice outcome. Whether the computerized characteristics of the A320 were an important element in that outcome seems uncertain. Langewiesche gives the airplane credit for smoothing out the slight ballooning in the last moments and easing it in the optimum position onto the water as Sullenberger held the stick full back, but given Sullenberger's abilities and good judgment, along with the weather and other circumstances, it seems likely that he would have accomplished the same thing in a Boeing, and that no autopilot or computer we can conceive of could have handled the emergency half as well.

(2010)

Questions

1. How does Salter build tension and maintain reader interest? Consider the structure of the article as well as his use of language.

2. What does this article say about the relative importance of technology and human skill? Do you agree?

3. Comment on the use of dialogue in this article.

4. After the events described in this article, Sullenberger was ranked second in *TIME Magazine*'s list of the "Most Influential Heroes and Icons of 2009." Do you think this is justified? Why or why not?

BIOGRAPHICAL NOTES

Addams, Jane (1860-1935)
American reformer and founder in 1889 of Hull-House, a Chicago settlement-house. Through her activities here, she created a strong social reform movement and was instrumental in the passage of several child labor and education laws. Written works include *Democracy and Social Ethics* (1902), *Twenty Years at Hull-House* (1910), and *A New Conscience and an Ancient Evil* (1912). In recognition of her reform efforts, Addams was awarded the 1931 Nobel Peace Prize.

Alvarez, Luis Walter (1911-88)
American experimental physicist and inventor, called "one of the most brilliant and productive experimental physicists of the twentieth century" by the *American Journal of Physics*. He received the Nobel Prize in Physics in 1968 for his innovations in the measurement and analysis of elementary particle interactions.

Alvarez, Walter (1940-)
Professor of Geology at the University of California, Berkeley, best known for his work with his father Luis Alvarez on the asteroid impact hypothesis explaining the extinction of the dinosaurs. His book *T. Rex and the Crater of Doom* (1997) details this discovery and its eventual acceptance in the scientific community. He is also the author of *The Mountains of St. Francis: The Geological Events That Shaped Our Earth* (2008).

Arambel-Liu, Stella (1974-2005)
Assistant Professor of Psychology at the University of New Hampshire.

Asaro, Frank
Nuclear chemist and Emeritus Senior Scientist at the Ernest Orlando Lawrence Berkeley National Laboratory.

Atwood, Margaret (1939-)
Atwood's collection of poetry *The Circle Game* won the 1966 Governor General's Award, and her critical book *Survival: A Thematic Guide to Canadian Literature* (1972) led to the entrenchment of Canadian Literature as a legitimate field of study in Canadian universities. Despite these lofty achievements, Atwood is perhaps best

known for her novels, including *The Edible Woman* (1969), *The Handmaid's Tale* (1985), *The Blind Assassin* (winner of the 2000 Booker Prize), and *Oryx and Crake* (2003).

Bacon, Francis (1561-1626)
English statesman and philosopher. During the reign of Queen Elizabeth I, Bacon was a member of British Parliament, and advanced to the position of Lord Chancellor during the reign of King James I. Bacon lost political favor in 1621, when he was convicted of accepting bribes and was imprisoned for a short duration. Bacon's written works include *Essays* (1597), *The Advancement of Learning* (1605), and *Novum Organum* (1620).

Baker, William Frazier (1953-)
American structural engineer and partner with the firm of Skidmore, Owings & Merrill. He is best known for his work on supertall buildings.

Barthes, Roland (1915-80)
French social and literary critic known for his writings on semiotics and structuralism. Written works include *Mythologies* (1957), *Elements of Semiology* (1967), *The Empire of Signs* (1970), and *The Luminous Room* (1980).

Beeman, Mark (1963-)
A neuroscientific researcher, Mark Beeman was investigating the right brain's contributions to understanding language when he recognized similarities with the type of thinking necessary to solve problems with sudden insight (experienced as Aha! or Eureka! moments). Together with co-author Ed Bowden, he began investigating insight in the mid-1990s, laying the foundation for the use of functional MRI to investigate the brain mechanisms of insight. The use of multiple measures of brain activity to uncover the unconscious processes underlying insight opened a new avenue to understanding this type of creative thinking.

Benedetti, Fabrizio (1956-)
Professor of Clinical and Applied Psychology at the University of Turin Medical School. A consultant for the Placebo Project at the U.S. National Institute of Health and a member of Harvard University's Placebo Study Group, he focuses his research on the functioning of the placebo effect.

Bowden, Edward (1958-)
Bowden is a teacher at Whittier Elementary School in Kenosha, Wisconsin.

Brand, Dionne (1953-)
Canadian author, film maker, and social activist known for her work in Canadian Black women's history and in fighting against racism. Written works include *Chronicles of the Hostile Sun* (1984), *In Another Place, Not Here* (1996), and *A Land to Light On* (1997). She was appointed Poet Laureate of Toronto in 2009.

Broyard, Anatole (1920-90)
An essayist and book reviewer for the *New York Times*, Broyard was also a writer of fiction. *Intoxicated by My Illness and Other Writings on Life and Death* was written mainly in the period between being diagnosed with metastatic prostate cancer in 1989, and his death the following year.

Cavanagh, Patrick (1947-)
An Ontario-born cognitive psychologist, Cavanagh researches vision at the Vision Sciences Laboratory at Harvard University and at the Laboratoire Psychologie de la Perception at Université Paris Descartes.

Cavendish, Margaret (Duchess of Newcastle) (1623-73)
The first English woman to write mainly for publication, she was both widely criticized and celebrated for her public disregard of social and literary conventions, particularly with regard to her views on the education of women. Works include *Poems and Fancies* (1653), *Philosophical and Physical Opinions* (1656), *Observations upon Experimental Philosophy* (1666), and a work of science fiction entitled *The Description of a New World, called The Blazing World* (1668).

Churchill, Sir Winston (1874-1965)
Prime Minister of the United Kingdom from 1940-45 and 1951-55, Churchill is most highly regarded for his leadership during World War II. A remarkable orator and prolific writer of memoirs and histories, he is also the only British Prime Minister to have been awarded the Nobel Prize in Literature.

Colloca, Luana (1977-)
Luana Colloca, MD, PhD is currently working at the National Institute of Health Department of Bioethics and at the National Center for Complementary and Alternative Medicine. Her research focuses on conceptual and empirical aspects of placebo phenomena.

Darnton, Robert C. (1939-)
Professor of European History at Princeton University specializing in eighteenth-century French history. His books include *The Great Cat Massacre and Other Episodes in French Cultural History* (1984), *The Kiss of Lamourette: Reflections*

in Cultural History (1989), and *The Case for Books: Past, Present, and Future* (2009).

Darwin, Charles (1809-82)

Born the son of an English doctor, Darwin himself attended medical school at the University of Edinburgh from 1825-27. During his later service as a naturalist aboard *HMS Beagle*, 1831-36, he observed the similarities and differences of various species, and was led to question the established position that species remained as God had first created them. Darwin delayed publishing his theory, but eventually presented it in *On the Origin of Species* in 1859.

Devlin, Tim (1954-)

Tim Devlin has more than twenty-five years experience as a journalist and broadcaster, with a special focus on social activism. He has recently served as Director of TRUCK, an artist-run gallery in Calgary, Alberta, and is a reporter for the CBC.

Donne, John (1572-1631)

Donne is widely considered to be the greatest of the metaphysical poets, and his poems are characterized by the use of elaborate conceits in examination of humankind's mortality and capacity to love. He was also a priest at St. Paul's Cathedral, and his celebrated sermons led him to be perhaps the most famous preacher of his age.

Du Bois, W.E.B. (1868-1963)

Du Bois was an African-American educator and historian, the founder of the Niagra Movement and the National Association for the Advancement of Colored People, and the editor of the NAACP journal *Crisis* from 1910 to 1934. Written works include *The Philadelphia Negro* (1899) and *The Souls of Black Folk* (1903).

Flanner, Janet (1892-1978)

Although an American, Flanner lived in Paris for most of her life. As a journalist, she provided reports and commentary on European culture and political affairs for five decades. Some of her most famous work includes her "Letter from Paris" column for *The New Yorker* and her important articles on Hitler's rise to power.

Franklin, Ursula M. (1921-)

Franklin, an experimental physicist and University Professor Emerita at the University of Toronto, is the author of many scholarly articles and several books, including *The Real World of Technology* (1989). She has served on both the National Research Council and the Science Council of Canada and is the recipient of more than ten honorary degrees.

Gladwell, Malcolm (1963-)
Malcolm Gladwell was born in England and raised in Canada. Since 1996 he has been a staff writer for *The New Yorker* magazine, and he is the bestselling author of *The Tipping Point* (2000), *Blink* (2005), *Outliers* (2008), and *What the Dog Saw* (2009).

Gopnik, Adam (1956-)
Adam Gopnik has been a contributor to *The New Yorker* since 1986. He has received the National Magazine Award for Essay and Criticism as well as the George Polk Award for Magazine Reporting. He is also a regular broadcaster for the Canadian Broadcasting Corporation, and is the author of *Paris to the Moon* (2000).

Gould, Stephen Jay (1941-2002)
Paleontologist, professor of geology and author of several books including *Ever Since Darwin: Reflections in Natural History* (1977), *The Panda's Thumb: More Reflections in Natural History* (1980), and *The Flamingo's Smile* (1985). In opposition to the gradualist theory of evolution, Gould originated the "punctuated equilibrium" theory, which proposes that the evolution of a species occurs through rapid changes in isolated populations, followed by long stable periods.

Gourevitch, Philip (1961-)
As a staff writer for *The New Yorker*, Philip Gourevitch was initially sent by that magazine to Rwanda in 1995 to study the aftermath of the genocide of the Tutsi minority. He stayed nine months in Rwanda and in neighboring Congo, and published the book *We Wish to Inform You That Tomorrow We Will Be Killed with Our Families* (1998). He was the editor of *The Paris Review* and is also the author of *A Cold Case* (2001) and *The Ballad of Abu Ghraib* (2008).

Greenblatt, Richard (1945-)
Scientist at Source Digital Imaging in San Diego.

Haberman, Jason (1978-)
Haberman is a postdoctoral fellow at Harvard University.

Harris, Judith Rich (1938-)
American author of numerous articles on the subject of childhood development. Senior author of *The Child* (1984) and *Infant and Child* (1992) and author of *The Nurture Assumption: Why Children Turn Out the Way They Do* (1998) and *No Two Alike: Human Nature and Human Individuality* (2006).

Harris, Marvin (1927-2001)
American anthropologist and theoretician known for his research in cultural materialism. Author of *The Rise of Anthropological Theory* (1968), *Cannibals and Kings: The Origins of Cultures* (1977), and *Cultural Anthropology* (1983).

Harris, Michael (1948-)
Canadian author and journalist. He hosts the radio talk show "Michael Harris Live" and is a columnist for *The Ottawa Sun*. His books include *Unholy Orders: Tragedy at Mount Cashel* (1991) and *Lament for an Ocean: The Collapse of the Atlantic Cod Fishery* (1998).

Hurka, Thomas (1952-)
Educated at the University of Toronto and Oxford University, Hurka is Chancellor N.R. Jackman Distinguished Professor of Philosophical Studies at the University of Toronto. He is the author of *Perfectionism* (1993), *Virtue, Vice and Value* (2001), and *The Best Things in Life* (2010). He is a frequent radio and television commentator and a contributor to *The Globe and Mail* newspaper.

Johnson, Samuel (1709-84)
English writer, lexicographer, and publisher of the periodicals *The Rambler* (1750-52) and *The Idler* (1758-60). A prolific writer, Johnson's major contributions to eighteenth-century literature were his *Dictionary of the English Language* (1755) and *The Lives of the English Poets* (1781). Johnson is the subject of one of English literature's most significant biographies, James Boswell's *Life of Samuel Johnson* (1791).

Justice, Daniel Heath (1975-)
Born and raised in the small gold mining town of Victor, Colorado, Daniel Heath Justice (Cherokee Nation) now calls Canada home, arriving in 2002 and becoming a Canadian citizen in 2009. A fantasy novelist as well as a literary scholar and editor, he teaches in the Department of English and the Aboriginal Studies Program at the University of Toronto. He lives with his husband, mother-in-law, and dogs in a log house near the shores of Georgian Bay in Huronia (Wendake), the traditional homeland of the Huron-Wendat peoples.

Kehoe, Alice Beck (1936-)
Alice Beck Kehoe, a professor of anthropology at Marquette University in Milwaukee, is the author of *The Ghost Dance: Ethnohistory and Revitalization* (1989) and of *North American Indians: A Comprehensive Account* (1992).

Kincaid, Jamaica (1949-)
Antiguan-born American novelist and Professor of Literature at Claremont McKenna College. Her writings, which often explore issues of colonialism, include the novels *Lucy* (1990) and *Annie John* (1985) and the essay collection *A Small Place* (1988).

King (Jr.), Martin Luther (1929-68)
African-American minister and leader of the American civil-rights movement in the 1950s and 1960s. King received the 1964 Nobel Peace Prize for his leadership of nonviolent civil-rights demonstrations. A charismatic speaker and author, King's books include *Stride Toward Freedom* (1958), *Why We Can't Wait* (1964), and *Where Do We Go From Here: Chaos or Community?* (1967). King was assassinated in Memphis, Tennessee.

Klein, Naomi (1970-)
Klein was born in Montreal and now makes her home in Toronto. She is a journalist whose work has appeared in such publications as *Harper's Magazine*, *The Nation*, and *The Guardian*. Her book *No Logo: Taking Aim at the Brand Bullies* (2000) has been translated into more than 28 languages, and her 2009 work *The Shock Doctrine: The Rise of Disaster Capitalism* was awarded the Warwick Prize for Writing.

Kolbert, Elizabeth (1961-)
American journalist and staff writer for *The New Yorker* best known for her work on environmental issues. She is the author of *Field Notes from a Catastrophe: Man, Nature, and Climate Change* (2006).

Korista, D. Stanton (1940-)
Civil-structural engineer. He retired in 2008 after a long career with the firm Skidmore, Owings & Merrill, where he continues to work as a consultant.

Kounios, John (1956-)
A researcher in cognitive psychology and cognitive neuroscience, Kounios was using behavioral research to investigate the perceived suddenness of insight when he recognized that brain EEG could provide information about the precise timing of the brain processes involved in solving problems with insight. With collaborator Mark Beeman, he continues to investigate the states and traits that are conducive to insights, and how insights alter subsequent cognitive processing. Kounios's findings have been reported in *The New Yorker*, *The Wall Street Journal*, and *Scientific American*.

Lai, Larissa (1967-)

Larissa Lai is a writer and cultural organizer, and Assistant Professor in Canadian Literature at the University of British Columbia. Her novel *When Fox is a Thousand* (1995) was nominated for the Chapters/Books in Canada First Novel Award in 1996. Her books since then include *Salt Fish Girl* (2002) and *Automaton Biographies* (2009).

Laurence, Margaret (1926-87)

Raised in Manitoba, Margaret Laurence lived in Ghana for some years in the 1950s before settling in Ontario. Her novels include *A Jest of God* (1966) and *The Diviners* (1974), both of which received a Governor General's Award, although *The Stone Angel* (1965) is often regarded as her finest novel. Her memoir, *Dance on the Earth*, appeared posthumously in 1989.

Lebowitz, Fran (1950-)

American journalist known for her irreverent humor and her satirical observations of urban living. In addition to numerous magazine contributions, she is the author of *Metropolitan Life* (1978), *Social Studies* (1981), and the children's book *Mr. Chas and Lisa Sue Meet the Pandas* (1994).

Lehrer, Jonah (1981-)

American science writer with a focus on psychology and neuroscience. He is a contributing editor at *Wired* and *Scientific American Mind*, and the author of *Proust Was a Neuroscientist* (2007) and *How We Decide* (2009).

Lessing, Doris (1919-)

British author best known for her insightful depiction of women's psychological experience and her engagement with radical political concepts. She has written both realistic and science fiction, and her works include *The Grass is Singing* (1950), *The Golden Notebook* (1962), *The Good Terrorist* (1985), and the *Canopus in Argos* series (1979-83). In 2007, she was awarded the Nobel Prize in Literature.

Lyell, Sir Charles (1797-1875)

Lyell was a Scottish geologist and developer of uniformitarianism (the theory that changes in the earth's form result from gradual and continual natural processes). Author of *Principles of Geology* (1830), Lyell and his theories influenced the work of Charles Darwin. Lyell is also considered a founder of stratigraphy, a method of classifying layers in the earth's surface.

M., Eliza (unknown)

Eliza M.'s exact identity is not known, but she was probably one of the Mfengu, a Xhosa-speaking people who were one of the first in Africa to convert to Christianity.

In the 1860s, she attended school at St. Matthew's Mission in the Ciskei in southern Africa.

Macdonald, Lady Susan Agnes (183-1920)
Born in Jamaica to wealthy British parents, Macdonald spent time in both England and Canada before marrying Canada's first Prime Minister Sir John A. Macdonald in 1867. Although much younger than her husband and without political experience, she nonetheless greatly enjoyed the excitement of Ottawa and the travel associated with his work. She wrote several articles on her travels and life in Canada for the London publication *Murray's Magazine*. After Macdonald's death in 1891, she became the Baroness of Earnscliffe, an estate in Ontario.

Martin, Emily (1944-)
Socio-cultural anthropology professor at New York University. Her work studies the effects of race, gender, and class on science and medicine in culture. Her books include *The Cult of the Dead in a Chinese Village* (1973), *The Anthropology of Taiwanese Society* (1981), and *Bipolar Expeditions: Mania and Depression in American Culture* (2007).

Marx, Groucho (Julius) (1895-1977)
Born in New York City, Groucho and his brothers appeared in vaudeville and films including *Animal Crackers* (1930), *Duck Soup* (1933), and *A Night at the Opera* (1935). Groucho's written works include *Groucho and Me* (1959) and *Memoirs of a Shaggy Lover* (1964).

McLeod, Neal (1970-)
Poet, painter, film-maker, and Indigenous scholar from James Smith Cree First Nation, Saskatchewan. His poetry publications include *Songs to Kill a Whitlow* (2006 winner of the National Aboriginal Poetry Award) and *Gabriel's Beach* (2008), and he is the author of *Cree Narrative Memory: From Treaties to Contemporary Times* (2007). He is a professor of Indigenous Studies at Trent University and the leader of the comedy troupe the Bionic Bannock Boys.

Michel, Helen (1932-)
Chemist, now retired from Lawrence Berkeley Laboratory at the University of California, Berkeley. She was among the first to use nuclear chemistry to date archaeological artifacts.

Milgram, Stanley (1933-84)
Milgram is regarded as one of the most important psychologists of the twentieth century, based mainly on his human obedience experiments at Yale University (1961-62). He is also noted for the small-world method, which became the

inspiration for John Guare's *Six Degrees of Separation*, and for an experiment on the effects of televised antisocial behavior. His books include *Obedience to Authority: An Experimental View* (1983).

de Montaigne, Michel Eyquem (1533-92)
French thinker and developer of the essay as a literary form. Montaigne's essays can be found in three volumes entitled *Essais* (vols. I & II, 1580, vol. III, 1588). Montaigne also published a translation of Spanish theologian Raymond the Second's *Theologia Naturalis* (1569).

Munro, Alice (1931-)
Award-winning Canadian writer known primarily for short stories characteristically containing themes of interest to women. Her short story collections include the Governor General's Award winning *Dance of the Happy Shades* (1968), and *Who Do You Think You Are?* (1978), as well as *The Love of a Good Woman* (1998), *Runaway* (2004), and *Too Much Happiness* (2009).

Ngugi wa Thiong'o (1938-)
Ngugi is East Africa's leading novelist and social critic. Originally named James Thiong'o Ngugi, the author changed his name in reaction to the effects of colonialism in Africa. His novels include *Weep Not, Child* (1964), *The River Between* (1965), *Petals of Blood* (1977), and *Devil on the Cross* (1980). Other works include *Homecoming* (1972), *Moving the Centre* (1993), and *Decolonising the Mind: The Politics of Language in African Literature* (1986).

Novak, Lawrence C. (1963-)
As a structural engineer, Novak was an Associate Partner with Skidmore, Owings & Merrill before he became the director of engineered buildings for the Portland Cement Association. He has received several awards for his papers on structural engineering.

Obama, Barack (1961-)
First African-American President of the United States, inaugurated in 2009. He received the 2009 Nobel Peace Prize.

Orenstein, Peggy (1961-)
American writer and editor best known for her memoir *Waiting for Daisy* (2007), which details her struggle with infertility. She is also the author of *Flux: Women on Sex, Work, Kids, Love, and Life in a Half-Changed World* (2000) and *SchoolGirls: Young Women, Self-Esteem, and the Confidence Gap* (1994). She is a contributing writer for *The New York Times Magazine*.

Orwell, George (1903-50)
Pseudonym of English political journalist and satirist Eric Blair; served with the Indian Imperial Police in Burma, 1922-27, fought with the Republicans in Spain, describing the experience in *Homage to Catalonia* (1938); author of *Animal Farm* (1945) and *Nineteen Eighty-Four* (1949).

Pepperberg, Irene (1949-)
Scientist known for her groundbreaking research in animal cognition, including intensive work with Alex, a remarkably intelligent African Grey Parrot, over the course of thirty years. She is the author of *Animal Cognition in Nature: The Convergence of Psychology and Biology in Lab and Field* (1998) and *The Alex Studies: Cognitive and Communicative Abilities of Grey Parrots* (2000), as well as the personal memoir *Alex & Me* (2008). She is a professor of psychology at Brandeis University and a lecturer at Harvard University.

Pollo, Antonella (1961-)
Italian neuroscientist and Assistant Professor at the University of Turin. Her current research focuses on the placebo effect on pain, neurological disorders, and muscular performance in athletes.

Putnam, Robert D. (1941-)
Professor of American politics, international relations, and public policy at Harvard University. Author of *Double-Edged Diplomacy: International Bargaining and Domestic Politics* (1993), *Making Democracy Work: Civic Traditions in Modern Italy* (1993), and *Bowling Alone: America's Declining Social Capital* (1995).

Reber, Paul (1967-)
Associate Professor at Northwestern University.

Rich, Adrienne (1929-)
Adrienne Rich's most recent books of poetry are *Tonight No Poetry Will Serve* (2011) and *Telephone Ringing in the Labyrinth* (2007). She edited *Muriel Rukeyser's Selected Poems* for the Library of America. *A Human Eye: Essays on Art in Society* appeared in April 2009. She was the 2006 recipient of the National Book Foundation's Medal for Distinguished Contribution to American Letters. She lives in California.

Royko, Mike (1932-97)
Syndicated columnist for the *Chicago Tribune*, known for his sympathy for the working-class, Royko won the Pulitzer Prize in 1972. He was also the author of an unauthorized biography of Mayor Richard J. Daley (1971) and collections of his own written work.

Rybczynski, Witold (1943-)
Rybczynski is a Scottish-born architect and planner. His written works include *Home: A Short History of an Idea* (1986), *The Most Beautiful House in the World* (1989), and *City Life: Urban Expectations in a New World* (1995).

Salter, James (1925-)
American novelist and short story writer. His works include the novel *A Sport and a Pastime* (1967), the short story collection *Dusk and Other Stories* (winner of the 1989 PEN/Faulkner Award), and the memoir *Burning the Days* (1997). He served twelve years in the U.S. Air Force, during which he fought in the Korean War.

Schlosser, Eric (1959-)
American investigative journalist known for his books *Fast Food Nation* (2000) and *Reefer Madness* (2003). His work has appeared in *The Atlantic Monthly*, *Rolling Stone*, *The New Yorker*, and *The Nation*.

Sedaris, David (1956-)
American humorist, comedian, and writer known for his short stories and autobiographical essays, published in best-selling collections such as *Me Talk Pretty One Day* (2000), *Dress Your Family in Corduroy and Denim* (2004), and *When You Are Engulfed in Flames* (2008).

Showalter, Elaine (1941-)
Showalter, a professor in the English department of Princeton University, is one of the founders of contemporary feminist criticism. Her works include *A Literature of Their Own* (1977), *The Female Malady: Women, Madness, and English Culture 1830-1980* (1985) and *Hystories: Historical Epidemics and Modern Culture* (1997).

Singer, Peter (1946-)
Singer, an Australian philosopher and professor at Princeton University, is known for taking a utilitarian approach to ethical issues involved in genetic engineering, abortion, euthanasia, and embryo experimentation. Singer's books include *Animal Liberation* (1975), *Practical Ethics* (1979), *How Are We to Live?* (1993), and *The Life You Can Save* (2009).

Stevenson, Jennifer (1980-)
Doctoral student at the University of Wisconsin-Madison.

Swift, Jonathan (1667-1745)
Swift was an Irish poet, fiction writer, essayist and political pamphleteer, best known for his satire aimed at political hypocrisy, literary pretension, and the folly

of human society. Key works include *Tale of a Tub* (1704), *A Modest Proposal* (1729), and *Gulliver's Travels* (1726).

Thoreau, Henry David (1817-62)
American naturalist and writer known for his individualist and transcendental philosophies. His most popular works include *A Week on the Concord and Merrimack Rivers* (1849) and *Walden; or, Life in the Woods* (1854). His posthumously published works include *Excursions* (1863), *Cape Cod* (1865), and *Faith in a Seed* (1993).

Twain, Mark (1835-1910)
Born Samuel Langhorne Clemens, Twain grew up in Missouri, and at 22 became a Mississippi river pilot. Five years later he began writing for a living, and was soon publishing humorous tales and delivering public lectures. After he married and moved to Hartford in 1870, Twain began to write the works for which he is now most famous, including *The Adventures of Tom Sawyer* (1876), *Life on the Mississippi* (1883), and *Adventures of Huckleberry Finn* (1884).

Wainaina, Binyavanga (1971-)
A Kenyan satirist and short story writer, Wainaina won the Caine Prize for African Writing in 2002. He is the founding editor of the literary magazine *Kwani?*, and his work has appeared in *The New York Times*, *Granta*, *The Guardian*, and *National Geographic*. He is also an expert on African cuisines, and has collected more than 13,000 traditional and modern African recipes.

Wilde, Oscar (1854-1900)
Born and raised in Ireland, Wilde attended Oxford University and then settled in London. His works include the novel *The Picture of Dorian Gray* (1890) and the plays: *Lady Windermere's Fan*, *A Woman of No Importance*, *An Ideal Husband*, and *The Importance of Being Ernest* (all 1892-95). In 1895 he was tried, convicted, and imprisoned on charges of homosexual behavior. After his release from Reading Jail, he left England for France, never to return.

Williams, Raymond (1921-88)
Prodigious Welsh author and pioneer in the field of cultural studies, Williams originated the concept of "cultural materialism." His written works include *Culture and Society* (1958), *The Long Revolution* (1961) and *Marxism and Literature* (1977).

Wente, Margaret (1950-)
Columnist for *The Globe and Mail* whose expression of conservative opinions often provokes controversy. She is the only journalist to have received the National Newspaper Award for column writing twice. A Canadian citizen born in the US, she

is also the author of *An Accidental Canadian: Reflections on My Home and (Not) Native Land* (2004).

Wollstonecraft, Mary (1759-97)

Wollstonecraft was an English writer and early advocate of women's rights, best known for her feminist work *A Vindication of the Rights of Woman* (1792). She was married to English philosopher William Godwin and was the mother of *Frankenstein* author Mary Wollstonecraft Shelley.

Woolf, Virginia (1882-1941)

Woolf was an innovative and influential English writer, whose novels include *Mrs. Dalloway* (1925), *To the Lighthouse* (1927), and *The Waves* (1931). She was also a literary critic and an early advocate of feminism, most notably in her book *A Room of One's Own* (1929).

ACKNOWLEDGMENTS

Luis W. Alvarez, Walter Alvarez, Frank Asaro, and Helen V. Michel, "Extraterrestrial Cause for the Cretaceous-Tertiary Extinction." Originally published in *Science*, Vol. 208, Number 4448, June 1980. Reprinted with permission from AAAS.

Margaret Atwood, "First Job" originally published in *The New Yorker Magazine*, April 2001. Copyright © 2001 O.W. Toad, Ltd. Reprinted by permission of the author.

William F. Baker, D. Stanton Korista, and Lawrence C. Novak, "Burj Dubai: Engineering the World's Tallest Building," originally published in *Structural Design of Tall and Special Buildings*, December 1, 2007. Copyright © 2007, John Wiley and Sons.

Roland Barthes, "The World of Wrestling" from *Mythologies* by Roland Barthes, translated by Annette Lavers. Translation copyright © 1972 by Jonathan Cape Ltd. Reprinted by permission of Hill and Wang, a division of Farrar, Straus and Giroux, LLC.

Fabrizio Benedetti, Antonella Pollo, and Luana Colloca, "Opioid-Mediated Placebo Responses Boost Pain Endurance and Physical Performance: Is It Doping in Sport Competitions?" from *The Journal of Neuroscience*, October 31, 2007, 27(44):11934-11939; doi:10.1523/JNEUROSCI.3330-07.2007). Copyright © 2007, the Society for Neuroscience.

Dionne Brand, "On Poetry," from *Bread Out of Stone* by Dionne Brand. Copyright © 1994 by Dionne Brand.

Anatole Broyard, "Intoxicated by My Illness," from *Intoxicated by My Illness* by Anatole Broyard, copyright © 1992 by the Estate of Anatole Broyard. Used by permission of Clarkson/Potter Publishers, an imprint of the Crown Publishing Group, a division of Random House, Inc.

Sir Winston Churchill, speeches to the House of Commons, 1940: "Blood, Toil, Tears and Sweat"; "We Shall Fight on the Beaches"; "This Was Their Finest Hour." Reproduced with permission of Curtis Brown Ltd., London, on behalf of The Estate of Winston Churchill. Copyright © Winston S. Churchill.

Robert Darnton, "Workers Revolt: The Great Cat Massacre of the Rue Saint-Séverin," from *The Great Cat Massacre and Other Essays in French Cultural History* by Robert Darnton. Copyright © 2009 Robert Darnton. Reprinted by permission of Basic Books, a member of the Perseus Books Group.

Tim Devlin, "Does Working for Welfare Work?" Originally published in *Alberta Views*, May/June 2000. Reprinted by permission of the author.

Janet Flanner, "Pablo Picasso," from *Janet Flanner's World: Uncollected Writings 1932-1975*, edited by Irving Drutman. Copyright © 1979 by Natalia Danesi Murray, reprinted by permission of Houghton Mifflin Harcourt Publishing Company. "Mme. Marie Curie (1866-1934)," originally published in *The New Yorker Magazine*. Copyright © The Estate of Janet Flanner. Reprinted by permission of The Estate of Michael de Lisio.

Ursula Franklin, "Silence and the Notion of the Commons." Originally published in *Musicworks* 59, Summer 1994. Copyright © 1994 by Ursula Franklin. Reprinted by permission of the author.

Malcolm Gladwell, "None of the Above: What I.Q. Doesn't Tell You about Race" originally published in *The New Yorker Magazine*, December 17, 2007. Copyright © 2007 by Malcolm Gladwell. "Priced to Sell: Is Free the Future?" originally published in *The New Yorker Magazine*, July 6, 2009. Copyright © 2009 by Malcolm Gladwell. Reprinted by permission of the author.

Adam Gopnik, "The Corrections: Abridgement, Enrichment, and the Nature of Art," originally published in *The New Yorker Magazine*, October 22, 2007. Copyright © 2007 by Adam Gopnik. Used with the permission of The Wylie Agency LLC.

Stephen Jay Gould, "Entropic Homogeneity Isn't Why No One Hits .400 Any More." Originally published in *Discover Magazine*, August 1986. Reprinted by permission of Rhonda Roland Shearer.

Philip Gourevitch, "We Wish to Inform You That Tomorrow We Will Be Killed with Our Families," from *We Wish to Inform You That Tomorrow We Will Be Killed with Our Families* by Philip Gourevitch. Copyright © 1998 by Philip Gourevitch.

Judith Rich Harris, "Where Is the Child's Environment? A Group Socialization Theory of Development." Originally published in *Psychological Review* 102:3, 1995. Copyright © 1995 by the American Psychological Association. Adapted by permission of the author.

Marvin Harris, "Pig Lovers and Pig Haters," from *Cows, Pigs, Wars, and Witches* by Marvin Harris. Copyright © 1974 by Marvin Harris. Used by permission of Random House, Inc.

Peggy Orenstein, "Stop Your Search Engines," originally published in *The New York Times Magazine*, October 23, 2009. Copyright © 2009 by Peggy Orenstein. Reproduced by permission of the author.

George Orwell, "Politics and the English Language," from *Shooting an Elephant and Other Essays* by George Orwell. Copyright © 1946 by Sonia Brownell Orwell and renewed 1974 by Sonia Orwell. "Shooting an Elephant," from *Shooting an Elephant and Other Essays* by George Orwell. Copyright © 1950 by Sonia Brownell Orwell and renewed 1978 by Sonia Pitt-Rivers. Reprinted by permission of Houghton Mifflin Harcourt Publishing Company.

Irene Pepperberg, excerpt from "The Next Horizon" from *Alex and Me: How a Scientist and a Parrot Uncovered a Hidden World of Animal Intelligence—and Formed a Deep Bond in the Process*. Copyright © 2008 by Irene Pepperberg. Reprinted by permission of HarperCollins Publishers.

Irene Pepperberg, Jennifer Vicinay, and Patrick Cavanagh, "Processing of the Müller-Lyer Illusion by a Grey Parrot (Psittacus Erithacus)," originally published in *Perception* 37(5) pp. 765-781. Reprinted with permission from Pion Limited, London.

Robert D. Putnam, "Bowling Alone: America's Declining Social Capital," from *Journal of Democracy* 6:1, January 1995. This article has been revised and expanded in *Bowling Alone: The Collapse and Revival of American Community* by Robert D. Putnam. Copyright © 2000 by Robert D. Putnam. Reprinted by permission of the author.

Adrienne Rich, "Taking Women Students Seriously," from *On Lies, Secrets, and Silence: Selected Prose 1966-1978* by Adrienne Rich. Copyright © 1979 by W.W. Norton & Company, Inc. Used by permission of the author and W.W. Norton & Company, Inc. "Invisibility in Academe," from *Blood, Bread, and Poetry: Selected Prose 1978-1985* by Adrienne Rich. Copyright © 1986 by Adrienne Rich. Used by permission of the author and W.W. Norton & Company, Inc.

Mike Royko, "Another Accolade for Charter Arms Corp." Originally published in *The Chicago Tribune*, 1980. © Tribune Media Services. All Rights Reserved. Reprinted with permission.

Witold Rybczynski, "One Good Turn: Why the Robertson Screwdriver Is the Biggest Little Invention of the Twentieth Century," from *Saturday Night*, July 29, 2000. This article has been revised and expanded in *One Good Turn: A Natural History of the Screwdriver and the Screw* by Witold Rybczynski. Copyright © 2000 by Witold Rybczynski. Reprinted by permission of the author.

INDEX

6,172 lb(s) de Rolland Opaque50
50% post-consumer
Environmental savings of the Cascades
selected products, compared to the industry
average for virgin products:

 26 trees
2 tennis courts

 28,120 gal. US of water
304 days of water consumption

 5,447 lbs of waste
50 waste containers

 17,002 lbs CO$_2$
emissions of 3 cars per year

 98 MMBTU
**478,660 60W light bulbs for one
hour**

51 lbs NOx
**emissions of one truck during 71
days**

Printed on Roland opaque 50% post-consumer EcoLogo certified paper,
processed chlorine free and manufactured using biogas energy.

50%

MIX
Paper from
responsible sources
FSC® C103567
FSC
www.fsc.org